GOVERNING THE HEARTH

MICHAEL GROSSBERG

GOVERNING THE HEARTH

LAW AND THE FAMILY IN

NINETEENTH-CENTURY AMERICA

THE UNIVERSITY OF NORTH CAROLINA PRESS

CHAPEL HILL AND LONDON

©1985 The University of North Carolina Press

All rights reserved

Manufactured in the United States of America

Library of Congress Cataloging in Publication Data

Grossberg, Michael, 1950–

  Governing the hearth.

  (Studies in legal history)

  Includes index.

  1. Domestic Relations—United States—History.

I. Title. II. Series.

KF505.G76   1985   346.7301'5'09   84-22107

ISBN 0-8078-1647-7   347.3061509

Portions of Chapter 4 appeared as "Guarding the Altar:
Physiological Restrictions and the Rise of State Intervention in
Matrimony," in *American Journal of Legal History* 26 (1982):
197–226, and portions of Chapters 7 and 8 appeared as "Who
Gets the Child?" in *Feminist Studies* 9, no. 2 (Summer 1983):
235–60, by permission of the publisher, Feminist Studies,
Inc.,% Women's Studies Program, University of Maryland, Col-
lege Park, Maryland.

Design by Carla S. Garrett

To Tina

CONTENTS

PREFACE

A specialized law of the family was one of the most significant products of the nineteenth-century legal order. Traditional Anglo-American ways of governing the family were transformed. By the end of the century a new set of rules, regulations, and practices had acquired the label "domestic relations."[1]

During the nineteenth century a series of policies blended tradition and innovation to form a distinctive American family law. Its nature and extent became the subject of protracted and often bitter public and private controversy and debate. The problems of family governance were greatly exacerbated by twin tendencies of the era: a reliance on the private family as the primary institution for confronting social and economic change, and a dependence on the law for resolving public and private disputes. Yet these also increased the importance of finding effective methods of governing the home. The struggle to meet these challenges produced a dynamic body of law.

At the center of domestic-relations law is the complex and vital relationship between two primary institutions and spheres of experience: the family and the law. Nineteenth-century changes had a profound effect on both. Innovations in family law did much to define the "modern family" as social historians classify the results of the fundamental household developments of the eighteenth and early nineteenth centuries. An American law of domestic relations was in turn the creation of a legal order whose institutions, ideology, and practices were being transformed into what legal historians consider "modern." Despite the changing relationships between these institutions, it is possible to identify one continuing reality: the family is in many ways a legal creation.[2]

My purpose is to explain the creation of American domestic-relations law. I have reconstructed its history by taking a broad approach that examines general policies developed over the entire nineteenth century and followed in most states, rather than dwelling on local or temporal peculiarities. Since domestic relations during the era was the province of the states, I have examined the major instruments of policy making within the American commonwealths: appellate court opinions; legislative acts; commission reports; political commentaries; and public and professional journals, treatises, and polemics. These have been drawn from the post-Revolutionary era to the early twentieth century.

I have not attempted to canvass family law fully, but rather have used a select number of topics to illustrate the character of the new American approach to family governance. Each topic has its own story, one that is distinctive but is related to the other branches of the increasingly intricate body of law that began to fall under the heading of domestic relations. Together, the topical chapters, each of which spans the century, indicate the dimensions of the nineteenth century's transformation of American family governance.

Family formation is the organizing focus of these chapters. Its mix of the controversial and the mundane reveals the central concerns that guided the creation of laws to govern the family. Part I examines the questions involved in the relations between husbands and wives; Part II those related to parents and children. These chapters not only unite the traditional categories of domestic-relations law—matrimony and parenthood—they also indicate the particular issues that dominated the law's major subfields.

Legal materials, especially formal legal records such as appellate opinions, legislation, and professional commentaries, are the basic sources of this analysis. Though admittedly such records reveal but part of the past, even of the legal past, it is an important part. Such records are especially valuable for a subject like family law, which was the conscious creation of professionals and laypersons intent on governing and protecting what was universally considered to be society's most vital institution. Examining these records broadly across time and space reveals both persistent regional variations and the symbiotic relationship that existed among the levels and branches of the legal order.

The exact impact of this new body of law on American households is beyond the scope of this study. Nevertheless, legal sources indicate quite clearly that domestic relations became a general category of American law because its authors fashioned policies that were spacious enough to accommodate the diversity of interests and issues thrust upon the law by the nation's political, economic, and social forces, yet cohesive enough to establish a national standard of domestic governance. As in so many areas of nineteenth-century law, these ends were achieved by carving out a special legal domain.

Judges figured prominently in the creation of domestic-relations law. Appellate opinions, in particular, offer the most thorough commentary on the law. They do so because one of the emerging realities of nineteenth-century family law was the primary role of the state judiciary in devising and applying its basic principles and policies. The unique nature of appellate opinions—their special character as public documents designed to persuade diverse audiences—also heightens their evidentiary value. In writing them, judges articulated their assumptions and ideas about family governance. The opinions thus reveal many of the fundamental values, fears, biases, and interests that governed the establishment of a distinctive category of law to govern the family.[3]

Even so, legal changes are difficult to document precisely. The incremental nature of most legal developments and the tendency of judges to mask doctrinal modifications behind a facade of continuity heighten the difficulties. I have dealt with these problems in part by relying on a descriptive analysis influenced by Karl Llewellyn and E. Adamson Hoebel's fascinating study of Native American law, *The Cheyenne Way* (1941). Their concept of the "case of trouble" was particularly useful:

> It is the case of trouble which makes, breaks, twists, or flatly establishes a rule, an institution, an authority. Not all such cases do so. There are also petty rows, the routine of law-stuff which exists among primitives as well as among moderns. For all that, if there be a portion of a society's life in which tensions of the culture come to expression, in which the play of variant urges can be felt and seen, in which emergent power-patterns, ancient security-drives, religion, politics, personality, and cross-purposed views of justice tangle in the open, that portion of the life will concentrate in the case of trouble or disturbance. Not only the making of new law and the effect of the old, but the hold and thrust of all other vital aspects of the culture, shine clear in the crucible of conflict.[4]

Cases of trouble, large and small, permeated nineteenth-century family law. Given the disposition of the era to turn major social and economic questions into legal issues, a phenomenon noted by observers from Tocqueville to Bryce, these friction points in domestic relations are very revealing. They point out methods of resolving conflict and adjusting values and interests to changing conditions. The cases analyzed in this study thus identify the questions that secured legal resolution and indicate the solutions that became basic principles of family law.

Three points give coherence to the topical chapters that follow. First, the end of the eighteenth century and the early nineteenth century was the time when jurists, legislators, litigants, and commentators most fundamentally redirected the governance of the American home. This formative era resulted in a republican approach to domestic relations, which laid the foundation for an Americanized family law. That body of law was then refined, extended, and modified over the course of the nineteenth century to produce the legal category of domestic relations. Throughout the century, the initial republican commitment remained a dominant force in the law. Second, legal developments substantially rearranged the balance of power within the home, and between family members and the state. Specifically, during the century, legal change diminished paternal authority, enlarged maternal and filial prerogatives, and fixed more clearly the state's responsibilities in domestic affairs. Third, the state judiciary supervised this reorientation of the law. Judges, especially appellate jurists, seized the institutional authority to govern the home. They became the public custodians of the family. In many vital ways, then, the American law of domestic relations was a judicial invention.

These fundamental circumstances of nineteenth century family law—a republican reorientation, a rearrangement of family power, and an assumption of authority by the judiciary—together produced an American way of governing the hearth.

ACKNOWLEDGMENTS

Obligations are part and parcel of family law; so too of the writing of its history. I would like to acknowledge mine.

My greatest debt is to Morton Keller, who patiently and with good humor guided this book from inception to publication. His insightful comments immensely improved not merely this study but also my understanding of the historical process. He helped me determine exactly what I wanted to say and to write it as well as I could. I am indebted as well to Morton Horwitz. His writing and teaching captured my imagination and cemented my interest in legal history. His advice during the early stages of this book was invaluable; as was that of Hendrik Hartog, whose extensive and incisive commentary on the project from beginning to end helped me clarify the critical issues of family law.

A number of colleagues unselfishly took the time to read drafts of this book. Their detailed criticism aided me in more ways than I can enumerate: Constance Backhouse, Edward Byers, Judith Taylor, Carl Ubbelohde and Ann Warren. I also benefited from the comments of several others on various aspects of the study: John Demos, Barry Levy, Bertram Wyatt-Brown, Jamil Zainaldin, and the members of the 1979–80 Wellesley College History Seminar and the Charles Riley Armington Interdisciplinary Seminar at Case Western Reserve University. My debt to a much larger group of scholars is evident in almost every footnote. Finally, the publication of this book would not have been possible without the support of its editor, G. Edward White. He endorsed the project at an early stage and has enthusiastically seen it to completion.

Neither could these pages have been written without other forms of assistance. Particularly useful were the services provided by the staffs of the Harvard Law School Library, the Goldfarb Library of Brandeis University, the Library of Congress (especially law librarian Lawrence Boyer), and the libraries of Case Western Reserve University. My research was assisted as well by the financial support of the Irving and Rose Crown Fellowship program of Brandeis University, the National Endowment for the Humanities, and the Charles Riley Armington Foundation on Childhood and Values of Case Western Reserve University. I would also like to thank the *American Journal of Legal History* for permission to reprint portions of Chapter 4 that first appeared under the title: "Guarding the Altar: Physiological Restrictions and the Rise of

State Intervention in Matrimony," 26(1982), 197–226; and *Feminist Studies* for the right to use material in Chapters 7 and 8 that first appeared as: "Who Gets the Child? Custody, Guardianship, and the Rise of a Judicial Patriarchy in Nineteenth-Century America," 9(1983), 235–60.

Despite this advice and assistance, I am of course responsible for the pages that follow.

My final obligation is to Tina Manuel. Without her constant encouragement and help I neither would have written this book nor would I understand its primary subject as well as I do.

I N T R O D U C T I O N

The supremacy of the law of family should not be forgotten. We come under the dominion of this law at the very moment of birth; whether we will or not. Long after infancy has ceased, the general obligations of parent and child may continue; for these last through life. Again we subject ourselves by marriage to a law of family; this time to find our responsibilities still further enlarged. And although the voluntary act of two parties brings them within the law, they cannot voluntarily retreat when so minded. To an unusual extent, therefore, is the law of family above, and independent of, the individual. Society provides the home; public policy fashions the system; and it remains for each one of us to accustom himself to rules which are, and must be, arbitrary.

James Schouler,
A Treatise on the
Law of Domestic Relations (1895)

CHAPTER 1

DOMESTIC RELATIONS
A LAW FOR REPUBLICAN FAMILIES

The "foundation of national morality must be laid in private families," declared Revolutionary lawyer and future president John Adams in 1778.[1] He and others looked to the law to ensure that families would perform their critical responsibilities. But when they looked to the law, their glance did not fall on a special category specifically designed to govern household affairs. On the contrary, laws dealing with the family were strewn across the legal landscape, some to be found in diverse statutes, others in common-law decisions on matters ranging from contracts to torts, still others in various ecclesiastical rules. Yet by the time John Adams's great-grandson Henry published his gloomy ruminations on his life's learning, the legal governance of the family had been transformed.

At the dawn of the twentieth century, domestic relations, as the domain of family law had come to be called, occupied a special place in the American legal order. It was described in voluminous detail in countless treatises, judicial reports, casebooks, and popular tracts. By the 1860s, legal-text author Joel P. Bishop, one of the first major expounders of family law, cautioned: "[A] practitioner who is familiar with every other department of our law, yet is unread in this, cannot give sound advice on questions coming within this department."[2] Bishop's warning documents one of the most significant legal and social developments to occur within the lifespans of the two Adamses: the creation of a distinctive American family law.

Throughout the nineteenth century the basic purposes of legal governance of the family remained fairly constant. In the eyes of the law, the family was as John Adams had visualized it: the primary institution of American society. Public authority was charged with ensuring family stability and guaranteeing the present use and future transmission of household property and other resources. But a fundamental reassessment, if not transformation, occurred within that continuing rationale. Judges, legislators, litigants, legal commentators, and popular critics spearheaded the changes. Their most profound revisions occurred in the first part of the century when they reformulated the English and colonial tradition of family governance and redefined the place of domestic relations within the legal order. Significant consolidation, refinement, and revision then went on throughout the century in a continuing effort to use the law to produce families of the sort that Adams had envisioned.

The Emergence of the Republican Family

A distinctive American family law has its most direct sources in household and legal changes of the late eighteenth and early nineteenth centuries. Identifying those changes and their role in shaping a new approach to family governance provides a necessary introduction to the history of nineteenth-century family law.

Historians have only recently begun to ferret out the details of post-Revolutionary family life. A composite picture of late eighteenth and early nineteenth-century households has emerged. Though the exact sources and timing of family change are difficult to determine, alterations in the households of the era occurred symbiotically with those social, economic, and political developments that marked the path toward a predominately bourgeois, capitalist society. The birth of that new society was not an easy one. Like other departures of the post-Revolutionary era, changes in family life entailed the substantial modification of traditional ways of life.

Through much of the colonial period, most colonists conceived of the family as part of a hierarchically organized, interdependent society rather than as a separate and distinct sphere of experience. Households were tightly bound to the rest of society by taut strings of reciprocity. Family and community were, a seventeenth-century author asserted, "a lively representation" of each other. Fittingly, the community not only had a deep and abiding interest in family life, but armed its agents with extensive powers to prevent homes from becoming disorderly or ineffective. A wide array of duties grew out of the public nature and communal obligations of households in an agrarian, mercantilist society. Family responsibilities ranged from economic production and the transmission of estates to craft training and dependent care. Though most fully defined as such in the New England provinces, throughout colonial

America the family was seen as a public institution tightly integrated into a well-ordered society: "a little commonwealth" in historian John Demos's succinct phrase.[3]

The colonial family's status as a vital link in the colonial chain of authority provided the major rationale for its internal organization. Replicating the surrounding society, the colonial household was hierarchical, patriarchal, and vested with overlapping and undifferentiated internal and external obligations. The community charged each male governor with the duty of maintaining a well-governed home and sustained his authority by granting him control of its inhabitants as well as of family property and other resources. Women and children, as subordinates and dependents in the corporate body, had limited capacity to engage independently in community life. Though the family was composed primarily of spouses and their offspring, apprentices, servants, "bound-out" youths, and other dependents often joined a household and served under its patriarch. A 1712 essay in *The Spectator*, an English journal with wide colonial readership, starkly described traditional patriarchal authority:

> Nothing is more gratifying to the mind of man than power or dominion; and this I think myself amply possessed of, as I am the father of a family. I am perpetually taken up in giving out orders, in prescribing duties, in hearing parties, in administering justice, and in distributing rewards and punishments. To speak in the language of the centurion, I say to one, Go, and he goeth; to another, Come, and he cometh; and to my servant, Do this, and he doeth it. In short, sir, I look upon my family as a patriarchal sovereignty, in which I am myself, both king and priest.[4]

Novel circumstances in the New World slowly but steadily undermined the ideal of the well-ordered family. The forced interdependence of rural, provincial life often gave women economic and social freedoms denied their European sisters. The availability of land and other commercial prospects weakened filial dependence on paternal largess, and maternal culture at times checked paternal authority. Demographic differences between the Old and New Worlds and between various provinces of British North America also altered the model of family life. The migration of single adults rather than families, higher mortality rates, and less effective ecclesiastical and civil establishments thus led to less ordered families in the Chesapeake than in New England.[5]

As modifications of the traditional ideal of the family accumulated with time, families became less and less willing to sacrifice domestic autonomy to the dictates of communal supervision. Individuals began to resist those community and family demands that might block their personal choices or their pursuit of material gain. Public officials were increasingly reluctant to curb generation or gender rebellions with the weapons of community authority.[6]

The gradual disintegration of the colonial ideal of the family left confusion and conflict in its wake. A process of redefinition began that reached its critical stages in the post-Revolutionary era. Led by middle-class households, families began to shed their public, multifunctional forms and stand apart in an increasingly segregated, private realm of society.

A series of interconnected changes marked the crucial transition of the family from a public to a private institution. The economic moorings of the household shifted from production toward consumption. Generational influences on family formation declined. New fertility patterns resulted in declining family size. A new domestic egalitarianism emerged to challenge patriarchy. Other alterations included companionate marital practices and contractual notions of spousal relations, an elevation of childhood and motherhood to favored status within the home, an emphasis on domestic intimacy as a counterweight to marketplace competition, and a more clearly defined use of private property as the major source of domestic autonomy.

A fundamental dichotomy flowed from these developments. The family and the outside world came to be viewed as separate entities, often pictured as bitter adversaries. Privatization spurred a new concept of the family: one in which the nation's households occupied a narrower place within secular society, but one in which heightened emotional and affective bonds and socialization duties were seen by almost all Americans as crucial to national well-being.[7]

The "republican family" is the label that identifies most precisely the context and content of the changes that began to alter American households in the 1780s and 1790s and into the next century. This label suggests both the particular American variant of a larger transformation of Western European family life and the persistent influence of its post-Revolutionary origins. As historian John Kasson has argued in his study of nineteenth-century technological values: "Republican ideology led finally beyond politics to a major coalescence and reorientation of American culture. The Revolutionary spirit charged virtually every aspect of life."[8]

Under the sway of republican theory and culture, the home and the polity displayed some striking similarities. These included a deep aversion to unaccountable authority and unchecked governmental activism, the equation of property rights with independence, a commitment to self-government, a belief that individual virtue could prevent the abuse of power, and a tendency to posit human relations in contractual terms that highlighted voluntary consent, reciprocal duties, and the possibility of dissolution. Most important, the American family, like the republican polity, suffered from the uncertainties of sovereignty and from the pressures of democratization and marketplace values unleashed by the Revolution's egalitarian and laissez faire ideology. The intimate relationship between political and family change is evident in the readiness of revolutionaries like Tom Paine to describe the crisis with Britain as a domestic quarrel. Indeed, American revolutionary ideology contained a fierce antipatriarchal strain.[9]

Shared post-Revolutionary origins made the period the formative era of both the republican family and the state. In a perceptive analysis of revolutionary rhetoric, literary analyst Jay Fliegelman suggests the consequences of that temporal connection: "The American revolution against patriarchal authority in the second half of the eighteenth century provided the paradigm by which Americans for the next two hundred years would understand and set forth the claims of both individual and national independence."[10] For the family, and especially for its law, republicanism was both a founding creed and a continuing frame of reference.

The advent of the republican family altered the place of each household member in society and law. Male authority remained supreme throughout the nineteenth century. Yet its scope narrowed as a result of challenges that grew more intense during the century. Egalitarianism encouraged the decline of deference to all social superiors, even patriarchs. Republican political ideology's reinforcement of individual worth and personal identity, the evangelical emphasis on equality before God, and the individual competitiveness and acquisitiveness unleashed by market capitalism fueled demands for greater autonomy in all relations, even domestic ones. A new respect for household dependents, and the inclination to seek individual identity and fulfillment in the home rather than the combative marketplace, also sparked challenges to traditional domestic authority. Self-government intensified intimate relations and encouraged greater reciprocity. Finally, affection began to replace status as the cement of domestic bonds.

From these profound developments came the creation of more explicit roles and responsibilities within republican households. Marriage came to be depicted in contractual terms and marital roles to fall into more clearly defined sexual spheres. As the home broke free from the world of work, the masculine responsibility for family support became more concrete while male household involvement atrophied. Domesticity became the stellar female attribute, the newly isolated home a woman's more exclusive domain.

By charging homes with the vital responsibility of molding the private virtue necessary for republicanism to flourish, the new nation greatly enhanced the importance of women's family duties. Studying the experiences of women in the Revolutionary era led historian Mary Beth Norton to conclude that the "revolutionaries' one unassailable assumption was that the United States could survive only if its citizens displayed virtue in both public and private life." At times "it even seemed as though republican theorists believed that the fate of the republic rested squarely, perhaps solely, on the shoulders of its womenfolk." Men were to complement women by being good providers, loyal companions, and effective if distant fathers. The segregation of male and female domestic responsibilities is evident in the mid-nineteenth-century complaint of women's rights advocate Samuel May:

> The terms in which the two sexes are generally spoken of seem to imply that men must of course go forth, take part in the collisions of political party, pecuniary interest, or local concernment; get themselves care worn, perplexed, irritated, soured, angry; while women are to stay at home, and prepare themselves with all the blandishments of maternal, sisterly, conjugal, or filial affection, to soothe our irritated tempers, mollify the bruises we have received in our conflicts with other men; and so prepare us to strive with renewed resolution, and bruise or get bruised again.[11]

A new perception of childhood also contributed to the post-Revolutionary redefinition of the home. Enlightenment ideas about human development and the influence of environment, affectionate ideas of child rearing, and the character of the new republican order transformed the perception of the young. Fliegelman in fact suggests that the "new parenting and the constitutional government were intimately related."[12]

During the nineteenth century, children came to be seen more explicitly than ever as vulnerable, malleable charges with a special innocence and with particular needs, talents, and characters. Consequently, authoritarian child rearing and hierarchical relations succumbed to greater permissiveness, intimacy, and character building. As with spousal relations, in the republican household parents and children became bound together by a new egalitarianism and by affection. Though other institutions such as the common school and the church shared its duties, molding the nation's young into virtuous republicans and competent burghers became more clearly the primary responsibility of the family. As the countless child-rearing manuals of the day warned, youthful minds and bodies would develop properly only in a special, sheltered home under the watchful guidance of concerned, informed parents. The widely held conceit that America represented the future and that youth must be reared successfully to fulfill the republic's manifest destiny magnified the significance of child rearing. In the child-centered homes that began to sprout within the nation's middle class, the parent-child relation, especially the newly created mother-child bond, became an all-important nexus.[13]

New sentiments about childhood and gender destroyed the mix of community and household that was central to the colonial family ideal. Its nineteenth-century republican replacement rested on clearly defined spheres and reciprocal obligations. By the first decades of the century, family had come to mean a separate social unit consisting of a worldly man, homebound woman, and their offspring. Most important, this republican household presented a facade of organic unity which masked the actual character of the family as a group of individuals each with his or her specialized roles and duties. The contrast between image and reality in nineteenth-century family life gave rise to some of the most dramatic and far-reaching legal controversies over the home.[14]

Divided by class, region, race, gender, and temporal variations in the rate of change, the republic experienced sharp and continuous conflicts generated by these family changes. But this bitter dissension should not cloud the central change in American homes: the emergence of the republican ideal of the family.

A middle-class creation, the republican family dominated household ideology and practice in an increasingly bourgeois nation. Historian Robert Griswold discovered its influence in his recent study of California divorce litigation from 1850 to 1890: "These records reveal that the companionate ideal did, indeed, affect the lives of rural men and women from all social classes. The legal documents and witness testimony make it clear that men and women from all social classes conceived of family relations in affective terms, placed a premium on emotional fulfillment in the family, considered women's opinions and contributions worthy of respect and consideration, emphasized male kindness and accommodation, and assumed that children were special members of the household in need of love and affection."[15] In other words, the reorganized family affected every class, region, and institution.

The Beginning of the "Crisis of the Family"

A conspicuous and persistent public obsession with the well-being of the American household was one of the most significant products of the republican family. "[I]f concern for the family was not new in the antebellum period," historian Ronald Walters surmises, "it nonetheless appeared from the mid-1820s onward in new guises and with striking variety, suddenness, and intensity." The family came to be a litmus test of social and economic change, he suggests, because it "and the relationships usually comprehended within it, were almost uniformly presented as vehicles of social and individual salvation." As early as 1791 David Ramsey warned that the nation would be in jeopardy if its families failed to subscribe to "industry, frugality, temperance, moderation, and the whole lovely train of republican virtues."[16]

By 1837 legal commentator David Hoffman spoke of "a reciprocal action and reaction constantly, though almost invisibly, existent between government and our firesides; and, if insubordination reigns in either, it is very certain, in a short time, to obtain in both."[17] A gnawing fear that such indeed was the case, propelled legions of self-appointed monitors of the hearth into action. Their surveillance of domestic affairs and increasingly apprehensive reports on the state of the family constantly thrust the household and its governance into the public and professional consciousness. By the 1840s they began to speak of a "crisis of the family" and to become a major force in the creation of laws to govern the new home.

Family reformers were a diverse lot. Their ranks included genteel reformers, social-purity advocates, clerical crusaders, philanthropic volunteers, social scientists, feminists, medical and legal professionals, and a host of others. The most determined of these united to save the republican family. Unable to comprehend fully the changes befalling a society in the midst of industrialization and sectional strife, these family savers often mistook effect for cause and treated deviations from the republican ideal as themselves sources of social and economic disruption. The progenitors of an increasingly varied and sophisticated line of reformers that would stretch well into the twentieth century, family savers sought to protect the home and thus the republic by turning the main tenets of the republican family ideal into a set of unbreakable commands. As historian William O'Neill has pointed out, by the "middle of the nineteenth century, Anglo-American society had formulated a moral code based on three related principles—the permanency of marriage, the sacredness of the home, and the dependence of civilized life upon the family. None of these ideas were new, but they did not become universally accepted until the Victorian era, when they quickly received such general support that men found it impossible to believe that customs had ever been otherwise."[18]

By mid-century, family critics warned that divorce and desertion, male licentiousness, and women's rights threatened the very fabric of the republic. Each departure from orthodoxy, they claimed, undermined needed domestic divisions of labor, sexual restraints, paternal authority, and household economic responsibilities. Though they often differed on tactics and goals, the growing corps of family savers united to decry excesses in the nation's household affairs. An overemphasis on personal welfare and private satisfaction was, they held, a menace to social cohesion because it fostered excessive individualism and self-indulgence. Such charges expressed a declining faith in contractualism and laissez faire economics as a guide to social relations. They forced a reevaluation of the role of public authority in household affairs.

In response came increasingly pessimistic calls for the elimination of family diversity and the imposition of orthodox republican ideals on all households. These demands were issued by voluntary associations like the New York Moral Reform Society, founded in 1834 to combat prostitution and the double standard; professional organizations such as the American Medical Association, which launched a campaign against abortion in the 1850s; and tracts on family life written by reformers like mid-century health advocate Dio Lewis. After the 1840s, then, pessimism and a growing demand for coercive legislation began to supercede an earlier toleration for deviant family practices as a romantic faith in human perfection and transcendent values faded. The shift in sentiment and reform strategy resulted in constant struggles over the family. These conflicts were not so much cyclical movements of reform and reaction as they were evidence of the everpresent concern for the state of the home that took a variety of expression.

The Civil War and its destructive impact on romantic reform, the advent of industrial capitalism and its attendant class and occupational struggles, and the twin forces of rapid urbanization and massive immigration intensified these fears. They added new strains to family life and new variety to family forms. Family savers of all stripes spoke of a dire urgency about the home, which slowly engulfed public debate over domestic relations for the remainder of the century.

The evolving character of family reform was evident in the program of action adopted by the newly formed American Social Science Association in 1865. Created by reform-minded men and women, primarily Republicans and liberal protestants, and often quite wealthy, the organization tackled a variety of family issues from women's domestic rights and juvenile justice to hygienic conditions and education. Its founding, historian William Leach argues in a recent assessment of mid-century feminism, "marked the movement of reform away from the romantic, individualistic, and laissez faire dispositions of the antebellum period and toward a new institutional, ameliorative reformism."[19]

This reformist search for order compelled family reformers to try and find a stable, broadly acceptable definition of the public interest in private households. Their efforts were part of what historian John Higham has called the mid-century transition from "boundlessness to consolidation."[20]

Founding a Republican Legal Order

As family practices and sentiments toward the home changed in post-Revolutionary America, the traditional Anglo-American system of domestic governance slowly unraveled. The republican family encouraged modifications in almost all of the doctrines, rules, and statutes that dealt with the household and its members. Yet alterations within the legal order itself proved quite as significant as family change in determining the nature and extent of those revisions. Legal practices designed for a relatively stable, homogeneous agrarian society were altered in the bustling, bourgeois nineteenth-century nation. That was as true for domestic relations as for commerce or crime. Consequently a distinctive American family law had its origins not only in a new household ideal but also in a refashioned legal order.

Colonial Americans had devised a legal system marked by overlapping and conflicting jurisdictions, mixed legislative, judicial, and administrative functions, lay officialdom, and localized authority resting in county courts or town meetings. Religious and mercantilist influences and the persistence of an antilegalism ensured that the law often placed communal needs over individual desires, cooperation over competition in market and social relations. Colonial law contained an uncertain and constantly changing blend of transplanted English practices and indigenous statutory and judicial deviations. Magistrates wove these into an informal pattern of legal, institutional, and customary practices. Few printed codes existed alongside the smattering of English legal texts, reports, and locally recorded cases. A small professional bar did begin to develop in the eighteenth century, but only after the decline of earlier lay opposition and the rise of royal legal patronage and more complex market transactions.

By the mid-eighteenth century, the more mature colonies, with their intricate social and economic relations, had produced hierarchical and differentiated legal systems and substantial numbers of attorneys. In some colonies, a process of Anglicization began in which the legal system tried to replicate England's. Even so, jurisdictional lines remained blurred, especially the appellate functions of courts and legislatures. Yet the informal, uncertain, community-centered priorities of the colonial legal system became increasingly unacceptable to the users of the law. What historian Gordon Wood has characterized as the "confusion and disorder of colonial law," generated distrust and conflicts it could not contain. But no systematic presentation of provincial law existed that could be generalized into a common legal culture.[21]

The Revolutionary generation resolved many of these difficulties by fundamentally transforming the place of the law in America. After years of legal debate and conflict, both Federalist attempts to create an elite-run legal system and radical Republican attempts to create a decentralized law had failed. They were cast aside in favor of what historian Richard Ellis has called "moderate republican" solutions, which first emerged in state constitutions and then the federal Constitution of 1787. Among its tenets were bicameral legislatures, institutional checks and balances, popular sovereignty, federalism, and an independent judiciary. These were designed to mute popular power, constrain governmental activism, and protect private rights, particularly property rights. Concurrent powers remained, but new constitutional arrangements promoted differentiation, specialization, and hierarchical lines of political authority.[22]

The judiciary and the bar benefitted immensely from the restructured polity. The courts' new status as an independent branch of government, the tacitly accepted power of judicial review, the wide degree of judicial freedom sanctioned by federalism, and the emergence of a franker style of appellate opinion writing, combined to give the post-Revolutionary common-law judges policy-making powers once denied the colonial bench and still withheld from their English brethren. Judicial power further grew as early nineteenth-century legislatures passed statutes that transferred authority over what had been private legislation such as corporate charters and divorces to individuals and the courts, professionals dedicated to common-law supremacy ousted lay judges, and the bench wrested control of trials from juries.

Following the lead of Alexander Hamilton, John Marshall, and other advocates of judicial curbs on popular authority, state and federal judges began to enlarge their jurisdiction. They did so through what legal theorist Karl Llewellyn termed the "grand style" of appellate reasoning. Judges took the lead in adapting the received tradition of economic and social governance to republican realities. The bench developed a clearer conception of the common law as an instrument for shaping economic and social policy. Colonial judges and politicians had distinguished between statutory law, which they held to be merely human constructions and thus transitory, and judicial doctrines, which they considered to be expressions of immutable legal principles. Those views fostered a distinction between making and declaring law that relied on legislation as the main response to changed conditions, and militated against judicial rule making. Post-Revolutionary lawyers blurred these distinctions by adopting positivist views that saw the common law primarily as a judicially forged instrument. As legal historian Morton Horwitz explains: "Law was no longer conceived of as an eternal set of principles expressed in custom and derived from natural law. Nor was it regarded primarily as a body of rules designed to achieve justice only in the individual case." Instead, he suggests, "judges came to think of the common law as equally responsible with legislation for governing society and promoting socially desirable conduct. The repeated early nineteenth century emphasis on law as an instrument of policy encouraged judges to formulate legal doctrines with the self-conscious goals of bringing about social change."[23]

Despite persistent complaints about the undemocratic and arbitrary nature of judicial power, the emergence and popular acceptance of legal instrumentalism profoundly affected political authority in nineteenth-century America. In particular, it helped to legitimize litigation as the society's primary method of settling disputes. During the first part of the century, according to legal historian Mark DeWolfe Howe, "the legislative responsibility of lawyers and judges for establishing a rule of law was far more apparent than it was in later years. It was clear to laymen as it was to lawyers that the nature of American institutions, whether economic, social, or political, was largely to be determined by judges. In such a period questions of private law were seen and considered as questions of social policy."[24] Generally unhampered by weak state executives and part-time legislators, judges at all levels of government became the most active agents of the state. They took the lead in devising policies governing social and economic life from railroads to families.

The judiciary encouraged the shift of policy making from public officials to private entrepreneurs and individuals. Judges assumed that facilitating individual accomplishment would add to the general good and the republican assertion of equal political and economic abilities. This vision of judicial responsibility was part of a larger political orientation of the era toward laissez faire economics and liberal politics. It rested on a division of the legal world into public and private spheres, which identified private will with the natural order and state action as artificial intervention. As one of its sages, Ralph Waldo Emerson, put it: "[T]endencies of the times favor the idea of self-government, and leave the individual, for all the code, to the rewards and penalties of his own constitution, which work with more energy than we believe whilst we depend on artificial restraint."[25]

Adapting colonial and English legal practices to the republican order proved to be one of the most exacting and critical tasks delegated to the bench in the refashioned polity. "Now that we have no negatives of Councils, Governors, and Kings to restrain us from doing right," Thomas Jefferson said of post-Revolutionary law reform, it is possible for the whole legal system to be "revised, adapted to our republican forms of government, and . . . corrected in all its parts, with a single eye to reason, and the good of those for whose government it was framed." Despite such pronouncements, Jefferson and others failed in their efforts to limit judicial discretion and banish what they considered to be the aristocratic common law. The already considerable weight of the nation's legal tradition guaranteed the continued usefulness of much of its English and colonial legal heritage. Each state enacted statutes that charged the legislature and the courts with selectively placing older rules and policies in proper republican codes and decisions. Toward a similar end, Virginian St. George Tucker issued the first of many Americanized versions of Blackstone's *Commentaries*. His, like the others, sought to reshape that digest to take account of American statutory and common-law deviations as well as the "newly adopted principles of republican government." American law thus became a mixture of English, colonial, and post-Revolutionary statutes and decisions.[26]

The demands of the rising republican legal order for unity and rationality also undermined an oral legal tradition and fostered the birth of an indigenous legal literature. Printed statutes, published case reports, and legal treatises and magazines proliferated after the 1790s. Connecticut lawyer Ephraim Kirby issued the first volume of American judicial reports in 1789. Other states and the federal circuits rapidly followed his lead, Rhode Island being the last to do so in 1847. These reports gave rapidly expanding local bars access to the decisions of their own and other states. Their availability sped the use of shared precedents and common policies and thus helped extend the policy-making powers of the appellate bench and the bar beyond jurisdictional boundaries.

Appellate reports by themselves could not, however, alleviate the endemic variations in the American legal order spawned by federalism, regional differences, and conflicting decisions and interests. Generations of treatise writers inspired by Blackstone took to the field to struggle against this legal chaos. Along with the *Commentaries*, which remained a primary source of law, treatises attempted to reduce judicial decisions to comprehensible sets of principles based on uniform standards of common-law reasoning and national sets of legal values. Treatises ranged from specialized tomes like Zephaniah Swift's 1810 digest of evidence to more general works in the Blackstonian mold. With the publication between 1826 and 1830 of James Kent's *Commentaries on American Law*, early nineteenth-century law writing reached its peak. American lawyers turned to this literature to locate solutions to cases brought them by clients; judges looked to it to resolve those disputes in as uniform a manner as they could. By organizing the maze of reports, the treatises helped create a judicially dominated national legal culture.[27]

Like the legal order itself, American legal literature had become by mid-century a dense thicket of minute topics described in majestic detail. The treatises expressed a larger scholarly concern with systemization. Treatise writers strove to rationalize the diffuse American legal culture and protect the policy-making prerogatives of the bench and bar by creating national doctrines. To do so they selectively arranged cases that conformed to their professional biases, commercial preferences, social values, and political commitments and often ignored regional differences and policy conflicts. Their goals at times compelled them to exaggerate the uniformity of American law.

More significantly, to forestall legislative tinkering with the common law, and to quiet popular resistance to some of its effects, these authors consistently depicted the law not as a set of policy choices but rather as an apolitical, scientific body of rules. In a profusion of detailed, practical texts that staked out the boundaries of their profession, they projected an image of the law as self-contained, autonomous, and free of class and other biases. These writers were not theoreticians so much as defenders and definers of professional rights, duties, and techniques. They helped create a common national legal culture. The treatises also buttressed the policy-making powers of the bench and bar by clothing judicial decisions in complex forms and language that concealed their capacity for arbitrariness. Attorneys Amasa Parker and Charles Baldwin summarized these lawyerly interests in their preface to the third edition of Tapping Reeve's *Law of Baron and Femme* (1816), the first American volume on domestic relations. After minimizing the impact of legislation on family law, they went on to insist that the cases "show great unanimity among the different courts, which could have been obtained only by a proper respect for the judicial decisions of sister states, and a sincere desire to build up a system of American law, uniform and harmonious as well as just and beneficent."[28]

Legal rules and doctrines codified in statutes, handed down in judicial decisions, and developed in legal treatises became crucial parts of a nineteenth-century political environment in which, as legal historian Lawrence Friedman has observed, "the official legal system began to penetrate deeper into society."[29] The transformed American legal order produced the laws that governed the republican family.

Creating a Republican Concept of Domestic Relations

Converging family and legal changes made the late eighteenth and early nineteenth centuries the formative era of American domestic-relations law. The timing was crucial. Family law came to rest on a common-law view of individual behavior that had a permanent impact on its doctrines and procedures. Historian John R. Aiken has described that notion as an image of "self-interest, of pressing one's legal rights against any individual or against society, *in personam* and *in rem*, regardless of the morality of one's cause. It is an image of a man not bound by any ethical considerations, but only law."[30] That legalistic standard of conduct freed individuals from communal supervision and allowed them—or perhaps compelled them—to rise or fall on their own actions. Its gradual diffusion through the society illustrates the law's republican roots and the period's glorification of the self-made man and individualistic tenets like risk taking, rational calculation, and strict internal discipline.

As a foundation for domestic governance, common-law thinking undermined traditionalism and increased the pressure for a more individualistic, private family law. It both ratified ongoing changes and initiated new ones. The nature of this reorientation is visible in Chancellor James Kent's description of the republican rejection of the old English policy of entailing land: "Entailments are necessary in monarchical governments, as a protection to the power and influence of the landed aristocracy; but such a policy has no application to republican establishments, where wealth does not form a permanent distinction, and under which every individual of every family has his equal rights, and is equally invited by the genius of the institutions, to depend upon his own merit and exertions."[31]

Once traditional family governance lost its privileged position, only the newly created republican state had the authority and legitimacy to oversee domestic relations. Yet turning to the state proved difficult for a society that enshrined individual and family autonomy and severely circumscribed the formal power of social sanctions and collective authority. The result was confusion and uncertainty over just how thoroughly to renovate the law.

The federal government played a minor role in answering that question. In the nineteenth century, the states assumed the task of forging a republican code of family governance.[32] That code emerged out of the solutions to household disputes ranging from inheritance claims and creditor demands to custody fights and nuptial challenges. These solutions came from courtrooms and legislative chambers from Maine to Florida and Ohio as well as from the pages of treatises like Reeve's *Law of Baron and Femme*. Family law's distinctiveness lay in new legal conceptions of matrimony and of parenthood. Changing definitions of these two fundamental elements of family law during the century provide an initial overview of the development of an American domestic-relations law.

Making Matrimony a Private Contract

Marriage law guarded the entrance to the republican household. In the 1790s Connecticut Supreme Court Reporter Jesse Root voiced the central assumptions of nuptial law when he declared that the idea that "one man should be joined to one woman in a constant society of cohabiting together, is agreeable to the order of nature, is necessary for the propagation of their offspring, and to render clear and certain the right of succession."[33] Root offered a lawyerly version of the popular belief that stable marriages performed critical roles in the society by producing healthy children, curbing sexual passions, and protecting private accumulation.

Faith in those assumptions never wavered. In 1888 the United States Supreme Court held out marriage as the "foundation of the family and society, without which there would be neither civilization nor progress."[34] Yet neither the law nor its assumptions remained static; on the contrary, they underwent constant revision in the effort to ensure that matrimony met its responsibilities.

The modification of nuptial law began because post-Revolutionary Americans repudiated the traditional conviction that compelling brides and grooms to submit to extensive community and family supervision best protected society. Ensuing uncertainty over just how tightly to regulate courtship and wedlock intensified the inquiry over the legal nature of matrimony begun in the New World by the Puritans. Judges, legislators, and law writers, the prime authors of domestic-relations law, readily accepted the need to specify public nuptial responsibilities. But they found it exceedingly difficult to formulate a durable allocation of public and private nuptial rights. The problems facing them in devising a broadly acceptable legal definition of matrimony related to the central difficulty of nineteenth-century marriage law: determining the boundaries between private nuptial rights and the state's marital responsibilities. Variations in legal definitions during the period reveal many of the broad ideas and interests that determined the way in which marriage was placed in a distinct American family law.

The definition of marriage as a private civil contract had deep roots in English legal tradition and colonial practice. The legacy of colonial legislation and custom, with its blend of Calvinism, Anglicanism, and English ecclesiastical law, remained important because it constituted the major statutory and judicial record for nineteenth-century lawyers. Though differing in many essentials, these sources emphasized the secular, contractual nature of matrimony while at the same time endorsing strict public nuptial vigilance. In most of the colonies communal had replaced ecclesiastical control, and the mutuality of the matrimonial pact was accepted. But while the effectiveness of community supervision waned with time, colonial law, like its English parent, highlighted the civil or public nature of the marriage pact.[35]

Post-Revolutionary views of matrimony evolved from, and reacted against, this heritage. Though the law continued to portray marriage as a civil contract, in a vital transition the accent shifted from the first word to the second. The new emphasis was on the consensual nature of marriage. It also reflected the broader use of contract as the central metaphor for social and economic relations in early nineteenth-century America. This occurred as part of the revolutionary change marked by "the gradual displacement of patriarchalism by contractualism." Contractualism gained strength from the same forces that were eroding the hierarchical conception of society. Rather than viewing the body politic as an amalgam of interdependent, status-defined groups, contract ideology stemmed from a world view whose lode star was the untrammeled autonomy of the individual will. Relations of all kinds were to be governed by the intentions, not the ascribed status, of their makers. The English philosopher Sir Henry Maine characterized this transition as the "movement from status to contract."[36]

In domestic relations, contractualism also was sustained by the new prominence given affection and reciprocity in family life. "If one word could be used to epitomize the republican conception of matrimony," historian Norton concluded, "that word would be 'mutual.'" A self-described "Matrimonial Republican" defined that new perception in the 1792 *Lady's Magazine*. She objected to the word "obey in the marriage service because it is a general word, without limitations or definitions." Instead, the writer insisted that the "obedience between man and wife, I conceive, is, or ought to be, mutual. Marriage ought never to be considered as a contract between a superior and inferior, but a reciprocal union of interests, an implied partnership of interests, where all differences are accommodated by conference; and decision admits of no retrospect."[37]

The contractual emphasis in marriage law rested on the one support common to all compacts, the consent of the parties. It also defined freedom in terms of resistance to state edicts and separated private from public spheres of action by consecrating the former and belittling the latter.

Nineteenth-century contract law assumed a place of its own in the legal order. An older, family-oriented contract law designed more to facilitate exchange than to allocate resources succumbed to laissez faire economics and liberal politics. A new individualistic and developmental idea of social protection and economic incentives led to the "will theory of contracts." The declared intentions of the parties would govern all bargains. The equities of a pact were left to the dictates of private conscience and calculation. The will theory assumed that all parties bargained equally and that the state had a circumscribed role in private agreements.

A will theory of marriage pacts came to the fore in post-Revolutionary America as well. It subjected matrimonial pledges and vows to a domestic relations variant of an imperialistic contract law.[38]

Religious jurisdiction, particularly the Roman Catholic belief in marriage as a sacrament, was the *bete noire* of those espousing the contractual foundation of matrimony. In 1816, Connecticut judge Tapping Reeve, a deist and ardent Federalist, used his volume on domestic relations to make clear the distinction between the two views: "There is nothing in the nature of a marriage contract that is more sacred than that of other contracts, that requires the interposition of a person in holy orders, or that it should be solemnized in a church. Every idea of this kind, entertained by any person, has arisen solely from the usurpation of the Church of Rome on the rights of the civilian."[39] Though in this way it was part of late eighteenth and early nineteenth-century disestablishment of religion, the contractual emphasis in marriage law primarily represented post-Revolutionary America's emphasis on individual rights: in this case, the right to contract marriage freely.

Marital unions were increasingly defined as private compacts with public ramifications rather than social institutions with roles and duties fixed by the place of the family in a hierarchical social order. A free-market notion of courtship and marriage also suggests the rise of an early nineteenth-century determination to make the law of domestic relations an ally, not a competitor, in the creation of a society grounded as much as possible in the bourgeois ideal of unregulated private competition and individual choice. What is more, matrimonial contractualism reinforced common-law authority over marriage, and thus encouraged judges to define the legal boundaries of nuptials.

Even so, marriage was never conceived of as a purely consensual agreement, despite the stridency of those like Reeve who waxed eloquent about its contractual nature. The varied but determined resistance to voluntary divorce and repeated assertions of state nuptial responsibility acted as constant reminders of the limits of matrimonial contractualism. Marriage remained simply too important to be left entirely to the invisible hand of the nuptial marketplace. Rather, a recurrent tension between public and private nuptial responsibilities persisted. Lawyers and laypersons, haunted by a fear of marriage lapsing either into individual anarchy or state coercion, repeatedly struggled to balance the two.

Marriage Revision

Late in the antebellum era, amid rising alarm about social disorganization, fed in part by the emergence of an obsessive concern with the nation's households, United States Supreme Court Justice Joseph Story made those distinctions clear. In 1841 he termed matrimony a contract in "the common sense definition of the word," but insisted that it was as well "something more than a mere contract. It is rather to be deemed an institution of society founded upon the consent and contract of the parties, and in this view has some peculiarities of its nature, character, operation, and extent of obligation, different from what belongs to ordinary contracts." The determination to find legal expression for the uniqueness of the marital agreement reflected the later era's extensive interest in nuptial regulation.[40]

Joel Bishop, a Whiggish Massachusetts law writer, took the lead in revising post-Revolutionary definitions of matrimony to accommodate rising mid-century concerns. In his 1852 *Commentaries on the Law of Marriage and Divorce*, Bishop tried to impose order on what had become a maze of judge-made and statutory law governing wedlock by clarifying the legal place of matrimony.

Bishop's treatise, the first major synthesis in domestic-relations law since Reeve's pioneering 1816 volume, showed the strides that American common lawyers were making in devising a distinct republican notion of family governance. It also indicated the distance the legal profession had traveled since the early decades of the nineteenth century. Where Reeve's concern had been with the aftershocks of the Revolution, especially the need to Americanize the English common law, Bishop's treatise was a contribution to the mid- and late nineteenth-century effort of law writers to rationalize a now diffuse American legal culture and protect the powers of the bench and bar.

The differences between the two legal volumes were evident in each's style and orientation. Reeve not only expressed a greater faith in the ability and virtue of republican legislators than did his law-writing descendant, he assumed a more obvious political and reformist stance. Consistently asserting his own judgments on issues of marriage law ranging from "popish priests" to nuptial fraud, Reeve embraced the overt policy making of the post-Revolutionary era and defined his task in broad political terms.

Despite his fervent Whig beliefs and antislavery background, Bishop masked his views with professionalism. He avoided personal statements and presented the law as a logical system he was merely elucidating. Where Reeve had pondered what law ought to be, his successor simply claimed to be presenting it as it was. In an 1882 revision of his widely used treatise on criminal law, Bishop took pride in the assertion that he admitted "nothing purely theoretical" into his law books. Such a statement revealed his own deep faith in law as a science and the professionalism with which his craft had come to defend its powers. Indeed, Bishop defined the legal author's role in idealized judicial terms: "A textwriter, like a judge, should principally endeavor to ascertain what the law is, in distinction from what it should be." He also relied on scientific analogies to explain the autonomous nature of the legal process and thus eschewed the more conscious political orientation of his predecessor. "We should bear in mind that the law is not a conglomeration of discordant decisions and utterances from the bench," Bishop lectured in an 1891 revision of his marriage-law treatise, "but a system of reason and doctrine which, however evidenced by the determinations of the courts and the words of judges and text-writers, is a complete harmony within itself, independently of these externals and surrounding."[41]

Treatise writing seemed such a needed endeavor that Bishop gave up his private practice to pursue it full time. As a popular writer dependent on the sale of his books, Bishop's works offer a number of telling examples of family law's theoretical and practical elements.

Bishop charged that blurring the differences between marital and other pacts made for legal confusion and perpetuated a misreading of the law's basic principles. He insisted that the common law had always considered matrimony to be more than a mere commercial agreement. To classify it as simply a contract was, as he phrased it, "as great a practical inconvenience as to call a certain well-known engine used for propelling railroad cars 'a horse,' and then add, 'but it differs from other horses in several important particulars,' which particulars of dissimilitude must be specially explained. It would be more convenient to use at once the term locomotive." He lamented that true legal principle has been lost by sloppy use of the now ambiguous contract label.[42]

Marriage and Divorce blazed a path through the legal jungle by highlighting the relationship initiated by matrimony. Relying on an obscure Scottish ruling, Bishop refined the legal definition of marriage:

> The word marriage is used to signify either the act of entering into the marital condition, or the condition itself. In the latter and more frequent legal sense, it is a civil status, existing in one man and one woman, legally united for life, for those civil and social purposes which are founded in the distinction of sex. Its source is the law of nature, whence it has flowed into the municipal law of every civilized country, and into the general law of nations.

In Bishop's view the social duties of marriage circumscribed its contractual nature independent of the agreement that created it.[43]

By repeating and perfecting this definition of marriage in numerous editions of his highly influential treatise, Bishop dominated the professional perception of this vital ingredient of family law. Oliver Wendell Holmes, Jr., even revised Kent's *Commentaries* in 1873 to define matrimony as a status rather than solely as a contract. In 1889 eighteen states retained statutory language defining marriage as a civil contract; but, as an attorney in one of them acknowledged, although "the domestic relations law of . . . New York says that marriage shall continue to be a civil contract, the phrase is practically meaningless." He went on to explain that since "marriage is the foundation of the family and the origin of domestic relations, which are considered of greatest importance to civilization and social progress, it is deemed to be a social institution, a status, and not a civil contract." Bishop's authoritative mixture of status and contract informed judicial opinions, statutes, and tracts well into the next century, thus illustrating the potent influence of treatise formulations. It proved so appealing because the definition offered a means of balancing the individualistic orientation of contract with the public concerns implicit in the status element, a symmetry increasingly demanded in nineteenth-century America.[44]

Bishop's qualification of nuptial contractualism mirrored the general decline of contract as a defining legal metaphor over the course of the century. Originally a residual category of law, contract swelled early in the century under the sway of laissez faire ideas and practices. The situation changed markedly after mid-century as the types of legal conduct governed by contract began to dwindle. Contract's domain shrank through internal legal changes, especially an effort by judges and lawyers to substitute objective for subjective standards and thus to reduce the flexibility and policy-making appeal of contract. But the most important reductions came through the creation of specialized legal categories for labor relations, insurance, social welfare, and other legal activities formerly considered primarily contractual in nature. The loss of each subject compressed contract law. Its receding dominion signalled an eroding faith in its individualistic, antistatist doctrines.[45]

Bishop's exercise in nuptial definition suggests that nuptials too would be redefined and then disengaged from the general body of contract law. Like the others, it began to be perceived by many of its authors and users as a special contract, one that was more public than pure contractual dogma would sanction. Bishop's stress on status typified a later nineteenth-century modification of the post-Revolutionary faith that individual virtue, self-interest, and voluntary reform would protect the commonweal. Reliance on the state to define and protect the public interest in nuptials began to qualify that conviction. Making room for a larger public presence in nuptials followed from the view that matrimony was too vital to society to be left far beyond the regulatory reach of the state.

As mid-century Americans chipped away at the contractual foundation of marriage law, it became ever more clearly a part of the emerging specialized field of domestic relations. But the post-Revolutionary republican base of nuptial law was never fully demolished. Marriage law remained wedded to the assumptions that individual choice was the norm, state intervention was only a last resort in special situations, and that the judiciary was charged with mediating disputes along the public and private boundaries of the law.

Launching an Attack on Patriarchy

The emergence of the freely contracting, autonomous individual as the ideal actor in early nineteenth-century legal thought permeated all domestic relations, not just nuptials. As Sir Henry Maine pointed out in a central postulate to his general evolutionary theory, the individual was being "steadily substituted for the family as the unit of which civil laws take account."[46] That process could occur only by thoroughly dismantling the legal concept of the traditional family as a patriarchal preserve and replacing it with one of the household as a collection of distinct individuals. Yet the transition was never complete. Like the republican family that it governed, post-Revolutionary law continued to proclaim a commitment to an idealized vision of household unity even though its policies often encouraged domestic fragmentation. The development of separate legal identities within the republican family thus was the second major defining element of nineteenth-century family law.

Post-Revolutionary views of spousal obligations, parenthood, and childhood led to attacks on the central tenet of the traditional legal assumption of family governance: the unity of family interests and rights. Colonial law had conceived of the family as an organism that had the husband/father at its head and his wife and children in its lower reaches. The law assumed the interests of the family to be inseparable and best represented by its patriarch. Patriarchy, though, stood for more than mere paternal supremacy within the home. It was as well an organizing model for the state, based on the control of all major forms of economic and political power by white, male heads of households. Patriarchy allowed these men to determine the place of women, children, and other subordinates. It fostered a definition of political authority and legal rights as the exclusive prerogative of household magistrates.[47]

In the home, patriarchy rested on the twin poles of marital unity and filial dependence. Through them the law denied wives and children legal independence. Under the traditional English definition of marital unity, as explained by Blackstone and other legal theorists, married women found their rights melded into those of their husbands. As Swift presented the doctrine in his 1810 digest, by "marriage the husband acquires all the rights, and succeeds to all the civil disabilities of the wife. They become one person in contemplation of the law; the existence of the wife is merged with that of the husband, and he has control of her person and property." Wives thus had no right to own property, sue, be sued, contract, or even to obtain the custody or guardianship of their children. Only antenuptial equity settlements could limit their husbands' control. Children faced similar restrictions. The law treated them as assets of paternal estates in which fathers had vested interests. As dependent, subordinate beings, their services, earnings, and the like became the property of their paternal masters in exchange for life and maintenance. Reciprocal rights and duties, such as the paternal obligation of support, qualified patriarchal dominion; but little legal space existed for separate identities within the well-ordered home.[48]

The realities of provincial life pummeled the unitary ideal of the family. The legal rights of married women, especially when they acted as surrogates for their husbands, increased. The availability of divorce in some colonies and domestic interdependence encouraged by colonial life in all of them also enhanced women's rights by increasing the presence of wives in the legal system and placing household and personal relations on a more contractual basis. The elimination of primogeniture and entail in several colonies and the existence of what may have been a higher concern for child welfare in the new settlements than in much of the Old World also elevated the status of colonial sons and daughters.

Yet such deviations hardly made the colonial era a golden legal age for either wives or children. Each departure occurred within a legal framework that stressed communal control, paternal supremacy, and maternal and filial deference. Colonial law retained, albeit in diluted form, the magistracy of the husband/father over his little commonwealth.[49]

The post-Revolutionary transformation of family governance forced a gradual redefinition of spousal and filial relations. Republican family law began to rest on the assumption that the family was a self-regulating, autonomous institution composed of distinct members, each with his or her own legal rights and identity. The rise of active women's rights and child welfare crusaders early in the nineteenth century created further pressures for change. Alexis de Tocqueville was but one of many who found that "one consequence of democratic principles [was] the subversion of marital power," and noted the decline of deference in intergenerational relations.[50] And while Anglo-American law traditionally relied on the bonds of affection and blood to augment public surveillance of households, early nineteenth-century legal ideas with their strong elements of antistatism went much further by consecrating the separation of the republican family and the state.

Timothy Walker, an Eastern-born, Harvard-trained lawyer and legal educator who made his career in Cincinnati, explained the legal redefinition of spousal and parental relations in his 1837 *Introduction to American Law*. His treatise, which earned him the title of the "American Blackstone," advocated greater freedom for women and children. Walker endorsed the retreat of the family behind private walls: "In a word, parental authority and filial obedience are left, as they should be, to the law which nature has written upon the heart. In very recent times we may discover the doctrine of non-interference, by legislators, in domestic affairs." He rejoiced that society finally valued personal liberty and recognized that "the world was too much governed; that the law interfered too much in matters which did not concern the public." Walker conceded that some "degree of government we must have, to preserve social order." But he proclaimed that "the less we have of it the better, provided that individuals will keep themselves in order. This is the happiest condition of society, in which the operations of government are the least felt in private affairs." His view of family/state relations rested on faith in republican virtue and a common-law vision of domestic rights. He assumed that each family member could assert and defend his or her rights, and that the state should breach domestic privacy only upon compelling evidence of family breakdown.[51]

As Walker suggested, republican domestic relations rested on marked alterations in the legal definition of spousal and parental roles. Kent's *Commentaries* provide evidence of the changing legal orientation. Whereas Blackstone, and even Swift, had stressed the merging of married women's interests with that of their husbands, Kent proclaimed that a new and "Christian" era had begun to provide "equality and dignity" for women and had done so in a way flattering to "the female character."[52] Such sentiments gradually led to a new concept of the husband/ father as more of an appellate judge than a colonial patriarch. Breaking the family ideal into its component parts created separate legal spheres in the home, which paralleled the social and economic ones at the heart of the republican transformation of the household. Consequently, enlarged maternal and filial rights within those spheres encouraged modifications of the theory of paternal stewardship.

Patriarchy retained its legal primacy, but more and more in republican America it described the governance of the home and not of the larger polity, as the family ceased to be a model for all relations. The domesticated concept of patriarchy depended on the segregation of worldly male from home-bound female functions and a clear demarcation between childhood and adulthood. It distinguished between male authority to govern the household and female responsibility to maintain it and nurture its wards. These demarcations perpetuated patriarchy in republican society.[53]

Guarding Homes

Compartmentalizing the home and sequestering it from public life refined the republican concept of domestic governance. Most significant, it created the potential for a more direct relationship between individuals and the state than had been possible when the traditional patriarchal family acted as a buffer between the two. Yet changes in family life and the legal response to them also contributed to mid-century anxiety about the home. In their 1862 revision of Reeve's *Baron and Femme*, editors Parker and Baldwin noted that innovations were underway in the laws governing married women. They concluded that such "changes are still in progress, and for many years to come the law on the subject will no doubt be in a 'transition state.' The result will probably be an entire revolution in the law affecting the rights and liabilities of married women."[54]

Such a prospect proved disquieting to many Americans who looked to the family as an anchor of social stability and material incentive. As a result, by mid-century the legal problem posed by changing definitions of spousal and parental relations came to parallel those in matrimony: reconciling a commitment to private family governance with a rising conviction that the state must ensure that families faithfully performed their essential responsibilities. Repeated confrontations within the legal system over efforts to define the scope of state power and the limits of family rights added to the confusion within domestic relations. They forced a reevaluation much like the reassessment of matrimonial contractualism.[55]

Legal disorder prompted another writer to enter the fray over the definition of family law. James Schouler became the leading late nineteenth-century authority on the law of spousal and parental relations. A Massachusetts native reared in Cincinnati, Schouler had a long and varied career as a teacher, historian, lawyer, and legal author. The Harvard-educated lawyer's achievements included the presidency of the American Historical Association. Like his contemporary Joel Bishop, Schouler's legal treatises embraced diverse subjects from personal property and bailments to wills. He published the *Law of Domestic Relations*, the first comprehensive treatise on the subject, in 1870. As Horwitz has persuasively argued, the appearance of a treatise in a new field "is almost always an important clue to when a specific subject area has begun to crystallize."[56] Schouler asserted that "domestic relations" had become "the well-sanctioned title of that law which embraces" the topics of his volume. The publication of his synthesis almost twenty years after Bishop's seminal treatise on marriage and divorce suggests that spousal and parental relations posed greater analytical and policy problems than matrimony.[57]

Domestic Relations demonstrated that Schouler, like Bishop and other legal commentators, was a synthesizer and a firm proponent of legal science. He too tried to hammer his topic into order by expounding its basic principles. Captured by the scientific ideal that so heavily influenced the emerging social sciences, Schouler portrayed himself as a legal scientist whose duty was to "analyze, classify, and arrange; from a mass of discordant material to extract all that is useful, separating the good from the bad, rejecting whatever is obsolete, searching at all times for guiding principles; and, in fine, to emblazon that long list of judicial precedents through which our Anglo-Saxon freedom broadens slowly down."[58]

His treatise, which quite consciously aped scientific methods and searched for eternal, objective standards, contrasted significantly with the more pragmatic public-policy tomes of early nineteenth-century writers like Reeve and Walker. Much like Bishop, Schouler prided himself on his professionalism. Not only did such an approach differ from the obvious policy-making concerns of a writer like Walker who championed law reforms in his *Introduction to American Law*, it also demonstrated the narrowed audience of late nineteenth-century treatises. Schouler wrote only for lawyers and judges.

In *Domestic Relations*, Schouler chided Blackstone, Reeve, and Kent for plunging into the subject without offering suitable analytical foundations. Schouler applied the designation "domestic relations" to the legal domain of the family. By insisting on a special place for the subject in the legal culture, his treatise was typical of mid- and late nineteenth-century efforts to differentiate legal topics.

After locating a legal category for the family, Schouler described domestic relations as a special blend of natural and positive law. The powerful, innate moral obligations that arose from matrimony and child rearing instilled a strong desire to preserve the home. They ensured that "scarcely anyone grows up without some knowledge of the general principles of law applicable to these topics, and particularly of the rights and duties as concern the person rather than the property. For positive law but enforces the mandates of the law of nature, and develops rather than creates a system." But Schouler conceded less primacy to natural instincts than had commentators such as Walker. Once formed, he contended, public interest in family success overrode domestic rights. "To an unusual extent," he explained, "is the law of the family above and independent of the individual. Society provides the home; public policy fashions the system; and it remains for each one of us to place himself under rules which are, and must be, arbitrary." Schouler granted greater legitimacy to public interests in the family than most earlier authors and, in certain areas, than some of his contemporaries like Bishop as well. Yet his common law allegiance also nurtured a skeptical attitude toward legislative innovation, and compelled him often to champion the courts as the rightful forum for domestic governance and policy making. In this way his presentation of spousal and parental relations vindicated domestic autonomy and common-law governance, and yet found room for state action when households departed from the republican family ideal.[59]

Definitions of domestic relations like Schouler's document some cardinal assumptions of family law that emerged in the nineteenth century. Each family member had distinct legal interests and rights drawn from his or her individuality, and the judiciary had the primary duty of resolving conflicts between them. This concept of the family, and the broad judicial powers it encouraged, upset traditional family law. In the past the family had been perceived to be a community of interests governed by a publicly accountable patriarch. The displacement of that concept fostered a legal climate dominated by clashes over the proper allocation of private and public domestic authority.

As a result, in nineteenth-century America, family law became the chief instrument of the republican state for determining the legal responsibilities of family members. In a society that placed great reliance on the law for settling conflicts, fixing status, and protecting wealth and authority, domestic-relations law helped establish the boundaries within which families formed and lived. It did so by occupying a position on the border between the public and private spheres of American society. Slowly it became the most personal aspect of public law, the most public aspect of private law.

Yet the law dealt with selected elements of domestic life. Most families did not become entangled in the legal system; generally, only couples or households riven by death or disputes resorted to the law. Antebellum Ohio legal writer Edward Mansfield's observation on marriage law can be applied to the entire corpus of domestic relations; he reminded the readers of his 1845 book on women's legal rights that the nuptial code was "too narrow in jurisdiction and too imperfect in its knowledge, to determine, regulate, or constrain those internal affections upon which, at last, the whole harmony and efficacy of the marriage relation depends. Too many expect from law more than law can give."[60]

But those rising expectations produced a dynamic law of the family that played a prominent role in defining and enforcing household roles, duties, and rights. Each of its branches helped locate the place of the family in the new American republic. The laws devised to govern courtship, nuptials, childbirth, and child custody—all vital methods of family formation—chronicle the creation of that American law of domestic relations.

PART ONE

MATRIMONY
COURTSHIP, NUPTIALS, PROHIBITIONS

Marriage is in every view the most important institution of human society, it involves the most valued interests of every class; awakens the thoughts and engages the care of nearly every individual; and how it may be entered into, or how dissolved, or what is the collateral effect of a dissolution, is a matter of almost constant legal inquiry and litigation.

Joel P. Bishop,
Commentaries on the
Law of Marriage and Divorce (1852)

CHAPTER 2

BROKEN PROMISES
JUDGES AND THE LAW OF COURTSHIP

The legal governance of a family sometimes began before the family was actually formed. The breach of a promise to marry could thrust courtship into the legal arena. Welcomed at first as a needed protection for virtuous women and restraint for duplicitous men, the action acquired an unseemly reputation by the end of the nineteenth century. Its declining fortunes make courtship a useful issue to begin an examination of American family law.

The engagement to marry has been a continuous source of perplexity in Anglo-American law not only because it attaches liability to lovers' vows but because it does so in problematic fashion. From its modern beginnings in the seventeenth century, the breach-of-promise suit has persisted as a curious legal action, a peculiar combination of contract and tort. Its mixed parentage stems from the suit's dual purposes of policing courtship and compensating nuptial victims.

Post-Revolutionary judges wove the action into the fabric of American family law as part of their larger attempt to fashion a republican code of domestic relations. The vagaries of the suit over the course of the nineteenth century illustrate the intricacies of domestic governance and the difficulties of defending the common law's individualistic, marketplace methods against shifting public sentiments toward lovers and the law.

A Common Law for Republican Courtship

Legislators rarely intruded into courtship. The bench translated court-ship into a common-law activity within their contractual scheme of marriage. According to Connecticut judge and legal authority Zephaniah Swift, engagements were "so far countenanced by our law, that if either party refuses to fulfill an executory contract of marriage, an action will lie in favor of the injured party for the recovery of damages, and courts have sometimes given large damages in such cases." The law left indi-vidual suitors free to make their own marital choices. But once matrimo-nial pledges had been exchanged, they became legally binding and actionable contracts. Since, as dictated by common-law governance, lovers policed their own courtship, the legal system came to the aid of the jilted man or woman only upon his or her complaint. It was in this way that the nominally public judicial forum was used as a means of private dispute resolution. The private right of a rejected lover to seek damages thus appeared "as natural as to allow an action for the breach of a contract to purchase merchandise."[1] That placed courtship within the purview and prejudices of the nineteenth-century bench, a fateful de-velopment.

Post-Revolutionary American lawyers incorporated the suit into the emerging body of family law by relying on English forms developed in the sixteenth and seventeenth centuries. Ecclesiastical courts had held jurisdiction over marital agreements, but canon law granted no damages for nuptial breach (though until 1753 the court could theoretically com-pel a reluctant lover to fulfill his or her nuptial promise). The developing writ of assumpsit served as the legal device for transferring jurisdiction to the common-law courts. Under assumpsit the breach-of-promise suit took on a mixed character. Originally an action to recover damages for an injury, assumpsit blossomed in sixteenth-century England as a means of enforcing simple, unsealed contracts. Its coverage came to include agreements that, like marital pacts, ought to have been completed. At the same time assumpsit retained a tortious nature—premised on the presence of deceit—thus providing the rationale for damages above those of regular contracts.[2]

The unique legal blend of the suit reflected as well the slowly evolving view of marriage as a simple, private contract. Lovers were allowed to make their own matches, but the suit afforded a legal remedy when one party failed to live up to the bargain. In much the same way, commercial law granted compensation for breached mercantile agreements. Thus, the breach-of-promise suit shared the commercial orientation of contract law. Marriage, and the nuptial promises that initiated it, were considered property transactions by the law's main users, the aristocracy and gentry. Nuptials often concluded intricate family negotiations and complex property settlements commenced for dynastic as much as individual purposes. The suit protected those property transactions and emphasized the public nature of matrimony by making its inception a legally binding act. The common-law courts' determination to protect property rights prompted their acceptance of the suit.

After the breach-of-promise suit won a place in English law, the crown's North American colonies became a fertile ground for the action. Since most colonists thought of matrimony as a public contract, requiring compensation for its breach seemed reasonable. And, as in the mother country, nuptial pacts often closed arduous bargaining among the elite over property and other financial details. Colonial Massachusetts judge Samuel Sewall gloated in his diary over crafty successes in arranging his own and his children's nuptials. Equally important, the breach-of-promise suit compensated forsaken men and women. A Massachusetts tribunal ordered: "Joyce Bradwicke shall giue unto Alex: Becke the some of xx^s for promiseing him marriage wthout her ffrends consent, & now refuseing to pforme the same." In a society that treated matrimony as a public act and family enterprise, broken vows naturally incurred legal penalties. Consequently, "if consent were once given and sealed by a contract in due form, it could not be lightly withdrawn."[3]

In post-Revolutionary America this commercial, property-bound legal tradition of courtship supervision became the basis for a new judicial approach to jilted lovers. Breach-of-marriage-promise suits allowed the courts to promote republican notions of marriage and gender responsibilities. This occurred as part of the reevaluation of matrimony itself. As Jay Fliegelman suggests in his study of the era's antipatriarchalism, the question as to "whether marriage was a property transfer between father-in-law and suitor or a sacred contract between lovers was a very real one in eighteenth century America—one that reflected a larger debate as to whether property or personal rights were more sacred, as to whether the possession of the former or the exercise of the latter conferred upon men a more real independence."[4] The breach-of-promise suit was one product of that debate.

In *Wightman* v. *Coates* (1818), Massachusetts Chief Justice Isaac Parker ended any doubt as to the suit's legitimacy and desirability. After a long engagement, a frustrated Maria Wightman had charged Joshua Coates with refusing to consummate his marriage promise. When her reluctant beau denied ever asking for her hand in marriage, she countered with a public exhibition of love letters. Parker used the lovers' quarrel to reconstitute the breach-of-promise suit along republican lines.

He began by quashing challenges to the suit's legality. After citing a number of English precedents to demonstrate its unquestioned acceptance by common lawyers, Parker quieted everpresent Anglophobic concerns by insisting that the action comported with American common law as well. The Federalist jurist buttressed his opinion by noting two post-Revolutionary cases that had unquestionably presumed the legality of the suit, and his own experience in litigating breach cases as a lawyer and trial judge.

Parker did acknowledge that by early nineteenth-century standards many previous cases had far more to do with finance than romance. But he neatly engineered a reconstruction of the suit to reflect the growing significance that his fellow citizens placed on affection as the cement of nuptials, asserting that the "loss sustained in other respects—the wounded spirit, the unmerited disgrace, and the probable solitude, which would be the consequences of desertion after a long courtship— were considered to be as legitimate claims for pecuniary compensation as the loss of reputation by slander, or the wounded pride in slight assaults and batteries." The New England jurist's common-law reasoning cloaked a fundamental alteration in the suit's logic and role. His devaluation of the commercial aspects of the breach and stress on the emotional losses of dashed nuptials aligned the suit more closely with the private ideal of the family and its transformation of gender roles. "Indeed," Parker contended, "there is no country in which the relative situation of the sexes, and their joint influences on society, would render such a principle more useful or necessary."

After establishing the legal soundness of the suit, Parker vigorously defended the necessity of awarding compensation for the violation of an agreement upon which the "interest of all civilized countries so essentially depends." The seriousness of the individual and community interests involved in matrimony justified damages for jilted lovers:

> When the female is the injured party, there is generally more reason for a resort to the law than when the man is the sufferer. Both have a right of action, but the jury will discriminate and apportion the damages according to the injury sustained. A deserted female, whose prospects in life may be materially affected by the treachery of the man to whom she had plighted her vows, will always receive from a jury the attention which her situation requires; and it is not disreputable for one, who may have to mourn for years over lost prospects and broken vows, to seek such compensation, as the law can give her.

Parker added the significant observation that it was in "the public interest, that conduct tending to consign a virtuous woman to celibacy, should meet with punishment which may prevent it from becoming common." Believing that common-law litigation provided the most effective combination of penalties and incentives for supervising engagements, he then ruled in Wightman's favor.[5]

The Massachusetts decision included themes that would reverberate in American breach-of-promise cases throughout the century.[6] Though a similar interest in compensating the emotional suffering caused by failed nuptial hopes arose in Britain, one late nineteenth-century English critic of the suit consoled himself with the thought "that [such suits] never in this country reached that phenomenal state which they apparently attained in the United States."[7] The American breach-of-promise suit achieved that state precisely because it echoed the central biases, concerns, and strategies of those who sought to govern republican families.[8]

Wightman v. *Coates* reveals how the post-Revolutionary judiciary used private law disputes to shape domestic relations policy. Breach-of-promise suits offered judges an opportunity to promote a free-market view of matrimony by giving them a common-law means of punishing nuptial transgressors. The action also permitted the courts to pursue a larger objective, promoting prudent legal behavior by creating special rules that affirmed the responsibility of every individual to fulfill voluntarily assumed responsibilities. They used the threat of judicially imposed punishment to deter the careless and the reckless. Judges could turn disputes into mediums for policy edicts because members of the bench like Parker repeatedly and consistently drafted opinions that went beyond the point at hand and issued expansive declarations touching on critical questions of domestic governance. In that manner, a New Jersey judge in 1797 summarized post-Revolutionary attitudes toward male suitors: "Let them be cautious in making no promises, except such as they intend to perform, or for the nonperformance of which they shall be liable to assign a sufficient reason, and they will be perfectly safe."[9]

Equally significant, the decision in the *Wightman* case showed how judges translated the period's assumptions about gender into binding legal rules. In post-Revolutionary America breach-of-promise suits became female actions. With its blend of contractual entrance and tortious exit, the suit elicited judicial and popular approval as an appropriate means of assuaging an injured woman's feelings within a privatized family law. A woman's right—or perhaps better put, a woman's need—to marry became the suit's primary social justification in a society that trumpeted marriage and motherhood as the most appropriate feminine vocations. In 1846 the Alabama Supreme Court asserted without fear of contradiction: "By strict rule the action is common to either sex, though in our country, a just regard to public morals has long since confined the action alone to the female sufferer."[10]

At a time when observers like Tocqueville marveled at the freedom given courting couples, nuptial liberty led to the judicial conclusion that the more independent, worldly male incurred greater legal liabilities while the politically and economically circumscribed female's liability declined. When her other male protectors left the field, judges stepped in to prevent female victimization. The revamped breach suit illustrates not only the pervasive influence of contractual ideology and romantic love on domestic relations, but more directly a new judicial recognition of the gap between the law's theoretical assumption of contracting equality between men and women and the reality of feminine powerlessness. As judges reassessed the place of women in the law, they began to view women as a dependent class with particular claims on the conscience of the bench and a special set of rights independent of either property ownership or male prerogatives. Such judicial reasoning meant that the will theory of contract was a peculiarly male concept, one that was less binding on women who entered agreements than men. This partial capacity of women was a continuing and significant feature of family law. But it took a variety of forms. Parker, assuming the cloak of feminine defender, succinctly described its meaning in breach-of-promise cases: "the delicacy of the sex, which happily in this country gives man so much advantage over women, in the intercourse which leads to matrimonial engagements, requires for its protection and continuance the aid of the laws."[11]

Lastly, Parker's reformulation of the breach-of-promise suit responded to post-Revolutionary judgments about marriage, especially the now triumphant ideal of romantic love. In 1802 a young Massachusetts woman happily declared that marriage could be a "galling chain. Souls must be kindred to make the bond silken. All others I call unions of *hands*, not *hearts*. I rejoice that the knot which binds me was not tied with my mercenary feeling and that my heart is not under the same subjection as my hand."[12] As affection and emotional commitment came to be seen as the sources, not the product of matrimony, traditional arranged marriages gave way to "sexual relationships based largely on the free choice of those involved; and . . . this kind of more personal and more romantic union steadily became more important."[13] But in staking out their claim over courtship, judges insisted that even personal relations were subject to contractual dictates. In the words of the Illinois Supreme Court: the "rules applicable to contracts of marriage do not differ materially from those governing contracts in general."[14] Early nineteenth-century judges like Parker reconstituted the breach-of-promise suit along these lines to place it securely in the emerging corpus of American family law. It is with these judges that the suit's history begins.

The Judicial Reception of the Suit

The significance of *Wightman* v. *Coates* for courting couples emerged in countless lawsuits thrashed out in courtrooms over the course of the century as appellate judges devised an American law of courtship. Across the nation these men demonstrated a striking uniformity in their construction and application of the law. By the late nineteenth century they had created an intricate body of legal rules that subjected disputed courtships to a set of peculiar common-law tests and penalties. Those rules were rooted in the judiciary's conception of proper antenuptial behavior.

Judges Create Rules for Courtship

The privacy of courtship was the initial obstacle facing judges determined to supervise nuptial selection. Especially after the decline of the banns (posted declarations of marriage required by traditional nuptial statutes), lovers rarely plighted their troth before a coterie of witnesses or in sealed agreements; often an explicit exchange of promises never took place. To surmount the secrecy of espousals, courts applied liberal evidentiary rules built on Lord Holt's 1704 ruling in *Hutton* v. *Mansell* that mutual promises of marriage need not be proven by direct evidence but could be authenticated by circumstantial proof. This freed courtship from a number of limitations usually applied to contracts, and highlighted the unique contractual nature of nuptials and the willingness of American judges to deviate from contractual uniformity when a larger goal—in this case protecting deserted brides—demanded it.

Chief Justice Parker's endorsement of the *Hutton* ruling in *Wightman* v. *Coates* underlines the point that despite repeated assertions of contractual similarities, judges never made courtship a captive of commercial law. The New England jurist contended that requiring public betrothal to gain access to the courts would give rise to "a state of public manners by no means desirable." He thought that courting couples, instead of having their pledges inferred from their conduct, would be "obliged, before they considered themselves bound, to call witnesses, or execute instruments under hand and seal, [and that] would be destructive of that chaste and modest intercourse which is the pride of our country; and a boldness of manners would probably succeed, by no means friendly to the character of the sex or interests of society." Parker had no interest in lifting the veil of privacy being lowered over this and other domestic relations.[15] The merger of strict contractual liability for men with loose evidentiary rules protected the privacy of courtship; it also ensured that males could not cover their broken promises with the intimacy of romance.[16]

Judicial laxity in admitting evidence of nuptial promises, and a refusal to demand strict corroboration of circumstantial evidence, imposed serious nuptial liabilities on men.[17] Darius Greenup experienced the severity of judicial vigilance in 1846 when the Illinois Supreme Court rejected his plea that Nancy Stoker had misconstrued his attentions. Along with a damage judgment, he received a judicial lesson in nuptial etiquette: in "the common language of the country, to court or to pay attention to a lady are synonymous. The latter is but a method slightly more refined and genteel of expressing the same thing."[18]

Self-policing and male liability dominated the judicial application of the common law to courtship; yet republican judges prided themselves on never extending liability without defenses to its imposition. Beyond demonstrating a mutually agreed upon termination to an engagement, bolting grooms claimed age as a defense. The latter evoked clashing judicial commitments: protecting women, shielding the young. Youth won out; American judges refused to hold young men fully liable for their romantic entanglements, in line with the common law's preferential treatment of minors (those under twenty one years of age). The exemption had been approved in one of the earliest English breach-of-promise cases, *Holt* v. *Ward Clarencieux* (1719), and was consistently reaffirmed in Anglo-American tribunals.[19]

The youthful exception flowed from a number of social considerations that influenced this and other branches of domestic relations law. Initially it offered protection to heirs of both sexes, who realized that their betrothed wanted property, not love. But increasingly it allowed minors more latitude in conjugal choices. It sanctioned the right of a young man to reassess the desirability of his potential life partner, a right denied his elders. The policy encouraged youthful romantic experimentation, but since the marriage age was high in America throughout the century, it mainly extended legal aid to youthful indiscretion. In effect it acted as a policy statement that made marriage, like everything else, a much more serious matter for those over twenty-one. These attitudes were so firmly entrenched in Anglo-American law and social mores that they provoked little debate.[20]

Only one other consistently effective defense was available to counter the judicial bias in favor of jilted women. A groom who bolted could justify his breach with evidence that his prospective bride was unfit for matrimony and motherhood. This ploy, which turned the chivalric sexual bias on its head, reveals the precariousness of women's legal powers when they depended on common-law forms drawn from bourgeois gender ideals and judicial paternalism.

In general, a nuptial version of *caveat emptor* governed courtship. Illinois Chief Justice Walter Scates pointedly informed one fickle groom of his responsibilities: "[A] suitor, with a full knowledge of the character of his lady-love, will be considered to have waived all objections to her on that account, by a promise of marriage. But it is otherwise, if the fact and her character be unknown."[21] Courts rejected out-of-hand the appeals of men who had not thoroughly investigated their brides before asking for their hands. Emmanuel McCauley paid the price when a court rejected the claim that his fiancée's drunkenness released him from a pledge. The court feared that if it accepted such a defense it would be "difficult to see why evidence may not be given of particular exhibitions of the numerous frailties of nature, such as gluttony, profanity, lying," and the like. A Massachusetts court even turned down a man's appeal that his prospective wife had not disclosed her black ancestry. Courts came to the aid of men whose testimony proved deception, not carelessness.[22]

But judges consistently recognized one womanly fraud: violations of the strict bourgeois code of feminine sexual morality. If a "shocked" man could prove that unknowingly he had pledged his love to a fallen woman, the courts set him free without penalty. After reversing a lower-court decision on the ground that evidence of a woman's sexual indiscretion had been improperly excluded, the Pennsylvania Supreme Court solemnly declared: "It is the legal as well as the moral duty of parties who plighted their mutual vows, and are looking to a marriage, to preserve themselves pure and blameless, and if a woman engaged to be married, will prostitute her person to another man, it will bar her action of breach of marriage contract."[23]

A determination to prevent wanton women from receiving compensation guided courts in assessing accused female litigants. Soiled virtue was unredeemable in the courtrooms of a society obsessed by declining standards of morality and actively trying to impose bourgeois standards of sexual propriety on men and women of all classes. *Denslow* v. *Van Horn*, an 1864 decision by the Iowa Supreme Court, spelled out the rigid code of sexual conduct maintained by the bench. Weighing a man's claim that his fiancée's sexual indiscretions justified his breach, Justice John F. Dillon sent the case back so that the evidence of her conduct could be given to a new jury. He acknowledged that the woman had maintained "for a long series of years an irreproachable character." Even so, Dillon, who as a major mid-century treatise writer championed common-law rights and responsibilities, argued that the jury deserved to know of her premarital behavior because a "woman who falls from virtue, no matter how artful the deception, or how distressing the circumstances, is, by the severe edict of society, dishonored."[24]

Eleven years later, the Pennsylvania Supreme Court uttered similar views while tossing out the breach-of-promise suit of a prostitute. After piously citing marriage as the relation on which the "whole happiness and prosperity of families—social order and social morality—the whole structure of our civilization, indeed, finally rest," the justices invoked the harsh sexual code: "It is enough to say that the law will not enforce a contract of marriage in favor of a party to it who is not fit to be married at all. A man is not bound by such a contract, if, in ignorance of her true character, he has entered into it with a woman who has earned an evil reputation by a vicious or reckless life." Other tribunals dismissed breach-of-promise suits in cases where a man proved that his lover had concealed the birth of an illegitimate child or acts of fornication with a number of men. Courts did not apply to fallen women the popular belief in the therapeutic effects of marriage, but instead treated them as unsalvageable victims of their own degeneracy.[25]

But before their judicial protectors abandoned them, discarded brides could try to refute accusations against their chastity. Recognizing that evidence of sexual misdeeds could be easily fabricated, the bench maintained its chivalric pose by subjecting the defense to stringent proof. Mere rumors or unsupported charges would not block the suit. In discarding the attempt of a South Carolina man to prove that his fiancée had engaged in intercourse with another man, a state equity court gave voice to its sense of the immense stake that women had in repelling false attacks on their chastity: "In such cases her rights, sensibilities, fate in life would have been left to the spirit of idle or malicious calumny." The court feared that "the craft of a whimsical and unscrupulous defendant might easily contrive the means of his own defense."[26] But when proven to satisfaction, male charges of feminine sexual lapses completely undermined the favored position of women. In 1805 the North Carolina Supreme Court made its sexual standards clear when it declared of a losing plaintiff: "[S]he held herself up to him as a chaste and undefiled woman. Upon this as a condition, he contracted and surely he is released from his engagement when she is found to be otherwise for the condition on her part is not complied with."[27]

But even with this defense, men found it quite difficult to prevail in breach-of-promise suits. Those who sought to reduce their liability looked to the final element of the suit, the damage award. Since marriage could not be decreed by judicial fiat, courts had to place a sufficient price on dashed marital hopes to soothe the injury and deter similar acts.

Damages for nuptial breaches emphasized the tortious, noncontractual strain of the suit. The law usually limited awards for the violation of commercial contracts to the value of the immediate loss. Despite its contractual base, courts treated a discarded nuptial vow differently. Judges refused to circumscribe damages, as one of them put it, by the "erroneous idea that the action must be governed by the same rules of construction as applied to all other contracts."[28] Instead, they adopted the more elastic damage measurement of torts. By doing so, the bench opened the door not only to compensation but to punitive and exemplary damages. This legal melding, and the judicial discretion it endorsed made breach-of-promise suits more like personal actions, such as slander or malicious prosecution, than failed commercial compacts. Judges thus granted compensation for the immediate loss and also for the wounded feelings, mental anguish, blighted affections, and damages to social standing associated with a broken courtship. Ohio lawyer Timothy Walker reported the results in his *Introduction to American Law* (1837): "[V]ery heavy damages are often received in such suits."[29]

Social and economic criteria guided the determination of proper compensation. An 1851 charge to a Rhode Island jury indicates the subjective nature of the inquiry:

> If a man promises to pay a sum of money and fails, the damages are the sum promised with interest from the date of the breach. But the damages here do not result in anything of a pecuniary nature. The amount, therefore, lies very much in your discretion. You will consider the injury to the plaintiff's feelings, her prospects, reputation, and her social position, and will give her just such damages as a girl like her, treated as she has been, ought to receive. You will consider what would have been her standing had the defendant married her and what is her situation now that he refuses.

The groom's wealth and the bride's reputation figured most prominently in these calculations. The wealthier the man, the greater his fiancée's loss; the nearer the woman to the society's ideal of a proper lady, the greater her injury and the higher her damages.[30]

The degree of a woman's injured virtue was the principal, and revealing, basis for arriving at damage judgments. Not surprisingly, accusations of improper sexual conduct were the primary means of lowering awards. In a society that subscribed to the "cult of true womanhood" and the double standard, women were particularly vulnerable to charges of sexual misconduct. If proven, such accusations in breach-of-promise cases lessened a woman's value as a nuptial prize and thus reduced her injury. A 1799 New York decision outlined the rationale for this. A defendant appealed a lower-court decision excluding evidence that he had broken the pact only after learning of "licentious conduct" by his fiancée. The court returned the case to be retried with the comment: "The object of this action is not merely compensation for the injury sustained, but damages for the loss of reputation. This must necessarily depend on the general conduct of the party subsequent to, as well as previous to, the injury complained of, and the damages to be recovered, as in actions of defamation, ought to be regulated by all the circumstances of the case."[31]

Class biases and sexual beliefs governed the application of the law. The contemporary ideal of the chaste lady was the model against which all female litigants were judged. In 1887 the Oregon Supreme Court upheld William Highfield's right to use evidence that his fiancée had been a prostitute to mitigate her award. The court approved the charge to the jury by a lower-court judge, which had authorized the jurymen to "take into consideration the character of the plaintiff, if it is subject to any criticism on your part, and if she is a woman of coarse manner, gross in her associations, and imprudent, careless, and reckless, in regard to her conduct and demeanor, these circumstances you may take into account in assessing damages; such a woman is not injured to the same extent by a breach of promise of marriage that one more confiding, retiring, and modest would be."[32]

Such evidence, however, tested the judicial determination to deny rewards to immoral women, and to ensure the protection of virtuous females. Judges resolved their dilemma by turning the legal tactic into a double-edged sword for men. Disenchanted lovers could freely attack the former object of their affections. But if their accusations proved false, purely malicious, or unsubstantiated, courts reclassified them as slander and raised the damages awarded. Similar policies were devised in divorce cases as judges began to consider husbands' false charges of their wives' infidelity as proof of mental cruelty. Through this legal fine tuning, the bench tried to aid the deserving and punish the wicked of both sexes.

Moreover, *caveat emptor* governed. If a man either participated in his fiancée's sexual misdeeds or failed to examine her character diligently, he received no aid from the bench. Justice Molton C. Rogers of Illinois told one disgruntled man who claimed that, too late, he discovered that his prospective bride had been a prostitute, that the law "does not confound, in the assessment of damages, the virtuous with the prostitute, but simply denies such distinction to one who has neither the taste nor the judgment to make it, or for other motives and influences has waived it by accepting as satisfactory the person and character of a prostitute."[33]

Seduction and the Shifting Bias of the Law

Treating the breach of a marriage promise as a tort also enabled the courts to award additional compensation for especially heinous conduct on the part of the deserting groom. Judges and juries exercised that option when a man broke off an engagement in a particularly demeaning manner. But a split in the judicial ranks over another matter—seduction—reveals a significant alteration of attitudes toward sexuality and female plaintiffs over the course of the nineteenth century.

Most post-Revolutionary judges rebuffed attempts by women to introduce evidence of seduction. They invoked the old common-law rule that a female could not file such a suit. Only a woman's father, guardian, or master could receive damages, on the basis of the legal fiction that they were the real sufferers since they stood to lose her services. An unmarried woman in the traditional hierarchical framework of the family was, in effect, a legal nonentity in any household in which she lived. Older sentiments toward sexual morality, which assumed both sexes to be willing, eager, and thus equally guilty participants in illicit intercourse, buttressed the legal restriction.[34]

South Carolina Judge Joseph Brevard relied on this latter view in 1804 to dismiss the claim of Rebecca Frost that her seduction by George Marshall, after his repeated pledges of love and proposals of marriage, warranted additional compensation. After the seduction Marshall spurned Frost, who subsequently gave birth to an illegitimate child. The mother then sued her former paramour. Despite evidence that Frost had been a virtuous woman prior to her relations with Marshall, Brevard denied her claim for additional damages. To do otherwise, he asserted, would allow a woman "to take advantage of her own frailty and turpitude; and might have a tendency to encourage lewdness, and the law might be in some measure subservient to the designs of artful women of loose morals, who may be inclined to sacrifice their virtue on slight solicitation, listening rather to the suggestions of their own libidinous passions, than trusting to the promises of a favored lover."[35]

In 1843 Chief Justice John Bannister Gibson of Pennsylvania, a mainstay of the state's Jacksonian Democracy, which resisted public incursions into all types of private conduct, dismissed another woman's plea. This litigant argued that her seduction and impregnation under false promises of marriage warranted additional damages because of the immense injury to her reputation and peace of mind. Gibson defended the law's refusal to distinguish between the motivations or moral culpability of either sex with the caustic observation: "Every girl who is silly enough to surrender her citadel of virtue to her lover, on the credit of

general professions of love, is silly enough to believe that she is going to
be married out of hand; and it must not be forgotten that professions are
not promises." Adhering to a dogmatic common-law construction of
individual responsibility under the ancient maxim *volenti non fit injuria*
(he [or she] who consents cannot recover injury), the court rewarded
sexual purity and punished sexual weakness.[36]

But a few antebellum judges began to question the assumption of
moral equality at the heart of the seduction policy. The 1807 Massachusetts decision of *Paul* v. *Frazier* accepted a woman's contention that
seduction and pregnancy merited additional compensation. Chief Justice
Theophilus Parsons, Parker's Federalist predecessor, delivered a disin-
genuous ruling in which he lamented that legislators had not provided a
remedy for women against their seducers, yet went on to declare that as
"the law now stands, damages are recovered for a breach of a promise of
marriage; and if seduction has been practiced under colour of that promise, the jury will undoubtedly consider it as an aggravation of the damages." Whether the ruling grew out of a particular common-law rule or
the judge's own observation of jury practices is not clear. But the opinion
appears to reflect a proclivity in New England to award additional
damages to seduced and discarded women.[37]

Though Parson's 1807 decision was ignored by most tribunals, the
Missouri Supreme Court in 1834 seized upon it to justify the granting of
higher damages in another breach-of-promise suit involving a pregnant
woman. Her beau had refused to marry her despite the fact that she had
borne their child. Acknowledging the weight of contrary authority, the
justices nevertheless wielded their discretionary powers to proclaim the
right to decide the case independently: "The argument attempted to be
urged, that to allow the evidence in such cases will encourage seduction,
can have no force." Instead they rested their decision on a new reading of
the judicial obligation to protect the public welfare by claiming that the
"only and obvious effect must be to induce persons to execute their
contracts of marriage, where seductions have ensued from them, for fear
of being compelled to answer in damages for the pain and ignominy
which the breach of such contracts would bring upon the victims of their
lust and fraud." The court also objected to the lack of a feminine right to
sue in such cases, thus adding its voice to a growing chorus in favor of
more distinct common-law prerogatives for women: "[N]or is it a reason
why the daughter should not be permitted to recover on the breach of a
marriage contract for a seduction procured under a cover of the contract,
that her father may give it in evidence and recover in his action for the
same seduction. Money can afford but a paltry and inadequate compensation for the loss of virtue and character to the child; or for the loss of
the child's society, and the peace and happiness of the family, to the

parent. They each suffer injuries to themselves, and for which they should have redress." A ringing dissent that charged the majority with using faulty precedents and forging bad policy went unheeded.[38]

The argument of the Missouri court won more and more converts in mid-century America. An 1850 decision in New York upholding an award of additional compensation to yet another pregnant woman suggests its appeal. Agreeing with their Missouri brethren that women had a separate legal personality and thus a right to assert their own claims, the New York judges relied on a 1783 English decision and the theories of English moral philosopher William Paley, who championed sexual restraint and feminine meekness, to distinguish between the moral guilt of the two sexes. They insisted that the "female and seducer do not stand on equal ground. She is the weaker party and the victim of his acts, and the seduction has been practiced upon her under the false color of a promise of marriage which he never intended to perform."[39]

This legal innovation was one aspect of the Victorian redefinition of sexuality. In their attempt to control sexuality, many Victorians stressed the passionlessness of normal women; some tract writers even denied women's sexual feelings. Judges not only accepted the new advice, they made the law conform to it. They used legal penalties to enforce a code of chaste sexual conduct on both men and women within the larger double standard. The bench appears to have been particularly determined to protect women from seducers. Jurists shared the opinion of women's rights advocate Samuel May who lamented the "ease with which the base, heartless seducer escapes the condemnation which his villany deserves; and the unforgiving censure with which his victim is pursued."[40] They redefined seduction as victimization that sprang from the passion and deceit of males; the passivity of women was newly emphasized, as was her instinct for a selfless life as wife and mother. According to the Illinois Supreme Court: "It is possible but hardly probable that a case may arise where the parties are equally guilty." By portraying sexual relations as inherently exploitive because of female dependency, the bench aligned the law with the Victorian campaign to restrain sexual excess.[41]

The new legal policy also promoted the differentiation of the family in republican family law. Judges granted women the right to claim damages for seduction as part of the separate legal identity they were devising for females. The bench refused to consider women as mere dependents with no distinct rights of redress when wronged. The conferral of legal independence for women in breach-of-promise cases paralleled the passage of legislation giving single women the right to sue their seducers. An 1845 petition from more than 5,500 Massachusetts citizens to make seduction a crime illustrates the popular support for penalizing violations of female chastity.[42] The seemingly contradictory recognition of feminine legal rights alongside sexual passivity and victimization was reconcilable only by the Victorian ideal of women, which consigned them to a separate sphere with its own combination of moral superiority, sexual control, and individuality.[43]

As seduction ceased to be considered an act of mutual consent, and women's subordinated status no longer blocked the plea, courts across the nation sustained the moral and legal right of women to claim additional damages. An 1880 Michigan ruling, *Bennett* v. *Beam*, explained the change. Mary Beam accused her lover of seducing her with the pledge that they would wed as soon as he finished constructing several buggies. No marriage bells rang, though horses hauled off the carriages. The court reaffirmed a judgment in Beam's favor with the added admonition:

> In many cases, the loss sustained for a breach of the agreement to marry may be but slight indeed; but never can this be the case where the life-long blight which seduction entails enters the case. Respectable society inflicts upon the unfortunate female a severe punishment for her too confiding indiscretion, and which the marriage would largely if not wholly have relieved her from. The fact of seduction should therefore go a great way in fixing the damages, as in no other way could amends be made to the plaintiff for the injury she sustained, or the defendant properly punished for his aggravated offence. It would seem also to be in full accord with the sense of justice implanted in the head of every right, high-minded person and therefore with the reason of the common law.[44]

Traditional ideas of equal capacity and guilt fell before the Victorian belief in women as victims of the uncontrollable passions of men.

The alteration in judicial attitudes and approaches toward seduction points out the central role that sexuality played in breach-of-promise cases. The use of female sexual indiscretion as a bar to the action revealed the judiciary's hostility to women who led immoral lives; the support courts gave to women who claimed seduction demonstrates how fault could be transferred to men. Since judges considered marriage to be the domestic prize sought by all women, they modified the law to keep sexual weakness (as distinct from immorality) from being unduly penalized. Female submission after a marriage promise was excusable and understandable; active sexual behavior without the pretense of a nuptial pledge was not. A complaint by Caroline Dall, a mid-century feminist and legal critic, captured the essence of the judicial approach to female sexuality: "In the eyes of the law, female chastity is only valuable for the work it can do."[45]

Judges Defend the Suit

The jury became the single most important element in the application of these legal rules to breach-of-marriage disputes. In such intimate, difficult-to-document affairs, the appellate courts sanctioned wide juror latitude in assessing the facts of each case and in setting damages. Judges refused to rein in the jury with the devices they used to curtail its role in commercial disputes. In breach-of-marriage-promise cases, the bench appears to have assumed that community standards would support the moral and legal purposes embedded in the general doctrines they laid down. As a result, one judge observed, jurors were "left to exercise a large discretion in awarding damages and courts have rarely felt themselves called upon to disturb their verdicts, and then, only where it is apparent from the great disproportion between the offense and the finding, that the jury acted under prejudice, partiality, or gross ignorance or disregard to their duties."[46]

As this comment suggests, the judges intervened only when jurors totally neglected to adhere to the common-law guidelines devised by the courts. The Pennsylvania Supreme Court explained why in 1849, when it refused the appeal of a man who seduced and then abandoned his lover, all the while promising her marriage "if anything happened": "It is true that juries, and sometimes courts, are occasionally carried away by feelings of indignation; but it is an honest prejudice, if prejudice it can be called, and if carried to excess it may be corrected by a motion for a new trial."[47]

The inability of a reluctant groom to mount an appeal received little consideration from the courts. Once broad directives had been issued, authority rested with local judges and jurors. During an era when only males filled the nation's jury boxes, breach-of-marriage-promise cases afforded them the opportunity to punish the sexual machinations and treachery of their brothers as well as to present themselves in the appealing role as the defenders of womanhood.

Only one mid-century tribunal, the Louisiana Supreme Court, directly questioned the judicial supervision of courtship. In 1850 the state's justices confronted their first breach suit. Maria Morgan sought damages from Stephen Yarborough after he broke off their engagement claiming that "unchaste and unladylike" conduct made her unfit to be his wife and the mother of his children. The court reluctantly affirmed a damage judgment in Morgan's favor. The justices, citing the state's civil-law traditions, complained that pressure from neighboring common-law states had forced Louisiana legislators to include the action in the state code. They proudly observed that the fact that no other breach-of-promise suit had reached the court "was creditable to our people," and concluded their opinion with the hope that "such actions may not become frequent."[48]

Few other courts shared these reservations. Judges and their allies among legal writers securely lodged the breach-of-promise suit in nineteenth-century common law. As the Louisiana court indicated, the suit struck a responsive chord in common lawyers. It encouraged the private regulation of courtship by using the courts to offset unequal bargaining power and to punish men who transgressed the free marriage market. Such an approach epitomized common-law governance of the family, fostering individual choice and responsibility under a protective judicial umbrella. Judges turned the law of courtship into a combination of risks, incentives, and responsibilities by treating an engagement as a special private contract governed by a unique blend of commercial, moral, and social concerns.

Legislators often demonstrated their agreement with this policy by codifying the judicial view. The New York code declared that a "promise of marriage is subject to the same rules as contracts in general, except that neither party is bound by a promise in ignorance of the other's want of personal chastity, and that either is released by unchaste conduct on the part of the other."[49] The statute went on to grant wide discretion to judges and juries in its application. It underscores a persistent reality of nineteenth-century domestic relations law, the willingness of legislators, the bench's main policy-making competitors, to codify judicial creations and to encourage the courts to fill in the interstices of a body of law believed best applied on a case-by-case basis. As a result, despite the frequent rhetoric of legislative-judicial confrontation and the widespread codification of family law, instances of cooperation, indeed of legislative deference, occurred throughout the era. These helped ensure that state codes were based on judicial solutions to domestic relations disputes.

Such institutional unanimity allowed the Indiana Supreme Court to deflect an 1877 frontal assault on the breach-of-promise suit. Samuel Short asked the court to cancel an award to his former fiancée. He claimed that neither English nor American common law recognized the action. After a thorough excursion into the suit's history, the court dismissed his appeal. "Indeed," it concluded, "the principle which upholds such action is as old as the principle which gives damages in any case for the breach of a contract."[50]

The Effort to Liberate Courtship from the Law

Auguste Carlier, a French observer of American mores, published a wide-ranging assessment of the new nation's nuptial customs in 1861. He subjected the breach-of-promise suit to particular scorn. "What a strange law!" Carlier exclaimed. "If it concerns the sale of the smallest corner of land, there must be a deed signed, sealed in the presence of a witness and recorded in a register. If it is a will, still more is demanded." Yet, the bewildered traveler noted, "for the most important act of life, the simplest tokens are sufficient to prove the existence of an engagement between the parties as if marriage did not involve consequences of fortune more important than a sale or a will." Carlier objected to the use of the suit to compel men, especially wealthy ones, to wed or pay damages. "In view of this excessive readiness of the law in the formation of marriage," he decried, "should we not be authorized in saying that it is aimed only at a promiscuous intercourse, designed to increase the population, without regard to moral considerations or to the future of the family?"[51]

Carlier's denunciation of the breach-of-promise suit found an increasingly receptive audience among mid-century Americans. For the first time, the suit came under sustained attack from a diverse assortment of critics, including lawyers, purity crusaders, and social reformers. They charged that it fostered a mercantile conception of courtship resulting in conjugal instability and domestic distress. The accusation that the breach-of-promise suit commercialized and thus devalued intimate relations was but one charge in a growing bill of particulars being drafted to indict common-law governance of the family. The most serious complaint was that the law too often sacrificed the public weal to individual desires and in doing so undermined the home. Legal critics charged family law with contributing to domestic disarray by instituting lax regulatory policies that failed to prevent dangerous or unstable families from being formed or perpetuated. They demanded that greater attention be paid the social impact of loosely governed nuptials and households, and feared for the law's inability to help maintain the social order.

In their effort to save the family, legal critics rightly concentrated on nuptial contractualism, the theoretical heart of marriage law. In the 1870s, Boston attorney and social reformer Frank G. Cook protested that the contractual emphasis of domestic relations allowed an "undue assertion of the rights of the individual at the expense of the rights of society." Abba Woolson, a prominent eastern feminist and president of the Boston Moral Education Society, cautioned in 1873: "[W]hatever tends to deteriorate the marriage relationship and consequently the home, tends to deteriorate the whole machinery of life, whether social or political." Domestic-relations law seemed to be such a malevolent force.[52]

Critics Challenge the Courts

Judges, the principal authors of family law, often were the target of these complaints. Even so, the conflict was one more of method than of conviction. Judges and their detractors shared a number of beliefs drawn from a shared republican vision of the family: in chastity, domesticity, rational love, and class compatibility. Their differences on how to enforce those values in courtship, matrimony, and family life reflected deepening disagreements over the proper scope of domestic governance. Breach-of-promise cases were merely one issue in this widening controversy.

As the intricacies of breach-of-promise decisions suggest, the courts adopted a case-by-case method of supervising courtship. In that way, they hoped to balance changing nuptial considerations with a firm commitment to common-law rights. But their critics demanded that new standards of assessing engagements replace what was held to be the privatism and crass commercialism in this and many other facets of family law. Attorney George Lawyer summarized this viewpoint in 1894:

> The maintenance of actions for the breach of the marriage contract so belittles and degrades the relation itself that the public is coming to look upon it as a matter of business alone. . . . The divine purpose is destroyed. The sacred institution has acquired a cash equivalent, and all its relations are cheapened and vulgarized. The rule, at best, is a quack nostrum. It stimulates rather than heals the disease. It assays to help the injured, but the guilty are shielded and benefited. . . . Blackmail is offered both opportunity and encouragement. It is an instrument often used to shatter honest reputations and to display vindictiveness. Misery is enforced where

there might have been happiness, and lives intended for good purposes are wrecked.[53]

So categorical a denunciation of the suit indicates that a new evaluation of matrimony led directly to the conclusion that courtship be released from common-law controls.

Divergent opinions on the breach-of-promise suit surfaced over the judicial policy of refusing to release men from their nuptial commitments when they claimed an honest change of heart. Samuel Neat entered such a plea in Massachusetts. The Supreme Judicial Court responded in 1880 with an angry retort that the defendant erroneously assumed that he had "the right, without the consent of the other party to the contract, to break off the engagement, without liability to make any compensation or indemnity, if he should come to the conclusion that the proposed marriage would not tend to the happiness of both parties." The judges dismissed that proposition as "equivalent to saying that the defendant has the right to secede from the contract, if he should be disinclined to fulfill it." Neat's argument that the marriage would not have been successful made little impression on a court that grounded rights in initial conduct, not later reflections. The same bench rejected another claim that irreconcilable religious differences justified the breach of a marriage promise.[54]

Yet, as sociologist Michael Gordon has discovered, most nineteenth-century marriage advisors considered religious agreement to be one of the most important factors in a successful union.[55] Guided by the common law, courts adhered to a policy that attached liability to choice no matter how compelling a man's refusal to wed might be. While there appears to have been a certain toughening of judicial attitudes toward female litigants late in the nineteenth century, judges made no attempt either to curtail drastically or eliminate a woman's right to be compensated for abandonment at the altar. Too many precedents, too many beliefs lay behind the suit for the bench to succumb to its critics.

But judicial resistance did not still the growing hostility. Critics singled out two elements of the breach-of-promise suit for special censure: sexual bias and jury complicity. Though judges and treatise writers maintained the facade of equal access, the domestic-relations authority James Schouler, who joined the suit's detractors, dwelt on the gap between theory and reality: "In practice, it is found that the suit . . . [is] almost exclusively a woman's weapon." That was so, he explained, "not, we may imagine, because those light perfidies are wholly on the man's part, nor necessarily because, when injured he feels his humiliation less, but rather on account of sexual differences in temperament and disposition, affecting the method of resentment."[56] Not only sexual partiality in the ability to seek legal redress, but the whole structure of rules upholding feminine claims came under attack. Yet critics did not want to make the suit, which one derided as "unmanly," available to both sexes. On the contrary, they pointed to its sexual bias as justification for the suit's abolition.[57]

The attack on sexual favoritism reflected a decided shift in sentiments toward female plaintiffs. Viewed earlier in the nineteenth century as the victims of male perfidy and passion and as paragons of wronged virtue, the female plaintiffs came under increasing suspicion by its end. Evolving Victorian visions of proper feminine behavior encouraged the belief that womanly modesty and passivity would make a virtuous lady blush at the thought of airing romantic intimacies in a public courtroom.

The Victorian commitment to a single standard of morality, so central to the era's conception of gender rights and responsibilities, is often assumed merely to have been aimed only at male conduct. But reformer Harter F. Wright argued: "No well-advised man would venture to call a woman to court for not fulfilling her promise to marry him. Yet no difference can be pretended between the case of the woman and that of the man. There are, indeed, women who say there is a difference—that a man can easily find a wife, and that his prospects are not blighted by a disappointment of this kind, but they are not the women to be listened to on such a question."[58] In fact there is little evidence of women publicly advocating the suit. Rather, the debate appears to have been carried on largely by men. In this instance, it was males who demanded an end to a legally sanctioned double standard.

As criticism swelled, women who filed breach-of-promise suits found themselves denounced as mercenaries who used the courts to gain lifetime sinecures. Marriage advisors, in particular, complained that the use of matrimony for economic or social advancement led to family instability. Glorifying romantic love as the only true source of conjugal bliss, minister and social reformer Henry Wright argued in *Marriage and Parentage* (1855) that "as a means to happiness, and a connecting link in that chain which binds us together, wealth is a nonentity."[59] A growing public consensus concluded that the suit was not worth its price; and, conversely, that those women willing to endure scandal, yellow journalism, and ill-repute must be fortune hunters or otherwise depraved.

Public concern had come full circle by the late nineteenth century. The fear aroused by the breach-of-the-marriage-promise suit was that good men could be abused when they were compelled to save their reputations from calumny either by marriage or by settling with a money-grubbing harlot out of court. Only those willing to risk their social standing would run the gauntlet of the breach suit. By the twentieth century a new stereotype had arisen: the suit was "normally brought by young and attractive but sophisticated women against mature and wealthy men, and there the plaintiff often wins a competence for life." The late nineteenth-century appellate record indicates a much greater diversity than this. It is peopled with pregnant servants, anguished farm girls, and duped daughters. Julia Kraxberger may well typify the judicial ideal of a wronged woman. Despondent when her fiancé told her he wanted to marry another, she gave him back his engagement ring. Her family minister, though, convinced her that "the marriage engagement could not be cancelled and that it was [her] religious duty to enforce it." In 1886, the Missouri Supreme Court refused to let the forfeiture of the ring block her damage suit. The justices instead insisted that her act be deemed merely a response to male fickleness understandable to the "mind of every true woman." Nevertheless, the stereotype began to dominate public attitudes, and helped sustain charges that the breach-of-promise suit undermined matrimony, thereby threatening society itself. As in so much of the agitation over family law, perception and prejudice, not empirical reality, most influenced the law.[60]

Dwindling support for a woman's right to be compensated for broken nuptial plans also reflected changing ideas about women's place in society. Late nineteenth-century America witnessed a small but noticeable widening of the social and economic opportunities opened to women along with a determined feminist movement. As positions in offices, retail stores, and government emerged and joined with vocations such as primary education that had accepted feminine workers earlier, more women entered the job force, many of them deciding to forego or at least postpone marriage. For other single women, greater social freedom and legal rights meant that the loss of an initial suitor posed less of a threat to future happiness than it might have earlier in the nineteenth century. Once unmarried women challenged the constraints of the female sphere, the legitimacy of special legal protections based on a set womanly role like the breach-of-promise suit came into question as well. As Harriet Daggett, a Louisiana law professor, put it early in the twentieth century: "This protection to women that at one time may have been a necessary and just thing now seems at times almost a travesty."[61] Though domesticity continued to be the bourgeois feminine social ideal, the accumulation of women's rights over property and other resources, changes in the marketplace, and further reductions in the functions of the home slowly undermined the legitimacy of the sexual partiality as well as popular support for the breach-of-promise suit. In explaining the impact of women entering the work force, historian Elaine May has noted that the "paradox of this 'emancipation' was that it increased individual moral responsibility rather than sexual freedom."[62] Courtship became one area where women had to protect themselves even more vigilantly.

Charges of jury complicity further inflamed fears of mercenary women. Critics of the action assailed jurymen for readily succumbing to the contrived suffering of litigating females and for measuring damages according to the beauty of the plaintiff and the pocketbook of the defendant. An English opponent of the suit, in an observation quickly reprinted and endorsed on the western side of the Atlantic, noted: "If the girl be pretty the jury generally gives her heavy damages; if she be unattractive, they often have a sneaking sympathy with the man."[63]

Such complaints echoed a growing dissatisfaction among some men with what they considered to be the favored legal status of women in the law. The popular Baptist minister Russell H. Conwell expressed such sentiments in his *Women and the Law* (1876). Though he cast himself as a defender of women's rights, Conwell attacked the legal bias in favor of female litigants. After praising the deference toward ladies inculcated in lawyers and judges through legal training, he observed:

> The jury, too, is composed of men—a fact oftentimes of the utmost importance to a woman, whatever may be said to the contrary. Jurymen, although less biased than lawyers, do naturally, in our land, incline toward leniency when the culprit is a woman. In a suit between a man and a woman for debt or damage, the man must calculate that the jury will give her the benefit of every doubt. There is a natural kindness in man toward a woman which does not live in his breast when he deals with men. And when he is called to say that she is telling the truth or falsehood, or is guilty or not guilty, his nature as well as his breeding leans toward her side of the case.[64]

Such assertions implicitly challenged the paternalistic role so readily assumed by judges in breach-of-promise suits, and the chivalric standards they embedded in the law.

Judicial Accommodation and the Limits of Reform

The bench was not immune to its critics. In the latter part of the century many judges narrowed the acceptable range of evidence that could be offered to juries as proof of nuptial pacts. A retreat from an expansive evidentiary policy in breach-of-promise suits was prominently signalled in an 1860 Massachusetts decision, *Russell v. Cowles*. The court overturned a judgment in favor of Mary Russell, who had relied on her own marriage preparations, such as buying clothes and furniture, to support her claim of a marital pledge. The justices refused to accede to the demand that a matrimonial agreement must be treated as an exception to the general rule that a person's acts could not be offered as evidence of their claims. Other courts supported the Massachusetts ruling.[65]

Two types of evidence came under judicial questioning. First, judges tried to separate mere courtship from espousals. They insisted increasingly that marital intent on the part of the couple be clearly proven. In 1872 the Illinois Supreme Court feared that if courtship and not actual promise of marriage had become the foundation of the suit, "it would be dangerous for an unmarried man to pay attention to an unmarried woman. Juries lean toward the woman and no man would be safe from the contrivances of an artful and designing female whose company might please him." That said, the justices remanded a case in which a woman's own statements to her sister constituted the only proof of a nuptial pact.[66]

The alteration in judicial thought on this question, and its implicit reassessment of breach-of-promise litigants, was elaborately set forth in a pivotal Michigan ruling, *McPherson* v. *Ryan* (1886). Despite a strong dissent accusing the majority of ignoring precedent and of judicial law making, the justices aligned themselves with what they recognized to be a modification of American common law. They conceded that the evidence offered in the case, the bride's statements to her friends, had been accepted as valid in many jurisdictions. But this time the court rejected it, warning:

> The plaintiff, as courts and juries must ever be constituted, has certain advantage over the defendant, without giving her the opportunity of fabricating by her acts and declarations, without his consent or knowledge, evidence to make a case against him. It would place almost every man at the mercy of an evilly disposed and designing woman. An adventuress would come into court and swear to a breach of the promise to marry, and then bring others of like ilk, her friends and intimates, to sustain her with stories she has told them in plan to further damages. There is no necessity of throwing open the doors of courts to such opportunities to work injustice. When the plaintiff has equal rights with the defendant to place fully before the jury the story of her wrongs aided, as she will ever be, by the sympathy accorded to the weakness and beauty of her sex—a sympathy which the most rigid administration of justice cannot prevent—right and equity demand that she no longer have the aid which the law refused in other cases.[67]

Other courts excluded such evidence as wedding preparations and the statements of the plaintiff's family when these had been made without the prospective groom's knowledge. Judges tightened the rules of evidence in response to assertions that laxity only encouraged abuse.[68]

The late nineteenth-century bench also trimmed the suit by refining the rules governing damages. Opposition to high awards existed both inside and outside the courts, particularly in cases where a woman had not been seduced. An 1882 decision by the Texas Supreme Court supported broad jury discretion in setting awards. But the justices stressed that a broken nuptial pledge did not, as many of their predecessors had seemed to assume, automatically qualify a woman for high damages. The judges cautioned: "[I]t is a well-known fact in everyday practical life, that the breach often affords as much satisfaction to the one party as to the other." Questioning feminine motives in instigating breach suits led the courts to demand that damages be based on actual, not imagined, injuries. In the same manner, judges granted men wide latitude in assaulting the character of their betrothed when attempting to lower awards.[69]

Yet the foremost accusation against the breach-of-promise action was that it undermined matrimony itself. An almost pathological fear of broken homes, a concern fed by constant reports of ever more divorces, helped rivet attention on the suit. The common-law ideal of fostering stable marriages by holding individuals to their nuptial pledges lost support. Attributing conjugal success to romantic love and individual happiness, the law's critics argued that the common law inhibited the formation of stable marriages. They condemned breach-of-promise suits as ill-advised curbs that corrupted courtship.

Opponents of the suit thus denounced legal rules that penalized socially valid reasons for terminating an engagement such as changed affections, incompatibility, and conflicting tastes. Almost all advisors on mate selection argued that courtship should be considered experimental, not legally binding, in order to ensure harmony in class, interests, taste, health, and religion, and thus successful marriages. Treatise writer James Schouler expressed this view in his text on domestic relations:

> The marriage state ought not to be lightly entered into. It involves the profoundest interests of human life, transmitting its complex influences direct to posterity, and invading the happiness of parents and near kindred. . . . From such a standpoint we view the marriage engagement as a period of probation, so to speak, for both parties, their opportunity for finding one another out, and if that probation results in developing incompatibility of tastes and

temperament, coldness, suspicion and incurable repugnance of one to the other, though all these may impute no vice to either nor afford matter for judicial determination, duty requires that the match be broken off. What, then, shall be the consequences to the party who takes the initiative?[70]

The dissolution of an engagement came to be seen by many professionals and laypersons as a non-legal injury; the incompatibility of lovers, they urged, was better left to other agencies than the courts. In 1894, the *Harvard Law Review* attacked the suit in these terms. Its editors charged that the suit coerced "the courts into a commercial view of what cannot properly be regarded as a matter of trade or dicker." They criticized the bench for bringing "feelings not properly the subject of judicial investigation into undue publicity" while rarely providing "a real remedy for the breach of legal obligation."[71]

These contentions reflected a new tendency to stress the limits of the contractual nature of marriage and thus the law governing nuptials. In 1850, two years before Joel Bishop's seminal exposition of marriage law, New York reformer Elisha Hurlbut declared that the classification of marriage as a civil contract stood as "the first grand error of the British and American law concerning marriage." Hurlbut, who fought for women's freedom from what he termed marital enslavement, used breach-of-promise suits to illustrate the corruption of matrimony caused by contractualism. He claimed that the law incorrectly considered an engagement "as a fair business transaction" of which the breach was "a civil injury." After elaborating on these failings, the reformer urged that the legislature, to which his appeal was addressed, banish the legal designation of marriage as a civil contract and instead consider it as "the holiest ordinance of the Creator's law."[72]

An isolated protest in the 1850s, Hurlbut's indictment won greater favor as the century came to a close. Attorney Martin Littleton pointedly criticized the mechanical application of contract to courtship in the 1916 *New York Times*. He lamented that "so long as they are both competent to contract and there has been no fraud, it does not make a particle of difference whether their motive was money, marbles, or jackstraws, a valid contract has been entered into, a contract which, if either party backs out, can be cashed in before a judge and jury." In an era in which the domain of contract law began to shrink, the *Harvard Law Review* decided that the breach suit was simply out of step with contemporary legal thought: "The similarity to other mutual agreements originally led the courts into allowing the action. As a fresh matter today it might well be doubted whether the commercial spirit is sufficiently apparent in the exchanged promises to show an intention of creating a contract in the sense of which contracts are enforced by the courts."[73]

The bench was not immune to these complaints either. Surging alarm over the transmission of hereditary defects in the late nineteenth century offered the judges an opportunity to add venereal disease to their list of valid justifications for breaking engagements. The North Carolina Supreme Court led the way in *Allen* v. *Baker* (1873). The justices objected to the leading decision on the subject, the English judgment in *Hall* v. *Wright* (1859). In that case, after a man had proposed but before his breach, he contracted a lung disease, which made marriage unhealthy for him. The English courts sustained his fiancée's suit on the ground that he could have partially fulfilled his pledge by giving her the status of wife and endowing her with his estate, even if he could not perform the sexual duties of matrimony.[74]

The North Carolina bench sternly rebuked the Britons for so easily equating the marital compact with a business agreement that could be partially fulfilled. The judges offered instead a proper republican vision of matrimony when they insisted that the English rule ran "contrary to the understanding of men generally, that the acquisition of property or social position, neither does nor should constitute a main and independent motive and inducement for entering into such a contract." The legitimate objects of marriage were gratification of natural passions, companionship, and children. A man unable to provide all of these should be legally excused from his pledge. That proposition applied even, as in the case before them, when the defendant had by his own "imprudence and sinful indulgence" contracted a disease, because it protected the complaining woman and any offspring she might have had. "The law will constrain no man to assume a position so full of peril," the court concluded, "as to have placed within his reach the lawful means of gratifying his pleasure, a powerful passion, at the risk of another's health or life, and the possibility of bringing into the world children in whose constitution the seeds of a father's sin shall lurk." This argument proved so compelling that the courts relaxed their contractual tests for breach suits. Judges thus partially allayed fears about their roles in courtship by joining their critics in the turn-of-the-century crusade for racial purity and the protection of women and children from male licentiousness and disease.[75]

Despite such concessions on particular elements of the breach-of-promise suit, only a few jurists broke from the ranks. One who did, an Illinois judge, made the pages of the 1874 *American Law Review*. In dismissing a breach-of-promise award of $1200 against Augustus Behrens for reneging upon his promise after he discovered that his bride would be accompanied by her mother, judge Robert Banyon declared:

Allow me to shake hands with you. I envy your firmness. There was a period in the life of this court . . . when it was in circumstances somewhat similar to yours. If it had had the moral courage which you possess, it would have saved about twenty-five years of misery and unhappiness. The alternative presented to this court was whether it would marry a young lady and her mother, or whether it would pay $125 in gold. The court was poor at the time. It was earning an unsatisfactory living at the restaurant business. It yielded. It took the young woman and mother-in-law and kept the $125. For a quarter of a century this court has regretted its hasty action. It is glad to meet a man who cherishes happiness more than he does money.

Banyon then fined Amelia Donnerschlog $10 and costs for "trying to bring a man into slavery to a mother-in-law."[76]

But such idiosyncratic judicial acts do not detract from the general judicial support of the breach-of-promise suit. The bench continued to endorse its creation with its own arguments of social utility: to punish love's transgressors, to vindicate the discarded objects of men's affections, to dissuade others from jilting their betrothed, to afford women legal solace for the loss of their rightful place in society. These commitments, made during the formative era of American family law, had become so interwoven with the judicial governance of the home that the courts would not back away from their self-imposed obligation to police courtship. Judges would modify the suit to meet new conditions, but they would not scuttle it. This judicial position represented not a mere formalistic effort to protect earlier policies, but rather a renewed determination that the suit was the most effective way of policing courtship.[77]

Legal Doubts

As the twentieth century dawned, judges found themselves under attack for their continued acceptance of the breach-of-promise suit. Their assailants accused them of using fallacious common-law reasoning and of failing to see the error of their ways and abolish the suit. The lawyers among them, as reformers steeped in the common-law tradition are wont to do, contended that the breach-of-promise suit had been erroneously founded in the law. Actually, they argued, the common law decidedly stood against the suit. What was more, its English sources had been soiled by commercial considerations that had been mistakenly applied to completely different social conditions in the New World. One such professional critic declared: "It is a notorious fact that in the early

English cases, even in actions for seduction of a wife or daughter, the courts were continually harping upon 'property rights' almost to the exclusion of rights of a higher nature."[78]

Others insinuated that the suit had been accepted in America not to aid feminine virtue but primarily to line the pockets of pettifogging lawyers. Georgetown University professor and legal author Harter F. Wright even tried to undermine the authority of *Wightman* v. *Coates* by attacking the character of the venerable Federalist Chief Justice Parker. Noting Parker's comment in the case that he had handled such litigation as an attorney, Wright likened him to the contemporary ambulance chaser: "[W]e do not attach great weight to the opinion on the point by a judge who catered to that class of business as counsel. It smacks strongly of self-justification."[79]

Critics of the suit, not surprisingly, turned to state legislatures, not courts, as the most promising agency of reform. After the mid-nineteenth century, domestic relations, like other broad areas of the law, ceased to be the almost exclusive domain of the bench and bar. Legislators, reformers from other professions, academic social scientists, and other critics began to lay claim to the shaping of family policy. Though stifled for much of the century by persistent localism and antistatism, opposition to tax increases, and other constraints, legislators and public officials under their direction began to assume a greater presence in this and other aspects of social and economic life. But the bench retained its dominion.

Relief did not come quickly or easily; common-law governance was too deeply implanted in the nation's still republican-rooted legal culture. Moreover, as the recurrent conflicts over codification in the period suggest, a persistent set of contradictory aims clouded the issue. A desire to rationalize the nation's diffuse common law and legislation and to constrain judicial powers often clashed with an equally fervent faith in judicial decision making and the bench's oversight of the distribution of wealth and authority. Convinced of the latter proposition by their craft's values, many lawyers, judges, and legal commentators vigorously defended the common law as the best means of protecting all institutions, including the family. They wanted power to be exercised through the courts, not through the legislature. Often on the defensive, the bench and bar struggled to retain hegemony over domestic relations during the rise of the regulatory state.

In 1900 the social climate surrounding the breach-of-promise suit had dramatically changed. The action was no longer popularly seen as the meritorious act of a mistreated woman. The public and professional consensus that supported the suit in colonial and early nineteenth-century America had evaporated. By the turn of the century, the breach-of-promise suit came to be regarded as legally sanctioned blackmail, a threat to marriage and the family. Though it still was used, its legal and social significance had fallen markedly. The social costs of the action ceased to justify its potential value for most jilted women.

Pressure for the abolition of the suit mounted, but it was not until the 1930s that a few states began to ban the action with statutes dubbed "Anti-Heart Balm Acts."[80] Even so, the suit remained available to most women in late twentieth-century America. The inability of reformers to dislodge the suit graphically illustrates the staying power of the creations of family law's formative era, and the ability of common lawyers to create enough autonomy for the law to protect their creations from shifting public attitudes and rising state activism.

Like many public-policy debates of the late nineteenth century, the struggle over the breach-of-promise suit had a mechanical quality to it. Each side reasoned downward from abstract assumptions about courtship, romance, and legal responsibility to concrete proposals for effectively using the law to promote successful engagements. Neither created an overwhelming case for its position, though the suit's defenders clearly ran afoul of an emerging popular view of courtship as an exploratory relationship. Yet the conflict over the suit ended in stalemate because no group could fashion a convincing definition of the public interest in courtship that would vanquish its opponents. As a result, breach of promise lingered on as a marginal suit for marginal women.

The suit's descent into a legal purgatory offers some initial evidence about the strength and the limitations of the nineteenth century's judicially dominated family law. Judges could in this case protect their creation, but could not assure its social legitimacy, no matter how carefully constructed and compartmentalized its rules. In a broader sense, the dwindling significance of the breach-of-marriage-promise suits documents one aspect of the marked revision of contractualism in all areas of late nineteenth-century family law. This occurred as a consequence of the tendency to look to public regulation as the proper solution to social controversies, a movement fundamentally at odds with the central tenets of a judicially dominated family law. These developments introduce forces at work in nineteenth-century domestic-relations law that will be more fully explored in the remaining areas of family formation.

CHAPTER 3

NUPTIAL LICENSE
THE REGULATION OF WEDDINGS

The difficulties that plagued the law of courtship stemmed largely from the immense significance that nineteenth-century Americans attached to matrimony. Anthropologist Claude Lévi-Strauss has noted that "every society had some way to operate a distinction between free unions and legal ones. Whatever the way in which the collectivity expresses its interest in the marriage of its members, whether through the authority vested in strong consanguinial groups, or more directly through the intervention of the state, it remains true that marriage is not, is never, and cannot be a private business."[1] Anglo-American society proved to be no exception.

When the English colonized North America, a sturdy tradition existed that distinguished between the marriages of those wed according to public forms and those that did not. Couples who observed nuptial formalities assured themselves of all the rights and privileges of matrimonial status. Irregular or clandestine marriages faced an uncertain reception because, as American legal authority David Hoffman suggested in 1836, the end of marriage could not be achieved "unless promiscuous intercourse be restrained."[2] In this sense the treatment of informal marriages in nineteenth-century America served as a litmus test of nuptial regulation in a society beset by conflicts between individual rights and public order.

The debate over informal marriages reflected a continuing tension between contractual freedom and state intervention. It produced generational solutions in marriage law, which were significantly different from those in the law of courtship. In the judge-dominated post-Revolutionary and antebellum eras, changes in the law stemmed from the bench's commitment to an Americanized common law and private decision-making. In this formative era of domestic-relations law, judges hoisted the banner of nuptial freedom and constricted public regulation of matrimony.

But as distrust of irregular marriage intensified, judicial priorities were called into question. In this case, unlike the debate over breach-of-promise suits, the bench's noninterventionist stance rather than its involvement fell afoul of family-law critics. Doubts as to the proper latitude to be given couples who flouted the law led to rising demands for greater public supervision of matrimony. These calls for reform in turn encouraged an expansion of the state's nuptial authority. As in many other areas of the law during the latter part of the nineteenth century, state after state shifted from an initial promotion of individual rights through eased marital regulations to the imposition of greater controls on those seeking matrimony.

These changes in the orientation of marriage law occurred in both of its primary categories, the rules governing the celebration of matrimony and the rules that established standards of nuptial fitness. The development of distinctive laws for wedding celebrations occupy this chapter, the creation of marriage standards the next.

Matrimony Becomes a Republican Right

Post-Revolutionary legal authorities were confronted with an ambiguous English and colonial legacy. English law demanded that brides and grooms negotiate a five-step nuptial course: espousals, publication of banns, execution of the espousal contract at church, celebration, and sexual consummation. Yet clandestine marriages flourished in early-modern England as dissenters, couples fleeing parental opposition, and others flocked to clergymen willing to perform private marriages for a fee. Scandalized critics assailed this lax nuptial law for causing property disputes, encouraging bigamy, and upsetting family continuity.[3]

Despite such opposition, couples who contracted and consummated their unions generally won legal recognition from the ecclesiastical courts that governed nuptials. But the gap between law and practice proved vexing for the English and their colonists.

Anglican officials had rejected the marital edicts of the Council of Trent (1543–63), which banned informal marriages by requiring the presence of a priest and other witnesses for a valid ceremony. They grudgingly accepted two forms of informal unions. The first—*espousals per verba de futuro*—consisted of an agreement to marry in the future followed by sexual intercourse, which transformed the future promise into immediate marriage. (This never gained acceptance in the colonies.) The second and most prevalent form—*espousals per verba de presenti*—turned a mutual agreement to be husband and wife made in public or private by a couple into a binding marriage. Church courts expressed their displeasure by retaining the power to fine couples who wed irregularly and subject them to religious sanctions. Even so, they treated informal matrimony far more leniently than did property-conscious common-law tribunals.

Lay courts did not disturb the legality of informal unions, but they refused to allow the parties and their children full property and inheritance rights. By separating legality from validity, the English created a system of nuptial regulation that placed severe penalties on those of property and wealth who wed clandestinely, but the system did not dissolve consummated unions. The law treated matrimony as a civil agreement subject to public controls.[4]

The English debate over clandestine marriages took a decisive turn in 1753. Lord Hardwicke's Marriage Act made religious ceremonies compulsory, and fixed formal requirements such as parental consent, registration, and published banns for all legal unions. Only Quakers, Jews, and members of the Royal Family were exempted. Though ecclesiastical courts retained some authority over nuptials until 1857, the new law tried to eliminate the marital freedom that church law had allowed. The Parliamentary debates made it clear that the propertied classes who governed England regarded marriage as an institution that must be subjected to rigid statutory controls. In the 1760s Blackstone encouraged further secularization of nuptial governance by rejecting entirely the view of marriage as sacramental and sacrosanct. In order to justify public controls, he defined matrimony as a civil contract.[5]

The English concept of marriage as the creation of positive law devalued individual rights by elevating public controls over private interests. Thomas Poynter, author of the leading English treatise on matrimony in the early nineteenth century, declared: "[W]ith the progress of society, marriage became a civil contract, regulated by laws, varying among nations, corresponding with different motives of public policy."[6] In England this relativistic notion of state marital authority became the foundation of strict public supervision of nuptials. Relying on a clear demarcation between licit and illicit sexual relations, marriage increasingly became "the gateway to respectability and stability" in nineteenth-century England.[7]

An Uncertain Colonial Nuptial Legacy

The difficulties of nuptial regulation were even thornier in colonial America. Nuptial freedom expanded due to the uncertainties of colonial life and such provincial innovations as the determination of all colonies but Maryland to offer betrothed couples a choice of civil or religious nuptial rites.

Colonial magistrates, like their English counterparts, made their preferences clear. Every province enacted a marriage code based on the five-step nuptial process of England, and then passed subsequent revisions aimed, like the North Carolina act of 1741, at "preventing clandestine and unlawful marriages."[8] Magistrates relied on parents and communities to police nuptials. Families had the major responsibility of guarding a ceremony that not only bound the bride and groom to one another but also united the couple's families. The customary right of parents, primarily fathers, to counsel and control family alliances continued in the colonies, particularly among the gentry. According to an English domestic-conduct guide popular in the provinces: "Children are so much the goods, the possessions of their parents, that they cannot, without a kind of theft, give themselves away without the allowance of those that have the right in them."[9] Though less potent among the propertyless classes and even among the gentry as economic opportunities widened, patriarchal authority over nuptials was the most effective check on nuptial freedom and protection against clandestine unions.[10]

So intertwined in colonial society were family and community that neighbors also had a supervisory role in the celebration of marriages. Demographic realities in many settlements, especially the high rate of adult mortality and large numbers of immigrants without families, heightened the importance of this traditional public responsibility. Statutory provisions prescribing wedding publicity were intended to ensure that anyone with an objection to a proposed marriage would know of the match and be able to come forward. Banns, initially the favored device, were premised on the right of parents, guardians, and neighbors to intervene in undesirable nuptial plans. Engaged couples initiated the community warning system by posting their intentions to wed in a conspicuous place for a specified number of days or weeks prior to their weddings.[11]

Most colonies also allowed licenses—special dispensations from magistrates giving the community's and family's blessing to a couple—in place of banns. Licensing engendered less publicity than banns, but nonetheless asserted the community's right to oversee the creation of a valid marriage. Benjamin Bowles's publication of a warning against the marriage of his ward in the 1756 *Virginia Gazette* illustrates the colonial notion of protecting public and family interests by stopping clandestine marriages:

> Whereas Sarah Holman, a niece of mine, under age, and to whom I am Guardian, hath lately an Elopement from me, and, as I believe, with an Intent to marry one Snead (alias Crutchfield), and as I think it will be greatly to her disadvantage, this is to give notice to all county court clerks not to grant them marriage license, and to all ministers not to marry them by publication of the Banns. I not knowing what part of the Colony they make resort to, to accomplish their Design, am obliged to make use of this method to prevent them.[12]

Those like Holman and her fiancée who violated the nuptial rules created to deter informal marriages faced varying forms of public disapproval. Fines, corporal punishment, and jailings were applied to offenders and their accomplices, especially compliant magistrates and ministers.

As in the mother country, neither legislative penalties nor family and community watchfulness prevented clandestine marriages. Ironically, the development of optional civil or religious rites and the spread of contractualism in marriage law may have encouraged informal matrimony, most notably among the many New Englanders and southern dissenters who questioned traditional religious and civic attitudes toward matrimony. In 1641 Massachusetts Bay authorities even had the responsibility of arraigning their governor, Richard Bellingham, for marrying without posting the banns.[13] Informal marriage also found precedent in the colonial practice of exempting Quakers from nuptial rules because they refused to take oaths.

Other couples, particularly in the traumatic early days of colonization and later on the frontier, may have had no choice since many colonies lacked a reliable corps of religious and lay officials. Growing resentment against the publicity that accompanied the banns and the rising costs of marriage fees, sometimes as high as a month's wages, may also have led many couples to bypass formal ceremonies. And the very minutiae of the provincial statutes may have awakened nascent antibureaucratic prejudices among the Scotch-Irish and other frontier settlers. In 1786 the Rev. Henry Addison, an Anglican minister in Maryland, admitted: "If the rule was Established here that no marriage should be deemed valid that had not been registered in the Parish Book it would I am persuaded bastardize nine tenths of the People in the Country."[14] A post-Revolutionary South Carolina lawyer echoed those sentiments when he acknowledged that his state's marriage laws never "extended any further

than about sixty miles from Charleston."[15] The coexistence of a determined government policy to make marriage a public act and of nuptial
practices that flouted the law continued in the New World as it had in the
Old.

The presence of informal marriage in colonial America may be clear
but its legal status was not.[16] After his examination of the issue in
colonial New England, historian Chilton Powell concluded in 1928 that
"although the first generation of Pilgrims adhered strictly to the regular
civil ceremony, the practice of common-law marriages after the manner
of the clandestine unions of England and the Continent soon became
more or less prevalent in the colonies; nor does any action seem to have
been taken by the courts to invalidate them." Massachusetts did formally
prohibit informal marriage in 1692, but Powell could find no evidence
that it had effect.[17]

The only widely known case on the subject outside of New England,
Cheseldine v. *Brewer*, points out the difficulties of determining the legal
response to informal marriages. This 1739 Maryland ruling upheld an
inheritance claim by accepting informal evidence of the heir's parents'
marriage. The case has been used to argue both that informal marriages
won legal support in colonial America, and that colonial courts merely
adopted the traditional common-law presumption of marriages from
evidence of cohabitation.[18] In all likelihood, though, the clouded distinction between legality and validity in English law and the uncertainty
engendered by the decentralized, informal colonial legal system led to
ad hoc, localized solutions. Despite the clear preferences of provincial
statutes, informal marriage probably received judicial acquiescence if
not endorsement, and thus the dual nuptial system lingered in the colonies after it had disappeared in the mother country.

Judges Differ over Marriages without Ceremonies

The post-Revolutionary American solution to "irregular marriage" was
entirely different from the British response. Instead of banning it, republican marriage law made matrimony much easier for a couple to enter,
rechristened "irregular marriage" as "common-law marriage," and significantly eased the rules governing proof of valid unions. Judges led the
way, indeed the new law of marriage was a judicial creation. The bench
acted from an Americanized version of the common law, which emphasized the private nature of contracts and relied on the self-regulation

implicit in such agreements for nuptial supervision. Legislatures generally seconded the bench's revision of the law governing the marriage ceremony.

As changes accumulated in the first half of the nineteenth century, American marriage law reflected, and in turn fostered, a republican ethos that weakened the public regulation of matrimony, whether by parents, the local community, or the state. It was derived from a faith in competitive individualism and voluntary choice, and relied on the initiative of aggrieved individuals for enforcement. The law asserted that the commonwealth was better served by judicially supervised self-regulation than by public scrutiny. It assumed that the evils produced by state intervention in the newly consecrated private sphere of life, in this case the right to marry, would far outweigh the inevitable problems arising from flawed human nature. In the realm of marriage law, this republican ethic was achieved through judicial ascendance over the legislative branch. However, the courts cast these self-serving results in the appealing, and convincing, rhetoric of promoting individual responsibility and liberty, free from state authority.

The judicial recognition of common-law marriage originated in a laconic, three-page 1809 New York decision, *Fenton* v. *Reed*. Though *per curia* [by the whole court], it is attributed to James Kent, then Chief Justice of the New York Supreme Court and soon to be the state's Chancellor before embarking on a career as the century's most influential law writer. In the suit, Elizabeth Reed sought judicial validation of her second marriage so that she could collect her husband's Revolutionary War pension. Her first spouse, John Guest, had deserted her in 1785. In 1792, after hearing rumors of his demise, she married Reed. Later that same year Guest returned, but did not reclaim his wife. Guest died in 1800 and Elizabeth continued to live with Reed until her second mate's death.

Invoking the ancient common-law rule against bigamy, Kent nullified Mrs. Reed's second match for the years before Guest's death. But he went on to hold that the continued matrimonial cohabitation of the couple after that time established a valid marriage under the common law. Kent brushed aside the fact that no new wedding ceremony had been performed, contending that "no formal solemnization of marriage was required. A contract of marriage *per verba de presenti* amounts to an actual marriage and is as valid as if made in *facie de ecclesiae*."[19] In 1826 Kent embellished his 1809 ruling in the second volume of his *Commentaries*:

> No peculiar ceremonies are requisite by the common law to the
> valid celebration of the marriage. The consent of the parties is all

that is required; and as marriage is said to be a contract *jure gentium*, that consent is all that is required by natural or public law. The Roman lawyers strongly inculcated the doctrine that the very foundation and essence of the contract consisted in consent freely given, by parties competent to contract. *Nihil proderit signasse tabulas si mentem matrimonii no fuisse constabit. Nuptias non concubitus, sed consensus facit.* This is the language equally of the common law and canon law and of common reason.[20]

Because the *Commentaries* became the primer for nineteenth-century American lawyers, Kent's rendition of common-law marriage came to enjoy wide dissemination.

As significant as Kent's invention of common-law marriage was his method of establishing its legal ancestry. The *Reed* decision relied on but a single English authority, and not at all on colonial law (perhaps because, as Chilton Powell suggests, the ruling "was obviously without precedent in America").[21] More to the point, Kent, like other aggressive post-Revolutionary proponents of common-law governance, wanted to insulate legal rules from the ebb and flow of popular opinion and political law making. Consequently, he invoked the weighty common-law authority of medieval English and continental lawyers such as Bracton, Coke, and Grotius, and even the Romans, in an attempt to bring the full force of the common-law tradition behind the doctrine. He later admitted the right of legislators to abolish common-law marriage by adding the caveat that informal unions were valid "in the absence of any civil regulations to the contrary."[22] But he tried to forestall legislative intervention by portraying his rule as the eternal expression of the common law.

Kent's innovation did not go unchallenged. Twice during the first decade of the nineteenth century the Supreme Judicial Court of Massachusetts upheld the Commonwealth's right to demand that its nuptial laws be fully observed. *Mangue* v. *Mangue*, an 1804 divorce suit by a disaffected wife, hinged on the existence of a valid marriage between the couple. They had exchanged nuptial pledges in the presence of a justice of the peace and signed a statement to that effect, but their union had not been solemnized by the magistrate. He had merely been recorded as one of the witnesses. In a terse decision, the court concluded that there could be no complete marriage without official administration of the vows by a recognized agent of the state.[23]

A more definite ruling came six years later. *Milford* v. *Worcester* resolved a dispute between those two towns over the support of the paupers Stephen and Rhoda Temple and their six children. If a valid marriage could be established, then Worcester was responsible for the whole family, because matrimony would have conferred Stephen's residence on his wife. After filing their marital intentions, the pair had stumbled across a justice of the peace in a tavern. They asked him to solemnize their bond. He refused, but they exchanged vows in his presence and then lived together as husband and wife. After a thorough examination of the common law and the state's nuptial code, Chief Justice Theophilus Parsons nullifed the marriage in what Powell said "might be taken as the reply of the Pilgrim fathers to this new and heretical doctrine" of common-law marriage.[24]

Parsons rejected Kent's central contentions. He too depicted marriage as a civil contract, but argued that its civil nature necessitated public supervision and sanction. Informal marriages might be valid in a state of nature, but Parsons insisted that once enacted, marital regulations became compulsory. He further claimed that the common law had never granted complete validity to clandestine marriages. "When our ancestors left England, and ever since," he declared in a revision of English marriage history, "it is well known that a lawful marriage there must be celebrated before a clergyman in orders." Reviewing the successive acts of the colonial general court, he concluded: "When, therefore, the statute enacts that no persons but a justice or a minister shall solemnize a marriage, and that only in certain cases, the parties are themselves prohibited from solemnizing their own marriage by any form of engagement, or in the presence of any witnesses whatever . . . the mutual engagement of the parties in this case, to take each other for husband and wife, in the room where the justice is present, he not assenting, but refusing to solemnize the marriage, is not a lawful marriage." Parsons urged that informal marriages be considered void even though they were not expressly prohibited as in England. Any other policy, he contended, would "render in a great measure nugatory all the statute regulations on the subject."[25]

Kent and Parsons parted company in their reading of law and public welfare, a division that dominated debate over the legality and desirability of common-law marriage and the lax public nuptial regulation it fostered. Both staunch Federalists, they sought to use the law pragmatically to maintain social order. Both also emphasized the role of matrimony in preserving social stability. But the means they chose were polar opposites. Kent argued that sanctioning voluntary nuptials provided the surest method of binding couples together. An acolyte of the common law, he regarded marriage as a private act, not a public event monitored by the state. The law should legitimate private marriage choices. Kent's promotion of common-law marriage also flowed from the desirability and necessity of judicial governance of marriage. A firm opponent of state regulation, he held that the bench better protected individual rights (particularly property ones), and thus social interests, than did the legislature.

Parsons held a more traditional view of matrimony as a public responsibility. Placing greater faith in government, he insisted that the commonwealth's authority to establish guidelines for matrimony was a necessary protection for society. The chief justice endorsed legislative direction as the most effective means of supervising nuptials. He cited prevention of immorality and fraud and protection of property rights as the dominant reasons for banning irregular marriages. "[E]very young woman of honor ought to insist on a marriage solemnized by a legal officer, and to shun the man who prates about marriage condemned by human law, as good in the sight of Heaven. This cant, she may be assured, is a pretext for seduction, and if not condemned will lead to dishonor and misery."[26] The arguments from both sides were refined and repeated well into the next century. The absence of consensus even among the judiciary demonstrates the vexing nature of the problem in republican society.

The Triumph of Common-Law Marriage

Kent and Parsons contended for the allegiance of their brethren. Kent triumphed. The vast majority of antebellum state courts accepted common-law marriage, as did influential treatise writers such as Tapping Reeve, Simon Greenleaf, and Joel Bishop.[27] Only a minority of courts, primarily in New England and the upper South, embraced Parsons's position. The only major antebellum legal writer to oppose common-law marriage was Parsons's son and namesake, who did so in an 1853 treatise on contracts. The disagreement, though, compelled the adversaries to defend their readings of the law.[28]

Proponents of common-law marriage used a set of interlocking social and legal arguments based on the assertion that marriage was (in the words of the Vermont Supreme Court) "one of the natural rights of human nature." By emphasizing the sanctity of individual nuptial rights judges, as did those in Ohio, could relegate nuptial regulations to the status of bureaucratic niceties that did not "profess to confer a right to marry, but only regulate the exercise of that right, the existence of which was presupposed." The New Jersey bench airily observed: "Fashion prescribes forms of celebration, and without attending to them, it may not be considered fashionable, but the laws of fashion bind only those who choose to be bound by them."

Judges also rendered nuptial statutes impotent by holding that if legislators had intended to outlaw informal nuptials, they would have expressly done so. The legislative inaction made the judicial reading of the law a self-fulfilling prophecy. The claim became a stock judicial idiom: nuptial laws were directory, not mandatory. Marriage, according to the Kentucky bench, "is nothing but a contract, and to render it valid, it is only necessary upon principles of natural law, that the parties should be able to contract, willing to contract, and should contract."[29]

Judges fortified their legal arguments with jeremiads against the harmful consequences of prohibiting informal marriages. Chief Justice John Bannister Gibson of Pennsylvania offered the strongest, and most frequent, argument in favor of common-law marriage: "It is not too much to say, that a rigid execution . . . [of colonial marriage regulations] would bastardize the vast majority of children which have been born within the state for half a century." He accepted that the laws may have been "wholesome when they were enacted," but contended that by 1833 they had become "ill adapted to the habits and customs of society as it now exists." Jurists like Gibson refused to upset years of cohabitation or deny family property rights merely to uphold public regulatory authority. While on the New Hampshire bench, the future Jacksonian Supreme Court Justice Levi Woodbury argued emphatically that common-law marriage enhanced rather than demeaned matrimony. "Under this view," he held, "the purity and sacredness of the marriage contract will remain not less but rather more inviolate, than under a different construction. For now the contract will never be annulled for any accidental or designed irregularity not extending to the essential grounds of the contract."[30]

A minority of the bench and bar stood with Parsons. A few went even further than Parsons and held licenses and parental consent necessary for a valid marriage. Theophilus Parsons Jr. articulated the concerns and convictions of these jurists when he asked in his 1853 treatise: "How can a contract be said to be regulated, not by the mere will of the parties, but by the provisions of law, if the mere will of the parties controls these provisions, and they have no force or effect whatever, if only the parties choose to disregard them?" To those who agreed with such sentiments, the social importance of matrimony mandated that it be formally sealed. In setting aside Woodbury's 1820 vindication of common-law marriage, the New Hampshire Supreme Court complained in 1848: "It is singular that the most important of all human contracts, on which the rights and duties of the whole community depend, requires less formality for its validity than a conveyance of an acre of land, a policy of insurance, or the agreements which the statute of frauds requires should be in writing." A public vow in front of an authorized agent of the state, argued opponents of common-law marriages, constituted the barest minimum protection for couples and the society.[31]

By advocating the preservation of a significant public role in marriage celebrations, these judges correspondingly narrowed the scope of individual nuptial rights and downplayed the social consequences of banning irregular marriages. The Tennessee bench acknowledged "the rights of innocent offspring to speak in such a case," but countered that "the rights of offended society must be heard" as well. This bench, and others like it, dwelt on what became a litany of common-law marriage evils: the specter of immoral cohabitation, consensual coupling and uncoupling, and endless property litigation. This minority reading of law and public policy reflected the persistence of an older ideal of protecting social order by the rigid enforcement of public standards on wayward individuals—a view that these jurists found perfectly compatible with republican legal ideas and commitments.[32]

The opponents of common-law marriage also received assistance from the mother country. In *Regina* v. *Millis* (1844), a divided House of Lords held that under the ecclesiastical and common law of England the presence of an ordained clergyman had always been essential to the creation of a valid marriage. Though their decision was later reaffirmed, the Lords' reading of law and history has been repudiated. According to the English legal historians Sir Frederick Pollock and Frederic W. Maitland: "[I]f the victorious case pleased the lords, it is the vanquished cause that will please the historian of the middle ages." Nevertheless, the opinion gave succor to the American dissenters.[33]

Expanding the Legal Freedom to Marry

The triumph of common-law marriage early in the nineteenth century, coming at a crucial time in the development of American family law, ensured that nuptial freedom would be one of the law's centerpieces. The ramifications of that commitment are evident, not only in the wide judicial acceptance of common-law marriage, but also in the complementary legislative tendency to relax statutory requirements as part of the pervasive republican effort to dismantle constraints on individual action. Though the legitimacy of public nuptial regulation stood unquestioned, legislators and judges simplified or eliminated key marriage-law provisions. Connecticut's Zephaniah Swift described the resulting tilt in the post-Revolutionary balance of nuptial power: "[M]easures may be taken to . . . stop all private and clandestine marriages; but if the marriage be celebrated without consent, or publication, it is valid, and the performer is only liable to penalty."[34]

Accordingly, legislators throughout the nation freed weddings from state controls. They lowered fees and authorized a widening number of religious sects, municipal officials, and judicial officers to perform marriages. Though it began in the colonial era, Connecticut's experience is typical. In 1694 ministers were allowed to officiate at marriages along with local magistrates. By 1702 both could exercise that right, but only within their towns. In 1783 their jurisdictions were extended countywide in the first post-Revolutionary revision. As a result of an 1820 act, ministers no longer had to be settled in a particular parish to marry couples. One year later marriages celebrated according to the rites of any sect were declared valid. An 1847 statute conferred matrimonial authority on all licensed ministers who had exercised their religious duties for over a year. Finally, in 1855 the legislature allowed every ordained minister in Connecticut who was engaged in religious work to solemnize a marriage.

The pace differed, but the other states also removed barriers created by colonial magistrates to ensure family and community nuptial surveillance. An 1843 Indiana act epitomized the legislative approach:

> When any marriage is solemnized, the ceremony of marriage may be according to such form or custom as the person solemnizing the same may choose to adopt; but in all cases, no particular form of ceremony shall be necessary, except that the parties shall declare in the presence of the person solemnizing the marriage, that they take each other as husband and wife; and no marriage solemnized before any person professing to be an officer or minister authorized by law to solemnize marriages, shall be adjudged to be void.

Eleven years later the state made its position even clearer by declaring that a marriage would not be void if the parties to it believed it legal when it was consummated.

These legislative changes had a double effect: they diminished the effectiveness of public regulation; and they provided easier access to formal ceremonies, thus lessening the need for clandestine alternatives. Freed from doctrinal, geographic, and bureaucratic controls, even formal nuptial ceremonies became an act between the betrothed and an agent of the state.[35]

As the major determiners of marriage law, judges used their interpretive powers to relax nuptial regulations still further. In 1818 the South Carolina bench dismissed a suit against a justice of the peace for marrying a couple in violation of a 1706 act confining that power to the clergy.

Justice John F. Grimke denigrated the statute as an antirepublican attempt to "establish the Episcopal Church in preference to all others." He argued that "since the establishment of our free constitution the act is totally inapplicable to our change of situation, and must therefore be considered obsolete."

Across the border in North Carolina, Chief Justice Ruffin undermined the original purpose of having a public representative at a wedding. In an 1852 bigamy decision he ruled that it was not necessary that a minister be "in charge of a church or the rector of a parish, or pastor of a particular flock." It was only essential that "he should have appeared to be a minister, capable of entering upon the duties of such a charge, according to the ecclesiastical economy of his church." Up north in New Hampshire, even before the state legislature allowed unsettled ministers to officiate at weddings, the state Supreme Court approved a marriage performed by a defrocked cleric. As judges and legislators whittled away at traditional checks on nuptial freedom, couples found it easier and easier to locate complaisant officials who would not pry into their private affairs.[36]

Publicity, which like local control was a community curb on matrimony, also faced the judicial and statutory ax. By the first decades of the nineteenth century most states had adopted a dual system of banns and licenses. But neither device served its original purpose of prodding parents, guardians, and neighbors into coming forward, of not holding their peace. Banns, best suited to communities with fixed populations committed to neighborly watchfulness, declined in use as the sense of corporate solidarity and willingness to abide by community decisions waned. The middle class and the gentry in particular dismissed the ancient controls as vulgar and unfashionable embarrassments as well as invasions of a newfound privacy. The mobility of individuals and families and urban growth also rendered public notice less and less effective.

Licenses emerged as the primary method of public surveillance. But even these administrative controls acquired a negative image among a populace that jealously shielded its activities from public inquiry and saw little need to follow nuptial directives. Resistance to license fees, which still meant posting a bond in many states, and administrative carelessness undermined licensing as a nuptial regulator. Efforts to strengthen the laws often died in legislative chambers. In North Carolina, an anti-common-law-marriage state, attempts by some of the state's leading politicians to enact a marriage-registration law failed four times in fifteen years. Only New England retained a semblance of community nuptial policing.[37]

The judiciary contributed to the devaluation of licenses by treating them as administrative aids instead of regulatory devices. According to the courts, licenses were to register, not restrict marriage. An 1857 New Hampshire decision chronicled the process. Jane Wood's father sued the minister who solemnized her marriage; the cleric had received a false certificate from the county clerk. But the court refused to disturb the union. The justices contended that prior to 1854 "the design and policy of the legislature seems to have been to give to the relatives and friends of the parties intending marriage, notice of their intentions." The 1854 act that eliminated banns and substituted licenses, they held, "seems to have abandoned entirely the policy of notice to relatives and others interested, and to have adopted instead thereof the simple procedure of securing somewhere, either before or after the marriage, an authentic record of the names, ages, and residence of those citizens in this state contracting marriage." This legislative and judicial concurrence acted upon the conclusion that communal controls no longer suited mobile individualistic mid-nineteenth-century Americans.[38]

Although parents, especially among the wealthy, exerted a powerful influence over their children's marriages, official backing for that power crumbled as the judiciary and local officials assumed many of the paternal duties formerly held by fathers. As for guardians, a writer in an 1845 legal journal observed that their opposition "may be macadamized by the court of chancery."[39] Parents who opposed their children's matches could use the law only to close the avenues by which the disobedient son or daughter might circumvent them; many succeeded.

Ministers and magistrates who joined a young couple without parental dispensations were repeatedly haled into court by disgruntled families. Judges refused to allow those officials to displace parents completely. The Pennsylvania high court so informed a justice of the peace who had exceeded his authority. The magistrate had solemnized the marriage of a pregnant fifteen-year-old. When her father sued, the magistrate pleaded to the court that "in such cases the constant practice has been for justices to marry the parties." Asserting that these "circumstances are proper for the consideration of the father, and no doubt, would always be duly weighed by him," the court sternly rebuked the local justice: "But to suffer them to be given in evidence, as a justification of the justice, would be transferring to the justice, that parental control over young women, which policy and nature have reserved to parents. As to the practice, it, being clearly unlawful, can be no justification." In this way parental nuptial authority became indirect; families only retained the right to hold public agents accountable for their carelessness.[40]

The Courts Put Old Rules to New Purposes

The continuing practice of irregular marriage, combined with unreliable public records and laissez faire government, made it difficult for couples to substantiate their marriages. However, judges placed the weight of the law behind those living as husband and wife. They did so by formally receiving into American common law the old rule that marriage could be presumed from the acknowledgements, cohabitation, and reputation of a couple.

Post-Revolutionary contractualism gave the common-law doctrine new vitality. Treating matrimony like a contract, a South Carolina chancellor asserted, made it "susceptible to an infinite variety of proof." That necessity arose from the fact that couples could "express their agreement by parol, they may signify it by whatever ceremony their whim, or their taste, or their religious belief, may select; it is the agreement itself, not the form in which it is couched which constitutes the contract." At the heart of the judiciary's incorporation of the presumption of marriage lay a persistent inclination to find matrimony whenever a man and a woman lived together. Since most cases invoking the presumption of matrimony involved the rights of widows and children to the estates of their husbands and fathers, this standard protected their claims against all but the most thoroughly documented attacks.[41]

In a clear policy decision favoring practice over form, courts refused to dissolve marriages and break up families for lack of evidence of a wedding ceremony. While turning away a woman's attempt to deprive her brother's widow of a share in his estate because there had been no formal rites, the New York bench asserted: "Society would not be safe for a moment, in this, the most sacred of its relations, if an open and public cohabitation as man and wife for ten years, continued with all the conventional usages of married life, and followed by the procreation of children, could be overturned by relating stale conversations and private statements of the husband as to the particular mode and the inception of the relation."

The bench disregarded warnings that domestic disorder might result from legal aid unwittingly granted to illicit unions, confident that it was capable of detecting immorality and that even more debilitating social evils would proceed from disbanding families. Pennsylvania Chief Justice William Tilghman, Gibson's Federalist predecessor, used the social reality of antebellum America to justify his 1816 decision reversing a lower-court ruling and awarding dower to a widow:

We have no established church. A certificate of the bishop, therefore, is out of the question. We have no law compelling the keeping of a register by all persons who perform the marriage ceremony. Our marriages are celebrated sometimes by clergymen, sometimes by justices of the peace and sometimes before witnesses, without the intervention of clergymen or justices. Many of our citizens are emigrants from foreign countries where they were married. Many marriages take place in parts of our country but thinly settled. To hold a woman, therefore, to proof of her actual marriage might be productive of great inconvenience, without any advantage.

Lax nuptial laws combined with a fervent belief in American exceptionalism to breathe new life into old common-law presumptions.[42]

By presuming marriage, judges could distinguish between two issues: the exact manner in which a marriage was formed and the evidence of its actual existence. In concentrating on the latter, they avoided the intractable question of formal and informal marriages. "[T]he only difference between a marriage celebrated by a formal ceremony and one not so celebrated," the New York Supreme Court explained, "is that in the former case regular celebration is conclusive proof of the mutual consent requisite to the validity of the marriage, while in the latter it is competent to rebut proof of the marriage by other evidence." In states that recognized common-law marriages, this presumption became the means by which such unions could be proved. More important, in the states that did not recognize common-law marriages, judges could use it to dodge the issue. One such jurist, Chief Justice Richmond Pearson of North Carolina, admitted that "as in this state there is no registry of marriages . . . frequently circumstantial evidence is the only mode of proving" a marriage. The result strengthened the legality of irregular marriage while undermining its opposition.[43]

The strands of this intricate judicial policy were brought together in an 1869 Pennsylvania decision. The state supreme court upheld the validity of a secret marriage between a University of Pennsylvania professor from an aristocratic Italian family and an Irish servant. Reversing a lower-court opinion denying the woman and her child the professor's estate, the justices proposed that "marriage, followed by the birth of issue, lies at the very base of the social fabric and of all good morals, and looking at the consequences to society we feel unwilling to suffer an acknowledged marriage and parentage of children to be overthrown by weak and inconclusive reasons drawn from the difference of position in life, and from conduct readily explained by the circumstances of the parties." Denying that the professor's decision to hide his marriage from his family invalidated it, the court solemnly declared: "Mystery may surround its origins, suspicion may linger in its circumstances, and slight doubt may disturb its clearness, but the policy of the state demands that this relation should not be lightly discredited and the issue bastardized." This policy was necessary, the justices concluded, "in a country where marriage is a civil contract and often unattended by ceremony or performed by a single officiating witness."[44]

New York offered a dramatic exhibition of the antistatist biases spawned by these nuptial policies. In the late 1820s a special commission revised the state code. The suggested changes included language that appeared to grant validity to formally solemnized unions only. During the interim between passage and implementation a controversy erupted over the proposal. Chancellor Kent, among others, argued that it would nullify common-law marriages. The revisers assured skeptics that their only intent had been to offer a statutory means for couples desiring to register their bonds. The new code, they insisted, did not abolish common-law marriage. Nevertheless, as Kent triumphantly reported in his *Commentaries*: "These regulations were found to be so inconvenient, that they had scarcely gone into operation, when the legal efficacy of them was destroyed, and the loose doctrine of the common law restored" by an act passed in April 1830. In New York, as in most states, courts and legislators united to promote matrimony by endorsing private, not public, regulation.[45]

Republican Nuptials

The French observer Auguste Carlier recognized the significance of the now triumphant republican notion of matrimony. "It is true," he admitted, "some people hold that the publicity of marriage is of no interest; that the union of individuals is their exclusive affair alone, and concerns no one else." The European visitor also acknowledged that such sentiments flowed from the "predominant view in America that the individual is superior to the community, and the latter should not exercise any restraints, except in rare cases, and from reasons of most serious moment." Even so, he strongly disapproved of the lax policies. Carlier's own evaluation of marriage revealed the deep gulf between his more traditional conception of domestic relations and that of the law in the nation he toured: "[M]arriage is the foundation of the family, and creates new relations between persons who have been strangers to each other, and hence come rights and duties of every nature, domestic, civil, political, and it cannot be too much protected as an institution most ancient and respectable of all, where morality is tempered by social condition."[46]

The legal acceptance accorded informal marriage reflected a view of matrimony quite at odds with Carlier's. By legitimizing private practice, marriage law strengthened the proposition that social order came through the validation of voluntary decisions rather than through regulated conduct. Though its sources differed, marriage law paralleled other antebellum legal policies that encouraged private decision-making. In particular, common-law marriage—what Powell calls the "utilitarian solution" to the problem of informal matrimony—reveals some central legal tendencies of the formative era of family law.[47] Common-law marriage gave the courts flexibility in governing nuptials and enhanced the judicial commitment to a common-law construction of domestic rights.

Moreover, loose nuptial regulation complemented the placement of marriage and other domestic relations in a special private realm of life. In doing so, it encouraged the flowering of republican nuptial mores, most notably mate selection based on romantic love rather than parental arrangements. Disagreements over the wisdom of recognizing informal marriages disclose the variety of solutions offered by the courts as they struggled to govern the republican family. But the debate also reveals the explicit policy views of all judges drawn into marriage disputes. Even more than in breach-of-promise cases, judges of all persuasions were doggedly, in the parlance of mid-twentieth-century judicial criticism, "result oriented."

The law ensured that informal marriage existed for those who wanted or needed it. Its underlying optimism (and paternalism) found expression in an 1860 Georgia decision. After declaring that the legislature could impose compulsory nuptial formalities whenever it chose, Chief Justice Joseph Lumpkin observed:

> For myself, I approve of the law as it is [without compulsory formalities]. True, it will sometimes be abused. What human law is not? Rarely however will the parties forego the benefits resulting from a compliance with the statutes. It adds so much both to the respectability as well as the security of the contract. I have never known of a self-solemnized marriage. But suppose one should occur; better for the parties, especially the female, that the law should be as it is. Her honor is saved and this is worth much more than everything, even life itself. All other contracts may be rescinded, and the parties restored to their former conditions; marriage cannot be undone.[48]

The official recognition of irregular marriages acted as a further step from the patriarchal families of the nation's colonial past, one more step toward the republican concept of the household as a voluntary collection of separate individuals. Anomalies existed, but by mid-century judicially inspired liberal rules governed nuptial rites in almost every state. The commonality of approach demonstrates the strength of the social forces that leveled the walls constructed earlier around the marriage ceremony.

A Marriage Reform Movement Challenges the Law

The tolerance of informal matrimony by jurists like Lumpkin evoked growing criticism in mid-century America. By the 1870s an organized reform campaign questioned the intent and methods of American family law. Reformers, legislators, social scientists, journalists, evangelical Protestants, and other interested parties assailed marriage law for its laxity and its failure to protect society from marital instability. Their attacks prompted a defense of nuptial law, most notably by the bench and its law-writing allies.

Out of the conflict came major alterations in the regulation of marriage, which cleared the way for greater state intervention into nuptials. By the first decades of the twentieth century, judicial dominion and nuptial privatism in marriage law had been significantly circumscribed, though not eliminated. The law retained its republican base, but to it had been added a new conception of "the public interest" in matrimony, which diluted its antistatism and common-law hegemony. The law slowly achieved a new institutional and policy balance as marriage regulation became a major controversy in post–Civil War America.

Marriage reform in late nineteenth-century America is an example of what social critic Stan Cohen has labeled a "moral panic." In an analysis of the British response to the youth movements of the 1950s and 1960s, Cohen argues that such mass phenomena erupt when a "condition, episode, person or group of persons emerges to become defined as a threat to societal values and interests; its nature is presented in a stylized and stereotypical fashion by the mass media; the moral barricades are manned by editors, bishops and politicians and other right-thinking people; socially accredited experts pronounce their diagnoses and solutions; ways of coping are evolved, or (more often) resorted to; the condition then disappears, submerges, or deteriorates." Sometimes panics pass and are forgotten. But other times, he suggests, the panic "has more serious and long term repercussions and it might produce changes in legal and social policy or even in the way in which societies conceive themselves." Such social scares offer a means of expressing deep-seated fears and help focus those concerns on the most visible symbols of the crisis, what Cohen terms "folk devils."[49] In nineteenth-century American domestic relations, panics over family life led to persistent efforts to compel deviant couples to adhere to orthodox republican matrimonial practices. Legal coercion became one of the most trusted weapons of reform.

The Case against Marriage Law

In 1888 the Massachusetts attorney and reformer Frank Gaylor Cook used the genteel pages of the *Atlantic Monthly* to put the marriage crisis into historical perspective. He sketched a portrait of a harmonious, pastoral past when "population was small, simple, and conservative" and "respect for law and conformity to the civil regulations almost universal" primarily because settlers "of the same race and faith usually dwelt together." These rude settlements had a "unanimity of sentiment in the protection of the common interest and the maintenance of social order." In that pristine time, of course, the "statutory forms for the celebration of marriage had been generally observed." Now, Cook lamented, all was chaos. The "widest diversity of race, religion, and sentiments existed among the populace." Cities multiplied, labor was "forsaking the fields" to congregate in factories and tenements, and even women faced new temptations as they worked outside the home and competed directly with men. The inevitable result: "industrial struggle and discontent and social evils are rife in the community."

Cook singled out lax marriage and divorce laws as the prime causes of the all-too-apparent social disintegration. Worried that the family, "the unit and source of society," might become a casualty of industrializing America, he declared that its integrity was "dependent no less upon its legal inception than upon its legal termination." Fearful that the more obvious problem of divorce would lull concerned Americans into a false sense of security about matrimony, he called upon all citizens alarmed by nuptial laxity to join the campaign for legal reform.[50]

George Eliot Howard personified the crusaders who answered Cook's call. A German-trained Stanford sociologist, he published a three-volume *History of Matrimonial Institutions* in 1904. It quickly became the era's authoritative statement on marital policy. Howard emerged as the major representative of a new constituency in family governance, the expert social scientist. Social scientists were able to create a place for themselves in the development and administration of domestic relations law because they offered appealing explanations of and remedies for the problems of industrial society. In the fight over the family, social scientists became a new source of authority taking their place alongside legal professionals, clerics, tract writers, and genteel reformers.

Howard argued that matrimony could be a success only when it united two competent, capable individuals who had judiciously chosen to bind themselves to each other. He accepted the right of individuals to abandon unhappy unions, but worried over the social costs of divorce. Howard hoped to find a proper balance between individual and social needs by using state authority to screen prospective husbands and wives effectively. "A good marriage code," he explained in a 1910 article, "tends to check hasty, clandestine, frivolous, and immature wedlock. A bad marriage law favors such unions, which so often end in divorce court." In common with most social scientists of the day, Howard strongly advocated a preventative approach to this social ill. Laws designed to prevent unsound unions from being formed, he contended, would be more effective and just than harsh divorce laws that tried vainly to keep troubled couples together.

Howard also shared the buoyant optimism of the period. The sociologist took issue with the old saw that "[y]ou can't make people better by law is a popular saying; but it is not true." He countered "[y]ou *can* make people better by law. For instance, good laws may remove temptations and create opportunities. A good marriage law is prevention—social prophylaxis; whereas a good divorce law is cure—social therapeutics." Instead of blindly encouraging all marriages, Howard wanted the law to make sure that only "sound" unions were consummated: "[B]ad marriages are the only marriages which divorce dissolves." Good matches would emerge from a progressive matrimonial code enacted at the behest of enlightened public opinion.[51]

Though they accepted the right of men and women to expect marital happiness, proponents of tighter nuptial regulation like Cook and Howard insisted that a new balance be struck between individual rights and public welfare. An 1892 opinion by the Washington Supreme Court offered a justification for more active involvement in nuptial rites: "There is a growing belief that the welfare of society demands further restrictions in this direction, and that this will find a voice in future legislation; that an institution of this kind, which is so closely and thoroughly related to the state should be most carefully guarded, and that improvident and improper marriages should be prevented. . . . Every thoughtful person would desire that this be so, even though in some cases it might seem to result in individual hardship."[52] As this suggests, the mid-century debate over informal marriage stirred a search for a new statement of the public interest in matrimony.

Trying to devise a broadly acceptable notion of public regulatory authority hampered most reformers in the era, and family savers proved to be no exception. They struggled in part because many reformers followed Cook's lead and couched their proposals in nostalgic terms. Yet their calls for more stringent state intervention rested on a new relationship between the individual and the state which bore little resemblance to the colonial bonds to which many reformers constantly referred. The hierarchical, patriarchal family no longer served as a buffer between people and public authority. Each citizen's legal identity now had its source in his or her individuality, not in family or community membership. Stronger nuptial controls would have to be applied directly by the state, not through the family or other intermediaries like the church. Marriage thus remained as judges had earlier defined it, an act between a man, a woman, and the state; but the law's critics now demanded room at the altar for the third party.

As in so many areas of conflict in an increasingly expansive, diverse, and class-conscious America, when moral suasion failed, family savers turned to state coercion. They demanded, often successfully, that public controls be substituted for private choice in the formulation of marriages. Yet reformers intent on expanding state authority continually clashed with judges, legislators, and others equally determined to limit state intervention into what they still considered the private domain, in order to protect the definition of public and private spheres carved out early in the century. Out of the ensuing struggle came a significant revision of public and private nuptial rights.

The Fight over Common-Law Marriages

"We have a right," Vermont minister M. H. Buckham proclaimed in the 1882 *International Review*, "to expect that every precaution shall be taken which law can devise to insure that the family shall be constituted with deliberation, with adequate maturity of judgment, with sufficient formality, to guarantee the full and free choice of the parties entering into it." Diagnosing legal laxity as the problem, reformers proposed regulation as the cure: publicity, formal ceremonies, registration. Since these were precisely the requirements nullified by common-law marriage, that practice became the symbol of what was wrong with existing marriage law and the prime target of its reform.

Opponents took up the cudgels of earlier critics like Chief Justice Parsons, and added some new complaints. They called common-law marriage misguided and pernicious, and charged it as well with spawning social anarchy and untrammeled individualism; these were serious accusations in a society thought to be suffering from what one reformer labeled "social disintegration."[53]

The foes of common-law marriage forced a reconsideration of its social consequences that paralleled the reassessment of breach-of-marriage-promise actions, but with different implications for the law. Arguments in favor of informal marriage began to lose their persuasiveness. Gordon A. Stewart reversed the prevailing priorities when he insisted that banning common-law marriage "by general statutory provisions might work hardship in some individual cases; but its existence works more harm to society and bastardizes more children than would enactment of stringent marriage laws, for parties would then be more careful and not enter into such relations without proof of marriage."

Howard agreed; in his 1904 study he exploded what he considered to be the fallacies of his opponents by patronizingly asserting, as experts did so easily, that it was far better

> that the children of a delinquent minority should bear the stain of illegitimacy than that the welfare of the whole social body should be endangered. For the same reason the supposed right of the individual must yield to the higher claims of society. In no part of the whole range of human activity is there such imperative need of state interference and control as in the sphere of matrimonial relations. In this field as in others we are beginning to see more clearly that the highest individual liberty can be secured only when it is subordinated to the highest social good.

Instead of aiding the virtuous, Howard and his allies contended, common-law marriage merely protected the disreputable acts of an immoral minority and bred blackmail, fraudulent estate claims, and sexual license.[54]

Howard's opposition to common-law marriage also illustrates the diversity and some of the inconsistencies of marriage-law reform. Unlike most family savers, he and a few others, especially feminists like Elizabeth Cady Stanton, paired their opposition to informal marriages with an endorsement of divorce as a needed outlet for men and women trapped in failed marriages. They championed stringent nuptial regulation as a better mechanism for policing domestic relations than strict divorce laws; indeed they looked to rational marriage as the only effective solution to the marital crisis. Contradictory aims like these permeated the movement and often sapped its energy and effectiveness.[55]

All critics of common-law marriage challenged its legitimacy. William E. Bullock indignantly reported that in spite of the "repeated lessons of history the contest between true and spurious marriage had to be renewed in this country" because the courts "flaunt again before the eyes of disgusted Christendom the scurrilous device of marriage *per verba, verba cum copula.*" He accused the bench of tending to "confuse the public mind as to the nature of true marriage" and thus engendering divorce. The attorney protested that the "existence of the rule as laid down by Chancellor Kent has never since been questioned, but the rule has often been criticized by the courts as opposed to morality, and the secret marriages to which it logically leads are condemned as suspiciously near the borderland of illicit intercourse." But due to judicial intransigence and ignorance, Bullock lamented, the only "remedy for the evils of common law marriage is to abolish it."[56]

Bullock's frustration with the courts was well warranted. To the reformers' amazement and dismay, common-law marriage remained deeply entrenched in American marriage law. It won the endorsement of several state supreme courts in the latter part of the century, and elicited the imprimatur of the United States Supreme Court in 1877. In giving its blessing to the Michigan wedding of a white man and an Indian woman who had not observed the state's nuptial forms, the justices declared that "such a contract constitutes a marriage at common law there can be no doubt, in view of the adjudications made in this country from its earliest settlements to the present day. No doubt States may take away a common-law right, but there is always the presumption that the legislature has no such intention, unless it be plainly expressed."

State jurists also expressed few doubts about common-law marriage. Justice Thomas M. Cooley of Michigan, whose best-selling *Constitutional Limitations* (1868) became the Bible of lawyers and judges battling state commercial regulation, gave common-law marriage his approval in an 1875 decision. Though better known for his defense of economic liberty, Cooley was equally insistent that legislatures refrain from unwarranted social regulation. A disciple of the law-as-science movement, Cooley considered common-law marriage one of the law's discoverable axioms, since it was, he declared in the 1875 case of *Hutchins* v. *Kimmell*, "the settled doctrine of American courts, the few cases of dissent, or apparent dissent, being borne down by the great weight of authority in favor of the rule."[57]

As Cooley acknowledged, dissenting opinions did exist among his brethren. Decisions against common-law marriage were handed down in the Federal District Court of Oregon (1870) and in the highest tribunals of Maryland (1871), West Virginia (1887), and Washington (1892) in cases of first instance. Despite the attempts of reformers to discredit the legal standing of common-law marriages, these decisions merely perpetuated the debate begun by Kent and Parsons.[58]

Judicial doubts regarding common-law marriage even turned up in a few of the states that accepted it. In New York, the birthplace of Kent's doctrine, one judge grumbled in 1869: "I wish it were in my power . . . to take away from the law, respecting the marriage contract, the reproach imparted to it." But however sympathetic such judges may have been to the complaints of reformers, their first commitment still lay with the common law, and they refused to support unilateral abolition of common-law marriage. As the Minnesota Supreme Court observed in 1896: "In view of the increasing number of common law marriage widows laying claim (in many instances, doubtless fraudulently), to estates of deceased men, it is a question whether the common law should not be changed; but with it the courts have nothing to do." Such jurists implicitly agreed with reformers that change must come from the statehouse, not the courtroom.[59]

Most of the bench and bar, though, endorsed common-law marriage not because of slavish adherence to precedent but rather because they agreed with the doctrine itself. Dwelling on the consistent opposition to informal marriage in New England, the Virginia lawyer W. D. Harris deplored the tendency to administer the law with "puritanic strictness." He argued that when a couple lived together, "public interest and the general welfare of society are better advanced by holding that they are in law, as well as in fact, husband and wife."

Advocates of common-law marriage like Harris did not believe that those who intended to live immoral lives would be deterred by strict codes. They insisted that it was better to suffer a few illicit unions than to risk injury and injustice to innocent couples and their children, and that the state had minimal nuptial responsibilities in republican government. "The State," New York City judge and former United States attorney Noah Davis argued in the 1874 *North American Review*, "should recognize the validity of all marriages between competent persons, made in any mode or form that indicates the making of a civil contract." He urged that legislators grant "the largest possible freedom to matrimony." The Mississippi Supreme Court made the point more succinctly in 1895 when it asserted that no court should nullify a marriage entered into openly and honestly "because of some wretched formality which has been overlooked or disregarded."[60]

Joel Bishop became the foremost opponent of state marital activism, writing impassioned defenses of common-law nuptial rights. In his popular treatise on matrimony, he castigated those who would deny marriage except when solemnized under special forms, and offered his own version of the decline and fall of Western civilization: "In proportion as a nation or state passes out of simple innocence and purity and into artificial rakishness, lust, and the debasement of real marriage, the laws put up their artificial barriers to matrimony in cumbersome forms which they rendered essential to legal marriage." Attacking legislative incursions into nuptial rights, Bishop used this history lesson to plead for a return to the simple common law. Trying to prevent the disintegration of legal and social support for common-law marriage, he implored: "Let us hope that the legislation of our states travelling not yet rapidly in this direction will pause and reverse its steps."[61]

Growing State Incursions into Nuptial Rights

Bishop's wish did not come to pass. On the contrary, the pace of legislation accelerated as reformers hammered away at nuptial laxity. They unleashed a barrage of criticism in the form of government surveys, muckraking press reports, legal and scholarly articles, and social science studies. The New England Divorce Reform League (later rechristened the National League for the Protection of the Family) assumed titular control of the campaign in 1881. Under the leadership of its executive secretary, the Congregational minister Samuel Dike, the League launched a concerted national drive for family-law reform through legislation and public education.

Dike, married and the father of four children, lost his congregation when he refused to officiate at the remarriage of an influential member of the church. Freed from the pulpit, he turned to reform. In 1881 Dike issued the League's rallying cry: "A thorough examination of the nature, the rights, and the place of the Family in civil society is the duty of the hour." He recruited a distinguished collection of board members, including Yale President Theodore Dwight Woolsey, Massachusetts attorney Cook, Dean E. H. Bennett of Boston University Law School, Frederic Stimson of the Harvard Government Department, the future reform mayor of New York City Seth Low, Yale Law professor Simeon E. Baldwin, and other professionals from the legal, scientific, and reform communities. Their object, as the League declared in 1881 and repeated in its yearly reports, was "to promote an improvement in public sentiment and legislation on the institution of the family, especially as affected by existing evils relating to marriage and divorce."[62]

Dike made the League the vanguard of the marriage-law reform movement. Tirelessly lecturing before professional and civic organizations, testifying to state legislative committees, writing articles and commentaries on the family question, compiling annual legislative assessments, and prodding other reformers into action, he became the major instigator of a broad-based effort to protect the family through tightened nuptial governance. In his constant attempts to rally support to his standard, Dike was fond of quoting British Prime Minister William Gladstone, who had declared in the 1889 *Nineteenth Century*: "[I]t seems indisputable that America is the arena in which many of the problems connected with the marriage state are in the course of being rapidly, painfully, and perilously tried out."

To ensure that the nation successfully met the challenge, Dike put together an organized campaign out of disparate reform efforts. Priding himself on the League's scientific methods, he condescendingly remarked in the 1898 report: "[S]pasmodic efforts at legal reform, popular crusades against some flagrant offense against decency, may have their value; but when their immediate occasion passes those who engage in them are too apt to forget the long and arduous task that remains—that of removing the roots of the special evil and cleansing the soil in which it grows." Taking a long-term, process view of reform strategy, Dike aligned the League with emerging social science approaches to domestic ills. He congratulated the League in the same report for its early recognition that "the great social movement of our day and our problem of the family are inseparably connected": a position that was now "the widely accepted principle of our best schools of sociology." These techniques turned the League into a clearinghouse for marriage and divorce data, and the center of a network of state nuptial reform lobbying and initiating educational drives.[63]

One of Dike's first major triumphs came in 1889 when he and his colleagues finally convinced Congress to fund a national survey of marriage and divorce laws. Dike insisted that the League take the lead in the use of "the scientific method in social reform"; and the survey reflected his faith in statistical information as a reform tool. The report was compiled by a like-minded reformer, United States Labor Commissioner Carroll D. Wright, former Massachusetts patent lawyer, state senator, and the first head of the state's Bureau of Labor Statistics. Examining state records on marriage and divorce between 1867 and 1889, Wright deplored the lack of reliable data on marriage. His survey concluded that most states kept such poor records that precise statistical analysis of the nation's nuptial practices was impossible. For a nation just entering the empirical age, data scarcity itself was an indictment of lax nuptial governance, as Dike constantly complained.[64]

The 1889 survey lent further credence to one of the major accusations leveled at existing nuptial governance: legal uncertainty. In an 1881 essay on the confusion of American marriage law, which won a New York University Law School prize, Charles Noble bemoaned "the contradictory and indefinite rules which come to us from various parts of the United States, when we ask this most fundamental of questions, 'What constitutes a valid marriage?' "[65]

Certainty was the goal of all those involved in the marriage question, indeed of the law itself. Most judges and lawyers held up the common law as the best device for securing certainty, but reformers like Dike and Noble demanded codification. Struggle between common law and codes had deviled the legal system since the first years of the republic, but primarily in issues involving criminal law and economic regulation. Now marriage became part of the codification battle.

A major barrier blocked legislative relief: the contractual emphasis in marriage law. The priority it gave individual nuptial rights buttressed the stunted public regulatory authority that reformers decried. Consequently, they stressed the other half of the legal equation, the status element of matrimony. Reverend M. H. Buckham, president of Dike's League, argued insistently that "the constitution of the Family is not merely a legal one; it is also moral. Marriage is not merely a contract, because to a contract there are two parties who remain two after as before the contract. Marriage is a union; They are not more twain, but one flesh." New York attorney Bullock made the point more forcefully by declaring that marriage "is as much a matter of public necessity if the race is to go on and the family to be preserved, as it is of individual consent in the selection of mates." By infusing the debate over marriage law with arguments that accentuated the contractual limits of matrimony, the reformers built support for the imposition of some restrictions on nuptial rights. Year by year, the League recorded legislative changes that compelled couples to wed formally, thus deterring irregular unions. By century's end, nearly every state had so revised its nuptial laws.[66]

These legislative changes laid the foundation for a new nuptial code. To ensure publicity, obtain accurate information on the state of matrimony, and regularize family status for estate and property purposes, most states began to require public notification of new unions. By 1907 twenty-seven states had procedures for the registration of marriages. The compilation of such vital statistics, long a practice in Europe, represented a marked deviation from traditional American resistance to state information gathering. John Wigmore, a Northwestern University law professor, noted in 1903 that "the deep-seated Anglo-Saxon individualism and its repugnance to state interference in family life and private affairs, has availed until comparatively recent times to leave its communities lacking in such an advantage." New York City offered a case in point; municipal officials "had difficulty getting the [marriage registration] system going twenty years after its passage in 1847." But the bureaucratic and reformist determination to document the exact condition of marriage and divorce gradually overwhelmed that traditional aversion. These reform efforts may well have coincided with a growing popular inclination to document legal actions of all sorts.[67]

As it had been previously, the formal ceremony became the primary mechanism for tightening public supervision of marriage. Reformers assumed that when a couple publicly exchanged vows, the seriousness of their new bonds would be clear to them. The marriage license was the primary device. It served a dual purpose: requiring examination of a couple's fitness for matrimony by a public official, and providing a means of recording marital information for statistical purposes. Licenses thus became the society's first line of defense against unwanted marriages, and signalled the end of legislative tolerance of unconfirmable matrimony. By 1906 only New York and South Carolina lacked code provisions requiring the acquisition of a license before a wedding. In 1892 Mississippi enacted the stiffest law. It held marriages void if celebrated without a license, and thereby eliminated a crucial statutory support for common-law marriage.[68]

Banns played an increasingly smaller role in nuptials as states began to rely on licenses. By the end of the century only Pennsylvania, Delaware, Maryland, and Georgia even authorized their use, a vivid illustration of the shift from the traditional policy of community watchfulness to the new one of bureaucratic responsibility. According to a European commentator on this transatlantic development: "[P]ublicity is no longer secured by the reading in the pulpit of promises of marriage. The State alone, with the concurrence of the press, can secure it."[69]

The change was accomplished by transforming the old banns into a new device—advance notice. Beginning with Maine in 1848, legislatures demanded that couples wait a prescribed period of time after being examined and before being wed. By 1940 over half the nation's states had adopted this safeguard. A pair of sociologists, Fred S. Hall and Mary Richmond, explained the significance of the reformulation of the banns in a 1929 survey of American matrimonial law:

> The earlier system of the banns was so devised, that if any impediment existed, others could interfere and bring forward their reasons for "forbidding the banns." The prevention of deliberate fraud is important, but far more important for both the protection of the state, and the welfare of the individual, is the boon of this additional, though brief, time for second thought. The state be-

comes able by this means to suggest that it has been called upon to sanction a contract, which, in so far as it is a civil contract at all, transcends all other civil contracts in value and significance.

After being granted a license by a public official, couples thus had a legally set time for reflection about their nuptial plans.[70]

The least successful reform was the attempt to control more tightly the number and qualifications of those authorized to perform weddings. Dike bitterly noted in 1886 that a "report, though almost incredible, is apparently well-founded that some clergymen have converted their privilege of solemnizing marriage into a trade and have their runners at ferries distributing bills and diagrams of the streets leading to their houses and hunting for couples with the diligence of a bunco-steerer." In spite of such revelations and the other alterations in nuptial rules, few states imposed severe restrictions on those conducting marriages. Several legislatures did make minor changes, such as placing geographical limits on the authority of magistrates. But they did not impose similar curbs on ministers nor reduce the number of marital celebrants. On the contrary, nuptial authority continued to be exercised by a dizzying array of public servants: New York granted the power to New York City aldermen, Tennessee to the speakers of the house and senate, Mississippi to county supervisors. Holding a public or religious office remained tantamount to a declaration of fitness for nuptial supervision.[71]

Only Massachusetts, which Dike constantly lauded as the national leader in nuptial reform, enacted a thoroughgoing change. Cook disclosed in 1886 the "surprising and disgraceful fact that there are in the city of Boston over a thousand justices of the peace with absolutely no special qualifications and hardly any responsibility but with full authority to represent society in the constitution of the most important civil relation, in which both the contracting parties and the State are supremely interested." In 1899 the state limited the number of authorized magistrates and required a special grant of matrimonial jurisdiction for those who remained. By 1922, only 257 such justices existed in the entire state.[72]

For the most part, though, reformers met only rebuffs in trying to convince state legislators to adopt the European practice of confining nuptial powers to a limited number of officials. Nor were they able to eradicate matrimonial entrepreneurs. The formal celebration of marriage remained localized and largely unregulated. Though a legally acceptable ceremony gradually became a standard practice, the actual mode of uniting a couple was left to them and an obliging celebrant. The business card of one justice of the peace graphically described the continuing nuptial reality:

If a man loves a girl,
    That's his business.
If a girl loves a man,
    That's her business.
If they want the knot tied,
    That's my business.[73]

The Judicial Defense of Common-Law Marriage

Though the august leaders of the bench and bar might have balked in claiming this justice of the peace as one of their own, his sentiments echoed theirs to a significant degree. Most lawyers and judges came to agree on the need for greater nuptial safeguards, but refused to accept significant expansion of state regulatory authority or reductions in the marriage responsibilities of the courts.

True, judges acknowledged, as they always had, that legislatures had the power to set the terms of nuptial regulation. But in most jurisdictions a gray area existed between legislation and judicial interpretation. This marital no-man's land and the uncertainty it fostered were chief complaints of reformers and jurists alike. In an 1881 compilation of Maryland family law, David Steward and Francis Carey offered the state's marriage laws as evidence for the proposition that "vague laws are as bad as no laws." Statutory reform narrowed the gap between code and common law, and an increasing tendency to solemnize formally and record marriages left the bench with a declining number of exceptional cases. Nevertheless, the bench did not concede its nuptial responsibilities. Judges staked out the perimeters of their jurisdiction and defended them against legislative incursions. Yet where their post-Revolutionary predecessors had cast off unrepublican restraints on nuptials, the late nineteenth-century bench concentrated on demarcating the exact boundaries of common-law nuptial rights.[74]

Judges preserved much of their discretion by retaining the axiom that marital regulations without explicit language making them compulsory were only directory. Most new statutes had been drafted vaguely enough to allow for flexible judicial interpretation. The Missouri Supreme Court expressed the late nineteenth-century judicial approach to nuptials in *State* v. *Bittick* (1890). The judges asserted that "all marriages should be entered into publicly before those authorized by law to solemnize them and place them upon the public records. But we are not here to make the law conform to what we think it ought to be, but to declare it as it is."

After that rather mechanical statement, the court discharged Hiram Bittick, who had been indicted for abducting and marrying sixteen-year-old Bertha Rice. The pair had hoped for a formal wedding, but Rice's mother withheld her consent, blocking their attempts to obtain a license. They performed their own ceremony at a friend's home and filed notice of their union with the county clerk. After reviewing marriage statutes passed in the state since 1857, the justices concluded that their legislative colleagues had never designated a license as absolutely mandatory to a valid marriage. Since no words nullifying irregular unions had been inserted in the code, they ruled that "we must conclusively presume that it was intended that the act shall be interpreted by the rule of this court. The legislature has the power to add these words at any time, but not the court." Seemingly submitting to the legislative will, the court in fact preserved its own discretion.[75]

Parents like Bertha Rice's mother who objected to the marriages of their children made extensive use of the nuptial code. As earlier in the century, most courts refused to terminate a union merely because a couple had failed to secure the consent of parents or other custodians. According to an 1872 reading of the law by the Illinois Supreme Court, statutory policy demanded the "encouragement, not the restraint of marriage." Consequently, it created "modes of its celebration at once simple, free from embarrassment, and adapted to the conditions, convenience and preference of every class of society." The only penalty, noted the justices, applied to agents of the state who failed to examine brides and grooms diligently. Parents could seek damages from such careless officials, but they could not void their offspring's new status. The North Carolina Supreme Court tried to ensure that public sentinels of marriage would recognize the gravity of their responsibilities by admonishing a county registrar who had issued a marriage license to a minor without evidence of parental consent:

> To all persons who believe that the welfare of human society depends largely upon the family relation and that the contract of marriage should be defended by careful and just laws for the purpose of guarding against legal impediments and to prevent the marriage of those under a certain age when the parties are presumed not to be able to contract, the duties of the Registrar of Deeds, the officer charged with the duty of issuing marriage licenses, seems most important and most solemn. . . . [H]e must exercise his duties conscientiously and not as a matter of mere form.[76]

Judges held these nuptial watchdogs to a vague standard of reasonable and diligent inquiry. In an 1890 pamphlet offering legal instructions to ministers who administered marriage rites, a New York attorney warned of unscrupulous couples, and proffered sage advice: "[B]e cautious in dealing with strangers." The courts adopted a case-by-case method of determining how well such suggestions were heeded.

Most important, neither the legislature nor the bench responded to the marriage controversy by reviving the strict family nuptial power formerly granted in Anglo-American law. The state now fulfilled that and many other parental responsibilities. After the *New York Times* called for legislation requiring licenses to prevent "the marriage of minors, now so frequent, and so frequently resulting in deception and unhappiness," an angry writer spoke for much of the legal fraternity when he declared in the 1874 *Albany Law Journal*: "Now the parents of this State, and of every other State on this side of the ocean, have given to minors the right to contract marriage. Parental consent is not legally necessary, and we say it should not be theoretically necessary." The lawyer added the telling coda that a parent "has no more right to control or dictate a child's marriage, than the child's religious tenets or his dreams." Revisions in regulations and judicial decisions maintained the status of marriage as an act between individuals, not families.[77]

Despite growing suspicion of the intentions of those who ignored statutory nuptial rites, the bench tilted the law in favor of couples whose habits and reputations demonstrated a commitment to matrimony. Courts retained the discretion granted them by the intricate common-law rules governing the presumption and proof of marriage, which allowed them to adapt nuptial laws to individual circumstances. Since most disputed marriages involved family and property rights, the courts persisted in their refusal to upset settled relations without strong evidence of illicit cohabitation. Dismissing the estate claim of a widow and her child, a New York judge declared in 1898 that the legal presumptions of marriage were "indulged in the interest of decency and clean living, because of the presumption which the law has for orderly and decent conduct as against illicitness. The inference is not made for the benefit of either party to the alleged contract." Even so, the common-law rules tended to qualify the new regulatory legislation.[78]

Nevertheless, as in the judicial evaluation of litigants in breach-of-marriage-promise suits, greater care appears to have been taken in late nineteenth-century courtrooms to detect and punish those who abused the law. Amid reformers' complaints of debilitating marital laxity, cries of rampant Mormonism, and acute fears of the spread of free love, the bench seems to have taken particular care to temper its earlier support of informal matrimony.

The Supreme Court of Kansas staked out the boundaries of nuptial freedom in an 1887 ruling that welcomed common-law marriage into the state. The justices sustained the conviction of E. C. Walker and Lillian Harman for illicit cohabitation. During their wedding the pair had proclaimed their hostility to conventional matrimony in terms reminiscent of those expressed at the 1848 wedding of the women's rights crusaders Lucy Stone and Henry Blackwell. Calling themselves Autonomists, the couple publicly declared their bond while repudiating all statutory controls on marriage. At the commencement of the ceremony, the bride's father read an elaborate statement of the sect's view of marriage as "a strictly personal matter." The bride and groom denied "the right of society, in the form of church and state to regulate it, or interfere with the individual man and woman in this relation." They dispensed with the traditional nuptial promise "to love and honor" each other, since this might not be possible to sustain. The groom also renounced his legal right to change his wife's name, take her property, and retain custody of their children. Instead, he promised her complete equality. The bride then pledged that her fidelity would be guided by her conscience. After these pronouncements were published in the sect's journal, local authorities arrested, convicted, and sentenced the pair to the county jail.

The ceremony repelled the state bench. Though the justices agreed that under the common law, nuptial regulations were merely directory, they refused to confer the status of common-law marriage on this union. Chief Justice Albert Horton thundered in his opinion: "They have lived together, but had no intention of creating that relation of status known and defined by law and by customs and usages of all civilized societies as marriage. Thus living together under such circumstances did not in law constitute a valid marriage." The court defended the state's nuptial authority and refuted the plea that Walker and Harman's civil rights had been violated. Instead, they assured the citizenry that the lax provisions of the law were amenable to reason.[79]

The reaction of the Kansas bench provides an apt illustration of historian William O'Neill's contention that the "notion that marriages ought deliberately to be made provisional was more disturbing than divorce itself to most Victorians." President M. H. Buckham of the Divorce Reform League took pains to argue that "in any case that two parties consent to marriage, reserving the right to terminate the relation on agreement so to do . . . the act would be condemned as an immoral one by the general moral sense of mankind." The Kansas court did its best to live up to that standard. In doing so, the justices implied that judicial support for common-law marital rights only protected those who innocently failed to adhere to statutory formalities, not those who deliberately defied public authority over matrimony and challenged majority beliefs. As the Missouri Supreme Court explained, the "cohabitation of a råke and a bawd will afford much less presumption of a marriage than would the cohabitation of an honorable man with a virtuous and refined woman. The one couple defy the sentiment of civilized mankind and the scorn of society, while the other renders perpetual obedience to an enlightened conscience." Judges considered it axiomatic that unions of those who adhered to middle-class values and life styles posed no threat to matrimony. They considered couples who deviated from or flouted bourgeois standards as menacing as did reformers.[80]

The common-law presumptions of matrimony were elaborate and ambiguous legal tools. Their continued existence left nuptial law in a state of flux despite the new codes. In some courtrooms the presumption of matrimony could be questioned only in the most blatantly unverified claims; in others, every alleged marriage was subjected to thorough investigation. In their continuing attempt to distinguish reputable legal relations from illicit ones, most judges insisted that a couple demonstrate not only that they had lived together but that their intentions had been matrimonial. They agreed with reformers that conferring legality on immoral couples weakened family life and threatened social order.

McKenna v. *McKenna*, an 1897 decision of the Illinois Supreme Court, reveals the prevailing judicial solution. Julia McKenna had lived with James McKenna for over thirty years, and borne several children. No longer able to endure his repeated but unspecified cruelties, she sued for separate maintenance. Her mate answered that no marriage existed between them. The judges "reluctantly" disregarded Julia's meager proof of cohabitation and repute, and explained to her the bench's ideal of nuptial security: "If parties wish to disregard the wise and wholesome regulation of the community as to forms of ceremony of marriage, they have the right to do so, and to make their marriage a matter of simple civil contract only; but in attempting to do so, they must see to it that such proof of the transaction is preserved as will enable courts to discover a valid marriage contract, vz., a definite agreement on the part of each followed by an assumption of the marriage status."[81]

Through concessions and adjustments, many late nineteenth-century judges marked off the boundaries of nuptial freedom more clearly than had their predecessors. In doing so they restrained rather than eliminated the bias in favor of informal matrimony implanted in the formative era of marriage law. This judicial stance did not indicate lack of concern with the law's responsibility to improve matrimonial conditions. On the contrary, few jurists would have disagreed with the sentiments of Mississippi judge Horatio F. Simrall in 1873: "The superstructure of society rests upon marriage and the family as its foundation. The social relations and rights of property spring out of it and attach to it, such as dower,

administration, distribution, and inheritance. All controversies, therefore growing out of marriage, assume the dignity and importance of
quasi public questions."

But the bench refused to obliterate the division between public and
private realms of life and make matrimony entirely a state question.
More than a mere formalistic acceptance of earlier precedents, the judicial reaction to the campaign for nuptial law reform represented the firm
determination that extensive public regulation of the marriage ceremony
was unnecessary and unwise. Thus the 1874 *American Law Journal*
labeled a Michigan statute requiring witnesses for a valid marriage "a
step backward in legislation," and then urged a different policy on the
nation: "[T]he conditions prescribed by law ought always to be as light
and plastic as prudence can sanction."

Such arguments testify to a persistent commitment by the bench and
bar to common-law rights and methods of conflict resolution, and an
equally fervent opposition to coercive state intrusion into private decision making. The judicial defense of common-law rights extended beyond economic activities to social actions such as informal marriage.
Thomas Cooley in his *Constitutional Limitations* argued that courts had
to intervene when legislatures threatened the "personal, civil, and political rights" of the nation's citizenry. In nuptial litigation, this judicial
definition of its responsibilities enabled the bench to reserve the right to
resolve special cases and thus maintain a large portion of its marital
authority. And the application of common-law nuptial rules revealed a
lingering judicial tolerance for matrimonial diversity that challenged the
statutory effort at marital uniformity.[82]

A New Balance

By the end of the nineteenth century, the law governing the celebration
of marriage had become a complex and uniquely American set of common-law rules and statutes. Though firmly constructed on the foundation laid in the formative era of family law, its initial commitment to
nuptial freedom had been significantly tempered by legislation expanding public supervision of nuptials. Charles Noble, in advocating the
institution of marriage registration laws, expressed in tortured prose the
central conclusion of the late nineteenth-century debate over nuptials:

> [N]o reasonable human being regarding marriage in the light in
> which it is usually regarded among civilized nations, could hold

as restraints such wholesome requirements and regulations as may be enacted to prevent not only the perpetration of the basest frauds and vilest seductions under cover of legal indefiniteness, but also the assumption of vague and dubious relationships, even though the requirements referred to necessitate some formality and the delay of a few days in consummating a desired marriage.[83]

The interplay of the professional and popular commitment to nuptial freedom and the reform demand for marital uniformity helped produce a new balance between individual rights and state responsibilities that dominated marriage law well into the twentieth century. The pockmarked path toward that new balance shows how difficult were the regulatory problems that marriage and other republican family relations posed for the nineteenth-century legal order. Too great an increase in state matrimonial regulation stirred the latent antistatism not only of the bench and bar but also of large segments of the public.

Philadelphia attorney Edmund O. Brown published a pamphlet in 1886 to ease the fears raised by a recently enacted mandatory marriage-license law. Because "many persons feel a delicacy, and hesitate in going before a clerk of the court to secure a marriage license," Brown reported, they fled to license-free New Jersey. To deter such flights, he assured betrothed couples that the clerks would ask only a few simple questions "which no honest person would be ashamed to answer." Brown also reminded his readers of the positive effects of formal rites, especially the added protection they gave estates. The uneasiness with which Pennsylvanians greeted marriage-license requirements suggests a broad public hostility to state interference with what had become a private compact.[84]

Continuing resistance to stringent public supervision influenced the drafting, application, and interpretation of the marriage-law revisions passed in most states in the second half of the nineteenth century. It may have forced rescission of stiff marriage statutes in states like Georgia and New York. Regional variations in the codes continued as well. New England, with its commonwealth tradition, enacted the earliest and most comprehensive regulations; parts of the South and Southwest had the least stringent. Everywhere, the law remained dependent on the initiative and competency of local officials and the willingness of couples to adhere to legal forms. To the dismay of reformers, even common-law marriage continued; though by the early twentieth century it, like breach-of-promise suits, met almost universal public condemnation. The 1918 *Minnesota Law Review* reported that such unions were "becoming quite a rare occurrence, and the instances in which [they are] being presented to the courts are fewer still." But common-law marriage remained a legal option in most jurisdictions. Uneven statutory development, a mixed public reception, and determined professional resistance: all prevented reformers from fully imposing the controls on nuptials that they insisted had become necessary to protect hearth and society.[85]

The opposition merely checked rather than defeated the reform drive, and thus helped ensure the new legal balance. Statutory inroads into the common law and persistent propaganda in support of formal matrimony led to nuptial regulations that combined the central tendencies of nineteenth-century marriage law. By century's end, most state marriage codes had made informal nuptials less desirable and less legally secure than they had been earlier, but those laws did not terminate the reign of individual choice in marital rites. Instead, the revised statutes and judicial opinions shifted the governance of nuptials away from self-policing and toward bureaucratic supervision. As a result, marriage ceased to be the concern only of the betrothed. The state had become an interested, active third party.

This obsessive concern with nuptials also found expression in the second category of marriage law, the rules setting the qualifications for men and women seeking matrimony. Yet unlike the limited increases in state authority over nuptial celebrations, public supervision of marital fitness increased steadily throughout the century. The development of these ever-more-stringent nuptial standards points to an acceptance of state intervention in certain areas of domestic relations, which added another dimension to the creation of a distinctive American family law.

CHAPTER 4

MATRIMONIAL LIMITATIONS
WHO'S FIT TO WED?

Marriage law guarded the altar not only by prescribing the rites necessary for a legal union, but also by establishing standards of fitness for brides and grooms. The statutes and common-law rules devised to deny certain individuals or couples the right to wed reveal particular moral, religious, social, and physiological traits considered fundamentally threatening to domestic life and social order. Indeed, these restrictions were a more positive and aggressive use of public nuptial authority in the republican legal order than the law governing marriage celebrations.

The power to protect society by preventing undesirable marriages was a sovereign right consistently invoked by American states. Even in post-Revolutionary Pennsylvania, where a statute made the promotion of matrimony an official state policy, the law included the caveat: "[A]ll marriages not forbidden by God shall be encouraged."[1] Matrimonial prohibitions thus tempered family law's commitment to nuptial freedom. They helped define the special contractual nature of marriage and the peculiar public responsibilities involved in family formation. Equally important, each category of the prohibitions had more consistent and uniform development than other titles in marriage law. They grew in number and severity over the course of the nineteenth century.

Consent was the basic criterion for determining marital capacity. Massachusetts legal author Francis Hilliard explained in his 1835 *Elements of Law*: "Marriage, being a contract, requires suitable contracting parties, and a free consent, to render it valid." In making such determinations, American marital prohibitions drew on common-law doctrines regarding void and voidable marriages.[2]

These complex, confusing rules originated in a statute passed under Henry VIII creating two main grounds for annulling marriages: civil and canonical. Civil prohibitions included infancy, want of reason, lack of free consent, or a previous marriage. Canonical constraints consisted of disabilities such as impotence, consanguinity, and affinity. The distinction was critical. Violations of civil prohibitions nullified marriages, but canonical transgressions merely rendered them voidable. Voidable marriages remained intact until legally challenged. If no questions were raised before the death of one of the spouses, then the marriage was fully valid. In England, which remained a "divorceless society" until 1857, these marital rules provided one of the few ways out of unwanted marriages.

But most American states established divorce proceedings early in the nineteenth century, and annulment procedures thus came to serve more as nuptial regulators than as outlets for matrimonial frustrations. In fact, most challenges to the capacity of individuals to marry in nineteenth-century America occurred after a marriage had been contracted. Attempts to annul such unions arose under two major circumstances. One of the spouses, an interested third party, or the state might challenge the legitimacy of a marriage; or the legality of a union might be called into question after the death of one of the partners. The second usually arose in a dispute over the deceased's estate. These conflicts not only accented the special contractual nature of marriage, they pitted the law's commitment to marital permanency against its responsibilities to police nuptial fitness.

Through the resolution of these disputes, American marriage restrictions grew into an intricate combination of statutes, common-law rules, and social customs. Its sources lay in changing popular and professional perceptions of the qualities needed for a successful marriage. The restrictions are best explained by tracing their nineteenth-century development in three broad areas: the antebellum adoption and expansion of traditional nuptial curbs; the addition of American innovations to the law; and the late nineteenth-century emergence of a coercive approach to all marital prohibitions. In each, judges and legislators sought a balance between individual nuptial rights and social protection. Even more than in the law governing the rites of marriage, that balance shifted dramatically over the course of the century. The law's priorities changed from an initial tendency to limit state policing of brides and grooms to a later determination to constrict nuptial freedom. Although marriage prohibitions did not undergo a total renovation, they were redrawn over the course of the century to more clearly emphasize that marriage was governed by public as well as private interests. The curbs point to a faith in state regulation less apparent in other areas of marriage law, but one that must be recognized to understand fully the character of American family law.[3]

The Adoption of Traditional Nuptial Prohibitions

Age-old English grounds for denying brides and grooms the right to marry formed the basis for this category of marriage law in post-Revolutionary America. Numerous restrictions identified a particular physiological, contractual, or moral liability deemed unacceptable in matrimony. The law considered each a violation of the consensual requirement of legal matrimony. Although the American application of the restrictions was not especially distinctive, republican overtones appeared as the antebellum legal system struggled to adapt its English and colonial heritage of nuptial regulation to contemporary needs and concerns. That perhaps mundane, but nonetheless vital, process itself was important in the creation of an American family law. So too were the implications of the century's most controversial violation of these traditional curbs, Mormon polygamy. The massive state regulatory power that was finally used to squelch the sect's peculiar practices suggests that even the traditional restrictions contained a latent faith in state authority, though one more apparent in the other areas of the law and later in the century.

Setting Physical Qualifications for Marriage

Physiological standards for matrimony were fundamental constraints on marital capacity in nineteenth-century America, as in most societies. Age, sexual integrity, kinship ties, and mental health formed a physical base line for assessing the nuptial fitness of individual men and women in all of the state codes of the newly independent nation. Infancy and impotence figured as the least controversial limits imposed on nuptial freedom. No judge, legislator, or public commentator disputed the use of age or sexual ability as a legitimate basis for nuptial proscriptions. But consanguinity, affinity, and sanity posed recurrent regulatory problems.

Youthful Marriages

Post-Revolutionary marriage law assumed that below a certain age, children could neither physically consummate a marriage nor intellectually understand its significance. Uncertainty lingered over the states' duty to accept marriages formed during the uncertain period between childhood and adulthood. The issue took on legal significance because matrimony customarily acted as a declaration of individual independence; and it also raised critical questions as to nuptial rights and state responsibilities.[4]

Early in the nineteenth century, the states resolved these uncertainties in favor of youthful freedom to wed free of public and parental restraints. Legislation and judicial decisions implemented this liberal policy by borrowing traditional English common-law nuptial-age demarcations. Under the common law, the magical age at which the law conferred nuptial rights on individuals was twelve for women and fourteen for men; parental control, however, continued to adulthood at twenty-one. Every American state adopted these age boundaries after the Revolution. According to Ohio editor and legal educator Edward Mansfield, writing in 1845: "It is obvious that there *is* an age, at which discretion would be wanting in respect to any contract. As this, however, varies in different countries and different individuals, the law has fixed an *arbitrary age*, before which marriage cannot be lawfully contracted." Unless altered by statute, these ages became part of American common law as well.[5]

Steeped in feudal strategies of property protection and based on commonsense notions of sexual development, common-law age rules attracted American judges and legislators on account of the protection they offered aberrant couples. Throughout the century, most middle-class Americans wed in their early twenties. The average marriage age did fall a bit at the end of the era, but only rarely did brides or grooms approach the common-law minimums. In 1816 the Connecticut judge and author Tapping Reeve, in expressing his approval of the common-law demarcations, observed that he had never "heard in this state of any marriage, when the persons married had not arrived at the age of discretion. I think it probable that such marriages would never receive any sanction from our courts. Such a contract, I apprehend, is void, upon principle, that it is a contract against sound policy; and *contra bonos mores*." Reeve's impression has been substantiated by a study showing that in 1774 only .9 percent of Connecticut males and 3.2 percent of females between the ages of ten and nineteen were married. Even these unions no doubt were clustered at the higher end of the age scale.

Though marriage ages were lower in the South, only the exceptional bourgeois couple wed before the groom was twenty-one and the bride twenty. Indeed, a reversal occurred; the lower classes abandoned a traditional custom of deferring matrimony and the middle classes embraced it. Changing market conditions and the influence of republican family values encouraged the shift. In the new nation, working class males could expect their highest incomes early in life, but their bourgeois counterparts aspired to a rising income. Equally influential were

attitudes associated with middle-class homes such as delayed gratification and rational calculation. Even so, both law and social policy protected youthful alliances by conferring legality on any union consummated after the wife reached twelve and her husband fourteen.[6]

There were a few attempts to raise the marriage age early in the
nineteenth century; their fates point out the antiregulatory bias of marriage law's formative era. In an effort to close the gap between expected
middle-class behavior and statutory prescriptions, several antebellum
legislatures increased the statutory age of marriage. New York's 1830
legislative attempt to set the minimum marriage ages at fourteen and
seventeen was reconsidered and repealed, as had been the threat to
common-law marriage. Critics like Chancellor James Kent vigorously
challenged the revision as a violation of common-law rights. Lucius
Chittenden, a Vermont lawyer who edited the second edition of Reeve's
Law of Baron and Femme, argued that such statutes rested on mistaken
notions of policy. Although he recognized that the acts might be "useful
to prevent early marriages," he urged that the better policy remained the
common law's vindication of individual choices and accountability. By
following it in Vermont, "a marriage below the age fixed by these
statutes is rarely, if ever, met with."[7]

Courts rendered other laws ineffective. In 1854 the Massachusetts
Supreme Judicial Court eviscerated an 1835 act similar to the aborted
New York statute. The justices issued a writ of *habeas corpus* to the
widow Susan Hervey and told her that she must release her thirteen-year-
old daughter who had wed Thomas Parton against her mother's wishes.
Mrs. Hervey's plea that the new Mrs. Parton had been deceived did not
convince the court, which admonished her: "[I]n regulating the intercourse of the sexes, by giving its highest sanctions to the contract of
marriage, and rendering it, as far as possible inviolable . . . and to
prevent fraudulent marriages, seductions, and illegitimacy, the common
law has fixed that period in life when sexual passions are usually first
developed as the one when infants are deemed to be at the age of consent
and capable of entering into the contract of marriage." The judges then
ruled that in the absence of a specific command from the General Court
declaring premature marriages void, they would consider legislative
standards to be "directory," not compulsory (as they did most statutory
controls).[8]

Most courts and legal commentators took the same position. As a
result, the law came to depend on individual self-policing rather than on
communal and parental supervision. The regulation of youthful marriage was left primarily to the dictates of courtship, personal calculations
of maturity and economic resources, and the moral and financial arguments of family and community. Age regulations thus contributed to

filial autonomy while undermining parental authority. If inability to support a family, fears of disinheritance, or strictures against hasty weddings did not extinguish the flames of youthful desire, then few legal barriers stood in the path of a young couple. A free-market view of a contract that most Americans assumed would be binding for life reflected the prevailing belief that social and personal influences could more effectively deter undesirable unions than would state intervention. According to Abba Woolson's 1873 study of *Women in American Society*: "[C]alculating parents in foreign lands bind their sons and daughters to the partners assigned them with no pretense of sentimental ties, and dispose of them as if they were so much merchandise." The American people, the educational reformer proudly announced, "are sensible enough to allow their children freedom of choice." But Woolson added a revealing coda: "[T]he young minds among us become so thoroughly imbued with the ambitions of their elders that there is no need to interfere."

Nuptial law also lent legal support to a more general social evolution hinted at by Woolson and described by the historian Daniel Scott Smith. He has identified a gradual movement from the "stable, parental-run marriage system" of the seventeenth and early eighteenth centuries to the nineteenth century's "stable, participant-run marriage system." The transition encouraged a reliance not on the state but on internalized restraint and individual conscience in choosing a mate. It meant, Smith suggests, that "property considerations were less critical to marriage choice after the Revolution than before." The general legal bias in favor of individual decision making, risk taking, and matrimony based on choice and affection also enhanced the nuptial rights of juveniles.[9]

Sexual Incapacity

Like age, sexual incapacity has been cause for terminating marriages in most societies. Nineteenth-century American popular and professional opinion dismissed homosexual unions out of hand; in them "none of the ends of matrimony would be thereby established." But each partner to a heterosexual union had to be "essentially complete in their sexual organization and capabilities." The remedy was rarely resorted to; only a few instances of marriages annulled for impotence were recorded in colonial America. But such actions had an uncertain legal standing. As a canonical prohibition, impotence made a marriage voidable within the lives of the parties. Since America had no ecclesiastical courts, many lawyers and judges argued that the courts needed statutory authority to invoke the restriction, a jurisdictional hesitancy that testified to the bench and bar's deep aversion to dissolving marriages.[10]

The New York chancery court voiced these reservations in the 1825 decision of *Burtis* v. *Burtis*. A woman claimed that her husband had been impotent from birth and had concealed the fact from her before their wedding. The husband's attorney argued that the court had no authority to grant an annulment in a state that granted divorce only for adultery; the opposing counsel countered that the chancery court had inherited all the powers of the English church courts. The Chancellor noted that four divorces had been granted in colonial courts and that two annulments had been issued for fraud. Yet he concluded that without an ecclesiastical tribunal all laws on divorce and annulments became matters of original jurisdiction, which could be enacted only by the legislature. "We have no judicature," he asserted, "authorized to adjudge, by a substantive and effectual sentence, that a marriage is illegal and to separate the parties. This court cannot, therefore, dissolve a marriage or decree a divorce for the cause of corporeal impotence." The opinion ended with the declaration that the adoption of ecclesiastical grounds for annulment by judicial fiat would subvert the state's rights to make its own marriage laws.[11]

These institutional concerns led most state legislatures to confer jurisdiction on the courts. New York lawmakers did so in 1828, three years after the *Burtis* ruling. A Pennsylvania act of 1815 declared that "if either party, at the time of the contract was and still is naturally impotent, or incapable of procreation, it shall and may be lawful for the innocent and injured party to obtain a divorce." The statutes treated impotence as a fraud, since by offering oneself for marriage each party implicitly guaranteed his or her ability to consummate the union. The law, however, offered redress only for sexual incapacity, not barrenness. It must be, physician Amos Dean wrote in *Medical Jurisprudence*, "absolute, organic, and arising from physical causes." These statutes represented a rare active use of legislative intervention in early nineteenth-century domestic relations.[12]

A widely reported 1836 New York ruling reveals the trepidation with which courts approached a suit perennially beset by difficulties of proof and emotion. In *Devanbaugh* v. *Devanbaugh* a dissatisfied husband claimed that his wife was totally incapable of sexual intercourse. At the first hearing, Chancellor Reuben Walworth stayed the proceedings until a medical examination could test the husband's contentions. He explained that

[i]n every case of this kind, it is necessary that the court should proceed with the greatest vigilance and care, not only to prevent

fraud and collusion by the parties, but also to guard against an honest mistake, under which they may be acting from the want of proper medical advice and assistance. From the very nature of the case, it appears to be impossible to ascertain the fact of incurable impotency, especially when the husband is the complaining party, except by proper surgical examination, by skillful and competent surgeons, in connection with other testimony.

When the hearing reconvened, the medical examiner testified that the wife remained a virgin and that she had an unusually strong hymen, which even if the couple were young and both "possessed all the vigor of youth," they could not breach. He expressed uncertainty about the possibility of curing the malady surgically. Since no other physical defects existed, the Chancellor decided that surgery could eliminate the problem and that, therefore, the woman did not suffer from incurable impotence. Even though the indignant wife now refused to live with her husband and declined to undergo such an operation, the court considered the dispute a private affair: "[It] is a matter to be settled with her own conscience and her lawful husband, as this court has no jurisdiction in any case to enforce the performance of her marital vows."[13]

The right to a sexually complete marriage partner became legally enforceable in American marriage law because of legislative intervention extending judicial jurisdiction. But judges acted only upon flagrant proof of physical incapacity and thus wielded their discretionary authority to bring the action in line with the bench's general aversion to dissolving marriages. It is also striking that men instigated most of these suits. That reversed the medieval practice, when women had filed proportionally more claims. Since the action was voluntary, the shift may indicate that by the onset of the Victorian era more women than men were willing to countenance an unconsummated marriage either from timidity or preference.[14]

Kin Restrictions

The other major physiological checks on marriage—kinship ties and sanity—raised more troubling problems for the legal system. They did so largely because each was considered a much greater threat to matrimonial success and social harmony.

Sexual intercourse between closely related individuals is banned in most societies; Anglo-American law's ominous term of "forbidden degrees" was inherited from medieval canon law. Like most such restrictions, it had a number of sources: the Biblical admonition in Leviticus, a determination to preserve family lineage, attempts to prevent sexual competition among family members, and fears of the physical effects of inbreeding. Truly incestuous marriages—that is, between parent and child, or brother and sister—provoked bitter and continual social and legal denunciations. Since such relationships are rarely formalized, the central legal and social issue for England and her colonies became the boundaries of the kinship nuptial ban.[15]

Colonial limits originated in Biblical commands and English canonical rules governing consanguinity and affinity. These family ties, the former created through blood bonds and the latter through matrimony, formed the basis of numerous, intricate distinctions, any one of which could be used to annul a marriage. Canon law prohibited the marriages of persons related by any degree of consanguinity, but it was primarily observed in the breach. In 1563 the Archbishop of Canterbury, Matthew Porter, gathered together various modifications of the taboo. His tables, confirmed in 1603, became the foundation for Anglo-American legislation on kin restrictions. The tables banned marriages beyond the third degree from a common ancestor (first cousin). In 1845 Cincinnati editor Edward Mansfield staked out the proper limits of the prohibition in republican America. Admitting that public welfare demanded some checks on consanguineous unions, he nevertheless asserted that "the holiness or unholiness of the matrimonial contract, in reference to ties of blood or other moral circumstances is not considered by law, but left entirely to the jurisdiction of ecclesiastical bodies or the restraint of conscience."[16]

Judgments like Mansfield's hastened the liberalization of many kin taboos in the first half of the nineteenth century. His comment, steeped in the era's contractual ideology, reflects some of its social and political sources. In a society that had disestablished religion and enshrined individual rights, most kin nuptials fell outside of the shrinking domain of public regulatory authority. Only a truly incestuous marriage posed a serious enough danger to warrant state intervention.

Such considerations compelled judicial action as well. Jurists like Chancellor Kent felt obliged to act even when the legislature had not. In an 1820 decision, ten years before his state enacted incest legislation, Kent incredulously asked: "Are the principles of natural law and of Christian duty to be left unheeded and inoperative because we have no Ecclesiastical Courts recognized by law, as specifically charged with the cognizance of such matters?" Where Walworth had hesitated in an impotence suit, Kent plunged in to argue that "prohibitions of natural law are of absolute, uniform, and universal obligation. They become rules of the Common Law, which is founded in the common reason and acknowledged duty of mankind, sanctioned by immemorial usages, and as such, are clearly binding." Restating his contentions in the *Commentaries* seven years later, Kent clarified the legal status of the forbidden degrees by deeming true incest a common-law taboo and other kin restrictions statutory directives.[17]

Legislative differences on the issue arose mainly as a result of first-cousin and affinal unions. The sociologist Bernard Farber has discovered two nineteenth-century kin systems. In New England and much of the older South a "Biblical System" based on English practice remained in place. It permitted first-cousin unions but banned marriages among various affines. At the same time a "Western American System" emerged in the new states of the Middle and Far West. Those regions proscribed first-cousin unions and authorized affinal ones. The regional difference is difficult to explain. It may lie in alternative responses to the problems of social stratification and economic development. The Biblical System helped sustain a highly stratified family-oriented social and economic order by providing a formal mechanism in which kin matrimonial alliances perpetuated concentrated economic power. The Western System promoted a more open society by encouraging marriages with a variety of outsiders and affines and thus expanding the distribution of family wealth. Regional variations thus may reflect the creation of nuptial policies by and for elites who differed in the way they used family alliances to protect or increase their wealth.[18]

In this instance the West prevailed; the major regulatory development of the early nineteenth century was the gradual reduction of controls on couples related by affinity. A growing number of statutes and judicial decisions dissolved such kin bonds after the death or divorce of one of the spouses. The pervasive character of this legal change was first evident in Massachusetts, Connecticut and Maryland statutes that reduced affinal restrictions in the late eighteenth century; other states joined them after 1800.[19]

The Vermont Supreme Court followed suit in an 1837 land dispute. The justices threw out an appeal by Amos Blodget, who had questioned the appraisal of some condemned property because one of the appraisers had married the sister of the owner's deceased first wife. The judges not only rejected that relationship as a ground for disqualification, but also repudiated the traditional common-law ban against the union of a widower and his deceased wife's sister: "though a man is by affinity, brother to his wife's sister, yet upon the death of the wife, he may lawfully marry his sister." Their ruling proceeded directly from the new assumption that matrimony united two individuals, not two families. Once the original bond ended, the remaining spouse was free to wed almost anyone he or she desired.[20]

A bitter debate in the Presbyterian Church over the issue underscores the waning influence of public controls on the marriages of individuals formerly related by affinity. Around 1840 the sect defrocked the minister of a Fayetteville, North Carolina congregation, Reverend Mr. Archibald McQueen, for marrying his deceased wife's sister. In an ensuing pamphlet war, all the disputants, some albeit grudgingly, conceded the propriety of the legislature's abstention from the issue. The pamphleteers instead quarrelled bitterly over whether or not the church itself should enforce the ban. One opponent of the restriction taunted his adversaries: "[I]f the prevailing public sentiment of this nation, sustained by the legislation of all the states but one [most likely he meant Virginia] is countenancing incest, we need to know it." Though McQueen finally won reinstatement in 1846, the debate indicated that traditional nuptial restrictions had to be defended on ground of public welfare, not merely accepted practice. In response to an inquiry about his position on the issue, the educational reformer Horace Mann gave voice to the sentiment of his age: "I regard the prejudice against marrying a deceased wife's sister, as not merely preventive of good, but as silly and superstitious."[21]

Even in the most litigated issue, marriages between uncles and nieces or aunts and nephews, the courts opposed strict public restraints. In 1858 the South Carolina Supreme Court refused to nullify the marriage of Edward Bowers and his brother's daughter, Elizabeth, in an estate fight. The court rebuffed an attempt by the children of Bowers's first marriage to deny Elizabeth dower rights because her marriage violated the ban on incestuous unions. Offering a judicial argument common in decisions refusing to dissolve marriages, the justices raised the specter of broken marriages and bastardized children to justify its allegiance to the common law. The judges concluded: "[E]xtreme cases of unnatural alliances may be supposed at which the moral sense could be offended, but hithertofore public sentiment if not private virtue has repressed all such evils." Though self-policing had failed to prevent the Bowerses' marriage, the South Carolina bench, like most of its antebellum counterparts, refused to rescind its endorsement of that system, paralleling its refusal to do so in other physiological challenges to marriage. Only the seemingly clear threat posed by truly incestuous marriage could breach the law's commitment to nuptial freedom.[22]

Mental Incompetence

Mental incompetence at the time of marriage represented as direct a threat to matrimony and society as did incest. It came to be recognized in post-Revolutionary America as an extreme deprivation of nuptial consent, even though traditionally the common law had refused divorce for insanity and only canon law had accepted imbecility as legitimate cause for annulment. Restrictions on the right of the insane to wed, instituted early in the nineteenth century, grew as much out of a post-Revolutionary attempt to prevent the victimization of the mentally ill as from a direct desire to inhibit their procreative powers. State legislators and judges used various common-law and statutory devices drawn from English ecclesiastical law, recent Parliamentary reforms enacted to protect the insane, common-law doctrines, and customary practices to develop a policy that demanded that a bride and groom be sane at the time of their wedding.[23]

This marital restriction became firmly entrenched in American law during the first decades of the nineteenth century. Reeve enlisted in the campaign by arguing in his 1816 *Law of Baron and Femme* that the "authorities teach us that marriage by an idiot, is valid; and assign as a reason why it should be so, that an idiot can consent to marriage. If his consent to this contract binds him, why is he not bound by other contracts to which he consents? If his want of understanding be such, that he ought not to be bound by other contracts, neither ought he to be bound by his contract of marriage." One year earlier the Massachusetts Chief Justice Isaac Parker asserted in an opinion that it was "reasonable that these unhappy persons, who are prohibited by law from making any binding contract for the merest pecuniary trifle, should be protected from the effects of a covenant of so high a nature." He even refused to succumb to the general judicial fear of dissolving marriages and bastardizing children. The traditional policy had been equally unfair, Parker insisted, since under it "that human being without reason, or their families, should be victims of the artifice of desperate persons, who might be willing to speculate on their misfortunes." By the contractual standards embedded in American family law, insanity violated the consensual requirements of matrimony.[24]

Neither the statutes nor the common law made a clear distinction between mental deficiency and insanity. Instead they formally restricted the nuptial rights only of those who at the time of their marriage demonstrated a clear inability to lead an independent existence. The ban thus prevented incompetent persons from being compelled to enter a relationship they could not comprehend and frustrated those who preyed on incompetents to gain access to their property. In applying the law, judges eschewed medical definitions of sanity for contractual ones. A subjective determination of whether the potential spouse could manage the common affairs of life and understand the meaning of matrimony served as the primary gauge of mental fitness for nuptials. Thus insanity too fell under the domination of the free marriage market.[25]

An 1850 New Hampshire ruling, *True* v. *Raney*, epitomizes the judicial approach. After a twenty-two-year-old woman had been abducted to Vermont and married, her parents sued to annul the union. They testified that their daughter could not wash or dress herself, spell or read, use money, tell time, knit or sew, and that—perhaps most telling to a New England jury—she did not know how to properly "get a boiled dinner." Affirming the dissolution of the marriage, Chief Justice John J. Gilchrist declared: "There is every reason to believe that no person so lamentably imbecile as this young woman appears to be, could have the remotest idea of the meaning of a contract for the performance of any of the ordinary duties of life, and still less of a contract of marriage."[26]

The sad plight of this New Hampshire woman suggests the severe level of incompetence necessary to invoke the curb, which consequently limited its use. Indeed, the policy was instituted over the dissent of some medical experts, including Isaac Ray, the leading authority on insanity in antebellum America, who objected to the simple legal standards used to judge mental competency. "In other contracts," Ray complained, "all the conditions and circumstances may be definite and brought into view at once and the capacity of the mind to comprehend them determined with comparative facility." But in nuptial pacts "there is nothing definite or certain, the obligations which it imposes do not admit of being measured and discussed, they are of an abstract kind and constantly varying with every new scene and condition of life." He therefore demanded a more stringent and scientific method of weighing mental fitness to wed.[27]

But Ray's contentions made little impression on the mid-century bench and bar. Significantly, although most laypersons and professionals believed that mental disabilities had hereditary origins, few acted on that belief to demand harsh constraints on the nuptial rights of the insane. The novelist Catherine Sedgwick, whose mother and brother suffered from mental illness, crossed swords with Horace Mann on this matter. He had lobbied to create the first Massachusetts lunatic asylum, and advocated stricter controls on the insane. Sedgwick responded in 1839 that Mann had failed to weigh the chance of insanity's being repeated in a family against the "certain misery" of inflicting the "heaviest curse that could fall upon . . . those whose families have thus been afflicted—of making them as lepers." Even if madness broke out in branches of a family, the novelist (famous for her stories of domestic tragedy) confidently asserted that "judicious physical education" and the observance of "sensitive laws, physical, moral, and intellectual" could "extirpate all disease." A society that resisted biological determinism, and that busily constructed asylums with an optimistic faith that even the hereditarily insane could be rehabilitated easily accepted a loose, contractual standard of mental capacity for matrimony. An aptly titled article in the 1845 *New York Legal Observer*, "Facetiousness of the Law—Husband and Wife," summarized the prevailing attitude: "[I]f want of reason really prevented a marriage from taking place, there would be an end to half the matches that are entered into."[28]

The balance in marriage law between the desire to prevent the victimization of the mentally ill and the determination to hold individuals to their marital pacts symbolized the early nineteenth-century approach to the issue of nuptial fitness. The result was the liberalization of traditional physiological curbs. As the Tennessee Supreme Court noted in 1857: "the annulment of other contracts would only affect property; but this would do that and more, it would tell upon the happiness, character, and peace of the parties. The appalling character of these consequences are well calculated to impress the courts with the solemn duty of requiring a clear case for the application of the general principles to this delicate and important contract." Antebellum judges and legislators generally acted in concert to create a hesitant approach to nuptial prohibitions.[29]

Preventing Nuptial Dishonesty

The contractual uniqueness of matrimony became clearer when spouses or their families claimed that nuptial consent had been induced involuntarily. Fraud was the most common and important form of marital entrapment. A plea of fraudulent marriage pitted the right of every bride and groom to enter matrimony free of coercion against the law's reluctance to disrupt consummated unions. The realities of courtship, in which men and women frequently misrepresented their character and social standing, only heightened the legal problem.

Like the English bench, which traditionally applied a narrow definition of marital fraud, post-Revolutionary American courts held couples to contractual standards that differed from those applied to commercial agreements. Judges translated the prevailing marketplace dictum, *caveat emptor*, into a nuptial maxim: "Let the suitor beware!" As the English legal author Thomas Poynter explained in his volume on ecclesiastical courts: "[T]he law expects that persons about to enter so important a contract as marriage, should for themselves use timely and effective diligence in order to obtain correct information on points which in general are considered materially to effect their future condition."[30]

But judges faced a difficult task in determining precisely how serious a misrepresentation justified the dissolution of a marriage and in measuring its consequences for the pair and their children. Conflicting pronouncements from post-Revolutionary Connecticut reveal the judicial dilemma.

The state's leading legal authorities, Tapping Reeve and Zephaniah Swift, advocated the application of general contract rules to matrimonial fraud. Reeve, the more dogmatic of the pair, wondered if "it be founded in justice, that the contracts which respect ordinary matters should be treated as void, when obtained by fraudulent practices, why then should a contract, the most important that can be entered into, be deemed inviolable, when obtained by such fraudulent practices?" He answered his own question by insisting that the "common sense of mankind must revolt at the idea" that when a man by an "abominable fraud, obtained the person of an amiable woman, and her property, that the law should protect such a contract, and give it the same efficacy as if fairly obtained." Instead, he argued that "a contract which is obtained by fraud, is, in point of law, no contract."[31]

But when faced with actual claims of fraud, the Connecticut Supreme Court resisted such an expansive definition. In an 1803 case, John Benton charged his wife Sarah with fraudulently claiming she was pregnant and inducing him to marry her rather than go to jail. The justices admitted that nuptial fraud could be broadly defined to include

> all those deceptive acts to which the sexes too frequently have recourse, with a view to obtain what they consider an advantageous marriage connection; or by professions of ardent affection, which they may not feel, or not in a degree to what they profess. These acts, though they meet with various degrees of indulgence, according to the circumstances, are still inconsistent with truth, sincerity, and may be, and often are, productive of serious mischief; they partake of the nature of fraud, and a marriage grounded on them is, in a sense, a *fraudulent contract*.

Nevertheless, they reasoned that if "the phrase be taken in this large sense, the statute would degrade the marriage contract, which, in its original design and institution, was to continue indissoluble during the joint lives of the correlates, and which is the pillar on which society itself is founded, to the level with the most trifling bargains." Concluding that a broad definition of marital fraud would subvert matrimony, lead to promiscuity, and cause manifold evils, the court sent Benton back to his wife and child.[32]

Almost thirty years later, the same tribunal reached a similar conclusion in a dispute between two Connecticut towns over the support of an impoverished family. The court upheld the marriage of Rhoda and Alanson Bryant, which had had the result of transferring her settlement from Guilford to Oxford. The justices waved aside the contention of poor-relief officers that Rhoda had misrepresented herself to her beau. Choosing between the narrow conception of fraud offered in the Benton ruling and the expansive one advanced by Reeve, they sustained the verdict of their predecessors "for the plain reason," Chief Justice Stephen T. Hosmer explained, "that it is a contract, the most important of any." He added that "ordinary contracts, which respect property only, may, with propriety and convenience, be tested by the rule of private justice; but the marriage contract, on which so much depends for the protection and maintenance and education of children, and in which the public have so essential a stake, demands a higher principle."[33]

Most nineteenth-century lawyers and judges agreed with the Connecticut bench. American courts remained hostile to all but the most persuasive claims of nuptial fraud. They rejected as untenable commonplace or lay ideas of marital fraud such as misrepresented character, temper, fortune, rank, or general health. As Chancellor Kent caustically remarked: "[T]he law makes no provision for the relief of blind credulity, however it may be produced."[34]

Nevertheless, the law remained vague and riddled with inconsistencies. One clear dividing line did emerge in a pivotal 1862 Massachusetts decision, *Reynolds* v. *Reynolds*. The case involved the contention of seventeen-year-old Michael Reynolds that his thirty-year-old bride Bridget had fraudulently concealed her pregnancy by another man. Empowered to act under an 1855 statute that granted the courts the authority to issue annulments for fraud, the justices used Reynolds's plight to refine its means of assessing the seriousness of nuptial misrepresentations.

The judges agreed with reigning precedents that stipulated that only a fraudulent "misrepresentation of some material fact" vitiated a pact. From that concurrence, though, came their new rule that the fraud must go to the "essence" of the marital agreement. That did not include trifles such as character or personal qualities; nor did a wife's mere promiscuity void a marriage: "Certainly it would lead to disastrous consequences if a woman who had once fallen from virtue could not be permitted to represent herself as continent and thus restore herself to the rights and privileges of her sex, and enter into matrimony without incurring the risk of being put away by her husband on discovery of her previous immorality." But the judges drew the line at pregnancy. Relying on several antebellum rulings, they argued that while mere immorality "relates only to her conduct and character prior to the contract," pregnancy "touches directly her actual present condition and her fitness to execute the marriage contract and take on herself the duties of a chaste and faithful wife." Logically, then, concealment of pregnancy at the time of marriage went directly to the "essentials of the marriage contract." It prevented procreation, imposed economic burdens on the husband, humiliated him, and violated his right to "require that his wife shall not bear to his bed aliens to his blood and lineage."[35]

Most state courts adopted the new measure of fraud. It quickly became a common-law dictum: "Fraud must go to the essentials of marriage." Alabama, Georgia, and North Carolina even codified the doctrine. But the English courts issued a scathing denunciation accusing the American courts of misreading the common law. In *Moss* v. *Moss* (1897), Sir Francis Jeune complained that nullifying a marriage because of a wife's concealed pregnancy treated the relationship too much like a commercial agreement. He instructed his American brethren that while "habitually speaking of a marriage as a contract English lawyers have never been misled by an imperfect analogy into regarding it as a mere contract. According to English law the only material circumstances by operation of which fraud vitiates a marriage is the reality of consent." By that the jurist meant the substitution of another person for one of the spouses, forced marriage, or marriage induced by a conspiracy.

Attorney Max Lee Friedman, an American exponent of the English position, also attacked the flexible, result-oriented approach to fraud taken in the *Reynolds* ruling and urged that couples be held to their vows. "Shall we put a premium in ill considered matches and hasty marriages, and allow every innocent fool to escape punishment for his own credulity and lack of precaution," Friedman queried, "or shall we require some few unfortunates to make a sacrifice for the good it will do to the community to have well-considered marriages, and unions not affairs of a day but a life-time?" Many judges no doubt agreed with the lawyer, but deemed that compelling a groom to accept a wife impregnated by another man was too great a sacrifice. The *Reynolds* rule came to dominate American marriage law because it provided the bench with a flexible instrument to gauge the severity of nuptial fraud without abandoning the judicial commitment to the promotion of nuptial voluntarism, marital stability, and feminine chastity.[36]

By mid-century the American judiciary had established a uniform approach to nuptial fraud that relied on contractual standards more stringent than those applied to commercial misrepresentations, but looser than traditional ones. The distinctive rules grew out of the bench's refusal to treat marriage agreements exactly like business pacts and its pragmatic, instrumental use of the law. Consistently, the courts interpreted the law to promote the creation, not the dissolution, of matrimony. Thus, judges weighed the standards for determining marital fraud like the *Reynolds* rule on the side of the preservation of marriage. James Schouler summed up the biases of nuptial law in 1873: "[C]*aveat emptor* is the harsh but necessary maxim of the law. Love, however indispensable in an aesthetic sense, is by no means a legal essential to marriage, simply because it cannot be weighed in the scales of justice."[37]

The Campaign against Mormonism

The last traditional restriction on nuptial rights protected monogamy, a matrimonial trait even more dearly valued than physical and mental competency or voluntary consent. It laid the foundation for the nineteenth-century concept of domestic relations, and served as the cornerstone of the republican family. The defense of monogamy through marital restrictions generally took the form of traditional common-law doctrines and statutes much like those in other areas of marriage law. Late in the century though, it culminated in one of the major domestic relations law confrontations of the century—the fight against Mormonism. Consequently, the ban on plural marriages reveals not only the central tendencies of the adaptation of traditional nuptial restrictions to the new republic, but also the emergence of a more aggressive enforcement of these prohibitions in post–Civil War America.

Bigamy, marrying one spouse while another mate still lives, was a canonical offense that had been made a crime by Parliament and American provincial assemblies. Though most post-Revolutionary bigamists had successive, not tandem, spouses, law and social thought united to label bigamy as polygamy, or plural marriage, and emphatically denounce it as immoral, heathen, and hostile to democratic institutions. Chancellor Kent dismissed polygamy as "exclusively the feature of Asiatic manners and of half-civilized life"; he thought it "incompatible with civilization, refinement, and domestic felicity." The South Carolina émigré and political theorist Francis Lieber feared that polygamy would reintroduce patriarchy and thus despotism into the new republic. Others worried that it would confine matrimony only to wealthy men who would quickly enslave women to satisfy their lust. Such degradation of American females, legal commentators constantly asserted, contradicted the republic's jealous concern for women's rights. In other words, even before serious challenges to monogamy arose, fierce legal and social opposition to plural marriage existed.[38]

Most of those who violated the monogamous standard did not contest its propriety. Rather, they wed a second time after either losing or leaving their first mates. Not uncommon events in a mobile and expansive nation, most bigamous unions were probably never discovered;

those that were, generally came to light when one of the parties tried to get out of the relationship or filed an estate claim.[39]

Every state outlawed bigamy and authorized criminal penalties. A 1705 Pennsylvania act made bigamy a punishable offense and ordered that violators be whipped, imprisoned for life, and have their second unions nullified. An 1815 revision tempered the law, but only by reducing the penalties and adding new protections for the property brought to a bigamous marriage by the innocent spouse. Judges proved no more sympathetic than legislators. The North Carolina Supreme Court asserted that "the law forbids" such a union because of its "outrage upon public decency, its violation of the public economy, as well as its tendency to cheat one into the surrender of the person under the appearance of right." The justices then sent John Patterson to prison because the father of his second bride had discovered a first Mrs. Patterson and several little Pattersons.[40] Bigamy became a routine element of American criminal codes, with harsh penalties and provisions for voiding the second union.[41]

Although bigamists were the most frequent evaders of the ban on plural marriages, the real challenge to the monogamous standard came from mid-century sexual radicals.[42] Resolutely believing in the possibility of human perfection, the Owenites, Shakers, Rappites, and other utopian groups held monogamy and the private family to be impediments to human progress. Under their sway, individual desires gained ascendancy over the needs of society itself; thus communal solidarity was sacrificed to personal self-interest. The utopians called for alterations in sexual relations ranging from the Shakers' doctrine of celibacy to John Humphrey Noyes's belief in group marriage.

The most successful utopian experiment, the Church of Jesus Christ of Latter Day Saints—the Mormons—defied the monogamous ban for over fifty years. Like many of the other groups, Mormons combined millennialism and communitarianism with a tendency to posit solutions to social problems in terms of changes in family organization. By not only practicing polygamy but raising it to a divine obligation, the Saints forced the legal system to weigh its preference for private nuptial decision making against its commitment to monogamy. As polygamy became a symbol of the mid-century family crisis, indeed a prime instigator of that "moral panic," the scales of justice tilted against the sect.[43]

Mormonism erupted in western New York under its first prophet, Joseph Smith. In a series of quasi-independent communities culminating in Nauvoo, Illinois, Smith tried to establish a theocracy based on the allegedly divine revelations of *The Book of Mormon*. He periodically supplemented the text with new revelations, one of which commanded the sect to follow the practices of the ancient Hebrew patriarchs and take multiple wives. He developed a complex theological justification for the practice based on the need for numerous offspring, so that each heavenly soul had an earthly repository. Dubbed "spiritual wifery," the doctrine turned child bearing and plural marriage into religious duties.

Though Smith did not publicize polygamy, rumors of unconventional sexual customs merely added to the apprehension among non-Mormons stirred by the sect's growing economic and political power and the fierce devotion it inspired among its followers. After pitched battles with local residents, devastating property losses, and the assassination of Smith by a mob of Illinois militiamen, Brigham Young led the Saints to the Great Salt Lake in 1847.[44]

In what became the federal territory of Utah, the Mormons created their version of a Biblical commonwealth. Though statehood became the primary political objective because of the sovereign authority conceded states under republican federalism, Young made a confrontation with the rest of the nation inevitable by publicly announcing the adoption of polygamy in 1852. The sect offered its theological justification in defense, and added that plural marriage was a social good because it prevented sexual immorality, especially prostitution, and guaranteed a place in a family for every individual. The Saints defiantly insisted that polygamy under Church regulation did not license lust. A second wife entered a Mormon family only after the first consented and ecclesiastical officials had certified the husband's moral and financial worth. Young also repeatedly argued that plural marriage was more virtuous than the tandem unions allowed in other American communities under the nation's lax marriage and divorce laws.[45]

Few were convinced. Public announcement of the practice confirmed earlier suspicions and revived traditional opposition to plural marriage. Sexual fantasies aroused by lurid stories reinforced a general disposition to condemn Mormon polygamy as legalized lust and prostitution and a direct threat to the American home. Many Saints wed sisters on the ground that it ensured domestic tranquillity, but in a country where many citizens still considered the marriage of a man with his deceased wife's sister a religious if not a legal wrong, such a practice reeked of incest. Reformers, such as Horace Greeley, who might have been sympathetic to the Saints' utopian philosophy, assailed the church for enslaving women. After a visit to Utah, the New York newspaper editor and social crusader objected to women's loss of civil rights and intellectual freedom under polygamy. The Saints' marital rites and theocratic politics condemned them in the eyes of most of the citizenry. The fledgling Republican Party added a denunciation of polygamy to its condemnation of slavery in its 1856 national platform.[46]

By moving to Utah, the Mormons made polygamy a federal problem.

Theocracy, polygamy, and statehood became intertwined difficulties for successive national administrations. But rabid public opposition to the Saints' nuptial experiment did not easily translate into effective policies. A protective umbrella of states' rights, religious freedom, individual rights, and the distraction of other national issues stymied federal efforts. But holes began to appear in that covering during the Civil War. Often linked with "Slave Power" as a threat to the nation's political and domestic institutions, the church theocracy was likened by many northerners to the southern gentry. More significantly, the war established political and public precedents for concerted federal action that, at least temporarily, overcame the persistent localism and aversion to state activism pervading the nineteenth-century polity. Out of these changed circumstances came a determined campaign to eliminate polygamy through a three-pronged assault by Congress, President, and federal courts. It began in the summer of 1862 when President Abraham Lincoln signed the Morrill Act, which declared polygamy illegal in all American territories.[47]

Lawsuits instigated under the Morrill Act, though, foundered on the noncooperation of males too poor to finance polygamous families and of most Mormon women. Upset at the law's ineffectiveness, President Ulysses S. Grant complained in 1871 that little had been done to destroy what he termed a "remnant of barbarism, repugnant to civilization, to decency, and to the laws of the United States." Congress tried again in 1874. The Poland Act increased federal control over territorial courts and juries in Utah by limiting the procedural rights of indicted Saints.[48]

The first test of the law came in that year. George Reynolds, Brigham Young's personal secretary, agreed to challenge the federal ban. Though it returned his case for retrial due to an illegally composed jury, the territorial supreme court (composed of non-Mormon federal appointees) curtly brushed aside Reynolds's central contention that the Morrill Act violated his first amendment right to religious freedom. The justices stated flatly that such an assertion had no foundation in "reason, justice, nor law." In a second appeal, the court sustained his conviction and sentence of two years at hard labor and a $500 fine. Reynolds turned to the United States Supreme Court for relief; again he met defeat.[49]

Although the justices remanded the case because of a technical error in the sentence, Chief Justice Morrison R. Waite's opinion eliminated the one foundation upon which an alternative to monogamy might have received constitutional protection, the right to religious liberty. While fully subscribing to the constitutional prohibition on persecuting individuals for their religious beliefs—which he termed "opinion"—Waite ruled that Congress could punish subversive and antisocial "acts." He then labeled polygamy "an odious practice" and rejected Reynolds's attempt to have it classified as a constitutionally protected theological belief. The Chief Justice relied on the traditional Anglo-American prohibition of bigamy and the contentions of Kent and Lieber to denounce plural marriage as illegal and un-American. Furthermore, he endorsed a broad definition of public nuptial authority by placing it "within the scope of the power of every civil government to determine whether polygamy or monogamy shall be the law of social life under its dominion." To permit plural marriage, the jurist concluded, would "make the professed doctrines of religious beliefs superior to the law of the land, and in effect permit every citizen to become a law unto himself." As Reynolds learned to his sorrow, that was an extension of nuptial freedom even the judiciary would not countenance.[50]

United States v. *Reynolds* cleared the way for a renewed assault on the Mormon theocracy. Under the prodding of Presidents Rutherford Hayes and James Garfield, and the determined lobbying of family savers and other social reformers, Congress passed the Edmunds Act in 1882. It increased the likelihood of polygamy convictions by making mere cohabitation rather than marriage with more than one woman a crime. The statute also used tactics that had proven successful in reconstructing the Confederacy. It disqualified jurors who had either practiced or expressed a belief in polygamy and denied the right to vote and hold office to polygamists. These provisions won the endorsement of the federal bench as proper exercises of federal authority. The Supreme Court added its endorsement in *Cannon* v. *United States* (1885) declaring that the cohabitation of a man and more than one woman "is not the lawful substitute for the monogamous family, which alone the statute tolerates."[51]

This concerted federal action suggests that polygamy was perceived as such a threat to the family that all obstacles to state intervention in domestic relations had to be thrust aside. Elizabeth Duffey detailed those evils in *The Relations Between the Sexes* (1876): "[I]t works injustice to women . . . it degrades both men and women, . . . it exalts sensual impulses over all others . . . it destroys the home, weakens the family, and . . . will ruin the state." When President Garfield demanded "the most radical legislation consistent with the restraints of the Constitution," he spoke for much of the nation.[52]

Congress responded in 1887 with the Edmunds-Tucker bill. It annulled the Mormons' articles of incorporation, confiscated most of the sect's assets, further enlarged the jurisdiction of the federal courts, and imposed test oaths on territorial citizens. The Saints attacked the bill as a flagrant violation of their constitutional rights and a blatant power grab by its Republican sponsors. Southern congressional delegations also denounced the act as a transgression of religious freedom and an illegal federal invasion of local rights. Representative Riesden T. Bennett of North Carolina argued that although "[p]olygamy is an evil . . . the Constitution should not be stabbed even through the disguise of scoundrels." Southerners urged that moral suasion and education, not force, be used to wean the Saints from polygamy. Early in the debate, Senator Joseph Brown of Georgia suggested that Vermonter Edmunds send 50,000 missionaries to Utah and thus convert the Saints to the "more refined, delicate, voluptuous, and attractive practices of the people of New England." But neither logic nor sarcasm stopped the bill.[53]

As court-appointed receivers began to confiscate church property under the Edmunds Act, the Saints again turned to the judiciary for relief. But the territorial courts and then the Supreme Court rejected a new tactic that couched the defense of polygamy in terms of the protection of property rights rather than religious liberty. Hoping to appeal to the deepest biases of a bench dedicated to safeguarding private property from legislative encroachments, the Mormons' attorney expressed his own abhorrence of polygamy, yet argued that "a firm belief in the rights of property and the protection of all persons in their rights to acquire and use and enjoy their property, compels the severest criticism and strongest condemnation of the high-minded acts of confiscation and spoilation" attempted by the statutes. In a split decision, the Court disagreed and labeled polygamy a criminal act that warranted an extraordinary federal response. Writing for the majority, Justice Joseph Bradley endorsed the right of federal officials to take the Saints' property and lashed out at the sect for refusing to abandon polygamy. Over the dissents of Justices Stephen Field and Lucius Q. C. Lamar and Chief Justice Melville Fuller, he announced that the "[s]tate has a perfect right to prohibit polygamy, and all other open offenses against the enlightened sentiment of mankind."[54]

Criminal prosecutions of almost 1,300 Mormons, financial destruction, and the combined assault of federal and local anti-Mormon politicians overcame the Saints' resistance. With the theocracy in shambles, President Wilford Woodruff renounced polygamy in 1890 and claimed divine support for the change. Once the sect's marital policy conformed to the national monogamous standard, federal officials returned its property and in 1894 granted Utah statehood. A mandatory constitutional proviso banning polygamy was the final shot in the campaign.[55]

The battle with the Mormons allowed the American legal system to arm itself with unusual power to enforce the nation's allegiance to monogamy. In a society increasingly obsessed by the character of family life, polygamy came to be seen as such a monumental menace to the nation's households that it encouraged an unparalleled federal intervention in the internal governance of a territory. Charles S. Zane, who presided over many polygamy trials as a federal judge, explained why in the 1891 *Forum*: "The immediate effect of the law often appeared very sad, and to justify it, it was necessary to look away, and ahead to a social system with a family consisting of one husband and one wife and their children, and the affections that arise from such relations."[56]

The potent regulatory weapons used in the crusade against polygamy usually remained in the sheath when judges and legislators adapted traditional nuptial restrictions to the governance of republican families. That was particularly true early in the century when nuptial volunteerism peaked and faith in state regulation faded. At no time did the bench apply these restrictions mechanically. Instead, judges assessed each transgression according to their own standards of nuptial fitness. Constructed in the first half of the century, the resulting system of restrictions was achieved by a flexible use of contractual standards supplemented by legislation. Though the prohibitions were heavily biased against the dissolution of existing marriages, the Mormon experience reveals that when brides and grooms posed too serious a challenge to the majority's beliefs and values, the bench and the state were quite willing to break-up offensive unions.

Americans Fashion Racial Restrictions

Throughout the nineteenth century, race provoked a much more determined use of state nuptial authority even than polygamy. Racism ran like a fault line through republican marriage law. Auguste Carlier spotted its impact: "Notwithstanding the great liberty allowed in contracting marriage, there is yet a very characteristic prohibition which should be here mentioned, as it is a trait in morals which proves how far the antagonism of the white to the other races has gone in America, even in those parts of the Union where slavery is prohibited."[57] He went on to describe various bans on interracial marriage.

Unlike most of the restrictions on marriage, the racial prohibition was an American innovation without English precedent. Its creation and persistence indicates that racism successfully and consistently overcame the law's powerful biases toward the promotion of matrimony. In the clash between racism and nuptial freedom, the latter always gave way.

This denial of matrimonial rights took two forms: bans on interracial marriages and prohibitions of slave unions. Each has its own history. In contrast to most of family law, though, the Civil War was a watershed for both. It gave new life to one and ended the other. The two restrictions point out forces that could enhance state authority in a generally anti-statist polity.

Antebellum Efforts at Racial Purity

Legal bars to interracial marriage originated in the economic incentive to treat blacks as a servile caste, and in the social aversion to legitimating racial mixing. Maryland in 1661 became the first of many provinces to enact such a ban. As settlers from the Atlantic seaboard streamed west after the Revolution, many interior states and territories placed racial prohibitions in state and territorial codes. During the nineteenth century, thirty-eight states and commonwealths had such restrictions at one time or another. Early in the period the ban became a regional phenomenon, with the most racially conscious states, generally in the South and West, formally prohibiting such unions, while those in the Northeast and Midwest made the more common assumption that private prejudice would accomplish the same result. Carlier shrewdly observed that "where the statute is silent, or even favorable to this sort of union, the force of prejudice is such that no one would dare to brave it. It is not the legal penalty which is feared, but a condemnation a thousand times more terrible."[58]

The formal ban on interracial unions had dubious legal standing because it lacked a common-law pedigree. This was evident in Bishop's 1852 *Commentaries*. An active opponent of slavery, Bishop nonetheless made a particularly revealing attempt to find a place for the racial curb in the common-law tradition. He cited with approval an 1841 Kentucky decision rejecting property claims based on the marriage of a white woman and a black man. The justices had ruled that because no formal proof of the union had been presented, they had to assume it had been "concubinage" rather than matrimonial. Bishop endorsed that reasoning by grouping the decision with an English opinion nullifying the alleged union of a countess and her footman. In that opinion, an English tribunal had accepted the aristocrat's contention that disparity of rank substantiated her claim of having "chosen to indulge in licentious passion rather than degrade herself from her high station by espousing her menial servant." Bishop's easy equation of American racial antipathies with British class prejudices illustrated not only the unceasing determination of American lawyers to find English roots for legal doctrines, but more important, the obvious correlation between class and race implicit in the racial prohibiton.[59]

Such legal sophistry made it clear that the regulatory power of the state was the most secure authority for the ban. The firm commitment of state-court judges to common-law nuptial rights made it impossible to impose the restriction without legislative initiative. Bridling at its powerlessness in 1842 to annul the inheritance rights of the children of a marriage between an emancipated black woman and a white man because it lacked a statutory ban, the South Carolina Supreme Court reluctantly agreed with the conclusion of one of the lawyers: "[A]lthough such marriages are revolting and justly regarded as offensive to public decency, they are not contrary to existing law." Similarly, after labeling interracial unions "degrading" and "repugnant to the institutions of society, and the moral law," the Kentucky Supreme Court in 1832 refused a Caucasian family's request that the definition of nuptial insanity be widened to include a white man's decision to wed a black woman. In a struggle between institutional commitments and racial ones, the courts retained their allegiance to the common law.[60] The willingness of most southern and a few northern legislatures to resolve the judicial dilemma by supplying statutes testifies to the powerful fear evoked by racial intermarriage.[61]

When such statutes existed, they won judicial endorsement. A dramatic turnabout by one of the eminent jurists of the Old South reveals the intense pressures on the bench exerted by concerns about racial "amalgamation" that threatened, in southern terms, social order and family legitimacy. North Carolina Chief Justice Thomas Ruffin faced two appeals in 1832 in which Caucasian grooms sought to annul their marriages with white women by charging nuptial fraud. The men claimed that their mates, with whom they had shared intimate premarital relations, had given birth to mulatto children and thus had falsely held themselves out as fit marital partners. In the first decision, Ruffin invoked the standard common-law rule, which demanded self-policing. He refused to annul Marville Scoggin's marriage: "There is in general no safe rule but this: that persons who marry take each other as they are."

But community sanctions about race mixing forced the Chief Justice to change his position. In the second opinion, Ruffin publicly acknowledged the public and professional opposition his first ruling had stirred. As a popularly elected judge and former speaker of the state assembly, he knew when to bow to the popular will. Though he admitted that his reading of the appeal brought by Jesse Barden against his wife Ann would have led him to issue the same verdict as in the Scoggins case, he modified the rule of fraud and dissolved the marriage. Ruffin ended the opinion with the frank declaration: "This is a concession to the deep-rooted and virtuous prejudices of the community on the subject." The judiciary's almost total approval of the racial ban, while at the same time jealously guarding other nuptial rights, exposes the singular ability of local values, in this case racism, to alter the commitment of the early nineteenth-century bench to a free marriage market.[62]

The Denial of Marriage to Slaves

Black nuptial rights suffered from white racism in an even more vicious way: antebellum slave codes prohibited matrimony. In the constant tension between the treatment of blacks as property and as human beings, marriage law ensured that slaves' domestic desires would not infringe on their masters' economic needs. Slave codes denied slaves the nuptial rights granted most other Americans through an extraordinary use of public authority.

Shortly after the abolition of slavery in the North, a benign view of northern bondage emerged as one of the sectional beliefs that would eventually tear the nation apart. This historical revisionism included the assertion that northern slave marriages had been treated with the dignity and respect that matrimony warranted rather than with the callous prohibition typical of the South.

Reeve contended that marriage emancipated northern blacks because slavery was so inherently inconsistent with marital rights and duties that masters must have assumed a grant of independence when giving permission. Others cited Samuel Sewall's successful amendment to the 1705 Massachusetts ban on interracial marriages as evidence of greater northern compassion: "[N]o master shall unreasonably deny marriage to his negro with one of the same nation." Jacksonian historian George Bancroft, Massachusetts antislavery Senator Charles Sumner, and Ohio abolitionist lawyer John C. Hurd were but some antebellum northerners who pointed to the acceptance of slave unions in most northern colonies (with the master's consent) as proof of the region's moral superiority.

The evidence of numerous slave marriages supported these assertions. However, actual practices may have differed significantly from the harmonious pictures northerners tried to paint. The records are strewn with forced separations of slave families despite the existence of legal marriages. And the lack of a master's consent totally nullified a slave's nuptial rights regardless of legal and social safeguards.[63]

An 1814 Pennsylvania decision suggests the tenuous legal standing of slave marriages even in the North. George Stephens sought a writ of *habeas corpus* to retrieve his slave wife. She had escaped from Maryland and married him in Pennsylvania. When her master came to reclaim her, they worked out a compromise in which she agreed to a three-year indenture in return for her freedom. Stephens challenged the bargain, asserting that his wife's legal subservience to him as a married woman precluded her from making a contract without his consent. After declaring the agreement to be in the woman's best interests, Chief Justice William Tilghman argued that "her situation is totally different from that of a free woman," and that therefore the common-law disabilities of coverture did not apply to her. Associate Justice Jasper Yates concurred, and insisted that "as a slave she could not enter into a [marriage] contract without her master's consent." Slave marriages were thus as dependent on white acquiescence in the North as in the South; the more favorable disposition of northerners to such unions did not alter that reality.[64]

The demise of slavery in the early nineteenth century freed northern blacks to wed one another and provided one more argument for the abolitionist protest against the peculiar institution. The importance invested in the issue by the opponents and defenders of slavery grew out of their shared belief that marriage required positive legal and contractual sanction. Without such legitimacy, a sexual union was considered only a casual connection between a man and a woman. By withholding the right to marry, southerners suppressed the right of their black charges to create families as whites defined them. The implications of that denial led each group to place great weight on the marital policy of slavery.[65]

The southern bench and bar developed a two-part justification for the ban. It addressed the fundamental contradiction of slavery, the status of slaves as humans and as property. Since the law held consent to be the one essential element of a nuptial contract, the denial of consensual ability to slaves rendered them legally incapable of forming that or any other legal relationship. Judges categorized slaves' legal status by placing them in the same nuptial category as infants or the insane. Second, slaves were ineligible for matrimony because of the incompatibility of marital rights and duties with those owed to masters. As one judge put it, slaves could not discharge domestic obligations without "doing violence to the rights of the owner." The master's needs overrode those of his charges. A perversion of the contractual logic used to extend marital rights to others thus became the legal foundation for upholding legislative acts barring slave marriages.[66]

Only one southern tribunal vested slave unions with legality. In 1819 the Louisiana Supreme Court decided that such marriages acquired an incipient set of rights:

> [I]t is clear, that slaves have no legal capacity to assent to any
> contract. With the consent of their masters they may marry, and
> their moral power to agree to such a contract or connection as that
> of marriage, cannot be doubted. But whilst in a state of slavery it
> cannot produce any civil effect, because the slaves are deprived of
> all civil rights, emancipation gives to the slave his civil rights, and
> a contract of marriage, legal and valid by the consent of the mas-
> ter and moral assent of the slave, from the moment of freedom,
> although dormant during slavery, produces all the effects which
> result from such a contract among free persons.[67]

This assertion most likely drew on the state's civil-law heritage, including the Roman slave custom of *contuberium*, which gave certain reciprocal marital rights to slaves after manumission.

As the shackles of slavery tightened, the Louisiana opinion not only
failed to influence other jurisdictions but elicited outright denunciation.
In 1825, perhaps in reaction to the ruling, the Louisiana legislature
reenacted its ban on slave unions and denied them any civil status
whatsoever. On the eve of the Civil War, the North Carolina Supreme
Court specifically repudiated the Louisiana decision. *Howard* v. *Howard*
(1858) quashed an attempt by the children of a slave marriage to share
equally in their father's estate with the offspring of his second and
formal union. In a burst of anti-Catholicism typical of the era, the court
chided the Louisiana bench for viewing marriage as a sacrament and not
a civil contract, as did the Protestant-influenced common law. The
justices then let loose the Old South's last barrage against the marital
rights of slaves:

> [T]he relation between slaves is essentially different from that of
> man and wife joined in wedlock. The latter is indissoluble during
> the life of the parties, and its violation is a high crime; but with
> slaves it may be dissolved at the pleasure of either party, or by a
> master of one or both, depending on the caprice or necessity of the
> owners. So the union is formed, and no ground can be conceived
> of, upon which the fact of emancipating can, not only drawn of it
> the unqualified relations, but by a sort of magic, convert it into a
> relation of so different a nature.

The court dismissed the notion of dormant rights as more of a "fanciful
conceit" than "the ground of a sound argument."[68]

Yet southern judges only denied the legality, not the reality, of slave
unions. In the Howard decision itself, the North Carolina bench conceded the existence of "a wide distinction between the cohabitation of

slaves, as man and wife, and an indiscriminate sexual intercourse; it is recognized among slaves, for as a general rule, they respect the exclusive rights of fellow slaves who are married." The judges also acknowledged the mixed motives behind the customary standing of slave unions: "[M]arriages are permitted and encouraged by owners, as well in consideration of the happiness of the slaves and their children, as because in many ways their interest as masters is thereby promoted." In 1853 the same court asserted that our "law requires no solemnization or form in regard to the marriage of slaves, and whether they 'take up' with each other by express permission of their owners, or from a mere impulse of nature, in obedience to the command 'multiply and replenish the earth' cannot, in contemplation of the law, make any sort of difference." Though recognized as humans with natural needs and subject to divine injunctions, the slaves' domestic arrangements occurred without benefit of law. Instead, the codes armed masters with complete legal dominion over the marital rights of their slaves.[69]

As the North Carolina opinions suggest, the denial of legality did not prevent slave marriages. On the contrary, most adults wed. Nor were their unions always instigated at the bequest of their masters. In the little breathing space that blacks created for themselves within the peculiar institution, marriage often became a powerful institution that softened the horrors of bondage. But the extensive rights of masters had a continuing impact on slave family life that cast a pall over all unions, whether voluntary or forced. Opponents and defenders of slavery would have agreed with Tocqueville's declaration: "There is a profound and natural antipathy between the institution of marriage and that of slavery."

Extending the full reciprocal rights and duties of matrimony to slaves proved impossible under the slave regime, despite the advocacy of slave marital rights by southerners such as Robert Toombs, George Fitzhugh, George Frederick Holmes, Henry Hughes, and John Belton O'Neal. As historian Eugene Genovese has explained: "The slave holders understood that such reforms threatened the economic viability of the capital and labor markets. No other issue so clearly expressed the hybrid nature of the regime; so clearly pitted economic interests against paternalism and defined the limits beyond which the one could not reinforce the other." In the 1930s an ex-slave registered his own recognition of that nuptial reality: "God made marriage, but da white man made de law." A slave preacher ended slave weddings with an even more frightful comment: "Till death or buckra part you."[70]

Reconstructing the Color Line after the Civil War

The legitimacy of the prohibitions against slave marriages and interracial unions fell into doubt when the collapse of the Confederacy and the emancipation of the slaves created a moral panic. The expanded legal personality of blacks created by Reconstruction civil rights legislation and constitutional amendments threatened to undermine the prewar structure of racial distinctions in matrimony. In the first decades after the war, judges and legislators reacted to that threat by devising a new racial policy that incorporated slave unions into the main body of nuptial law while maintaining—indeed reinforcing—the prohibition against interracial marriages.

Slave Unions

Although their response to most black demands for legal rights was negative, southern whites readily granted the matrimonial requests of their former charges. The prevailing belief that marriage civilized and controlled the brutish nature of all people encouraged the use of formal matrimony as a remedy for the widespread immorality and promiscuity that whites believed to prevail among blacks. The Florida commission that drafted the state's repressive black code proclaimed that the "only inherent evil of the institution of slavery in the Southern states," was the lack of legal matrimony. The commissioners and other whites were quite willing to redress that particular wrong.[71]

Even more compelling, blacks themselves eagerly desired legal unions. As northern armies liberated them, many ex-slaves used all available means to reunite and maintain their families. Although some blacks deserted slave marriages, many others wandered across the South searching for lost family members. They seized the opportunity to legalize customary slave ties. Not only did they believe in matrimony, they also wanted to fortify their domestic relationships with as many legal protections as possible. As a result, blacks swamped public officials with demands to validate old and new unions.

At first, authorities responded to this groundswell with makeshift devices. Union army officers, missionaries, local officials, and others conducted mass marriage ceremonies. Later, with the reorganization of southern governments, came more orthodox solutions. Every southern state, as well as Congress, passed validation statutes or constitutional provisions conferring formal legitimacy on marriages begun under slavery. Most of them simply declared slave marriage legal if the couple continued to cohabit as husband and wife when the law went into effect; a few required the registration of slave unions. Freed slaves quickly took advantage of the laws. In 1866 over 9,000 couples registered their marriages in seventeen North Carolina counties.[72]

Almost as rapidly, legal disputes over the status of slave unions made their way to the appellate courts through litigation involving estates, criminal complaints (generally for bigamy), and divorces. As had other American tribunals in similar circumstances, southern courts willingly ratified legislative provisions. Invoking the acts and the nation's common law of marriage, judges easily integrated slave marriages into the law. The Alabama Supreme Court expressed the spirit in which the bench received the acts in an 1881 dower suit. It upheld the claim of a slave wife who lived with her husband until he left in 1865, and married another woman. Upholding the union under an act passed a few months before the husband left, the justices declared: "The ordinance commends itself to the moral sense, is eminently just, conservative of social order, promotive of morality, and preservative of the legitimacy and rights of innocent offspring of the preexisting union it ratifies. There is no room to doubt the power of the convention to enact it; and it belongs to the class of legislation which, when employed for such beneficial purposes, deserves the highest judicial consideration."[73]

The limits of this judicial tolerance emerged in Alabama when slave unions became entangled in the vicious warfare of Reconstruction politics. In 1870 a Republican-dominated state Supreme Court declared that slave marriages had always been valid while it resolved the estate fight between the children of Cassius Swanson's two wives. He had wed both women while he was a slave. "Marriage," the justices argued in *Stikes* v. *Swanson*, "is undoubtedly a natural right and slavery did not deprive the man in this condition of all his natural rights. So far as was consistent with his status, these were allowed." In a further revision of the Old South's past, the court elevated the customary unions of slaves into binding marriages by categorizing them as "quasi marriages. The unhappy condition of the parties only intervened to prevent these marriages from being perfect in the highest legal sense." In dividing the estate between the two sets of children the Republican jurists went on to repudiate the entire line of antebellum cases that denied the legality of slave marriages: "The former decisions were made in the interests of slavery. This interest is now overturned, and these cases deserve little weight."[74]

Although the Alabama court reaffirmed its position four years later, when Redeemers carried the state, both rulings were overturned. In *Cantelou* v. *Doe* (1876), an estate fight between the children of a man's slave wife and those of the woman he married after emancipation, a new set of judges rejected what they considered to be an attempt to undermine the already mythical Old South. After listing the numerous decisions rejecting the legality of slave unions, they curtly declared: "We prefer to follow the earlier decisions of this court . . . and we thereby overrule the latter two decisions, so far as they conflict with our former rulings." By linking themselves to their antebellum predecessors, the court cast aside the one significant postwar effort to confer full legality on all slave unions. The United States Supreme Court backed the Redeemers in 1875 by declaring that it had been "an inflexible rule of the law of African slavery, wherever it existed, that the slave was incapable of entering into any contract, not excepting the contract of marriage."[75]

The 1877 *Virginia Law Journal* offered a way to reconcile the common law with antebellum slave doctrines and customs. Its solution rested on a stereotyped white vision of slave family life: "In view of the casual and fleeting character of the cohabitation during the lives of the parties, in many cases, among slaves, and that there was no obligation, save a moral one, to a permanent union, there is some difficulty in presuming that the parties entertained in the first instance the matrimonial purpose, so to speak, and in making the subsequent cohabitation after freedom have the effect of changing their contubernial relation into a perfect marriage." The journal urged that "this ought to be a question of fact in each case; subject, however, to the principle that the law favors marriage, and the circumstances being ambiguous, such an interpretation ought to be put on them as will consist with moral rather than an illicit connection between the parties." Most courts followed this approach. In doing so they upheld most contested slave marriages without violating the memory of the Old South.[76]

When trying bigamy indictments or probate disputes, judges generally ruled that marital cohabitation after emancipation and the passage of a validation act made a slave union legally binding. These cases stirred the paternalistic sentiments of the bench. In an 1869 bigamy trial, one Georgia judge cautioned: "It is true, that under the peculiar circumstances surrounding them, a moralist will not judge upon them harshly, and it is perhaps a wise policy not to inflict upon them severe penalties for failing as in most instances they did, to comprehend the sacredness of the marital ties." Another Georgia bigamy trial in 1881 gave the bench an opportunity to instruct the new citizens in their nuptial responsibilities. After emancipation an ex-slave had deserted his adulterous mate and wed another woman. The court upheld the legality of the first union and sustained the indictment. The justices lectured the defendant on his civic obligations: "[H]is wife was unfaithful, he got mad and married again without a divorce. Being a free citizen, he must act as one, carrying the burdens, if he so considers them, as well as enjoying the privileges of his new condition." In a region dominated by paternalistic white males and where the belief in black promiscuity masked fears of black sexuality, the judiciary's mixture of concern and exhortation was easily grafted onto marriage law.[77]

Antimiscegenation Laws

Slave marriages posed difficulties for the post–Civil War legal system, but ones solvable by relying on the now immense body of American marriage law. Interracial marriage, on the other hand, quickly became the most sensitive and complex legal area of black-white relations. The determination of whites to retain class and sexual hegemony over their former bondspersons gave a renewed urgency to earlier fears spawned by interracial marriage.

The mere possibility of granting such unions legitimacy led to the coining of a new word in 1864, "miscegenation." It soon became synonymous with interracial sexual relations, matrimonial or otherwise. In election campaigns, legislative debates, and other social and political gatherings in Reconstruction America, opponents of Republican rule pointed to miscegenation as the logical and heinous result of endowing blacks with political rights.

Miscegenation became the Democratic equivalent of the Republicans' "bloody shirt." President Andrew Johnson appealed to the deepest racial fears of all whites when he justified his veto of the Civil Rights Act of 1866 by arguing that "if Congress can abrogate all state laws of discrimination between the two races in the matter of real estate, of suits, and of contracts generally, may it not also repeal the State laws as to the contract of marriage between the two races?" Frequent Republican denials of any intention to legalize interracial marriage were to no avail. One Illinois Republican even took pains to announce in the congressional debate on the Fourteenth Amendment: "I deny that it is a civil right for a white man to marry a black woman or for a black man to marry a white woman." To ensure that such unions did not occur, legislatures in the South and a few midwestern states used the agitation over miscegenation to reenact antebellum statutes prohibiting interracial marriage or to pass new legislation. Lawmakers hoisted chivalric banners, claiming that the laws protected white womanhood, the "fetish of the postwar era."[78]

It fell on Reconstruction state courts to integrate the revitalized ban into postwar marital governance. Judges responded by creating a sturdy legal breakwater that stood for almost a hundred years. The justices of the North Carolina supreme court expressed the sentiments of the southern bench toward miscegenation quite explicitly in an 1869 decision that upset the marriage of a black man and a white woman: "The emancipation of the slaves has made no alteration in our policy, nor in the sentiments of our people." In declaring the pair guilty of fornication and adultery, the court rejected an attempt to use Reconstruction legislation to lower marriage law's racial barriers. It ruled decisively that the enactments had not been "intended to enforce social equality, but only civil and political rights." The justices concluded with a stern warning to those who planned to use the courts to change the law: "[I]f the terms [of the acts] were doubtful, the policy of prohibiting the intermarriage of the two races is so well established and the wishes of both races so well known, that we should not hesitate to declare the policy paramount to any doubtful construction."[79]

These and other state judges defended the prohibition with two interlocking arguments. First, they joined the growing retreat from a full contractual definition of matrimony. This process of redefinition led to the classification of marriage as more a legal status than a contract. Courts and treatise writers like Bishop redefined marriage to lay a foundation for a new balance in which the state played a larger role. Judges now waxed eloquent about the uniqueness of matrimony and the inherent right of each state to determine marital capacity. The judiciary's special pleading prevented the new contractual abilities of freed blacks from undermining racial curbs. In particular, it forestalled the classification of matrimony as a civil, rather than a social, right under Reconstruction legislation.

The Texas Court of Appeals addressed the issue directly when it ruled on Charles Frasher's petition to overturn his conviction for violating the state antimiscegenation law by marrying a black woman. The judges dismissed his claim that the Fourteenth and Fifteenth Amendments and the Civil Rights Bill of 1866 made the ban an unconstitutional deprivation of individual rights. Citing Bishop as an authority, they threw over the ban a cloak of new cloth, manufactured from states' rights and the privileged status of marriage by claiming that marriage was "not a contract protected by the Constitution of the United States or within the meaning of the Civil Rights Bill." On the contrary, they asserted that "marriage is more than a contract . . . it is a civil status, left solely by the Federal Constitution and the law to the discretion of the states under their general power to regulate their domestic affairs." After dogmatically asserting the prohibition's legality, the court granted Frasher a temporary reprieve from his four-year prison term by sending the case back with the demand that definite proof be offered of his wife's race.[80]

The judiciary also argued that society had to be protected from the serious social and physiological effects of interracial unions. This contention drew on a growing and increasingly influential body of racist scientific thought and pessimistic views of heredity. In an 1878 case, the justices of the Kentucky Supreme Court confirmed the legislature's right to regulate interracial marriage, contending that dropping the ban would "legalize intermarriage between the races, deteriorating to the Caucasian blood and [be] destructive of the social and legislative decorum of States." The racial ban thus fell under a growing postwar judicial disposition to accept enlarged state supervision of health and safety as a pretext for greater nuptial regulation.[81]

Aaron and Julia Green discovered this to their dismay when Redeemers on the Alabama Supreme Court overturned yet another ruling of their Republican predecessors. The earlier court had pronounced the racial intermarriage ban to be an unconstitutional violation of the contractual rights conferred on blacks by the Civil Rights act of 1866. The new jurists called homes the "nurseries of the States," and wondered "[who can] estimate the evil of introducing into their most intimate relations, elements so heterogeneous that they must naturally cause discord, shame, disruption of family circles, and estrangements of kindred? While with their interior administration, the State should interfere but little, it is obviously of the highest public concern that it should, by general laws adapted to the state of things around them, guard against disturbances from without." Julia Green, a Caucasian, spent two years in prison for having violated the southern hearth.[82]

As separation became the chief goal of American race laws, more and more states added antimiscegenation statutes to their codes and constitutions. From 1880 to 1920, when white racial phobia reached unprecedented heights, twenty states and territories strengthened or added antimiscegenation laws. Moreover, though five states had repealed the ban during the 1880s, none did so from 1890 to 1920. By 1910 Harvard Professor Frederic Stimson could write: "Marriage may be forbidden or declared null between persons of different races, and the tendency to do so is increasing in the South, and is certainly not decreasing in the North. Indeed, constitutional amendments are being adopted and proposed having this in view, 'the purity of the races.' "[83]

Other nonwhite minorities found themselves barred from marrying whites as the racist tide peaked. Indeed, the West replaced the South as the most restrictive region of the nation by adding Asians to the prohibited roster.[84] The corrosive racial environment ended what had been the most conspicuous anomaly among nuptial prohibitions, a grudging tolerance for Indian-white marriages.

Through much of the nineteenth century whites had designated Native Americans as a special people, one much less sexually and economically threatening than blacks. There was consequently less pressure to ban marriage, particularly in the antebellum era when such white dignitaries as the Revolutionary war hero Patrick Henry and Georgian William H. Crawford, the 1824 presidential candidate, publicly advocated Indian-white marriages and state judges upheld their legality. Native customs such as easy divorce and bride purchase did draw criticism, but neither a legislative nor a judicial disposition to stigmatize Native Americans with formal marital prohibitions existed in most states.[85]

By the 1870s, Francis Wharton, a legal-treatise writer, noted a change in the racial climate, observing that marriages of whites with Indians had not been "questioned until recently." Gradually the immunity of such unions weakened. Four states banned them by the end of the century: Arizona, North Carolina, Nevada, and Oregon. One critic, attorney Isaac Franklin Russell, even tried to explode the happy myth surrounding the marriage of John Rolfe and Pocahontas: "[N]o one will say the experiment thus made of the intermarriage of the redman and the paleface was a success." On another front, Congress attempted in 1888 to eliminate what was thought to be an incentive for Indian-white matrimony by denying reservation property rights to most Caucasian marriage partners.[86]

By 1916 twenty-eight states and territories prohibited various forms of interracial marriages. These bans represented an uncompromising determination to limit individual marital freedom and increase state nuptial authority over racial matters. In 1873 Schouler described the unique role of race in marriage law: "[T]he manifest tendency of the day is toward removing all legal impediments of rank and condition, leaving individual tastes and social manners to impose the only restrictions of this nature. But the race barrier has a strong foundation in human nature, wherever marriage companionship is concerned." Most northern states relied on that aversion, as muckraker Ray Stannard Baker explained in a widely read 1910 study of the color line: "[A]lthough there are no laws in most Northern states against mixed marriages, and although the Negro population has been increasing, the number of intermarriages is not only not increasing, but in many cities, as in Boston, is decreasing. It is an unpopular institution." Almost two-thirds of the nation codified its unpopularity.[87]

Recognizing the legality of interracial unions, in the view of many white critics, would have offered at least tacit support for racial and social equality in domestic relations. As racial segregation became even more inflexible with the appearance of "Jim Crow" laws, marriage was singled out by the most stringent restrictions. More statutes banned interracial marriage than any other form of racially related conduct. A 1910 study of racial discrimination categorically labeled the ban as the one restriction "which has not been confined to the South, which has in large measure escaped the adverse criticism heaped upon other race distinctions."[88]

Part of the popular appeal of antimiscegenation laws stemmed from their supposed ability to protect the "racial purity" of all families. As early as 1868 a white delegate to a Mississippi constitutional convention defended his proposed ban on interracial marriage with "scientific" arguments of a sort that would become a compelling force in family law for the rest of the century:

> [W]hereas the fact has been demonstrated by physiologists and long since settled as an axiom in science, that the progeny resulting from intermarriage between the white and black races, are very liable to a character of hereditary diseases; that the children of pure white or pure black unions are not subject to diseases incurable in this nature, and, most destructive to human life; that the general intermarriage of the two races occupying the South will inevitably result in the destruction of both, and it should be the settled policy of all good men of both races, who desire the perpetuation and prosperity of their respective races, to discontinue such comingling.[89]

As such contentions won wider approval, the ban on interracial marriage provided a model for a dramatic transition in American marriage law: the imposition of scientific restrictions on brides and grooms.

Late Nineteenth Century Attempts to Prevent "Unfit" Marriages

After mid-century, a determination to apply more rigorous tests of nuptial fitness undid the commitment to contractual rights that had governed the post-Revolutionary creation and application of marriage restrictions. As the social optimism of that earlier nuptial liberalism faded, and the apparently harmful effects of nuptial freedom spawned widespread apprehension, matrimonial prohibitions grew in number and restrictiveness. Like its companion piece, the campaign against common-law marriage, the demand for stricter standards of marital eligibility succeeded in augmenting contractually based nuptial restrictions with curbs drawn from other sources. Feminist-clergywoman Anna Carlin Spencer, a leader in the American Purity Alliance and the American Social Hygiene Association, argued for the prevention of "so many from marrying who are not physically, morally, or economically able to make marriage a social advantage."[90]

As the controversy over the prohibitions centered on an effort to forestall the marriage of the hygienically "fit" with the "unfit," science exerted a powerful influence on the legal assessment of nuptial capacity. Scientific explanations and solutions to social issues like marital fitness rose in popular and professional esteem because, as historian Barbara Rosenkrantz has said: " 'Science' became for the physician, the sanitary engineer, and the laboratory investigator, a goal as well as a procedure, which gave it the authority of higher law and removed it from criticism."[91] It did so for the lawyer too. The seemingly apolitical, authoritative aura of science made it a potent instrument of reform. In marriage law, science strengthened the drift from optimism to pessimism in the construction and use of nuptial prohibitions. Legislators infused with a new sense of urgency used scientific arguments to justify greater constraints on the right to wed. These laws challenged the common-law reliance on consent as the major test of nuptial fitness.

The Campaign against Youthful Marriage

The attempt to raise the statutory age of marriage discloses an increasingly acrimonious debate over marital eligibility. During the middle and late nineteenth century, attacks grew on the lax regulation of youthful marriages. The continued reliance on the common-law nuptial ages of twelve and fourteen drew special censure. In an 1884 *North American Review* article, Noah Davis reviled the common-law standard as "not a fit or decent one for this country." Other critics, like the Social Purity Alliance, singled out youthful brides and grooms as prime sources of marital instability. In 1901, George Howard, soon to be president of the American Sociological Association, summarized almost fifty years of protests against lax marriage age regulation: "[M]ajority is the law's simple devise for securing mental maturity in the graver things of life. Is not wedlock as serious a business as making a will or signing a deed?" His question implied the legal answer and his dissatisfaction with it. Howard, who crusaded for numerous progressive causes, called youthful matrimony a "fruitful source of evil" and urged legislators to deny it legal recognition.[92]

Youthful marriage not only stood accused of violating the middle-class ethic of sexual restraint but also of posing a biological threat to society. The domestic adviser Dio Lewis described the results of early marriages in *Chastity, Or Our Secret Sins* (1874): "[S]tunted growth and impaired strength on the part of the male; delicate if not utterly bad health in the female; the premature old age or death of one or both; and a puny, sickly offspring." After several decades of agitation, attorney Albert Swindlehurst repeated Lewis's contentions in the 1916 *Harvard Law Review*: "[It] is the noble mission of medical science to strengthen and preserve the weak; that of the legislature to stay the evils at its course, and to say that, in so far as the law can effect it, future generations shall be of sound mind and body, imbued with all the qualities which make for natural greatness." In this manner, the campaign against youthful marriages drew support from the attempt to make science an important means of weighing nuptial fitness.[93]

Many lawmakers responded by imposing greater restraints on youthful nuptials. A series of acts beginning around 1850 and increasing in scope and frequency a few decades later succeeded in raising the national statutory age of marriage to sixteen for women and eighteen for men. The Indiana progression proved fairly typical; it began with a codification of the common-law ages in 1830, then revised them to fourteen and seventeen in 1843, and the new legislative norm of sixteen and eighteen was reached in 1877. By 1906 only seventeen states and territories still clung to the common law.[94]

These revisions were part of a broader reassessment of the place of the young in American life. Persuaded by educators, physicians, and reformers, legislators began to segregate youths through compulsory school laws, and to provide special courts for them with vast discretionary power over status offenses and dependency, as well as to limit nuptial freedom. The law thus fostered a Victorian concept of youthful development and marital conduct by prolonging childhood and saving children from themselves and their misguided parents through the forced imposition of self-restraint, educational advancement, delayed gratification, and domesticity. Critics of the family believed that these traits held the key to marital bliss, and should be mandated by coercive state action.[95]

These new marriage-age laws, like many other post–Civil War legislative interventions into what previously had been considered private matters, received a mixed judicial review. They posed a challenge to the reigning judicial view of the right to wed. Many jurists and their professional allies retained a striking, if increasingly anachronistic, faith in the social utility of youthful nuptial freedom. As Francis Wharton, a major legal theorist of the era, put it, encouraging early marriage had become "as much a part of the distinctive policy of the United States as to discourage such marriages [was] part of the distinctive policy of Europe." He urged the courts to "sustain matrimonial capacity in all cases of persons arrived at puberty."[96]

Confronted with disputes over the scope of the vaguely worded age regulations, judges often had to choose between the settled common-law policy of limited state interference and new legislative restrictions. Where they could use their discretion, they usually chose the common law. The bench treated marriages as voidable when one or both parties wed below the new statutory ages. If the union continued after the spouses reached these ages, it became permanent. The Supreme Court of Nevada followed this reasoning in finding the 1869 marriage of Jennie C. Dirks valid even though she had wed three years under the new statutory age of sixteen. The court considered the ceremony before a justice of the peace "a valid binding contract."[97]

In an 1876 bigamy appeal, the Alabama Supreme Court expressed its disagreement with the reformers by favorably comparing violations of the age curbs to infractions that the judges considered much more serious. It swept aside Thomas Beggs's attempt to have his first marriage declared null and void because he had wed when he was below the statutory age of seventeen. The justices concluded that the legislature had not intended to punish such transgressions as severely as other violations, such as the ban on incestuous unions. They contended that a marriage earlier than the "age of consent may be indiscrete, may disturb the peace of families and may subject youth and inexperience to the acts of the cunning and unscrupulous, but it is wanting in the vicious and corrupting properties of the incestuous connection which contravenes the voice of nature, degrades the family, and offends decency and morals."[98]

These opinions reflected the persistent judicial endorsement of self-regulation and the judicial determination to oversee, and if necessary repel major legislative invasions of nuptial law. In his *First Book of Law* (1868), a primer for would-be law students, Bishop singled out marriage-age restrictions as an example of misdirected statutory initiatives. After quoting at length physiological arguments against early marriage and the call for legislative intervention by moral philosopher George Coombe, Bishop hastened to add that the "law does not approve of the marriage; it merely, in some instances, keeps its fingers out of other people's messes." He concluded that "if 'a girl of fifteen' thinks she can violate any law of nature with impunity, the blame should not be taken all away from her parents and instructors, and placed upon the law of the land."[99]

The inconclusive debate over curbing youthful matrimony through legislation revealed the difficulty of activating public authority in late

nineteenth-century America, particularly when the acts to be banned did
not invoke the intense and uniform condemnation that sustained state
intervention in polygamous or interracial unions. Nevertheless, judges
and legislators slowly established a new balance between state authority
and individual rights that reduced youthful freedom by raising the formal
age of marriage. But it was a balance in which the young and the courts
retained marked discretionary powers. The state's regulatory authority,
though enhanced, remained less extensive than in the case of interracial
marriage. Although the specific interests and concerns varied in each
case, similar revaluations of state power and contractual freedom occurred in all nuptial prohibitions.

The Hygienic Invasion of Marriage Law

Only prejudices as potent as racism or monogamy could dislodge
the commitment to individual choice embedded in nineteenth-century
American marriage law. The fear of transmission of hereditary defects
through marriage became such a primary concern after mid-century. A
scientific pessimism first evident in the antebellum defense of the racial
ban and then in the debate over nuptial ages slowly spread, undermining
the social confidence in nuptial privatism that had been a pillar of liberal
marriage law and the aversion to state intervention. The "environmental-
ism and optimism which had characterized mid-century discussions of
heredity," historian Charles Rosenberg has pointed out, "was gradually
replaced in the 1880s by a growing biological reductionism and emphasis on authoritarian solutions." The use of marriage prohibitions to ban
unions that appeared to pose hereditary threats resulted. Penal reformer
Charles Reeve expressed such sentiments in his 1888 address to the
National Prison Association, one of the era's most powerful reform
organizations. Attributing the weakness and deformities of the "dependent classes" to "erroneous and perverted" marriages in which many a
"viciously diseased man or woman was being permitted to procreate," he
condemned both the law and public indifference.[100]

Incest Fears

Alterations in the content and the defense of kin prohibitions offer clues
to the way in which new biological fears reoriented the law. In each of
the numerous editions of his treatise on marriage law, Bishop advanced a

definitive explanation of kin restrictions. Yet where the 1852 volume had relied on traditional justifications for the ban, a revised edition twenty years later used medical arguments to question the very propositions he had so confidently put forward in the earlier work:

> Marriages between persons closely allied in blood are apt to produce an offspring feeble in body, and tending to insanity in mind. They are everywhere prohibited; but the more common reason assigned for the prohibition is, that the toleration of them would impair the quiet of families, jeopardize female chastity, and hinder the formation of favorable alliances. And while this reason appears utterly insufficient of itself, it shows how in the world's history, the promptings of the nature of man frequently carry him in the right direction even where his mere intellect fails to discern the path. [101]

Though the relaxation of affinal restrictions continued unimpeded, the longstanding antipathy to consanguineous unions revived and expanded as biological fears intensified. Heightened interest in the consequences of kin unions eroded support for individual nuptial rights and encouraged public intervention. Legislative attempts to ban those kin marriages that seemed the most threatening led to greater statutory uniformity.

By the end of the century, two significant developments had occurred. First, the number of states banning first-cousin marriages increased significantly. The statutory changes were another way in which the Western System of kin restriction achieved dominance. The passage of these curbs, despite a continuing debate over the actual physiological effects of such marriages, reveals a new inclination to take no chances with heredity. Dio Lewis asserted without qualification that "the products of" marriages "within the second and third degrees" are "proverbially feeble and delicate." His declaration was spawned in an increasingly cautious and often repressive legal environment in which an earlier romantic belief in human rationality and the possibilities of change through moral suasion gave way to "social darwinism and scientific fatalism."

Second, states devised more comprehensive nuptial codes bringing all possible family members within the incest ban. Respect for the sanctity of the family grew so intense that even adopted children found themselves under statutory supervision; the new laws prohibited marriages between adopted children and their new parents or siblings. In addition, most states reversed traditional practice and declared incestuous unions void rather than merely voidable. By 1900 every state prohibited marriages of blood relations. Most ended the prohibition at first cousins, but many went a step further to second cousins. This dramatic rejection of self-policing offers graphic evidence of the late nineteenth-century conclusion that the free marriage market had failed to protect society from major biological threats. Only more vigorous state regulation could provide adequate security.[102]

Rising apprehension over the biological and social effects of incestuous marriages also eroded judicial support for contractual rights. Most cases coming before the bench continued to be property fights arising from uncle-niece or aunt-nephew marriages. Thus judges generally had to resolve estate disputes and did not have the opportunity to prevent the formation of biologically dangerous unions. The judiciary interpreted the acts in such a way as to retain the discretion to use common-law rules in applying the more rigorous curbs. Legal authors like Bishop encouraged such interpretations by arguing that the best protection for society lay in judge-dominated rather than legislative-directed marriage rules. His advice echoed a widespread determination in the bench and bar to protect the authority over nuptials that had been won earlier in the century.[103]

An 1863 Pennsylvania decision was typical. John Parker married his niece in 1856, but had kept the ceremony a secret. He died in 1861, a year after a new act prohibiting such marriages, and his wife and his mother vied for his estate. The state supreme court followed the advice offered by Bishop, interpreting the statute in the light of common-law precedents. The justices ruled that because the law contained no express clause declaring such marriages void, they would apply the common law and treat the incest transgression as irrelevant after Parker's death. They defended their ruling as a needed protection for legitimacy and inheritance claims based on functioning marriages. But the judges took it upon themselves to reject publicly an earlier faith that self-policing would control the problem: "We cannot refrain from stating that such connections are destructive of good morals and should not only be frowned upon by the community, but very severely punished; and this is unquestionably the view of our criminal code."[104]

In his 1865 *Book of Nature*, John Aston noted that "it is well known that marriage between near relatives produces unhealthy and imperfect children, but the causes of such a result are not generally understood." By 1900 scientific uncertainty had disappeared and with it a legal tendency to tolerate kin violations in defense of contractual rights. Sociologist George Arner thus could confidently predict in 1904: "[W]hen rational marriage laws prohibit the marriages of the diseased and the degenerate, the problem of consanguinity will cease to be of vital importance."[105]

Mental Fitness

Biological fears also tipped the legal scales used to measure mental fitness for matrimony. A continuing belief in the hereditary sources of mental illness, the failure of asylums' promised cures, and the new faith in scientific solutions to social ills, combined with growing apprehension about the American family, to shift the focus of professional and lay interest from rehabilitation to prevention. As alarm over mental illness mounted, reformers argued that stringent and well-enforced marriage standards for conjugal fitness would prevent the birth of feebleminded—a new and pejorative term—children. Even that arch foe of the active state, legal treatise writer Christopher Tiedeman, declared that if "the blood of either of the parties to a marriage is tainted with insanity there is imminent danger of its transmission to the offspring, and through the procreation of imbecile children the welfare of the state is more or less threatened."[106]

However the courts offered little comfort to interventionist reformers. Applying legal rather than medical standards, they preferred case-by-case determinations of nuptial sanity to a general definition. As the Mississippi Supreme Court declared in 1872 after it refused to annul the marriage of William and Mollie Smith because of Mrs. Smith's insanity: "We have not seen a case where the presence of the taint of hereditary insanity . . . has of itself been held to be the cause of dissolving the marriage." Both explicit legislation and convincing new arguments would be necessary to alter the bench's reading of the law.[107]

The source of these new arguments was eugenics. Eugenically inspired nuptial laws, though erected on the scaffolding created by canonical and common-law impediments to matrimony, constituted a major legal departure. They arose from a new assumption, that physical defects in themselves abrogated nuptial rights because the state was obliged to defend itself against unhealthy offspring and the pollution of the marriage bed by disease. In 1910 political scientist Frederic Stimson pinpointed the essence of the change: "To-day we witness the startling tendency for the State to prescribe whom a person shall not marry, even if it does not prescribe whom they shall. The science of eugenics . . . will place on the statute books matters which our forefathers left to the Lord."[108]

The eugenics crusade, which crested between 1885 and 1920, had a direct and longlasting effect on marriage law. Under its sway, restraints on individuals afflicted with mental and physical maladies reoriented the traditional physiological impediments to matrimony. The additions ensured that nuptial prohibitions contained explicit medical as well as contractual means of assessing nuptial fitness.

Though courts continued to interpret the new standards in terms of older common-law rules biased toward the promotion of matrimony, the laws gradually became incorporated into matrimonial governance and practice. Proponents emphasized their social neutrality; attorney Joseph Chamberlain declared: "Recent legislation limiting the right to marry is based not on historic rules or race feeling but on scientific fact." On that foundation, physical eligibility became a powerful new test of marital capacity.[109]

Advocates of hereditary restrictions touted them as necessary weapons to defend the nation from degeneration. Feminist and pioneering social scientist Elizabeth Cady Stanton declared in 1879 that the "law of heredity should exclude many from entering the marriage relation." Ten years earlier she had insisted that only those "who can give the world children with splendid physique, strong intellect, and high moral sentiment, may conscientiously take on themselves the responsibility of marriage and maternity." By the 1870s, many feminists, like Stanton, demanded hygienic controls on matrimony along with sanitary reforms, boards of health, and the introduction of physiological and hygienic education in the nation's schools. Similarly, sociologist George Howard complained in 1904 that "under pleas of 'romantic love' we blandly yield to sexual attraction in choosing our mates, ignoring the welfare of the race." Appealing for a "higher standard of conjugal choice," he contended that experience "shows that in wedlock natural and sexual selection should play a smaller and artificial selection a larger role." Here, he declared, "the state has a function to perform."[110]

Howard's plea discloses both the goals and limits of the eugenic marriage law movement. The full program could only be achieved by treating marriage as state-controlled mating. The very breadth of such a proposal doomed it to legal oblivion; few reforms requiring massive increases in state power succeeded in late nineteenth-century America. Nevertheless, major alterations did occur as part of the larger revision of nuptial liberalism.

In 1895 Connecticut enacted a reform-inspired statute. It banned the marriage of feebleminded, imbecilic, and epileptic men and women under forty-five years of age, and imposed a minimum three-year prison sentence on violators. Dr. George H. Knight, the Superintendent of Connecticut's School for Imbeciles, explained the act's assumptions to the 1899 National Conference of Charities and Corrections. He asserted that such laws "strike a blow directly at the root of what is called the law of individual right, but I claim that the mentally unfit have no right to reproduce themselves [and] that which they will not, cannot, do for themselves, the law of the land must do for them. The sane, normal, everyday people of this country must have a chance."

The Connecticut Supreme Court willingly incorporated the act into its supervision of wedlock. In 1905 it approved the dissolution of Marion and Roy Gould's marriage. Marion Gould claimed that her husband had hidden his epilepsy from her. The justices rejected Roy's contentions that the new law unconstitutionally abridged private rights: "Laws of this kind may be regarded as an expression of the conviction of modern society that disease is largely preventible by proper precautions, and that it is not unjust in certain cases to require the observation of these, even at the cost of narrowing what in former days was regarded as the proper domain of individual rights."

The Connecticut action encouraged the legislatures of Kansas (1903), New Jersey and Ohio (1904), and Michigan and Indiana (1905) to impose similar restrictions. By the 1930s forty-one states had enlarged the common-law tests of mental capacity with statutes that used the terms lunatic, feebleminded, idiot, and imbecile. These acts, and complementary judicial opinions, indicate a willingness to retreat again from the common-law defense of contractual rights, this time in reaction to perceived biological threats to public safety.[111]

Medical Restrictions

During the final decades of the nineteenth century, apprehension over the transmission of hereditary defects and contagious diseases, especially venereal disease, inflamed the public mind. Reformers bombarded the nation with statistical studies claiming that disease had reached epidemic proportions and with terrifying stories of women and children ruined by male sexual deviance and disease. Because the "welfare of the human race is largely bound up in the health and reproductive capacity of the wife and mother," New York City medical professor Prince A. Morrow pleaded in a 1904 polemic, the "sanitation of the marriage relation becomes the most essential condition of social preservation." A leading member of the hygienic wing of the Social Purity Alliance, he lamented that through "its instrument, the law, the State affords the injured wife the doubtful remedy of separation or divorce, but it does not protect her from this injury." Morrow traced this "callous indifference" to popular acceptance of the inevitability of "evil" and to the cynical assumption that the "communication of disease in marriage" remained a "matter between husband and wife with which society has nothing to do." The physician demanded a state ban on diseased grooms.[112]

Diatribes like Morrow's against male licentiousness helped forge an alliance between medical experts and women reformers that had as a major goal the institution of a single standard of domestic morality, and consequently the restriction of traditional male sexual liberties. In *Chastity*, Dio Lewis remarked that "most men don't believe that the marriage contract is binding upon both parties, they have their own 'little irregularities' and joke about them; but let a wife lapse, and the husband howls with rage." Lewis called for "a common standard of virtue for both sexes"; and counseled women: "If the man who offers you his heart and hand is of a household which has been visited by insanity, consumption or epilepsy, you are a reckless woman if you do not hesitate ere you accept him." In an address to the 1892 Congress of Women, Clara Holbrook Smith was even more emphatic. After insisting that in "light of today's revealment a person is criminal who does not look after the purity of the blood," she asserted in unequivocal terms: "If you are unscientific you will condemn my next statement, the 'Destroyer' of a home, whether it is a home that now exists or a home that could have existed, should be put to death. The law of Leviticus, when interpreted by science, is none too severe." These critiques linked male disease and immorality with nuptial individualism. They helped create a medically based domestic moral code that increased the dependence of the family on therapeutic experts like Morrow and on laws with expanded state authority to intervene in family life.[113]

In 1899 Michigan legislators passed an act barring persons infected with syphilis or gonorrhea from marrying and imposed a criminal penalty on violators. By the 1930s over twenty-six states and territories had enacted similar measures. Generally the statutes provided for criminal punishment and fines when an individual knowingly wed while infected.

The campaign for medical restrictions in marriage law did not end with the passage of these acts. Reform shifted from deterrence to prevention. As early as 1876 Elizabeth Duffey had urged that when "a man and a woman are about to marry, let each present themselves for examination in regard to health by a competent physician, who should decide whether they are proper candidates for parentage." In 1913 Wisconsin became the first state to heed such advice when it required prospective grooms to submit to medical tests. Critics complained about the unreliability of the tests and claimed that they violated individual rights. But disease-inspired fears, improved detection, greater documentation, and growing popular faith in therapeutic regulation drowned these objections. As other states followed Wisconsin's lead—and began to include brides—prenuptial medical examinations became standard procedure.[114]

The new nuptial controls elicited general judicial approval as valid exercises of state police power over matrimony. Many judges hedged their acceptance by incorporating the acts into traditional common-law disabilities, thus retaining a significant degree of discretion. The bench tended to categorize violations as frauds rather than criminal transgressions, unless expressly compelled to do so by statute or indictment.

The Massachusetts Supreme Judicial Court followed that path in the 1898 case of *Smith* v. *Smith*. Emma Smith sued for an annulment, having discovered her husband's syphilitic condition on their wedding night. He denied it, but a doctor confirmed her fears. Traditionally illness could not be considered a nuptial fraud since couples pledged to "take each other in sickness and health." But a series of decisions by the same court, beginning with the 1862 *Reynolds* v. *Reynolds* ruling, had held that nuptial violations which went to the "essence" of the matrimonial agreement qualified as fraud. The court considered Smith's act such a violation. It pledged that no woman would be asked "to sacrifice herself to incurable disease and to blight her posterity." Tellingly, Schouler equated the right of a woman to shed her tie to a man infected with venereal disease to the male right to an annulment if his wife proved to be pregnant by another.[115]

Sterilization, the most extreme eugenic measure, crowned the effort to curtail the nuptial freedom of the unfit. By permanently preventing the mentally, physically, and morally defective from procreating, reformers hoped to allow these unfortunates to rejoin society and enjoy the solace and controls of matrimony without endangering society. Indiana passed the first act in 1907. It authorized the sterilization of confirmed criminals, idiots, imbeciles, and rapists in state institutions upon the approval of a board of experts. By 1931 twenty-seven states had enacted some form of mandatory sterilization. The acts varied widely in scope; most included the feebleminded and imbecilic.[116]

As the most drastic invasion of nuptial rights, mandatory sterilization generated intense controversy. Courts in Indiana and New York declared their statutes unconstitutional deprivations of the right to due process and equal protection of the law. A federal tribunal overturned a Nevada act, terming it cruel and unusual punishment. Repeal or neglect eliminated other statutes or rendered them ineffective. But in 1927 the United States Supreme Court approved the sterilization of eighteen-year-old Virginian Carrie Buck, who, like her mother and daughter, was classified as feebleminded. Justice Oliver Wendell Holmes, Jr., who in 1881 had insisted that public policy must sacrifice the individual to the general good, confidently asserted in this decision: "It is better for all the world, if instead of waiting to execute degenerate offspring from crimes, or to let them starve for their imbecility, society can prevent those who are manifestly unfit from continuing their kind." He unequivocally declared that "three generations of imbeciles are enough."[117]

Holmes's endorsement of the most radical invasion of what had been earlier considered a private right aptly symbolized and summarized the new tenor of legal restrictions on marriage. Most of the curbs retained a bias against the dissolution of marriages and state restrictions on the right to wed; but legislators, judges, and reformers achieved another new balance between public regulation and individual rights in the law. It was different from, but as significant as, the new orientation of the laws governing nuptial celebrations and breach-of-marriage-promise suits. Each revision made the point that, in republican family law, matrimony was a species of public as well as of private law. Related developments occurred in the other major category of domestic relations: parenthood.

P A R T T W O

PARENTHOOD
BIRTH, LEGITIMACY, CUSTODY

The next domestic relation which we are to consider, is that of parent and child. The duties that reciprocally result from this connection are prescribed, as well by those feelings of parental love and filial reverence which Providence has implanted in the human breast, as by the positive precepts of religion, and of our municipal law. . . . The duties of parents to their children, as being their natural guardians, consist in maintaining and educating them during the season of infancy and youth, and in making reasonable provision for their future usefulness and happiness in life, by a situation suited to their habits, and a competent provision for the exigencies of that situation. . . . The duties that are enjoined upon children to their parents are obedience and assistance during their own minority, and gratitude and reverence during the rest of their lives.

James Kent,
Commentaries on American Law, II (1826)

CHAPTER 5

CONTRACEPTION AND ABORTION
WHO CONTROLS THE WOMB?

Nineteenth-century family law guarded parenthood, the other entrance to the republican family, as jealously as it did nuptials. The relations between parents and children, however, highlight different aspects of the law. In particular, the contractualism so influential in marriage law was diluted for a number of reasons: the obvious dependency of all children; the assumed dependency of wives; the varied impact of class, race, and ethnicity; and the particularly strong popular and professional animus against state intervention into these relations. Consequently, although many of the concerns and developments evident in nineteenth-century marriage law arose in this second category of domestic relations, the law of parents and children had its own characteristics as well. The interplay of shared and distinct features in the two fields of American family law will be examined in three vital topics of the law of parents and children: birth, legitimacy, and custody.

Childbirth unearths a fundamental ambiguity of nineteenth-century America: the coexistence of public opposition to family limitation along with a widespread resort to family planning. Indeed, the incongruity of even applying those terms to the era suggests the gulf between thought and practice, one never to be bridged during that period.

The increasing use of two forms of family limitation, contraception and abortion, turned the governance of birth into a public controversy. It is hardly surprising that these practices engulfed the legal system in controversy. Legislators and judges tried to make the society's ideals and practices compatible and to overcome a powerful aversion to involving the state in these most intimate of parental decisions. This task proved impossible.

Out of the resulting social and institutional struggles came complex and often contradictory laws and doctrines. Early in the nineteenth century, the law's original bias toward childbirth yielded to powerful pressures compelling the middle class to limit the size of its families. But in the 1840s and 1850s the growing resort to family limitation sparked a powerful reform drive that succeeded in instituting a dogmatic pronatal policy by the end of the century. Thus halting attempts to regulate childbirth evolved into a regulatory strategy that condemned as criminal all forms of family limitation but reserved its harshest treatment for abortion.

Even so, the law never fully subscribed to pronatalism in practice as much as it seemed to in rhetoric. Like the general public, judges and legislators found it difficult to refute the charges against family limitation, but they foundered in their attempts to end the practice. As a result, the constant tension between ideal and use became embedded in the law itself. That legal reality allowed husbands and wives to retain a significant degree of legal freedom to plan the size of their families throughout the nineteenth century.

The emergence of a distinctive American law on childbirth, therefore, reveals a legal commitment to parental rights that became a domestic relations counterpart to family law's endorsement of nuptial freedom. This commitment was evident in all areas of the law of parent and child. In childbirth, it became an influential factor as pronatalism came to dominate the law governing contraception and abortion late in the antebellum era. The overlapping yet separate development of the laws governing these forms of family limitation document an everpresent struggle between regulation and choice, one that led to statutory policies often at odds with family practice and fostered a widening gap between public policy and private conduct.

The Law Endorses Parental Choice in Antebellum America

At the heart of the nineteenth-century controversy over family limitation lay the quiet determination of American mothers and fathers to reduce the number of children they reared. They initiated what historical demographers now designate the "demographic transition": a reduction in family size that characterized most Western nations. In America, white female fertility, the critical measure of family size, declined in each decade of the century, falling from 7.04 in 1800 to 3.56 a hundred years later. This reversal of the colonial situation of extremely high birth rates gave the nation one of the lowest fertility rates of Western society, a profound change resulting from the conscious choice of large numbers of men and women. The figures suggest that a powerful popular desire to control childbirth was deeply embedded in the republican family.[1]

Although the exact sources of that new disposition remain uncertain, some characteristics of the republican household offer clues and indicate its legal ramifications. These include the child-centered nature of the republican home in which numerous offspring seemed to inhibit proper child care; the rise of what historian Daniel Scott Smith terms "domestic feminism," or the determination of women to assert their individuality and household authority by regulating pregnancy and marital sexuality; the economic incentives of market capitalism in which large families seemed a burden and in which moderation and self-control became prized virtues; the companionate nature of republican matrimony, which fostered the separation of sexual pleasure from protection; and the emerging American insistence on overcoming what had previously been considered natural forces beyond human control. These changes transformed the issue of childbirth.[2]

Birth Control Enters Family Law

Though it is difficult to pierce the privacy surrounding family limitation, at the beginning of the nineteenth century, husbands and wives apparently still relied on age-old methods of birth control such as delayed marriage, breast feeding, and abstinence (as well as *coitus interruptus* and other active contraceptive practices). The growing determination to control fertility encouraged innovation; the popularizer of one method, douching, ignited the first legal confrontation over contraception.

A Massachusetts country doctor, Charles Knowlton, published the first American medical treatise on contraception in 1832. His reading of Robert Dale Owen's *Moral Physiology: A Brief and Plain Treatise on the Population Question* (1830), a polemic espousing birth control as a means of restructuring sexual relations on more humane and equitable lines, and his experiences as a youth, husband, and medical practitioner, stirred Knowlton. After an early manhood fraught with sexual tensions, Knowlton found solace in matrimony. But the birth of several children severely strained his economic resources and his wife's health. After witnessing similar economic despair and medical complaints among many of the young couples he treated, the doctor seized upon contraception as the solution to their common dilemma.[3]

Knowlton's slim volume, *Fruits of Philosophy*, offered the most detailed explanation of contraception and reproduction popularly available in the English language. He wrote the volume in a forthright, easy-to-understand style. Though he relied on Owen's theoretical arguments, the importance of *Fruits of Philosophy* lay in its practical information. But that advice proved his undoing. The *Boston Medical Journal* reacted to the volume sternly: "The less is known by the public at large, the better it will be for the whole moral community." Local officials responded more aggressively: Taunton, Ashfield, and Cambridge indicted Knowlton for peddling obscenity. His publisher, the Bostonian freethinker Abner Kneeland (the last man to be tried in the Bay State for blasphemy), also ran afoul of the law for distributing *Fruits of Philosophy*.[4]

When officials brought Knowlton before Massachusetts judges, however, there were no common law precedents or statutory directives labeling the distribution of contraceptive information as either immoral or illegal.[5] The doctor protested that he had written *Fruits of Philosophy* to improve health and morality, not injure them; he described his book as the "most useful book in the English language," encouraging "early marriage, and thus diminishing prostitution." The physician claimed far-reaching benefits from following his advice: less poverty, fewer illegitimate births, and improved feminine health. He defended women's access to such information against charges that it would corrupt them. Knowlton also protested that theoretical tracts like Owen's were sold and circulated without legal impediments.[6]

Knowlton's defenses failed. He could not overcome the repeated charge that his volume promoted illicit sexual relations. One prosecuting attorney retitled *Fruits of Philosophy* as the "Complete Recipe how the trade of a Strumpet may be carried on without its inconveniences or dangers." The Taunton court fined him $50 and $27.50 court costs, Cambridge sentenced him to three months of hard labor in the house of corrections, and East Cambridge added another jail sentence. Only in his hometown of Ashton did two hung juries lead to his acquittal. None of the courts accepted his plea that contraception was a fit subject for public discussion. Though Knowlton received support from free-thought journals and their supporters, his cause stirred little public sympathy.

The republican legal system translated popular pronatalism into a policy that deemed contraception information criminally obscene. Only an 1847 Massachusetts obscenity statute turned that tendency into a formal prohibition. Knowlton's arraignments and convictions prior to the act's passage indicates the character of the policy: the law would be used not to punish contraception directly, but rather to halt the dissemination of birth-control devices and knowledge. That course of action placed schizophrenic popular sentiments into the law. For most Americans, birth control remained a private affair, but its public advocacy became associated with indecency and sexual radicalism. Perfectionist reformers like Owen, John Humphrey Noyes, and others stressed family limitation in their attempts to reshape society. The identification of birth control with radicalism and its legal designation as obscene marked the subject fit only for underground discussion and private practice.[7]

The reception of Knowlton's book documents this divergence of thought and practice. Three thousand copies of *Fruits of Philosophy* were printed in the first eighteen months, ten thousand by 1839. By 1881 over 277,000 copies had been published in the United States and Britain, and reprints had appeared in Europe. In 1856 Dr. William Alcott, an opponent of birth control, admitted in his *Physiology of Marriage* that Knowlton's tract enjoyed wide circulation and was "in vogue even now in many parts of our country, it is highly prized." That popularity placed severe constraints on prosecutions. For much of the century, birth control remained beyond the reach of the law.[8]

Abortion Becomes a New Crime

Abortion began to vie with contraception as a method of family limitation early in the nineteenth century. It had two main appeals: its effectiveness at a time when contraceptive techniques were neither reliable nor always obtainable; and its availability as a way for wives to unilaterally terminate a pregnancy. Unlike birth control, though, abortion was burdened with a restrictive legal legacy. Contraception was regarded as vaguely disreputable and immoral, but abortion, under certain circumstances, was a crime. In colonial America, abortion, much like infanticide, was the traditional resort of women seduced or abused by men. But the growing determination of middle-class wives to regulate family size changed its social character. The middle classes embraced abortion in the late 1830s and early 1840s, when historian Carl Degler discovered, "the modern child-centered family in which the woman was the moral guide and guardian was establishing itself." Disagreements over a married woman's right to terminate a pregnancy ignited one of the most bitter legal controversies of the nineteenth century.[9]

In post-Revolutionary America, abortion was regarded as an immoral, but not basically dangerous, practice of seduced women. Theodoric Beck, the Philadelphia doctor who wrote the nation's first authoritative treatise on medical jurisprudence, insisted in 1827 that the "practice of causing abortion, is resorted to by unmarried females, who through imprudence or misfortune, have become pregnant, to avoid the disgrace which attaches to them from having a living child." He admitted that "sometimes it is even employed by married women, to obviate a repetition of peculiarly severe labour pains, which they may have previously suffered," and that "abortion is not always associated with crime and disgrace; it may arise from causes perfectly natural and altogether beyond the control of the female."[10]

The law deemed a newborn child to be a full legal person, so its destruction was homicide. But the uncertain status of the fetus plagued the legal system. Locating the point at which the embryo became a human being had perplexed physicians, theologians, philosophers, and lawyers for centuries. Antebellum Americans inherited a medieval common-law formula drawn from the gestation phenomenon called "quickening." A fetus quickened when its mother felt its first movements in the womb. Thomas Aquinas is credited with first attributing life to the fetus at this point of its development; the time at which, he argued, a rational soul entered the embryo. Before animation, according to theological and customary practice, the fetus was not a person and its destruction was not murder. The use of quickening to distinguish criminal from legal abortion meant that under the law a woman had complete dominion over her womb until the first fetal movements, generally in the fourth or fifth month of pregnancy.[11]

Only those who aborted a quickened fetus were punished by the ecclesiastical courts. In the thirteenth century, when Aquinas was making his distinctions, Bracton incorporated the crime into the English common law as an act of homicide. But in a revision by Lord Coke, abortion after quickening became "a great misprison" or what now might be called a misdemeanor. Blackstone summarized these developments: "Life . . . begins in contemplation of law as soon as an infant is able to stir in the mother's womb. For if a woman is quick with child, and by a potion or otherwise, killeth it in her womb; or if any one beat her, whereby the child dieth in her body, and she is delivered of a dead child; this, though not murder was by ancient law homicide or manslaughter. But Sir Edward Coke doth not look upon this offence in quite so atrocious a light, but merely as a heinous misdemeanor." In any event, under the common law as it passed over to the colonies, criminal abortion could only occur after a fetus had quickened; aborting an unanimated fetus was not an indictable offense.[12]

English legal uncertainty ended with the passage of Lord Ellenborough's Act of 1803, which made abortion a statutory offense. The preface to the act's section on poisoning read in part: certain "heinous offenses, committed with intent to destroy the Lives of His Majesty's Subjects by Poison, or with Intent to procure the Miscarriage of Women . . . have been of late so frequently committed; but no adequate Means have been provided hitherto for the Prevention and Punishment of such

Offenses." The statute, part of Ellenborough's effort to inject more rigor into the law by increasing its severity, prohibited the use of poisons to induce abortions and made prequickened abortions criminal acts, though not capital crimes like postquickened ones. The act was the first attempt in Anglo-American law to regulate abortion by statute and to punish the termination of pregnancies before quickening.

This English development had little immediate effect on abortion in most of the United States. Unquestionably, abortion was used in colonial settlements, but, as in so many areas of family law, its legal standing is unclear. The first definitive statement came in an 1812 Massachusetts decision, *Commonwealth* v. *Bangs*. Isaiah Bangs was indicted for assaulting and beating his pregnant lover and for administering an abortifacient to her in a desperate attempt to prevent the birth of their bastard child. The state's highest court, invoking the common law, freed Bangs: "There can be no sentence upon this verdict. The assault and battery are out of the case, and no abortion is alleged to have followed the taking of the potion; and if an abortion had been alleged and proved to have ensued the averment that the woman was quick with child at the time is a necessary part of the indictment." In the absence of statutory revisions, the *Bangs* ruling elicited the endorsement of other courts as the proper exposition of the law. As long as abortion occurred before animation, it remained legally and morally justifiable in post-Revolutionary America.[13]

As part of a general codification of the criminal law (a process which reflected an aversion to judicial discretion, which was without parallel in other areas of the law, and was based on Revolutionary complaints of royal abuses) American legislators began to make abortion a statutory offense in the 1820s. The early statutes merely codified the common law. Connecticut enacted the first statute in 1821 as part of a general criminal-code revision. Like Lord Ellenborough's Act, which influenced it, the statute punished only those who administered a poison or an abortifacient to a woman.

But the New England legislature rejected the English criminalization of prequickened abortion and instead punished with life imprisonment for murder only those who aborted an animated fetus. The act thus codified existing legal beliefs and the conventional medical wisdom that abortion by drugs posed the greatest danger to women. Missouri (1825) and Illinois (1827) passed similar laws.

All of these statutes, like those in the mother country, punished the abortionist only. Indeed, they assumed a mother could not be her own abortionist. Though the midwestern acts did not cite the quickening distinction, quickening remained the only legally recognizable method of proving pregnancy. These first laws, which became statutory models, used the common law of abortion more to protect women from the ill effects of abortifacients than to restrict access to abortion. Equally important, legislative acceptance of the quickening doctrine remained the legal foundation for abortion policy.[14]

While Americans were enacting their first abortion statutes, the English were strengthening their existing law. In 1828, after a Parliamentary committee concluded that the 1803 bill had been poorly drafted, Lord Lansdowne's Act replaced it. Though the new bill reduced the penalties for criminal abortion, it penalized instrument-induced abortions for the first time. An 1837 act went further, and abolished the quickening doctrine. In that year, the first of Queen Victoria's reign, all references to quickening fell victim to the legislative ax; abortion at any time during pregnancy became illegal. Both statutes punished the intent to commit abortion whether the woman involved was pregnant or not. What was more, the British legislation appeared to make the mother criminally liable.[15]

These stringent laws won few American converts. Most of the state laws passed in the 1830s and 1840s either expressly or implicitly followed the quickening doctrine, and classified abortion as a misdemeanor. The most significant American contribution to abortion law widened, rather than reduced, access. In 1828 the New York legislature included that state's first abortion law in a general code revision. It departed from prevailing policy by legalizing therapeutic abortions; that is, terminating a pregnancy at any time if proven "necessary to preserve the life of such women, or shall have been advised by two physicians to be necessary for that purpose." Though such an exception had been hinted at in Lord Ellenborough's Act, the New York statute constituted the first example of the priority that early abortion statutes gave to protecting the mother's health. Whether under the common law or the new statutes, through the first four decades of the nineteenth century, abortion before quickening continued to be legally available to American women.[16]

Judges Protect Early-Term Abortions

Judges generally confronted abortion only after a disaster, often a death, had occurred. Until the passage of more comprehensive statutes, the *Bangs* holding of 1826 blocked prosecutions for prequickening abortions, as the New Jersey Supreme Court pointed out in 1849. The state had charged Eliakim Cooper with assault on an unquickened fetus because he performed an abortion on its mother. The prosecutor argued that the mother's consent did not matter because the criminal act had been against the child. Citing Blackstone, Chief Justice Henry Green invoked the quickening doctrine: "In contemplation of law life commences at the moment of quickening, at that moment when the embryo gives the first physical proof of life, no matter when it first receive it." After an elaborate discussion of English common law, Green acquitted Cooper with the assertion that as long as the mother assented and was not quick with child, abortion prior to quickening was not illegal.

But in acknowledgement of the growing furor over abortion, Green expressed a willingness to have the common law legislatively altered, a sentiment paralleled in antebellum family law only by the judicial reaction to miscegenation, incest, and polygamy: "If the good of society requires that the evil should be suppressed by penal inflictions, it is far better that it should be done by legislative enactments than that courts should, by judicial construction, extend the penal code or multiply the objects of criminal punishment." The Chief Justice's unwillingness to judicially alter the law coincided with the post-Revolutionary aversion to punishment for nonstatutory crimes that hastened the codification of criminal law, and was evidence of the mid-century bench's unwillingness to depart from established common-law rules. This decision and others like it placed the onus of change on the legislature.[17]

Though quickening continued to be the chief dividing line in abortion cases, the new statutes altered the character of abortion prosecutions and thus of judicial responsibilities. The most dramatic development came in New Jersey. The volume of reports containing the *Cooper* ruling included a special note: "This decision induced the legislature to amend the criminal code, so as to make the offense in question a crime."[18]

The 1849 act had its first judicial test nine years later when Leonard Murphy appealed his conviction for advising a woman about abortifacients. Chief Justice Green heard his appeal, as did Daniel Haines, who as governor had signed the new law and joined the bench after his term of office. Assigning the opinion to himself, Green repeated his *Cooper* decision interpretation of the common law, and then noted that the state had altered the law after his ruling. The chief purpose of the statute was to remedy the "mischief" of the "supposed defect" in the common law, that procuring or attempting an abortion was not indictable unless the woman was shown to be quick with child. "The design of the statute," Green ruled in quashing Murphy's appeal, "was not to prevent the procuring of abortions so much as to guard the health and life of the mother against the consequences of such attempts." The defendant's guilt did not depend on the success or failure of the abortion or "whether the fetus is destroyed, or whether it has quickened or not." As other judges reached similar conclusions in states with specific laws against attempted abortions, the quickening doctrine lost some of its influence on abortion prosecutions, and attempts to perform or solicit abortions became separate crimes.[19]

Equally important, in interpreting and applying the statutes judges took pains to exonerate the women involved. In the *Murphy* opinion, Chief Justice Green declared that the "statute regards her as the victim of the crime, not as the criminal, as the object of protection, rather than of punishment." Chief Justice Isaac Redfield of Vermont expressed similar sentiments in *State* v. *Howard* (1859). William Howard, a physician, had been indicted for performing an abortion on Olive Ashe, a twenty-year-old single woman. The state's star witness, the victim's sister, had described Olive's agonizing death from hemorrhaging after the operation.

Redfield ruled that the prosecution did not have to prove that the fetus had become animated, and held that the act penalized attempted abortions and made the death of the woman a felony. He went on to excuse Olive from complicity in her own demise. The purpose of the statute was to protect the mother and the fetus. "The life and health of the mother, and the probability of future offspring are so seriously put at hazard by such a transaction when produced by mechanical means," the jurist maintained, "that it is not easy to determine precisely which is the more important in the statute, to prevent injury to the child or to the mother." The law recognized, Redfield exclaimed in a paternalistic statement that suggested a new concern about childbirth, that "the evil of such a practice, and the teaching of mothers, or thus attempting to teach them, the facility with which they may escape the perils of child bearing and the consequent responsibilities, and the impediments to a life of ease and vicious indulgence, are among the most pernicious consequences of such abominable practices, and are no doubt properly to be regarded as fairly coming within the evils to be considered in fixing the construction of the statute and its probable object and purpose." Howard went to prison.[20]

Mid-century jurists Green and Redfield viewed women who had abortions as victims, not accomplices, despite the obvious voluntary nature of the act. As in the judicial response to seduction under the cover of a marriage promise, the bench refused to consider women and men equally liable participants in sexually related crimes. Instead of coconspirators, the bench depicted women as the prey of abortionists who enticed them to act against their better instincts by appealing to their peculiar weaknesses. The diminished criminal responsibility of women reflected their special legal status, one repeatedly characterized by a partial capacity. They were not as bound as men by their actions. This was true not only in the contractual facets of family law but also in its criminal elements. The result in abortion prosecutions, women designated as victims, was a boon to females seeking abortion. They had only to weigh the physical and moral risks involved (considerable though they may have been) since the criminal penalties would fall on the abortionist.

Nor did the abortion statutes seriously alter the bench's conception of the legal standing of a fetus. As in the *Cooper* decision, some prosecutors cited the legal rights accorded children *in esse* (unborn), to argue that under the common law, fetuses should be considered as persons from their conception. From the late eighteenth century on, common-law courts, first in England and then in America, granted equal property rights to children born after the death of their kin. These decisions held the unborn child to be, in the words of a 1795 English opinion, "clearly within the description of 'children living at the time of his decease.'" Francis Wharton cited these cases in his treatise on criminal law to argue that the quickening distinction in fetal development was at variance with medical knowledge and legal principles. Dr. Horatio Storer, who was the foremost medical opponent of abortion in mid-century America, argued: "We have seen the mistaken basis, as regards the criminality of abortion, on which the common law is founded, and while it recognizes the distinct existence of the fetus for civil purposes, it here considers its being as totally engrossed in that of the mother."[21]

But these challenges to the common-law description of the fetus made little headway in mid-century courtrooms. New Jersey Chief Justice Green expressed the prevailing judicial opinion when he argued that while it was "true, for certain purposes, [that] the law regards an infant as *in being* from the time of conception, yet it seems nowhere to regard it as *in life*, or to have respect to its preservation as a living being." Under these judicially imposed distinctions, a fetus enjoyed rights only in property law and then only if successfully born. It had no standing in criminal law until quickening, and none at all in tort. The law highly prized children, not fetuses.[22]

As judicial attitudes toward fetal legal personality suggest, quickening continued to play a significant role in abortion litigation, especially in the question of intent. Most of the early abortion statutes were vague. Without explicit statutory language, intention remained dependent on proof of fetal animation.

Judicial treatment of Maine's 1840 abortion law points out how the question of intent could undermine abortion prosecutions. A jury convicted James H. Smith of the murder of Berlingera D. Casswell. It sentenced him to life imprisonment at hard labor for performing an instrument abortion and then trying to hide Casswell's body in a brook after her death from the operation. The statute made abortion a crime whether the fetus had quickened or not. But it also stipulated that the state had to prove the defendant's "intent to destroy such child."

In his 1851 appeal, Smith argued convincingly that the operation on Casswell had not been intended to produce an abortion but to treat other ailments. Chief Justice John Tenny acknowledged that the statute had removed the necessity of proving quickening, but decided that under the common law only fetal animation could be used to prove that the abortionist knew his victim was pregnant. Since the prosecution had not mentioned quickening in the indictment, Tenny freed Smith.

By mandating proof of an intention to abort a fetus, the courts made abortion prosecutions very difficult. In Massachusetts, for instance, between 1849 and 1857 the state prosecuted thirty-two abortionists, but failed to win a single conviction.[23]

The Battle over Abortion Begins

Legislators reacted to the paucity of abortion convictions by revising the criminal codes. There ensued a legal tug-of-war over abortion that stemmed not so much from ideological conflicts as from differing institutional commitments and constituencies. Several states enacted more restrictive statutes in the 1840s and 1850s in an effort to close loopholes uncovered in litigation. Under these acts the first significant crackdown on abortionists began.[24]

Though many of the codes remained vague and poorly drafted, courts sometimes willingly participated in the antiabortion drive by using discretion and legislative intent to strengthen the hand of the prosecution. Decisions in Indiana (1845) and New York (1853) held that the state did not have to name the drug an abortionist supplied a woman or even prove it a noxious substance to secure a conviction. In 1860 the Massachusetts Supreme Judicial Court broadly interpreted the state abortion law in rejecting an appellant's claim that the prosecution had improperly introduced his business card as evidence to convince the jury that he operated as an abortionist. The card read: "F. H. Barrows, magnetic and electrical treatments for all female weaknesses, lecurrhoea, suppression, cancer, tumor, etc." The court declared that in "such cases cards and circulars of a defendant have been held admissible in evidence if they tend to show that the defendant holds himself out as a person whose business it is to procure abortions. It is not to be expected that cards and circulars of this kind will state in precise terms, or that their meaning will not be more or less disguised." But judicial support for the prosecution of abortionists was limited by rulings insisting upon procedural correctness.[25]

Neither statutory revisions nor judicial concessions stemmed the tide of women seeking abortions. New York City provides a graphic example in the person of Madame Restell, the most notorious and, most likely, the wealthiest abortionist of the era. Restell, an English immigrant born Caroline Lohman, began providing her services in the 1830s. By the 1840s she had become a city fixture. She operated out of a huge brownstone on Fifth Avenue near St. Patrick's Cathedral, and accumulated a fortune. Her ads brazenly proclaimed: "Madame Restell, as is well known, was for thirty years Female Physician in the two principal female hospitals in Europe—those in Vienna and Paris—where, favored by her great experience and opportunities, she attained that celebrity in those great discoveries in medical science so specially suited to the female frame. . . ." Women from all classes bought her medicines and flocked to her clinic.[26]

The law, though constantly tightened, failed to deter her. She was arrested in 1841 under the state's 1828 statute, but only charged with minor infractions. By the mid-1840s she had opened branch offices in Boston and Philadelphia and was conducting a booming mail-order business. After the passage of a more rigorous statute in 1845, authorities indicted her for giving abortifacients to Maria Bodine, a woman impregnated by her employer. Assistant District Attorney Jonathan Phillips demanded a conviction from the jury so that the "community will no longer be cursed with one who disgraces her sex, forgetting that she is a mother, disregarding at once divine and human laws, [and] has amassed a fortune in the daily perpetuation of a crime which violates and annuls one of the most sacred ordinances of Almighty God." He called on the male panel to meet its responsibility: "It is for you as jurors, as husbands, fathers, and brothers, to say whether these monstrous crimes are to continue."

They did their duty by convicting Madame Restell of a misdemeanor. The state supreme court did its part as well. It denied her appeal despite clear evidence that one juror had been influenced by newspaper accounts.[27] Orson Squire's *Love and Parentage* (1844) deplored the results: Madame Restell faced imprisonment but "her lawyer stayed the proceedings by a bill of exceptions, and now she rides over one of her judges, tosses up her beautiful head, and says in effect, 'behold the triumph of virtue!' Instead of a linsey woolsey petticoat . . . she is gloriously attired in rich silks and laces, towers above her sex in a splendid carriage, snaps her fingers at the law and all its pains and penalties, and cries out for more victims and more gold."[28]

Abortion also continued because of a public ambivalence evident in an 1856 Iowa slander case. A neighbor accused Julia Abrams of being "a bad woman," having "destroyed with instruments one or two children," and taking medicine to kill others. Abrams sued the neighbor for slander and won in the lower courts. But her neighbor argued that in the absence of claims for special damages, an action for slander could only be grounded on accusation of an actual crime. The state supreme court agreed with the contention that prequickened abortion did not constitute such a crime under Iowa statutes. The justices relied on slander precedents and the criteria they and other jurists used to evaluate female actions, standards that placed a high priority on sexual virtue: "To say of her that she was a common tattler, or liar, or that she indulged in the use of profane or vulgar language; that she was a drunkard, or the like, would reasonably, if believed, have a tendency to bring her into disrepute, but such words would not be actionable *per se*. But to impute to her a want of chastity is to charge her with the want of that, without which the female is necessarily and certainly driven beyond the circle of virtuous friends and acquaintances." Because it refused to classify abortion as a serious immoral act, the court reversed Abrams's victory. The Alabama Supreme Court reached the same conclusion in a similar case. Only in New York, where laws more tightly regulated abortion, did a court sustain a slander judgment based on a charge of abortion.[29]

In Iowa, the *Abrams* decision did provoke a physician to campaign successfully for a tighter abortion law.[30] But its real significance lies in the light it shed on the mid-century status of abortion. By suing for slander, these women in effect declared that accusations of abortion constituted such a slur that their reputations had to be publicly cleansed of the taint. The relatively benign judicial response indicates that judges did not rank abortion with sexual immorality, and other foul deeds worthy of compensation. This mixture of repulsion and acceptance permeated law and society. In many ways abortion was like prostitution. Both were seen as reprehensible but necessary to middle-class life, which neither should nor could be admitted, legalized, or eliminated. Instead, there was half-hearted, occasional punishment of prostitutes and abortionists, not their clientele.

The abortion laws also reflected a tendency to codify existing criminal law rather than to indulge in judicial innovation. This tendency proceeded from strong demands that statutes be used to curb judicial discretion. Rather than perpetuate the ambiguous and therefore, according to republican dogma, potentially repressive common law of crimes, only acts clearly codified as illegal were to be punished, a policy the United States Supreme Court declared in 1812 as "long since settled in public opinion." The demise of common-law crimes was part of a quest for legal certainty and predictability through statutes rather than judicial opinion. Moreover, codification furthered the gradual reliance on penal codes as arbiters of morals in an increasingly secularized and diverse society. Law became the medium that dictated behavior. But as the abortion statutes reveal, legislators assumed this power in domestic (and most other) matters hesitantly and relied on the courts for fine tuning.[31]

Mid-Century Childbirth

Abortion and contraception entered the mainstream of American family life during the first half of the nineteenth century. They helped the republican family control its size and thereby attain its nurturing, refuge, and spousal goals as well as enhance its efforts to domesticate sexuality and accumulate capital. According to historian Carl Degler, in this era, abortion "was more like contraception—an interference with a natural process but no more closely related than that to murder and manslaughter."[32]

Yet the public advocacy of contraception by sexual radicals and reformers, and even by some writers of domestic advice tracts who championed voluntary motherhood, had no proabortion counterparts. The practices also had quite different receptions by the legal system. Unlike birth control, abortion became the center of a gathering legal storm. Disagreements over the legal and medical status of the fetus led to unparalleled disputes in controversies over birth control. Though both methods of family limitation continued to be widely available, they held different positions within American society and its law.

Still, the legal reaction to both birth control and abortion demonstrates a high regard for domestic privacy, which became a fixture of family law during its formative era. Although both family limitation methods violated cherished moral and social beliefs, statutes and judicial opinions hesitantly and ineffectively infringed on the right of husbands and wives to control their reproduction. Instead, that prerogative, much like the right to wed, remained generally available to mid-century Americans who chose to exercise it.

Contraception and Abortion Become Obscenities

Family limitation flourished under the mid-century umbrella of social and legal tolerance. The falling fertility rates of white married women—from 5.21 in 1860 to 3.56 at the end of the century—are the most eloquent commentary on the choices made by husbands and wives. The wide use and legal acceptance of family limitation shocked opponents into action in the 1850s and 1860s. Physicians, purity reformers, and other family savers organized the opposition. They accused those who used abortion and birth control of putting indulgence over responsibility, encouraging sexual immorality and family instability, violating natural laws, and abandoning divinely ordained family duties. Opponents of birth control and abortion branded both as crimes against God, nature, and society; they demanded that the practices be made crimes under the law as well.[33]

Such charges rested upon republican family ideals that were subscribed to by most husbands and wives. But the persistent decline in family size indicates that reformers addressed an ambivalent public. Reformers represented only one side of a complicated debate. Much of the other side spoke not in pamphlets and speeches but in silent practice. The resulting clash of ideal and reality made childbirth an unresolvable controversy in the last half of the nineteenth century.

The Spread of Antiabortion Agitation

All methods of family limitation met with opposition, but critics reserved their deadliest salvos for abortion. Reverend John Todd of Boston labeled it "fashionable murder." Dramatic changes in its incidence frightened its opponents and fueled their outrage. All observers, regardless of their perspective, agreed that the abortion rate rose significantly after 1840. In the most comprehensive analysis of the issue, historian James Mohr calculates that abortions increased from approximately one for every twenty-five or thirty live births to as high as one abortion for every five or six births by the 1850s and 1860s. White, Protestant wives from the middle and upper classes in all regions of the nation were responsible for the surge in abortion. No wonder, then, that a group of Buffalo, New York physicians lamented that abortion had been "brought to the very heart of every family."

Abortion had become a huge, profitable business catering to all classes, but directed primarily at bourgeois women. Singling out abortion as a "conjugal sin," Augustus Gardner in 1876 treated the practice as a direct assault on the family, and more particularly on the natural responsibility of wives to bear children: "We can forgive the poor, deluded girl—seduced, betrayed, abandoned—who, in her wild frenzy, destroyed the mute evidence of her guilt. We have only sympathy and sorrow for her. But for the married shirk, who disregards her divinely-ordained duty, we have nothing but contempt, even if she be the lordly woman of fashion, clothed in purple and fine fashion. If glittering gems adorn her person, within there is a foulness and squalor."[34]

The intensifying controversy over abortion encouraged a therapeutic invasion of family law by the medical profession and its allied domestic experts. They began to assert control over all health issues involving the family as part of their evolving conceptions of professional expertise and social pathology. Abortion raised problems akin to those involved in the question of nuptial fitness and generated a complementary response from doctors and family advisors.

Mohr argues that medical professionalism was the primary influence on the development of abortion law during this period. Though such a contention ignores the interrelated and diverse array of groups involved in family saving, doctors did play a critical role in this issue. The demands of medical practitioners that birth should not be left to unscientific midwives, poorly trained irregular doctors, and especially not to commercial vendors of abortion won a receptive hearing. Organized doctors charged that self-taught, irregular doctors who performed abortions downgraded medical practice and lowered the profession's image. The American Medical Association (AMA), formed in 1847, took the lead in agitating for more stringent abortion laws.[35] Abortion-law reform became one of the means by which doctors established a monopoly on health care.

Boston obstetrician and gynecologist Horatio Robinson Storer led the physicians' crusade. His 1865 essay, "The Criminality and Physical Evils of Forced Abortions," won a gold medal and cash prize from the AMA. Two years later he became a vice president of the association. He published his essay as a popular tract, *Why Not? A Book for Every Woman*, and followed it with an 1869 companion volume, *Is it I? A Book for Every Man.*

The two polemics were typical of the genre, portraying abortion as the product of feminine weakness and male lust. In another volume, Storer argued that regular physicians neither condoned nor performed abortions, that only professional abortionists and their helpers engaged in the practice. He urged that professional physicians be entrusted with the problem because "medical men are the physical guardians of women and their offspring" and their "peculiar knowledge" in "all obstetric matters [should] regulate public sentiments and . . . govern the tribunals of justice."[36]

Physicians such as Storer, convinced by their professional training that abortion at any time during pregnancy should be made criminal and that women should be disabused of their complacency on the subject, singled out the quickening doctrine as their target. They dismissed animation as a relic of religious superstition, what an Albany medical professor in 1850 called an "absurd distinction." Storer and colleague Franklin Fiske Heard argued that scientific logic and experiments, let alone common sense, "would lead us to the conclusion that the fetus is from the very outset a living and distinct being." Dr. Andrew Nebinger, president of the Philadelphia County Medical Society, confidently declared that exploding the myth of quickening would "in a brief cycle very perceptibly diminish, and finally almost entirely prevent the commission of the crime of abortion." James Ashton insisted, in the same 1865 volume that urged hereditary controls on marriage, that abortion and "miscarriage, being in collision with nature's laws, should never be resorted to except in extreme cases, and then only under medical advice."[37]

Antiabortion physicians invaded the domain of their fellow professionals, the bar. They criticized the criminal law for being drafted in scientific ignorance, too lenient, easily evaded, and loosely enforced. Storer and Heard in 1868 wrote the strongest brief in favor of tighter abortion laws, *Criminal Abortion: Its Nature, Its Evidence, and Its Law*. They claimed that legal laxity spawned public indifference. Statutes, they complained, "are so worded as almost wholly to ignore foetal life, to refuse it protection, to insure their own evasion, and by their inherent contradictions to extend the very crime they were framed to prevent." Consequently, "in the sight of the common law, and in most cases of statutory law also, the crime of abortion, properly considered does not exist; the law discussing and punishing a wholly supposititious offense, which not only does not exist, but the very idea of whose existence is simply absurd." They demanded that abortion at any time during pregnancy be made a felony.[38]

Indictments of abortion based on a roughly similar bill of particulars filled the pages of medical journals, religious publications, genteel magazines, and the popular press. The *New York Times* labeled it "The Evil of the Age." Abortion foes agreed with Storer and Heard that laws must be passed making "its detection more probable" and "its punishment more certain." According to Nebinger, abortion would be abolished only when "the power of the Legislature, the courts, and all legal instrumentalities" had been "enlisted in the good work of crushing out the accursed crime."[39]

Legislators responded with statutory tinkering, producing more comprehensive acts with stiffer penalties. Massachusetts passed the first separate abortion statute and a few states even mandated punishments for women seeking abortions in direct response to the discontent over legal laxity. But the laws remained a patchwork of differing details.

Most troubling to abortion foes, the quickening doctrine retained a place in the codes. Some states used it as proof of pregnancy. Others like California enacted laws that penalized abortion only when the woman was demonstrably pregnant and thus invited judicial application of the quickening doctrine. Only New Hampshire, Wisconsin, and New York penalized women seeking abortions by 1860. Michigan and Minnesota adopted the therapeutic exception, which accepted abortion to save the life of the mother. But in 1860 thirteen states carried no abortion bans in their codes. Statutory reform thus failed to appease the law's critics.[40]

The vagaries of the legislative process in New York illustrates the influence of the antiabortion forces during the last half of the century. Statutes in 1845 and 1846, which punished the death of the mother of the quickened fetus as second degree manslaughter, made procuring or attempting an abortion on a pregnant woman punishable acts, and subjected women seeking abortions to criminal penalties, failed to satisfy legal critics.

Between 1863 and 1869 the *New York Times* gave prominent coverage to ten abortion stories, five of which involved the death of the women, and editorialized against laws allowing abortionists to go unpunished. The presiding judge in the 1862 decision of *Cobel* v. *People* supported reformers' complaints when he railed from the bench against ineffective statutes that failed to penalize abortionists who used surgical instruments rather than drugs. In 1867 the state medical society joined the antiabortion chorus by passing a set of resolutions prefaced by a stern declaration: "[F]rom the first moment of conception, there is a living creature in process of development to full maturity. . . . [A]ny sufficient interruption to this living process always results in the destruction of life. . . . [T]he intentional arrest of this living process, eventuating in the destruction of life (being an act with intention to kill), is consequently murder. . . ." The petition, which the physicians forwarded to the legislature, requested that abortion advertising be banned and that abortion at any time during pregnancy be penalized.[41]

New York lawmakers responded with two enactments. In 1868 they banned advertisement and dissemination of abortifacients and services, as well as contraceptives and other materials defined as obscene. During the next legislative session an act modified the quickening rule by stipulating that no abortion could be performed on a "woman with child" (in place of the existing phrase, a "woman with quick child"). It also punished all abortions as second-degree manslaughter and made attempted abortions, regardless of pregnancy, a misdemeanor. Finally the statutes held accomplices to be equally liable with the actual abortionists.

The acts did not satisfy antiabortion groups, particularly the Medico-Legal Society of New York which continued to press for even tougher laws. Graphic press accounts of two publicized events stiffened their resolve: Thomas Evans's indictment for using instruments to abort the fetal twins of Ann O'Neill; and Jacob Rosenzweig's arrest for the abortion-caused death of a beautiful young woman found in a trunk in a railway station. In the Rosenzweig prosecution a judge called for legislation to make the use of drugs or instruments on a woman with child first-degree murder. In 1872 the legislature responded, classifying abortion a felony, and even defined voluntary abortion by a pregnant woman a felony. The statute strengthened the ban on advertising abortion services and devices by prohibiting their sale and manufacture.[42]

Legal difficulties caused by the constant modification of the quickening rule led to one final piece of legislation. These emerged in the appeal of abortionist Evans, which reached the bench just as the governor signed the 1872 act into law. The state appeals court overturned Evans's conviction on the ground that the lower-court judge had incorrectly charged the jury when he informed them that the 1868 act penalized abortion as felonious manslaughter at any time during gestation, regardless of pregnancy or quickening. Echoing countless jurists before him, Justice Theodore Allen ruled that although "physiologists claim that life starts from the moment of conception, the law still retained the common law distinction on fetal development." Quickening, he maintained, continued to be the only legal means of distinguishing a fetal child from an embryo. "It is not the destruction of the fetus, the interruption of that process by which the human race is propagated, that is punished by the statute as manslaughter," he decided, "but it is the causing of death of a living child."[43]

Allen's invocation of the quickening doctrine had a direct impact on the New York legislature. In 1881 lawmakers made prequickened abortion criminally punishable, but subject to less severe punishment than abortions performed after quickening.[44]

Though few states went as far as New York in using legislation to try to halt abortion, most enacted tougher codes. The statutory foothold that antiabortion had achieved during the 1830s and 1840s was secure by the century's end. The quickening doctrine was retained to structure penalties, but all abortions and attempts at abortion were penalized. Bans on the advertising and sale of abortion services and information reduced their public presence. Legislatures generally exempted the therapeutic abortion, further solidifying the medical profession's control over reproduction. Only Connecticut, New York, California, Minnesota, Indiana, and the territory of Arizona subjected women seeking abortions to criminal penalties. Without question, antiabortion had become the official policy of American law at the dawn of the twentieth century.[45]

Most state laws were passed under the prodding of forces similar to those in New York. In the most intense period of legislation, from 1860 to 1880, physicians and other family savers pressured state lawmakers to stiffen abortion bans. Significantly, antiabortion groups were not the only ones pressing legislators to police more actively the public health and safety. During the high tide of antiabortion legislation, other statutes set new standards for job safety, food processing, and the sale of cigarettes to minors. Lawmakers also took more concerted action against quack and patent medicines. Health problems were being redefined as public, not private responsibilities, thus hastening the domination of health policy debates by physicians and other social welfare professionals.[46]

Contraception Becomes a Major Crime

Although statutes prohibiting various forms of abortion had been on the books since the 1820s, there were few explicit restrictions on contraception until the 1870s. But federal and state acts labeling both abortion and contraception obscene capped the growing determination of family savers to ban all forms of family limitation. Augustus Gardner described contraception as yet another conjugal sin: "The most prolific causes for the injury to the public health of the age, are the methods which have for their aim, the prevention of having children." Though he sympathized with women's fears about childbirth and rearing large families, Gardner confidently insisted that efforts made "to avoid propagation, are ten thousand-fold more disastrous to the health and constitution, to say nothing of the demoralization of mind and heart. . . ." He unhesitatingly declared that the employment of contraceptive practices "must produce a feeling of shame and disgust utterly destructive of the true delights of pure hearts and refined sensibilities. They are suggestive of licentiousness and the brothel, and their employment degrades to bestiality the true feelings of manhood and the holy state of matrimony." Gardner's colleague William Wallings denounced contraception in *Sexology* (1876), but he admitted that the practice had become "so universal that it may well be termed a national vice, so common that it is unblushingly acknowledged by its perpetrator, for the commission of which the husband is even eulogized by his wife and applauded by her friends, a vice which is the scourge and desolation of marriage. . . ." Gardner, Wallings, and their followers looked to the criminal law for relief.[47]

Self-appointed purity campaigners led the drive against contraception. New Yorkers created the first purity society in 1872, the New York Society for the Suppression of Vice. Though founded and funded by elite city residents such as banker Morris K. Jessup, who also headed the YMCA, the society's point man for purity reform was a little known ex–dry goods salesman, Anthony Comstock. The son of devout Connecticut parents, he tried unsuccessfully to make his fortune as a businessman in New York City. The flagrant vices he encountered in the city shocked him into a highly publicized vigilante campaign. It culminated in his appointment as the antivice society's chief agent, thus launching his career as late nineteenth-century America's self-avowed savior of public morals.

Comstock regarded the feeble statutes then on the books as the weakest link in his war on vice. The legislation at his disposal consisted of the 1868 New York act prohibiting the circulation of obscene materials and a similar federal ban. He termed both toothless. After federal judge Samuel Blatchford failed to convict Frank Leslie, editor of *Day's Doings*, for advertising "fancy" books, gaming materials, and contraceptives on the grounds that federal law did not apply to newspapers, Comstock began to lobby for tougher laws. In 1872 he convinced the antivice society to send him to Washington to press for a rigorous national statute.[48]

In Washington the vice crusader succeeded beyond his wildest expectations. Armed with a display case of vice paraphernalia and vivid tales of his fights with the panderers of obscenity, Comstock enlisted the aid of Vice President Henry Wilson and Supreme Court Justice William Strong to draft a new obscenity law. The bill passed with little debate and became law on 1 March 1873. Its swift enactment may indicate the difficulties of defending practices so at odds with popular values. Resistance would come in the law's implementation, not its passage.

The act's primary purpose was to ban the circulation and importation of obscene materials through the national mails. Specifically included on the list of banned goods was every article designed, adapted, or intended "for preventing conception or producing abortion, or for indecent or immoral use; and every article, instrument, substance, drug, medicine, or thing which is advertised or described in a manner calculated to lead another to use or apply it for preventing conception or producing abortion, or for any indecent or immoral purpose. . . ." The act set punishment at a $5,000 fine, one to ten years at hard labor, or both. Federal authorities capped the statute's passage by appointing Comstock a special postal agent charged with enforcing the law.[49]

The federal act, quickly dubbed the Comstock Law, was the centerpiece of the drive against obscenity, but purity crusaders also prodded state legislators into action. Antivice societies, and after 1885 the Social Purity Alliance, succeeded in persuading twenty-two legislatures to enact general obscenity laws and another twenty-four to specifically ban birth control and abortion.

One year after their victory in Washington, Comstock and the New York antivice society rewrote their state code along the lines of the federal statute. An assemblyman, who later became a member of the purity organization, shepherded the bill through the legislature, aided by Comstock's vigorous lobbying. The act defined abortion-inducing drugs as immoral and indecent, and prohibited their sale. In 1881 a legislative revision banned the sale and manufacture of contraceptives as well. However, the law included a vague physicians' exemption for reasons of health. Finally, in 1887 the prohibitions were extended to advertising. Under Comstock's prodding, New York had enacted some of the nation's most stringent legal curbs on the transmission of information and services to control reproduction.[50]

Comstock also enlisted the citizenry of Massachusetts in the cause. In 1878 he helped form the New England Society for the Suppression of Vice. This organization, which later became the Watch and Ward Society, included representatives from New England educational and religious institutions. It pushed the state legislature into enacting an 1879 act "Concerning Offenses against Chastity, Morality, and Decency." Passed with little dissent or debate, the law also banned the distribution and sale of family limitation information and devices.[51]

Connecticut legislators took the most drastic action the same year. Promoter Phineas T. Barnum, chairman of the Joint Standing Committee on Temperance, drafted the obscenity statute. Comstock and the antivice societies do not appear to have played a major role in the deliberation on the bill, but Barnum and his allies held comparable views. In fact, they obtained a provision banning the use as well as the sale of contraceptives. This was the first instance of such a prohibition, which paralleled the state's attempt to penalize women seeking abortions. Though the 1879 ban had been part of a general obscenity statute, the lawmakers detached it in 1887 and made it a separate offense.[52]

The federal act was the most important weapon in the purity crusade against contraception. But the Little Comstock Laws, as they came to be

called, reveal the depth of determination to close every possible avenue
for traders in obscene materials. The opposition to banning the free flow
of such information and devices was meagre. Only religious liberals and
advocates of freedom of the press voiced dissent, and they were a small,
unheeded minority. The author of *Chastity*, Dio Lewis, expressed the
prevalent view. He recognized the pressures compelling many couples to
practice contraception: "[W]hen the health of the mother is doubtful, the
family cash-box empty, or a predisposition to some grave malady inherited, they will ask how conception may be prevented or the next baby
postponed." Nevertheless Lewis applauded Comstock's effort to stop the
purveyors of such services: "We need a thousand such young men to
hunt up these wretches, in all parts of the country. Under the [Comstock
Law], which is now in force, and under state laws which happily are now
moving forward to enforce the national act, any friend of virtue, male or
female, may quickly bring to justice these whelps of sin. It seems hard
that decent men are not allowed to shoot them on sight as they would
shoot a mad dog."[53] These strident calls for a vigilante citizenry drowned
opponents of the obscenity legislation. Though the anticontraception
drive lacked some of the fervor of the antiabortion crusade, by the end of
the century both practices were banned as obscenities.

The Courts and the Defense of Family Limitation

All contenders in the family limitation struggle agreed that the fate of the
effort to use legislation to eliminate abortion and contraception would be
decided in the nation's courtrooms. Unsatisfactory common-law judgments had spurred reformers into action, and helped define their tactics
and statutory goals. The right of husbands and wives to control the size
of their families had never been explicitly endorsed by the judiciary or
other common law authorities. On the contrary, they had joined other
policy makers in promoting childbirth. But the judiciary's allegiance to
common-law precedents and its support for private decision making and
domestic privacy, particularly the bench's refusal to consider contraception and abortion before quickening as common-law crimes, were barriers to reform success. The new statutes forced the late nineteenth-
century bench to reconsider its position on both issues by extending the
police power and criminal authority of the state over childbirth choices.
The acts and the reformers' efforts to depict abortion and contraception
as unsavory and undesirable practices did succeed in winning judicial
support, but it was hedged with caveats.

Judges Weaken Antiabortion Laws

Antiabortion crusaders found it easier to secure legislation than to ensure its enforcement. Lingering sentiments in favor of prequickened abortions and against vigorous prosecutions persisted well into the late nineteenth century. Judicially imposed evidentiary rules again stirred complaints of legal laxity. Comstock often bemoaned the lenient treatment given abortionists; he arrested eleven in Chicago only to see the courts release them with small fines. The vice crusader wrote in dismay of one case: "An old man, very feeble, but an unscrupulous old villain and abortionist. The evidence was of the most positive character. For some unknown reason the Judge fined the worst abortionist but the smallest fine and no imprisonment."[54] Gradually, though, the passage of more stringent legislation, the vehemence of abortion foes, and the accumulation of judicial decisions combined to reduce the scope of legal tolerance, and enthroned antiabortion as the dominant policy of all branches of the legal system.

Storer and Heard, who wrote *Criminal Abortion* in large part to elicit the support of the bar, called for a joint professional campaign against abortion. "Lawyers and physicians," they urged, "should stand to each other, in medical-legal matters, as associates and working together for the common good of society, rather than adversaries liable to be thought endeavoring to make the worse appear the better reason. The crime of unjustifiable abortion is now recognized by both professions as of frequent occurrence, and as going too often unwhipped of justice." But differing professional roles and constituencies made cooperation problematic. Physicians and lawyers joined the antiabortion crusade, but the doctors took the lead while their professional colleagues were often circumscribed by their preexisting allegiances to legal forms.[55]

Judges did not publicly question the authority of legislators to proscribe abortion, any more than they did the lawmakers' right to regulate matrimony. But the appellate reports were filled with acquittals and reversals of abortion convictions because of the judicial insistence on balancing statutory demands with the dictates of common-law rules of evidence and criminal defendant rights. In the reformers' judgment, the courts seemed unwilling to recognize that the magnitude of the evil required a suspension of routine practices and the imposition of extraordinary penalties.[56]

The cautious approach taken by the bench was particularly evident in the judicial insistence that the procedural rights of abortionists be recognized. Judges repeatedly overturned convictions if indictments failed to specify the proper crime, jury charges were erroneous, or introduction of character witnesses had not been allowed. They scrutinized murder and manslaughter convictions with particular care.

The Michigan Supreme Court took such a position in the appeal of Nathan J. Aiken, who had been convicted of aborting the fetus of Mary Noel. The indictment charged him not only with abortion but with negligent care after the miscarriage, when Noel had died. The court overturned the conviction because Aiken had been tried for two charges simultaneously, the evidence for one prejudicing the other. The justices defended their decision with a lesson in legal ethics:

> It must be remembered that, however heinous the crime, and however difficult it may be to establish it by the usual and approved means of procedure, and no matter how firmly the public prosecutor and the community at large may be satisfied of the guilt of the accused, and even though in fact he may be guilty, the rules and methods of trial, permitted to be relaxed or disregarded in his particular case with perhaps the laudable object and desire that justice may be done, must nevertheless, as a natural consequence of the ways of our jurisprudence appear hereafter, as so relaxed or disregarded, as precedents to be used against all persons accused of crime, to vex the innocent as well as the guilty. There is therefore no safety and no justice in allowing the supposed merits of a particular case to override and set aside even for a moment, the barriers that our Constitution and laws have hedged about the citizen when arraigned and put upon trial for an alleged crime.[57]

Judicial caution should not be construed as support. Late nineteenth-century abortion decisions are also filled with denunciations of the practice. In *Lamb* v. *State*, the Maryland Supreme Court discharged the abortionist John Lamb despite clear proof of his deed; the state had erroneously charged him with a crime not in the statutes. The judges sternly noted that the act "described in the second count which dealt with abortion drugs is extremely immoral and very offensive to the sensibilities of all virtuous people, but we have no power to make a law for its punishment." Nor did the judicial commitment to the common law mean that legal rules were bent to free abortionists. Though solicitous of procedural rights, judges did not purposely dull abortion statutes as they seem to have done in many areas of nuptial law. Thus in turning away Harry Moothart's plea of innocence based on the claim that he had merely sent, not administered, an abortion drug to Martha Marr, the Iowa Supreme Court declared that "any other construction would defeat the plain intent of the statute." It feared that doing so would grant "evil-disposed persons" the power "to carry out their criminal intents with impunity by sending a drug, instrument, or other means of producing miscarriage through the mail or other channels of conveyance."[58]

Judges earned the wrath of antiabortion groups, but their procedural reversals of abortion convictions merely highlighted the major obstacle facing prosecutors: building a convincing case. The very conditions associated with the crime made it difficult to prove. Abortions were generally voluntary, performed in the privacy of a clinic, home, or hotel room, and kept secret by all those involved. Unless the woman herself filed a complaint or died, the state had a difficult time gathering evidence. The criminal-law standard of reasonable doubt and a jury bias in favor of defendants—a bias that may have more accurately reflected popular sentiments than did the new statutes—simply heightened these difficulties. As a physician complained in the 1860s: "[I]t is now given as a reason of non-prosecution by public prosecuting officers that a jury could not be found in Boston to convict for this crime, even in the most flagrant and indisputable cases of maternal death." However exaggerated, the character of the crime threw up roadblocks to successful prosecution.[59]

Murky evidence was a particular problem for local authorities trying to convict abortionists. Pittsburgh officials indicted W. (his or her name was kept secret) in 1871 for trying to abort the fetus of Jennie S. Scott. W. advised Scott to use violent exercise. She tried to do so by repeatedly jumping off a ladder. Although the state abortion code did not specifically include that method among the acts it banned, the court upheld the legality of the indictment. But the jury could not agree on W.'s guilt and he (or she) went free.

Four years later in Illinois, Trevlar Slattery was convicted of performing an abortion on his wife. He had beaten her, and appealed the conviction claiming that he had only intended to punish his wife, not induce her to abort. The court accepted this defense by interpreting the statute as "evidently aimed at professional abortionists, and at those who, with the intent and design of producing abortion, shall use any means to that end, no matter what those means may be, but not at those who, with no such purpose in view, should, by a violent act, unfortunately produce such a result."[60]

While antiabortion forces tried to tighten the law through legislative lobbying, prosecutors used briefs and oral arguments to win judicial interpretations of the codes and common law more favorable to the state. They secured judicial approval for using circumstantial evidence linking abortionists to their crimes. In 1874 the Maryland bench upheld the conviction of Susan Hays despite her appeal that evidence disclosing that she ran a bordello had prejudiced the jury against her. The court ruled that the state had properly introduced the fact to show the jury that the scene of the crime had been one well calculated to prevent its detection. Similarly, Massachusetts courts allowed the state to introduce medical instruments designed for performing abortions by analogizing them to burglar's tools, which were admissible in theft and robbery trials.[61]

Circumstantial evidence could help convict an abortionist, but prosecutors generally required stronger evidence to sustain an indictment. In desperate need of witnesses who could verify abortion charges, the woman or her body became the prosecution's prize catch. Yet women had an uncertain legal standing in abortion cases. A woman's corpse could usually be used to substantiate an indictment, but defense lawyers objected to the live testimony of women who had sought abortions. Like reformers, they argued that such females were accomplices in the deed. Storer and Heard contended that the "mother almost always is an accessory before the fact, or the principal, and should not, as now, be allowed almost perfect immunity. There is no valid reason for such entire exemption, unless we allow that all pregnant women are from that very fact more or less insane." They demanded that there "be a certain measure of punishment for the mother, even if it be not so severe as for other parties engaged." But few legislatures heeded either appeal.[62]

Cleaving to their longstanding paternalistic depiction of women as victims of sex-related crimes, most judges repelled attorneys' charges of complicity and reformers' complaints about immunity. In upholding the conviction of John Snow, the Massachusetts Supreme Judicial Court declared that the "act makes [abortion] criminal without regard to the consent of the person upon whom it was performed." Nor did abortion destroy a woman's credibility as a witness in the eyes of the judiciary. In 1880 the Texas Court of Appeals emphasized that point in passing on Dr. J. Watson's appeal from a conviction for aborting the fetus of Mattie Snook. The justices admitted that there "has been some contrariety of opinion and decision in the courts on this subject," but argued that the "rule that she does not stand legally in the situation of an accomplice but should rather be regarded as the victim than the perpetrator of the crime is one which commends itself to our sense of justice and right, and there is certainly nothing in our law of accomplices which should be held to contravene it."[63]

Despite court warnings that the woman's testimony should be heard with an awareness of her participation in the deed and the view of some jurists that the abortee's testimony alone should not convict an abortionist, judges continued to view women as passive victims. Law Professor John Wigmore endorsed that approach in his authoritative treatise on evidence: "[In] sexual crimes the other person—usually the woman—

may not be an accomplice, according as she is, by the nature of the crime, a victim of it or a voluntary partner in it. Thus in adultery, the other party may well be deemed an accomplice; and so also, perhaps in incest; but the woman is not an accomplice in rape under age, seduction, or abortion; nor the participant in sodomy." As in these other crimes, the special legal capacity of women, the Victorian belief that women were unwilling participants in most sexual acts, and the prosecutorial need for evidence brushed aside other considerations. Indeed, women became star witnesses in abortion trials.[64]

The bench aided prosecutors by accepting statutory revisions classifying attempted abortions as separate and distinct crimes. By punishing attempted abortions, legislators closed off one of the most effective defenses to the crime.[65]

An 1894 decision in Texas illustrates the effectiveness of the statutory tactic. After discovering her pregnancy, Livie Brown went to a man named Cave for abortion drugs. He advised her to try a number of substances: calomel, an unknown red liquid, a mysterious dark one, and finally turpentine. None worked and Brown bore the child. After its birth, Cave offered to pay Brown for her sexual favors. Enraged, she went to local authorities and had him arrested as an abortionist. Cave appealed his conviction, arguing that he was not culpable since the drugs had been ineffective. But the state court of appeals declared that if "the means shall fail to produce abortion, the offender is nevertheless guilty of an attempt to produce abortion, provided it be shown that such means were calculated to produce that result." Several state tribunals further enhanced the effectiveness of this prosecutorial tool by holding that the drug did not even have to be an abortifacient.[66]

The only remaining form of legalized abortion, the therapeutic exception, underscored the health and safety interests of abortion legislation. Most state abortion laws exempted abortions performed to save the life of the mother. As the Supreme Court of Ohio pointed out in 1866, the therapeutic exception provided one of the few valid defenses to the crime: "The statute does not declare every procurement of an abortion to be an offense; but does so only when it is not done for the purpose of saving the life of the mother. The absence of this necessity is, then, so far descriptive of the crime, that the offense can not be established without proof that such necessity did not exist." Because most statutes demanded that physicians monitor such operations, they also testified to the increasing stature of professionalized doctors, as well as the legislative tendency to delegate to them greater decision-making authority.[67]

Still, the role of physicians in abortion was controversial. Many abortion foes from outside of the medical profession complained that doctors too readily assisted women in getting rid of unwanted children.

In *Marriage and Parentage*, Henry Wright sadly reported that physicians, "instead of urging men to control their passions, direct their attention to discovering means to prevent conception and procure abortion. To kill her babe, the mother endangers herself and she resorts to medical advisors to help her destroy her child with safety to herself." Edward Bond Foote, the son of a well-known radical physician, Edward Bliss Foote, and himself a trained physician and a proponent of birth control and women's rights, agreed with Wright. He further claimed that his professional colleagues not only performed abortions, but often went unpunished out of official deference to their medical judgment while the nonphysician abortionist faced trial and a prison term. Foote noted that the latter was "apt to be looked upon as a 'butcher' lacking the requisite skill in a delicate business self-assumed," while regular doctors got "the full measure of the law" and if "of sufficient high standing or having political influence" could expect to be "leniently treated" through some "ready loophole of the law or in the evidence." Regular doctors, particularly those in the forefront of the antiabortion effort like Storer, rejected such charges and placed the blame for most abortions on professional abortionists, midwives, and female physicians.[68]

A measure of the effectiveness of physicians' pleas of immunity comes from the 1880 prosecution of Orlando Bradford in New York City. Claiming to be a trained physician, the defendant insisted that the abortion that had led to the death of Sarah Conners had been performed to save her life. After the lower courts rejected his defense, Bradford turned to the appellate bench. The New York Court of Appeals responded by placing the burden of proof on the "professional man" to demonstrate that an abortion had been necessary to preserve the mother's life. Restricting the defense to physicians, the court conceded them the professional discretion to make such decisions: "It is not at all likely that courts in the administration of justice would require more, in explanation of the operation performed, to overcome the existing penalty than that an honest judgment was exercised declaring the necessity of resorting to an instrument for the purpose of relieving the mother or saving the child." Bradford could not provide such evidence and his conviction stood, as did those of other defendants whose assertions of therapeutic necessity judges and juries decided had been fabricated. Even so, as Foote had correctly complained, the bench generally deferred to physicians and accepted their expanding control over reproduction and fetal life in the absence of compelling evidence of actual criminal conduct, a deference they withheld from others indicted for abortion.[69]

The most far-reaching legal victory of the antiabortion forces demonstrates the physicians' power: the relegation of the quickening doctrine to a cobwebbed corner of the common law alongside other relics of the legal past. The assault on the doctrine, begun in the 1830s, continued into the late nineteenth century. In 1887 Isaac M. Quimby, head of the AMA's section on medical jurisprudence, blamed the nation's high abortion rate on the "fallacious idea that there is no life until quickening takes place." He lamented that quickening had become the "foundation of, and formed the basis of, and been the excuse to ease or appease the guilty conscience which had led to the destruction of thousands of human lives." Such contentions won more and more converts.[70]

An 1880 decision of the North Carolina Supreme Court suggests how the bench began to bypass the quickening rule. The justices upheld the conviction of Jacob F. Slagle for administering abortion-inducing drugs to Eva Bryson. Though the indictment alleged that Bryson had been "quick with child," the court waived the need to prove that by interpreting the law to mean that "it is not the murder of a living child which constitutes the offense, but the destruction of gestation by wicked means and against nature." The judges thus ruled all abortions illegal. By making abortionists culpable regardless of fetal animation or even pregnancy, legislatures joined courts in invalidating the quickening doctrine. The retreat from the old policy reached its high point in 1882 when the Massachusetts Supreme Judicial Court officially interred the *Bangs* decision, which had legalized prequickened abortions fifty years before.[71]

Although no longer used to distinguish legal from criminal abortion, the quickening doctrine enjoyed a second legal life as the basis for determining the punishment meted out to abortionists. Statutes still relied on a developmental theory of fetal growth to impose higher penalties on the destruction of a well-developed fetus. In *The Physiology of Marriage* William Alcott explained why: "[T]here [is] something particularly shocking in those cases of destruction which approximate to maturity of the embryo, especially when the results are accomplished by poison, or by surgical instruments." Others were concerned over the greater danger to women from late-term abortions.[72]

The Missouri Court of Appeals in 1883 overturned the conviction of Charles R. Emerich, who stood accused of using an instrument to abort a pregnant employee. Indicted for first-degree manslaughter after the woman died, Emerich argued that he should have been charged with a misdemeanor. The court agreed, noting that the "advance of science shows that the term 'quickening' as indicating the beginning of life in the foetus, has no foundation in physiology, yet the common-law writers held, that life began only when the woman became 'quick with child.'" The justices decided that the state legislature had intended the old common-law doctrine to determine the penalties for criminal abortion. They offered three variants of the crime: the willful killing of a quickened fetus by an injury to the mother constituted manslaughter in the first degree; the death of a quickened fetus or the mother done with the intent to destroy the fetus was manslaughter in the second degree; the mere attempt to perform an abortion fell in the category of a misdemeanor. Without proof of the deceased woman's pregnancy, the justices concluded that Emerich could only be convicted of a misdemeanor.[73]

By the end of the century, the quickening doctrine had been stripped of its ancient authority. But this development did not raise the fetus to the legal status of the infant in abortion law. Though punished with increasing severity, the destruction of a fetus never gained the standing either of infanticide or homicide. On the contrary, the fetus could acquire full legal status only upon live birth. Instead of placing the fetus alongside other legal persons, the law generally created a special legal niche for the unborn. In the law of abortion, this led to the conclusion that a fetus could be destroyed without incurring the legal punishment reserved for the murder of an actual person.[74]

The transformation of the quickening doctrine was the kingpin in the larger reformulation of abortion law. It signalled the end of legalized abortion, save for the therapeutic exemption. According to historian Degler, when seen against "the broad canvas of humanitarian thought and practice in Western society from the 17th to the 20th century," including such developments as reduced use of the death penalty, the peace movement, and the abolition of torture and whipping as criminal penalties, "the expansion of the definition of life to include the whole career of the fetus rather than the months after quickening is quite consistent."[75]

But this enlargement of the definition of life occurred at the expense of the legal emancipation of women. By the end of the century American abortion law codified the role of women as child bearers. Statutes and judicial decisions declared that denying birth to a fetus was a crime: a legal determination that made the womb part of the public domain. Legislators and judges had created a formidable arsenal to use against criminals who intruded into that restricted area.

However, greater ideological and legal unanimity in the law neither eliminated abortion nor quieted antiabortionists. In a 1910 polemic the St. Louis physician Frederick J. Taussig decried the appalling number of criminal abortions, which he estimated at 80,000 a year in New York City and 6,000 to 10,000 in urban centers like Chicago. While in theory the crime was "punished by a severe penalty," in actuality it was "practically never punished." Calling the enforcement of abortion laws "sadly inefficient in this country," he reported that "even in the face of evidence that to any fair-minded person would be incontrovertible" the chances for conviction were only one in ten. He blamed the situation on a lingering belief in quickening, the difficulty of mounting a successful prosecution, and the indifference of judges and jurors.[76]

Nor did debate over the legitimacy of state regulation cease. An anonymous author in the 1889–1890 *Medical-Legal Journal* attacked the new abortion codes as dead letters that took away the right of married women to control the size of their families and of unmarried women to avoid disgrace. Though this critic disavowed abortion, he or she argued that abortion legislation unfairly legislated private morality into public law. Chicago physician and medical professor Junius C. Hoag offered a quick reply, arguing that the law reflected the actual sentiments of the nation: "The law is a constant monitor. . . . [T]he clergy and all other educators may fail in their duty to properly instruct the people, but we still have left instruction in the law. The man who would remove the barrier to crime, lays the axe at the very root of civilization, the home." Though the law did not eradicate criminal abortion nor root out its social and economic sources, it did, as Hoag suggested, formally denounce the practice and, more concretely, made it legally hazardous and morally questionable.[77]

The Federal Campaign against Birth Control

Unlike abortion, which became an object of attention on all levels of government, contraception fell primarily under the purview of federal authorities. In fact, the dominant role of national officials made anti–birth-control laws quite unusual in a polity that left domestic relations issues and most other social policy questions to the states. But the Comstock Law proved to be the most effective mechanism for combating contraception because purveyors depended on the postal service to transport their merchandise.

Judge John F. Dillon of the federal district court in Missouri took pains to distinguish between federal and state responsibilities in an opinion quashing the conviction of a contraceptive dealer trapped by a Comstock agent: "Congress has, it is conceded, no power to make criminal the using of means to prevent conception, or to procure abortion, etc., in the several states. That power belongs to the respective states." Yet only Connecticut banned the actual use of contraceptives. Most little Comstock laws repeated the federal classification of birth control as obscene and relied on penalizing their sale and advertisement.

The Pennsylvania Supreme Court staked out the limits of the state's effort in *Commonwealth* v. *Leigh* (1881). The justices ordered prosecutors to amend an indictment against a defendant charged with selling instruments for contraceptive purposes because the state code prohibited only their advertisement, not their sale or use. "The legislature," the court declared, "had in view the injury that might be done to ignorant people by the use of such instruments, if their whereabouts and description should be blazoned to the community by manner of publication referred to." Since officials fought contraception in the mailroom, not in the bedroom, the federal court became their main arena.[78]

Though the exact intent of the Congress and state legislatures in declaring contraception obscene was, as always, uncertain, that approach became a widely used method of combating unwanted behavior in late nineteenth-century America. The definitional elasticity and moral rigidity of obscenity statutes made them an attractive method for curtailing practices difficult to regulate in other ways. The passage of the Comstock legislation with little debate reflects the delicacy of the subject as well as a broad acquiescence in, if not approval of, banning obscenities of all sorts. Because contraception did not raise the health and safety issues so central to the abortion debate, its public discussion and legal treatment centered more directly on issues of decency, morality, and obscenity.

As they had in the 1832 Knowlton prosecution, judges approved classification of contraception as obscene. Comstock's biographers concluded that "his success in court would have been impossible but for the fact that many men upon the bench were wholly of his mind in matters relating to obscenity." Comstock capitalized on these shared values by appealing to the judges' own concept of their role and the proper use of the law: "[The courts] ought to be, the schools of public morals."[79]

The Comstock law surmounted its first legal hurdle just seven months after its enactment. The federal district court in New York City upheld the conviction of John Bott, a physician, for mailing a powder he credited with contraceptive and abortive powers. District judge Robert D. Benedict, who would become Comstock's most reliable judicial ally, rejected Bott's defense that the substance was ineffective. The judge asserted that "Congress has exclusive jurisdiction over the mails, and may prohibit the use of the mails for the transmission of any article." "Any article of any description," Benedict concluded in a blanket assertion of federal regulatory power rarely heard from the bench, "whether harmless or not, may therefore, be declared contraband by mail, by Act of Congress, and its deposit thereby made a crime."[80]

New York was a hotbed of antivice agitation and the home of the nation's leading purity crusader, but judicial approval of the Comstock law extended far beyond its borders. Three years after the *Bott* decision, a federal court in Nevada used the act to strike down a favorite ploy of the contraception business, ambiguous ads. Federal authorities had indicted E. D. Kelly for carrying an advertisement in his newspaper soliciting replies from "all married ladies" with sexual problems and promising quick remedies. Circuit judge Lorenzo Sawyer relied on Massachusetts Chief Justice Lemuel Shaw's opinion in the Abner Kneeland blasphemy case to hold that courts were authorized to interpret unclear language according to its context and obvious import. He asked rhetorically: "Is it possible for anybody to read this advertisement and not understand that he can find medicine, advice, and treatment at the place mentioned, for the purposes which are by statute forbidden?" Kelly's appeal he dismissed with the frank declaration: "It is not to be expected that a quack doctor will advertise in plain express terms, that he will furnish the means for the prevention of conception, or to procure abortion."[81]

Federal rulings such as this shielded the Comstock law from assaults on its constitutionality and the scope of its jurisdiction. Later amendments to the statute, including an 1897 addition banning the importation of contraceptives and their deposit at freight offices for interstate shipment, also won judicial approval as valid exercises of the federal power to regulate commerce. The judiciary's endorsement of the ban on mailing contraceptives was part of its broader acceptance of obscenity legislation. Taking its lead from English decisions, the bench relied on the first substantive Anglo-American definition of obscenity, devised by Lord Chief Justice Cockburn in the 1868 case of *Queen* v. *Hicklin*: "[T]he test of obscenity is this, whether the tendency of the matter charged as obscenity is to deprave and corrupt those whose minds are open to such immoral influences, and into whose hands a publication of this sort might fall."[82]

American judges used the "Hicklin Rule" to support the constitutionality of obscenity prosecutions in the federal courts. The Supreme Court endorsed the principle as well when in 1877 it upheld the conviction of Orlando Jackson for mailing lottery tickets. Justice Stephen Field, in an unusual unilateral evocation of federal regulatory power, argued that in excluding various articles from the mails, "the object of Congress has not been to interfere with the freedom of the press, or with any other rights of the people; but to refuse its facilities for the distribution of matter deemed injurious to the public morals." As to the constitutionality of the Comstock law, Field tersely declared, "we have no doubt." In 1891 a federal district court in Kansas summed up the bench's expansive definition of obscenity when it described as obscene anything "offensive to the common decency and modesty of the community."[83]

Let loose by Congress, state legislatures, and the courts, vice hunters prowled the nation sniffing out their prey. Posing as customers or using decoy letters, federal agents and local societies purchased proscribed items and then arrested sellers. By Comstock's own account, contraceptives represented only a small part of a war on obscenity, which included the arrest of gamblers and pornographers, the banning of Tolstoy's disapproving tale of infidelity, *The Kreutzer Sonata*, a pamphlet urging total chastity, and a medical text on physiology written by an eminent Harvard scientist.

Spacious definitions and adamant intentions made inevitable the placement of contraceptives on the target list. Comstock in fact caught his most famous victim with a birth-control ploy. Having been warned not to tangle with the infamous Madame Restell, he took her capture as a personal challenge. In the guise of an impoverished father, Comstock pleaded for contraceptive information because his meager finances could support no more children. When she obliged, he arrested her. Faced with the almost certain prospect of jail at the age of 67, Restell slit her throat with a carving knife. Comstock experienced no remorse: "a bloody end to a bloody life."[84]

Purity reform did stir opposition both because it relied on state activism and because it employed unsavory methods. After Restell's suicide, Comstock used a similar ruse to arrest Dr. Sarah Chase of Boston for selling vaginal syringes. But he overstepped when he compared her to Restell in court testimony. A juryman asked if Comstock intended to drive Chase to suicide as well; the panel acquitted the Boston physician.

The vice hunters' tactics proved self-defeating when they aroused public hostility to the purity campaign. Comstock obtained the conviction of a longtime foe, Ezra Heywood, a feminist and former Garrisonian abolitionist who championed openness and education in sexual matters, for publishing *Cupid Yokes*, a tract against monogamy. But President Rutherford B. Hayes was forced to pardon the aged, infirm ideologue in response to an organized campaign for his release. Even so, resistance to the purity movement was sporadic and limited in impact. The broad challenge to the obscenity laws as unconstitutional infringements on civil liberties mounted by freethinkers and sexual radicals failed to elicit popular support.[85]

An 1876 decision by Judge Benedict, the New York federal jurist, illustrates the chilling effect of the obscenity laws. Dr. Edward Bliss Foote, whose son had denounced the hypocrisy of antiabortion physicians, was arrested in 1875 when he sent birth-control information in response to a decoy letter. Though a graduate of a Philadelphia medical school, Foote had never been licensed and practiced in an unorthodox manner. His career disturbed both the antivice societies and professionalized physicians. He publicly supported free-thought, civil liberties, women's rights and birth control, and had established a publishing firm that issued tracts on health care and contraception. After his arrest, Foote wrote that it "is my conscientious conviction that every married woman should have it within her power to decide for herself just when and just how often she will receive the germ of a new offspring."

Benedict not only upheld Foote's conviction; he went out of his way to place the law squarely against the prescription of contraceptives by physicians:

> It is plain that an attempt to exclude information given by medical men from the operation of the statute would afford an easy way of nullifying the law. If the intention had been to exclude the communications of physicians from the operation of the act, it was certainly easy to say so. In the absence of any words of limitation, the language used must be given its full and natural significance, and held to exclude from the mails every form of notice whereby the prohibited information is conveyed.

Dismissing any distinction between reputable and quack providers of contraception, he ruled that all were prohibited from using the mails. Foote received a fine of $3,500 and court costs, which added up to $5,000. He later declared that it had been his "duty to enter a solemn protest as a physician to this piece of meddlesome impertinence on the part of hasty lawmakers who have inconsiderately obeyed the behests of mistaken moralists." But he admitted that he could not continue to provide birth-control information until a "change in our Congressional and State laws" occurred. Designating contraception as an indecent, criminal subject had relegated it to underground discussion.[86]

An 1885 New York slander case is illustrative. Emily Halstead, an instructor in the sewing department of the Central New York Institution for the Deaf, accused the school principal of slander. Before the Institution's board of trustees, he had charged her with sending a birth-control circular, which he called a "dirty, obscene letter," to his house. He claimed the letter had "cost himself and his wife much pain" and demanded and received Halstead's dismissal. The instructor sued and won a verdict of $1,200. On appeal, a New York court ruled that mailing such a circular was indeed a misdemeanor under state law, and that charging a person with the "commission of an indictable offense involving moral turpitude, is slander *per se*."[87] In such an atmosphere, questioning the Comstock laws was courageous, repeal impossible.

During the early years of the twentieth century, however, the effort to legalize and disseminate contraceptives became increasingly respectable. Organized activity began in 1915 with the formation of the Birth Control League. Contraception became a single-issue reform, distinct both from radical politics and from civil libertarianism. Using judicial test cases, legislative lobbying, and public relations ploys, this new group of reformers gained support for their protest against the ban on contraception. Margaret Sanger, whose abandonment of early socialist sympathies enhanced her appeal to the middle class, emerged as the leading advocate of birth control. By the 1920s the movement had developed a broad base that even included Abraham Jacobi, president of the AMA and political radical Emma Goldman. But it had little immediate effect.[88]

Legislators and judges retained their veto on the dissemination of birth control materials and information. Indeed, Congress strengthened the federal ban in 1908. By the 1930s eight states specifically prohibited the flow of contraceptive information while the rest acted through broadened obscenity laws. Contraception remained a taboo subject, even though, much like prohibition, the statutes expressed a moral standard clearly at odds with actual practices. One distressed New York assemblyman reneged on an agreement to introduce a birth-control reform bill with the excuse that it "would do me an injury that I could not overcome for some time." Birth control, no matter how essential family limitation had become to the republican family, still violated the nation's code of proper domestic behavior. Fears aroused by the immigration of seemingly fecund non-Protestant women, charges of race suicide leveled against non-immigrant mothers who regulated their child bearing, and the everpresent concern over changes in gender responsibilities reinvigorated the stigma attached to the practice.[89]

The constitutionality of the ban was also impenetrable. In *Commonwealth* v. *Allison* (1917) the 1879 Little Comstock law of Massachusetts won judicial vindication. Local officials arrested Van Kleeck Allison, the scion of a wealthy New York family attending Columbia University, for distributing two contraceptive leaflets to workers at a factory gate: "Why and How the Poor Should Not Have Many Children" and "Don't Have Undesired Children." A defense committee used his case to challenge the state ban, urging the court to recognize the medical necessity of contraception in some cases and its moral, social, and economic necessity in others. Their arguments did not sway Chief Justice Samuel Ruggs, who used the Hicklin Rule to uphold Allison's conviction. He argued that anticontraception laws were manifestly "designed to promote the public morals and in a broad sense the public health and safety. Their plain purpose is to protect purity, to preserve chastity, to encourage continence and self-restraint, to defend the sanctity of the home, and thus engender in the state and nation a virile and virtuous race of men and women."[90]

True, there were occasional fissures in judicial support. New York and

Cleveland judges in 1916 released women who claimed that they had to steal to feed their children. In their opinions, the jurists argued for the wider use of birth control to ease such family problems. Using a technique that political scientist C. Thomas Dienes calls "judicial martyrdom," Margaret Sanger and her sister secured several convictions for violating the contraceptive ban in order to marshal support. In Margaret Sanger's 1918 case, Justice Frederick Crane of the New York Court of Appeals construed the state law, which included a new legislative reform of the ban permitting a licensed physician to give birth control advice for the "cure or prevention of disease," to include not merely ailments like venereal disease but any general health problem. Massachusetts courts granted a similar exemption to Dr. Antoinette Knoelow for exhibiting but not selling contraceptives.[91]

Such judicial revisions of the Comstock laws in the early years of the twentieth century eased somewhat the legal restrictions on contraception, but they also demonstrated the formidable opposition facing birth-control advocates. The medical exemption, like the therapeutic qualification in abortion statutes, equated sexual rights with medical authority. Even in the most tolerant states contraceptives remained classified as indecent articles permissible only on the recommendation of a reputable doctor. Birth control continued to be an obscene subject banished from polite society. In 1917 Frederick A. Blossom wrote in the *Medical-Legal Journal* that to champion the idea that "every wife should have the right to regulate the size of her family is an argument which would reduce marriage from the institution it is now, or at least is presumed to be, to an institution the purpose of which would not be the raising of a family but the gratification of sexual desire."[92]

Legal Differences

Anthony Comstock had labeled as abortionists everyone who advocated or dealt in family-limitation materials and services. That characterization reflected a general nineteenth-century tendency to link contraception and abortion, although abortion was always considered the greater evil. But the ties binding them together frayed noticeably by the turn of the century.

Medical reformers and their allies, who portrayed family limitation as an assault on home and nation, continued to denounce both methods. But they reserved their harshest condemnations and most zealous efforts for the antiabortion crusade. Dr. John Stoddard, in an article urging the suppression of abortion, linked the practice with infanticide. He called it "foeticide" and demanded it be made a capital crime "if maliciously committed."

Even sexual reformers tended to agree. The free speech advocate D. M. Bennett, one of the Comstock's most strident foes, declared that abortion "cannot be justified by any moral, right-minded person, but the too rapid increase of population and the experience of preventing it by safe and legitimate means, is a question which will demand the serious attention of future philosophers, physicians, and legislators." He added that there were "thousands of children brought into the world that would be better for themselves and for the world if they never entered it. If conception, in these cases had been prevented, no wrong would have been committed." His comment suggests how reformers who advocated a single sexual standard and the right of women to regulate marital sexuality resolved their ambivalence toward active fertility control.[93]

The growing inclination to distinguish between abortion and contraception was evident, too, in popular conduct. The middle-class desire to regulate family size did not subside nor did its inherent uneasiness over the practice. But increasing numbers of couples turned to contraception rather than abortion to limit the number of children they would rear. After the 1870s the sales of abortion drugs and services declined, while those of contraceptives rose. An even more telling indication of changing sentiments was the changing abortion clientele. End-of-the-century court cases and popular reports suggest that once again abortion had become the resort of single women rather than their married sisters. Wives still had abortions, but birth control seems to have become the chief means of reproductive control.[94]

The dramatic change in popular practice and opinion had a clear relationship to and implications for the legal system. Since the 1830s the law judged both obscene, but singled out abortion for far greater penalties. This paralleled social opinion and practice. The women's rights advocate Elizabeth Duffey, who promoted voluntary motherhood as a means of female economic and social liberation, contended in 1876 that contraception was a benign activity; women who practiced it were "free from blame and simply taking advantage of the law which nature and nature's God have enacted in her behalf. . . ." Few reformers would have said the same about abortion. Edward Bond Foote made the point explicitly: "[P]hysicians and laymen take liberties with the law, and where it becomes a necessity to decide between lawful abortion and unlawful contraception, they prefer to break the man-made law against contraception rather than the natural law against abortion."[95]

Thus in the first half of the new century, contraception became the focal point of legal disputes over family planning, with courtrooms the

forums of debate. This reflected the legal reality that artificially terminating a pregnancy remained a crime, though artificially inhibiting conception was only a social wrong. A fertilized egg had the right to join a
family, unfertilized eggs had not.

Moreover, the greater moral and legal legitimacy of contraception
as compared to abortion reinforced the judicial inclination to supervise closely all legislatively authorized invasions of family privacy and
household decision making. That disposition was evident in the tendency to punish purveyors rather than users of family-limitation devices
and materials. It also became apparent in the greater tolerance of judges
toward the practice.

The pattern of the institutional response to the aggressive campaign
against all forms of family limitation is significant as well. Unlike many
issues in marriage law, there appears to have been fairly wide agreement
within all branches of the legal system that reproductive rights should be
regulated. Even so, shared values did not guarantee uniform policies. As
they did in marriage law, legislators responded more decisively to the
pressures of reformers than did judges, who retained their self-pro-
claimed commitments to maintaining doctrinal and institutional continuity as well as protecting the family. The law of childbirth reveals limits of
institutional cooperation that even shared beliefs could not overcome. It
also underscores the wariness with which family law approached questions of family membership and autonomy and the rising pressure on the
law to hold parents more accountable for the nation's domestic life.

BASTARD RIGHTS

RECOGNIZING A NEW FAMILY MEMBER

The legal measures that separated legitimate from illegitimate children generated controversy just as did those that distinguished between fetus and infant. Bastards, as Anglo-Americans traditionally classified both children born out of wedlock and adulterine offspring, had long faced legal barriers to full family membership. These obstacles had been constructed to protect family lineage and resources, and to promote matrimony by penalizing misbegotten offspring, thus enhancing the status of the lawfully born.

In post-Revolutionary America, though, illegitimate children became an object of legal reform. Chancellor Kent's *Commentaries* documented the changes underway by the 1830s: "This relaxation in the law of so many states of the severity of the common law, rests upon the principles that the relation of parent and child, which exists in this unhappy case in all its native and binding force, ought to produce the ordinary legal consequences of that consanguinity." Bastardy law in the new republic never fully jettisoned two perennial influences: fiscally conservative local authorities anxious to control child-support costs and a deeply ingrained prejudice against extramarital sexual relations. But growing concern over the welfare of illegitimate children, produced in large part by republican views of children, combined with a grudging conferral of rights on their mother to transform the law.[1]

The reorientation of bastardy law raised a fundamental issue in nine-teenth-century family law: individual versus family rights. Enlarging the legal status of illegitimate children entailed a redefinition of the legitimate family. In particular, it raised anew a fundamental but troublesome question for the republic: was the individual or the family the basic unit of society?

No definitive answer ever came from the nineteenth-century legal order, but a generational response did. It came first in a series of post-Revolutionary and antebellum changes that created a new legal place for the bastard. These changes were followed, though, by the limited success of a late nineteenth and early twentieth-century reform drive to expand the rights of illegitimates even further.

The widely acclaimed changes in the legal status of bastards during the century demonstrate the transforming potential of child welfare in family law; correspondingly, the limits of reform point out the potency of the law's commitment to an orthodox vision of the republican household. In the end, the goal of the most determined advocates of bastards' rights, abolition of all legal discrimination against children born out of wedlock, failed because it came to be seen as too direct a threat to the integrity of the legitimate family; that is, a wedded couple and their offspring and heirs. Nonetheless, a transformed bastardy law added another dimension to republican domestic relations; one that, unlike many matrimonial innovations of the law's formative era, was never to be repudiated.

The Colonies Inherit a Repressive Heritage

At the outset, bastardy-law reform required drastic changes in traditional Anglo-American policies. Colonial legislators followed the mother country's illegitimacy laws, which had two primary purposes: to repel the challenges that bastardy posed to established family organization and property distribution, and to prevent the public from being saddled with the costs of rearing children born outside wedlock. The law used matrimony to separate legal from spurious issue. It defined the latter as *"filius nullius,"* the child and heir of no one. The bastard had no recognized legal relations with his or her parents, particularly not those of inheritance, maintenance, and custody. Nor did the illicit couple have any rights or duties toward their spurious issue. The only heirs of bastards were those of their own bodies.[2]

The English refusal to follow the Continental civil law and allow children to be legitimated by the subsequent marriage of their parents underscores the use of law to repress bastardy by punishing those star-crossed infants. Though ecclesiastical courts adopted the Continental rule, common-law tribunals held that only children born after nuptials could claim inheritance rights. An English child thus could be legitimate in one court, while propertyless and illegitimate in another. In 1236, at the Merton Parliament, the Bishops urged the Law Barons to reconsider and adopt the civil-law policy. They refused, as did their descendants, who clung to the common-law rule until the twentieth century. Indeed, this rejection gained new significance as bastardy law became secularized and the common-law courts no longer relied on ecclesiastical authorities to determine legitimacy.

Common lawyers assumed, as Blackstone explained, that to do otherwise "is plainly a great discouragement to the matrimonial state; to which one main inducement is usually not only the desire of having *children*, but also of procreating lawful heirs." He and other defenders of the common law opposed the civil-law procedure because they feared that it would lead to uncertainty over parentage, engender fraud, upset proper legal relations among legitimate family members, and topple the natural order of family membership beginning with the male head and followed by his wife, first son, second son, and so on down the line. The *filius nullius* not only existed outside of the family order and hence the legal order, but posed a sufficient threat to be barred at any cost.[3]

Fittingly, the one major modification of the law in favor of illegitimate children did much more to aid parish rate-payers than bastards. The Poor Law of 1576 decreed that the parents of an illegitimate child had to pay for its upbringing, thus relieving the public of those costs. The bastard became the charge of poor-law officials who could compel support but not family membership. The statute also subjected the parents to criminal penalties for their acts.

The Elizabethan Poor Law and its related common-law definition of the bastard applied in the North American provinces as well. Colonial officials transferred to the New World the English policy of using illegitimate children to enforce proper sexual conduct, protect public solvency, and aid the patriarchal distribution of property. The Atlantic migration of the law ensured that the bastard and its mother bore the brunt of punishment and social ostracism, without compensating rights or benefits.[4]

But bastardy proceedings and attitudes toward illegitimate children sustained a subtle but significant modification in the provinces: the focus of prosecutions shifted away from an initial effort to punish sin and toward a narrowed emphasis on limiting the public costs of bastardy. Because bastardy proceedings were at once criminal complaints pursued under fornication statutes and civil matters, men and women charged with parenting a bastard found themselves subjected to criminal penalties such as fines and whippings, as well as being liable for maintenance costs.

As this direct form of the enforcement of sexual propriety declined, local officials concentrated their efforts on recovering support costs by prosecuting single mothers and the fathers. They let other institutions police premarital sexuality. Historian Hendrik Hartog has found such a change in tactics in the Middlesex County Court of General Sessions fornication prosecutions. By the 1750s the proceedings in that Massachusetts tribunal had been "largely reconstructed as a form of public welfare law. They became a way of allocating the costs of illegitimacy." Similarly, many provincial assemblies reduced the severity of criminal punishments while they sharpened the tools available to ferret out putative fathers. Revised bastardy statutes used harsher penalties to compel women to name the father of their baseborn children, granted local officials the right to prosecute if an impoverished mother failed to go to court, and made the father more clearly responsible for support. These acts and complementary judicial policies skewed the rules of evidence, and paternity proceedings in general, toward conviction.[5]

The change in orientation encouraged the community interest in keeping baseborn offspring off the public rolls. Thus persons of means could escape paternity hearings through out-of-court settlements that saved local officials from providing for child support. Bastardy penalties fell most heavily on those who could not afford such settlements. Servants, especially women and blacks, suffered most as they faced longer indentures and greater penalties. Men of wealth and influence, often imbued with the tradition of *droit de seigneur*, could either disregard bastardy proceedings or treat the penalties as the nominal cost of sexual play. Lesser men had to scramble to work something out or fall under the control of the poor laws and face the loss of property or liberty.[6]

The shift in bastardy prosecutions occurred against a colonial American backdrop of changing sexual standards, escalating rates of premarital pregnancy, challenges to an active state regulation of sexual behavior, the emergence of more affective notions of child rearing, and, perhaps, lower illegitimacy rates. Historian Robert Wells has found an interest in the welfare of illegitimate children among colonials that apparently did not exist in England. The admittedly scanty evidence, he concludes, suggests that many provincial Americans had become "unwilling to punish children for the sins of their parents." He cites the willingness of Virginia and Rhode Island to grant bastards inheritance rights, statutes in other colonies equalizing the period of service of black and white indentured bastards, and the political success of such notable illegitimates as Alexander Hamilton and William Franklin (Benjamin's son), the last royal governor of New Jersey.[7]

The new social and legal climate surrounding illegitimacy found vivid expression in the plea of Polly Baker, the heroine of a Benjamin Franklin satire. Standing before a local court facing her fifth bastardy indictment, Baker told the magistrates of her poverty, and claimed that she had always led a moral life and supported her children. She lashed out at the law and its presumed morality, insisting that only religious bodies could legitimately punish her for moral transgressions. Ridiculing legal pretensions, she asked the bench: "But how can it be believed that heaven is angry at my having children, when to the little done by me towards it, God has been pleased to add his divine skill and admirable workmanship in the formation of their bodies, and crowned it by furnishing them with rational immortal souls." Baker, who blamed her troubles on a local magistrate who had seduced and then jilted her, concluded her plea with a defiant declaration:

> What must poor young women do, whom custom has forbid to solicit men, and who cannot force themselves on husbands, when the laws take no care to provide them any; and yet severely punishes them when they do their duty without them; the duty of the first and great command of nature, and of nature's God, increase and multiply; a duty, from the steady performance of which, nothing has been able to deter me; but for its sake I have hazarded the loss of public esteem, and have frequently endured public disgrace and punishment; and therefore ought, in my humble opinion, instead of a whipping, to have a statue erected in my memory.

Baker's plea reflects the twin interests that came to dominate bastardy law in the nineteenth century: public costs and child welfare. That combination set the stage for a fundamental revision of American illegitimacy law.[8]

The Creation of a Republican Bastardy Law

In the decades after the Revolution, judges and legislators could not, and did not attempt to, rid family law of bastardy. The intent, Tapping Reeve explained in 1816, was evident in the major legal disability imposed upon illegitimate children, the lack of family-membership rights: "I apprehend this rule to be partly founded in that anxiety which the law everywhere exhibits, to secure domestic tranquility, and partly in policy, to discourage illicit commerce betwixt the sexes. If a bastard might inherit either to his father or his mother, where they had married, and had a family of children, it might be a real source of domestic uneasiness."[9]

But a rising inclination to protect the welfare of illegitimate children eroded the legal barriers. The penalties of bastardy were diminished by narrowing the legal domain of illegitimacy, creating new means of legitimating baseborn children, and giving bastards their first substantive legal rights as family members. This occurred at the dawn of the nineteenth century, a period during which, historian Daniel Scott Smith argues, bastardy declined and the nation experienced "strikingly low illegitimacy ratios." For this and other reasons, then, the pain of bastardy was eased in the new republic.[10]

Reducing the Chances of Becoming or Staying a Bastard

A strong reluctance to stigmatize children as illegitimate pervaded post-Revolutionary family law and helped instigate the changes in bastardy law. This sentiment found a number of expressions, from the use of liberal marriage rules to the adoption of simple methods of legitimation.

By accepting the validity of irregular unions, especially by creating common-law marriage, the courts greatly diminished the likelihood of children being branded as baseborn. The two policies complemented one another; indeed, a recurrent attraction of common law marriage was the prevention of illegitimacy. In an 1829 decision Supreme Court Justice Joseph Story declared: "It is well known that in cases of pedigree, the rules of the law have been relaxed in respect to evidence, to an extent far beyond what has been applied to other cases. This relaxation is founded upon principles of convenience and necessity." As in matrimony, the lack of reliable records, the informal legal habits of the citizenry, and the conflicting laws and customs of the populace encouraged the bench to adopt liberal evidentiary standards. The role of juries in these disputes, a Pennsylvania judge urged, was to "make every intendment in favor of plaintiff's legitimacy, which was not necessarily excluded by proof."[11]

The judiciary's disinclination to use marriage law to bastardize children was also in an English legal tradition that prized family integrity over domestic affection. The English had a body of rules that made it extremely difficult to bastardize the child of a married woman. Under the early common law, only uncontroverted proof that a husband had no sexual access to his wife prior to the child's birth could rebut the presumption of legitimacy. According to Blackstone, nonaccess could be established only if the husband had been "out of the kingdom of England, or, as the law somewhat loosely phrased it, *extra quatuor maria* [beyond the four seas], for above nine months, so that no access to his wife can be presumed, her issue shall be bastards." This meant that mere evidence of a husband's absence could not be used to bastardize a child born to his wife. In the agonizing conflict between a man's right to limit his paternity only to his actual offspring and the right of a child born to a married woman to claim family membership, the common law, first in England and then in America, generally made paternal rights defer to the larger goal of preserving family integrity.[12]

Judges in both nations gradually widened the acceptable range of evidence that could be offered by spouses, and placed restraints on the "four seas rule." But the law retained a strong bias against ruling the children of married women illegitimate. Particularly in an age before blood tests, the difficulty of proving paternity, and the presumption of legitimacy granted children born in wedlock, meant that the judicial refusal to allow a married couple to testify on the question reinforced both ends of bastardy law. It protected children from illegitimacy and helped local officials guard their purses. As another Pennsylvania tribunal candidly admitted in 1857: "It is true that the same reasons are not always given for the rule. In some of the cases it is said to be founded upon the question of interest, and in others upon a question of policy; but whatever may be the reason for the rule, whether good, bad, or indifferent, the rule itself is an inflexible one, and in no event can the wife be permitted to prove the non-access of her husband." Adulterine bastardy stood condemned as one of the most reprehensible acts a wife could commit, but her punishment remained separate from that of her child. As a Virginia judge noted in 1811, the bench "only tolerates an inquiry going to show that the husband could not possibly have been the father."[13]

In a complementary action, legislators declared the offspring of annulled marriages to be legitimate. Under the common law an annulment not only severed marital bonds but, by treating the union as if it had not existed, bastardized the children produced by the couple. American lawmakers began to reject that policy and follow the more benign civil-law doctrine of putative marriage, which granted legitimacy to the children of parents who had wed unaware that an impediment existed to their union. American legislation, contrary to the common law, proceeded from the conviction that the parents' sins should not be visited on the innocent issue, a bastardy-law variation of the republican creed of individual rights and responsibilities.[14]

The character of the change is evident in post-Revolutionary Virginia. A pathbreaking 1785 statute legitimated the offspring of voided marriage. Part of a general republican revision of the state code, directed by Thomas Jefferson among others, the law passed judicial scrutiny in the 1804 case of *Stones* v. *Keeling*. In his opinion, St. George Tucker, who had included the new rule on annulled marriages in his Americanized edition of Blackstone a few years before, endorsed the deviation from the common law.

The case concerned William Keeling who, before the passage of the 1785 act, had wed Arthalia Arbuckle while her former husband from an annulled marriage was still living. The Keelings had two daughters; William had had a son from a first marriage. Keeling died after his son. An inheritance fight then broke out between the daughters and his son's widow, centering on the legitimacy of the two girls. To Tucker the daughters' plight was "a strong case to show the sense of the legislature, that the turpitude, or guilt of the marriage, should not break upon the heads of their innocent offspring." He rejoiced that "the general policy of our law" proved to be "much more favourable to bastards, than the law of England." Tucker dismissed the contention of the widow's attorney that the act only encouraged bigamy and reduced the inducement to marry. As did other advocates of change in bastardy law, Tucker insisted that the fate of the parents and their children be treated separately. This jurist, a committed republican, argued that the "legislature certainly meant not to encourage fornication, or incestuous marriages, and yet it has expressly legitimated the offspring of both."

Tucker's endorsement had one major caveat. Once again racism limited family-law reform. In response to an assertion that the statute would legitimate the children of a void interracial marriage, he assured his fellow white citizens that the racially blind terms of the new law were to be "construed and understood in relation only to those persons to whom that law relates; and not to a class of persons clearly not within the idea of the legislature when contemplating the subjects of marriage and legitimacy."[15]

The Virginia statute and Tucker's opinion set a pattern for the liberalization of bastardy law throughout the nation. Some states, such as Kentucky in 1796, simply enacted the Virginia statute *in toto*; in others change resulted from the more complex process of legal diffusion, the spread of innovations from one jurisdiction to another that occurred in other areas of the law as well. And since the acts were in derogation of the common law, judges often construed them strictly.

The legislation thus varied from state to state. Most acts included annulments for causes such as fraud, but differences persisted in applying the reform to the children of incestuous or bigamous unions. And, as Tucker had suggested, in states where interracial marriages were banned, the offspring of dissolved unions that had crossed the color line remained bastards.

But the desire to temper the severity of the law by legitimating the children of annulled marriages triumphed in more and more statehouses and courtrooms. The Texas Supreme Court captured the child-centered, individualistic spirit of the change in an 1850 ruling: "[T]he rights of the children do not depend on the legality or illegality of the marriage of the parents. If there be a crime, if there be an offense against the laws in such marriages, they are considered unconscious of the guilt, and not the proper subject for the infliction of its retributive consequences."[16]

In an even sharper break with English legal tradition, post-Revolutionary legislatures legitimated children born unequivocally out of wedlock. Disavowing the English reliance on blood and matrimony as the sole sources of parenthood, they revised bastardy law in light of republican attitudes toward the family. The statutes indicate a legislative inclination to create new relationships and roles that often acted in tandem with judicial innovation. From that convergence came legislation that created the first of several alternative methods of family formation beyond the traditional use of private legislative acts of adoption; legitimate birth thus ceased to be the only path by which a child could legally enter a family.

Given the liberty to reevaluate existing policies, American lawmakers reversed the decision of the English barons at Merton and adopted the civil-law proposition that the subsequent marriage of its parents legitimated a child. Virginians did so first in the pioneering 1785 statute, which included the declaration: "where a man, having by a woman one or more children, shall afterwards intermarry with such woman, such child or children, if recognized by him, shall be thereby legitimated." Louisiana, the first former civil-law colony to enter the union, merely continued the continental practice.

The new policy spread slowly. In his 1823 *Abridgement of American Law*, Nathan Dane acknowledged the existence of the new approach, but reported that the common law still prevailed in "our states generally." The jurisdictions that clung to the older policy of using bastardy law to enforce sexual morality took heart, no doubt, from the remark in Chancellor Kent's *Commentaries* that "a recent traveller, of great intelligence and of a high moral tone considers that legitimation of bastards by the subsequent marriage of the parents, as of a very immoral tendency, and an encouragement to the increase of spurious issue."[17]

Increasingly, though, such traditional arguments fell before denunciations of the common-law policy as an aristocratic, property-conscious English view by which a heartless monetary interest in maintaining established lines of descent overruled compassion and common sense. Timothy Walker, for one, considered that the "justice and humanity" of the new acts "cannot fail to strike every mind." He dismissed the common law as "cruel and unreasonable" because it visited "the sins of the parents upon the unoffending offspring of their unlawful intercourse." This law reformer from Cincinnati held up the civil law as "wise and humane" because it gave "to such parents the strongest of motives to repair, by subsequent marriage, the wrong they will otherwise have done." To Walker, and many others, "such improvements in the law cannot be too much commended, cannot fail to purge the law of a multitude of doctrines unsuited to the present state of civilization."[18]

Matrimony offered the simplest and most socially acceptable method of legitimating children. But legislatures, in their zeal to protect children from the disabilities of bastardy, began to authorize other means as well. Once again civil and common law provided conflicting strategies. Under the common law only a special act of Parliament could legitimate a child. Like divorce and other forms of family change through legislative petition, it was expensive, difficult, and rare. In both England and America the process reflected a continuing uneasiness with the thought of creating family bonds between a child and a father who would not or could not wed its mother. Spanish civil law, in a far simpler procedure, granted fathers the right to legitimize their bastard offspring by a notarial act. Though the civil law revealed the biases of its creators by excluding adulterine bastards from its benefits, it did allow a father to acknowledge his illegitimate children without fear of disrupting established domestic arrangements or forming new ones. Moreover, it demonstrated a much greater willingness than the common law to separate legal status from property rights. Precursors of legalized adoption, these private acts were the first procedures available to create nonmatrimonial but legally binding family ties.

As befitted their legal heritage, common-law states initially followed the English model, while states that had formerly been civil-law colonies utilized the civil-law procedure. But unlike most areas of commercial and even family law, the civil law edged out its English competitor as private acts gave way to administrative procedures for legitimation (much as they did in divorce and incorporation). An 1858 Wisconsin statute stipulated that "every illegitimate child shall be considered the heir of the person who shall, in writing, signed in the presence of a competent witness, have acknowledged himself to be the father of such child."[19]

When this statutory creation, the legitimated bastard, demanded not merely a place at the hearth but also a share of the family estate, litigation ensued. Such a plea set against each other two of the deepest commitments of the post-Revolutionary bench: the private use and distribution of property, and the promotion of child welfare through family membership.

Judges were extremely cautious in allowing bastardy reform to upset an existing scheme of family inheritance. When the evidence clearly indicated a man's desire to legitimate his illegitimate child, the courts generally aided his intentions. Judges appeared to be particularly sympathetic to children legitimated by their parents' weddings. Tucker, in an 1805 appellate decision, sustained the inheritance rights of Henry Sleigh, who had been legitimated by the marriage of his parents and his father's acknowledgment two years after his birth. Ruling that the act applied to all children whether their parents had wed before or after its passage, Tucker concluded that the 1785 statute had meant "not only to encourage marriages after the passing of the law, but to protect and provide for the innocent offspring of indiscrete parents, who had already made all atonement in their power, for their misconduct, by putting the children, who the father recognized as his own, on the same footing as if born in wedlock."[20]

Private legislative acts of legitimation, however, often drew judicial inquiries. In 1835 the Tennessee Supreme Court was called upon to consider an inheritance claim based on a private act that decreed that Robert Searcy "shall in all respects, both in law and equity, be upon an equal footing with the other children." Justice Jacob Peck expressed reservations as to the procedure: "Such partial and limited legislation, not intended to give a general rule by which a whole community shall be governed, but passed with a view to a special case, has generally been looked upon with suspicion." He suggested that the terms of the act seemed too broad "to create in the illegitimate child an inheritable quality; a quality which takes away a portion of the rights of the heirs proper [of the father] by dividing the estate with the illegitimate child." He accepted the contention of the legitimate children's counsel that "if it is permitted men to adopt into the family by act of assembly, children of pleasure, it may follow that such orphans may be thus adopted, and their estates become partible between different families, or go to the foster father of his children, in exclusion of actual brothers and sisters, or other blood relations on whom the law casts the estates." Peck's decision echoed the common law's age-old determination to protect property rights by maintaining illegitimacy as a legally valid form of discrimination.[21]

Since many of the private acts legitimating children were poorly drafted and vague in the rights they conferred, Peck's reaction was not uncommon. But as the new family member became a more common legal personality, the courts became more accommodating. Twenty years after Peck's ruling, the Tennessee Supreme Court upheld the inheritance rights of legitimated children. In *Swanson* v. *Swanson* (1855), the progeny of a man who had legitimated his four bastard children, two by legislative act and two by formal written petitions, fought over his estate. Both procedures had specifically included inheritance rights. Acknowledging that the "severity of the common law, in its condemnation of the policy of legitimation, has been a good deal relaxed in several of the American states," the Tennessee court held that the "legitimation of persons born out of wedlock, is to be regarded, then, not only as a settled, but, likewise, as rather a favored policy, in the legislation of this and other states of the union." Consequently, the courts "in the exposition of the statutes conferring this right, whether they be general or private acts, are to give them at least a fair and reasonable, if not a liberal construction." The bench in Tennessee and other states slowly accepted the creation of legal but, by traditional common-law standards, artificial families.[22]

The Creation of a Bastard Family

If a bastard could not gain entrance to the father's family, then the child dwelt in a kind of legal purgatory, "as if he were dead and his relatives had never existed."[23] The illegitimate child's only "rights" were to support from the poor-law authorities, and to the customary practice of being left in the care of its mother for its first years of life. In a fundamental legal departure, republican bastardy law lessened these disabilities by creating a new legal household and binding it together with inheritance rights. It did so by turning the customary bonds between the bastard and its mother into a web of reciprocal legal rights and duties.

The judiciary began the change by supporting the right of mothers to the custody of their children born out of wedlock. Paternalistic English law granted fathers the custody of all legitimate children; it simply assumed that illegitimate offspring were outside of the legitimate patriarchal household and thus of custody law. In his 1810 digest of the law of evidence, Zephaniah Swift described the ambiguous status of illegitimates: "Though in legal contemplation a bastard has no relations, yet his mother is considered his natural guardian, has the custody and control of him, and is bound to educate and maintain him. In a moral view, he is considered the child of his mother, so far as their intermarriage would be unlawful, and sexual intercourse between them unlawful. The putative father has no power or control." Ignoring the confused and conflicting decisions and dicta on the subject in English reports, American judges in the first decades after the Revolution expanded maternal legal rights in an effort to enhance the welfare of illegitimate children.[24]

Mothers' custodial rights over their illegitimate children grew out of legal disputes between the parents. Writs of *habeas corpus* issued at the insistence of one parent charging his or her former lover with illegally detaining the child made the problem a legal issue. Under the legal fiction that such detention amounted to imprisonment, judges wielded the discretionary authority to decide which parent had the valid claim.

Two widely cited decisions in the first decade of the nineteenth century helped establish the maternal right. The custody of Charles Wright stood at issue in the 1806 Massachusetts case of *Wright* v. *Wright*. His parents married after his birth, but in Massachusetts the wedding did not then make him legitimate. After their divorce, Charles's mother kept the boy. She later remarried and Charles's father filed a writ *de homine replegiando* [recovering a man]. Losing in the lower courts, Paul Wright appealed. His counsel argued that "no difference" existed between the case of Charles and "that of legitimate children, who always remain in the custody of the father after a divorce."

Justices Samuel Sewell, Theodore Sedgwick, and Chief Justice Theophilus Parsons rejected that assertion in *seriatum* opinions. Sedgwick asserted that the "marriage of the natural parents gave to the husband, in a certain degree, a right to the custody of the child. But the divorce, which dissolved the marriage, annulled that right, and the child remained with the mother in the same manner, and under the same right as before the marriage." Parsons concurred, arguing that in "legal contemplation, a bastard is generally considered as the relative of no one. But to provide for his support and education, the mother has a right to the custody and control of him, and is bound to maintain him, as his natural guardian." The chief justice supported that contention, observing that the law recognized that family bonds existed between the two when it imposed the incest ban on them. Without citing English precedents, the court ruled that the maternal duty of support created the same right to the custody of illegitimate children as comparable paternal responsibilities did to legitimate ones.[25]

A year later, the New York courts, facing a similar dispute, issued an even more emphatic endorsement of maternal rights. A man claimed that the mother and stepfather of his illegitimate nine-year-old daughter had been mistreating her. He relied on English decisions supporting the primacy of paternal custody rights, particularly after a child passed the seven-year-old age of nurture. His former lover denied the charges of abuse, and cited other English precedents rejecting the custody demands of fathers. Reviewing the issuance of a writ of *habeas corpus*, the judges ruled that "the only question before the court is who has the legal right to the child." They answered their query with an admittedly pragmatic interpretation of the law that combined the new republican faith in maternal care with a typical post-Revolutionary assertion of judicial authority over the allocation of domestic rights: "[I]n the case of illegitimate children, and especially as to females, the mother appears to us to be the best entitled to the custody of them; but this right is not of such a nature as to prevent the court from interfering to take the infant from the custody of the mother, under special circumstances of ill-treatment." Finding no evidence of abuse, they dismissed the writ and in so doing cemented an identification of maternal legal rights with child welfare and judicial descretion that remained intact for much of the rest of the century.[26]

The policy won the support of most state courts in the new republic. Kent's *Commentaries* nationalized the rule by portraying maternal preference as an uncontroverted doctrine of American common law. The Chancellor simply explained that the mother of a bastard "has a right to the custody and control of it as against the putative father, and is bound to maintain and support it as its natural guardian; though perhaps the putative father might assert a right to the custody as against a stranger."[27]

The formal conferral of custody rights on mothers with illegitimate children won widespread support because it wove together three fundamental beliefs of the post-Revolutionary bench. First, as Parsons noted, the common law traditionally used correlative duties and privileges to bind families together. Since both nature and the poor laws attached the bastard to its mother, judges concluded that the mother deserved commensurate rights.

Second, maternal preference found its origins in the "cult of domesticity" that pervaded nineteenth-century American culture. These sentiments put immense pressure on legal authorities to place children with their mothers whenever possible. Though women always had been saddled with child care, antebellum legal and social thought so thoroughly and single-mindedly linked women with domesticity—indeed confused womanhood with motherhood—that motherhood became a weapon, a double-edged one perhaps, to secure legal rights such as custody. Always qualified by the degree to which a woman fit the society's model of a proper mother, these sentiments strengthened the claims of unmarried women in custody fights. Ironically, the thoroughly paternalistic English judiciary assisted by providing the clear, if sometimes ignored, policy that children under seven belonged with their mothers. The woman's maternal instinct, judges argued, tilted the scales of justice in her favor.

Finally, new ideas about child welfare reinforced the judicial preference for maternal custody. The legal authority for this was an unlikely source, a repudiated opinion of the English commercial-law reformer Lord Mansfield. In *Rex* v. *Delaval* (1763), a dispute over the custody of a seduced eighteen-year-old female apprentice, Mansfield ruled that a writ of *habeas corpus* bound the courts "*ex debito justitiae* to set infants free from improper restraint; but they are not bound to deliver them over to anybody nor give them any privilege. This must be left to their discretion according to the circumstances that shall appear before them."

American judges used this broad discretionary power to settle custody battles according to their determination of child welfare.

Most fully elaborated in custody decisions involving legitimate children and reduced to common-law shorthand as the "best-interests-of-the-child doctrine," the new rule was also applied in custody cases involving illegitimate children. After citing the *Delaval* opinion, a New York judge in 1849 explained the judicial calculation used to determine custody. He stressed that in "making such election for the child, its welfare is chiefly, if not exclusively to be had in view. The rights of parental authority are to be regarded no farther than they are consistent with the best good of the child." Custody disputes in the new republic thus became discretionary hearings in which the judge balanced the newly recognized legal rights of the mother against his assessment of the needs of her child. This legal framework encouraged mothers and fathers to hurl charges and countercharges of neglect, abandonment, and abuse against each other. The bench settled the contests by abrogating to itself the discretion to decide a child's future. Maternal rights prevailed unless a clear case of unfitness could be proven against the mother.[28]

These changes in custody law primarily aided those mothers who could support their offspring. However, other post-Revolutionary modifications of the common law did ameliorate somewhat the plight of poor women. According to early English poor laws and the common law, a bastard's place of settlement was the town where he or she was born, since illegitimates belonged to no legally recognized household. If the mother was a transient, poor-law officials could separate the pair by ordering the child to stay in the parish of its birth and sending the mother back to her place of settlement. American statutes changed this settlement policy.

The Connecticut Supreme Court faced a dispute between the towns of Canaan and Salisbury over the support of a pauper and her bastard child in 1790. It decided that although "by the laws of England, a bastard is settled where born, unless the mother is illegally thrust out; yet by the laws of this state a bastard is settled with the mother, and this is agreeable to the law of nature and reason." Twenty-five years later, a Massachusetts ruling related the settlement laws to the newly created family unit of a mother and her illegitimate children. In a support suit between the towns of Petersham and Dana, Chief Justice Parker used the *Wright* opinion to argue that since the mother of a bastard child had "the rightful custody of his person, and that she is bound to support and maintain him, he is of course part of her family, wherever she may go. A provision of the legislature, therefore, that his settlement shall be the same as hers, until he makes one for himself, is in no degree inconsistent with the relation, by our law, subsisting between a mother and her illegitimate child." Kent added the rule to his *Commentaries* as yet another example of the relaxation of bastardy law and of the law's commitment to keeping families together.[29]

Nevertheless, the legal rights of an impoverished mother with illegitimate children continued to be precarious, as they were for all paupers in a society that abhorred, feared, and penalized dependency. The legislature could at any time enlarge or revoke those prerogatives, and judicial discretion could whittle them down. Eventually most states adopted the new settlement provisions. But until they did so, wandering, indigent mothers could lose their children. An Ohio woman did in 1832 when the State Supreme Court blocked her attempt to retrieve her child from poor law authorities in Chagrin after her marriage and move to Bloomfield. In resolving the fiscal fight at the center of this and other settlement disputes, the courts balanced children's needs with taxpayers' concerns. Moreover, once a child passed the age of nurture maternal custodial rights were subject to the demands of local fiscal needs. Bastards, like other poor youths, were apprenticed to get them off the public rolls. Maternal rights and child welfare did make inroads into the poor law of bastardy, but in general, solvent mothers probably benefitted more from the new legal protections than did their less fortunate sisters.[30]

The new domestic unit of mother and illegitimate offspring also found legal support in inheritance, an age-old common-law method of uniting parents and children. For property-conscious common lawyers, inheritance cemented domestic bonds by creating a common interest in preserving the family heritage and resources. Not surprisingly, the English attempt to discourage illegitimacy and premarital intercourse included a denial of inheritance rights to bastards. Blackstone pointed approvingly to that stance as a significant difference between the common and the civil law. On the continent, he noted, "a bastard was likewise capable of succeeding to the whole of his mother's estate, although she was never married; the mother being sufficiently certain, though the father is not. But our law, in favor of marriage, is much less indulgent to bastards." In post-Revolutionary America the attraction of what appeared to be the humane, but not indulgent, civil law encouraged states to repudiate English policy as feudal, aristocratic, and antidemocratic.[31]

Once again Virginia's 1785 statute led the way. That act formally decreed that bastards "shall be capable of inheriting or transmitting inheritance on the part of their mother, in like manner as if they had been lawfully begotten of such mother." This change, perhaps more than any other in the state's bastardy law, reflects the republican nature of the revisions. As historian Stanley Katz has argued persuasively, the reform in Virginia's inheritance laws in the 1770s and 1780s blended natural rights theory and legal positivism in pursuit of a more equalitarian method of family property distribution. In an assessment of the statutory changes which not only aided bastards but officially renounced primogeniture and entail, Jefferson explained their larger implications:

> I consider these 4 bills . . . as forming a system by which every fibre would be eradicated of antient [sic] or future aristocracy; and a foundation laid for a government truly republican. The repeal of the laws of entail would prevent the accumulation and perpetuation of wealth in select families, and preserve the soil of the country from being daily more & more absorbed in Mortmain. The abolition of primogeniture, and equal partition of inheritances removed the feudal and unnatural distinctions which made one member of every family rich, and all the rest poor, substituting equal partition, the best of all Agrarian laws.

Similarly, the legislature in post-Revolutionary Delaware prefaced an act rescinding the double share granted to the eldest son with the declaration that "it is the duty and policy of every republican government to preserve equality amongst its citizens, by maintaining the balance of property as far as it is consistent with the rights of the individual." The search for such a balance of egalitarianism and individual liberty ensured the inclusion of bastards in the inheritance reforms. Though illegitimate children never achieved the inheritance rights of legitimate offspring, the barriers keeping them outside a legally recognized family began to crumble.[32]

By the 1830s Kent reported that thirteen states had joined Virginia in modifying their inheritance laws to aid bastards: Vermont, Connecticut, New York, North Carolina, Alabama, Georgia, Tennessee, Kentucky, Louisiana, Missouri, Indiana, Ohio, and Illinois. By mid-century, Massachusetts, Texas, and Maryland had joined them. These statutes established direct lines of inheritance between the mother and her illegitimate child. But their provisions varied widely.

Many, like those of Virginia, appeared to elevate the bastard to the legal position of the woman's legitimate children. But others contained more restrictions. The laws of Georgia and New York, for example, allowed the child's uncles and aunts to be its heirs only if it died without others in its line of descent. New York also granted an illegitimate child the right to claim his or her mother's estate only if the child had no legitimate heirs who could later demand the property. The Massachusetts act stipulated that the bastard could not "claim, as representing his mother, any part of the estates of her kindred, either lineal or collateral." In the former civil-law province of Louisiana, the illegitimate offspring of adulterous or incestuous unions failed to gain inheritance rights, and other bastards had to be recognized by their mothers before they could inherit.[33]

Thus even though those born out of wedlock gradually won the right to become their mother's heirs, federalism spawned variety, and most legislatures refused to eliminate completely the inheritance disabilities of these children.

Judicial interpretations of the laws reveal a similar constrained liberalism. Unprecedented modifications of the common law compelled judges to stake out the boundaries of maternal descent. State courts differed over the right of the mother to claim the inheritance of their illegitimate issue, and over the status of similar claims by her lineal and collateral heirs. The judiciary's cautious approach was expressed by the highest court of the land. In 1820 the staunch Federalist Justice Bushrod Washington interpreted the pioneering Virginia statute in *Stevenson's Heirs* v. *Sullivan* to mean that bastards could not inherit from their siblings and mothers could not claim the estates of their illegitimate issue. Despite the reforms, he insisted that illegitimate children remained "bastards." They have "neither father, brother, or sister." The only alteration in their rights he conceded was the claim on maternal estates obviously prescribed by the act. Beyond that, bastards remained outside their mothers' families.[34]

Washington's opinion was but one of a number of decisions qualifying the new inheritance laws. The same year Justice Ruffin of North Carolina held that legitimate children could inherit the estates of their mothers' bastard children, but that the illegitimate siblings had no such reciprocal rights. He argued on quite practical grounds that it was "manifest, that the moral and political considerations which exclude bastards from the succession to the mother, when there is legitimate issue, have no force to exclude the legitimate from succession to a bastard brother." Eleven years later the Ohio Supreme Court, citing the *Stevenson* decision, ruled that a mother's collateral heirs had no claim on the estate of her illegitimate child. And in 1849 a Maryland tribunal decided that a mother could not inherit her illegitimate son's estate. The justices contended that the legislative revision of the common law giving bastards the right to inherit as if born lawfully in wedlock accrued to their benefit only: "[T]o permit her to share in the distribution, unless it be within the express terms of the act, would be to sanction, not discourage illicit connections."[35]

But Connecticut Supreme Court decisions granting bastards inheritance rights by judicial fiat rather than legislative act suggest an alternative judicial disposition. In *Brown* v. *Dye* (1795), the court awarded an illegitimate child the estate of her legitimate half-brother who had died intestate and without other heirs. The court supported its determination by arguing that the common law of England, "which has been urged in this case, is not to be mentioned as an authority in opposition to the positive law of our state, and nothing can be more unjust than that the innocent offspring should be punished for the crimes of their parents by being deprived of their right of inheriting by the mother, when there doth not exist among men a relation so near and certain as that of mother and child." Later decisions in the state repeatedly confirmed and then enlarged upon the opinion to include all maternal family members. In 1825 one justice declared with proper judicial rectitude: "[I]t has been discovered in this state that a bastard is the child of his mother, and capable of inheriting estate and deriving settlement from her."[36]

Reeve and Kent endorsed Connecticut's stance as the proper exposition of American law.[37] The liberal view of bastard rights elicited judicial converts, most notably in 1837 when the Virginia Court of Appeals rejected the *Stevenson* decision. All three justices wrote lengthy opinions explaining their disagreements with the Supreme Court, Justice Tucker's being the most compelling.

He asserted that Bushrod Washington had misunderstood Virginia's post-Revolutionary spirit and cleaved too closely to the English common law. "After the termination of the revolution," he observed, "when a revision and radical change of much of our system of jurisprudence became indispensable, other counsels prevailed as to the law respecting bastards as well as in relation to inheritances generally." The elimination of primogeniture and the creation of inheritance rights for bastards became part of a republican legal code because "our law of descents was formed in no small degree upon the human affections; and the legislature very justly conceiving that the object of our laws of descent was to supply the want of a will, and that it should therefore conform in every case, as nearly as might be, to the probable current of those affections which would have given direction to the provisions of such will." The justices agreed that their legislative colleagues intended the bastard to become a member of the maternal family, sharing in property as well as in household affairs. The intent of the law, they concluded, had been to "abolish this distinction, to a certain extent, between legitimate and illegitimate children; and to endow the latter with inheritable blood on the part of the mother."[38]

The initial statutes and subsequent judicial decisions conferring family membership and property rights on illegitimate children laid the foundation for their distinct place in American family law. At a crucial period in the development of the new nation's governance of domestic relations, the illegitimate child began to have its own set of guaranteed rights and responsibilities. Legislators and judges carved out that place by using the welfare of the child and the rights of the mother to sever the link between punishment for sexual immorality and rights to family membership. Illegitimacy never ceased to blight children's lives. But bastards with the "good fortune" to be born to women able and willing to care for them were afforded unprecedented opportunities to escape some of the degradation of birth outside wedlock.

The Poor Laws Resist Change

Amid these reforms, the continuing legal disabilities of illegitimates and their parents cast light on the purposes of family law in its formative era. In particular, they reveal that the gradual relaxation of some of the most onerous forms of discrimination did not sever the longstanding connection between bastardy law and poor law. The use of illegitimacy to police sexual conduct did wane, but other traditional goals of the law remained. The opportunity to be legitimated or to enter the maternal family made it easier for illegitimates to commandeer parental aid, and thus relieved community resources of unwanted burdens. If parents could support their baseborn issue, then they could elude bastardy law; not so, however, those who, because of poverty, were dependent upon public aid.

Most significant, reform did not alter the basic character of bastardy proceedings. The preoccupation of these hearings with paternal support underscored the state's vital interest in fixing paternity upon some man and thus obtaining child support. Despite growing maternal rights, paternity hearings (as the name implies) continued to rest on the assumption that support was a male obligation, which the republican faith in domesticity only reinforced. Explicit legislation and established common law rules protected taxpayers more than children. There was little room for change or innovation.

Statutes, such as an Ohio 1805 act, relied on paternal support obligations to protect the state and its unwed mothers from the economic burden of rearing bastards. In doing so, bastardy laws held the community and the mother to be victims of male lust and irresponsibility. The Ohio legislature eliminated a woman's right to claim damages in an 1824 revision; but in that state, and most others, such changes merely clarified the status of putative fathers as debtors and criminals.

Paternity hearings, like their subject, were bastardized legal creations. Post-Revolutionary judges repeatedly insisted on classifying them as civil proceedings, but they retained the trappings of criminal trials because of their dual objectives of determining paternity and compelling support. A Kentucky man discovered the implications of this hybrid when the state supreme court rejected his plea that men arraigned on bastardy charges be granted the rights of defendants in a criminal trial. The judges informed him that "the case of bastardy cannot be considered as a criminal prosecution; nor the order for the maintenance of the child, in the nature of a criminal penalty." Instead they asserted the nineteenth century version of traditional paternalism: "[The] true object of the law seems to be, to enforce upon the unfeeling father, the performance of a natural duty for the easement and benefit of the mother, at whose instance the prosecution be instituted or carried on."[39]

Eight years later the Connecticut Supreme Court explained the changes underway in the law more fully. In contrast to the colonial era, there was "no public wrong . . . to be redressed; no offender punished; but a sum of money for the infant's maintenance is all which the statute contemplates." Thus in paternity suits, as Reeve accurately put it, "the object is wholly civil; but the proceedings are altogether in a criminal dress." As in breach-of-promise suits, this reorientation of the law helped secure convictions.[40]

The hybrid nature of bastardy proceedings eased the most vexing problem facing local authorities: identifying the father. The need to do so in order to secure child maintenance was balanced by recognition that men could easily be victimized by false paternity accusations and tenuous evidence. Colonials had treated a woman's accusation as tantamount to conviction. But this summary approach was less appealing in the rights conscious new republic.

Paternity hearings usually boiled down to accusatory battles between the former lovers. Though witnesses could offer evidence of the couple's general behavior and the child could be brought in to prove its resemblance to the father, most cases succeeded or failed on the testimony of the parties. Because they were considered civil proceedings, the woman merely had to establish a preponderance of the evidence in favor of paternity. The right of the parties to testify did, however, reflect a gradual change in the rights of litigants. In this suit, as in many others, the old common law prohibition of the testimony of interested parties faded away. The new conviction that justice demanded the presentation of all relevant information fueled the change.

The North Carolina legislature also expressed this new attitude toward litigants when in 1814 it modified a 1741 bastardy law to allow men the option of having a jury trial. Thirty-five years later, Justice Frederic Nash endorsed the change, but emphasized the precarious nature of a man's rights in such legal actions: "[Y]ou may, if you please, submit the question of your guilt to a jury, but if you do so, the burden of showing your innocence shall be on you; for the examination of the woman shall be sufficient to convict you, unless you show you are not the father of the child." By transforming paternity into an issue of fact to be determined by a jury, authorities had gone as far as they would in balancing paternal rights with community interests. Only the introduction of blood tests and other scientific procedures in the next century significantly altered these hearings.[41]

Men apprehended for fathering an illegitimate child could try to prove their innocence by contending that their accuser had given birth to the offspring of another man. But the judiciary's solicitude for wronged female virtue and their desire to affix financial responsibility severely limited this defense, much as it did in breach-of-promise suits. Judges normally excluded evidence of a woman's sexual behavior, as the Vermont Supreme Court did in 1832 when it barred the introduction of testimony that the plaintiff had been a prostitute. Such a defense, they declared, "supposes that none but prostitutes are found in this situation. This cannot be a correct supposition, undoubtedly some are seduced and ruined, with no connection with any but their seducer." Only clear proof that the woman had slept with another man around the time of conception convinced a jury to release a defendant.[42]

A criminal law approach to bastardy trials pervaded support provisions as well. Post-Revolutionary statutes either retained colonial procedures or made minor modifications to more easily apprehend men trying to elude paternity charges. All loopholes were plugged. Such was the case, to take the most extreme example, in an 1860 Maryland revision that created a special mechanism to allow sightless or speechless women to institute paternity hearings.[43]

Putative fathers found themselves subject to arrest, compulsory trials, detainment, and property restraints until they assumed support, with the economic condition of the mother serving as the main index of a man's liability. They were not compelled, however, to treat bastards as members of their households. The purpose of paternity trials, unlike that of bastardy-law reforms, was to relieve local taxpayers, not to alter the economic or social standing of the mother or her child.[44]

An 1845 Pennsylvania decision that accepted the legality of a private child-support bargain between the parents of an illegitimate child summarized early nineteenth-century bastardy proceedings. The decline of morality prosecutions for parenting a bastard freed women to make such pacts. Chief Justice John Bannister Gibson argued that a father's pledge of aid should be considered an equitable consideration for the mother's dropping paternity proceedings, even though provincial statutes had declared it illegal and void. He admitted that there had been "a time when fornication and bastardy stood on the foot of every other offense, and when an agreement to stifle the prosecution of it would have been an illegal consideration. Originally the principal object attempted by the punishment of it was the correction of the offender." But post-Revolutionary legislation reversed colonial practice. "Thus the offense, like assault and battery, with which it was associated in that statute, became little more than a private wrong; and when the legislature authorized the parties to treat it as such between themselves, the contract between them certainly became legal, so far as they were individually concerned." Thus the demise of illegitimacy proceedings as a means of directly enforcing sexual propriety resulted in streamlined procedures for protecting public coffers as well as enhanced legal protection of maternal rights and child welfare.[45]

New Rights

By the middle of the nineteenth century a new combination of interests held sway in bastardy law. It did so because illegitimate children had come to be considered less of a threat to social order, sexual morality, and domestic life, and more compelling objects of compassion. Post-Revolutionary legal authorities responded to an unstable mix of concerns for the public purse, child welfare, and maternal rights. The rights of the newly created family unit of mother and illegitimate child coexisted uneasily with the fiscal interests of local officials.

Bastardy law thus continued to be a tangle of legal and social contradictions. But it does illustrate some early nineteenth-century innovations that shaped American family law. Legislatures and courts not only formalized what had been customary rights, but also expanded those rights through creative legislation and judicial decisions. Imbued with post-Revolutionary America's increased respect for the individual, they enlarged the law's concept of a family to include the bastard and its mother, and revamped the common law to aid children who sought legitimacy. A new conviction was being woven into American family law: voluntarily assumed domestic relations provided the most secure foundation for family success.

Bastardy Law and the Process of Legal Diffusion

The changes in American bastardy law begun after the Revolution gradually spread across the nation. From their tenuous footholds in states such as Virginia, they entered the legislative codes of almost every jurisdiction. The central tenets of these innovations—the child's right to membership in a maternal-family network, the right of women to claim parental prerogatives when they bore illegitimate children, and state interest in the finances rather than the morals of putative fathers—became orthodoxy. Even amid the late nineteenth-century controversies over the family, they retained their appeal.

However, though no retreat or repudiation occurred, they represented the high point of bastardy-law innovation. Consolidation and refinement, not further reform, characterized late nineteenth-century bastardy law. The alterations had so thoroughly recast legal perceptions of illegitimacy that received tradition no longer provided sure guidance. Lawmakers now wrestled with their implications: just how far should the traditional common-law concept of bastardy be diluted and how extensively should illegitimate children be assimilated into paternal and maternal families?

The gradual diffusion of post-Revolutionary bastardy-law reforms through the American legal system is a graphic example of one of the salient features of late nineteenth-century family law, incremental development. As in many areas of the law, innovations became orthodoxies as they elicited the endorsement of increasing numbers of legislators, judges, and commentators. Consequently, their history became the vital but mundane story of refinement and consolidation; the zeal that infused the earlier era of reform is missing.

The unequivocal support given these revisions illustrates one aspect of the dynamics of family-law diffusion. From the vantage of 1900, Frank Fessenden recounted the transformation of illegitimacy in the *Harvard Law Review*: "Acts of legislation and judgments of courts abound in evidence of the zealous care which the public exercised over children. [These children] belong to the public no less than to the parents." Indeed the federal circuit court in New York had eight years earlier used an inheritance dispute to declare that the presumption of matrimony had been "indulged with special cogency when the legitimacy of the offspring is the issue of judgment."

Several states, California, Georgia, Oregon, Montana, Oklahoma, Louisiana, and the Dakotas among them, codified the presumption of legitimacy. Others stipulated that only one of the spouses or their descendants could challenge an offspring's pedigree, abrogating an old common-law rule granting anyone that right. Louisiana went the furthest and allowed a husband only a month or two after an infant's birth to deny paternity. The Illinois Supreme Court granted a legitimated woman her parents' estate, and then declared that the "presumption and charity of the law are in . . . the child's favor, and those who wish to bastardize him must make out the fact by clear and irrefragable proof. The presumption of law is not lightly repelled."[46]

But it was in the interstices of bastardy law that problems unresolved earlier in the century reemerged. Thus the doctrine that the child of a married woman could not be bastardized without overcoming immense difficulties continued to puzzle the architects of the law. Lord Mansfield's influential dictum had demanded that "decency, morality, and policy" preclude husbands and wives from bastardizing their issue by testifying as to their lack of sexual access. The Pennsylvania Supreme Court defended the doctrine in a pauper dispute: "Many reasons have been given for this rule. Prominent among them is the idea that the admission of such testimony would be unseemly and scandalous; and this, not so much from the fact that it reveals immoral conduct upon the part of the parents, as because of the effect it may have upon the child, who is in no fault, but who must nevertheless be the chief sufferer thereby. That the parents should be permitted to bastardize the child is a proposition which shocks our sense of right and decency." The Michigan Supreme Court, after barring the testimony of a woman who had been raped and whose husband had been too ill to engage in sexual intercourse, offered the consolation of Montesquieu's *The Spirit of the Laws*: "The wickedness of mankind makes it necessary for the laws to suppose them better than they really are. Thus we judge that every child conceived in wedlock is legitimate, the law having a confidence in the mother as if she were chastity itself." By continuing to deny married couples the most effective means of establishing the illegitimacy of a child, the courts placed child welfare above parental rights, thus ignoring the growing conviction of jurists that litigants had the right to present all evidence that supported their causes.[47]

Critics had attacked the doctrine barring spousal testimony on sexual access as inconsistent and unfair from the first days of the republic. John Wigmore, the late nineteenth century's reigning authority on the law of evidence, revived the dispute in his seminal treatise. He insisted that Lord Mansfield had created a doctrine without the aid of precedent, the perennial complaint of lawyers when policy is at issue. Wigmore argued that in bastardy cases, as in other litigation, all the pertinent facts should be admitted. He condemned as absurd and unwise the inability of married persons to compile and present the full evidence on the question of access. Wigmore contended that the rule allowed immorality and indecency under the pretext of preventing them: "The truth is that these high sounding 'decencies' and 'moralities' are mere phrasical afterthoughts, invented to explain an otherwise incomprehensible rule and there is just as little reason or policy to maintain it."

But Wigmore found few allies because such disputes pitted the rights and interests of family members against each other. Some courts did limit the doctrine's use, and the Kansas Supreme Court actually followed the law professor's advice and abolished it. But in turn-of-the-century America the doctrine still served the law's larger purposes of limiting bastardy.[48]

Concurrently, statutory methods devised early in the century to legitimate children appeared in more and more statute books. By 1900, over forty states pronounced legitimate the offspring of voided marriages or unions consummated after the child's birth. The gradual diffusion of the new methods of legitimation signalled the triumph of post-Revolutionary convictions that bastards should be bound to their natural parents and provided with a home and family rights whenever possible.[49]

Inheritance rights, however, remained a thorny issue. Statutes conferring such rights were complex, vague, and differed in significant details from state to state. Their complications reveal a continuing reluctance to confer on the bastard full rights to the paternal family's property unless the father had married the child's mother. In Nebraska, the most extreme case, not only did illicit couples have to wed but they had to bear additional children before their baseborn issue could inherit.

Judges expressed similar misgivings. In 1885, Mary Jane Owen had filed a claim in Wisconsin on her natural father's estate despite her mother's bigamous marriage. In a careful balancing of interests, the state supreme court commented that the legal power to ease the burdens of such children "is a very just and humane provision, and serves to mitigate somewhat the severity of the old law, which visited upon the children the sins of their parents." Only by dwelling on the innocence of the offspring could the courts (like their legislative colleagues) justify this invasion of family property.[50]

Judicial predispositions to aid bastards were put to the test most clearly in disputes arising from the rubble of slavery and the fight over Mormonism. Slave codes had declared the offspring of enslaved couples to be, in the awkward language of a Tennessee judge, "not legitimates." Reconstruction legislation validating customary slave unions legitimated the issue of such marriages. Legislators and judges proved as solicitous of the fate of emancipated children as they were of ex-slave husbands and wives. Here too, white Southerners acted out of a sense of equity as well as a conviction that the newly freed blacks would be best integrated into postwar Southern life by being legally grouped into families. And emancipated blacks grasped legal methods of legitimating their children as eagerly as they seized ways to sanctify their marriages.[51]

Southern courts, which handled most of these controversies, liberally construed the legitimation laws. They interpreted them as applying not only to the offspring of couples who had continued to live together as husband and wife after emancipation, but also to the children of slave unions in which one or both of the parties had died before acquiring their freedom. The Arkansas Supreme Court summarized judicial inclinations when granting a surviving sibling, whose paternity was disputed, the right to his deceased brother's estate. The father had died before emancipation, but the judges upheld the claim by relying on state acts legitimating the children of void marriages and validating slave marriages. Finding an early judicial disposition to "save the innocent offspring of void marriages from the inconvenience and odium of illegitimacy," the court contended that the language of the Reconstruction enactment was

> remedial in nature, and in the circumstances of which the court can take cognizance, it would be a very narrow, and exceedingly literal construction of this act to exclude from its scope those children, whose parents, although now dead, had cohabitated as husband and wife, and recognized them as their offspring. The act is not in derogation of the common law. It is in aid of it—applying its rules of inheritance to what was really a new people, amongst whom there had been formerly no marriages, no property, nor any rules of inheritance whatever. It had in view the complete homologation of all *legal* rights of all classes in the State, as distinct from *political* rights—the latter coming through the Federal constitution and acts of Congress.

Only when a slave couple had separated after emancipation did the courts hesitate to legitimate their children. According to the Alabama Supreme Court, the state's 1867 statute did not "and could not, legitimate offspring of the earlier and discontinued cohabitation, or import to them the capacity to the inheritance" of a man who later lived with a second wife.[52]

The courts were even more disposed to accept legislation allowing the subsequent marriage of parents because it removed the stain of bastardy from the offspring. An 1875 Maryland ruling upholding the estate claims of legitimated adulterine bastards typified the judicial integration into American family law of the new statutes removing children from the bastardy rolls. A father had parented six children in an adulterous affair. When his wife died, he married his mistress and acknowledged their offspring. The state supreme court ruled that "the main purpose and intent of the enactment we are now considering [first enacted in 1825], was to remove the taint and disabilities of bastardy from the unoffending children, whenever their parents did marry, without regard to the deepness of guilt on the part of the parents, in which they were conceived and born." Though children had to establish that their parents' marriages had occurred, the courts usually accorded them full family inheritance rights once they did so. That policy, the Maryland bench claimed, exhibited "a continual advancement, and a breaking away from those antiquated English maxims, in the direction of human progress and liberal thought." Equally important, the act of humanity did not upset settled lines of descent or create competing sets of heirs when parents atoned for their sins.[53]

Legal protection of the innocent offspring of illicit relations suffered a most severe test, though, when the children of polygamous Mormons claimed the new legal rights of legitimated bastards. They lost in anti-Mormon territorial courts, but found support from the United States Supreme Court.

A territorial act of 1852 had allowed illegitimate children acknowledged by their fathers to inherit paternal estates. In *Chapman v. Handley*, the territorial supreme court ruled that the provision violated the Edmunds Act because it tended to "support, maintain, and countenance polygamy" by lessening the penalties inflicted on the issue of second marriages. An attorney's plea that innocent children should not be punished for parental sins, usually so persuasive, went unheeded. Instead, the judges argued that "[it] must be understood that Congress was legislating against polygamy as an institution; that it intended to disapprove of all that tended to establish, support, countenance, or maintain it; sought to lessen and prevent injustice to illegitimate children by breaking up and destroying the system that applied to and produced them."

A sharp dissent attacking the majority for judicial law making and illogical argumentation also failed to move the majority but they did convince the United States Supreme Court. Writing for a unanimous court in an 1891 decision, *Cope v. Cope*, Justice Henry Billings Brown refused to treat the territorial act differently from similar state statutes:

> Legislation for the protection of children born in polygamy is not necessarily legislation favorable to polygamy. There is no inconsistency in shielding the one and in denouncing the other as a crime. It had never been supposed that the acts of the several States legitimating natural children, whose parents intermarry after their birth had the slightest tendency to shield or countenance illicit cohabitation, but they were rather designed to protect the unfortunate children of those who were willing to do all in their power to right a great wrong. So, if the act in question had been passed in any other jurisdiction, it would have been considered as a perfectly harmless, though perhaps indiscreet exercise of the legislative power, and would not be seriously claimed as a step toward the establishment of a polygamous system.

In response, the territorial court reversed its previous ruling. Congress was not so easily persuaded. It amended the Edmunds Act to eliminate the inheritance rights of polygamous children born after its implementation. Though those rights were restored in 1896 after the Mormons abandoned polygamy, this last struggle over the morality of legitimation reveals the persistence of traditional links between sexual morality and bastardy law. The fact that those states that had banned interracial marriage refused to legitimate the children of such unions merely confirms the pattern.[54]

The same process of gradual incorporation characterized the most innovative creation of post-Revolutionary bastardy-law reform, the newly legalized household of mother and illegitimate offspring. James Schouler proclaimed in 1870: "There is scarcely a State in the Union which has not departed widely from the policy of the English common law; and statutes, which happily have required as yet very little judicial interpretation, perpetuate the record of our liberal and generous public policy toward a class of beings who were once compelled to bear the inequities of the parent."

Reciprocal inheritance rights under the intestacy laws, the most common modification of the common law, were the strongest legal bonds between blood relations. By 1886 thirty-nine states and territories had granted bastards the right to share in maternal estates; by 1930 the number had risen to forty-nine. Though the acts varied, they generally treated the illegitimate child as if it had been born lawfully. But the state codes split almost evenly on the issue of allowing spurious children to share in the estates of their mothers' other kin. Though more and more legislatures took that step, continued resistance spoke of a widespread uneasiness about removing all the disabilities of bastardy.[55]

The judicial treatment was similar. An 1865 Pennsylvania decision upholding statutory changes made a decade earlier is illustrative. The state supreme court granted the right of two illegitimate children to share in their mother's estate along with their legitimate siblings. The justices asserted that birth in "wedlock is no longer the criterion, but blood relationship. The bastard and the lawful child now have a like capacity." They also shunted aside complaints that the legislative acts promoted sexual immorality and discouraged matrimony. The court publicly doubted that the law would cause illicit conduct and reminded its readers that the "fiery torrent of passion seldom stops to consider consequences." It concluded with a declaration of the law's moral legitimacy: "While the law leaves them the frown of society and bitterness of shame, it is unwilling to add beggary to their misery by refusing them a share in the property of that one parent who is often more sinned against than sinning, and whose mother's heart yearns toward the child of her misfortune."

As with most of the widely adopted bastardy-law reforms, this course posed little threat to established domestic property rights, since an illegitimate child likely to receive a legacy tended to remain with his mother and to be incorporated into her family. Similarly, further legislative revisions and judicial rulings allowed women and those of their bloodline, especially the bastard's siblings, to share in each others' estates. Nevertheless, vague legislation and cautious judicial opinions meant that the full inclusion of illegitimate children in the maternal legal family came very slowly.[56]

The gradual approach was evident in the courts' treatment of the other major legal instrument used to bind the mother to her illegitimate offspring: custody rights. The bench retained the right to make the delicate choice of child placement by relying on the broad discretionary powers granted it under the best-interests-of-the-child doctrine. Lewis Hochheimer, in an 1889 treatise on the law of *habeas corpus*, explained the logic of granting the courts what had traditionally been considered a patriarchal authority: "[N]o one is entitled to the possession as a matter of mere right or claim. The welfare and happiness of the child itself constitutes the paramount consideration in the determination of controversies affecting its custody." Statutory provisions codifying maternal custody rights to illegitimates were rare, as law professor Ernst Freund explained in 1919, "the assumption being that the mother will keep her child"—rare, too, because of the general reliance on the common-law courts to settle custody disputes. Consequently, as Hochheimer noted, "the power of courts, whether of law or of chancery to intervene in such cases is no less extensive than in the case of legitimate children."

The North Carolina Supreme Court in 1883 dogmatically set forth its own view of how those powers should be used: "As touching the right of custody of children, the doctrines of the common law have been greatly weakened of late, and courts pay less regard to the strict legal rights of parents, even than they were wont to do, and look more to the interests, moral and physical, of the infants themselves—making it, indeed, their paramount consideration." Supremely confident of their ability to make such determinations, judges ensured that the custodial rights granted to mothers of illegitimate children remained judicially supervised common-law preferences rather than legal prerogatives.[57]

Consequently, the appellate bench restricted itself to issuing general guidelines for assessing the interests of bastards, which were then applied by lower and trial courts case by case. The guidelines ordered tribunals to evaluate the fitness of potential custodians, as well as the child's age, health, sex, education, and prospects. The Nebraska Supreme Court summarized the law's priorities in 1891: "If the mother is dead, the court should, as far as possible, provide for the safety and welfare of the child. While in such case the father may be trusted with its nurture and care, if he was not a suitable person or should himself or others ill-treat the child during its minority, it would be the duty of the court to so modify the judgment that the amount due thereon for its support and maintenance should be paid to some person who would, in good faith, provide it with necessaries and a home." As with most discretionary rights, custodial ones could be lost through evidence of immoral or abusive conduct.[58]

Furthermore, parents who relied on poor relief for sustenance lost a significant portion of their custodial rights. Poor-law officials who furnished support often acquired the right to place the child where they saw fit. An Indiana statute, for example, authorized overseers of the poor to bind out as apprentices all poor children whose parents were dead or unable to maintain them. Protection of the taxpayers' pocketbooks reinforced the general conviction that proper child nurture required guardians capable of providing material support for their charges. As the Vermont Supreme Court asserted (without intentional irony), the illegitimate child "has the same rights as any pauper when its custody is shifted from one keeper to another." In this situation, as in many others within domestic relations, the law fostered a system of clashing individual rights and state interests that demanded judicial oversight and discretion.[59]

Bastardy proceedings themselves, however, continued to be immune from nineteenth-century reform. The suit's nature and purpose were described succinctly by Ohio lawyer William M. Rockel in the 1884 *Central Law Journal*: "The proceedings is entirely regulated by statutes in the different states, and nowhere is the mother criminally liable. These statutes are mere police regulations, enacted solely to prevent the maintenance of the bastard child from becoming a public charge. A majority of the decisions hold that the proceedings is a civil one, and that the rules of evidence governing civil actions are to be applied."[60] Bastardy suits still troubled local officials, but only because they continued to face the age-old problem of locating putative fathers and compelling them to support their spurious issue. That overriding concern stifled innovation.

Neither the virulent racism nor the repressive sexual beliefs of late nineteenth-century America deterred local authorities from seeking financial relief. An 1867 ruling of the Kentucky Supreme Court turned away an attempt by a black man to use his second-class citizenship as a shield in a bastardy complaint. He argued that from 1850 to 1866 only unmarried white women could instigate bastardy hearings, and that therefore the charge against him, filed at the insistence of a single black woman, must be thrown out. But the judges rebuffed his legal sophistry with their own, declaring that the object of the 1866 civil rights acts had been "to confer upon this recently liberated class comprehensive civil rights, not only against each other, but all classes and individuals, whilst it did secure more extended and perfect rights against individuals of their own race than against the white race." Such an application of the law ensured that racial discrimination would not unduly harm public budgets.[61]

Nor did female sexual misdeeds, otherwise so damaging to women, protect men in paternity suits. If a putative father proved that another man could have been the father of the disputed child he might be released, but common-law evidentiary rules and legal bias clearly continued to favor his accusor. Information about the woman's general sexual reputation remained inadmissible in bastardy proceedings despite changing views of sexual morality and women's culpability—alterations that had begun to undermine the favor with which the bench viewed women who filed breach-of-marriage-promise suits or demanded rights based on common-law marriages. Rather, the object of the law, Ohioan Rockel maintained, was "not to punish or reward the mother but it is to maintain the child, and in order to meet the full ends of the law the bastard child of a prostitute should be afforded the same protection as any other." He linked this exception to the law's general notion of female victimization: "A woman whose general reputation for chastity is good, is as likely to be the mother of a bastard as one whose reputation for chastity is unsavory. Experience has taught us that prostitutes seldom bear children and that the majority of unmarried women who become the mothers of children are those whose reputations have always been above suspicion."[62]

The same logic reinforced the legal assumption of paternal financial responsibility, and deflected demands for maternal support. The North Carolina Supreme Court in 1872 refused a man's contention that his former lover could afford to support their illicit infant with little aid from him. Admitting that the "mother may be rich and abundantly able to maintain the child," the justices nevertheless held that the "common law imposes no such liability on her, at least after the child passes the age of nurture, and the statute intended to impose that duty on the father, where it more properly belongs." The refusal to hold parents equally liable for support was now orthodoxy as was the conviction that men should be penalized as sexual predators and held accountable because of their assumed superior economic status.[63] Ernst Freund's 1919 description of American illegitimacy law would have been applicable a century earlier:

"It is apparent that the law of bastardy is controlled by standards of poor relief. In any event the alimony is measured by the mother's and not the father's position in life, and although the law may not express it that way, it is in the nature of an assistance to her."[64]

A New Drive to Reform Illegitimacy Law

Despite the legal changes of the nineteenth century, it became evident that a point existed beyond which the law would not be used to assist children born out of wedlock; indeed the post-1850 American obsession with improving family life reinvigorated the use of the law to separate illegitimate from legitimate offspring. When a call for further reductions in the disabilities of bastardy arose late in the century, the efforts of this new generation of reformers only served to underscore the persistent attraction of illegitimacy.

The reformers exposed the problem at the heart of bastardy law: whether the individual or the family was the unit to be protected by the law. Reformers, like most of those who tackled the issue, divided over the question. They struggled to find a way to aid these children without undermining the home as a social institution; a task many came to see as inherently contradictory. Their efforts led to a number of reform proposals, most of which relied on greater state intervention to alleviate the problems facing illegitimate children. As a result of this search for a delicate balance, the law continued to be an uneasy blend of individual rights granted bastards and special protections for the legitimate family.

The harrowing plight of pauper bastards in turn-of-the-century America, despite the diffusion of post-Revolutionary reforms, aroused the child-saving brigades of the family protection movement. They renewed the campaign to lessen the penalties of illegitimacy.

In 1882 the pioneer progressive social reformer Florence Kelley, then a student at Cornell, optimistically traced the century's legal progress: "The illegitimate child's position is somewhat modified by direct legislation; but, apart from the recognition by statute of his need and right to be in his mother's custody, and to have her responsible for his maintenance, his status improves with every growth of legislation touching children as individuals removed from the domestic relations and directly responsible to the State." She listed some of these improvements: equal treatment of illegitimate and legitimate paupers, training offered in the growing number of public schools, tightening restrictions on child labor, and prohibitions on buying liquor and obscene literature. Kelley added:"[S]o far is his condition assimilated to that of the legitimate child that the statement is now true that the chief legal disadvantage of the illegitimate child is his inability to inherit."[65]

Other reformers may not have been as sanguine as Kelley as to the improved condition of illegitimate children, but they shared her assumption that further reform for these and other young citizens rested on their recognition as autonomous individuals and their ability to establish separate relationships with the state. Some visionaries began to argue that only the abolition of the legal concept of bastardy itself could remove the stigma marking these innocent children. But most reformers recognized, as historian Morton Keller has suggested, that "the social and moral implications of illegitimacy were too unsettling to accord the child full rights." Once again, the belief that discriminatory laws reinforced legitimate families and deterred spurious birth inhibited reform efforts. The issue provoked a clash within the family-saving cadres.[66]

Investigation of the squalid cities of industrial America by muckrakers and progressive urban social reformers ignited the conflict anew. They uncovered shocking evidence of mistreatment and death among the nation's illegitimate waifs, higher rates of infant mortality among them than among lawfully born children, and a thriving market offering bastard children for sale and barter.

The new United States Children's Bureau estimated the magnitude of the problem in a 1915 survey. Approximately 32,400 illegitimate children were born that year, or about 1.8 percent of all live births. Other investigations demonstrated that most illegitimate children and their mothers faced the world with few resources beyond the meager aid provided under poor laws or by charities. The Bureau's 1914 examination of illegitimacy in Boston found that only 13 percent of illegitimate births resulted in paternity hearings and a mere 7 percent in actual maintenance awards. More disturbing, reformers in Chicago concluded that through abandonment and neglect fully a third of the known 3,000 illegitimate children born in 1914 had not survived their first year. Boston officials surmised that 60 percent of all bastards appeared on the rolls of public and private charities in their first year of life.[67]

In response to these frightening findings, as historian Susan Tiffin has argued in a survey of Progressive era child-saving activities, reformers turned to the judicially created "bastard family":

> [While] the normal family unit was considered ideal and reformers had no intention of undermining this structure by encouraging illegitimacy, they came to feel that it was possible to approximate the family unit by keeping mothers and babies together. Just as they encouraged widows and deserted wives to keep their families in-

tact, so they suggested that unmarried mothers should not give up their children. This, it was claimed, would benefit both the children, who need mother love, and the women, who would be helped to become respectable, responsible people.

One reformer, Kate Waller Barrett, made the point quite directly: "[I]f we cannot have the trinity which God intended—husband, wife, child— we can have the other trinity—mother, child, home—that has a mighty potency in it for good."

A minority of radical reformers demanded that bastards be accorded the same legal rights as legitimate children to ensure insofar as possible that they be cared for during childhood and trained for a productive future. Reformers were fired by the conviction that there "may be illegitimate parents but there can be no illegitimate children." These sentiments encouraged full use of the arsenal of progressive reform: national conferences, model legislation, reformist tracts and articles, local surveys, legislative lobbying, and popular propaganda.[68]

Scandinavian developments provided a further stimulus for change. Norway's epochal Children's Rights Law of 1915 advanced a coherent reform program. Among other things, the act decreed that upon a finding of paternity a child had the rights to both parents' names, to inherit from each of them and their kin, and to claim support and education from the parent granted custody. Less appealing to American sensibilities were provisions requiring mandatory paternity hearings and giving the child whose paternity was disputed the right to aid from all of the men who might have been its father. These smacked of excessive state coercion in a society that consistently balanced the public needs with defenses of private rights, usually deferring to the latter.

American reformers endorsed the act as a necessary first step in placing bastards on an equal footing with legitimate children. An editor of the 1915 *Columbia Law Review* proclaimed that the "Norwegian statute accomplishes in a direct manly way a much needed reform at which American courts and legislatures have hinted and connived, but to which they have not given their support." He reviewed the reforms that had spread across the nation during the nineteenth century, and concluded that "all these things are a tacit acknowledgment of the inexpedience and injustice of disposing of the bastard with the summary brutality of the common law." Dismissing contentions that discrimination against bastards promoted stable families, he maintained, that "[o]nly by holding parents strictly to account can promiscuous propagation be restrained by law; and only by granting to the unfortunate bastard the same rights against his progenitors to which his legitimate brother is entitled, can justice be done to him."[69] Philadelphia attorney W. Logan

McCloy agreed: "[There] would seem to be no just reason why, after a jury had adjudged a man to be the father, he should be allowed to escape all responsibility beyond the order of the court, while at the same time the child is limited to inheritance from the mother alone, a right which, in these cases, is usually of no practical significance whatever."[70]

Two states, Arizona and North Dakota, did adopt the Norwegian model, declaring all children the legitimate offspring of their natural parents and thus entitled to support and education as if they had been born in legal wedlock. But no other states followed suit; the limits of the reform movement had been reached.

The illegitimacy laws of most states continued to be characterized by solicitousness for putative fathers: safeguards against blackmail, and protection of paternal rights—minimal statutory levels of support, brief periods during which maternal claims could be pressed, and evidentiary constraints such as the North Dakota rule that mothers could not be sworn in as competent witnesses in the event of a father's death. Piecemeal reform of legislative codes did continue but, as one Maryland reformer admitted ruefully, "the interests of the state were still the motivating force behind the new provisions." In his state, the reforms, enacted in 1912, clearly had no intent other than relieving pressure on the public purse; the statute stipulated higher monthly support payments than previously demanded, raised from seven to twelve the ages of mandatory support, and transferred the responsibility of hospital care during confinement from the public to the father. Other states acted similarly.[71]

Perhaps the most successful reform was symbolic. Slowly the word "bastard" disappeared from statutes and legal proceedings; in its place came the milder phrase "child born out of wedlock."

New Protectors

The most profound changes in the fate of illegitimate children occurred neither in courtrooms nor legislative chambers, but rather through the gradual exertion of control over bastardy by social workers and welfare bureaucrats. Illegitimate children and their mothers had long been subjected to the supervision of poor-law officials, and impoverished bastards traditionally had been treated more as wards of the state than offspring of their parents. But that power had been used primarily to support and protect town coffers.

As welfare professionals took up the cudgel for these unfortunates, the policy objectives of bastardy law were called into question because their strategies of philanthropic intervention tended to rank the interests of individual children over those of the family as an institution, often at the expense of the parental rights. Berkeley Davis's sweeping declaration in "The Passing of Illegitimacy" is typical: "[T]he state has the obligation to inquire officially into the circumstances of the child's birth, to protect him against the greatest cruelty to which childhood can be exposed, the suffering which comes from not knowing its parentage." An official of the Children's Bureau also explained the social workers' mandate: "to hold paramount the welfare of the child born out of wedlock; to recognize the responsibility of the state for the protection of the rights and best interests of such a child; to consider it the duty of the state to afford better protection to the unmarried mother and to bring the father of her child to justice."[72]

Minnesota pioneered a new bureaucratic approach in 1917, creating a state board authorized to safeguard the interests of illegitimate children, establish paternity in disputed cases, and secure for the misbegotten the care received by the lawfully born. The statute also modified the common law to deny men a defense predicated on proof that the mother in question had engaged in sexual relations with other men around the time of conception. The act mandated paternal support for illegitimate children until the age of sixteen, in amounts left to judicial discretion, and authorized a minimum jail sentence of ninety days for men who violated paternity decrees.

This tough statutory language had little immediate impact. A 1924 study of illegitimacy in the state discovered that paternity actions had been instituted in only a third of known cases and court support orders issued in only a sixth. Even so, over half the fathers had failed to meet their obligations. Equally important, the act's intended aim of keeping the mother and child together had failed in many cases. Investigators determined that only 35 percent of the children studied in 1921 were still in their mother's custody by the time they reached their second birthdays. Other states established similar boards and encountered similar difficulties. Indeed, the reliance of social workers on adoption, foster homes, and severing natural bonds as necessary child-saving techniques exemplified a tension in bastardy policies themselves over the priority to be given individual or family interests.[73]

Professional social welfare was a house divided. Bastardy-law reform on the Scandinavian model threatened disruption of the autonomous family, America's bulwark against disorder. Many welfare reformers chose the family when confronted with a choice. Thus Bradley Hull, the agent of a Cleveland humane society, warned his colleagues in 1919: "I think that between the two, there should be an unmistakable preference shown for the marriage status. And I think entirely aside from the legal question, if you put the illegitimate child on a basis of equality with the child born of the man's wedded wife, there is a great source of danger." An indignant Minnesota delegate countered with the cry: "They are all children are they not?" But Hull would not give ground. He retorted: "Yes, but there is something more. The question is, is the child or the home to be the unit of the state? If you are going to make, as far as the economic basis is concerned, the status of the unmarried mother and her child equal to that of the married woman and her child, you are going to do something to unsettle society."[74]

Hull had laid bare one of the most profound issues in domestic relations, the conflict between using the law to support individual rights and to buttress the family as a separate institution. Uncertainty, an underlying fear that compulsory legitimation and equality for illegitimates would ultimately undermine paternal property rights and the family itself and encourage blackmail and sexual immorality, tilted the conference (and the law) in Hull's direction. Throughout the national debate over bastardy law, as in the complementary campaign to abolish common-law marriage, there ran a constant theme: the persistent willingness to sacrifice the interests of the illegitimate child to a majoritarian vision of society's larger needs. A New York court made the point explicitly in 1917: "Illegitimate children are not favored by law and have only such property rights as are expressly granted by statute."[75]

In the end, the continuities in nineteenth-century bastardy law were as important as the innovations. Emma O. Lundberg's 1926 assessment is both accurate and telling: "[I]n practically all states, up to the present time, it has been held incompatible with the interest of the legal family to place the child of illegitimate birth upon an equality with the children born in wedlock with respect to his claims upon the father."[76] By 1900 bastards had been freed from the disabling status of *filius nullius*. But the high regard in which nineteenth-century America held the legitimate fruits of matrimony underscores the uneasiness with which it confronted the issues of bastard rights and welfare. Ironically, the expanded rights granted legitimate children in the nineteenth century contributed to the plight of children born out of wedlock.

CUSTODY RIGHTS
WHO GETS THE CHILD?

The notable changes in legal rights of illegitimate children reveal one aspect of the republican recasting of the law of parent and child. Other elements emerged in the treatment meted out to legitimate children. Freed from the restraints imposed on bastardy law by concern over sexual immorality and rate-payer solvency, innovation in child custody was even more rapid and thorough. New custody standards gave republican domestic-relations law yet another opportunity to group individuals into proper families.

A difficult legal concept to define, child custody involved the right of a parent or someone acting as a parent to control a minor: a volatile mix of parental and filial interests, rights, and duties. Custody disputes arose after separation, divorce, death, or public intervention disrupted a family. Such disputes involved three main protagonists: one or both natural parents, a third party or the state, and the child. Out of their resolution in nineteenth-century American courtrooms came a novel custody law of which the highest priority was the child's interests as determined by the judiciary. In that law the bench took to its logical conclusion the republican vision of the family as a collection of individuals each with his or her own needs and rights.[1]

Alterations in custody law began in the formative era of domestic-relations law. As the focus of custody disputes became a nurture-based definition of child welfare, the traditional means of allocating child-rearing responsibilities were less and less acceptable. The declining appeal of apprenticeship and other traditional methods of placing out children and the rising concern for child welfare encouraged custody-law innovation.

The changes proceeded directly from the republican vision of the family. Post-Revolutionary Americans abandoned the hierarchical concept of the family that had dominated English common law and colonial practice. Concurrently, they displayed a new faith in women's innate proclivities for child rearing and in developmental notions of childhood. The impact of these changes on custody law was remarkable. Traditional paternalistic custody rules and practices disappeared; an entirely new standard of child placement took their place.

Prerepublican Anglo-American law granted fathers an almost unlimited right to the custody of their minor legitimate children. Moored in the medieval equation of legal rights with property ownership, it assumed that the interests of children were best protected by making the father the natural guardian and by using a property-based standard of parental fitness. Custody law held children to be dependent, subordinate beings, assets of estates in which fathers had a vested right. Their services, earnings, and the like became the property of their paternal masters in exchange for life and maintenance. Literary critic Jay Fliegelman summarized the stark reality of the traditional law of parent and child: "[T]he debt is owed nature not nurture."[2]

These assumptions lingered on in the new republic. The influential University of Maryland law professor David Hoffman explained the dual nature of paternal authority in his 1836 *Legal Outlines*. First was "the injunction imposed on parents by nature, of rearing, and carefully watching over the moral, religious, and physical education of their progeny, and the impracticality of advantageously discharging that duty, unless children yield implicit obedience to the dictates of parental concern, seeing that they are not of sufficient age and discretion to limit the measure of their submission or obedience." Second was "the presumed consent of the offspring." Hoffman explained the latter point:

> The parent shows himself ready, by the care and affection manifested to his child, to watch over him, and to supply all his wants, until he shall be able to provide them for himself. The child, on the other hand, receives these acts of kindness; a tacit compact between them is thus formed; the child engages, by acts equivalent to a positive undertaking, to submit to the care and judgment of his parent so long as the parent, and the manifest order of nature, shall coincide in requiring assistance and advice on the one side, and acceptance of them, and obedience and gratitude on the other.

Professor Hoffman also emphasized that these parental rights conferred authority primarily on the father:

> If parental power arose not in truth from these principles, but from some fancied property given to the parent in his offspring, by the

act of propagation, it would seem to follow, as a natural illation, that this authority would appertain in the largest degree to the mother, since she not only has the pains and deprivations incident to gestation and parturition, but is the principle sharer in the cares which succeed the birth. Yet it is the father who holds and exercises the principal authority. . . .

The mother, Blackstone had insisted several decades earlier, "was entitled to no power, but only to reverence and respect." Consequently, a husband had a paramount right to custody and also the power to appoint a testamentary guardian and thus extend his authority beyond the grave.[3]

Few inroads into the paternal bias of custody law had been made during the colonial period. The settlers' assumptions were traditional, as in the 1641 *Body of Liberty* of Massachusetts Bay: "No man shall be deprived of his wife or child . . . unless by virtue of some express law of the country established by the General Court and sufficiently published." However, paternal custody rights were never absolute and local courts always had the right to overrule them. It is also likely that many women gained the custody or guardianship of their children without specific legal justification. But the practices and customs that departed from English ways were not institutionalized.[4]

However modified by republican child-rearing beliefs, paternal power reigned supreme as long as a nineteenth-century American family remained together. But family disruptions allowed legal authorities to step in and reformulate child-custody procedures and priorities.

Their new approach to custody relied on two English innovations. During the contentious seventeenth century, when the crown was often accused of abusing feudal wardships, English chancery courts assumed increasing jurisdiction over the welfare and property of minors. They did so by expanding the old doctrine of *parens patriae*. Under it, the courts assumed sovereign custodial power over children and other dependents in the name of the crown. They used these powers mainly to ensure the orderly transfer of feudal duties. Chancellors hesitated to rely on the doctrine to override the custody rights of a child's natural parents. Yet they did begin to act more vigorously in custody disputes involving parents accused of being grossly immoral or heretical.

The development of *parens patriae* into a means of challenging paternal custody rights went on more rapidly and fully in North America. It capped a larger change in the legal standing of children and parental rights. Gradually a father's custody power evolved from a property right to a trust tied to his responsibilities as a guardian; his title as father thus became more transferable. The latter momentous insight was yet another example of the antipatriarchal ethos embedded in republican family law.

It was reinforced in the revolutionary era by "the new definition of a true parent as one who forms a child's mind rather than one who brings a child into the world." Armed with the authority of *parens patriae*, the courts could, and did, circumvent the common law's traditional paternal biases.[5]

Lord Mansfield provided the judiciary with a means of redirecting the law. He issued a number of decisions authorizing the use of writs of *habeas corpus* in custody disputes. The most influential decision, *Rex v. Delaval* (1763), also became the primary precedent American judges used to increase the custody rights of the mothers of illegitimates. Under it and similar rulings, the courts could award custody by examining a child's interests rather than by merely assessing the legitimacy of parental claims.[6]

Judicial discretion, when linked to republican sentiments toward the family, enabled post-Revolutionary state judges to rewrite the common law of custody. As they did, a republican custody law emerged; first in scattered decisions early in the nineteenth century and then in an increasingly intricate and expansive body of rules as the period came to an end. Three interrelated developments chronicle these innovations: the use of child nurture to circumscribe paternal custody rights and expand maternal ones; the reliance on the interests of children to increase the legal rights of surrogate parents; and the creation through the invention of adoption of an artificial family based on volunteerism, not blood.

The Creation of the "Best-Interests-of-the-Child" Doctrine

In 1809 a South Carolina equity court heard Jennette Prather's demand for a separation from her husband and the custody of her children. She charged her mate with living openly in adultery. The judges easily complied with her first request, but hesitated in granting the second. Chancellor Henry De Saussure was mindful, he said, of the father being the children's "natural guardian, invested by God and the law of the country with reasonable power over them. Unless his parental power has been monstrously and cruelly abused, this court would be very cautious in interfering with the execution of it." The court finally denied the errant husband his full parental rights. It gave the custody of an infant daughter, though not of the older children, to Jennette. In doing so, the judges acknowledged that they were treading on uncertain legal ground.[7]

The ambivalence of the South Carolina court reveals the conflicting pressures on the post-Revolutionary bench generated by custody disputes between mothers and fathers. Traditional male authority over the family remained a fundamental tenet of family law. But a growing concern with child nurture and the acceptance of women as more legally distinct individuals, ones with a special capacity for moral and religious leadership and for child rearing, undermined the primacy of paternal custody rights.

The Courts Create New Custody Rights

The *Prather* opinion also shows how judicial discretion could be used to restrict paternal rights and align the law with new gender beliefs. Judges like those on the South Carolina court began to enlarge their authority to determine if a father had so clearly abused his domestic authority that custody should be forfeited. They used the era's faith in the innate child-rearing capacities of women as counterweights to paternal economic and political power and judicial policy-making prerogatives as counterbalances to domestic patriarchy. Judicial innovations like *Prather* v. *Prather* spread throughout the nation by winning the support of more and more state judges. Custody rulings increasingly devalued paternally oriented property-based standards, emphasizing instead maternally biased considerations of child nurture.

This rearrangement of custody preferences occurred as the state judiciary resolved suits triggered by separation, divorce, and death. The exact incidence of marital dissolution in early nineteenth-century America is difficult to determine. Though in the popular mind, marriage remained a contract for life and its breakdown a source of shame, the number of divorces rose steadily, as no doubt did separations. Divorce records in New Jersey disclose that between 1788 and 1799 only thirteen formal marital dissolutions occurred, but in 1860 alone eighty-six couples formally severed the marital knot. A liberalization of divorce and separation statutes occurred as well. Much like the change in child legitimation procedures, divorce came to be seen as an act that should be routinely available and under the direction of the bench, not the legislature. Pennsylvania became the first state to make the change in 1816; other states followed gradually.[8]

Attempts by the bourgeois white women involved in these collapsing marriages to secure superior rights for motherhood constituted the strongest assault on paternal custody rights. These mothers used their newly enshrined domestic virtues as a wedge for extending the legal boundaries of their sphere. Their efforts sparked spousal, legislative, and judicial battles over child custody and guardianship that sped legal change.

A Pennsylvania couple discovered the subtleties of the emerging American law of custody in 1813. Joseph Lee petitioned for the custody of his children after he obtained a divorce from his adulterous wife Barbara. The husband contended that his wife's misdeeds and subsequent marriage to her paramour in violation of a state ban on such unions disqualified her from rearing the couple's seven- and ten-year-old daughters. Chief Justice William Tilghman, citing the *Delaval* decision to legitimize his assumption of discretion, expressed the court's "disapprobation of the mother's conduct." But he noted that her care of the two girls had been faultless. "[O]ur anxiety is principally directed," he explained, "to the children. It appears to us, that considering their tender years, they stand in need of the kind of assistance which can be afforded by none so well as a mother." Consequently, "It is on their account . . . that exercising the discretion with which the law has invested us, we think it best at present not to take them from her."

The court monitored the situation, however, and three years later Joseph triumphed. Tilghman again relied on the court's determination of filial needs, now ruling the girls' maturity rendered them less dependent on maternal nurture. Invoking his power to place children, the judge argued that two potential wives should not be reared by a mother who had flaunted the marital vow. "At the present they may not reflect upon it," the jurist concluded, "but soon they will, and when they inquire why it was that they were separated from their mother, they will be taught, as far as our opinion can teach them, that in good fortune or bad, in sickness or health, in happiness or misery, the marriage contract, unless dissolved by the law of the country, is sacred and inviolable."[9]

The judicial disposition to emphasize child welfare in determining custody began to refashion the preferences of the common law. The "best interests of the child" became a judicial yardstick used to measure all claims for children. Its dramatic impact is most apparent in the resolution of disputes between the natural parents for their children.

The mother who was an injured party in a divorce was an early beneficiary of these shifting standards. In 1815 Chancellor Kent granted a bed-and-board divorce (a formal separation) and custody of a six-year-old girl to a woman who proved to the court's satisfaction that her mate drank habitually and physically abused her. The awards of child custody to women in such suits strengthened the judicial tendency to equate motherhood with child care.[10]

By the 1820s traditional paternal custody rights had declined so precipitously that some judges began to seek a means by which fathers could be given presumptive but not absolute rights. An 1834 Massachusetts decision suggests the bench's quandary. Samuel Thatcher secured a writ against his wife Mehitabel and her father Wales Briggs for the return of his son. Mehitabel had left her husband without benefit of formal legal proceedings and returned to her parents' home, complaining bitterly that Samuel's drinking made life unbearable and left him unfit to be a husband or father. Chief Justice Lemuel Shaw denounced the judicial encouragement of the unauthorized separation of husband and wife that he thought resulted from granting women who had not obtained divorces or legal separations custody of their children. He upheld the discretionary right of judges to use the "good of the child [as the] prominent consideration" in awarding custody of "a child of tender years," but ruled that only where a man was proven unfit—he cited the example of a vagabond—could mothers claim custody. In general, "the father is by law clearly entitled to the custody of his child." In this case, Samuel Jr. was returned to his paternal abode.[11]

These issues became more acute as divorce ceased to be a legal rarity, and most likely the province of the wealthy. As divorce became more common and percolated downward in the American class structure, parental custody disputes may have become more complicated. The inability of workingclass fathers, and many middle class ones, to secure corps of nurses and servants, as wealthy men could, is but one example of the new issues thrown up by the changing demographics of nineteenth century divorce.

Treatise writers began to devise new balancing tests for assessing competing parental custody claims. Chancellor Kent noted and accepted the changes in custody law in his influential *Commentaries*. Maintaining that a "husband was the best judge of the wants of a family," he nevertheless cited Lord Mansfield and a number of American decisions to contend that paternal custody rights could be overruled when, as he put it, "the nature of the case appears to warrant it." The jurist accepted the diminution of paternal rights, despite his sentiment that the father is "the independent . . . Lord of [his] fireside." Joseph Story reached a similar conclusion in his treatise on equity. He paid homage to the traditional ideal of patriarchy, but in fact urged judges to examine the fitness of each parent when selecting a custodian, admitting his own inclination to place a girl of "very tender years" with her mother.[12]

By the 1830s legislators began to codify these judicial innovations. In an 1830 code revision, the New York legislature recognized that husbands and wives were leaving one another despite the state's strict divorce laws. Unwilling to leave child custody to informal agreements, they authorized women to apply for writs of *habeas corpus* to let the courts settle the placement of the child. In one of the first judicial tests of the law, a vice chancellor declared in 1840 that the legislature had "neutralized the rule of the common law as annulling the superiority of the *patria potestas* and placing the parents on an equality as to the future custody of the children, even if it does not create a presumption in favor of the wife." Massachusetts passed a similar statute in the 1840s with an even more explicit charge to the courts: "[T]he rights of the parents to their children, in the absence of misconduct, are equal and the happiness and welfare of the child are to determine its care and custody."[13]

A widely publicized custody fight in the 1840s between Ellen Sears, the daughter of a wealthy Boston manufacturer, and the Baron D'Hauteville, a Swiss nobleman, spelled out the implications of these legal developments. The pair parted over the wife's dissatisfaction with her husband's filial dependence and his refusal to spend part of each year in America with her family. Fearing that the Baron might try to seize his heir, a son born in Boston, the mother searched the Atlantic coast for a maternal custody haven. Eventually she chose Philadelphia because appellate court rulings in Pennsylvania favored mothers. The state bench vindicated her choice when it rebuffed her husband's challenge to its jurisdiction over the boy, and then rejected his argument that paternal custody rights are paramount in the absence of clear proof of unfitness.

In a careful amalgamation of English and American decisions, the state supreme court argued that "the reputation of a father may be stainless as crystal, he may not be afflicted with the slightest mental, moral, or physical disqualification from superintending the general welfare of the infant . . . and yet the interest of the child may imperatively demand the denial of the father's right, and its continuance with the mother." Such was the situation with the two-year-old boy before them, the judges asserted. They concluded with a paean to motherhood: "[N]ot doubting that parental anxiety would seek for and obtain the best substitute which could be procured, every instinct of humanity unerringly proclaims that no substitute can supply the place of her, whose watchfulness over the sleeping cradle or waking moments of her offspring is prompted by deeper and holier feelings than the most liberal allowance of a nurse's wages could possibly stimulate." The court ordered the child to stay with its mother. John Cadwallader, the victorious woman's attorney, aptly summarized the growing gender orientation of custody law: "Everyone knows that a father is unfit to take care of an infant; physically unfit and unfit by reason of his avocations."[14]

A Massachusetts lawyer published an anonymous pamphlet in protest. He attacked the contention that a wife could be granted custody without proving her husband had violated his spousal or fatherly duties. The unity of the husband and wife, he claimed, blocked such an outcome. Married women had no separate custody rights, just as they had none to sue or make a contract. Questioning the judiciary's growing authority over child placement, the attorney charged that the Pennsylvania decision represented "nothing less than an assumption of power by a court . . . to determine the domestic arrangements of a man's family."[15]

Joel Bishop's 1852 treatise on marriage law took that judicial responsibility for granted. A father's right, he explained, "is not an absolute one, and is usually made to yield when the good of the child, which, especially according to the modern American decision, is the chief matter to be regarded, requires that it should." Parental rights were constrained by the new legal assumptions that "children are not born for the benefit of the parents alone, but for the country; and, therefore, that the interest of the public in their morals and education should be protected"; and that "children, though younger in years have themselves an interest more sacred than their parents, and more deserving of protection." Bishop asserted in conclusion that "no parent has properly an interest in the mere custody of a child."[16]

Child Welfare and Republican Guardianship

Similar reasoning led post-Revolutionary judges and legislators to reassess guardianship. Fathers continued to be considered the proper legal guardians of children. Most states codified paternal guardianship with few alterations from English practice. Even Thomas Jefferson's liberal revision of the Virginia statutes took paternal testamentary power for granted. Many men apparently appointed their wives, but the law's longstanding premise was retained in the new republic: children should be distributed as men saw fit. Tapping Reeve made that point by noting that mothers "during coverture, exercised authority over their children; but in a legal point of view, they are considered as agents for their husbands, having no legal authority of their own. After the death of the husband, they often have this authority. Indeed, it is an immaterial inquiry whether they possess this authority in character of parent, mistress, or guardian."[17]

Even when a mother managed to secure the guardianship of her children, the law placed special restrictions on her authority. Compared to fathers, mothers had less claim to their children's services, less control of their property, fewer defenses to removal from office, and inferior custody rights. The law made custody dependent on support, and the general assumption that widows lacked financial independence undermined their demands for guardianship, as it did many other feminine claims. Diminished guardianship merely echoed the plight of widows in early nineteenth-century America. More often than not they were viewed as objects of pity and feared as potential drains on community resources. Consequently, unlike in Colonial America, widows, to an even greater extent than other women, were seen as persons in need of protection rather than as individuals with valid claims for legal rights such as custody.[18]

However, the new approach to child placement in custody litigation compelled judges and legislators to reformulate maternal guardianship. In 1835, when a New Jersey mother challenged the school selected by her son's testamentary guardian, an equity judge pointedly reminded the woman of her legal impotence. After a father appoints a testamentary guardian, he lectured, "the natural right of the mother must yield to the will of the father. It is paramount and testamentary guardianship is considered a continuation of the father's authority." But his court did not suffer from such constraints. Expressing distrust of the guardian's choice, he used his discretionary powers to act in the boy's best interests, and in that way complied with the mother's request.[19]

Judges rewrote guardianship law not only by circumscribing paternal power but also by enlarging maternal authority. For example, the traditional common-law rule that remarriage extinguished maternal guardianship fell afoul of judicial sentiments. Their newfound faith in women's child-rearing instincts led jurists to question the assumption that a remarried woman's maternal responsibility would be superseded by the deference and affection she owed her new husband. In 1852 the Virginia Court of Appeals upheld the guardianship petition of a newly remarried woman against her former father-in-law. The state code allowed a mother to request the guardianship of her children after her husband's death, and the justices decided that the "right was not lost by her remarriage, there being no legal guardian to the child; and the facts and circumstances disclose nothing which would induce the court, in the exercise of its discretion, to deprive her of the custody." In issuing a similar ruling, an Alabama judge explained: "[I]t is safe to presume . . . that a mother . . . would be more careful of the moral, intellectual, and physical well-being of her children than any other person in the world." Such instances of judicial rule making narrowed the gulf between maternal and paternal guardianship by placing both firmly within the bench's ever broadening discretionary domain.[20]

Feminist Protests against the New Custody Law

Judicially inspired custody and guardianship changes shifted the child placement authority to the courts more than they changed the subordinate legal status of married women. Post-Revolutionary egalitarianism, popular democracy, and capitalist individualism significantly enlarged the capacity of most white males, but relegation to a special feminine sphere excluded wives and mothers from many of those benefits. Within their sphere, though, married women's legal prerogatives did increase. That was particularly true of child-related rights because the canons of domesticity demanded that husbands defer to their wives in household matters and submit to feminine moral guidance. Married women gained a foothold in the law primarily in the form of protection for their special domestic responsibilities in republican households. The rapid enactment in mid-century America of laws protecting married women's property thus represented the demands to free all forms of wealth for use in the market and the desire to shelter women and children from dissolute husbands more than they did attempts to turn wives into independent legal actors. As one critic quite accurately noted in 1867: "[A]ll early legislation for women was founded, not on her own rights, but on those of her husband and children and the State over her." A maternal custody preference was one of these new legal privileges.[21]

Many advocates of women's rights acted from the same assumptions as did judges and legislators; they merely wanted to secure the tenuous and contingent new legal privileges by statute. Their demands embodied what Canadian historian Linda Kealey terms "maternal feminism"; that is, although these women protested the "private/female and public/male dichotomy that characterized much of nineteenth century middle-class life," their critique of society did not include a total rejection of middle-class values. Instead they advocated "a transferral of private/female 'virtues' into the public/male sphere."[22]

In this vein, the "Declaration of Sentiments" issued at the first women's rights convention in 1848 assailed men for framing the law of child custody after separation and of guardianship in disregard of the "happiness of women—the law in all such cases going upon the false supposition of the supremacy of man, and giving all powers into his hands." Thereafter, custody and guardianship figured prominently in every women's rights meeting and political campaign.

An 1854 address to the New York legislature set forth the basic arguments advanced in support of equal custody rights. The petition pleaded for the special nurturing abilities of women: "There is no human love so generous, strong, and steadfast as that of the mother for her child." It attacked the law for being "cruel and ruthless" because man, "in his inordinate love of power," used it to defy nature's command to give children to women. Gamblers and rum sellers had more secure legal rights to their children than did mothers. "By your laws," it concluded, "the child is the absolute property of the father, wholly at his disposal in life and at death." Its authors demanded that the legislature give mothers a superior right to their children.[23]

Unlike the incremental adjustments to parental custody and guardianship rights made by the judiciary, the mass campaign for maternal rights generated a mixed, often hostile reaction. Two mid-century examples suggest why judicial control won greater popular and professional support than did statutory reform.

In 1852 at a stop in Vermont an elderly man and a sheriff boarded a Massachusetts-bound train in which Clarina I. Howard Nichols, a women's rights campaigner, was traveling. When the pair attempted to seize the young children of a female passenger, Nichols rose to the woman's defense proclaiming: "It means my friends that a woman has no legal right to her own babies; that the law-givers of this Christian country (!) have given the custody of the babies to the father, drunken or sober, and he may send the sheriff . . . to arrest and rob her of her little ones! You have heard sneers at Women's Rights. This is one of the rights—a mother's right to the care and custody of her little ones." Learning that the husband in question had transferred his custody rights to his own father, Nichols explained that a recent Massachusetts appellate decision held that only a father could take children away from their mother. The aroused passengers threw the two men off the train; when the mother reached Massachusetts she got a favorable custody ruling from a local magistrate.[24]

Demands for formal custody rights secured by statute often met a far cooler public response, as was evident in an 1854 *New York Tribune* account of a women's rights rally. When a woman demanded statutory custody and guardianship rights, male hecklers greeted her with cries of "Oh dry up!," "Bow-wow!," "Waugh!," "Hiss-s-s-s!," "Get out!" A more reasoned expression of the same sentiments appeared in lawyer-historian James Schouler's 1870 treatise on domestic relations. Discussing legislative changes in married women's legal status, he argued: "The danger to be apprehended from all legislation of this sort is that it will weaken the ties of marriage by forcing both sexes into an unnatural antagonism; teaching them to be independent of one another, and to earn their own living apart; whereas God's law points to the family and the mutual intercourse of man and woman as among the strongest safeguards of human happiness." Schouler declared that the law should provide "honorably, faithfully, and generously against all possible misfortune," and teach a wife to "lean upon the stronger arm of her husband, and to look to man for guidance."[25]

Many opponents of women's rights resisted all significant changes in the legal status of women, not just those such as suffrage that would have clearly extended feminine authority outside the home. The Massachusetts women's rights advocate Samuel May identified those worries in an 1869 tract: "The greatest difficulty to overcome is not that most men are unwilling to do complete justice to the sex, or that the majority of women care nothing for this object; but it is simply a superstitious dread lest a change so radical could unsettle all the foundations of society and bring down the whole fabric in ruins." Sewall might well have been referring to someone like Schouler who, the next year, apprehensively predicted that with complete female emancipation "the idea of unity in domestic government—of domestic government at all—becomes weakened." Dr. William H. Wallings was even more explicit in *Sexology*: "[T]he attainment of women's rights will prove the establishment of babies' wrongs."[26]

Women's rights advocates countered these charges with the twin themes of equity and motherhood. They demanded that the law consider motherhood the equal of fatherhood. Feminist Lucinda Chandler contended that the "law perpetuates one of the errors of barbarism which science has exploded and which experience is constantly disapproving, viz., that the father alone is the creative power." Similarly, in an 1877 address to voters and legislators, the New York State Women Suffrage Society denounced laws that treated married women "as criminals by taking from them all legal control of their children, while those born outside of marriage belong absolutely to the mothers." Feminists were outraged by this disparity between the custody rights of mothers of illegitimate children and those of married women. Caroline Dall, a social reformer and attorney, decried that differential status as a violation of the natural rights of women because the "natural dependence of the child on the mother" expresses "the obvious laws of nurture, natural and spiritual, entitling a good mother" to have custody of her child.[27]

Little came of the feminist agitation for rights protected by statute. Indeed, the lure of judicial supervision was so strong that it eventually frustrated the movement's early victories. New York, the seat of the most organized women's rights effort, passed the first major reform act in 1860. It enlarged married women's property rights and declared a wife to be the "joint guardian of her children along with her husband, with equal powers, rights, and duties in regard to them, with her husband." The lawmakers retreated almost immediately, amending the act in 1862 to require that husbands had only to obtain their wives' consent before appointing testamentary guardians or indenturing their children. Looking back at this legislative backsliding from the early twentieth century, feminist Bell Squire remarked bitterly: "Ponder on this, all of you who think that the liberties of women are safe in the keeping of the other sex! Reflect on this, all of you who think chivalry of sex is all sufficient to guard the rights of those who in the nature of things cannot defend their rights by force of arms!"[28]

New York judges had much earlier integrated the legislation into their custody determinations so as to preserve, indeed augment, their own power to govern domestic relations. A state tribunal rejected a mother's contention that the 1860 act gave her independent custody rights. The justices held that her rights could be exercised only in conjunction with her husband unless she proved him to be an unfit father and spouse. "The common law remains, except as modified by the joining of the wife with him." Determining that she had failed to prove her estranged husband to be an unfit father, they denied her petition.[29]

There were, of course, successes. In 1869 Ann H. Connelly convinced New Jersey legislators to equalize parental rights; she was driven to act after losing a custody battle with her ex-husband. But in a scathing 1910 polemic against sexual biases of the law, *What Eight Million Women Want*, feminist Rheta Childe Dorr described the political reality of custody law. She reported that the year before, a bill to equalize guardianship in California had been defeated with the same arguments used "in Massachusetts and New York a quarter century ago." These were, she lamented, that if wives "had the guardianship of their children, would anything prevent them from taking the children and leaving home? What would become of the sanctity of the home, with its lawful head shorn of his paternal legitimacy?" Such contentions stymied legislative reform.[30]

In 1900 only the District of Columbia and nine states gave mothers the statutory right to equal guardianship. Most American commonwealths continued to grant the father testamentary powers, though many had begun to insist on maternal consent to the choice. By refusing to formalize maternal custody privileges, legislators left the issue to the common-law creations of the bench, ensuring that judicial judgments of parental fitness and child welfare, not statutes, determined custody rights. It was one more instance of a disposition to rely on judicial discretion to protect women.[31]

Judges Devise Republican Custody Standards

In an 1858 self-help manual, *Every Woman Her Own Lawyer*, attorney George Bishop explained that the law empowered the bench to "give custody to the party that, in the court's judgment, is most competent to bring them up with advantage to the children themselves and benefit to society." As Bishop's explanation intimates, declining paternal rights were not automatically supplanted by maternal ones. On the contrary, the law reduced the rights of parenthood generally. Courts applied judicially created standards of child welfare and parental fitness in order to take the ultimate decision of child placement out of the hands of both parents. Those standards included the best interests of the child, tender years, established ties, and priority to the innocent party in separation and divorce proceedings. These rules often biased custody determinations toward mothers; as important, they made clear the extraordinary increase in the bench's domestic authority.[32]

The "tender years" rule is an apt illustration of the growing body of rules devised by the courts to enhance their new powers. It decreed that infants, children below puberty, and youngsters afflicted with serious ailments should be placed in a mother's care unless she was proven unworthy of the responsibility. Under it, mothers gained a presumptive claim to their young children, as in an 1860 New Jersey codification of the judicial creation: "[T]he mother is entitled to the custody of her children under the age of seven unless it affirmatively appears that, in her custody, they would be exposed to either neglect, cruelty, or the acquisition of immoral habits and principles." Nine years after the act's passage it won the full endorsement of the state court of errors and appeals. The justices declared that "it is not the dry, technical right of the father, but the welfare of the child which will form the substantial basis of judgment."[33]

The tender years doctrine institutionalized Victorian gender commitments. After mid-century, courts extended the policy by insisting that daughters of all ages were best cared for by their mothers. An 1876 Alabama divorce decision explained the rationale for broadening the rule. A woman, whose name the court refused to divulge, sued for divorce, charging cruelty. The court refused her petition, but accepted the fact that the pair would continue to live apart. Agreeing that the woman had sufficient cause to do so, and to have custody of her daughter, the justices proclaimed: "All must feel, that no greater calamity can befall an infant daughter, than a deprivation of a mother's care, vigilant precept, and example. A mother's sympathy and culture exerts an influence on her life and character, perceptible only in its results. Therefore, courts are reluctant to deprive her of the custody of her infant daughter and but seldom if ever, do so, unless misconduct is imputable to her."[34]

The doctrine achieved, in part, what the feminist agitation for statutory reform had sought: the presumptive right of women (or at least, women judged to be fit) to the custody of children in need of maternal nurture. But it proved to be a double-edged sword for women, revealing the weakness of using the argument of maternal instincts as a foundation for women's rights. Judges could, and did, award to fathers the custody of children deemed to need a "masculine" domestic environment. Courts often split custody by giving fathers the care of older sons and mothers that of daughters and younger children. The Virginia Supreme Court considered such an action necessary in one case because, after the "tender nursing period has passed," it became time for the masculine duty of training a boy for life outside the home. Though the policy led to the separation of siblings, it was rooted in the widespread conviction that specific gender skills and responsibilities should be transferred from mother to daughter, from father to son.[35]

The tender years doctrine required the courts to devise broad standards for maternal fitness, ones then used in all custody deliberations. Legislators thrust this role on the bench as well. An 1853 Pennsylvania act allowed judges to give women child custody when their spouses proved to be abusive or poor providers as long as the mother afforded the child "a good example." Similarly, an 1895 code revision qualified equal child-care rights with the stipulation that a mother could exercise them only on the condition that she be "qualified as a fit and proper person to have the control and custody of said child." Such acts not only put the issue back in the courts, but they indicated a wariness about maternal fitness that accompanied all legal extensions of married women's sphere.[36]

The courts resolved the question of what constituted a fit mother by relying on what had become a family-law fiction of the reasonable woman. The Supreme Court of Georgia used that standard in 1854 to refuse the custody demands of an adulterous mother. In response to her spouse's petition for a writ of *habeas corpus*, she claimed that his cruelty and lack of financial support had forced her to flee with her daughter and take refuge with another man. The justices sustained a lower-court ruling that the child's welfare would best be served by being returned to her father. They observed that while "there may be no difference in the sins of the man and woman who violate the laws of chastity," in "the opinion of society it is otherwise." Accordingly, when a man committed adultery, he did not automatically lose the respect of the community; his children would not necessarily be excluded from association with "decent people" and "may be educated to become good and useful members of society." Adhering rigorously to the sexual double standard, the court reminded its audience that with "the frail female" the outcome was quite different. Having violated the marriage contract, the wife inevitably found herself reduced to "utter and irredeemable ruin, where her associations are with the vulgar, the vile and the depraved. If her children be with her, their characters must be, more or less, influenced and harmed by the circumstances which surround them."[37]

Economic dependency limited maternal rights under the bench's fitness standards as well. Boston attorney and Portia Law School Professor Lelia Robinson explained the dilemma facing women who sought custody of their children in *The Law of Husband and Wife, Compiled for Popular Use* (1899). She emphasized the continued judicial faith in paternal authority, due not only to "the strong, half-conscious weight long custom brings to bear on a judge's mind, but also because it is so generally the case that the money, property, income, means of support, and education are in the father's possession rather than the mother's." Robinson readily agreed that the courts would deprive unfit fathers of custody and give it to their virtuous wives ("provided their influence and character is good"), but feared that such men could easily evade court-ordered support payments. The inability of women, and communities, to collect such aid testifies to the soundness of her concern; this was a problem that was not solved in spite of the spate of desertion laws passed around the turn of the century.

Legal changes that increased maternal rights could not overcome the economic reality of feminine dependence. Maternal preference consequently could be a hollow right or a ticket to genteel poverty. New economic rights, such as the married women's property acts, only partially alleviated the plight of mothers intent on keeping their children.[38]

Divorce and the New Custody Law

The most direct, and longlasting, impact of the refinements in custody law symbolized by the tender years doctrine came in divorce. The act itself became much more common for Americans of all classes during the latter part of the nineteenth century; horrified family savers considered it a primary source of household and thus social disarray. Tighter divorce codes, in tandem with more stringent marriage regulations, failed to stem the tide. During the last decades of the century, divorce rose at a rate of over 70 percent. By 1900 courts handed down more than

55,000 divorce judgments each year. As historian William O'Neill has pointed out, the surging demand for divorce reflected the increasingly intimate, emotional nature of marriage. No longer a mere partnership, over the course of the nineteenth century it became a bond based primarily on affection and thus one that would all the more easily disintegrate as feelings changed. By officially dissolving a marriage rather than informally separating, the parties freed themselves, in most states, to enter another union formally, and protected their property and domestic rights—including custody.[39]

Divorce remained an adversary process in which one spouse sued the other claiming injury. The most widely used and sanctioned grounds were adultery, desertion, cruelty, and drunkenness. With the exception of adultery these generally were charges made by wives, and during the period women won a customary right to file for divorce. In the late nineteenth century, more than two-thirds of all divorces were granted to women; child-custody awards often accompanied those decrees. In his study of rural California divorce litigation from 1850 to 1890, historian Robert Griswold determined that "female petitioners received custody in 91 percent of their suits, men in just 37 percent." Similarly, in her analysis of New Jersey and Los Angeles divorce records for the years 1880 and 1920, historian Elaine May discovered that "in cases of divorce, even if the husband filed suit, custody of the children almost always went to the wife."[40]

By 1867, thirty-three of thirty-seven American jurisdictions had substituted judicial for legislative divorce. These grants of domestic authority to the bench included a large discretionary power to award custody. Though judges constantly reaffirmed their allegiance to paternal supremacy, they used assertions of equity and children's welfare to equalize custody rights.[41]

Fault became the major criterion for awarding custody. In an 1891 revision of his treatise, Joel Bishop argued that "because one who has done well or ill in the marriage relation will be likely to do the same in the parental, all courts lean palpably to the innocent parent in the divorce when determining the consequential custody of a child." Because women had chivalrously been accorded a customary right to file for divorce, fault was a boon to maternal custody rights.

The Mississippi Court of Errors and Appeals articulated the rationale. Louisa Cocke had been granted a divorce after proving her husband John's adultery, but no disposition of the couple's three-year-old son had been made. Louisa remarried and John demanded the child, claiming a father's paramount custody rights. The court denied his writ: "After divorce, the welfare of the child is the governing consideration. By the misfortune of its parents, it must be deprived of the care and attention of both of them which were due it, and it generally must be committed to one of them. It would be most unjust both to the child and to the mother that it shall be committed to the keeping of an unworthy father, whose misconduct may have caused the divorce from the mother, thereby inflicting a double wrong upon her as well as an injury upon the child." The legal right of the father was "at an end." The "father should not be permitted, when his own violation of duty has produced a dissolution of the marriage tie, to deprive the mother of her child to which she was entitled by fidelity to the marriage vow." Fault could also prevent men from regaining custody of their children in later hearings to modify divorce decrees.[42]

As in all areas of family law, maternal rights deferred in divorce custody deliberations to the double standard. According to the Wisconsin Supreme Court, "a woman who has been guilty of adultery is unfit to have the care and education of children, and more especially of female children." Jennie Crimmins had been divorced by her husband Thomas for adultery. In 1882 she sought access to her children, complaining that Thomas had not only won custody of their children, but also deprived her of visiting rights. A New York court piously proclaimed that by her act she had ceased to "have any right to the care, control, education, or companionship" of the children. It called the idea of forcing Thomas to admit her into the "purity of the family . . . repugnant to every assessment of virtue and propriety." The judges lectured the now childless woman that a mother was usually granted custody rights on the "natural supposition that her virtues, and the affection which she has for children, qualify her for the discharge of this duty." In her case, "the sins of her life" justly led to a denial of those rights.[43]

However, Victorian morality sometimes yielded to judicial concern for child welfare. Another New York ruling awarded a mother custody in an adultery case: "[T]he right of the husband here to the custody of the child seems . . . to be absolute, unless the good of the children themselves requires some other disposition." Judges could at their discretion invoke the tender years rule to nullify evidence of unfitness; the rule permitted the bench to distinguish a woman's parental fitness from her marital errors. Schouler took the point to its logical conclusion in an early twentieth-century revision of his domestic relations treatise:

> The physical, moral, and spiritual welfare of the child is the only safe guide in cases of the custody of the child in divorce proceedings. The love of the mother for her child, regardless of conditions and environment, has been proven by the history of the ages,

and while her devotion can be counted upon unfailingly, it is sad to say that sometimes the tie between father and child is a different matter, and requires the strong arm of the law to regulate it with some degree of humanity and tenderness for the child's good.[44]

Maternal Preference

By the last quarter of the nineteenth century, traditional paternal custody and guardianship rights had been superseded in America; judicial decisions and complementary legislation had established a new orthodoxy, maternal preference. The chances of mothers gaining control of their children were greatly enhanced, and late in the century they became even more secure as a result of the prolongation of childhood through compulsory schooling and the emerging concept of adolescence. In an 1881 decision, the Philadelphia Court of Quarter Sessions succinctly summarized the evolution of Pennsylvania's rulings on paternal custody rights:

> We do not look upon the wife and the children as mere servants to the husband and father, and, as therefore held, subject to his will so long as he does not transcend the power of an absolute master. We do not hold that though a husband drive his wife from his house by his crimes or his cruelty, still he is entitled to take away from her the custody of her children. We do not look upon the parental authority as one to exercise merely for the profit of the parents, though it may be so abused, but for the advantage of the child. . . . The substantial reality of the old common law right has faded almost to fiction, under the ameliorating influences of modern common law of Pennsylvania.

However, within that modern law, the bench had the final authority to determine the fate of a child when its parents parted. In such cases, judges exercised what equity law author John Norton Pomeroy termed their "enlightened discretion."[45]

Surrogate Parents Gain Greater Custody Rights

The capacity of child nurture to reorient custody law was nowhere more apparent than in the way it began to chip away at traditional assumptions that the bond of blood constituted the surest guarantee of proper child care. Judges used their expanding discretionary authority over child placement to revise the automatic preference given natural parents. In the post-Revolutionary era they began to scrutinize the qualifications of everyone who claimed child custody, biological parents as well as those who assumed child-rearing duties as foster parents, either at the request of a natural parent or the state. Courts were encouraged to do so by republican antipatriarchalism, which separated office from character and thus cleared the way for a broad legal definition of a fit parent.

As the antebellum bench extended greater legal protection to surrogate parents, judges operating on their vague fictional model of the fit parent further solidified the hold of the best-interests-of-the-child doctrine on American custody law. Yet they did so with at times contradictory results, ones that indicate some of the gender and class limitations of these legal changes. These are evident in judicial decisions involving surrogate parents, especially decisions that dealt with private and public apprenticeship. The extension of rights to surrogate parents illustrates how family-law doctrines could have quite different effects depending on the claimants; in particular, they reveal the debilitating impact of poverty and deviancy on parental rights under the new child nurture standards.

Judges Dilute Natural Parents' Rights

Custody fights between natural parents and surrogate child rearers brought out the clashing rights and obligations of fathers, mothers, and those who stood *in loco parentis*. The common law's allegiance to family integrity included a deep aversion to the private relinquishment of custody by a parent. As a New Jersey chancery court said in 1846: "[T]he care and custody of minor children is a personal trust in the father, and he has no general power to dispose of them to another." Yet many antebellum fathers, and mothers, did just that. Judicial involvement commenced when the parent changed his or her mind, demanded the child back, and the surrogate parent refused. The courts then had to resolve some of the most intricate, heart wrenching of all family law disputes. As they did, post-Revolutionary and early nineteenth-century judges established new surrogate parents' rights, ones enlarged by their successors.[46]

A judicial inclination to rely on child nurture as the prime means of assessing these clashing claims of parenthood appeared as early as 1796, in the Connecticut decision of *Nichols* v. *Giles*. The state supreme court dismissed a writ of *habeas corpus* issued on behalf of a man whose wife had left him and taken their three-year-old daughter to her family home. The judges concluded that because the child's "intemperate, property-less father could not properly care for her," she should remain with her grandparents. They relied on the *parens patriae* doctrine, which allowed courts to withhold custody from unfit fathers who had transferred or abandoned their children. During the next century, judges broadened their authority by enlarging their definition of a child's interests.[47]

Paternal custody rights were the major casualty, as an 1816 New York decision suggests. A father attempted to regain his daughter; she and her mother had sought refuge with her maternal grandparents after the family had sustained several financial crises. At first the father had frequently visited the girl, but his attention waned. The child was reared and educated by her grandparents after her mother died. Chief Justice Smith Thompson seized upon rulings by Lord Mansfield and the Pennsylvania bench in deciding the child's fate: "From the affidavits which have been laid before the court, little doubt can be entertained that it will be more for the benefit of the child to remain with her grandparents than to be put under the care of her father; and if this court has any discretion in such case, it will no doubt be discretely exercised by permitting the child to remain where she is."[48]

Eight years later Justice Story faced an almost identical case, except that before her death the wife in this case had extracted a promise from her husband to leave their daughter with her maternal grandparents. Denying his pledge, Elisha Williams secured a writ to retrieve the girl. The paramount right of the husband, Story insisted, "is not on account of any absolute right to the father, but for the benefit of the infant, the law presuming it to be for his interest to be under the nurture and care of his natural protector, both for maintenance and education." Courts settled custody disputes with regard to the "real permanent interests of the infant"; Williams had no "absolute, vested right in the custody."[49]

Contrasting Georgia's and Ohio's decisions illustrates the standards of nurture and parental fitness that judges were devising to resolve these private custody disputes. More specifically, it points out the masculine ideal of proper parenthood spawned by republican family ideology, one which highlighted economic success and domestic propriety.

The Georgia case involved the 1836 claim of a well-respected physician to his three-month-old child. The mother had died in childbirth, and on her deathbed made her husband agree to let her parents raise the girl. But the doctor soon disagreed with his in-laws' child rearing, and demanded the return of the baby. Superior Court Judge Robert M. Charlton issued the writ, asserting the bench's authority to settle custody disputes. "All legal rights, even those of personal security and liberty, may be forfeited by improper conduct," he maintained, "and so this legal right of the father to the possession of his child must be made subservient to the true interests and safety of the child, and to the duty of the State to protect its citizens of whatever age." Deciding that both parties appeared to be responsible custodians, Charlton deferred to the father's superior claim.[50]

The Cincinnati Superior Court treated Stephen Ball's 1848 assertion of parental rights much less respectfully. The judicial record shows him to be a stereotypical example of the failed male, and that fathers too were judged on their ability to be loving, nurturing parents. Indeed, fathers were quite vulnerable to attacks on their parental abilities because they were not assumed to be innately endowed with nurturing qualities. In this case, Ball abandoned his daughters and their mother when he and his father quit their carpentry trade to join the millennial Millerite movement. Without support, Ball's family moved in with his wife's parents. Ball's wife died. He joined the Shakers, and then sought custody in order to have the girls raised by his sect.

Judge William Johnston argued that the right to custody flowed from the parental responsibility to clothe, feed, and educate a child. "Separate from the duty of providing," he sternly lectured, "the right to custody does not exist." The Shakers' communal child-rearing practices, which demanded that parental ties be broken and that all children be raised by special caretakers, repelled the judge. Under such a system, he contended, the Shakers, not Ball, would actually receive custody; something that neither the grandmother nor the judge thought to be in the child's best interests. Johnston then summarily rejected what he characterized as Ball's attempt to "sever them from the bosom of their grandmother and from his own bosom, and plant them in the cold ascetic bosoms of the 'female caretakers,' and transfer all his rights, title, and interest in the child which God had given him, to total strangers." Such plans, the judge ruled, proved Ball's parental unfitness and could not counter the grandmother's "moral lien."[51]

New Ties

By mid-century the judiciary had used custody law to give greater legitimacy to newly formed family relationships. Parental rights to custody remained superior, but they were subject to much greater supervision as judges demanded, and secured, the right to weigh assertions of parental rights against their evaluation of the character and benefits of the new arrangements for the child. The courts wielded their discretionary power through policies whose effect was to compel parents to demonstrate that their children would be better off with them than in their surrogate homes.[52]

A very influential ruling, *Chapsky* v. *Wood* (1881), by the future Supreme Court Justice David J. Brewer when he sat on the Kansas Supreme Court, helps clarify the status of surrogate families. The dispute involved the conflicting custody claims of a father and his deceased wife's family. On her deathbed, Mrs. Chapsky had made her mate pledge that he would give their daughter to her sister. After letting the foster mother care for his child for five and a half years, Chapsky tried to reclaim her to allow his kin to rear the girl.

Brewer rhetorically deferred to paternal custody rights. He also refused to consider the transfer of child custody as the equivalent of a commercial contract in which the seller lost his or her interest in the merchandise. The justice then invoked the best-interests-of-the-child rule. He argued that such an assessment was particularly necessary when a parent allowed his child to form new family ties: "[W]hen reclamation is not sought until a lapse of years, when new ties have been formed and a certain current given to the child's life and thought, much attention should be paid to the probabilities of a benefit to the child from the change. It is an obvious fact, that ties of blood weaken, and ties of companionship strengthen, by lapse of time; and the prosperity and welfare of the child depend on the ability to do all which the prompting of these ties compel." Because of the responsibility of the bench to heed the needs of children, the claims of the surrogate parents had to be given as much consideration as those of the natural ones.

After careful investigation, Brewer and his colleagues concluded that the girl should be left in her present home. The child appeared to be healthy, happy and properly cared for. Fearful of the ill effects of a change, he urged: "'Let well enough alone,' is an axiom founded on abundant experience." Though he unearthed no evidence of the father's unfitness to be a parent, Brewer did assert that he had a "coldness, a lack of energy, and a shiftlessness of disposition, which would not make his personal guardianship of the child the most likely to ripen and develop her character." Nor did the judge think that Chapsky's family had offered any compelling evidence of great concern for the girl. He contrasted those "facts" to the warm family care given the child in her aunt's home. Brewer even dismissed as irrelevant the father's greater wealth. The court ordered the girl to remain with her new mother.[53]

Mothers, too, lost their custody rights and their legal standing as nature's preferred parent when they let their children remain too long with surrogate families. The Rhode Island Supreme Court used the new "established ties" doctrine in 1888 to deny a remarried mother the right to take her son from his paternal uncle. The justices did not "feel called upon to sunder the ties that have been permitted to grow up, believing that the happiness of the boy and rights and feelings of his foster parents will be best subserved by leaving custody where it now is." They did not "doubt the mother's love for her child," but decided that denying her writ would do less "violence to interests and affections."[54]

By equating newly formed surrogate family ties with natural ones, judges placed their faith in the preponderant benefits of a stable home for any child. As a California judge remarked in 1878: "I am of the opinion that a child should, as far as possible, have the influences of home life; that the State is interested in having those influences surround and impress its future citizens." Though never applied mechanically, the policy encouraged the bench to use its child-placement powers to leave apparently happy and healthy children where they were and thus devalued the rights of natural parents.

In the 1881 decision of *Verser* v. *Ford*, a custody dispute between the father and maternal grandparents of a three-year-old girl, the Arkansas Supreme Court described the conditions under which courts assumed the power to deny parental custody claims: "It is impossible to define them, further than to say that they should be of such urgency as to overcome all considerations based upon the natural affections and moral obligations of the father." Despite the justices' insistence that arbitrarily taking a child from its father would be "intolerably tyrannical as well as Utopian," when the court weighed the girl's delicate health and the soothing maternal care given her by the grandmother against the "inexperienced efforts of a father" and the unknown "sense of duty" of a stepmother, the scales of justice once again tipped in favor of the surrogate family.[55]

The Texas Supreme Court in 1894 summarized this revision of parental rights in custody law by likening parental authority to a trusteeship subject to public oversight:

> The State, as the protector and promotor of the peace and prosperity of organized society, is interested in the proper education and maintenance of the child, to the end that it may become a useful instead of a vicious citizen; and while as a general rule it rec-

ognizes the fact that the interest of the child and society is best promoted by leaving its education and maintenance, during minority, to the promptings of paternal affection, untrammelled by the surveillance of government, still it had the right in proper cases to deprive the parent of the custody of the child when demanded by the interests of the child and society.

In the case before them, the justices held that a two-year-old girl should remain in the custody of her foster parents, in whose care she had been almost since her birth.[56]

Apprenticeship and Private versus Public Custody Disputes

The early nineteenth-century reorientation of custody law also began to influence apprenticeship, one of the oldest of Anglo-American family relationships. In apprenticeship contracts, masters pledged training and support in exchange for the promise of a child's personal service. Like other forms of bonded servitude in traditional society, indentures created a familylike legal tie in which apprentices assumed the role of family members and masters held the title of surrogate parents. Fathers and, upon their death, mothers could indenture their children voluntarily because the right to an offspring's services carried with it a corollary authority to assign those services to another. The master then stood *in loco parentis*, receiving the child's services in return for parental support, nurture, and education. But unlike the normal parent-child relationship, apprenticeships were created by signed agreements. They could also be forced upon a parent by poor-law authorities after a finding of parental neglect or failure, so-called public indentures.

Colonial apprenticeships had been conceived of largely in terms of paternal responsibility, filial subordination, and hierarchical social arrangements. Within that scheme, they served a variety of functions for all classes, ranging from moral and cultural training to poor-law relief. In the boom and bust antebellum economy, with its growing reliance on the self-regulating market and entrepreneurs, independent labor swept aside many older forms of overt workplace dependency. As a result, family-based apprenticeship became an increasingly anomalous economic relationship. Concurrently, changing family attitudes—the importance of mother-child bonds, prolonged childhood, and the home as nursery and refuge—undermined the attractions of indentures. The creation of public schools in the North also undercut the role of apprenticeship as a training medium. The emergence of factory labor, especially its use of armies of untrained children and immigrants rather than artisans and the general decline of the skilled trades, reinforced these developments.[57]

The effects of these changes were profound. The parental responsibilities of the master and the filial obligations of the apprentice withered as their relationship came to be deemed primarily one of employer and employee. More important, preexisting class biases in apprenticeship law and practice were solidified. Private, voluntary indentures narrowed to a method of vocational training; its custody disputes fell within the broad outlines of the law's nurture-biased doctrines. Involuntary indentures remained a question of poor-law relief, and existed uneasily with the new demands of custody law. The differing fates of these two forms of indentures graphically illustrate the corrosive effect of dependency on legal rights. Middle-class domestic-relations law emphasized private common-law rights and freedom from state intervention except in the case of socially threatening conduct such as abortion. But the family law of the lower classes used dependency to abridge individual rights and to sanction broad public controls. The dual system of apprenticeship reveals some of the class boundaries of republican family law.[58]

Voluntary Indentures

The family framework of apprenticeship did survive the American Revolution. Tapping Reeve reminded his readers in 1816 that the master stood *in loco parentis* to his apprentice. Kent later claimed that the relationship, "if duly cultivated under a just sense of the responsibility attached to it, and with the moral teachings which belong to it, will produce parental care, vigilance, and kindness on the part of the master, and a steady, dutiful, faithful, and reverential disposition and conduct on the part of the apprentice." The statutory demands of voluntary apprenticeship agreements were well established. State codes insisted upon a written indenture, the consent of both the parent and, if older than fourteen, the apprentice, termination at the age of twenty-one for males and eighteen for women, and means of redress if either party violated the pact. Domestic trappings and statutory requirements made voluntary apprenticeship quite compatible with the emerging child-centered law of custody. But they may have lessened the attraction of the apprentice system in the post-Revolutionary marketplace.[59]

The formal continuation of colonial apprenticeship devices in fact masked basic changes. As historian Bernard Bailyn has observed: "Officially, legally, the assumption continued that the master stood *in loco parentis*, that his duties included all those of an upright father, and that the obligations of apprentices remained, as sanctified in law and tradition, filial in scope and character. But both sets of obligations were increasingly neglected as both sides responded to the pressures of the situation." In the first place, parents were less attracted to the idea of putting their children out. As the parental home became enshrined as the irreplaceable locus of child nurture, apprenticeship no longer seemed an appropriate means for socializing the young. The demands of the competitive marketplace induced masters to question the value of assuming parental responsibilities toward young workers. Generally, post-Revolutionary America was an inhospitable place for the traditional practice, as the repeal or neglect of laws prohibiting apprentices from being enticed to leave their masters and the failure to enforce runaway apprentice laws testify. But the codes continued to demand that masters act like parents and apprentices like children.[60]

The courts struggled to reconcile these contradictory demands. Apprenticeship disputes proved particularly troublesome because, as so often happened, the cases pitted against each other two major judicial commitments: to use the common law to promote child welfare, and to encourage economic individualism. Apprenticeship rulings exemplify the judicial perplexity over the proper way to incorporate a traditional relationship into the new order.

The child-centered nineteenth-century bench stressed the rights of apprentices over those of masters and parents. In an 1811 decision, a New York court applied the pivotal *Delaval* custody ruling to indentures by giving children who had reached the age of discretion the chance to choose between their masters or their parents. In 1816 Justice Story took a similar position in a case involving a father's attempt to enlist his son in the army and gain the enlistment bounty, against the child's will. Denying that the father had a property right in his children which he could assign to others for his own profit, Story declared:

> The custody of minors is given to their parents for their maintenance, protection, and education; and if a parent, overlooking all these objects, should, to answer his own mercenary views, or gratify his own unworthy passions, bind his child as an apprentice upon terms evidently injurious to his interests, or to a trade, or occupation, which would degrade him from the rank and character, to which his condition and circumstances might fairly entitle him, it would be extremely difficult to support the legality of such a contract.

Using similar logic, the *American Law Register* in 1853 questioned whether the "condition of a child is so far analogous to that of the slave that a father could bind him for his own gain." The "better adjudication," concluded the journal, "is decidedly in favor of confining the authority of the father in this respect within more reasonable limits, and allowing the child to exercise some choice where its own interests are at stake." As the best-interests-of-the-child doctrine helped to expand mothers' rights over their children, so did the insistence on filial consent to indentures use child welfare to constrain the traditional prerogatives of fathers and masters.[61]

The child-centered bias of the bench led judges to highlight the domestic character of indentures. Thus the Connecticut Supreme Court refused to award compensation to a master whose apprentice had run away claiming that the man had not only failed to instruct him in the art of wagon making but had also forced him to work on the Sabbath: "By express covenant, the master was bound to instruct him in his art or mystery, and to feed and clothe him. As a master stands *in loco parentis*, he is under a higher obligation to instruct him in the principals of morality and religion. But instead of performing his paramount duty, this master compelled his apprentice, unnecessarily to work on the Lord's day. From such an apprenticeship it was a right—it was the duty of the ward to escape and of the guardian to rescue him." Masters like the Connecticut wagon maker learned the hard way that courts would insist that they treat their apprentices like family members, not mere employees.[62]

The inherent conflict between the traditional concept of apprenticeship and the realities of antebellum economic life arose with particular clarity in disputes over the right of a master to assign his apprentice to another person. That had been a longstanding practice; apprentices had even been listed among the assets of bankrupts in colonial America, used as payment for debts, and considered as part of estates. Judges frowned on such transfers, and held them to be violations of personal trusts not assignable to others. Reeve termed these practices "incompatible with the nature of the contract, which is altogether fiduciary. The master is one in whom the parent of the apprentice has such confidence, as induces him to place under his care his child." He admitted that transfers were a "usual practice in this country," but contended that they had never "been sanctioned by the decision of any court."[63]

Early and repeatedly, appellate judges followed Reeve's lead and refused to countenance the assignments. In the 1811 Massachusetts case of *David* v. *Coburn*, involving the transfer of an apprentice house joiner, Judge Theodore Sedgwick ruled it void as a violation of a parental trust:

> That a father, during the minority of a child, should have a power to dispose of a requisite portion of his authority for the purposes

of education and instruction, is frequently important and necessary for the welfare of the child; but in doing this, a due regard to
the interest of his child will render him cautious to what hands he
confides the trust; and for this purpose a wise and prudent parent
will be as anxious about the moral qualities of the man, to whom
he delegates his authority, as to his competency in other respects.
But all his attention in this regard would be useless, if the master
might immediately transfer or assign his authority to another.

In a similar case, Chief Justice Tilghman of Pennsylvania refused to be
swayed by the argument of commercial development. Nullifying the
transfer of an apprentice from England to the United States, he declared
that, as for "the policy of encouraging manufacturers to emigrate from
Europe, by permitting them to retain their apprentices, it is a consideration by which this court must not be influenced." Only when the
apprentice, the parents, and the master agreed, would courts validate the
assignment of indentures. But this may have served only to lessen
further the attraction of indentures to masters.[64]

Though apprenticeship continued to elicit judicial endorsement as a
virtuous method of child rearing, its twin objects of support and training
increasingly were thought of as separate activities better left to other
agencies and institutions. An 1835 decision by Tilghman's successor,
the Jacksonian Democrat John Bannister Gibson, indicates the mid-
century status of voluntary apprentices. Gibson cast aside the colonial
law requiring that apprentices live with their masters. Declaring it to be
his responsibility to "interpret statutes so far as to fit them to business
and habits of the time," Gibson decided that because apprentices had
become more akin to wage laborers than children, they no longer had to
live with their masters. This view of the young apprentice as a free wage
laborer eroded the domestic underpinnings of apprentice law. In an
increasingly functionally segmented legal system, it hastened the transfer of apprenticeship from the domain of the family to that of labor.[65]

Poor Apprentices

Involuntary apprenticeship thrived much longer in nineteenth-century
America than did voluntary apprenticeship. In part, this disparity is not
surprising. Arrangements for involuntary apprenticeships were made
almost exclusively by poor-law overseers, public officials whose primary concern was to reduce the burden of poor relief for local rate-

payers. The welfare of the apprenticed children figured only secondarily in their calculations. Nineteenth-century poor-relief officials differed little from their colonial counterparts; the apprenticeship agreements they negotiated seem much the same as pre-Revolutionary ones.

The innovations of custody law did little to alter this continuing reality. The bench did, to be sure, apply its doctrines—the best interests of the child, denial of parental property rights in children—equally for voluntary and involuntary apprentices. In an 1838 dispute over a son's wages between a violent, drunken, indigent father and a sea captain, Samuel Ware, a federal district judge in Maine, insisted that custody rights were conferred on parents solely for "the benefit of the child." Consequently,

> [W]hen a parent abuses this power, or neglects to fulfill the obligations from which its results, he forfeits his rights. . . . If instead of treating his child with tenderness and affection, and bringing him up in habits of industry, sobriety, and virtue, he treats him with such cruelty that he cannot be safely left in his custody; or corrupts him up to immorality and profligacy, the protecting justice of the county will interpose and deprive him of the exercise of a power, which having been allowed for the benefit of the child is perverted to his injury and perhaps his ruin. There are many cases in which the court of chancery in England has interposed its authority and taken children from the custody of their fathers who have abused their paternal authority, and placed them under the care of persons proper to have the control of them, and to superintend their education. I am not aware that any doubt exists that the courts in this country have similar authority.

Any other course, the judge maintained, would be tantamount to treating children as parental property. But "children do not become property of the parents. As soon as a child is born, he becomes a member of the human family, and is invested with all the rights of humanity."[66]

Statutes and judicial directives transferred parental responsibilities for these children from parents to masters. Most state codes required that poor apprentices be taught the rudiments of an education, such as reading, writing, and (for males) arithmetic. Masters could also have their powers revoked for cruel treatment, failure to instruct the apprentice in a trade, and other violations of their parental office. The courts even insisted that a poor-law indenture did not convert the child into a servant. They also resisted attempts of masters to sell or assign their apprentices. These formal protections approximated those governing voluntary indentures and posed an ideal of apprenticeship as unbiased and classless.[67]

Ironically though, doctrines that ameliorated the condition of voluntary apprentices served to exacerbate the plight of involuntary ones. The main reason seems to be that the courts often held parental poverty to constitute an unfit environment for a child. In an 1817 parental challenge to the poor laws, Justice Robert Duncan of Pennsylvania asserted that the public authority to bind out poor waifs "must, in its nature, be compulsory in its execution; it requires not the agency or the cooperation of the father or the child." He premised this denial of commonly granted parental rights on the ground that impoverished parents had proven themselves to be less capable than the courts and local officials in determining their child's best interests. Rather, the law, "humanely and wisely" conferred on public representatives the "direction and management of the poor child." The Indiana Supreme Court agreed in an 1841 ruling: "Overseers of the poor have no right to meddle with the children of living parents, unless they be found unable to maintain them."[68]

Judicial investigations of the home—necessary in other custody cases to determine what environment served the best interests of the child— served different ends when dependent paupers were before the bench. Judges, like most propertied Americans of the nineteenth century, assumed that dependent poverty was but one component of an unsalubrious nexus: ignorance, moral license, idleness. In this context, the judiciary's commitment to child welfare was a mandate to disqualify the parental home.

The canon that parents had no automatic right to their children thus had a malign effect in these cases. Invariably such cases involved a parental plaintiff challenging public-welfare authorities who had arranged an indenture. The presumption of parental fitness that guided the judiciary in other custody cases simply did not hold for parents dependent on poor relief. Regularly the courts found for the public authority, the poor-relief officials whose guiding principle was fiscal austerity.

The vast power granted local officials under the poor laws emerged quite clearly in an 1835 Vermont decision. The state supreme court prevented a widow from retrieving her son from his master even though the child had fled his new household and his mother now claimed she could support him. "It is true," the justices admitted, "that the probable advantage of the child is also to be consulted; but as the power vested in the overseers is a power in derogation of parental rights, and may sometimes operate with great severity upon the prospect and fortunes of the child, it should be confined to those cases which come within the evident intention and policy of the statute." Not only did this case fulfill that standard, but sufficient others did, to make poor-law indentures a continuing element of American custody law for the rest of the century.[69]

Thus, consistently the reality of poor-law apprenticeship belied the legal ideal. Protective laws were subject to widely fluctuating enforcement, not only among states but also localities, because of the wide discretionary powers granted community authorities. Moreover, poor apprentices as children "of the public," in the words of a New Jersey justice in 1819, could not veto particular indentures as could youths bound out voluntarily. Statutory requirements mandating practical and moral training appear to have been ignored with impunity, as was evidence of physical and sexual abuse. In some communities, poor children continued to be auctioned off to the lowest bidder along with other paupers. Freed black children endured the most drastic curtailment of rights. States like Kentucky, Missouri, and Indiana passed laws eliminating the educational requirements of their indentures. In other jurisdictions, masters received the right by statute to indenture black children regardless of parental finances. Poor-law indentures, especially for blacks, resembled involuntary servitude.

As happened in many cases, judicial doctrines that appeared to liberate individuals were in reality double-edged swords. When applied to vulnerable sectors of the population, they merely liberated the individual to confront the unmediated power of the state and the market. As historian Maxwell Bloomfield has argued, by the 1840s apprenticeship had been robbed of much of its meaning and instead of "providing useful vocational training for the children of all classes, the apprenticeship system now functioned largely as a device for the recruitment and exploitation of young paupers."[70]

Judicial authorization for state intervention in dependent poor families, so counter to the bench's general antebellum tendencies, may well have been encouraged by the asylum movement. Social reformers held out the promise of community regeneration through state intervention. Old institutions that had perpetuated misery and crime would be replaced by new public institutions of reform and rehabilitation. It was an easy corollary that dependent poor families should be superseded by state-provided benign environments.[71]

In *Ex Parte Crouse* (1838), the most influential antebellum judicial analysis of newly created children's asylums, the Pennsylvania Supreme Court relied on the poor-law variant of custody law to uphold the right of the state to remove children from unsuitable households. The justices did so in the appeal of Mary Ann Crouse's father, who contested his daughter's commitment to the Philadelphia House of Refuge. She had been placed there by local officials after her mother petitioned that Mary

Ann had become incorrigible. Her father argued that this constituted imprisonment without a trial and thus violated her constitutional rights. The justices disagreed:

> The object of charity is reformation, by training its inmates to industry; by imbuing their minds with principles of morality and religion; by furnishing them with means to earn a living; and, above all, by separating them from the corrupting influences of improper associates. To this end, may not the natural parents, when unequal to the task of education, or unworthy of it, be superseded by the *parens patriae*, or common guardian of the community? It is to be remembered that the public has a paramount interest in the virtue and knowledge of its members, and that, of strict right, the business of education belongs to it. That parents are ordinarily entrusted with it, is because it can seldom be put into better hands; but where they are incompetent or corrupt, what is there to prevent the public from withdrawing their faculties, held, as they obviously are, at its sufferance? The right of parental control is a natural, but not an unalienable one. It is not excepted by the declaration of rights out of the subject of ordinary legislative power, which, if wantonly or inconveniently used, would soon be constitutionally restricted, but the competency of which as the government is constituted, cannot be doubted.

At the same time the justices defended minors' rights by stressing the rehabilitative influence of the institution: "The House of Refuge is not a prison, but a school." Placement in the institution did not constitute a violation of her rights; on the contrary, it served her best interests because she "has been snatched from a course which would have ended in confirmed depravity; and, not only is the restraint of her person lawful, but it would be an act of extreme cruelty to release her."[72]

The Pennsylvania ruling suggests that the courts were quite willing to use dependency to redefine domestic relations. Mary Ann not only continued her stay in the House of Refuge, she could later be indentured by the institution. Poverty and deviations from middle-class family standards left homes like the Crouses' continually open to the effort to place children in households that most closely approximated the republican ideal of a socially beneficial family. The law governing forced apprenticeship, like other forms of poor law, acted on the assumption that dependency abrogated common-law rights. It placed the poor and deviants in a dependent legal position that matched their economic, material, and cultural ones. As with race, family law treated them with special, and generally repressive, treatment. Thus although voluntary apprenticeship fell into desuetude and its legal provisions were incorporated into the labor law of a capitalist republic, involuntary apprenticeship remained embedded in the poor law, subject to the republican assumption that dependent poverty disqualified its victims from the full rights of citizenship.

Adoption and the Creation of a New Legal Family

Apprenticeship disputes, public and private, were part of the broader problem of the surrogate parent. The relationships formed through voluntary or involuntary transfers of parental care could not be complete relinquishments of family authority and obligations; conflicts were inevitable. Not so, however, with the most far-reaching innovation of nineteenth-century custody law: the American law of adoption. It provided a legal mechanism for completely severing the bonds created by birth and replacing them with binding artificial ties. The new legal device allowed the formation of families brought together by choice and affection, not nature. As such, it was the greatest extension of republican family law's antipatriarchalism and child-nurture priorities since it assumed that parental authority could be irrevocably transferred.

The Mid-Century Enactment of Adoption

Although adoption had long been part of Western legal culture in civil-law nations, English common law had refused to accept complete transfers of parenthood. Civil-law adoption had its roots in Roman procedures designed primarily to aid the adopting patriarch. It enabled a man to avoid the extinction of his family and to perpetuate its religious rites. Although English legal historians Pollock and Maitland believed that early Britons also used a form of adoption, by the early modern era the stance of English common lawyers could be summarized in the terse statement of Glanville: "Only God can make a heres [heir], not man."

English reluctance stemmed from two major sources. First, the solicitude of the common law for the property rights of blood relatives made the concept of allowing unrelated heirs to join in family succession quite foreign to English jurisprudence. This fear for the safety of inheritance rights dominated common law discussions of the issue into the twentieth century. Second, the availability of alternative forms of child placement such as apprenticeship, voluntary transfers, and other quasi-adoptive devices, lessened the need for a formal means of permanently placing children in new households.[73]

The animus against adoption was carried to the colonies as part of the cultural baggage of English immigrants. Only the gradual diffusion of child-welfare considerations into custody law, the lessened appeal of alternative devices, and concern about regularizing inheritance rights could alter this age-old aversion. Without these developments, adoption was unattractive to common lawyers; with them it became irresistible in America by the 1850s.

Adoption replaced other voluntary and involuntary transfers of parental authority, in which the duration and extent of family legal ties had not been precisely determined.[74] Some agreements had been tantamount to adoption, but even they were insecure. In the 1857 case of *Van Dane* v. *Vreeland*, the New Jersey Supreme Court upheld the validity of a forty-year-old contract between a father and his brother in which the father had exchanged custody rights to his son for a promise that the boy would be given full family status and inheritance rights in his uncle's home. After hearing the uncle's natural children's challenge to the agreement, the justices contended:

> It is said that the character of the agreement is such that the court ought not to entertain a bill upon it. There is no consideration of public policy which should forbid the court's countenancing such an agreement. Considering the situation of the parties, and their circumstances in life, it was beneficial to all the parties, and cannot be considered as injudicious or unreasonable. The father made a beneficial arrangement for his offspring, and the uncle's affections were satisfied by the adoption of a son. The agreement is alleged to have been unreasonable, because it deprived the uncle of the free disposal of his property. But this is not so. It provided him with a son, and only obligated him, in the disposal of his property, to make such a provision for the child of his adoption as might reasonably be expected from parental obligation and affection.

The adopted son did win, but the cumbersome and tenuous nature of this method of securing family membership clearly limited its usefulness and spawned fears about child welfare and inheritance rights.[75]

Early nineteenth-century Americans could avail themselves of an alternative. As in other areas of family law, private acts could be used to surmount common-law barriers. In Massachusetts, the legislature enacted 101 bills altering the domestic status of children between 1781 and 1851. Most merely changed a child's name, no doubt finalizing an informal assumption of parent-child relations. One act explained that the new parent had "supported said child for the five years last past, and still expects to provide for the support and education of the child and to make him heir to your petitioner." Much more formal was the bill passed by the General Court through which Harriet Augusta Sumner became Harriet Augusta Robinson. The law included the signed petition of the new mother pledging to make Harriet her legal heir and stipulating that the "child forever hereafter may reciprocally bear" to her "the same legal relations as though the said Mary Robinson had been the mother of said child."

Such petitions reflect a growing conclusion that only by formally binding a child to a surrogate parent could the waif become a full member of the new household. Like divorce, legitimation, and other species of private legislation, these acts also document the penetration of formal legal consciousness in the populace. And with the others, they came to be seen more as judicial issues than as legislative matters. Time consuming and expensive, these acts constituted the only formal means available to Americans for creating an artificial family.[76]

Even the civil-law states Louisiana and Texas exhibited an animus against adoption. Although the practice had been valid in both states, republican legislators restricted adoption when given the opportunity to draft their own codes. Louisiana's first body of laws in 1808 placed curbs on adoption, and an 1825 revision abolished it altogether.

The rejection may have been another instance of common-law imperialism, and have reflected contemporary dissatisfaction with adoption in France. In 1809 a correspondent in the *American Law Register* reported that only the intercession of Napoleon had kept adoption in the French code. The writer termed the practice one not "grounded on either the general feelings of human nature, or on any rational rules of artificial society." He cited with approval opponents of adoption who charged that it only created ill will within families without replacing natural parental feelings. The Emperor had offered a traditional defense of adoption as a necessary means of enabling a family name and its property to be preserved and of providing domestic comfort for childless couples. Even so, the French code limited adoption to persons over fifty without children or legitimate descendants, and who had cared and supported the child for at least six years. The child had to reach majority, but even then could reclaim a place in his or her natural family. This restrictive conception of adoption spread to most civil-law nations and their colonies.[77]

Thus Louisianans could adopt children only by private act and notorial endorsement; the process paralleled the private act in common-law states. An 1858 challenge in Louisiana to one of these laws led to the only significant legal interpretation of private adoption acts to come out of an antebellum courtroom. *Vidal* v. *Comagere* (1838) involved an act that allowed Pierre Jean Baptiste Vidal and his wife to adopt Adele, a seven-year-old orphan. The couple had been caring for the child, and the statute merely formalized their relations; a codicil stipulated that the pair considered Adele to be their heir and entitled to full domestic legal rights. Pierre died shortly thereafter, and some of his nieces and nephews disputed Adele's right to claim anything more than maintenance from the estate.

Chief Justice E. T. Merrick, a transplanted Ohioan who became a civil-law expert, rejected the relatives' arguments. Taking a broad view of the private act, he interpreted it in the light of the civil law of adoption and the commonsense use of the word. A narrow reading should be rejected because it "cannot be presumed that a formal exertion of the sovereign power was made for trivial reasons." Merrick also refused to construe the act strictly on the grounds it was in derogation of inheritance law. He concluded that the couple intended Adele to "enjoy the same rights, advantages, and prerogatives, as if she had been the issue of the marriage of the parties to the act, and their legitimate child." This opinion influenced the interpretation of private acts in common-law states as well as in former civil-law colonies, and demonstrated once again the judicial tendency to uphold voluntarily assumed domestic obligations. It also underscored the precariousness of rights secured under special procedures.[78]

Enacting Adoption

A favorable climate for the institution of adoption emerged in mid–nineteenth-century America as a result of the problems associated with other forms of child placement, the gradual refinement of nurture-based custody law, confusion over inheritance rights, and the everpresent plight of homeless, neglected, and delinquent children. The acts fell into two rough categories. The first group, those enacted in Mississippi in 1849, Vermont and Texas in 1850, Tennessee in 1851–52, Missouri in 1857, and Iowa in 1858, resembled the old civil law of adoption. But in 1851 Massachusetts had taken another track. Its statute, which soon became the national model, created a means of establishing an artificial bond between a parent and child that closely approximated the legal ideal of republican domestic relations.

The act made adoption a legal procedure, and charged the courts with making sure that the new parents were of "sufficient ability to bring up the child, and furnish suitable nurture and education, having reference to the degree and condition of its parents, and that it is fit and proper that such adoption should take place." All natural family ties were dissolved, and replaced by relations with the adopted parents. Pennsylvania, the second state to enact such a child-centered adoption law, offered an even more explicit indication of its source. Its 1853 statute dictated that courts were to be satisfied that the "welfare of such child will be promoted by such adoption."[79]

Adoption spread at a phenomenal rate. It quickly displaced other forms of custody transfers, particularly apprenticeship. The appeal of the new device was evident in Louisiana, where the earlier constitutional ban succumbed to an 1864 declaration that the "legislature may enact general laws regulating the adoption of children . . . but no special laws shall be enacted in relation to particular or individual cases." Similarly, in the report accompanying the draft of a civil code for New York, the legal codifier David Dudley Field and his colleagues urged enactment of adoption: "The total absence of any provision for the adoption of children is one of the most remarkable defects of our law. Thousands of children are actually, though not legally, adopted every year; yet there is no method by which the adopting parents can secure the children to themselves except by a fictitious apprenticeship, a form which, when applied to children in the cradle, becomes absurd and repulsive. It is, indeed, so inappropriate a form in every case that it is rarely resorted to."

Field and the others supported their call for adoption by claiming that existing legal procedures with their bias toward the rights of natural parents inhibited the efforts of child-saving reformers. They contended that there were "very many childless parents who would gladly adopt children, but for their well-founded fears that they could never hold them securely." The more successful the child turned out to be, the more likely, as shown by "facts within the knowledge of almost everyone," that the natural parents would "reclaim the child as soon as any money can be made out of it."

Though the New York legislature rejected their plea, California responded. By century's end resistance to adoption had been overcome in almost every state. New York joined the ranks in 1873.[80]

Some of the sources of its appeal are revealed in *The Law of Adoption*, written in 1876 by William H. Whitmore to assist a Massachusetts legislative committee considering revisions of the state's pioneering law. Whitmore lamented that "the whole subject is one which has received little discussion from writers upon legal topics, except so far as it was part of the civil law, and very few decisions have been made under any of our state laws." He discovered that adoption's welfare ties and similarity to civil-law procedures made it suspect to common lawyers. After noting that all "legislation about it has been made from the philanthropic standpoint," he insisted that the "whole idea of creating children by act . . .

may even be said to be repugnant to" the common law. Whitmore questioned adoption's social implications as well, worrying that vague provisions might result in too casual a relationship between adoptees and their new parents. Swayed by emerging scientific theories on heredity, he warned: "[T]he fact that the subjects of adoption are so largely taken from the waifs of society, foundlings, or children whose parents are depraved and worthless; considering also the growing belief that many traits of mind are hereditary and almost irradicable; it may be questioned whether the great luxury of the American rule is for the public benefit." More pointedly he advised the legislature that the statutes could be used by fathers to adopt their illegitimate offspring, and thus remove "a great barrier to illegal connections." These concerns echoed the fears of many family savers, as did Whitmore's caveat that spinsters might adopt children, thus upsetting lines of descent and undermining the family.

Whitmore ended his analysis by calling for greater statutory uniformity and vigilance. He endorsed the child-saving aspects of adoption, but urged lawmakers to make sure that natural families were not unnecessarily disrupted by adoption. The newly formed households should ease, not inflame social disorder. His conclusion was pessimistic: "Evidently as the matters stand, the attempts of philanthropists to cure a small evil may have resulted in a serious injury to the rights of many persons."[81]

Judges Create a Special Legal Place for Adopted Families

Late nineteenth-century adoption statutes and judicial rulings wove the thread of Whitmore's analysis into the fabric of American family law. The creation of permanent, albeit artificial, families realized some of the most cherished goals of American family law. It was depicted as a panacea for the ills besetting American households: adoption created new families to take the place of failed ones. But judges and legislators approached it warily, anxious that the rights of all parties—the state included—be safeguarded.

Legislators created adoption but the courts used their powers of policy making and dispute settlement to actually define the artificial family. The bench's own creation, child-centered custody rules, served as the guide. Many of the statutes had in fact relied on the doctrines and their assumption of broad judicial discretion, for the language to be used to set standards of fitness for adoptive parents. The Massachusetts act and its imitators required that judges be satisfied that the new parents were able to furnish proper nurture and education, and that their assumption of custody was "fit and proper." Pennsylvania went further, specifying that judges be "satisfied that the welfare of such child will be promoted by such adoption." Connecticut insisted that the creation of the new household be "in the public interest." Pennsylvania judge Arthur Cummin offered a complementary reading of the intentions of the new procedure in 1888: "The purpose of our adoption act is to promote the welfare of the child to be adopted."[82]

The process by which these objectives were realized is clearly illustrated in the judicial reaction to two different issues: the powers of natural parents, and the limits of inheritance rights. The severing of natural bonds often proved to be the most painful and trying aspect of adoption. Adoption statutes generally required the consent of the natural parents. Since adoption, unlike transfers of custody, permanently dissolved natural families, parental consent had far greater implications. In a 1911 review, Almon G. Shepard warned: "[T]o take a child from his parents and consign him absolutely to the care and control of another is a serious step for a court to take, a step which should never be taken except after a full and complete hearing, and then only for clearly good reasons. Except in such cases, the necessities and well-being of the social state do not require the severing of the parental tie, and is more to be conserved by protecting and fostering it."[83]

Typically hesitant in the face of statutory alterations of domestic rights, judges insisted upon evidence either of parental notification and consent, or of unfitness to discharge their natural duties, as in the 1893 Wisconsin Supreme Court case of Mary Schiltz. She had been placed for adoption after her father's desertion and her mother's death, but John Schiltz returned and contested the action. The justices sustained his claim, and ordered a new hearing:

> The contention that the county court could, without notice to the plaintiff or opportunity to him to defend against the charge of abandonment, grant an order depriving the plaintiff of his most sacred natural rights in respect to his child, so jealously guarded and protected by the laws, offends against all our ideals respecting the administration of justice, and is opposed to the principles which lie at the foundation of all judicial systems not essentially despotic in their character and methods of procedure.

They held the adoption to be a violation of the parent's right to due process under the fourteenth amendment. Widows, mothers of illegitimate children, guardians, and juvenile institutions were also given their day in court to dispute adoptions.[84]

As they did with other custody claims, adoptive and natural parents were judged by child-welfare standards of parental fitness. California, like most states, waived parental consent "from a father or mother deprived of their civil rights or adjudged guilty of adultery, or of cruelty, and for either cause divorced, or adjudged to be a habitual drunkard, or who has been judicially deprived of the custody of the child on account of cruelty or neglect." Leaving children in the care of adoptive parents for an extended time also led to a forfeiture of natural parent rights. Judges relied on their own rules to determine whether children would be better off in artificial families than in natural ones. Indeed, creating such an alternative had been the primary intent of adoption.[85]

Statutes and court decisions used tests of adoptive parental fitness, and strict eligibility standards to make the artificial family approximate the legal ideal of a proper natural one in age, race, affection, and legal authority. The Tennessee Supreme Court observed: "It is difficult to see, upon any rule of construction, or of policy, why all the powers possessed by a natural father should not be exercised by him, who, by adoption of a minor, assumes the relationship of parent." The courts endorsed the right of adoptive parents to change a child's name, move its settlement and residence, and receive its earnings, all in an effort to make the artificial household replicate a natural one.[86]

Inheritance rights within artificial families posed more fundamental questions about the nature of adoption. In his 1876 analysis, Whitmore predicted that it was "not sufficient merely to state that a man may adopt a child to be to all intents and purposes his own, but to prevent endless complications it is necessary to enact in what degree this child shall be substituted in other relations to persons other than the adoptive parents." He emphasized that the problem was of "great importance in all questions of inheritance, since the adopting parent is often but the medium of transmission of property acquired by persons neither cognizant of nor consenting to the act of adoption." Since the law jealously guarded the transmission of family property, inheritance disputes revealed the extent to which adoptive families differed from natural ones.[87]

Each adoption statute alluded to inheritance, but too often it was in vague, confusing, and contradictory language despite an obvious intent to routinize the confused inheritance rights of adopted children. The judiciary's reaction was reminiscent of its response to innovations in bastardy law and in married women's rights. Judges endorsed the child-centered concept and goals of adoption, but qualified its invasion of common-law property rights.

Inheritance claims by adopted children were the most heavily litigated adoption issue. This litigation reveals the estate interests that competed with child welfare concerns in the creation of adoption. The Supreme Court of Missouri expressed the typical judicial sentiment toward these suits in the 1906 case of *Hochaday* v. *Lynn*: "Adoption being unknown to the common law and in derogation of it . . . statutes of adoption have always been more or less strictly construed." The justices contrasted the restrictions placed on the rights granted adopted children with the liberality that governed the transfer of custody to the adopting family. They invoked the authority of treatise writers who classified the new bond as an "artificial relation" or a "quasi-parental relation" to illustrate the "frosty attitude" of the law toward the inheritance rights of such children.[88]

Adoption law enabled children to join families, but judicial restrictiveness initially denied them a full legal membership in their adoptive households. Guided by their commitments to property rights and child nurture, the courts viewed adoption primarily as a welfare device, not as a mechanism for rearranging established lines of descent.

Most inheritance disputes testing these sentiments involved conflicts between the adopted child and relatives of the adopting parents, with blood relations challenging the artificial bond when it upset their expectations. The courts often used a strict construction of the statutes to aid the challengers, insisting on total compliance with the legislatively mandated adoption process. In *Long* v. *Hewitt* (1876), the Iowa Supreme Court refused to validate an adoption because the presiding judge had died before signing the adoption papers, and the adopting father had died in the interim. Though the adoption had been approved by the child's natural father, and the girl had been living with her new family, the justices argued that "courts of equity cannot dispense with all the regulations prescribed by a statute; for otherwise, equity would in effect defeat the very policy of legislative enactments."[89]

In 1873 attorney J. B. Varnum had pleaded for expanded inheritance rights for adopted children in the *Albany Law Journal*, after Governor John Dix had successfully lobbied to have inheritance rights stricken from the proposed New York adoption law. Varnum called for legislation that would "compel persons of property, who adopt children, either to provide for them in some way or if they do not want to do that, to formally say so by will." He feared that it had become "a case of not infrequent occurrence, that a child is trained up tenderly and in luxury, and then left in utter poverty, because the adopted parent had made no will. In the case of a daughter it works much hardship."[90]

As adoption became more common and less unsettling in the last decades of the nineteenth century, Varnum's arguments became more acceptable to judges and legislators alike. Eventually, adoptees' inheritance rights were seen as the logical culmination of the new relationship. Thus the New York legislature amended its 1873 adoption law in 1887, substituting the phrase "including the rights of inheritance" for the initial provision that had read "excepting the rights of inheritance."

A parallel judicial conclusion came from the Wyoming Supreme Court in 1893. The justices resolved a dispute over the estate of Michael Powell that pitted his siblings against his adopted daughter Emily. Powell's kin claimed that Emily's natural father had not endorsed the deed of adoption, thus rendering it invalid. She argued that he had abandoned her and that her mother had legitimately signed the documents. The judges heartily endorsed the addition of adoption to the state code: "[T]he right is a beneficial one to both the public and to those immediately concerned with its exercise." They praised it also for brightening the homes of childless couples as well as for rescuing orphans and needy children from lives of ignorance and vice. Consequently, they declared: "[I]n cases of this kind it is not the duty of the courts to bring the judicial microscope to bear upon the case in order that every slight defect may be found for declaring invalid an act consummated years before; but rather approach the case with the inclination to uphold such acts, if it is found that there was a substantial compliance with the statute." Ruling that Emily's father had lost his custody rights, and her mother had full authority to place her out for adoption, Emily was declared to be the lawfully adopted child and heir of Michael Powell.[91]

The child-centered biases of family law overcame the initial resistance to granting adopted children the right to inherit from their new fathers and mothers, but the apparent incompatibility of the adoptees' status with the interests of the law slowed extension of these rights. Thus adoptive children were denied the right to claim the estates of their new parents' blood relations. The courts and some legislatures took it upon themselves to protect the inheritance rights of consanguineous relatives who had not taken part in the adoption.

The Pennsylvania Supreme Court in a typical decision refused to allow an adopted child to benefit from testamentary bequests to its new parents. In rejecting the attempt of an adopted daughter to share in a bequest from her maternal grandfather, the court held: "[H]is gift of the remainder was to the children of his daughter Theresa Clark, and the heirs of her children. Adopted children are not children of the person by whom they have been adopted, and the Act of Assembly [of 1855], does not attempt the impossibility of making them such." The Ohio Supreme Court was even more explicit in 1898 when it concluded that the word "issue" in the state code referred to a person "of the blood of the testor and of the deceased child or other relative by birth. Adoption does not make the adopted child of the blood of its adopter, nor of the blood of his ancestors."[92] Some courts issued more flexible rulings, but in most cases the late nineteenth-century bench refused to regard the adopted child as a full legal member of its new family.[93]

The adopted child's anomalous legal position was apparent in judicial refusals to sever completely the natural ties of inheritance. A few states, Connecticut for example, stipulated that adopted children could not claim their natural parents' estates. But in the absence of explicit legislation, many courts granted them that right; it was another instance of narrow judicial reading of adoption statutes, but in this case the interpretation benefitted adoptees. The Supreme Court of Iowa explained: "[T]hey are the children of their natural parents, and the act of adoption does not deprive them of the statutory right of inheriting from their natural parents, unless there is a statute which in terms so provides." Some judges even endorsed the right of natural parents to inherit the estate of children that they had placed out for adoption. At times courts preferred those claims over the appeals of adopting parents.[94]

By giving priority to blood relations rather than adoptive ones, the courts maintained their allegiance to the domestic ideals of the common law and to a view of adoption as a custody device more than a total transfer of family membership. The adopted child, much like the illegitimate one, was consigned to a special legal status.[95] Joseph Newbold explained the resulting early twentieth-century reality of adoption in the 1927 *Minnesota Law Review*: "In the United States, adoption is a technical term that does not have the broad, unrestricted meaning which it had in the civil law, which was that a personality was destroyed and in its stead the creation of a new person as the natural son of the adopting father. The fact remains that an adopted son is not a natural son, but something else, and consequently, the status of the adopted child is not the status of a natural child."[96]

Adoption as an Instrument of Child Saving

By 1900 adoption was widely accepted and the creation of artificial families routine. But adoption retained the child-welfare orientation so influential in its creation. Most adoptees came from the ranks of dependent, neglected, and delinquent children; and innovation affected the process more than the status of adoption. Beginning with Michigan in 1891, states mandated stricter controls over adoption procedures, and insisted on thorough investigations of the natural and adoptive homes. Gradually professionalized social workers and child-care experts assumed control as part of their broadening efforts at family saving.[97]

A few decades earlier, reformers began to reject the solution of special children's asylums for the rehabilitation of wayward and dependent youths. They called for the replacement of institutional treatment with familylike methods such as apprenticeship, foster homes, and similar devices for placing out children.

As the movement increased in numbers and lobbying effectiveness, particularly with the establishment of urban organizations dedicated to the prevention of cruelty to children modeled on the first such society created in New York City in 1873, it secured passage of a series of child-protection acts. These included child-labor regulations aimed at removing children from the workforce; compulsory-education laws, which extended the period of youthful intellectual and cultural training; vice laws, which penalized adults for selling liquor, tobacco, or obscene materials to children; and higher-ages-of-consent statutes to protect the virtue of young women. Along with the protective legislation came new public assistance to the family in the form of stiffer support and desertion laws passed to catch roving men, and the rapid enactment of mother's pension statutes designed to stabilize the financial condition of one-parent families.[98]

Juvenile courts were a logical product of the movement. These specialized tribunals entered the urban legal system in the last decade of the century. The Chicago Bar Association extolled the pioneering 1899 Illinois act, lauding its methods and goals: "The whole trend and spirit of the act is that the State, acting through the Juvenile Court, exercises that tender solicitude and care over its neglected and dependent wards, that a wise and loving parent would exercise with reference to his own children under similar circumstances." The courts monitored parents and children, enforcing the new standards of family life and overseeing arranging the removal and treatment of children from homes that failed.[99]

Like most post–Civil War reform efforts, these measures were designed to save families. They sought to keep a child from being taken from his home by compelling parents to provide suitable education, clothing, food, and moral instruction. If that failed, though, one New York City reformer clamored in 1893 for the right of the state to "enter the privacy of every family, to carefully investigate the manner in which the children are provided for, physically, morally, and intellectually and, in every case, where the requirements fall below a prescribed standard, to remove the children and place them under the control of the state. Statutes in every state authorized such actions. But the family bias of the reform drive compelled the placement of children in as homelike an environment as possible. Harvey Rice, the trustee of a Cleveland industrial school, declared triumphantly that "so rapid is the transfer of the child to homes that very few remained for a year in the institution. There is no purer or holier influence on earth than that which surrounds the family altar."[100]

These reformers were inspired, as their predecessors had been, by concern for the plight of "children in need" and fear of the social threat that neglected, abused, homeless, or delinquent children represented. The shape these solutions took was primarily determined by the class and ethnic biases of the reformers. The bourgeois family ideal was the standard against which actual families were measured, and the mandate for intervention in families that deviated. The growing web of laws and procedures was justified, according to Homer Folks, a late nineteenth-century child-welfare reformer and chronicler of dependency laws, by "philanthropic instincts" and "the fact that neglected childhood is a menace to the state." Boston reformer Miriam Van Waters deftly explained the sentiment of the child savers in a 1927 volume fittingly entitled *Parents on Probation*: "Our goals of child protection have changed entirely since the time of Blackstone. Parents no longer can shield themselves behind *natural* rights. A new sense of chivalry toward childhood must be developed in communities; adults who pose stumbling blocks to the welfare of children, must be removed no matter how much pain it causes them."[101]

Reform legislation made it easier for public authorities to intervene in private homes; adoption ensured that the change in these children's lives would be permanent. In apprenticeships, placing-out systems, foster homes, and institutional care, the natural and thus the legal bonds remained. Adoption severed both, created new domestic relationships, and consequently added to family law the startling idea that parents could completely and permanently lose their children. It became the favored form of state aid to children taken from their natural homes.

Adoption thus embodies some of the major innovations—and limitations—of the republican custody law created in the nineteenth century. Devised in part to alleviate the welfare and estate difficulties attributed to other child-placement measures, it testified to a dawning concept by legal authorities of children as separate, if naturally dependent, individuals with their own needs and interests. Judges and legislators created a set of adoption rules that devalued natural ties if they were deemed to stand in the way of the bench's notions of proper child rearing. Only after parental fitness had been redefined by standards of child welfare and nurture, was the common law's repugnance to non–blood bonds cast aside and artificial homes permitted to supplant natural ones.

Child Custody at the End of the Century

Custody-law innovations during the formative era in domestic relations dominated family law for the rest of the century. The basic principles and priorities of the earlier period continued to guide the law, especially the use of child-welfare standards and of class and sexually biased parental fitness principles. These resulted in new legal notions of parental and filial legal relations.

Reverend Minot Savage, a leader of the Social Gospel movement, explained the altered domestic legal balance when he told parents in 1892: "You have no personal, selfish right at all over your children. You have invited an immortal to come into your temporary keeping; and you have only the right to treat that as a reverant trust committed to you for awhile, which you are to discharge with the highest and noblest sense of responsibility which you can attain." In the same year, the kindergarten pioneer and children's author Kate D. Wiggins described the independent standing of the child produced by complementary legal and social change: "Who owns the child? If the parent owns him—mind, body, and soul—we must adopt one line of argument; if, as a free-will human being, he owns himself, we must adopt another. In my thought, the parent is simply a divinely appointed guardian, who acts for his child until he attains what we call the age of discretion, that highly uncertain period which arrives very late in life with some persons and never arrives with others."[102]

Savage and Wiggins spoke for a republican household in which child rearing had become the most vital responsibility. As legislators and judges subscribed to this idea of the home, they circumscribed parental (particularly paternal) sovereignty, and expanded filial and maternal rights. At the turn of the century, this led the legal educator and progressive reformer Ernst Freund to declare that parental authority was "a power in trust. . . . The authority to control the child is not the natural right of the parents; it emanates from the State, and is an exercise of police power." Custody law had been completely reformulated to reflect that legal reality.[103]

American custody law over the course of the nineteenth century thus had rearranged spousal rights. Mothers gained new powers as custody and guardianship rights became part of the new legal domain of married women. Through the best-interests-of-the-child doctrine and its offshoots, women won the right to go to court, fight for and often obtain their children. The attorney Charles Savage took note of the trend in the 1883 *American Law Register*, when he postulated that in all areas of the law "the irresistible movement is in the direction of the most perfect legal equality of the married partners, consistent with family unity." The caveat, however, hinted at boundaries of the newly constructed maternal legal sphere.[104]

Debates, often bitter, over the proper household balance of power continued. The terms of the debate are reminiscent of the American revolutionaries' challenge to the English theory of indivisible political sovereignty. Antifeminists echoed the Tories when they contended that there must be an ultimate locus of power within the home, and that nature had ordained the patriarch as that sovereign. Madeline H. Dahlgren, a member of an anti–women's suffrage association, used that argument in testifying before a Congressional committee:

> The family . . . is the foundation of the State. Each family is represented by its head, just as the State ultimately finds the same unity, through a series of representations. Out of this comes peace, concord, proper representation, and adjustment—union. The new doctrine, which is illusive, may thus be defined: Marriage is a mere compact, and means diversity. Each family, therefore, must have separate individual representation, out of which arises diversity or division, and discord in the corner-stone of the State. Gentlemen, we cannot displace the corner-stone without destruction to the edifice itself!

Similarly, with complete emancipation within the home, Schouler maintained, the "idea of unity in domestic government—of domestic government at all—becomes weakened."[105]

However compelling such arguments may have been—and they proved attractive enough to the panicked late nineteenth-century middle class to stifle many increases in maternal and filial rights—they met the same fate as had Tory beliefs. A republican solution to household sovereignty accepted divided authority, and looked to the bench to resolve the inevitable disputes. Consequently, married women's custody rights, like so many other maternal prerogatives, remained a discretionary privilege usable only after domestic discord had undermined paternal authority. They constituted yet another example of the dependent nature of feminine rights in nineteenth-century family law; married women had a partial legal capacity, which illustrated the continued refusal of the legal order to grant them full membership. The law retained, in the words of the 1883 *American Law Review*, "a sort of legal guardianship over the power and property of women." Custody law transferred that guardianship from husbands to judges.

Thus the feminine legal rights attached to coverture expanded significantly in nineteenth-century America. But the ideal of judicially dependent rights, which was, as historian Linda Kerber has perceptively observed, antirepublican by its very nature, was never dropped. Alterations in the law increased married women's legal abilities, but like many initial maternal rights that had depended on equity, these common-law and statutory prerogatives remained tied to judicial discretion.[106]

The great increase in judicial discretion over child placement sanctioned by nineteenth-century custody-law transformed the legal measures used to gauge parental fitness as dramatically as it did spousal rights. The widespread desire to use the law to encourage proper family life led to statutory directives and judicial decisions that subjected parents and children to ever-tightening controls. Innovations—from the tender years doctrine to the juvenile court—carried with them notions of children's welfare needs, parental fitness, and codes of parental duties, which reduced the legal autonomy of the home. Such innovations authorized the courts to weigh claims for children's interests against legal rules emphasizing household integrity and social stability. The standards placed all parents—including mothers—and custodians at the mercy of judicial assessments of their capacity to rear the nation's future citizens.

Definitions of those nurturing duties were intricately elaborated. Roscoe Pound, the founding father of sociological jurisprudence, explained why in an 1916 article, "Individual Interests in Domestic Relations":

> In modern times the individual interests of the child came to be given greater weight. Today certain social interests are chiefly regarded. These are on the one hand a social interest in the maintenance of the family as a social institution and on the other hand a social interest in the protection of dependent persons, in securing to all individuals a moral and social life and in the rearing and training of sound and well-bred citizens for the future. The parent's claim to the custody of the child and to control over its bringing up has come to be greatly limited in order to secure these interests.[107]

Custody Rules

These developments expose the central tenets of American custody law as it emerged out of the nineteenth century: each family member had distinct legal interests, and the judiciary had the duty to resolve disputes between them. This adversarial view of the family, and the broad discretionary judicial powers it encouraged, constituted yet another way in which traditional family law was upset by republican beliefs and practices. Custody, like many other legal policies, had rested on a view of the family as a community of interests governed by a male patriarch. The displacement of that ideal initiated many of the major domestic innovations of the century. Among other things, it ensured that parental fitness, not paternal rights, would be the focus of custody disputes and that judges would assume part of the paternal responsibility, formerly the province of the father.

Perhaps the best summary of the new level of judicial sovereignty comes from a judge. Robert Grant served as a probate judge in Boston for over thirty years. Known in his own day mainly as a writer of romantic novels, Grant today is best remembered as a member of the commission that upheld the convictions of Sacco and Vanzetti. Judge Grant learned the law at Harvard Law School in the 1870s, when the innovations of the antebellum era had become legal commonplaces. In 1919, near the end of his career, he published a volume on family law. It acknowledged the sexual biases of custody law: "[T]he attitude of the courts where parents battle over children has inclined so steadily toward the mother that, unless she has shown herself wanton or exceptionally recreant or heartless, she is not likely to be separated from them." Yet, Grant feared that the "pendulum has swung so far in the opposite direction and the theory of paternal ownership been so completely discredited that the boot is sometimes upon the other leg, and women are heard asserting that they own their children because they bore them, and ought under no circumstances to be deprived of them—a complete reversal of the original injustice."

To let women know their place, the judge asserted the judicial ideal of child placement:

> [M]other-love, though set upon a pinnacle in the conscience of modern courts, must yield to a higher consideration, the well-being of her offspring. Where the custody of children is concerned the only enemy which the modern woman has to fear is her own unfitness. This is more apt to be challenged by the social workers and charitable societies, who might be called liaison officers of the courts of domestic relations, than by masculine ill-will. The beneficent body-guard, who probe into and bring to the attention of the court the conditions which menace the child, serve as a buffer between it and maternal Bolshevism.

Thirteen years earlier, Grant had expressed similar sentiments a bit less ponderously, when he offered a local bar association a poetic description of the judicial powers he so confidently exercised:

A probate Judge who outlives you
May break your will—yes tax it too.
. . . .
Concerning other things,
His power outrivals that of kings,
Your children, when you prove unfit,
Are whisked away by sovereign writ.
In short, it may truly be said,
He has you living, he has you dead.
The moral is, as on you trudge
Propitiate the Probate Judge.[108]

C O N C L U S I O N

For let it be borne in mind that, while in ruder forms of government more power was left with the Family itself for its own protection, the State has now taken to itself most of the old *patria potestas* and other forms of family autonomy, and assumed the maintenance of all rights pertaining to the Family. We have, therefore, as citizens the right to hold the State to a strict account for the discharge of the obligation thus assumed.

M. H. Buckham,
"The Relation of the Family to the State,"
International Review (1882)

CHAPTER 8

A JUDICIAL PATRIARCHY

FAMILY LAW AT THE TURN OF THE CENTURY

During the nineteenth century, domestic-relations law became the nation's chief means of governing the hearth. Charged with settling conflict, allocating power and resources, and fixing status and rights in society's most important institution, family law assumed a vital responsibility. The sagging bookshelves of courts, law libraries, attorneys' offices, governmental agencies, and private philanthropies bore mute but visible testimony to the results: an ever denser American law of domestic relations.

James Schouler offered a summary of the law in the 1895 revision of his treatise *Domestic Relations*: "The law of the family is universal in its adaptation. It deals directly with the individual. Its provisions are for man and woman; not for corporations or business firms. The ties of wife and child are for all classes and conditions; neither rank, wealth, nor social influence weighs heavily in the scales. To everyone public law assigns a home or domicile, and that domicile determines not only status, capacities, and rights of the person, but his title to personal property." Family law eluded Schouler. The intense public and private interests, conflicts, and fears spawned by the republican family and its governance generated a body of law that defied simple summation.[1]

American family law was not easily reducible to a set of clear and certain propositions. It was an amalgam of complex, often contradictory policies devised amid shifting concerns to govern every aspect of family life from courtship to probate. In it, innovations of the law's formative era lay side by side with revisions tacked on later in the century. Some of those changes were incremental and limited, like the refinements in the best-interests-of-the-child doctrine; others were abrupt and basic, like the eugenics-inspired nuptial restrictions. And within domestic-relations law, jurisdictional diversity and doctrinal inconsistency persisted, though it narrowed during the century. All in all, the regulatory presence of the state in family law had significantly increased by 1900, yet public authority continued to be tempered by a dogged commitment to the law's initial faith in family autonomy and private decision making.

This legal welter is best summarized by identifying its principal architect, the judiciary. Judicial domination was one of the most fundamental realities of nineteenth-century domestic-relations law. Its origins lay in the post-Revolutionary era when traditional Anglo-American family governance began its final decline. Only the state had the authority and legitimacy to be the regulator of the hearth. But in a society that cherished limited government and personal choice in all legal relations, especially family ones, state regulation was suspect. Consequently, the assumption of authority over the home by the individual states substituted an antagonistic relationship for the colonial ideal of harmony between the big and little commonwealths. The judge became the buffer and referee between the family and the state.

Over the course of the nineteenth century, trial and appellate judges became the primary domestic-relations agents of the expanding republican state. They assumed those powers in a special way. Judges were new kinds of patriarchs, ones invested with a power over some domestic relations that rivaled that of their predecessors. They used the broad discretionary authority conferred on them by equity and common-law procedures, and conceded by legislative inertia, to rewrite the laws governing the allocation of resources, rights, and duties within the home and between family members and the state. As the major arbiters of nineteenth-century family governance, judges took the lead in framing and applying the growing body of American domestic-relations law. Family law became their patriarchal domain.[2]

Though patriarchy had a broad range of meanings, it is the most precise label for the particular approach of the nineteenth-century bench to domestic relations. Most important, patriarchy best explains the way judges themselves viewed their role in domestic relations law. It was their vision that gives this new role its true meaning. The designation judicial patriarchy also indicates that part of the consciousness of these men, and part of their power, stemmed from their ability to divide the world into various categories and assume different poses in each; these ranged from patriarch to promoter to policeman. Patriarchy helps locate one variant of this consciousness. In judicial hands, the law became a distinctive set of doctrines and policies which mixed traditionalism with innovation. Judicial power was greatest in the law's formative era, but the courts retained significant authority over family governance throughout the century. The image of patriarchy helps to clarify and summarize American family law as it emerged from its first century and entered its second.

The Sources of Judicial Dominion

Judicial control of domestic relations sprang from the very nature of American governance of the home. Judges, reformers, legislators, and the others drawn into the popular debate over domestic relations often propounded different ideas of order, utility, and propriety in family governance; yet all of their views were firmly rooted in middle-class ideology and interests. They differed little in values, visions of proper family life, or class allegiances despite their at times vitriolic rhetoric. Policy disagreements among them stemmed more from differences in their training, governance responsibilities, professional commitments, and assessments of the seemingly endless family crisis. Judicial patriarchs dominated family law because within these institutional and intraclass rivalries judges succeeded in protecting their power over the law governing the hearth. The sources of the court's patriarchal authority were thus deeply embedded in the governing order of nineteenth-century America.[3]

Judicial Allegiance to the Common Law

The judiciary's patriarchal role had its roots in the common law. In part, it grew out of traditional equity powers like *parens patriae*. But more influential were nineteenth-century judicial commitments to common-law doctrines, methods, and power. These allegiances helped dictate domestic-relations policies and procedures. Prime among them were the bench's belief in the legitimacy, indeed the superiority, of common-law decision making as a source of public policies.

The potent influence of these commitments was evident in the strident partisanship of Joel Bishop. Throughout the second half of the nineteenth century, the writer was the most resolute defender of the judiciary's domination of domestic relations. In addition to his highly influential treatises on the law of marriage and divorce, Bishop wrote a number of books and pamphlets attacking legislative encroachment on the common law and the courts.[4]

A two-volume assessment of the law of married women published in 1871 was Bishop's most sustained indictment of legislative change. In it he railed against statutory reform and pled that the common law be allowed to adapt slowly to changing sentiments and conditions. Invoking the old common-law dictum that law cannot change behavior, he championed judge-made doctrines as the most effective and least disruptive way of accommodating new social demands such as women's rights: "[E]xperience proves that the habits make the law, and not the law habits; and that it is unnatural, and it tends to disturb the just repose of the community, to press forward a reform in either of these directions much in advance of the other." It was far better for all concerned, he urged, to let the bench decide when the "habit of thought and the consequent opinions prevailing have changed."[5]

In an 1888 pamphlet, *Common Law and Codification*, Bishop offered an even more explicit analysis, which placed judicial domestic-relations authority in the context of larger professional beliefs:

> Our common law is a particular system of reason. It is one of the great departments of our government structure; and the study, practice, and administration of it produce that training of the reason necessary to the carrying on of the government in other departments. Statutes are not reason, they are mere command. And if we convert our common law of reason into statutes, we in effect abolish reason in things legal and governmental, so that our whole system of government and law becomes a wreck. Such is the end of total codification. A partial codification works this result in part,—the eclipse is not total.

He recognized the existence of popular complaints against the legal order, but attributed most of them to ignorance and demagoguery. Bishop prayed that the public would not "bury the entire body because upon it are a few warts."[6]

Bishop painted in greater detail than most of his professional colleagues a common picture of the judicial process, one that the bench and bar repeatedly advanced to fend off statutory and other invasions of domestic-relations law. In pointed contrast to legislation, defenders of judicial authority stressed the courts' more personal case-by-case method of resolving private disputes and setting public policy. The trend toward popular election of judges merely reinforced this judicial authority.

In an 1871 article, Vermont Chief Justice Isaac Redfield emphasized a second element in that defense. He, like the vast majority of lawyers and judges, firmly believed a fundamental distinction existed between the common law and statutes. Redfield drew on that difference to assert that a "lawyer in the legislature is no more in the profession than a merchant, a banker, or a mechanic." Despite the obvious policy-making powers of the bench, this separation of professional roles allowed lawyers like Redfield and Bishop to regard common-law and judicial interpretations of statutes as a less partisan endeavor than legislation and therefore more worthy of popular support. Such a portrayal immeasurably enhanced the appeal of judicial policies and helped secure a dominant voice for the courts in all areas of economic and social policy, including domestic relations. It encouraged a conception of judges involved in family disputes as stern but just fathers.[7]

One other pervasive tendency of the nineteenth-century common law, to separate and categorize, also strengthened the hold of the courts on domestic-relations law. In this, as in all branches of the law, the judiciary adopted a particular approach, one rooted in the vision of each realm of legal practice as a special part of law and society. This functional and ideological line drawing had substantive results. Much of the judiciary's strength in nineteenth-century America flowed from its ability to use the common law to respond distinctively to diverse concerns. A specialized domestic-relations law was one of those responses; the judicial patriarchy was its chosen medium of expression.[8]

The emergence of domestic relations as a special category of the law thus was part of the larger movement of the legal order toward specialization. Not only did the legal system become a thicket of rules, procedures, and institutions; more important, each segment spawned its own set of interests and techniques. Consequently, in spite of repeated assertions of the law's conceptual uniformity, republican family law was never a mere offshoot of the legal order's more dominant commercial branches; the relationship between the two was much more complex and symbiotic. Though often influenced by concerns similar to those that guided commercial law—in particular, a judicial determination to promote economic development, protect common-law rights, advance private decision making, and deflect state activism—domestic relations law had its own biases, commitments, and interests as well.

In domestic-relations law, then, the broader use of the law to enhance the nation's maturing republican, capitalist order had its own meaning. Family law was derived from a singular responsibility: to promote and protect the republican family and its constellation of economic, social, cultural, and class interests. This particular mission helped define the distinct role of the courts in family governance; it created the basis for the judicial patriarchy. The uniqueness of domestic relations was apparent in the law's primary set of governing influences: gender biases, racial and ethnic animosities, domestic-relations individualism, child nurture beliefs, household economics, and idealized visions of the bourgeois family. These had far more of a direct impact on family law than they did on commercial law. Moreover, though entrepreneurial concerns were far from absent in domestic-relations law, they were filtered through these other influences.[9]

The movement toward specialization encouraged the construction of domestic-relations policies tailored to the needs of the household and its members as determined by the complex interaction of the law's users, creators, and critics. The tortured evolution of the rules guarding the entrance into the family offers a vivid demonstration of the creation of one portion of this new body of law. It suggests that in the tangled webs of agreement and disagreement among the authors of domestic-relations law not only did the judiciary have a controlling role but that the courts developed a particular orientation in addressing family questions.

Domestic relations became an influential body of law through its specialization. During the nineteenth century, a new self-consciousness emerged in the law. Statutes, judicial decisions, legal commentaries, and even reform tracts portrayed the family as a distinct institution and its governance as a particular branch of the law. These distinctions were not merely refinements in the century's pervasive demarcation of the public and private spheres of life. They testified to the designation of judge-dominated family governance as a critical and distinctive aspect of nineteenth-century American society and its governing order.[10]

Legislators Defer to Judges

The judiciary's secure place in nineteenth-century domestic-relations law also had its origins in the limitations of its main competitor, state legislatures. For much of the century, limited tenures, fiscal conservatism, bureaucratic ineptitude, and persistent antistatism combined with recurrent scandals and repeated deference to the bench to stifle legislative initiative. Legislators acted inconsistently and then generally in crisis issues like abortion and miscegenation. Indeed they often helped clothe judges with patriarchal robes, as Elinor Nims explained in a 1928 analysis of Illinois adoption law: "[T]he trend of modern legislation has been to make the court equal to enforcing the duties of the father and to provide a way whereby the state could insure . . . the care, protection, and support which a physically able and morally responsible parent would provide."[11]

Judicial ascendancy occurred as well because its case-by-case methods of policy making seemed more attuned to the needs of American families embroiled in disputes over estates, child custody, and the myriad of family controversies that disrupted households. Legislative action was denigrated as too general and cumbersome to govern properly something as intimate as domestic relations. Even the bench's critics tended to agree. Attorney Lelia Robinson did so in her 1899 book on spousal rights. Though quite critical of judicial paternalism, Robinson preferred the courts' discretionary methods to legislative directives. She endorsed the best-interests-of-the-child doctrine and thought that there was "great difficulty in attempting legislation upon the subject. It is so hard to tell what will be the best for the children." A judicial assessment, she like so many others concluded, was far more likely to serve a child's interests than a legislative command.[12]

Equally important, judicial dominance of domestic relations grew out of an abiding commitment to local control that lay at the heart of nineteenth-century American family law. An expression of the nation's persistent localism, opposition to national jurisdiction over the family stemmed from the deep-seated republican aversion to centralized government in general, and more particularly its lingering localist corollary that state policy makers and community officials best understood the dynamics of family life. The states tenaciously clung to their right to govern the home in the face of recurrent attempts at national uniformity. Overturning a writ of *habeas corpus* in an 1890 child custody dispute, United States Supreme Court Justice Samuel F. Miller declared unequivocally: "The whole subject of domestic relations of husband and wife, parent and child, belongs to the laws of the States and not the law of the United States."[13]

Ironically, perhaps, state domestic-relations chauvinism struck another blow at legislative authority by encouraging a reliance on the courts to harmonize the law of the disparate members of the union. The judicial form of uniformity sanctioned domestic-relations diversity and championed common-law rights over legislative directives. It arose out of conflicts between state family policies. Judicial solutions took two forms: a loosely arranged set of national domestic relations doctrines such as common-law marriage or the best-interests-of-the-child doctrine, and a set of rules devised to settle jurisdictional disputes that fell within the legal category of the conflicts of law. In either case, state jurisdiction allowed the courts the discretionary right to evaluate legislation in terms of national common-law priorities.[14]

The results were most telling in marriage law. Amid the confusion of state nuptial policies, the courts constructed a series of rules that sanctioned the evasion of most statutory controls on matrimony. Guided by their doctrine that local law should prevail, judges gave their blessing to couples who shopped for a forum that would accept their match. Only the most determined state policies, such as antimiscegenation, secured any extraterritorial authority. Bishop's presentation of the rule in his mid-century treatise reveals its debilitating impact on marriage legislation:

> If individuals, desiring to be married, find the laws of the country in which they are, forbidding the union within the territorial limit of the country,—find the statute law prescribing certain forms which they choose not to follow, or defining who may enter the relation, and they are not within the definition,—yet find a law, not of statutory regulations, but equally a law in their own country, under which they are able to superinduce the status upon themselves in some way say, by going into another state or country, they simply follow a proper impulse of nature and a rule of the highest reason, while also they follow the law of their own country in availing themselves of their privilege of marrying abroad. They do not, in any just sense of the expression, commit a fraud upon their own laws.

Efforts by reformers to strengthen nuptial regulation by eliminating the right to evade state law met with little success. Their attempts to pass complementary state legislation, congressional acts, and federal amendments generally failed. Instead, judicially devised rules that deferred to state sovereignty and relied on the courts to adjust statutory differences prevailed in marriage and most domestic relations.[15]

Protestors against Family Law

The courts held their own against their critics as well. Resistance to judicial domination of the law, often expressed in drives to revise common-law policies, sparked many of the controversies and alterations in domestic relations after its formative era. A defiant declaration from an 1880 women's rights conference came from one major group of opponents: "The theory of a masculine head to rule the family, the church, or the State is contrary to Republican principles and the fruitful source of rebellion and corruption." Criticism of the subordinate status of women and other dependents in domestic-relations law persisted as long as the demand for equal family rights conflicted with judicially administered policies; it was fed by the obvious gap between republican ideals, especially the aversion to dependency, and the limited legal rights of women and children. Lelia Robinson, the Boston lawyer, even suggested boldly that a few female judges might alter the very content of family law.[16]

More frequently, judicially dominated domestic-relations law came under indictment for failing to live up to its self-appointed goals of producing stable households and self-reliant individuals than for its inability to secure domestic equity. After 1830, when the republican family had been defined as a set of orthodox practices and beliefs, reformers became the leading critics of domestic-relations law. Intent on altering household governance by expanding state regulatory authority, they often clashed with judges and the bench's professional, legislative, and other allies. The judiciary and its supporters were determined to blunt intervention into what had been considered private calculation and to protect the public and private spheres of life carved out early in the century. The excessive individualism and regulatory reluctance sanctioned by these judicial commitments deeply troubled the family savers.

Reverend Samuel Dike of the National League for the Protection of the Family voiced a typical complaint in 1889: "[L]aw is vastly less careful of domestic interests as affected by marriage and divorce, than it is of the transactions and records of real property! The American people surely should not long permit property to gain the ear of legislation more readily than the family." But the citizenry did just that; and in so doing encouraged judicial policies predicated on the differences between commercial and domestic-relations law.[17]

Even reform measures that altered family law could result in changes quite different from the ones family savers envisioned; indeed they often reinforced the bench's influence over family governance. In a study of turn-of-the-century divorce litigation, historian Elaine May found that the reliance of reformers on coercive legal measures to protect the family not only "ushered in a new trend in government intervention that would accelerate through the twentieth century," but by "expanding the bureaucratic network" they fed "the very monster that gave rise to their anxieties. As governmental structure reached further into individual lives, it undercut the voluntaristic methods the Protestants had hoped to restore."

Child-labor reformer Florence Kelley reflected this confusion in an 1882 article. She confidently asserted that legal reforms had dethroned the common law's commercial concept of childhood and begun to act in "guarding all children without reference to the family, diminishing paternal power, and making the child more and more nearly the ward of the state." At the same time she felt free to claim that the "child's prime safeguard is the family, and whatsoever strikes the family wounds the child." Kelley's declarations reveal the reformers' incompatible objectives: trying to preserve republican individualism and economic liberalism, while creating a more cooperative community and active state.[18]

The major product of family saving was an interventionist strategy that relied on a therapeutic approach to family problems. The designation of troubled homes as diseased, and the state and the helping professions as agents of therapy permeated late nineteenth-century reform. Consequently, reformers developed and applied a public set of household standards that fostered a new type of dependency, one with its own system of rewards and punishments. Support for such action was widespread. Chicagoan Lucinda Chandler, a vice-president of the National Women's Suffrage Society and proponent of family limitation, insisted that "the state must be in its legislation and its political operation a supplement to the integrity and moral righteousness of the home, or it will inevitably disintegrate and become a destroyer of the home."[19]

Despite the new restraints imposed by family-saving legislation and more vigorous protective agencies, these institutional changes added to the attraction of the judiciary's patriarchal methods of family governance. Unlike the reformers, the courts relied less on direct compulsion and more on the subtle coercion of the common law. In a polity congenitally suspicious of state activism and constantly fearful that government might overstep its legitimate bounds, the courts' patriarchal approach found consistent support. In fact, the bench assumed a new role as the major institutional check on the therapeutic state.

Equally important, family savers suffered from their own intrinsic weaknesses. The most thoughtful reformers were sincere men and women who raised vital questions about family governance. But too often they were guided by narrow beliefs about proper republican family life and adhered to unrealistic ideals of household uniformity. As a result, they continually lapsed into racism, xenophobia, gender and age discrimination, and class repression. Unwilling to accept the diversity of American family life, they often turned to coercion to induce family conformity. But reforms that required massive increases in state authority sapped the strength of the movement. They overreached the possible bounds of change and stirred the latent hostility to state activism that so pervaded the citizenry. Only on subjects that evoked widespread public anxiety, such as miscegenation, abortion, or venereal disease, could these tactics succeed.[20]

Isaac Redfield probed the sources of opposition to reform in an 1872 article. The piece was a lengthy endorsement of *People* v. *Turner*, an Illinois Supreme Court decision two years before, declaring an 1867 child-saving act unconstitutional. The statute had authorized the apprehension of any child between the ages of six and sixteen who "is a vagrant, or is destitute of proper parental care, or is growing up in mendicancy, ignorance, idleness, or vice." Redfield's analysis provides an insight into the general judicial aversion to such measures.

Redfield accepted the benevolent intent of such reform legislation: "[R]eformers of all ages have mainly been well-intentioned men, who had the highest good for the greatest number deeply at heart." Even so, his judicial skepticism led him to accuse them of devising schemes based on narrow interests and a ready resort to coercion:

> We have no evil will towards reformers of any class. The love of reform comes always from the best of purposes; from a desire to have others participate in the beauty and excellence which we have found for ourselves. But we cannot disguise the fact, as we look back, across the dark tract of the ages, that reformers, in all times and in all countries, invoke the aid of force and compulsion in some form. They sincerely believe themselves entitled to exercise the strong arm of the law, in order to bring about some greater good, or in some shorter period, than could otherwise be accomplished. The time for the resort to the fagot or the gibbet or the rack or the wheel, has indeed passed away; at which we all rejoice. But in doing so, we are in danger of forgetting, that those who invented and exercised these engines of reform were animated by the same spirit as ourselves—the doing of good to those who were too ignorant or too perverse willingly to accept their highest good at our hands.

The New England jurist then hinted darkly that acts like the failed Illinois statute had "an ominous squint toward the children of Roman Catholic parents, and of the multitudes of poor emigrants yearly coming to our shores."

Redfield questioned the legitimacy of such legislative coercion: "There is a wide field of debatable ground between the dominion of punishment for crime and that of mere improved culture, in which it will be a long time before any exact definition of jurisdiction or of the distribution of service between the voluntary and compulsory fields can be satisfactorily fixed." Such suspicion of reform motivation and technique permeated the nineteenth-century bench and bar. It supported a cautious treatment of statutory changes and strengthened the judiciary's faith in its own methods and commitments, which in turn buttressed the judicial patriarchy.[21]

As the only policy makers with a broad concept of domestic relations, judges held the upper hand in all contests over the construction of the law. The bench retained the power to do so, in part, because judges wielded an essentially negative governmental weapon. Unlike legislators or reformers, they could block or dilute family-law changes by appealing to procedural rules or common-law dictums, without having to devise a new durable conception of an active state that could transcend the law's initial promotion of self-interest over community needs.

Gender Roles and Judicial Power

Judicial hegemony over domestic relations continued as well because the bench's patriarchal role rested on more than institutional developments. To a significant degree, the courts' power had its origins in nineteenth-century gender alliances and castes, especially the rigid segregation of worldly males and home-bound females. The judicial patriarchy represented a refined and revised legal version of the distinction between the male authority to govern the home and the female responsibility to maintain it. By seizing the power to define the legal abilities of married women, and other family members, judges helped perpetuate, albeit in altered form, patriarchal authority within republican society. The judicial acquisition of patriarchal powers stemmed from the traditional assumption that married women lacked the economic and intellectual independence to act without male supervision (and thus needed special protection), combined with the new faith in separate and mutually exclusive spheres so central to the organization of the republican family.[22]

These prevailing notions of family governance and gender capabilities helped to define the particular powers of the bench in domestic relations. Judicial creations such as the best-interests-of-the-child doctrine or breach-of-marriage-promise rules illustrate their influence on the creation of domestic-relations law. Such policies reflected the partial capacity that was the central reality of women's place in nineteenth-century family law.

Wives and mothers were free to contract, but unlike men they were not always bound by their agreements. Conversely, whereas in Blackstone's *Commentaries* male rights *a fiori* meant that married women had none, nineteenth-century family law recognized rights in dependency, or perhaps more accurately rights separate from property. As the main family beneficiaries of the rights consciousness embedded in republican legal ideology, married women came to be considered as a quasi-independent class with particular claims on the conscience of the courts. This legal shift resulted in the critical distinction between dependent legal powers based on judicial discretion, and independent legal rights assertable by women themselves.[23]

In the hands of the judicial patriarchy, that dichotomy proved crucial to feminine status in American domestic relations law. It led to double-edged family policies. Judges recast the law to aid wives and mothers who successfully performed household responsibilities such as child rearing and to compensate them for the travails of courtship and matrimony, while at the same time invoking their authority to check radical alterations in the subordinate legal status of women. Judicially inspired changes in domestic relations thus allowed for an expanded feminine presence in the legal order, but in a way that ensured that women's domestic powers would not be translated into extensive external political and economic authority. These legal developments point to a persistent reluctance to grant women superior legal powers, especially statutorily protected legal rights.

Unquestionably, in republican domestic-relations law, women and their children gained new legal footholds. Granted significant legal identities for the first time in Anglo-American law, these former family dependents secured for themselves a much more independent place in the law of the home and the community. Florence Kelley pointed out that nowhere in Blackstone's *Commentaries* had there been "a hint that the common law regarded the child as an individual with a distinctive legal status." But by 1882 the law had been compelled to recognize "the child's welfare as a direct object of legislation apart from the family."[24]

The same could be, and was, said of wives and mothers. In 1918, attorney Mary Greene even attacked feminists for failing to recognize the changed legal status of married women. She contended that feminist demands for family-law reform were fundamentally misdirected because they ignored the vast powers conferred on women by the judiciary. Greene maintained that further change was not necessary, the courts had aided wives and mothers as much as the law could. As Greene insisted, the source of legal change was critical; it was as significant as the changes themselves. Blackstone had been exiled from American family law by a judicial patriarchy whose dominion over the legal rights of all family members perpetuated and reinvigorated paternal governance of the home.[25]

The traditional purpose of family law—producing stable families— and male governance proved inseparable in the republican legal order. When a household patriarchy became untenable, a judicial one arose. The resulting dilution of paternal rights and creation of judicially dependent maternal and filial legal prerogatives allowed judges to assume the mantle of patriarch. The degree to which the judiciary displaced domestic patriarchs was evident in the mid-century complaint of southern apologist George Fitzhugh. An admirer of the seventeenth-century political theorist Sir Robert Filmer, a resolute defender of patriarchalism,

Fitzhugh lamented in 1857: "Riots, mobs, strikes, and revolution are daily occurring. The mass of mankind cannot be governed by law. More of despotic discretion and less of law is what this world wants. . . . There is too much law and too little Government in this world." Here too Fitzhugh championed a lost cause.[26]

The Impact of the Judicial Patriarchy

The persistence of patriarchy in its new guise proved to be critical to the shaping of nineteenth-century domestic-relations law. It allowed judges to supervise the laying of a republican base for American family governance and oversee later renovations.

Doctrines such as common-law marriage and the tender years rule, along with the bench's intricate standards of proper domestic conduct and legitimate state intervention, had the power to organize professional and popular conceptions of domestic-relations law. Though their influence is not reducible to mathematical analysis, these judicial creations were far more than elitist proscriptions, meaningless literary expressions, or idiosyncratic appellate directives. In the law, language is an instrument of power. These doctrines and standards established an intellectual and political language that helped set the agenda for debates over the family and law. By providing the terms for discussion and controversy, the legal language of domestic relations helped shape their results. The resort to analogy, metaphor, fiction, and precedent thus not only enabled the courts to respond to new conditions, but allowed judges to do so in a way that ensured that their legal instruments retained their potency. The durability of domestic-relations doctrines and standards immeasurably strengthened the hold of the judicial patriarchy on family law.[27]

Although legal language established the terms of family law, the common law's adversarial methods set the context. The most obvious effect was a tendency to define the family as a collection of distinct legal personalities rife with potentially antagonistic relations: husband versus wife, parent versus child, state versus father. When many innovations of domestic-relations law's formative era came into question, the adversarial concept of the family dictated that legal revision would be approached as a form of dispute resolution. Family law debates, particularly late in the nineteenth century, were consequently punctuated by military metaphors that stirred visions of pitched battles being fought over the nation's homes. The adversarial approach to domestic relations encouraged such depictions; it also tended to distort the actual character of legal change by highlighting cases of trouble and camouflaging more mundane, but important modifications and alterations of the law. More important, the adversarial nature of domestic-relations law impeded a clear articulation of the public's role in family governance by placing the focus on individual rights and common-law authority and thus obscuring legitimate community interests.

In a paradoxical way, judicial domination of domestic-relations law also limited the possibilities of significant reform. The steadfast commitment of the bench to the basic tenets of family governance established in the law's formative era meant that legislatures would be the main avenue of subsequent reform. Recognizing that, reformers descended on state houses late in the nineteenth century to prod legislators into action. Thanks to their efforts, state domestic-relations codes grew thicker and thicker. Yet judicial hegemony over the law was so pervasive that in most cases modifications came in piecemeal fashion, often merely codifying judicial doctrines and standards. Equally significant, the bench's intricate framework of family governance gave judges a unique ability to integrate statutory changes into their ongoing procedures and policies. Though direct and fundamental legislative interventions into family law, such as adoption provisions or antimiscegenation acts, did compel the bench to modify significantly its governance of domestic relations, these were exceptional developments. Most of the acts filling the codebooks relied far more on judicial discretion than state regulation to govern the family.

Statutory revision thus narrowed but did not upset the patriarchal powers of the courts. In some cases, legislation even strengthened the bench's hold on domestic relations. As historian Richard Hofstadter noted: "[T]he development of regulative and humane legislation required the skills of lawyers and economists, sociologists and political scientists, in the writing of laws and in the staffing of administrative and regulative bodies. Controversy over such issues created a new market for the books and magazine articles of the experts and engendered a new respect for their specialized expertise. Reform brought with it the brain trust." Patriarchal judges were charter members of that august monopoly.[28]

Indeed a statutory creation and one of the most uniformly praised progressive reforms, the juvenile court constituted the apogee of the judicial patriarchy. Welcomed with open arms by their appellate brethren, juvenile-court judges presided over a tribunal that stood as the most explicit assertion of the bench's peculiar family-law powers. In a 1909 description of the court, social worker Henry Thurston stressed that special authority: "[T]he juvenile court has simply the parental and human problem of trying to do just what the child needs to have done for him." A year later, corporation lawyer Bernard Flexner described the juvenile-court judge as "an elder brother, offering encouragement and helpful advice as to how the home may be improved and the environment of the children and of the family generally sweetened and purified." As the first head of the Cook County Juvenile Court, Judge Richard Tuthill of Illinois put this paternalistic approach into practice. He would "talk with the boy, give him a good talk just as I would my own boy." Granted broad discretion under purposely vague statutes dealing with youthful crime and dependency, the juvenile-court judge assumed a patriarchal role first devised by the judiciary in the decades after the revolution. The rapid establishment of juvenile courts in early twentieth-century America demonstrates just how appealing that judicial role had become.[29]

The Continuing Legacy of Nineteenth-Century Family Law

Out of the intricate interplay of two of nineteenth-century America's most vital and dynamic institutions, the family and the legal order, came a remarkable corpus of law. Fundamental changes during the formative era of domestic-relations law established a distinctive American method of governing the home. Never a static body of rules, over the course of the century and beyond the law underwent constant, though selective, changes. Its peculiar blend of public and private rights and duties established a system of family governance that became a critical element of the social and legal order.

Perhaps the most enduring product of the distinctive domestic-relations law hammered out in nineteenth-century America was the legal concept of the family as a collection of separate legal individuals rather than an organic part of the body politic. This occurred at the expense of traditional notions of paternal sovereignty and household legal unity. The older concept of the family, evident in the legal maxim "the husband and wife are one, and that one is the husband," gradually declined as the distinct legal personalities of married women and their children developed. In an analysis of family governance in France, sociologist Jacques Donzelot has persuasively argued that "[f]amily patriarchalism was destroyed only at the cost of a patriarchy of the State." In republican America, the state's new paternal authority was delegated to the bench; judges used their patriarchal powers to forge direct relationships between each family member and the state. These legal identities breached the home's protective walls and vitiated its role as a buffer between the state and each occupant of the household.[30]

Critics and proponents alike recognized the fundamental nature of this legal development. In 1900 Reverend Samuel Dike pessimistically commented at length on the change:

> We do not recognize the Family at all in our National Constitution. It appears in our State laws only as an object of some care, but not as an element of our political power. Politically the family is not in sight. We are purely individualistic, giving no recognized place to the paternal idea of Germany, nor to the altruism on the part of the elder brother, as in Great Britain. . . . The perils of democracy in the domestic institution are a part of the price we pay for our political system. Looking intently at the work of the individual we have taken too little notice of the work of the Family in making the individual. It is possible that the contrasts we are fond of showing between our domestic morality and that of others may be less significant of our security than we think. The fear of [British Prime Minister William] Gladstone for our future centered largely upon our ability to protect the family.

Though he reached the same conclusion, sociologist Arthur Calhoun enthusiastically proclaimed the passing of what he termed "patriarchalism and familism." His 1917 history of the American family summarized the fundamental shift in household governance: "The subsidence of the family as the arbiter of life is the culmination of the movement of political democracy which has made the individual the social unit." Calhoun felt compelled to add that the "new view is that the higher and more obligatory relation is to society rather than to the family; the family goes back to the age of savagery while the state belongs to the age of civilization." Whether their fellow citizens rejoiced with the sociologist or fretted with the minister, it is clear that by encouraging the legal primacy of the individual, domestic-relations law had become the primary public medium for governing the republican family.[31]

Because of the varied interests at work within nineteenth-century family governance, the law did not develop along a clearly linear path. Instead, it constantly blended innovation with traditionalism. Family law was a mix of common-law rules, statutory commands, and private practices and prejudices. Each reflected the dominant forces that came to bear on domestic relations, ranging from intense racial antipathies and extreme fiscal fears to gender biases and antibureaucratic sentiments. As a result of its peculiar chronology, domestic relations retained a certain undefinable quality; it was as much the sum of its many parts as it was a finely honed legal subject.

These complex sources produced a powerful body of law. Nineteenth-century family law's major doctrines remained largely in place until the late twentieth century. Agitation over the law declined significantly after the second decade of the twentieth century; but it erupted once again in the 1960s, embroiling many of the basic elements of nineteenth-century domestic-relations law in bitter controversy. An increasing number of conflicts have appeared: couples protesting statutory restrictions on matrimony and cohabitation; women objecting to criminal penalties on contraception and abortion; children attacking paternalistic controls on their legal rights; parents assailing legally sanctioned state regulation of their homes; fathers questioning maternally biased custody rules. These complaints have renewed an old debate over republican governance of the home.

As a new set of reformers, legislators, judges, and litigants enter the fray, the continued influence of nineteenth-century domestic-relations law becomes apparent. The law's detractors and its defenders have voiced concerns and relied on arguments strongly reminiscent of the skirmishes over the family that broke out in the 1840s and continued through the nineteenth century. Not surprisingly, contemporary protests have centered on the legislative innovations of the late nineteenth century, and challengers have achieved their greatest successes in courtrooms. These triumphs suggest that the judicial patriarchy still reigns. Major breaches in the law have come in the form of federal and state appellate decisions endorsing individual domestic-relations rights and undermining statutory controls on miscegenation, birth control, abortion, and child saving. As they had earlier, judicial decisions have become symbols and slogans of the debate; Loving, Gault, Griswold, Parnum, and Roe stand for more than mere court rulings, they represent victories and defeats in the latest family-law campaigns. Once again, as well, state legislatures and the Congress become the principal targets of those who insist that only coercive laws can save the American home and protect treasured family orthodoxies.[32]

Late twentieth-century family-law controversies are not evidence of historical stasis or circularity. Far from that, they are the products of important changes in the home and the law. Indeed, the dominant role of the United States Supreme Court and the Congress in these struggles indicates that major institutional developments have occurred in domestic relations since the turn of the century. But the nature of continuing debate over family governance reveals the powerful legacy of nineteenth-century domestic-relations law. In many ways it continues to supply the terms of debate, especially in contests over abortion, sexual equality, nuptial freedom, child welfare, and judicial authority over the family. The lingering influence of those earlier policies suggests just how fundamental were the changes of the nineteenth century. Though contemporary actors are but dimly aware of the fact, they are merely the latest players in a legal drama the history of which stretches back to the first days of the republic. From that era to this, governing the hearth has been too vital to the social order to long remain out of the limelight.

A B B R E V I A T I O N S

AAPS	*American Academy of Political and Social Science*
ABAJ	*American Bar Association Journal*
ABFJ	*American Bar Foundation Journal*
ABS	*American Behavioral Scientist*
AHR	*American Historical Review*
AJLH	*American Journal of Legal History*
AJS	*American Journal of Sociology*
AlaLR	*Alabama Law Review*
ALJ	*Albany Law Journal*
ALRec	*American Law Record*
ALReg	*American Law Register*
ALRev	*American Law Review*
AM	*Atlantic Monthly*
AQ	*American Quarterly*
Arena	*The Arena Magazine*
AS	*American Scholar*
ASR	*American Sociological Review*
AStJ	*American Studies Journal*
BayLR	*Baylor Law Review*
BCRev	*Birth Control Review*
BJS	*British Journal of Sociology*
BULR	*Boston University Law Review*
CalLR	*California Law Review*
CC	*Case and Comment*
CinLR	*Cincinnati Law Review*
CLJ	*Central Law Journal*
CLQ	*Cornell Law Quarterly*
CM	*Century Magazine*
ColLR	*Columbia Law Review*
CWH	*Civil War History*
CWRLR	*Case Western Reserve Law Review*
Forum	*The Forum Magazine*
FS	*Feminist Studies*

GaHQ	*Georgia Historical Quarterly*
GeoLJ	*Georgetown Law Journal*
HCQ	*History of Childhood Quarterly*
HLR	*Harvard Law Review*
HM	*Harper's Magazine*
IaLB	*Iowa Law Bulletin*
IaLR	*Iowa Law Review*
ICLQ	*International and Comparative Law Quarterly*
IlLR	*Illinois Law Review*
IR	*International Review*
JAH	*Journal of American History*
JCL	*Journal of Comparative Legislation*
JFL	*Journal of Family Law*
JHId	*Journal of the History of Ideas*
JIH	*Journal of Interdisciplinary History*
JLS	*Journal of Legal Studies*
JMF	*Journal of Marriage and the Family*
JNH	*Journal of Negro History*
JSH	*Journal of Southern History*
JSocH	*Journal of Social History*
LCP	*Law and Contemporary Problems*
LLJ	*Law Library Journal*
LN	*Law Notes*
LoyLR	*Loyola Law Review*
LQR	*Law Quarterly Review*
LSR	*Law and Society Review*
LT	*Law Times*
MdLR	*Maryland Law Review*
MHM	*Maryland Historical Magazine*
MinnLR	*Minnesota Law Review*
MissLJ	*Mississippi Law Journal*
MLJ	*Medico-Legal Journal*
MLR	*Michigan Law Review*
MP	*Marxist Perspectives*
MVHR	*Mississippi Valley Historical Review*
NAR	*North American Review*
Nation	*The Nation Magazine*

NebLR	*Nebraska Law Review*
NCHR	*North Carolina Historical Review*
NCLR	*North Carolina Law Review*
NEHGR	*New England Historical and Genealogical Register*
NEQ	*New England Quarterly*
NLR	*Northwestern Law Review*
NYLF	*New York Law Forum*
NYULR	*New York University Law Review*
OH	*Ohio History*
OreLR	*Oregon Law Review*
PAH	*Perspectives in American History*
PLJ	*Pittsburgh Law Journal*
PP	*Past and Present*
PSM	*Popular Science Monthly*
PSQ	*Popular Science Quarterly*
SAQ	*South Atlantic Quarterly*
SCaLR	*South Carolina Law Review*
SCLR	*Southern California Law Review*
SLR	*Southern Law Review*
Soc	*Societas*
SoR	*Social Research*
StanLR	*Stanford Law Review*
StLLJ	*St. Louis Law Journal*
UChiLR	*University of Chicago Law Review*
UCLALR	*University of California, Los Angeles Law Review*
UColLR	*University of Colorado Law Review*
UPLR	*University of Pennsylvania Law Review*
VaLJ	*Virginia Law Journal*
ValLR	*Valparaiso Law Review*
VaLR	*Virginia Law Review*
VaLReg	*Virginia Legal Register*
VLR	*Vanderbilt Law Review*
WMLR	*William and Mary Law Review*
WMQ	*William and Mary Quarterly*
YLJ	*Yale Law Journal*

N O T E S

Preface

1 In the following pages I will use the terms "family law" and "domestic-relations law" as interchangeable labels for the body of laws relating to the organization of the family and the legal relations of its members. Though neither phrase was widely used in much of the nineteenth century, domestic relations became the dominant title of the law by the end of the period and family law an equally used term in the twentieth century. In England, neither the field nor the titles were accepted as separate areas of the law until the twentieth century.

2 This volume is based on research first presented in the form of a dissertation and some of the issues and legal developments in nineteenth-century family law are more fully examined in the thesis. See Michael Grossberg, "Law and the Family in Nineteenth-Century America," (Ph.D. diss., Brandeis University, 1979). For discussions of some historiographical issues on the topic see Michael Grossberg, "Guarding the Altar: Physiological Restrictions and the Rise of State Intervention in Matrimony," *AJLH* 26 (1982):197–226; Grossberg, "Who Gets the Child? Custody, Guardianship, and the Rise of a Judicial Patriarchy in Nineteenth-Century America," *FS* 9 (1983):235–60.

3 For assessments of the strengths and weaknesses of appellate reports as historical evidence and of the character of the American appellate bench see G. Edward White, "The Appellate Court Opinion as Historical Source Material," *JIH* 1 (1971):491–509; and Robert A. Kagan, Bliss Cartright, Lawrence M. Friedman, and Stanton M. Wheeler, "The Business of State Supreme Courts, 1870–1970," *StanLR* 30 (1977):121–56.

4 *The Cheyenne Way* (Norman, Okla., 1941), p. 29. For general discussions of these issues see Richard Abel, "Law Books and Books About Law," *StanLR* 26 (1973):175–228; and David Engel, "Legal Pluralism in an American Community: Perspectives on a Civil Trial Court," *ABFJ* (1980):425–54.

Chapter 1

1   John Adams, *Diary and Autobiography of John Adams*, ed. L. H. Butterfield, et al. (Cambridge, Mass., 1961), 4:123.

2   Joel P. Bishop, *First Book of Law* (Boston, 1868), p. 216.

3   William Gouge quoted in John Demos, *A Little Commonwealth, Family Life in Plymouth Colony* (New York, 1970), p. x; and see generally Edmund S. Morgan, *The Puritan Family* (Boston, 1944); Morgan, *Virginians at Home* (Williamsburg, Va., 1952); David Rothman, *The Discovery of the Asylum, Social Order and Disorder in the New Republic* (Boston, 1971), pp. 10, 16–17; Lorena S. Walsh, " 'Till Death Do Us Part': Marriage and the Family in Seventeenth-Century Maryland," in *The Chesapeake in the Seventeenth Century: Essays on Anglo-American Society*, ed. Thad W. Tate and David L. Ammerman (Chapel Hill, N.C., 1979), pp. 126–52.

4   Quoted in Julia P. Spruill, *Women's Life and Work in the Southern Colonies* (Chapel Hill, N.C., 1938), p. 44.

5   Kenneth A. Lockridge, *A New England Town: The First Hundred Years* (New York, 1970); Phillip Greven, *Four Generations: Population, Land, and Family in Colonial Andover, Massachusetts* (Ithaca, N.Y., 1970); Russell R. Menard, "Immigrants and Their Increase: The Process of Population Growth in Early Colonial Maryland," in *Law, Society, and Politics in Early Maryland*, ed. Aubrey C. Land, Lois Green Carr, and Edward C. Pappenfuse (Baltimore, 1977), pp. 88–110; Darrett B. Rutman and Anita H. Rutman, " 'Now-Wives and Sons-Law': Parental Death in a Seventeenth-Century Virginia County," in *The Chesapeake in the Seventeenth Century*, pp. 153–82.

6   David H. Flaherty, *Privacy in Colonial America* (Charlottesville, Va., 1970), pp. 54–59; Nancy F. Cott, "Eighteenth-Century Family and Social Life as Revealed in Massachusetts Divorce Records," *JSocH* 10 (1976):35; James A. Henretta, "Families and Farms: Mentalité in Pre-Industrial America," *WMQ*, 3rd series, 35 (1978):3–32.

7   Barbara Laslett, "The Family as a Public and Private Institution: An Historical Perspective," *JMF* 35 (1973):480–92; Kirk Jeffrey, "The American Family as a Utopian Retreat from the City," *Soundings* 55 (1972):21–41; John P. Demos, "The American Family in Past Time," *AS* 13 (1974):442–46; Eli Zaretsky, *Capitalism, the Family, and Personal Life* (New York, 1976); Carl Degler, *At Odds, Women and the Family in America from the Revolution to the Present* (Oxford, 1980), chap. 1.

8   John Kasson, *Civilizing the Machine, Technology and Republican Values, 1770–1900* (New York, 1970), p. 5.

9   Gordon Wood, *The Creation of the American Republic, 1776–1787*

(Chapel Hill, N.C., 1969); Eric Foner, *Tom Paine and Revolutionary America* (New York, 1976).

10 Jay Fliegelman, *Prodigals and Pilgrims, The American Revolution Against Patriarchal Authority, 1750–1800* (New York, 1982), p. 267.

11 Mary Beth Norton, *Liberty's Daughters, The Revolutionary Experiences of American Women, 1750–1800* (Boston, 1980), pp. 243, 247–48; Samuel May, *The Rights and Conditions of Women* (Boston, 1869), p. 6. For discussions of changes in gender roles and ideas see Nancy Cott, *The Bonds of Womanhood: "Woman's Sphere" in New England, 1780–1835* (New Haven, 1977); Barbara Welter, "The Cult of True Womanhood, 1820–1860," *AQ* 18 (1966):151–74; Linda Kerber, *Women of the Republic, Intellect and Ideology in Revolutionary America* (Chapel Hill, 1980); Degler, *At Odds*, chaps. 2–7.

12 Fliegelman, *Prodigals and Pilgrims*, p. 161.

13 Bernard Wishy, *The Child and the Republic: The Dawn of Early American Child Nurture* (Philadelphia, 1968); Robert Bremner, et al., eds., *Children and Youth in America: A Documentary History* (Cambridge, Mass., 1970), vols. 1, 2; Daniel Calhoun, *The Intelligence of the People* (Princeton, N.J., 1973), pp. 134–205.

14 Lise Vogel, "The Contested Domain: A Note on the Family in the Transition to Capitalism," *MP* 1 (1978):50–73; Bertram Wyatt-Brown, *Southern Honor, Ethics and Behavior in the Old South* (New York, 1982), especially Part II; Gerda Lerner, "The Lady and the Mill Girl: Changes in the Status of Women in the Age of Jackson," *AStJ* 10 (1969):5–15; Caroll Smith-Rosenberg, "Beauty, the Beast, and the Militant Woman: A Case Study in Sex Roles and Social Stress in Jacksonian America," *AQ* 33 (1971):562–84; Clifford E. Clark, Jr., "Domestic Architecture as an Index to Social History: The Romantic Revival and the Cult of Domesticity in America, 1840–1870," *JIH* 7 (1979):33–56.

15 Robert Griswold, *Family and Divorce in California, 1850–1890* (Albany, N.Y., 1982), p. 5.

16 Ronald Walters, "The Family and Antebellum Reform: An Interpretation," *Soc* 3 (1973):224; Ramsey quoted in Norton, *Liberty's Daughters*, p. 243.

17 David Hoffman quoted in Maxwell Bloomfield, *American Lawyers in a Changing Society, 1776-1876* (Cambridge, Mass., 1976), p. 91.

18 William O'Neill, *Divorce in the Progressive Era* (New Haven, Conn., 1967), p. 89.

19 William Leach, *True Love and Perfect Union, The Feminist Reform of Sex and Society* (New York, 1980), pp. 798–99; and see Thomas Haskell, *The Emergence of Professional Social Science, The ASSA and the Crisis of Authority* (Urbana, Ill., 1977).

20 John Higham, *From Boundlessness to Consolidation: The Transforma-

tion of American Culture, 1848–1860 (Ann Arbor, Mich., 1969). For general descriptions of the family crisis see Wishy, *The Child and Republic*, pp. 120–22; Daniel Walker, "Victorian Culture in America," in *Victorian America*, ed. Daniel Walker (Philadelphia, Pa., 1976), p. 13; John Demos, "Images of the Family, Then and Now," in *Changing Images of the Family*, ed. Virginia Tufte and Barbara Myerhoff (New Haven, Conn., 1979), pp. 49–55; Paul Boyer, *Urban Masses and Moral Order in America, 1820–1920* (Cambridge, Mass., 1978), pp. 18–120.

21 Wood, *Creation of the American Republic*, p. 299. For general descriptions of colonial legal development see Lawrence Friedman, *A History of American Law* (New York, 1973), Part I; John M. Murrin, "The Legal Transformation: The Bench and Bar of Eighteenth-Century Massachusetts," in *Colonial America*, ed. Stanley N. Katz (Boston, 1st ed., 1971), pp. 415–48; William Nelson, *The Americanization of the Common Law, 1780–1860* (Cambridge, Mass., 1975), pp. 13–63; David T. Konig, *Law and Society in Puritan Massachusetts, 1629–1692* (Chapel Hill, N.C., 1979); Anthony Gregg Roeber, *Faithful Magistrates and Republican Lawyers: Creators of Virginia Legal Culture, 1680–1810* (Chapel Hill, N.C., 1981); William E. Nelson, *Dispute and Conflict Resolution in Plymouth County, Massachusetts, 1725–1825* (Chapel Hill, N.C., 1981).

22 Richard Ellis, *The Jeffersonian Crisis: Courts and Politics in the Young Republic* (New York, 1974), pp. 21–24, and see especially Part III.

23 Morton Horwitz, *Transformation of American Law, 1780–1860* (Cambridge, Mass., 1977), p. 30, and see generally chap. 1. Though the Horwitz thesis about legal change has been subjected to vigorous criticism, it remains the most useful framework for examining post-Revolutionary legal change. For a helpful assessment of the historiography of the period see Hendrik Hartog, ed., *Law in the American Revolution and the Revolution in the Law* (New York, 1981), especially the concluding essay by Hartog, "Distancing Oneself from the Eighteenth Century: A Commentary on Changing Pictures of American Legal History," pp. 229–57.

24 Mark DeWolfe Howe, "The Creative Period in the Law of Massachusetts," *Proceedings of the Massachusetts Historical Society* 69 (1947–50):237.

25 Ralph Waldo Emerson, *The Selected Writings of Ralph Waldo Emerson*, ed. Brooks Atkinson (New York, 1979), p. 433. For general descriptions of the legal changes of the Revolutionary era see Friedman, *A History of American Law*, pp. 93–137; G. Edward White, *The American Judicial Tradition* (New York, 1976), chap. 1; James W. Ely, Jr., "Law in Republican Society: Continuity and Change in the Legal System of Post-Revolutionary America," in *Perspectives on Revolution and Evolution*,

ed. Richard A. Preston (Durham, N.C., 1979), pp. 46–65; William E. Nelson, "Officeholding and Power Wielding: An Analysis of the Relationship Between Structures and Style in American Administrative History," *LSR* 10 (1976):191–219; Karl Llewellyn, *The Common Law Tradition* (Boston, 1960); G. Edward White, *Patterns of American Legal Thought* (Indianapolis, 1978), pp. 18–37.

26   Thomas Jefferson quoted in Wood, *Creation of the American Republic*, pp. 300–1; William Blackstone, *Blackstone's Commentaries, With Notes of Reference to the Constitution and Laws of the Federal Government and of the Commonwealth of Virginia*, ed. St. George Tucker (Richmond, Va., 1803), 1:x–xi; and see generally Roeber, *Faithful Magistrates*; Charles Cullen Thomas, "St. George Tucker and the Law in Virginia, 1720–1804," (Ph.D. diss., University of Virginia, 1971).

27   Friedman, *A History of American Law*, pp. 282–92.

28   Tapping Reeve, *Law of Baron and Femme*, ed. Amasa Parker and Charles Baldwin (Albany, N.Y., 3rd ed., 1862), p. v; and see Horwitz, *Transformation of American Law*, pp. 144–45, 244, 257–58; White, *American Judicial Tradition*, chap. 2.

29   Friedman, *A History of American Law*, p. 99.

30   John R. Aiken, "Utopia and the Emergence of the Colonial Legal Profession: New York, 1664–1710, A Test Case," (Ph.D. diss., University of Rochester, 1967); and see Bloomfield, *American Lawyers*, chap. 2.

31   James Kent, *Commentaries on American Law* (New York, 1826–30), 4:20; and see Stanley N. Katz, "Republicanism and the Law of Inheritance in the American Revolutionary Era," *MLR* 76 (1976):1–36.

32   "Note: Federal Jurisdiction of 'Domestic Relations Cases,'" *JFL* 7 (1967):309–17.

33   1 Root xxvvi (Ct. 1789–1793); and see also Paul H. Jacobson, *American Marriage and Divorce* (New York, 1951).

34   Maynard v. Hill, 125 U.S. 190, 210 (1888).

35   For English marriage law see Blackstone, *Commentaries*, 2:433–34; R. H. Hemholz, *Marriage Litigation in Medieval England* (London, 1974); Thomas Poynter, *A Concise View of the Doctrines and Practices of the Ecclesiastical Courts* (London, 2nd ed., 1825), especially pp. 1–6. For colonial marriage law see George E. Howard, *A History of Matrimonial Institutions*, 3 vols. (Chicago, 1904), vol. 2, chaps. 11–15; Richard Morris, *Studies in the History of Early American Law* (New York, 1930), pp. 126–27; Sumner Powell, *English Domestic Relations, 1487–1653* (New York, 1917), pp. 44–49, 53–54.

36   Edwin G. Burrows and Michael Wallace, "The American Revolution: The Ideology and Practice of National Liberation," *PAH* 6 (1972), 287; Sir Henry Maine, *Ancient Law* (London, 1861), p. 100; and see generally Ronald H. Graveson, *Status in the Common Law* (London, 1953).

37 Norton, *Liberty's Daughters*, pp. 234; "Matrimonial Republican" quoted in Norton, *Liberty's Daughters*, p. 235.

38 Horwitz, *Transformation of American Law*, pp. 160–210. For a full description of the development of American contract law see Lawrence M. Friedman, *Contract Law in America* (Madison, Wis., 1965). For cases adopting these ideas see Dumarsely v. Fishly, 3 A. K. Marsh. 368 (Ky. 1820–21); Holmes v. Holmes, 6 La. 463 (1834).

39 Reeve, *Law of Baron and Femme* (New York, 1816), p. 307; and see Zephaniah Swift, *A System of the Laws of the State of Connecticut*, 2 vols. (New Haven, Conn., 1795), 1:184; Fornshill v. Murray, 1 Bland. 479, 481 (Md. 1828).

40 Joseph Story, *Commentaries on the Conflicts of Law* (Boston, 1834), p. 100; Kent, *Commentaries*, 2:139; and see Maguire v. Maguire, 7 Dana 181 (Ky. 1838); Dickson v. Dickson, 1 Yerg. 110 (Tenn. 1826); Townsend v. Griffin, 4 Harr. 440 (Del. 1843–47); Parde v. Cirahon, 4 Fla. 23 (1851).

41 Joel Bishop, *Commentaries on the Law of Married Women* (Boston, 1871), 2:3; *New Commentaries on the Law of Marriage and Divorce*, 2 vols. (New York, 1890).

42 Bishop, *Commentaries on the Law of Marriage and Divorce* (Boston, 1852), p. 35.

43 Ibid., p. 25. For a discussion of Sir Henry Maine's use of the term see W. S. Holdsworth, *A History of English Law*, 17 vols. (London, 1903–70), 3:457.

44 Frederick C. Hicks, "Marriage and Divorce in State Constitutions of the United States," *AAPS* 26 (1905):145–48; James Kent, *Commentaries on American Law*, ed. Oliver Wendell Holmes, Jr. (New York, 12th ed., 1873), 3:121, note 1. For examples of the reliance on Bishop and his status definition of matrimony see James Schouler, *A Treatise on the Law of Domestic Relations and Infancy* (Albany, N.Y., 3rd ed., 1882), pp. 806–9; Carroll D. Wright, "A Report on Marriage and Divorce in the United States, 1867 to 1886," U.S. Labor Department (Washington, D.C., 1889), p. 25; Hugo Hirsch, "Popular and Legal Views of Marriage and Divorce," *CC* 21 (1914–15):10–13; Fred S. Hall and Mary Richmond, *Marriage and the State* (New York, 1929), pp. 332–36; George J. Bayles, *American Women's Legal Status* (New York, 1905), p. 47.

45 Friedman, *Contract Law in America*, pp. 20–24; and see Grant Gilmore, *The Death of Contract* (Columbus, Ohio, 1974).

46 Maine, *Ancient Law*, p. 140.

47 For discussions of patriarchy see Gordon J. Schochet, *Patriarchalism in Political Thought* (New York, 1975); Janet Rifkind, "Toward a Theory of Law and Patriarchy," *Harvard Women's Law Journal* 3 (1980):83–95;

Paul Conner, "Patriarchy: Old and New," *AQ* 17 (1965):48–62; Fliegelman, *Prodigals and Pilgrims*.

48   Zephaniah Swift, *Digest of the Law of Evidence in Civil and Criminal Cases*, 2 vols. (New York, 1810), 1:18; and see George Haskins, *Law and Authority in Early Massachusetts* (New York, 1960), pp. 82–83, 195–96; Arthur Calhoun, *A Social History of the American Family*, 3 vols. (Cleveland, 1917), 1:71–83; Demos, *A Little Commonwealth*, Part I; Morgan, *Puritan Family*, chaps. 2, 3.

49   Greven, *Four Generations*; C. Ray Keim, "Primogeniture and Entail in Colonial Virginia," *WMQ*, 3rd series, 25 (1968):545–86; Bloomfield, *American Lawyers*, pp. 91–104. For clashing views on the status of women in colonial America see Norton, *Liberty's Daughters* and Kerber, *Women of the Republic*.

50   Alexis de Tocqueville, *Democracy in America*, trans. Henry Reeve, 2 vols. (New York, 1889), 2:221–24.

51   Timothy Walker, *Introduction to American Law* (Philadelphia, 1837), pp. 232–33; and see M. Paul Holsinger, "Timothy Walker: Blackstone of the Republic," *OH* 84 (1975):145–57.

52   Kent, *Commentaries on American Law*, 2:187; and see Reeve, *Baron and Femme*, p. 289.

53   For a thorough discussion of these issues see Albie Sachs and Joan Hoff Wilson, *Sexism and the Law: Male Beliefs and Legal Bias in Britain and the United States* (New York, 1978).

54   Reeve, *Baron and Femme*, 3rd ed., p. iii.

55   For historical assessments of some of these conflicts see O'Neill, *Divorce in the Progressive Era*; Christopher Lasch, *Havens in a Heartless World, the Family Besieged* (New York, 1977); James C. Mohr, *Abortion in America* (New York, 1978); Morton Keller, *Affairs of State* (Cambridge, Mass., 1977), chaps. 12, 13; Linda Gordon, *Women's Body, Women's Right, A Social History of Birth Control in America* (New York, 1974).

56   Morton Horwitz, "Part III—Treatise Literature," *LLJ* 69 (1976):461.

57   James Schouler, *A Treatise on the Law of Domestic Relations* (Boston, 1870), pp. 4–5.

58   Ibid., p. 21.

59   Ibid., pp. 5, 9.

60   Edward Mansfield, *The Legal Rights, Liabilities, and Duties of Women* (Cincinnati, Ohio, 1845), p. 49.

Chapter 2

1   Robert C. Brown, "Breach of Promise Suits," *UPLR* 77 (1928–29):247.

2   W. S. Brockelbank, "The Nature of the Promise to Marry: A Study in Comparative Law," *IlLR* 41 (1946):1, 4; Robert Helmholz, *Marriage Litigation in Medieval England* (London, 1974), pp. 31–36; "Clapcarols v. DeCastro," *ALR* 43 (1909):759; James Barr Ames, "The History of Assumpsit," *HLR* 2 (1888):1–55; Frederic W. Maitland, *The Forms of Action* (London, 1909), pp. 68–70.

3   George E. Howard, *A History of Matrimonial Institutions*, 3 vols. (Chicago, 1904), 2:200–3; Samuel Sewall, *The Diary of Samuel Sewall*, 2 vols., ed. Thomas M. Halsey (New York, 1973), 1:300, 2:828; and see generally Stretcher v. Parker, 12 Car. Rep. 21 (1639); Holcroft v. Dickenson, Carter 233 (1672); Harrison v. Cage, 5 Mod. 411 (1698); Holt v. Ward Clarencieux, 2 Str. 937 (1732); Foulkes v. Sellway, 3 Esp. 235 (1800); Potter v. Debos, 1 Stark 82 (1815); Geoffrey May, *The Social Control of Sexual Expression* (New York, 1931), pp. 248–49; Julia Spruill, *Women's Life and Work in the Southern Colonies* (Chapel Hill, 1938), pp. 151–55; Edmund Morgan, *The Puritan Family* (Boston, 1944), pp. 82–84; Ronald H. Graveson and F. L. Crane, eds., *A Century of Family Law* (Cambridge, 1957), pp. 28, 37, 137, 144; John Adams, *Legal Papers of John Adams*, 3 vols., ed. L. Kinvin Wroth and Hiller B. Zobel (Cambridge, Mass., 1965), 1:8.

4   Jay Fliegelman, *Prodigals and Pilgrims* (Cambridge, 1982), p. 131.

5   Wightman v. Coates, 15 Mass. 2, 2–4, 3 (1818).

6   See generally Harter F. Wright, "Actions for the Breach of a Marriage Promise," *VaLR* 10 (1924):361–65.

7   J. Dundas White, "Breach of Promise of Marriage," *LQR* 38 (1894): 137.

8   Homer Clarke, *Law of Domestic Relations* (St. Paul, Minn., 1968), pp. 2–3.

9   Peppinger v. Low, 1 Halst. Law 384, 386 (N.J. 1797).

10 Kelly v. Renfro, 9 Ala. 325 (1846). A similar transition occurred in England.

11 Wightman v. Coates, 15 Mass. 3 (1818); and see Nancy Cott, *Bonds of Womanhood* (New Haven, Conn., 1977), pp. 77–83; Carl Degler, *At Odds* (New York, 1980), chap. 2; Ronald W. Hogeland, " 'The Female Appendage': Feminine Life Styles in America, 1820–1860," *CWH* 17 (1971):101–14.

12 Quoted in Cott, *Bonds of Womanhood*, p. 18.

13 James Henretta, *The Evolution of American Society, An Interdisciplin-*

ary Analysis (Lexington, Mass., 1973), p. 133.

14 Greenup v. Stoker, 8 Ill. 202, 212 (1846); and see Burks v. Shain, 2 Bibb. 341 (Ky. 1811).

15 Wightman v. Coates, 15 Mass. 2 (1818); and see Nathan Dane, *A General Abridgement and Digest of American Law*, 9 vols. (Boston, 1823–29), 8:297–98.

16 Admitting circumstantial evidence of marriage promises rested in large part on another dimension of the judiciary's paternalistic approach to female litigants, a shared (and applauded) belief in female modesty. A late eighteenth-century New Jersey opinion, Peppinger v. Low, 1 Halst. 384, 386 (1797), articulated the prevailing assumption. Substantiating female espousals was very difficult, the court insisted, because of the "privacy with which these arrangements are almost universally made, the natural timidity of the sex, and the general customs and opinions of the world, which seem to restrain the woman from making use of those open and direct avowals of a marriage contract which may sometimes be proved upon a man, render this degree of testimony almost impossible." The court then ruled that the woman could use her own declarations to others to establish her claims. Excluding such testimony, the justices argued, would prevent women from being on the "same or equal footing with men" and thus violated the judicial attempt at gender equity in domestic governance. See also Moritz v. Melhorn, 13 Pa. 331 (1846).

17 Ellis v. Guggenheim, 20 Pa. 287 (1853); Thurston v. Cavenor, 8 Ia. 155 (1859); Kelly v. Renfro, 9 Ala. 325; Whitcomb v. Wolcott, 21 Vt. 368 (1849); Whetmore v. Mell, 1 Ohio St. 26 (1852); Hubbard v. Bonsteel, 16 Barb. 360 (N.Y. 1853); Ray v. Smith, 9 Gray 141 (Mass. 1857).

18 Greenup v. Stoker, 8 Ill. 202, 211 (1846); and see Hoitt v. Moulton, 2 N.H. 586 (1850). Though they tilted the rules of evidence to aid women, judges were not completely insensitive to male entreaties about the problems of circumstantial evidence, see for example Lecky v. Bloser, 24 Pa. 401; Conrad v. Williams, 6 Hill 444 (N.Y. 1844); Munson v. Hastings, 12 Vt. 346 (1839).

19 Holt v. Ward Clarencieux, 2 Str. 34 (1719); and see Evans v. Terry, 1 Brev. 80 (S.C. 1802); Hunt v. Peake, 5 Cowen 475 (N.Y. 1826); Conaway v. Shelton, 3 Ind. 334 (1852); Frost v. Vought, 37 Mich. 65 (1877).

20 Willard v. Stone, 7 Cowen 21 (N.Y. 1827); Warwick v. Cooper, 5 Sneed 659 (Tenn. 1858). The most striking example of the bench's commitment to promoting matrimony by compelling proper contractual behavior was the refusal to accept either the existence of a prior marriage or of another nuptial promise as a valid defense. In each case the use of the law to coerce actual matrimony was out of the question; rather both acts were treated as frauds on the innocent woman. Only if she knew of the

other connection would courts reject her claims. See Blattsmacher v. Saal, 29 Barb. 22 (N.Y. 1858); Cropsey v. Ogden, 1 Kern. 228 (N.Y. 1854).

21   Butler v. Eschleman, 18 Ill. 44, 45 (1856). For the application of contractual standards to commercial behavior see Lawrence Friedman, *A History of American Law* (New York, 1973), pp. 234–35.

22   Button v. McCauley, 38 Barb. 413, 415 (1862); Van Houten v. Morse, 162 Mass. 414 (1894). For the consistent nineteenth-century application of these policies see Healey v. O'Sullivan, 6 Allen 114 (Mass. 1862); Stevenson v. Pettis, 12 Phila. 468 (Pa. 1877); Noice v. Brown, 10 Vroom 133 (N.J. 1876); Simmons v. Simmons, 8 Mich. 318 (1860); Reish v. Thompson, 55 Ind. 34 (1876); Haviland v. Halstead, 34 N.Y. 643 (1866); Wade v. Kalbfleisch, 58 N.Y. 282 (1874); Liechtweiss v. Treskow, 21 Hun. 487 (N.Y. 1880); Stone v. Appel, 12 Bradw. 582 (Ill. 1883).

23   Lecky v. Bloser, 24 Pa. 401, 407 (1854); and see Woodward v. Sellamy, 2 Root 354 (Conn. 1796); Johnson v. Caukins, 1 Johns. Cas. 116 (N.Y. 1799); Boynton v. Kellogg, 3 Mass. 189 (1807); Palmer v. Andrews, 7 Wend. 141 (N.Y. 1831); Snowman v. Wardwell, 32 Me. 275 (1850); Willard v. Stone, 7 Cowen 21 (N.Y. 1827); and Robert Griswold, *Family and Divorce in California, 1850–1890* (Albany, N.Y., 1982), pp. 66–70.

24   Denslow v. Van Horn, 16 Ia. 476, 481 (1864); and see William Alcott, *The Physiology of Marriage* (New York, 1855), p. 51.

25   Van Storch v. Griffin, 77 Pa. 504, 506 (1875); and see Bell v. Eaton, 28 Ind. 468 (1867); Sprague v. Craig, 51 Ill. 288 (1869); Hunter v. Hatfield, 68 Ind. 416 (1879).

26   Capehart v. Carradine, 4 Strob. Eq. 42, 46 (S.C. 1849).

27   Gaskill v. Dixon, 2 Hayw. 350 (N.C. 1805); and see Keith Thomas, "The Double Standard," *JHId* 20 (1959):195–216.

28   Baldy v. Stratton, 11 Pa. 316, 324–25 (1840); and see Johnson v. Travis, 33 Minn. 231 (1885).

29   Timothy Walker, *Introduction to American Law* (Philadelphia, 1837), p. 233; and see Chesley v. Chesley, 10 N.H. 327 (1839); Greenleaf v. McColly, 14 N.H. 303 (1843); Arthur Calhoun, *A Social History of the American Family*, 3 vols. (Cleveland, 1917), 2:216.

30   Perkins v. Hersey, 1 R.I. 493, 495 (1851); and see Tobin v. Shaw, 45 Me. 331 (1858); Coryell v. Colbaugh, 1 N.J. Law 77 (1791).

31   Johnson v. Caukins, 1 Johns Cas. 116, 117–18, 119 (N.Y. 1799).

32   Kelly v. Highfield, 15 Ore. 277, 189 (1887); and see Burnett v. Simpkins, 24 Ill. 265 (1860); Woodward v. Bellamy, 2 Root 354 (Conn. 1796); Willard v. Stone, 7 Cowen 21 (N.Y. 1827); Palmer v. Andrews, 7 Wend. 142 (N.Y. 1831); Green v. Spencer, 3 Mo. 225 (1834); Denslow

v. Van Horn, 16 Ia. 476 (1864); Smith v. Braun, 37 La. An. 225 (1885); Simmons v. Simmons, 8 Mich. 318 (1860); Burtis v. Thompson, 42 N.Y. 246 (1870); Collins v. Mack, 31 Ark. 684 (1877); Royal v. Smith, 40 Ia. 615 (1875); Vanderpool v. Richardson, 52 Mich. 336 (1883); Miller v. Hayes, 34 Ia. 496 (1872); Lawrence v. Cooke, 56 Vt. 187 (1868); Schrekengart v. Ealy, 16 Neb. 510 (1884); Holloway v. Griffith, 32 Ia. 409 (1871).

33 Butler v. Eschleman, 18 Ill. 44, 46 (1856), and see Griswold, *Family and Divorce in California*, p. 72.

34 John Demos, *A Little Commonwealth* (New York, 1970), pp. 152–54, 157–59; Howard, *Matrimonial Institutions*, 2:180–6; Howard Gadlin, "Private Lives and Public Order: A Critical View of Intimate Relations in the United States," *Massachusetts Review* 17 (1976):304–6.

35 Frost v. Marshall, 2 Brev. 114, 115–6 (S.C. 1804).

36 Weaver v. Bachert, 2 Pa. 80, 81–82; and see Burks v. Shain, 2 Bibb. 341 (Ky. 1811); Hay v. Graham, 8 W. & S. 27 (Pa. 1844); Perkins v. Hersey, 1 R.I. 493 (N.J. 1851); Baldy v. Stratton, 11 Pa. 316 (1849); Tapping Reeve, *Law of Baron and Femme* (New York, 1816), pp. 241–43.

37 Paul v. Frazier, 3 Mass. 71, 73 (1807); and see Zephaniah Swift, *A System of Laws of the State of Connecticut*, 2 vols. (New Haven, Conn., 1795), 1:188; Whalen v. Laymen, 2 Blackf. 194 (Ind. 1828).

38 Green v. Spencer, 3 Mo. 225, 227 (1834).

39 Wells v. Padgett, 8 Barb. 323, 325–57 (N.Y. 1850); and see Martin v. Feen, 3 Doug. 211 (1783); William Paley, *The Principles of Moral and Political Philosophy*, 2 vols. (London, 5th ed., 1788).

40 Samuel May, *The Rights and Legal Condition of Women* (Boston, 1809), p. 11; and see Degler, *At Odds*, chap. 11; Dio Lewis, *Our Girls* (New York, 1871), p. 181; Gadlin, "Private Lives and Public Order," 317–20.

41 Tubbs v. Van Kleek, 12 Ill. 446, 465–66 (1874); and see Fidler v. McKinley, 21 Ill. 308 (1859); Theophilus Parsons, Jr., *The Law of Contracts*, 2 vols. (Boston, 1853–55), 1:553.

42 Cited in James Mohr, *Abortion in America* (New York, 1978), pp. 121–22.

43 Daniel Scott Smith and Michael S. Hindus, "Premarital Pregnancy in America, 1640–1971: An Overview and Interpretation," *JIH* 5 (1975): 553–62; Caroll Smith-Rosenberg, "Beauty, the Beast, and the Militant Woman," *AQ* 33 (1971):563–64; Charles Rosenberg, "Sexuality, Class, and Role in Nineteenth Century America," *AQ* 25 (1973):138–48.

44 Bennett v. Beam, 42 Mich. 346, 351 (1880).

45 Caroline Dall, *The College, the Market, and the Court* (Boston, 1867), p. 293; and see Espy v. Jones, 37 Ala. 379 (1861); Sayer v. Schulenberg, 33 Md. 288 (1870); Smith v. Braun, 37 La. An. 225 (1885); Haymond v. Saucer, 84 Ind. 3 (1882); Bird v. Thompson, 96 Mo. 424 (1888); Kurtz

v. Frank, 76 Ind. 594 (1881); Wilds v. Bogan, 57 Ind. 453 (1877); Kniffen v. McConnell, 30 N.Y. 285 (1864); Cotes v. McKinney, 48 Ind. 562 (1874); Giese v. Schultz, 53 Wis. 462; Ibid., 65 Wis. 487 (1886); Ibid., 69 Wis. 521 (1887); William Bullock, *The Law of Domestic Relations of the State of New York* (Albany, N.Y., 1898), p. 250.

46 Fidley v. McKinney, 21 Ill. 308, 316 (1859).

47 Baldy v. Stratton, 11 Pa. 316, 325 (1849); and see Wilcox v. Gree, 53 Barb. 639 (1854); Waters v. Bristol, 26 Conn. 398 (1857). On the curtailment of jury power see Morton Horwitz, *The Transformation of American Law* (Cambridge, Mass., 1977), pp. 141–43.

48 Morgan v. Yarborough, 5 La. An. 316, 323; and see Harriet Daggett, "The Action for the Breach of the Marriage Promise," in *Essays on Family Law* (Baton Rouge, La., 1935), pp. 43–44.

49 Cited in Charles J. MacColla, *Breach of Promise, Its History and Social Considerations* (London, 1879), p. 32. For general discussion of legislative cooperation see Frances Hilliard, *Elements of Law* (New York, 1835), pp. 5–7.

50 Short v. Stotts, 58 Ind. 29, 35 (1877).

51 Auguste Carlier, *Marriage in the United States* (Boston, 1867), pp. 42–43.

52 Frank G. Cook, "Reform in the Marriage Celebration," *AM* 61 (1888): 681; Abba Woolson, *Women in American Society* (Boston, 1873), p. 82; and see William Leach, *True Love and Perfect Union* (New York, 1980), pp. 86, 231.

53 George Lawyer, "Are Actions for Breach of the Marriage Contract Immoral?" *CLJ* 38 (1894):272.

54 Coolidge v. Neat, 129 Mass. 146, 149–50 (1880); Grant v. Willey, 110 Mass. 356 (1869); and see Kraxberger v. Roiter, 9 Mo. 404 (1886); Prescott v. Guyler, 32 Ill. 312 (1863); Herbert F. Goodrich, "Iowa Decisions on Breach of Marriage Promise," *IaLB* 4 (1918):170–71.

55 Michael Gordon, "The Ideal Husband as Depicted in the Nineteenth-Century Marriage Manual," *Family Coordinator* 18 (1969):288.

56 James Schouler, *A Treatise on Domestic Relations*, 2 vols. (New York, 6th ed., 1906), 2:1518, 1529; and see Joel Bishop, *New Commentaries on Marriage and Divorce*, 2 vols. (New York, 1891), 1:80; David J. Pivar, *The Purity Crusade* (Westport, Conn., 1973); Sondra R. Herman, "Loving Courtship or the Marriage Market? The Ideal and its Critics, 1871–1911," *AQ* 25 (1973):235–52.

57 "Action for Breach of Promise of Marriage," *ALReg*, N.S., 1 (1872):65–73.

58 Wright, "Actions for the Breach of the Marriage Promise," 370–71; and see Calhoun, *Social History of the American Family*, 2:216.

59 Henry Wright, *Marriage and Parentage or the Protective Element in*

Man, as a Means to his Elevation and Happiness (Boston, 2nd ed., 1855), p. 204.

60 Brown, "Breach of Marriage Promise Suits," 474; Kraxberger v. Roiter, 91 Mo. 404, 409 (1886); and see "Damages of a Breach of Promise of Marriage," *ALJ* 10 (1874):342–43.

61 Daggett, "The Action for the Breach of Marriage Promise," 41.

62 Elaine May, "The Pursuit of Domestic Perfection: Marriage and Divorce in Los Angeles, 1890–1920," (Ph.D. diss., UCLA, 1975), 214; and see Calhoun, *Social History of the American Family*, 3:95; Caroll Smith-Rosenberg, "The Hysterical Woman: Sex Roles and Role Conflict in Nineteenth-Century America," *SoR* 39 (1972):652, 655–58.

63 White, "Breach of Promise of Marriage," 141.

64 Russell H. Conwell, *Women and the Law* (Boston, 1876), pp. 18–19.

65 Russell v. Cowles, 15 Gray 582 (Mass. 1860).

66 Walmsey v. Robinson, 63 Ill. 41, 42–43 (1872).

67 McPherson v. Ryan, 59 Mich. 33, 39 (1886).

68 Miller v. Rosier, 31 Mich. 475 (1875); Cole v. Holliday, 4 Mo. Ap. 94 (1877); Graham v. Martin, 64 Ind. 567 (1878).

69 Glasscock v. Shell, 57 Tex. 215, 223–24; and see Sauer v. Schulenberg, 33 Md. 288 (1870); White v. Thomas, 12 Ohio St. 312 (1861); Leavitt v. Cutler, 37 Wis. 46 (1875); Von Storch v. Griffin, 71 Pa. 240 (1872); Hunter v. Hatfield, 68 Ind. 416 (1879); Simpson v. Black, 27 Wis. 206 (1870).

70 James Schouler, *Domestic Relations*, 6th ed., 2:1529; and see James Schouler, "Breach of Promise," *SLR* 7 (1881):65.

71 "Recent Cases," *HLR* 7 (1894):372.

72 Elisha Hurlbut, *Essays on Human Rights* (New York, 10th ed., 1875), p. 149.

73 Martin Littleton quoted in Calhoun, *Social History of the American Family*, 3:223; "Recent Cases," *HLR* 7, 372.

74 Hall v. Wright, 96 Eng. C.L. Rep. 746 (1859).

75 Allen v. Baker, 86 N.C. 91, 96–98 (1873); and see Sander v. Coleman, 97 Va. 690 (1899); Goddard v. Westcott, 82 Mich. 180 (1890).

76 Robert Banyon, "Donnerschlog v. Behrens," *ALRev* 9 (1874–75):151–52.

77 See for example, Homan v. Earle, 53 Barb. 267 (N.Y. 1873); Prescott v. Guyler, 32 Ill. 312 (1863); Tefft v. Marsh, 1 W. Va. 38 (1864); Nichols v. Weaver, 7 Kan. 373 (1871); Blackburn v. Mann, 85 Ill. 22 (1877); Collins v. Mack, 31 Ark. 684 (1877); Lahey v. Knott, 8 Ore. 198 (1879); Wagenseller v. Simmers, 97 Pa. 465 (1877).

78 "Some Defenses to Actions for Breach of Promise of Marriage," *Law Notes*, O.S., 3 (1899–1900):209.

79 Wright, "Actions for the Breach of the Marriage Promise," 376; and see

generally Brocklebank, "The Nature of the Promise to Marry," 199, 204–5, 209, 113; Brown, "Breach of Promise Suits," 497; Wright, "Actions for the Breach of the Marriage Promise," 362–63; Goodrich, "Iowa Decisions," 166; *Reports of the American Bar Association* 43 (1918):45.

80 Nathan P. Feinsinger, "Legislative Attack on 'Heart Balm,'" *MLR* 33 (1935):979–1009.

Chapter 3

1 Claude Lévi-Strauss, "The Family," in *Man, Culture, and Society*, ed. Harry L. Shapiro (New York, 1956), p. 142.

2 David Hoffman, *Legal Outlines* (Baltimore, 1836), p. 147.

3 See generally Lawrence Stone, *The Family, Sex, and Marriage in England, 1500–1800* (New York, 1977), Part IV, chaps. 6–8.

4 Sir Frederick Pollock and Frederic W. Maitland, *The History of English Law*, 2 vols. (London, 1895), 2:364–85; Frederic W. Maitland, *Roman Law and Canon Law in the Church of England* (London, 1898), pp. 38–40; Richard Helmholz, *Marriage Litigation in Medieval England* (London, 1974), pp. 4, 25, 30–31; T. E. James, "The Court of Arches During the Eighteenth Century," *AJLH* 5 (1961):55–66.

5 William Blackstone, *Commentaries on the Laws of England*, 4 vols. (London, 1765–69), 2:433–34; and see George Howard, *A History of Matrimonial Institutions*, 3 vols. (Chicago, 1904), 1:339–447; David Engdahl, "Proposals for a Benign Revolution in Marriage Law and Marriage Conflicts Law," *IaLR* 55 (1969):57–58.

6 Thomas Poynter, *A Concise View of the Doctrines and Practices of the Ecclesiastical Courts* (London, 2nd ed., 1825), pp. 1–6.

7 Jeffrey Weeks, *Sex, Politics, and Society: The Regulation of Sexuality Since 1800* (New York, 1981), p. 24, and see generally chap. 2. Though modified in the early nineteenth century, ecclesiastical controls continued until 1857; see generally Margaret K. Woodhouse, "The Marriage and Divorce Bill of 1857," *AJLH* 3 (1959):260–75.

8 Howard, *Matrimonial Institutions*, 2:252, and see generally chaps. 12–14; John E. Semonche, "Common Law Marriage in North Carolina: A Study in Legal History," *AJLH* 9 (1965):324–41; Otto E. Koegel, *Common Law Marriage and its Development in the United States* (Washington, D.C., 1922), pp. 54–123; Howard, *Matrimonial Institutions*, 2: 121–263.

9   Quoted in Julia Spruill, *Women's Life and Work in the Southern Colonies* (Chapel Hill, 1938), p. 314.

10 John Demos, *A Little Commonwealth* (New York, 1970), pp. 154–59; Daniel Scott Smith, "Parental Power and Marriage Patterns: An Analysis of Historical Trends in Hingham, Massachusetts," *JMF* 35 (1973):419–28.

11 Susan Norton, "Marital Migration in Essex, Massachusetts, in the Colonial and Early Federal Period," *JMF* 35 (1973):407–8; Lorena Walsh, " 'Till Death Do Us Part': Marriage and the Family in Seventeenth Century Maryland," in *The Chesapeake in the Seventeenth Century*, ed. Thad Tate and David L. Ammerman (Chapel Hill, 1979), pp. 127–31.

12 Quoted in Edmund S. Morgan, *Virginians At Home* (Williamsburg, Va., 1952), pp. 34–35; and see Spruill, *Women's Life*, p. 145; Koegel, *Common Law Marriage*, pp. 56–59. For a description of a typical gentry wedding see Allan Kulikoff, " 'Throwing the Stocking,' A Gentry Marriage in Provincial Maryland," *MHM* 71 (1976):516–21.

13 Chilton Powell, "Marriage in Early New England," *NEQ* 1 (1928):331.

14 Henry Addison, quoted in Walsh, " 'Till Death Do Us Part'," 130, note 9.

15 Quoted in Howard, *Matrimonial Institutions*, 2:261.

16 Frank G. Cook, "The Marriage Ceremony in the Colonies," *AM* 61 (1888):352–62; Semonche, "Common Law Marriage in North Carolina," 336–39; Maxwell Bloomfield, *American Lawyers in a Changing Society, 1776–1876* (Cambridge, Mass., 1976), pp. 92–94.

17 Powell, "Marriage in Early New England," 333.

18 Cheseldine v. Brewer, 1 Harris and McHenry 152 (Md. 1739); Koegel, *Common Law Marriage*, pp. 76–77; Howard, *Matrimonial Institutions*, 2:262–63, 3:180.

19 Fenton v. Reed, 4 Johns. 52, 53 (N.Y. 1809). Kent's reading of the law and his legal reasoning have been subjected to sustained criticism. Critics have concentrated on his sources. Since New York had few nuptial regulations, Kent relied on the common law for support. Only one of the three English decisions he cited, Collins v. Jessop, though, even partially sustained his position. The other two cases, Morris v. Miller and Reed v. Passer, merely contained dicta that cohabitation and repute of marriage raised the presumption of matrimony. None of the cases granted full legal standing to an irregular marriage. See Koegel, *Common Law Marriage*, pp. 80–81; Frank G. Cook, "The Marriage Celebration in the United States," *AM* 61 (1888):521; Stuart Stein, "Common Law Marriage: Its History and Certain Contemporary Problems," *JFL* 9 (1969):277–79.

20 James Kent, *Commentaries on American Law*, 4 vols. (New York, 1826–30), 2:75.

21   Powell, "Marriage in Early New England," 334.

22   James Kent, *Commentaries on American Law*, 5th ed., (New York, 1838), 2:87.

23   Mangue v. Mangue, 1 Mass. 240 (1804).

24   Powell, "Marriage in Early New England," 334.

25   Parsons did concede that noncompliance with minor provisions, such as banns or license, would not nullify a marriage. Milford v. Worcester, 7 Mass. 48–58 (1810); see also Cook, "The Marriage Celebration in the United States," 523–24; Stein, "Common Law Marriage: Its History," 277–79.

26   Milford v. Worcester, 7 Mass. 58.

27   Judicial decisions in support of common-law marriage include Hantz v. Sealy, 6 Binn. 405 (Pa. 1814); Rodebaugh v. Sanks, 2 Watts 9 (Pa. 1833); Vaigeur v. Kirk, 2 S.C. Equity, 640 (1817); Londonderry v. Chester, 2 N.H. 268 (1820); Dumarsely v. Fishly, 3 A.K. Marshall 368 (Ky. 1821); Wyckoff v. Boggs, 2 Halst. 138 (N.J. 1824); Holmes v. Holmes, 6 La. 463 (1833); Graham v. Bennett, 2 Cal. 503 (1852); Hargroves v. Thompson, 31 Miss. 211 (1856); Askew v. Dupree, 30 Ga. 173 (1860); and see also Simon Greenleaf, *A Treatise on the Law of Evidence*, 3 vols. (Boston, 3rd ed., 1852), 2:442–44; Joel Bishop, *Commentaries on the Law of Marriage and Divorce* (Boston, 1852), pp. 133–39.

28   Judicial decisions opposing common-law marriage include Bashaw v. State, 1 Yerg. 177 (Tenn. 1829); Grisham v. State, 2 Yerg. 589 (Tenn. 1831); State v. Samuel, 2 Dev. and Pat. 177 (N.C. 1836); State v. Patterson, 2 Ire. 346 (N.C. 1836); State v. Hodgskins, 19 Me. 155 (1841); Northfield v. Plymouth, 20 Vt. 582 (1848) and Dumbarton v. Franklin, 19 N.H. 257 (1848), both of which overturned earlier approvals; Theophilus Parsons, Jr., *The Law of Contracts*, 2 vols. (Boston, 1853–55), 2:76; *Acts of Kentucky* (1849–51), pp. 212–16 which overturned judicial approval of common-law marriage. In Jewel v. Jewel, 1 How. 219 (U.S. 1843), the United States Supreme Court divided evenly on the issue and gave no opinion.

29   Newbury v. New Brunswick, 2 Vt. 151, 159 (1829); Carmichael v. State, Ohio St. 553, 560 (1861); Pearson v. Howey, 6 Halst. 12, 18 (N.J. 1829); Dumarsely v. Fishly, 3 A.K. Marshall 368, 375 (Ky. 1821); and see Holmes v. Holmes, 6 La. 463, 470 (1833); Graham v. Bennett, 2 Cal. 503, 506; Tapping Reeve, *Law of Baron and Femme* (New York, 1816), pp. 199–200; Hargroves v. Thompson, 31 Miss. 211, 215.

30   Rodebaugh v. Sanks, 2 Watts 9, 10–11 (Pa. 1833); Londonderry v. Chester, 2 N.H. 268, 281 (1820); and see Vaigneur v. Kirk, 2 S.C. Des. Equity 640, 643–45, 646 (1806).

31 *The Law of Contracts*, 2:76; Dunbarton v. Franklin, 19 N.H. 257, 264–65 (1848).

32 Bashaw v. State, 1 Yerg. 177, 196 (Tenn. 1829). Such posturing was possible in part because many of these decisions involved criminal complaints for bigamy or murder, cases which did not involve children, and disputes in which the couples were clearly living illicitly. See generally State v. Samuel, 2 Dev. & Bat. 177, 181 (N.C. 1836); Dunbarton v. Franklin, 19 N.H. 257, 265 (1748); Ligonia v. Buxton, 2 Greenl. 102 (Me. 1822); State v. Hodgskins, 19 Me. 155 (1841); State v. Patterson, 2 Ire. 346 (N.C. 1842).

33 Pollock and Maitland, *History of English Law*, 2:372; and see Beamish v. Beamish, 9 H.L. Cas. 274 (1861); Joel Bishop, *Commentaries on the Law of Marriage and Divorce* (Boston, 2nd ed., 1856), pp. 129–35.

34 Zephaniah Swift, *A System of Laws for the State of Connecticut*, 2 vols. (New Haven, Conn., 1795), 1:189.

35 Connecticut legislation is analyzed in Howard, *Matrimonial Institutions*, 2:394; and Roberts v. State, 2 Root 381 (Conn. 1796). For the Indiana policies see Indiana Revised Statutes 1843, Chap. 35, art. 1, Sec. 4; Indiana Revised Statutes 1852, Chap. 168, Sec. 1; State v. Carr cited in Robert Adgate, "Nineteenth Century Indiana Law on the Formation of Marriage: Contract or Status?" (Unpublished seminar paper, Indiana University Law School, Spring, 1981). For other examples of legislative relaxation of the law see Howard, *Matrimonial Institutions*, 2:412, 416–17, 458; Frederic J. Stimson, *American Statute Law* (Boston, 1886), pp. 664–82; Guim Griffis Johnson, "Courtship and Marriage in Antebellum North Carolina," *NCHR* 8 (1931):398.

36 Watson v. Blaylock, 2 Mills 351 (S.C. 1818); State v. Bray, 35 N.C. 289 (1852); Londonderry v. Chester, 2 N.H. 268 (1820); and see State v. Kean, 10 N.H. 347 (1839); Kent v. State, 8 Blackf. 163 (Ind. 1846–47); State v. Pierce, 14 Ind. 302 (1860); Pearson v. Howey, 6 Halst. 12 (N.J. 1829). For opposing decisions see Ligonia v. Buxton, 2 Greenl. 102 (Me. 1822); Brunswick v. Litchfield, 2 Greenl. 28 (Me. 1822); Lewiston v. Yarmouth, 5 Greenl. 66 (Me. 1827).

37 Johnson, "Courtship in North Carolina," 397–98; William Nelson, "The Early Laws of New Jersey and the Influences Bearing on their Formation" in his *Documents Relating to the Colonial History of New Jersey* (Paterson, N.J. 1900); p. cxvi; Helen I. Clarke, *Social Legislation: American Laws Dealing with the Family, Children, Dependents* (New York, 1940), p. 85; Howard, *Matrimonial Institutions*, 2:401–3, 441–52, 481–97.

38 Wood v. Adams, 35 N.H. 32, 39, 40 (1857). The Kentucky Supreme Court, for example, also feared that strict enforcement of license laws

would "vitiate a great proportion of the marriages of the country," Dumarsely v. Fishly, 3 A.K. Marsh. 368, 272 (Ky. 1820); and see Bashaw v. State, 1 Yerg. 177, 184 (Tenn. 1829); Gatewood v. Tunk, 3 Bibbs. 246 (Ky. 1813); State v. Watts, 10 Ire. 369 (N.C. 1849); State v. Robbins, 6 Ire. 23 (N.C. 1845); Johnson, "Courtship in North Carolina," 396.

39 "Facetiousness of the Law—Husband and Wife," *The New York Observer* 3 (1845):155.

40 Macklin v. Taylor, 1 Add. 212, 213 (Pa. 1794). The New Jersey Supreme Court even assumed the role of family counselor in helping parents acclimate themselves to the new situation. It advised them that sometimes "the best way of preventing an unhappy attachment is not to oppose it too violently but seem to assent, in order to recover the lost confidence of a child, and win him back to respect for wholesome advice," Wyckoff v. Boggs, 2 Halts. 138, 139–40 (N.J. 1824); and see Worley v. Walling, 1 Har. & John. 208 (Md. 1801); Bennett v. Smith, 21 Barb. 439 (N.Y. 1856); Zieber v. Boos, 2 Yeates 321 (Pa. 1798). Chief Justice Gibson of Pennsylvania spelled out the limits of the judicial relaxation of nuptial supervision in 1835. He told a clergyman who had asserted that provisions for parental consent were obsolete: "[I]t never has been doubted that the requirements must have been complied with in order to save the penalty, though not to legalize the marriage," Heffenstein v. Thomas, 5 Rawle 209, 211 (Pa. 1835); and see Ellis v. Holl, 2 Aiken 41 (Vt. 1826); U.S. v. McCormick, 26 Fed. Cas. 1059 (D.C. 1802); Stansbury v. Bertron, 7 W. & S. 362 (Pa. 1844); Bolin v. Shiner, 12 Pa. 205 (1849); Caroon v. Rogers, 6 Jones 240 (N.C. 1858); State v. Cain, 6 Blackf. 422 (Ind. 1843); White v. State, 4 Ia. 449 (1857); Robinson v. English, 10 Casey (Pa. 1859); Robinson v. English, 10 Casey 324 (Pa. 1859); State v. Ross, 26 Mo. 260 (1858); State v. Wainwright, 12 Mo. 410 (1849); Harvey v. Bush, 2 Penning. 529 (N.J. 1812); Hall v. Williams, 14 S. & R. 286 (Pa. 1826); Huston v. Ayres, 1 Add. 346 (Pa. 1797); Lorwill v. Kirby, 14 Ohio 1 (1846); Vaughan v. McQueen, 9 Mo. 330 (1845). Parents also had the right to be compensated for their loss. Judges did not discount the grief and hardship parents endured, they only blocked efforts to overturn consummated unions. Another Pennsylvania decision explained why this palliative was offered to families. Rebuffing a minister's claim that a parent must demonstrate his actual loss to be compensated, the court declared: "This penalty is given to the person or persons aggrieved; but the grievance to be redressed is not necessarily an actual and specific damage, it being sufficient that the marriage is an unjustifiable interference with the relation existing between the parent and his offspring, and, in that aspect, a grievance in contemplation of the law. To say nothing of the education and nurture superseded by the obtrusion of a new relation into

the family, the deprivation of the right gone by forever, to participate by counsel and advice in the formation of a connexion involving the happiness or misery of the child, may be numbered in the severest injuries that can be inflicted on a parent," Donahue v. Dougherty, 5 Rawle 124, 127–28 (Pa. 1835); and see Bucanan v. Thorn, 1 Pa. 431 (1845).

41   Fryer v. Fryer, Rich Cas. Equity 85, 93, 92 (S.C. 1832); and see Kuhl v. Knaver, 7 B. Monroe 130 (Ky. 1846). In 1812 a Connecticut justice upheld a widow's claim for dower by accepting evidence of matrimonial cohabitation and reputation: "I am of the opinion that it was proper to accept such evidence. I take it to be fully settled both in this state, and in Great Britain, that the fact of marriage may be proved by evidence of this kind," Hammack v. Bronson, 5 Day 290, 293–94 (Conn. 1812). For other uses of these presumptions see Taylor v. Robinson, 29 Me. 323 (1840); Boatman v. Curry, 25 Mo. 434 (1857); Donnelly's Heir v. Donnelly, 8 B. Monroe 113 (Ky. 1847–48); Taylor v. Shemwell, 4 B. Monroe 575 (Ky. 1844); Taylor v. Swett, 3 La. 33 (1831); Cole v. Langley, 14 La. An. 770 (1859); Sellman v. Bowen, 8 Gill & John. 50 (Md. 1836); Fleming v. Fleming, 8 Blackf. 234 (Ind. 1846); Tarpley v. Poage, 2 Tex. 129 (1847); Thorndell v. Morrison, 25 Pa. 326 (1855); Hull v. Rawls, 27 Miss. 471 (1854); Henderson v. Cargill, 31 Miss. 367 (1856); Albertson v. Smyth, 2 Penning. 358 (N.J. 1809).

42   Tummalty v. Tummalty, 3 Bradf. 369, 371–72 (N.Y. 1855); Chambers v. Dickson, 2 S. & R. 475, 477 (Penn. 1816); and see Bannister v. Henderson, 1 Quincy 119 (Mass. 1765); Houpt v. Houpt, 5 Ohio 539 (1832); Mitchell v. Mitchell, 11 Vt. 134 (1839); Crozier v. Gano, 1 Bibb. 257 (Ky. 1808); Chapman v. Cooper, 5 Rich. 452 (S.C. 1852); State v. Hasty, 42 Me. 287 (1856); Succession of Prevost, 4 La. An. 347 (1849). Class and sexual standards guided these judicial determinations. The judicial concept of proper feminine behavior proved particularly important. As a North Carolina judge declared in a 1799 property dispute: "There was in this case no positive proof of a marriage, but there were circumstances advancing to create a belief that a marriage has taken place; they have lived together for a long time, as man and wife, had several children, and the witnesses say that she was a woman of irreproachable character before these things happened [a family fight]. If so, a presumption arises that she would not have cohabited with the other defendant unless a marriage had been previously solemnized," Fetts v. Foster, 2 Hayw. 102 (N.C. 1799); and see Starr v. Peck, 1 Hill 270 (N.Y. 1841); Caujolle v. Ferrie, 26 Barb. 177 (N.Y. 1857).

43   Clayton v. Wardell, 4 Comst. 230, 232 (N.Y. 1832); Archer v. Haithcock, 6 Jones Law 421, 422–23 (N.C. 1859). Despite their stern pronouncements against informal marriages, all of the dissenting courts adopted the presumptions in favor of matrimony, indeed the Massachu-

setts legislature even codified the rules in 1841; see Fetts v. Foster, 2 Hayw. 102 (N.C. 1825); Whitehead v. Clinch, 2 Hayw. 3 (N.C. 1797); Bannister v. Henderson, 1 Quincy 119 (Mass. 1765); Newburyport v. Boothbay, 9 Mass. 414 (1812); Means v. Welles, 12 Met. 356 (Mass. 1847); Chiles v. Drake, 2 Met. 146 (Ky. 1859); Johnson v. Johnson, 1 Cold. 626 (Tenn. 1860); Stevens v. Reed, 87 N.H. 49 (1858); Northfield v. Vershire, 33 Vt. 110 (1860); Stein, "Common Law Marriage: Its History," 280–82; Semonche, "Common Law Marriage in North Carolina," 347.

44 De Armaell's Estate, 2 Brew. 239, 246 (Penn. 1869). The fervor with which courts used these rules to support established marriages did not, however, preclude their never-ending battle against immorality. Though given a lower priority in the more secular republic than in colonial America, the court's role as moral watchdog did not disappear. If a relationship clearly had begun illicitly, the couple had to offer strong evidence that their bond had become matrimonial in order to qualify for legal rights. Though marriage could begin in private, once consummated it had to be open and public. In the same vein, courts cautioned couples that informal marriages, though legal, made it more difficult for them to establish the validity of their marital claims; see Rose v. Clark, 8 Paige 574, 582 (N.Y. 1841); Cockrill v. Calhoun, 1 Nott. & McCord 285 (S.C. 1818); Fryer v. Fryer, Rich Cas. Equity 85 (S.C. 1832); Letters v. Roberts, 3 Western Law Journal 368 (Ohio 1850); Turpin v. Public Admin., 2 Bradf. 424 (N.Y. 1853); Hyde v. Hyde, 3 Bradf. 509 (N.Y. 1856); Cram v. Burnham, 5 Greenl. 213 (Me. 1828); Grotgen v. Grotgen, 3 Braf. 373 (N.Y. 1855).

45 Kent, *Commentaries on American Law*, 2:287. The modification read: "For the purpose of being registered and authenticated according to the provisions of this Title, marriages shall be solemnized by the following persons," and then a list was attached, *2 New York Revised Statutes, 1827–28*, 139; *3 New York Revised Statutes, 1836*, 661; and see Fred S. Hall, "Common Law Marriage in New York State," *ColLR* 30 (1930): 6–9.

46 Auguste Carlier, *Marriage in the United States* (Boston, 1867), p. 36.

47 Powell, "Marriage in Early New England," 334.

48 Asken v. Dupree, 30 Ga. 173, 190 (1860); and see David Langum, "Expatriate Domestic Relations Law in Mexican California," *Pepperdine Law Review* 7 (1979):47.

49 Stan Cohen, *Folk Devils and Moral Panics* (London, 1972), p. 9. I discovered Cohen's study in Weeks, *Sex, Politics, and Society*, pp. 14–15.

50 Cook, "The Marriage Celebration in the United States," 530; and see Beecher W. Watermore, "Marriage and Divorce Laws," *ALJ* 67 (1906):

163–66; Edmund Bennett, "Marriage Laws," *Forum* 3 (1887):228; Glenn C. Gillespie, "Remedial Legislation Affecting Marriage and Divorce," *Michigan State Bar Journal* 3 (1924):129, 132.

51 George E. Howard, "Social Control of Domestic Relations," *AJS* 167 (1910):815, 816–17, 816; and see William O'Neill, *Divorce in the Progressive Era* (New Haven, 1967), pp. 174–79.

52 In re McLaughlin's Estate, 4 Wash. 570, 591 (1892).

53 M. H. Buckham, "The Relation of the Family to the State," *IR* 13 (1882):63; and see Frank G. Cook, "Reform in the Celebration of Marriage," *AM* 61 (1888): 681–82; Isaac Van Winkle, "Marriage," *ALJ* 17 (1875):441–8; Samuel Dike, "Status of Marriage and Divorce," *PSQ* 4 (1889):228.

54 Gordon A. Stewart, "Our Marriage and Divorce Laws," *PSM* 23 (1883): 228; Howard, *Matrimonial Institutions*, 3:184.

55 William Leach, *True Love and Perfect Union* (New York, 1980), pp. 171–79; and see "Marriage," *CLJ* 3 (1876):486; Clarke, *Social Legislation*, p. 79; Erroll C. Gilky, "Validity of Common Law Marriage in Oregon," *OreLR* 3 (1923–24):46–48; Robert Black, "Common Law Marriage," *CinLR* 2 (1928):114–15.

56 William E. Bullock, *The Law of Domestic Relations of the State of New York* (Albany, N.Y., 1898), pp. 33–34, iii–iv; and see Cook, "Marriage Celebration in Europe," *AM* 61 (1888): 245–46, 263; "Editorial: Slave Marriage," *VaLJ* 1 (1877):643–44; Cook, "The Marriage Celebration in the United States," 532, 527–30; Koegel, *Common Law Marriage*, 80–81, 113; Robert C. Brickell, "Common Law Marriage," *ALRev* 44 (1910):208.

57 Meister v. Moore, 97 U.S. 76 (1877); Hutchins v. Kimmell, 31 Mich. 126, 130–31 (1875); and see Bishop, *Commentaries on Marriage and Divorce*, 2nd ed., pp. 130–33. For decisions in support of common-law marriage see Carmichael v. State, 12 Ohio St. 553 (1861); Blackman v. Crawfords, 3 Wall. 175 (U.S., D.C., 1865); Campbell v. Gullatt, 43 Ala. 57 (1869); Jones v. Jones, 28 Ark. 19 (1872); Port v. Port, 70 Ill. 484 (1873); Blanchard v. Lambert, 43 Ia. 228 (1876); State v. Worthingham, 23 Minn. 528 (1877); Williams v. Williams, 46 Wis. 464 (1879); Teter v. Teter, 101 Ind. 129 (1885); State v. Walker, 36 Kan. 297 (1887); Bailey v. State, 36 Neb. 808 (1893); Israel v. Arthur, 18 Col. 158 (1893).

58 In rejecting a woman's claim that a common-law marriage entitled her to dower, the Washington Supreme Court stated its policy assumptions quite clearly. Though the justices agreed that marriage "ought to be encouraged in all legitimate ways," they argued that "if the statutory requisites are dispensed with, it would, to some extent, set a premium upon illicit intercourse." On the contrary, by "adhering to the statutory

provisions all objectionable cases of this kind are eliminated, parties are led to regard the contract as a sacred one, as one not lightly to be entered into, and are forceably impressed with the idea that they are forming a relationship in which society has an interest, and to which the state is a party," In re McLaughlin, 4 Wash. 570, 590 (1892). And see Holmes v. Holmes, 1 Abb. 525 (U.S. C.C. Ore. 1870), but see Estate of Megginson, 21 Ore. 387 (1891); Denison v. Denison, 35 Md. 361 (1871); Beverlin v. Beverlin, 29 W.Va. 732 (1887); Bennett, "Marriage Laws," 228; Arthur Calhoun, *Social History of the American Family*, 3 vols. (Cleveland, 1917), 3:220.

59 Van Tuyl v. Van Tuyl, 57 Barb. 235, 237 (N.Y. 1869); Hulett v. Carey, 66 Minn. 327, 338 (1896); and see Sorenson v. Sorenson, 68 Neb. 483 (1903).

60 W. D. Harris, "Essentials of a Valid Marriage in Virginia," *VaLReg* 6 (1900):608; Noah Davis, "Marriage and Divorce," *NAR* 139 (1884):31; Crawford v. State, 73 Miss. 172, 178 (1895); and see Matney v. Linn, 59 Kan. 613 (1898); Tarett v. Negus, 127 Ala. 301 (1899); Comly's Estate, 185 Pa. 208 (1898); Galveston, Harrisburg, and San Antonio R. R. Co. v. Cody, 20 Tex. Civ. App. 520 (1899); "The Contract of Marriage," *ALJ* 9 (1874):401–2, "Note," *YLJ* 28 (1918):102–3.

61 Joel Bishop, *New Commentaries on Marriage and Divorce*, 2 vols. (Boston, 1891), 1:165–67. For a critique of Bishop, which argues that his definition of marriage was in fact conducive to greater legislative regulation see Henry T. Blake, "The Gospel of Marriage According to Bishop," *IlLR* 13 (1918–19):34–41.

62 *Report of the National League for the Protection of the Family* (Boston, 1891), p. 6. This was a summary report that included the League's history, policy decisions, and membership.

63 Gladstone cited in *Report of the League, 1898* (Boston, 1899), pp. 7, 12; Dike's comments on sociology in *Report of the League, 1888* (Boston, 1889), p. 15; and see *Report of the League, 1895* (Boston, 1896), pp. 8–10.

64 Carroll D. Wright, *A Report on Marriage and Divorce in the United States, 1867-1886* (Washington, D.C., 1889); Dike, "Status of Marriage and Divorce," 592–614.

65 Charles Noble, *A Compendium of the Laws on Marriage and Divorce* (New York, 1881), p. 28.

66 Buckham, "The Relation of the Family to the State," 64; Bullock, *The Law of Domestic Relations*, p. ii; *Reports of the League, 1886–1913*.

67 Wright, *A Report on Marriage and Divorce*, 190–97; John Wigmore, *Treatise on the Law of Evidence* (Boston, 1905), 2:2001; Thomas Monahan, *The Pattern of Age at Marriage in the United States*, 2 vols. (Philadelphia, 1951), 1:143.

68 Howard, *Matrimonial Institutions*, 3:190; U.S. Bureau of the Census, *"Special Reports: Marriage and Divorce, 1867–1906"* (Washington, D.C., 1908–1909), 186–88; William L. Snyder, *The Geography of Marriage* (New York, 1889), p. 20; Schouler, *A Treatise on the Law of Domestic Relations*, 6th ed. (New York, 1920), 2:1463; Chester Vernier, *American Family Laws*, 4 vols. (Stanford, Ca., 1931–38), 1:46, 59–81; Mary Richmond and Fred S. Hall, *Marriage and the State* (New York, 1929), pp. 9–119.

69 Quoted in Cook, "Reform in the Celebration of Marriage," 686.

70 Clarke, *Social Legislation*, p. 87; Richmond and Hall, *Marriage and the State*, p. 116, and see pp. 107–10; see also Ernst Freund, *Administrative Powers Over Persons and Property* (Chicago, 1928), pp. 508–9. Though the belief became more widespread that formal nuptials were necessary to protect family life adequately, a persistent refusal to inhibit matrimony was evident in the new license regulation. Enforcement continued to be dependent on penalties, not nullification. While forty-eight states and territories required licenses by 1907, only seventeen of them imposed fines for the failure to record the application. Lax official inspections and judicial constraints also stymied strict regulation. U.S. Bureau of the Census, "Marriage and Divorce, 1889-1907," 187, 106.

71 Dike's comments are in *Report of the League, 1886* (Boston, 1887), p. 8. Information on marriage powers can be found in Howard, *Matrimonial Institutions*, 3:187–90; Cook, "Reform in the Celebration of Marriage," 687–90; Richmond and Hall, *Marriage and the State*, pp. 222–36.

72 Cook, "Reform in the Celebration of Marriage," 685; Howard, *Matrimonial Institutions*, 2:390; Richmond and Hall, *Marriage and the State*, p. 221.

73 Quoted in Richmond and Hall, *Marriage and the State*, p. 223.

74 David Steward and Francis Carey, *A Digest of the Law of Husband and Wife as Established in Maryland* (Baltimore, 1881), p. 161; and see Maynard v. Hill, 125 U.S. 190, 193 (1888); Robinson v. Redd's Admin., 43 S.W. 435 (Ky. 1897); Toon v. Huberty, 104 Cal. 260 (1894); Hinckley v. Ayres, 105 Cal. 357 (1895); Sharon v. Sharon, 67 Cal. 185 (1885); Ibid., 75 Cal. 1 (1888); Ibid., 79 Cal. 633 (1889); Ibid., 84 Cal. 424 (1890); Rugh v. Ottenheimer, 6 Ore. 231, 237 (1877); State v. Madden, 81 Mo. 421, 423 (1884); Howard, *Matrimonial Institutions*, 2:467–70.

75 State v. Bittick, 103 Mo. 183, 192 (1890); and see State v. Brown, 119 N.C. 825 (1896); Williams v. Walton and Whann Co., 9 Houst. 322 (Del. 1892); Holen v. State, 35 Tex. Crim. Rep. 102 (1884); Campbell v. Beck, 52 Ala. 584 (1869); Lewis v. Ames, 44 Tex. 319 (1875).

76 Gilbert v. Bone, 64 Ill. 518, 521–22 (1872); Agent v. Willis, 124 N.C.

29, 31–32 (1899); and see Maggett v. Roberts, 112 N.C. 71 (1893); Haggin v. Haggin, 35 Neb. 375 (1892); Chapman v. Chapman, 11 Tex. Civil App. 392 (1895); Hunter v. Milan, 41 Pa. 332 (1899); Gardiner v. Mancester, 88 Me. 249 (1896); Baughman v. Baughman, 29 Kan. 283 (1883); State v. Dole and Ball, 20 La. An. 378 (1868); Sabalot v. Populus, 31 La. An. 854 (1879). Attempts to assert community authority over nuptials fared little better. Neither interested members of the community nor parents could use their disfavor to nullify a consummated union. The Massachusetts Supreme Judicial Court even upheld a slander conviction against a minister who had been urged by a bride's father to impugn the character of her fiancé, Joannes v. Bennett, 5 Allen 169 (Mass. 1862).

77   Theodore Baumeister, *The Law of New York as to the Solemnization of Marriage by Clergymen* (New York, 1890), p. 8; *The New York Times* and the attorney are cited in "Contract of Marriage," *ALJ* 9 (1874):401–2; and see "Note," *ALJ* (1874):370; Schouler, *Domestic Relations*, 6th ed., 2:1463.

78   Hynes v. McDermott, 91 N.Y. 451, 459 (1898); and see Redgrave v. Redgrave, 38 Md. 93, 97 (1873); Proctor v. Bigelow, 38 Mich. 282, 283 (1878).

79   State v. Walker, 36 Kansas 297, 298–300, 313 (1887); and see Bishop, *Commentaries on Marriage and Divorce*, 2nd ed., pp. 137–38; "Law Regulating the Forms of Marriage in the United States," *ALRev.*, N.S., 3 (1864):120; Peck v. Peck, 155 Mass. 475 (1892); In re Ruffino, 116 Cal. 304, 313 (1897).

80   O'Neill, *Divorce in the Progressive Era*, p. 106; Buckham, "The Relationship Between the Family and the State," 64. If the manner in which a couple treated one another, their mode of living together, and the reputations they had created among their families and friends sufficiently demonstrated a commitment to matrimony, then the courts steadfastly supported their claims. Teter v. Teter, 88 Ind. 494 (1883); Miller v. White, 80 Ill. 580 (1875); Canadian and American Mortgage and Trust Co. v. Bloomer, 14 Wash. 491 (1896); Richard v. Brehm, 73 Pa. 140 (1873); Greenwalt v. McEnelley, 85 Pa. 352 (1877); Grieve's Estate, 165 Pa. 126 (1895); Durning v. Hastings, 183 Pa. 210 (1897); Richwell v. Tunnicliff, 6 Barb. 408 (N.Y. 1862); People ex. rel. Commissioner of Public Charities and Corrections v. Bartholf, 24 Hun. 272 (N.Y. 1881); Betsinger v. Chapman, 88 N.Y. 487 (1882); Budington v. Munson, 33 Conn. 481 (1866); Soyer v. Great Falls Water Co., 15 Mont. 1 (1894); Womack v. Tankersley, 78 Va. 242 (1883); Case v. Case, 52 Cal. 568 (1878).

81   McKenna v. McKenna, 73 Ill. App. 64, 87 (1897). The persistent reliance of judges on common-law presumptions did not imply a lack of

concern for marital stability but rather a distinct institutional policy as to how to achieve conjugal permanency. Hooper v. McCaffery, 83 Ill. App. 341, 358 (1898); Bowman v. Bowman, 24 Ill. App. 165 (1887); Kansas Pacific R.R. Co. v. Mill, 2 Col. 442 (1874). The only exception to the use of cohabitation and repute to validate a marriage contract was in criminal cases. There was a split between states that accepted such evidence and those that demanded formal proof. For examples see Ryan v. State, 17 Ala. 80 (1877); State v. Clark, 54 N.H. 456 (1897); State v. Seals, 16 Ind. 352 (1861); Wigmore, *Treatise on Evidence*, 2:1948–54. A new watchfulness was apparent in the late nineteenth-century bench. In contrast to their antebellum brethren, judges later in the nineteenth century appear to have been more intent on ensuring that the virtuous were rewarded with marital legitimacy. In deciding these cases, the judges clearly considered it axiomatic that those who adhered to middle-class values and life styles posed no threat to matrimony, while those who flouted bourgeois standards threatened domestic order. See for example, Wright v. Wright, 48 How. Pr. 1, 7 (N.Y. 1874); Van Dusan v. Van Dusan, 97 Mich. 70, 72 (1893); In re Brush, 49 N.Y. Supp. 803, 805–6 (1898); Waddingham v. Waddingham, 21 Mo. App. 609, 621 (1886); Taylor v. Taylor, 10 Col. App. 303 (1897); Bates v. Bates, 27 N.Y. Supp. 872 (1894); Commonwealth v. Dill, 156 Mass. 226 (1892); Norcross v. Norcross, 155 Mass. 425 (1892); Estate of Beverson, 47 Cal. 621 (1874); Hunt's Appeal, 86 Pa. 294 (1878); Port v. Port, 70 Ill. 484 (1873); Crymble v. Crymble, 50 Ill. App. 544 (1893); Hulett v. Carey, 66 Minn. 327 (1896); Yardley's Estate, 75 Pa. 207 (1874); Eldred v. Eldred, 97 Va. 606 (1899); Chapman v. Chapman, 16 Tex. Civ. App. 382 (1897); Nixon v. Wichita Land and Cattle Co., 84 Tex. 408 (1892); Floyd v. Calvert, 53 Miss. 37 (1876); Wilson v. Allen, 108 Ga. 275 (1899); Brooke v. Brooke, 60 Mich. 464 (1884); Williams v. Kilburn, 88 Mich. 279 (1891); Erwin v. English, 61 Conn. 502 (1892); Poole v. People, 24 Col. 510 (1898); Leach v. Hall, 95 Ia. 611 (1895); Physick's Estate, 2 Brew. 179 (Pa. 1862); Strauss' Estate, 168 Pa. 561 (1895); Cargile v. Wood, 63 Mo. 501 (1876); "Good Faith as a Test of Common Law Marriage," *MLR* 9 (1910–11):54–58; Koegel, *Common Law Marriage*, p. 116; Bishop, *New Commentaries*, 1:132–34.

82 Wilkie v. Collins, 48 Miss. 496 (1873); "Contract of Marriage," *ALJ* 9 (1874-75):401–2; Thomas M. Cooley, *A Treatise on Constitutional Limitations* (Boston, 1868), p. 355; and see Bissell v. Bissell, 55 Barb. 325 (N.Y. 1869); Alan Jones, "Thomas M. Cooley and 'Laissez Faire' Constitutionalism: A Reconsideration," *JAH* 53 (1967):751–71; G. Edward White, *The American Judicial Tradition* (New York, 1876), pp. 115–22.

83 Noble, *A Compendium on the Laws on Marriage and Divorce*, p. 43.

84 Edmund Q. Brown, *Marriage in Pennsylvania Under the New License Act* (Philadelphia, 1886), pp. 3, 6; and see Elizabeth Duffey, *The Relations of the Sexes* (New York, 1876), pp. 61–62.

85 Koegel, *Common Law Marriage*; "Cohabitation as Essential to a Common Law Marriage," *MinnLR* 3 (1927):428. And see Howard, *Matrimonial Institutions*, 2:444–45, 3:182; Hall, "Common Law Marriage in New York," 1–11; Vernier, *American Family Laws*, 1:45–170; Lawrence M. Friedman, *A History of American Law* (New York, 1973), p. 435.

Chapter 4

1 Quoted in George Howard, *Matrimonial Institutions*, 3 vols. (Chicago, 1904), 2:481. Georgia was the only other state to encourage matrimony legislatively. More generally, the courts rebuffed every agreement or condition that inhibited nuptials. The Supreme Court of New Jersey dismissed a claim for $1,000 by a man who had agreed to end his marital plans in exchange for cash. The court held that the agreement had no legal standing and violated public policy: "Marriage rests as the foundation not only of individual happiness but also of the prosperity, if not the very existence of the social state, and the law, therefore, frowns upon and removes out of the way every rash and unreasonable restraint upon it, whether by penalty or inducement," Sterling v. Sinnickson, 2 South. 891 (N.J. 1820); and see "Conditions in Restraint of Marriage," *ALJ* 3 (1871):406–7; "Note," *HLR* 10 (1896–97):372–73; Nathan Dane, *A General Abridgement and Digest of American Law*, 9 vols. (Boston, 1823–29), 2:302. The only exception to this policy was the right of a husband to stipulate that his property be transferred to another heir if his widow remarried.

2 Francis Hilliard, *The Elements of Law* (New York, 1835), p. 15.

3 The sources of the law were equally perplexing. Originally the distinction between void and voidable marriages arose in an attempt to separate the property concerns of the common-law courts from the moral interests of ecclesiastical tribunals. But by the reign of Henry VIII this jurisdictional conflict was joined with the desire of many Britons, most notably the King himself, to find a way around the common law's refusal to dissolve marriages. For general discussions of these issues see Herbert I. Goodrich, "Jurisdiction to Annul a Marriage," *HLR* 32 (1918–19):806–24; Richard Helmholz, *Marriage Litigation in Medieval England* (London, 1944), p. 62; Paul S. Goda, "The Historical Evolution of the Concept of Void and Voidable Marriages," *JFL* 7 (1967):297–307; Da-

vid F. Engdahl, "Metaphysical Metaphysics and English Marriage Law," *JFL* 8 (1968):381–97. Early in the nineteenth century, disagreements arose over whether or not American courts had jurisdiction over annulments without specific authorization. The subject had come under ecclesiastical law in England and the right of American courts to use such rules was unclear. The problem was generally resolved by equating ecclesiastical courts with equity courts or by express legislation. For some cases which discuss the problem see Wightman v. Wightman, 4 Johns. 343 (N.Y. 1829); Burtis v. Burtis, 1 Hopk. Ch. 557 (N.Y. 1825); Gathings v. Williams, 27 N.C. 487 (1845); Smith v. Smith, 5 Ohio St. 32 (1855); Harrison v. State, 22 Md. 468 (1863).

4   Henry Swinebourne, *A Treatise on Spousals or Matrimonial Contracts* (London, 1686), pp. 18–28, 34, 47–49; William Blackstone, *Commentaries on the Laws of England*, 4 vols. (London, 1765–69), 1:436; Helmholz, *Marriage Litigation*, pp. 98–99; Sir Frederick Pollock and Frederic Maitland, *A History of English Law*, 2 vols. (Cambridge, 1895), 2:390–92; T. E. James, "The Age of Majority," *AJLH* 4 (1960): 31–32; Joseph E. Kett, *Rites of Passage, Adolescence in America, 1790 to the Present* (New York, 1977), chap. 1.

5   Edward Mansfield, *The Legal Rights, Liabilities, and Duties of Women* (Cincinnati, Ohio 1845), p. 239.

6   Tapping Reeve, *The Law of Baron and Femme* (New York, 1816), p. 200; the information on Connecticut marriages can be found in Thomas Monahan, *The Pattern of Age at Marriage*, 2 vols. (Philadelphia, 1951), 1:103; Norma Basch, *In the Eyes of the Law* (Ithaca, N.Y., 1982), p. 133; Rosser H. Taylor, *Antebellum South Carolina* (Chapel Hill, N.C., 1942), p. 61.

7   Lucius Chittenden quoted in Reeve, *Baron and Femme*, 2nd ed. (New York, 1846), p. 200n. In addition to New York, several other states also passed acts between 1830 and 1860, which hiked nuptial age requirements. Reeve, *Baron and Femme*, 2nd ed. (New York, 1846), pp. 200–1; Ibid., 4th ed. (New York, 1862), pp. 313–14.

8   Parton v. Hervey, 1 Gray 119, 121 (Mass. 1854); and see Goodwin v. Thompson, 2 Greene 329 (Ia. 1849); Koonce v. Wallace, 7 Jones 194 (N.C. 1859); Governor v. Ractor and Ryford, 10 Hump. 57 (N.C. 1849); Joel Bishop, *Commentaries on the Law of Marriage and Divorce*, 2nd ed. (Boston, 1856), p. 162. There was only one significant dissent to the use of the liberal common-law age levels. In 1851 the Supreme Court of Ohio upheld the state's new statutory age requirements in a bigamy trial. The justices argued that "each state must for itself, by fixed and reasonable rules, regulate the matter with regard to its own peculiar circumstances." Arguing that the common-law ages merely represented an English attempt to protect estates, the court urged

that in Ohio "such a regulation would be poorly adapted to a state of society like our own, where no such policy is to be promoted, where fidelity to the marriage vow has all the sanctity of a religious sentiment, and where all the experience has shown that the blessing of the marriage relation can only be realized when entered into with the utmost freedom of choice, and between persons of mature judgment and discretion," Shafner v. State, 20 Ohio 1, 4-5 (1851).

9 Abba Woolson, *Women in American Society* (New York, 1873), p. 60; Daniel Scott Smith, "Parental Power and Marriage Patterns, An Analysis of Historical Trends in Hingham, Massachusetts," *JMF* 35 (1973):426; and see Pool v. Pratt, 1 D. Chip. 252 (Vt. 1814); Aymar v. Roff, 2 Johns. Chan. 49 (N.Y. 1817); *American Jurist* 20 (1839):275–76; Arthur Calhoun, *A Social History of the American Family*, 3 vols. (Cleveland, 1917), 2:12, 22, 28–32; Guim Johnson, "Marriage in Antebellum North Carolina," *NCHR* 8 (1931):394–95.

10 Bishop, *Commentaries on Marriage and Divorce*, 2nd ed., pp. 185, 191–92; and see Zephaniah Swift, *A System of Laws for the State of Connecticut*, 2 vols. (New Haven, 1795), 1:440; Helmholz, *Marriage Litigation*, pp. 87–90; Marvin M. Moore, "Defenses Available in Annulment Actions," *JFL* 7 (1967):239, 252; Theodoric Beck, *Elements of Medical Jurisprudence*, 2 vols. (Philadelphia, 1823), 1:159–61.

11 Burtis v. Burtis, 1 Hopk. Chan. 557, 567, 568 (N.Y. 1825).

12 Beck, *Medical Jurisprudence*, 1:162; the Pennsylvania and New York statutes are cited in Amos Dean, *Medical Jurisprudence*, 2nd ed. (Albany, N.Y., 1873), p. 41; and see James Kent, *Commentaries on the American Law* (New York, 1826–1830), 2:77, 105, 113. Proof was the major legal problem in these cases. Medieval courts had developed the test of triennial cohabitation to determine sexual ability. If at the end of three years a wife remained a virgin, the marriage was annulled. Though English courts retained this customary device until the middle of the nineteenth century, American judges began to use other tests. The New York divorce law of 1830 required that claims of impotence be filed within the first two years of a marriage. In place of the older policy, couples were allowed to offer proof of sexual maladies as soon as they became known. The change appears to have been the product of two factors: a growing conviction that mandating three years of unblissful matrimony produced unnecessary social and family problems, and an increasing judicial reliance on medical determinations of sexual adequacy. Thus medical testimony replaced the traditional lay inspections relied upon in England and colonial America to test complaints. Bishop, *Commentaries on Marriage and Divorce*, 2nd ed., pp. 197, 203–5; Keith v. Keith, Wright 518 (Ohio 1834).

13 Devanbaugh v. Devanbaugh, 5 Paige 554, 557; 6 Paige 175, 177–78

(N.Y. 1836); and see Newell v. Newell, 9 Paige 25 (N.Y. 1841). In these, as in most matrimonial cases, the judicial reluctance to dissolve existing marriages threw the onus of proof on the complaining party. In Keith v. Keith, for example, an Ohio Court finally annulled a marriage when a woman who had been married for a year and a half had a team of medical inspectors examine her husband. They discovered he had undeveloped genitals, Keith v. Keith, 1 Wright's Reports, 518 (Ohio 1834); and see Bascomb v. Bascomb, 25 N.H. 267 (1852); Ferris v. Ferris, 8 Conn. 166 (1830); Norton v. Norton, 2 Aiken 188 (Vt. 1827); Simon Greenleaf, *A Treatise on the Law of Evidence*, 3 vols. (Boston, 3rd ed., 1852), p. 253; Dane, *Abridgement of American Law*, chap. 46.

14 Helmholz, *Marriage Litigation*, pp. 87–90; Charles Rosenberg, "Sexuality, Class, and Role in Nineteenth Century America," *AQ* 25 (1973): 131–53.

15 Zephaniah Swift, *Digest of the Law of Evidence*, 2 vols. (N.Y. 1810), 1:19; Talcott Parsons, "The Incest Taboo in Relation to Social Structure," in *The Family*, 2nd ed., ed. Rose Lauber Coser (New York, 1974), pp. 13–30; Michael P. Einbinder, "Comment: The Legal Family, A Definitional Analysis," *JFL* 13 (1973):782; Frederic P. Stokes, "The Incestuous Marriage, A Relic of the Past," *UColLR* 36 (1964):473–74. For an example of a case involving true incest see Cook v. State, 11 Ga. 53 (1852).

16 Mansfield, *The Legal Rights of Women*, p. 236; and see Pollock and Maitland, *History of English Law*, 2:386–89; Helmholz, *Marriage Litigation*, pp. 77–87; Thomas Poynter, *A Concise View of the Doctrines of Ecclesiastical Courts*, 2nd ed. (London, 1825), pp. 85–113; Julia Spruill, *Women's Life and Work in the Southern Colonies* (Chapel Hill, N.C., 1938), pp. 141–43; Howard, *Matrimonial Institutions*, 2:212–16, 398–99, 433–35; Samuel Sewall, *Diary of Samuel Sewall*, ed. Thomas M. Halsey, 2 vols. (New York, 1973), 1:285, 333–34, 349; 2:658.

17 Fenton v. Reed, 4 Johns. Chan. 343, 346, 347, 350 (N.Y. 1820); Kent, *Commentaries on American Law*, 2:82–85; and see Carl Degler, *At Odds* (New York, 1980), pp. 104–9.

18 Bernard Farber, *Kinship and Class* (New York, 1971), chap. 3. For a comment on Farber's analysis see Peter D. Hall, "Marital Selection and Business in Massachusetts Merchant Families, 1700–1900," in *The American Family in Social-Historical Perspective*, ed. Michael Gordon (New York, 1973), pp. 101–14. For discussions of first-cousin unions see Reeve, *Baron and Femme*, pp. 202–4; Timothy Walker, *Introduction to American Law* (Philadelphia, 1837), p. 409; Bishop, *Commentaries on Marriage and Divorce*, 2nd ed., pp. 181–82; Blodget v. Brinsmaid, 9 Vt. 27 (1837); State v. Shaw, 3 Ire. 532 (N.C. 1843); Paddock v. Wells, 2 Barb. Chan. 331 (N.Y. 1847); Spear v. Robinson, 29 Me. 531

(1849); McClellan v. Kennedy, 3 Md. Chan. 234 (1852); but see also Moore v. Whitaker, 2 Har. 50 (Del. 1835).

19 Howard, *Matrimonial Institutions*, 2:214, 397, 334–5; Dr. Strahan's Opinion, 2 Va. Col. Dec., Baradell's Rep. 320 (1820); Commonwealth v. Leftwich, 5 Rand. 83 (Va. 1827); Commonwealth v. Perryman, 2 Leigh 717 (Va. 1830).

20 Blodget v. Brinsmaid, 9 Vt. 27, 30 (1837). England did not permit such marriages until 1907; see Jeffrey Weeks, *Sex, Politics, and Society* (London, 1981), pp. 30–31; and see Bishop, *Commentaries on Marriage and Divorce*, p. 184; Kent, *Commentaries*, 2:85n; Kelly v. Scott, 5 Gratt. 479 (Va. 1849); Winchester v. Hinsdall, 12 Conn. 87 (1837).

21 Quoted in Parsons Cooke, *The Marriage Question: Of the Lawfulness of Marrying the Sister of a Deceased Wife* (Boston, 1842); Horace Mann quoted in *Letters of the Right Reverend Bishop McIlvaine of Ohio and Other Eminent Persons in the United States of America in Favor of Marriage with a Deceased Wife's Sister* (London, 1852), p. 7; and see Domesticus, *The Doctrine of Incest Stated with an Examination of the Question of Whether a Man May Marry his Deceased Wife's Sister* (New York, 1817); Clericus, *The Arguments of Domesticus on the Question of Whether a Man May Marry his Deceased Wife's Sister* (New York, 1817); Colin McIver, *An Essay Concerning the Unlawfulness of a Man's Marrying his Sister by Affinity* (Philadelphia, 1842); Johnson, "Marriage in Antebellum North Carolina," 385–86.

22 Bowers v. Bowers, 10 Rich Eq. 551, 555 (S.C. 1858); and see Ward v. Dylaney, 23 Miss. 410 (1852); Hutchins v. Commonwealth, 2 Va. Cas. 331 (1823); Bonham v. Bagley, 7 Ill. 622 (1845); Sutton v. Warren, 10 Met. 451 (Mass. 1845); Kelley v. Neely, 12 Ark. 657 (1852); State v. Barefoot, 2 Rich. Law 209 (S.C. 1845).

23 Blackstone, *Commentaries*, 1:438–39; T. E. James, "The English Law of Marriage," in *A Century of Family Law*, ed. Ronald A. Graveson and F. L. Crane (Cambridge, 1957), pp. 30–31; David Rothman, *The Discovery of the Asylum* (Boston, 1971), pp. 109–28; Norman Dain, *Concepts of Insanity in the United States, 1789–1865* (New Brunswick, N.J., 1864).

24 Reeve, *Baron and Femme*, p. 201; Middleborough v. Rochester, 12 Mass. 363, 365 (1815).

25 Wightman v. Wightman, 4 Johns. Chan. 343 (N.Y. 1820); Kent, *Commentaries*, 2:76; Bishop, *Commentaries on Marriage and Divorce*, 2nd ed., p. 148; Dain, *Concepts of Insanity*, pp. 49, 198, 208–9.

26 True v. Raney, 21 N.H. 53, 54–55 (N.H. 1850).

27 Isaac Ray, *A Treatise on the Medical Jurisprudence of Insanity*, ed. John Harvard [1838] (Cambridge, Mass., 1962).

28 Catherine Sedgwick quoted in Dain, *Concepts of Insanity*, p. 180; "Fa-

cetiousness of the Law," *New York Legal Observer* 3 (1845):156; and see Rawdon v. Rawdon, 28 Ala. 565, 568 (1856).

29   Cole v. Cole, 5 Sneed. 57, 59 (Tenn. 1857). The court added: "If the exceptional conduct of either widows or widowers, when they become anxious to marry, is to be regarded as delusion our lunatic asylum might have to be much enlarged. Eccentricity of conduct, or peculiarities of manners does not constitute insanity." See also Anonymous, 4 Pick. 32 (Mass. 1846); Jenkins v. Jenkins, 2 Dana 102 (Ky. 1834); Crump v. Morgan, 38 Ire. Eq. 91 (N.C. 1843); Foster v. Means, Speer's Eq. 569 (S.C. 1844); Clements v. Mattison, 3 Rich. 93 (S.C. 1846); Keyes v. Keyes, 22 N.H. 553 (1851); Powell v. Powell, 27 Miss. 783 (1854); Elzey v. Elzey, 1 Houst. 308 (Del. 1857); Little v. Little, 13 Gray 264 (Mass. 1859); Atkinson v. Medford, 46 Me. 510 (1859).

30   Poynter, *Doctrines of Ecclesiastical Courts*, p. 140; and see "Fraud: Is it a Ground for Dissolving Marriage Contracts?," *PLJ*, O.S., 23 (1876): 163; Bishop, *Commentaries on Marriage and Divorce*, p. 151.

31   Reeve, *Baron and Femme*, p. 206; Swift, *A System of Laws*, 1:190.

32   Benton v. Benton, 1 Day 111, 113 (Conn. 1803).

33   Guilford v. Oxford, 9 Conn. 321, 327 (1832).

34   Kent, *Commentaries*, 2:78. The fault line in judicial determinations of fraud appears to have been the moral culpability of the disaffected spouse. The issues were most vividly presented in the emotionally charged annulment cases involving concealed or uncertain pregnancies. Many of these disputes stemmed from marriages entered into only after the groom had been threatened with bastardy proceedings. By marrying he could have the indictment quashed. Applying the strict contractual standard evident in the *Benton* case, most courts refused to nullify these unions even if the husband proved he had been deceived. Judges acted on the assumption that the wedding acted as an admission of guilt and a waiver of rights. For various judicial reactions to such cases see Hoffman v. Hoffman, 30 Pa. 417, 424 (1858); Jackson v. Winne, 7 Wend. 47 (N.Y. 1831); Frith v. Frith, 18 Ga. 273 (1855); Montgomery v. Montgomery, 3 Barb. Chan. 132 (N.Y. 1848); Moss v. Moss, 2 Ired. 55 (N.C. 1841); Scroggins v. Scroggins, 3 Dev. 535 (N.C. 1835); Scott v. Schufelt, 5 Paige 43 (N.Y. 1835); State v. Murphy, 6 Ala. 765 (1844); Baker v. Baker, 13 Cal. 87, 103–4 (1859); Ritter v. Ritter, 5 Blackf. 81, 84 (Ind. 1839); Morris v. Morris, Wright 630 (Ohio 1834); Nancy Cott, "Divorce and the Changing Status of Women in Eighteenth Century Massachusetts," *WMQ* 33 (1976):598–99. If couples did not live together and had no children or the union was immediately repudiated or never consummated, courts were less reluctant to dissolve the marriage and use a more expansive definition of fraud. See for example Sloan v. Kane and Grant, 10 How. Pr. 66 (N.Y. 1854); Robertson v. Cole, 12 Tex.

356, 364 (1854); Respublica v. Hevice, 3 Wheeler Crim. Cases 505 (N.Y. 1825).

35 Reynolds v. Reynolds, 3 Allen 605, 606–11 (Mass. 1862). For a discussion of the case see Bishop, *Commentaries on Marriage and Divorce*, 5th ed., pp. 156–67.

36 Moss v. Moss, L.R. 263 (1897); Max Lee Friedman, "Fraud and the Marriage Contract," *ALRev* 32 (1898):571. Both common-law decisions and the statutes that followed the Massachusetts bench decreed that when a husband had premarital intercourse with his mate, there could be no fraud. Nor could the misrepresentation of incontinence by the bride before marriage be used by a husband to annul a marriage. Except for pregnancy, *caveat emptor* continued to rule the common law of fraud. Two states, Virginia and Maryland, modified the common law by legislation granting courts the power to dissolve a marriage if the husband discovered his bride had had illicit relations with other men before their marriage. For the gradual diffusion of the *Reynolds* rule see Carris v. Carris, 24 N.J. Eq. 516 (1873); Allen's Appeal, 99 Pa. St. 196 (1881); Harrison v. Harrison, 94 Mich. 559 (1893); Sinclair v. Sinclair, 57 N.J. Eq. 222 (1898); Dawson v. Dawson, 18 Mich. 335 (1869); Seilheimer v. Seilheimer, 40 N.J. Eq. 412 (1885); Foss v. Foss, 12 Allen 26 (Mass. 1866); Crehore v. Crehore, 97 Mass. 330 (1867); Tait v. Tait, 22 N.Y. Supp. 597 (1893); Leavitt v. Leavitt, 13 Mich. 452 (1865).

37 James Schouler, *A Treatise on the Law of Domestic Relations* (Boston, 1870), p. 36; and see Bishop, *New Commentaries on Marriage and Divorce*, 2 vols. (New York, 1891); 1:194; Tomperts' Ex'rs v. Tomperts, 13 Bush. 326 (Ky. 1877); City v. Williamson, 10 Phila. Rep. 176 (Pa. 1873); Lewis v. Lewis, 41 Minn. 124 (1890). Similar rules were applied to claims of duress and force.

38 Kent, *Commentaries*, 2:177; Francis Lieber, *Manual of Political Ethics*, 2 vols. (New York, 1820), 2:9; and see Swift, *A System of Laws*, 1:186–87; William Paley, *The Principles of Political and Moral Philosophy*, 2 vols. (London, 5th ed., 1788), 1:351, 295, 2:293–94; Blackstone, *Commentaries*, 1:436, 4:163–64.

39 Lawmakers did try to suppress bigamy and initially they took an expansive definition of the crime. In their efforts to defend monogamy, a number of states created a new prohibition: they banned the remarriage of the guilty party to a divorce. As an innovation on the common law, courts generally required legislative authorization. After legislators acted, courts generally upheld the restriction's social utility and legality. See Cropsey v. Ogden, 11 N.Y. 228 (1854); West Cambridge v. Lexington, 1 Pic. 507 (Mass. 1823); Barber v. Barber, 16 Cal. 378 (1860).

40 The Pennsylvania legislation is discussed in Griffith v. Smith, 1 Pa. Legal Journal 479 (1842–43); and Howard, *Matrimonial Institutions*,

2:398, 436–37, 476; State v. Patterson, 2 Ire. 346 (N.C. 1842); and see Martin's Heirs & Adm'r v. Martin, 22 Ala. 86, 103–5 (1853); Higgins v. Breen, 9 Mo. 497 (1845); William v. Oates, 5 Ire. 535 (N.C. 1841); Robbins v. Potter, 11 Allen 588 (Mass. 1866); Baker v. People, 2 Hill 325 (N.Y. 1842); Janes v. Janes, 5 Blackf. 141 (Ind. 1839). Bigamous marriages were held to be void in most states. They conferred no marital rights on either party and the children of such unions were illegitimate. However, Louisiana and Texas adopted the civil-law doctrine of putative marriage. Under it, if one of the parties to a marriage had acted in good faith, not knowing that the other had a previous marriage, then the innocent victim and any children were entitled to the full civil benefits of matrimony along with the first family. Missouri adopted a similar provision which declared that the children of bigamous unions were legitimate. This modification of the common law was later accepted as part of the reformation of bastardy law in many states. But the common-law states refused to grant bigamous spouses property rights. Smith v. Smith, 1 Tex. 621 (1846); Lee v. Smith, 18 Tex. 141 (1856); Abston v. Abston, 15 La. An. 137 (1860); Summerlin v. Livingston, 15 La. An. 519 (1860); Hubbell v. Inkstein, 7 La. An. 252 (1852).

41 The law's preference for matrimony and bias against disrupting homes, though, helped lessen the strictness even of this policy. Following the lead of a 1603 Parliamentary act, which included a title reinvesting matrimonial rights on those whose partners had been absent or unheard of for over seven years, most states incorporated a nuptial escape clause in their codes. These acts, dubbed Enoch Arden laws (after the heroic sailor of a Tennyson poem who returned from the sea to find his wife remarried and then left without revealing himself), freed the parties from criminal liability even if the original spouse returned. This took the law one more step away from the ecclesiastical ideal of matrimony as an indissoluble bond. The appeal rested on the certainty the acts provided for abandoned spouses and their utility to the bench as one more way of aiding couples to wed in good faith. See for example the discussion in Woods v. Adm'r of Woods, 2 Bays 476, 478–79 (S.C. 1802). Tennessee and Pennsylvania had unique provisions. They gave the returning spouse the right to choose between reclaiming his or her former spouse or accepting the new situation. Bishop, *Commentaries on Marriage and Divorce*, p. 171. And see Samuel Adams, "Two Score and Three of Enoch Ardens," *JFL* 5 (1965):159–69. To aid them, courts accepted the statutes and used the common-law presumption that an individual was considered dead if absent for more than seven years. When the presumption of death and innocence clashed, the courts often sided with the contested marriage and presumed the first spouse to be dead. Commonwealth v. Mash, 7 Met. 474 (Mass. 1844); Northfield v. Plymouth, 20

Vt. 582 (1848); State v. Gibbon, 38 Mass. 313 (1860); Valleau v. Valleau, 6 Paige 207 (N.Y. 1836); Spears v. Burton, 31 Miss. 547 (1856); Cropsey v. McKinney, 30 Barb. 47 (N.Y. 1859); Greensborough v. Underhill, 12 Vt. 604 (1839); Jackson v. Claw, 18 Johns. 346 (N.Y. 1820); Fenton v. Reed, 4 Johns. 52 (N.Y. 1809).

42   Other challenges came in the form of opposition to strict nuptial regulation. The most frequent target was the ban on the remarriage of divorced persons. Opponents considered it ill advised and a hindrance rather than an aid to marriage. See for example Henry Wright, *Marriage and Parentage*, 3rd ed. (Boston, 1855), p. 202; Bishop, *Commentaries on Marriage and Divorce*, p. 175; Commonwealth v. Putnam, 1 Pick. 136 (Mass. 1822); People v. Hovey, 5 Barb. 117 (N.Y. 1849); Reed v. Hudson, 13 Ala. 570 (1848); Cox v. Combs, 8 B. Monroe 231 (Ky. 1848); Park v. Barron, 20 Ga. 702 (1856).

43   Raymond Lee Muncy, *Sex and Marriage in Utopian Communities in Nineteenth Century America* (Bloomington, Ind., 1973); Kimball Young, *Isn't One Wife Enough?* (New York, 1954).

44   Muncy, *Sex and Marriage*, pp. 122–43; Sydney E. Ahlstrom, *A Religious History of the American People* (New Haven, Conn., 1973), pp. 501–9; Young, *Isn't One Wife Enough?*, pp. 88–102; David Brion Davis, "The New England Origins of Mormonism," in *Mormonism and American Culture*, ed. Marvin S. Hill and James B. Allen (New York, 1972), pp. 13–28; Leonard Arrington, "Early Mormon Communalism," in ibid., pp. 37–58; David Brion Davis, "Some Themes of Counter Subversion," in ibid., pp. 59–73; Stanley S. Invins, "Notes on Mormon Polygamy," in ibid., pp. 101–4; Sidney Ditzion, *Marriage, Morals, and Sex in America: A History of Ideas* (New York, 1953), pp. 215–20.

45   Howard Lamar, "Statehood for Utah: A Different Path," in *Mormonism*, ed. Hill and Allen, pp. 128–29; Klaus Hansen, "The Political Kingdom as a Source of Conflict," in ibid., pp. 12–21. For a discussion of the particular Mormon approach to the law see Orma Linford, "The Mormons, the Law, and the Territory of Utah," *AJLH* 23 (1979):213–35.

46   Davis, "Some Themes of Counter Subversion," in *Mormonism*, ed. Hill and Allen, pp. 67–70; Ditzion, *Marriage, Morals, and Sex*, p. 210; Lamar, "Statehood for Utah," in *Mormonism*, ed. Hill and Allen, pp. 130–31.

47   The treatment of the Shakers offers a revealing contrast to that of the Mormons. The sect's adoption of celibacy was condemned as unhealthy and immoral. Several states even passed laws authorizing divorce if a person's mate joined the group. Nevertheless, Shakers did not suffer widespread persecution. They were even admired for their personal sacrifice and religious commitment. Sexual denial was quite different

from sexual deviation. The Saints, who flouted the society's most dearly held marital beliefs, engendered a commensurate opposition. For a general analysis of the Mormons' political troubles see John R. Wunder, "Freedom from Government," in *Values of the American Heritage: Challenges, Case Studies, and Teaching Strategies*, ed. Carl Ubbelohde and Jack R. Fraenkel (Washington, D.C., 1976), pp. 84–108.

48 U. S. Grant cited in *A Compilation of the Messages and Papers of the Presidents, 1798–1900*, 10 vols., ed. James D. Richardson (Washington, D.C. 1909), 2:151; and see Lamar, "Statehood for Utah," in *Mormonism*, ed. Hill and Allen, pp. 132–33; Muncy, *Sex and Marriage*, pp. 144–55; Ray Jay Davis, "The Polygamous Prelude," *AJLH* 6 (1962):6–9.

49 U.S. v. Reynolds, 1 Utah 226, 227 (1874); U.S. v. Reynolds, 1 Utah 319 (1876).

50 Reynolds v. U.S., 98 U.S. 145, 162–67 (1878).

51 Cannon v. U.S., 116 U.S. 55 (1885). The courts also upheld most procedural tactics used in the crusade against the Mormons, though only after statutory changes accommodated common-law provisions. For example, the courts upheld statutes making cohabitation with more than one woman a crime to avoid the problems of spousal immunity from testifying. See for example, Miles v. U.S., 103 U.S. 304 (1881); In re Snow, 102 U.S. 274 (1886); Snow v. U.S., 346 (1886); Murphy v. Ramsey, 114 U.S. 15 (1885); Davis, "Polygamous Prelude," 9–18.

52 Elizabeth Duffey, *The Relations Between the Sexes* (New York, 1876), pp. 83–84; James Garfield cited in *A Compilation of the Messages of the Presidents*, 7:560, 606.

53 Bennett and Brown quoted in A. M. Gibson, "Have the Mormons Any Rights?" (undated pamphlet in Goldfarb Library, Brandeis University, Waltham, Mass.); Lamar, "Statehood for Utah," in *Mormonism*, ed. Hill and Allen, p. 137.

54 Church of Latter-Day Saints v. U.S., 136 U.S. 1 (1890) in *Landmark Briefs and Arguments of the Supreme Court of the United States: Constitutional Law*, 15 vols., ed. Phillip B. Kurland and Gerhard Casper (Arlington, Va., 1975), 10:123; Church of Latter-Day Saints v. U.S., 136 U.S. 1, 50.

55 Mormons who had settled in adjoining territories met similar legal suppression. Their smaller numbers afforded them even less protection. Test oaths were adopted in several territories to enforce statutes stripping Mormons of their rights to vote and hold office. These laws were upheld by local and federal courts. The determination of non-Mormons to combat polygamy and to curtail the political and economic power of the Saints led to continuous battles before and after statehood in these areas.

For test oath cases see Davis v. Beason, 133 U.S. 333, 341–42 (1889); Wooley v. Watkins, 2 Id. 555 (1889); Innis v. Bolton, 2 Id. 407 (1888); Davis, "Polygamous Prelude," 18–23.

56 Charles S. Zane, "The Death of Polygamy in Utah," *Forum* 12 (1891–92):371; and see Ernst Freund, *The Police Power* (Chicago, 1904), p. 64; Frederic J. Stimson, *Popular Law Making* (Boston, 1910), pp. 306–7.

57 Auguste Carlier, *Marriage in the United States* (Boston, 1867), p. 87.

58 Ibid.; and see Hugh Davis' Case, 1 Laws of Va. 146 (Henning. 1823); Robert Sweet's Case, 1 Laws of Va. 552 (Henning. 1823); Jonathan L. Alpert, "The Origins of Slavery in the United States, The Maryland Precedent," *AJLH* 14 (1970):189, 209–12; James Johnston, *Race Relations in Virginia and Miscegenation in the South* (Amherst, Mass., 1970 reprint of 1934 Ph.D. dissertation), pp. 165–84; Lorenzo Greene, *The Negro in Colonial New England, 1620–1776* (New York, 1942), p. 208; Harvey M. Applebaum, "Miscegenation Statutes: A Constitutional and Social Problem," *GeoLJ* 53 (1964):49–50.

59 Bishop, *Commentaries on Marriage and Divorce*, 2nd ed., pp. 74–75. The Kentucky case was Armstrong v. Hodges, 2 B. Monroe 69 (Ky. 1841); the English was Forbes v. Countess of Strathmore, Ferg. Cons. Law Rep. 113; and see Blackstone, *Blackstone's Commentaries*, ed. Tucker (Richmond, Va., 1803), 2:434, 438.

60 Bowers v. Newman, 2 McMullen 472, 491–92 (S.C. 1842); Patton's Heirs v. Patton's Ex'r, 5 J.J. Marsh. 389 (Ky. 1831). The North Carolina Supreme Court was not as fastidious as its neighboring tribunal. The state's lawmakers had neglected to include the racial ban in the 1836 revised statutes. Two years later they remedied their error. But when a black man and a white woman tried to take advantage of the time lapse, the court held that since their marriage took place before 1836 their cohabitation during the brief statuteless period did not validate their union, State v. Hooper, 5 Ire. 201 (N.C. 1844). For cases applying the ban see Butler v. Boarman, 1 Har. & McHenry 371 (Md. 1770); Butler v. Craig, 2 Har. & McHenry 214 (Md. 1787); Shorter v. Boswell, 2 Har. & McHen. 359 (Md. 1808); Shorter v. Rozier, 3 Har. & McHen. 238 (Md. 1794); Commonwealth v. Isaacs, 5 Ran. 634 (Va. 1826); Tindall v. Johnson, 5 Mo. 179 (1838); State v. Fore and Chestnut, 1 Ire. 378 (N.C. 1841); Black and Manning v. Oliver, 1 Ala. 449 (1840); Succession of Minvielle, 15 La. An. 342 (1860); State v. Brady, 9 Hump. 74 (Tenn. 1848); Tindall v. Johnson, 5 Mo. 179 (1838).

61 Massachusetts was one of the few states to buck the statutory trend. Repeal of its statutory ban on interracial marriages proceeded directly from its role as a seedbed for antislavery agitation. Abolitionists and others pointed out the incompatibility of the ban with opposition to

slavery. A series of petitions culminated in the 1843 repeal even though many legislators argued, in terms that foreshadowed the separate-but-equal doctrine of the 1896 Plessy v. Ferguson case, that since the law applied equally to both races neither was stigmatized. Iowa in 1851 and Kansas in 1857 passed similar repeals. These antebellum actions, although they did little to alleviate the customary barriers to interracial unions, did help turn the formal prohibition into a sectional phenomenon and suggest how deep the opposition to state nuptial regulation ran. Massachusetts House of Representatives, Report No. 28 (Feb. 18, 1839); Ibid., No. 74 (April 3, 1829); Ibid., No. 46 (March 6, 1840); Massachusetts Acts and Resolves (1843), 40; Louis Ruchames, "Race, Marriage, and Abolition in Massachusetts," *JNH* 40 (1955):250–73; Leon Litwack, *North of Slavery* (Chicago, 1961), pp. 105–6; Applebaum, "Miscegenation Statutes," note 51. The more common response, to enact a ban, is chronicled in Theodore Soreson, "Legislation: Nebraska's Miscegenation Statute," *NebLR* 35 (1948–49):475–77; Henry W. Farmham, *Chapters in the History of Social Legislation in the United States to 1860* (New York, 1838), pp. 216–17.

62 Scroggins v. Scroggins, 3 Dev. 535 (N.C. 1832); Barden v. Barden, 3 Dev. 548, 550 (N.C. 1832).

63 Reeve, *Baron and Femme*, p. 340; Samuel Sewall quoted in Howard, *Matrimonial Institutions*, 2:215–26; and see Loiver v. Sale, Quincy 29, note 2 (Mass. 1762); Edgar J. McManus, *A History of Negro Slavery in New York* (Syracuse, N.Y., 1966), pp. 65, 177–78.

64 Commonwealth v. Clements, 6 Binney 206, 211 (Pa. 1814); and see Greene, *Negro in Colonial New England*, pp. 192–201; John C. Hurd, *The Law of Freedom and Bondage*, 3 vols. (Boston, 1858), 1:287; Arthur Zilversmit, *The First Emancipation: The Abolition of Slavery in the North* (Chicago, 1967), pp. 9–10; Marbletown v. Kington, 29 John. 1 (N.Y. 1822); Jackson v. Lervey, 5 Cowen 397 (N.Y. 1826); Howard, *Matrimonial Institutions*, 2:218, 223.

65 Herbert Gutman, *The Black Family in Slavery and Freedom, 1750–1925* (New York, 1976), pp. 61–62.

66 Frank and Lucy v. Denham's Adm'r, 5 Litt. 330, 331 (Ky. 1824); and see Melinda and Sarah v. Gardner, 24 Ala. 719 (1854); Gutman, *Black Family*, p. 291.

67 Girod v. Lewis, 6 Martin 559 (La. 1819).

68 Howard, *Matrimonial Institutions*, 2:160; Howard v. Howard, 6 Jones 235, 239–40 (N.C. 1858); and see Maxwell Bloomfield, *American Lawyers in a Changing Society* (Cambridge, Mass., 1976) pp. 109–10.

69 Howard v. Howard, 236; Alvany v. Powell, 1 Jones Eq. 35, 39–40 (N.C. 1853); Thomas R. R. Cobb, *An Inquiry into the Law of Negro Slavery in the United States of America* (New York, 1858), pp. 242–46; State v.

Smith, 9 Ala. 990 (1846). And see generally Opinion of Daniel Dulaney, 1 Har. & McHenry, 560–63 (Md. 1758); Frazier v. Spear, 2 Bibb. 385 (Ky. 1811); State v. Samuel, 2 Dev. & Batt. 177 (N.C. 1836); Alfred v. State, 37 Miss. 296 (1859); Williams v. State, 33 Ga. Supp. 85 (1864). A Maryland act of 1777 did grant slaves the right to marry with their masters' consent, but no civil rights accompanied this privilege; see Jones v. Jones, 36 Md. 447 (1872). Other states conceded such marital rights as limits on a slave spouse's ability to testify against his or her mate, but few had the force of law behind them. These legal incursions into black marital rights even extended to free black couples. Free blacks were permitted to wed each other, but this right was couched in terms that ensured that their marriages posed no threat to the slave system. See for example, Kyler v. Dunlap, 18 B. Monroe 561 (Ky. 1857); Taylor v. Swett, 3 La. 33 (1831); Stover v. Boswell's Heir, 3 Dana 233 (Ky. 1835); Akin v. Anderson, 19 Ga. 229 (1856); Bryan v. Walton, 14 Ga. 185 (1853); State v. Roland, 6 Ire. 241 (N.C. 1846); Coleman v. State, 14 Mo. 157 (1851); Eugene Genovese, *Roll, Jordan, Roll: The World the Slaves Built* (New York, 1974), pp. 398–413.

70 Tocqueville quoted in Gutman, *Black Family*, p. xxi; Genovese, *Roll, Jordan, Roll*, p. 53; ex-slave quoted in Gutman, *Black Family*, p. 284; slave preacher quoted in Genovese, *Roll, Jordan, Roll*, p. 481; and see C. Peter Ripley, "The Black Slave Family in Transition: Louisiana, 1860–65," *JSH* 42 (1975):369–70; John Blassingame, *The Slave Community: Plantation Life in the Antebellum South* (New York, 1972).

71 Quoted in Morton Keller, *Affairs of State* (Cambridge, 1977), p. 218; and see Peter Kolchin, *First Freedom* (Westport, Conn., 1972), pp. 58–62.

72 Gutman, *Black Family*, pp. 426, 6, 14–15. Such legislative validations had been used by several antebellum states to remove the cloud of uncertainty over the marriages of large groups of people. Connecticut had used such a law to validate the marriage of couples who had been wed by unauthorized clergymen, Tennessee to ease the doubts of those whose marriages had not been formally complete, and Texas to give legal backing to informal colonial unions called "bond marriages." In 1813, New York had even passed a law granting slave marriages validity. See Howard, *Matrimonial Institutions*, 2:426–27; Goshen v. Stonington, 4 Conn. 224 (1821); Thomas Cooley, *Constitutional Limitations*, 5th ed. (Boston, 1883), pp. 372–73; Bennett L. Smith, *Marriage by Bond in Colonial Texas* (Dallas, 1972); William Bullock, *The Law of Domestic Relations in New York* (New York, 1898), pp. 34–36. The reconstruction marriage acts are reprinted in 39 Cong., 2nd Sess., Senate Execu. Docs., No. 6, 1866–67, 124–25, 170–209; and see Texas Constitution of 1869, Art. II, sec. 27; Mississippi Constitution of

1868, Art. xii, 621-22; Virginia Constitution of 1870, Art. XI, sec. 9.

73 Washington v. Washington, 69 Ala. 281, 285 (1881); and see Estill v. Rogers, 1 Bush. 62 (Ky. 1866); Stewart v. Munchandler, 2 Bush. 278 (Ky. 1867); Hall v. U.S., 92 U.S. 97 (1875); Dowd v. Hurley, 78 Ky. 260 (1880); James v. Mickey, 26 S.C. 270 (1886); U.S. v. Route, 33 Fed. 246 (U.S. Es. Mo. 1887); Diggs v. Wormley, 21 D.C. 477 (1893); Green v. Norment, 5 Mack. 80 (D.C. 1886); Thomas v. Holtzman, 18 D.C. 62 (1888); Scott v. Raub, 88 Va. 721 (1892); Butler v. Butler, 161 Ill. 451 (1896); Scott v. Lairamore, 17 Ky. Law Rep. 613 (1895); Lewis v. King, 180 Ill. 111, 259 (1899); Renfrow v. Renfrow, 60 Kan. 277 (1899); Commonwealth v. Omohyandro's Adm'r, 2 Brew. 298 (Pa. 1870); Davenport v. Caldwell, 10 S.C. 317 (1877).

74 Stikes v. Swanson, 44 Ala. 633, 636, 637 (1870).

75 Cantelou v. Doe, 56 Ala. 519 (1876); Hall v. U.S., 92 U.S. 27 (1875). Haden v. Ivery, 51 Ala. 381 (1874) had reaffirmed the *Stikes* decision. For similar developments in Texas see Clements v. Crawford, 42 Tex. 601, 603 (1875), which overturned Honey v. Clark, 37 Tex. 686 (1872–73).

76 "Editorial," *VaLJ* 1 (1877):641, 650; and see Andrews v. Paige, 3 Heisk. 653 (Tenn. 1871); Jones v. Jones, 36 Md. 447 (1872); Pierre v. Fontenette, 25 La. An. 617 (1873); Ross v. Ross, 34 La. An. 860 (1882); State v. Harris, 63 N.C. 1 (1868); McKnight v. State, 6 Tex. Ap. 158 (1879); State v. Adams and Reeves, 65 N.C. 636 (1882); Succession of Pearce, 30 La. An. 1168 (1878); Adams v. Adams, 57 Miss. 267 (1879); Dickerson v. Brown, 49 Miss. 357 (1873).

77 King v. State, 40 Ga. 244, 247 (1869); Williams v. Williams, 39 Ga. 260, 263 (1881); and see State v. Harris, 63 N.C. 1, 4-5 (1868).

78 "Bloody Shirt" from Alfred Avins, "Anti-Miscegenation Laws and the Fourteenth Amendment: The Original Intent," *VaLR* 52 (1965):1227; Johnson and Illinois Republican quoted in Cong. Globe, 39th Cong., 1st Session, pt. 2, 1680 (1866); Ibid., pt. 1, 632; Forrest G. Wood, *Black Scare, The Racist Response to Emancipation and Reconstruction* (New York, 1968), p. 143, and see generally pp. 53–79, 143–53; and see Applebaum, "Miscegenation Statutes," 1229; R. Carter Pittman, "The Fourteenth Amendment: Its Intended Effect on Anti-Miscegenation Laws," *VaLR* 43 (1964):92; Paul C. Palmer, "Miscegenation as an Issue in the Arkansas Constitutional Convention of 1868," *Arkansas Historical Quarterly* 24 (1965):99–119; Vernon L. Wharton, *The Negro in Mississippi, 1865–1890* (Chapel Hill, 1947), pp. 150, 227–29; Malcolm C. McMillan, *Constitutional Development in Alabama, 1798–1901: A Study in Politics, the Negro, and Sectionalism* (Baton Rouge, La., 1955), pp. 139–52; Charles S. Magnum, Jr., *The Legal Status of the Negro* (Chapel Hill, 1940), pp. 242–43.

79   State v. Hairston and Williams, 63 N.C. 451, 452, 453 (1869). This decision was reaffirmed in State v. Reinhardt, 63 N.C. 547 (1869).

80   Frasher v. State, 3 Tex. Ct. of App. 263, 276 (1877); and see Doc Lonas v. State, 3 Heisk. 287 (Tenn. 1871); State v. Gibson, 36 Ind. 389 (1872); State v. Jackson, 80 Mo. 175, 176 (1883); Scott v. State, 39 Ga. 321 (1869); Bishop, *New Commentaries on the Law of Marriage and Divorce* (Boston, 1891), 1:286; Jack Greenberg, *Race and American Law* (New York, 1959), p. 344. The racial prohibition also won judicial endorsement as nondiscriminatory legislation since both races were prevented from crossing the color line. Though the United States Supreme Court never directly decided the constitutionality of the antimiscegenation laws in the nineteenth century, it did uphold laws against interracial sexual relations on the grounds that the penalties applied equally to members of both races, Pace v. Alabama, 106 U.S. 583 (1882). And see State v. Jackson, 80 Mo. 175.

81   Bowlin v. Commonwealth, 2 Bush. 5, 8–9 (Ky. 1867); and see Scott v. State, 39 Ga. 321, 333; State v. Jackson, 80 Mo. 175, 179 (1883); State v. Gibson, 36 Ind. 389, 404 (1871).

82   Green v. State, 58 Ala. 190 (1877); and see McMillan, *Constitutional Development in Alabama*, pp. 105, 139–40. Postwar state courts used these interlocking arguments to support the constitutionality of the bans on interracial marriages. The acts withstood assaults by couples contending that they violated the constitutional clauses on contracts, privileges and immunities, equal protection, and due process, as well as the Civil Rights Act. See generally Adelbert Hamilton, "Miscegenatic Marriages," *CLJ* 13 (1881):121–24; Applebaum, "Miscegenation Statutes," 50–57.

83   Stimson, *Popular Law Making*, p. 313; and see George Fredrickson, *The Black Image in the White Mind* (New York, 1971); Schouler, *Domestic Relations*, pp. 28–29.

84   Stimson, *American Statute Law* (Boston, 1886), p. 662; U.S. Census Bureau, "Marriage and Divorce, 1889–1906"; Chester Vernier, *American Family Laws*, 4 vols. (Stanford, Ca., 1931–38), 1:204–9; Gilbert T. Stephenson, *Race Distinctions in American Law* (Boston, 1910), p. 82; Magnum, *Legal Status of the Negro*, pp. 252–53, 239.

85   Johnston, *Race Relations*, pp. 269–92; Samuel Sewall, *Diary of Samuel Sewall*, 1:532; Winthrop D. Jordan, *The White Man's Burden, Historical Origins of Racism in the United States* (New York, 1974), p. 83; Felix Cohen, *Handbook of Federal Indian Law* (New York, 1942), p. 79; Wells v. Thompson, 13 Ala. 793, 802 (1848); State v. Melton and Byrd, 1 Busbee 49 (N.C. 1852); Johnson v. Johnson's Adm'r, 30 Mo. 72 (1860); Morgan v. McGhee, 24 Tenn. 12 (1844).

86   Francis Wharton, *A Treatise on the Conflicts of Law*, 3rd ed. (Philadel-

phia, 1875), p. 148; Isaac Franklin Russell, "The Indian Before the Law," *YLJ* 18 (1908–09):331; and see Fredrick Hoxie, "Beyond Savagery: The Campaign to Assimilate the American Indian, 1880–1920," (Ph.D. diss., Brandeis University, 1977), 609–10; McPherson v. Commonwealth, 28 Grat. 939 (Va. 1876); La Riviere v. La Riviere, 77 Mo. 512 (1883); In re Wilbur's Estate, 8 Wash. 35 (1894); Estate of Walker, 5 Ariz. 70 (1896).

87   Schouler, *Domestic Relations*, pp. 28–29; Ray Stannard Baker quoted in Magnum, *Legal Status of the Negro*, p. 99; and see "Note: Intermarriage with Negroes, A Survey of State Statutes," *VaLReg*, N.S., 13 (1927): 311–12; Albert E. Jenks, "The Legal Status of Negro-White Amalgamation in the United States," *AJS* 21 (1916):666–78; George Schuman, "Miscegenation: An Example of Judicial Recidivism," *JFL* 8 (1968):69–78; State v. Tutty, 41 Fed. 753, 762 (C.C.S.D. Ga. 1890).

88   Stephenson, *Race Distinctions*, p. 78.

89   *Journal of the Proceedings of the Constitutional Convention of Mississippi* (Jackson, Miss., 1871), p. 199.

90   Anna Carlin Spencer, "Problems of Marriage and Divorce," *Forum* 48 (1912):196, and see generally 188–204; see also Leach, *True Love and Perfect Union* (New York, 1980), p. 179.

91   Barbara Rosenkrantz, *Public Health and the State, Changing Views in Massachusetts, 1842–1936* (Cambridge, Mass., 1972), p. 77.

92   Noah Davis, "Marriage and Divorce," *NAR* 139 (1884):32; George Howard quoted in Fred S. Hall and Brooke, *American Marriage Laws* (New York, 1916), p. 18; and see W. C. Robinson, "The Diagnostics of Divorce," *Journal of Social Science* 14 (1881):136; Rosenberg, "Sexuality, Class, and Role," 137.

93   Dio Lewis, *Chastity, or Our Secret Sins* (Philadelphia, 1874), p. 56; Albert Swindlehurst, "Some Phases in the Law of Marriage," *HLR* 30 (1916):148; and see William Alcott, *The Physiology of Marriage* (New York, 1855), pp. 22–30.

94   Indiana Revised Statutes, 1831, 1843, 1877; U.S. Census Bureau, "Marriage and Divorce, 1889–1906," 188; Ibid., "Marriage and Divorce, 1867–1886," 28–31; Stimson, *American Statute Law*, pp. 665–66.

95   Monahan, *Pattern of Age at Marriage*, 2:333–38.

96   Francis Wharton, *Conflicts of Law*, 3rd ed., pp. 332, 305, 354.

97   Fitzpatrick v. Fitzpatrick, 6 Ne. 63, 66 (1870).

98   Beggs v. State, 55 Ala. 108, 112–13 (1876); and for judicial discussions of nuptial ages see People v. Slack, 15 Mich. 193 (1867); People v. Schoonmaker, 117 Mich. 190 (1898); Eliot v. Eliot, 77 Wis. 634 (1890); Ibid., 81 Wis. 295 (1892); State v. Cone, 86 Wis. 498 (1893); Fisher v. Bernard, 65 Vt. 663 (1893); Hardy v. State, 37 Tex. Crim. Rep. 55

(1897); Williams v. Hodges, 101 N.C. 300 (1888); Wall v. State, 32 Ark. 565 (1877).

99   Joel Bishop, *First Book of Law* (Boston, 1868), p. 20; and see Bishop, *Commentaries on Marriage and Divorce*, 2nd ed., pp. 161–67; Bishop, *New Commentaries*, 1:249; Schouler, *Domestic Relations*, pp. 32–33; Christopher Tiedeman, *A Treatise on the Limitations of the Police Power in the United States* (St. Louis, 1886), pp. 124, 131–32, 146.

100 Charles Rosenberg, "The Bitter Fruit: Heredity, Disease, and Social Thought in Nineteenth Century America," *PAH* 8 (1974):223; Charles Reeve quoted in Anthony Platt, *The Child Savers* (Chicago, 1969), p. 24. The new social analysis proved so compelling that Alexander Graham Bell, a pioneer in the treatment of the deaf, began to argue for curbing the nuptial rights of those with impaired hearing. Alexander Graham Bell, "Marriage," *Science* 17 (1891):160; but see Edward Allen Fay, *Marriages of the Deaf in America* (Washington, D.C., 1898).

101 Bishop, *Commentaries on Marriage and Divorce*, 5th ed., (1873), pp. 273–74; and see Albert Swindlehurst, "Impediments to Marriage," *ALRev* 51 (1917):407, 409–20; William Wallings, *Sexology* (Boston, 1876), p. 9.

102 Lewis, *Chastity*, p. 75. The statutes are chronicled in Donald K. Pikens, *Eugenics and the Progressives* (Nashville, Tenn., 1968), pp. 45–46; Stimson, *American Statute Law*, pp. 666–67; Vernier, *American Family Laws*, 1:173–87; and see O. S. Fowler and L. N. Fowler, *Hereditary Descent, Its Laws and Facts Applied to Human Improvement* (New York, 1908), pp. 136–43.

103 Harrison v. State, 22 Md. 468, 491 (1863); Walter's Appeal, 70 Pa. St. 392 (1872); Cummings v. State, 36 Tex. Crim. Rep. 256 (1896); Boylan v. Deinzer, 45 N.J. Eq. 485 (1889); Central R.R. & Banking Co. v. Roberts, 91 Ga. 513, 517 (1893).

104 Parker's Appeal, 44 Pa. St. 309, 312 (1863).

105 John Aston, *The Book of Nature* (New York, 1865), pp. 50–52; George B. Arner, "Consanguineous Marriages in the American Population," *Columbia Studies in History, Economy, and Public Law* 31 (1908):95; and see Benjamin H. Hartogensis, *Rhode Island and Consanguineous Jewish Marriages* (Publication of the American Jewish Historical Society, No. 20, 1911), pp. 137–46.

106 Tiedeman, *Police Powers*, p. 530; see also Peter Tylor, "Denied the Power to Choose: Sexuality and Mental Defects in American Medical Practice, 1850–1920," *JSocH* 10 (1977):472, 479; and for an examination of the issue of medical versus contractual proof see St. George v. Biddlefield, 70 Me. 593 (1885); and see Wright, *Marriage and Parentage*, pp. 14, 73–74; Vernier, *American Family Laws*, 1:188–96; Helen I. Clarke, *Social Legislation* (New York, 1940), pp. 92–93.

107 Smith v. Smith, 47 Miss. 211 (1872); and see Waymire v. Jetmore, 22
     Ohio St. 271, 273–74 (1872); Baker v. Baker, 82 Ind. 146 (1882);
     Roether v. Roether, 180 Wis. 24 (1923); Goshen v. Richmond, 4 Allen
     458 (Mass. 1862); Wiser v. Lockwood, 42 Vt. 720 (1870); Lloyd v.
     Lloyd, 66 Ill. 87 (1872); Banker v. Banker, 63 N.Y. 409 (1875); Wertz v.
     Wertz, 43 Ia. 534 (1876); Powell v. Powell, 18 Kan. 371 (1877); Ball v.
     Bennett, 73 Ga. 784 (1884); Unity v. Belgrade, 76 Me. 419 (1884);
     McCleary v. Barcalow, 6 Ohio Cir. Ct. Rep. 481 (1891); Forman v.
     Forman, 24 N.Y. Supp. 917 (1893); Nonnemacher v. Nonnemacher, 159
     Pa. 634 (1894); Sims v. Sims, 121 N.C. 297 (1897); Orchardson v.
     Cofield, 171 Ill. 14 (1898); Payne v. Burdette, 84 Mo. Ap. 332 (1900);
     for cases that questioned the dominant trend see Brown v. Westbrook, 27
     Ga. 102 (1859); Hamaker v. Hamaker, 18 Ill. 137 (1856); and see
     Bishop, *New Commentaries*, 1:252–80.
108 Stimson, *American Statute Law*, p. 327; and see generally Mark S.
     Haller, *Eugenics* (New Brunswick, N.J., 1963), especially pp. 141–43.
109 Joseph P. Chamberlain, "Eugenics and the Limitation of Marriage,"
     ABAJ 9 (1923):429.
110 Stanton quoted in Leach, *True Love and Perfect Union*, pp. 31, 33–35;
     Howard, *Matrimonial Institutions*, 3:258; and see Clarke, *Social Legis-
     lation*, p. 92; Chamberlain, "Eugenics and Limitation of Marriage,"
     429.
111 Public Acts of Connecticut, 1895, p. 667; Knight quoted in *Proceedings
     of the National Conference of Charities and Corrections*, ed. Isabel C.
     Barrows (Boston, 1899), p. 306; Gould v. Gould, 78 Conn. 242 (1905);
     Jessie Spaulding Smith, "Marriage, Sterilization, and Commitment
     Laws Aimed at Decreasing Mental Deficiency," *Journal of Criminal
     Law and Criminology* 5 (1914):365–66; Vernier, *American Family
     Laws*, 1:190–95.
112 Prince A. Morrow, *Social Disease and Marriage* (New York, 1904),
     pp. 20, 331–32; and see George Howard, "Social Control of Domestic
     Relations," *AJS* 10 (1910):814–15; Thomas Speed Mosby, "Eugenics,"
     CC 22 (1914–15):22–24; F. B. Smith, "Ethics and Disease Since the
     Late Nineteenth Century: The Contagious Diseases Acts," *Historical
     Studies* 15 (1974):118–35.
113 Lewis, *Chastity*, p. 220; Clara Holbrook Smith, "Home-Side of Prog-
     ress," in *The Congress of Women*, ed. Mary Kavanagh Didham (Chi-
     cago, 1894), pp. 333, 335; and see Dr. Mary Donahue, "Preventative
     Medicine," in ibid., pp. 737–38; Minot Savage, "The Rights of Chil-
     dren," *Arena* 6 (1892):8–9; Rose Falls Bres, *Maids, Wives, and Widows,
     The Law of the Land and of the Various States as it Affects Women* (New
     York, 1918), pp. 57–60; Leach, *True Love and Perfect Union*, p. 97.
114 Duffey, *Relations Between the Sexes*, p. 307. The statutes are discussed

in Schouler, *Domestic Relations*, 6th ed., 2:1350–51; Mary Richmond and Fred S. Hall, *Marriage and the State* (New York, 1929), pp. 58–63; Clarke, *Social Legislation*, pp. 92–98; Vernier, *American Family Laws*, 1:199–203; Stimson, *American Statute Law*, pp. 327–28. For a general discussion of marriage fitness tests see Fred S. Hall, *Medical Certification for Marriage, An Account of the Administration of the Wisconsin Marriage Law* (New York, 1921); Dr. R. W. Schufeld, "Needed Revisions of the Law of Marriage and Divorce in the United States," *MLJ* 15 (1898):231–39; Francis Galton, "Studies in Eugenics," *AJS* 11 (1905–06):7, 11; Charles H. Huberick, "Venereal Disease and the Law of Marriage and Divorce," *ALRev* 37 (1903):226–36; Edward W. Spenser, "Some Phases of Marriage Law," *YLJ* 25 (1915–16):58–65.

115   Smith v. Smith, 171 Mass. 404, 407 (1898); Schouler, *Domestic Relations*, 5th ed., p. 34; and see Morrow, *Social Disease*, pp. 318–22. For a general discussion of the era's more expansive definition of nuptial fraud see Bishop, *Commentaries on Marriage and Divorce*, 5th ed., pp. 153–56; Leonard C. Crouch, "Annulment of Marriage for Fraud in New York," *CLQ* 6 (1920–21):401–9; Frank C. Fessenden, "Nullity of Marriage," *ALRev* 23 (1899–1900):116–23; Bishop, *New Commentaries*, 1:193–236.

116   Haller, *Eugenics*, pp. 130–41; Morrow, *Social Disease*, pp. 366–69; Chamberlain, "Eugenics and the Limitation of Marriage," 429; Pikens, *Eugenics and the Progressives*, pp. 86–101; Charles B. Davenport, *Heredity in Relation to Eugenics* (New York, 1915), pp. 256–59.

117   Oliver Wendell Holmes, Jr., *The Common Law* (Boston, 1881), p. 37; Buck v. Bell, 274 U.S. 200; and see Haller, *Eugenics*, pp. 140–41.

Chapter 5

1   Robert V. Wells, "Family History and the Demographic Transition," *JSocH* 9 (1975):1–19; for the most thorough recent summary of demographic developments see Carl Degler, *At Odds* (New York, 1980), chap. 8.

2   Daniel Scott Smith, "Family Limitation, Sexual Control, and Domestic Feminism," in *Clio's Consciousness Raised*, ed. Mary Hartman and Lois Banner (New York, 1974), pp. 121, 123.

3   The most comprehensive assessments of birth control in nineteenth-century America are Linda Gordon, *Women's Body, Women's Right, A Social History of Birth Control in America* (New York, 1974); Norman

Himes, *Medical History of Contraception* (Baltimore, Md., 1926); Peter Freyer, *The Birth Controllers* (New York, 1966).

4   Charles Knowlton, *Fruits of Philosophy* (Boston, 1832); Robert E. Riegel, "The American Father of Birth Control," *NEQ* 6 (1933):470–90; *Boston Medical Journal* cited in Bruno Gebhard, "Medical Pioneers in Contraception, I: Charles Knowlton, M.D. 1800–1850," *Ohio State Medical Journal* 58 (1962):290; and see Freyer, *Birth Controllers*, pp. 99–106.

5   Post-Revolutionary American courts and legislatures departed from traditional Anglo-American common law by authorizing prosecutions for the dissemination of materials considered indecent or obscene. Obscenity had not been a separately indictable offense under the common law; it fell under the criminal law only when coupled with blasphemy, sedition, or a tendency to provoke a breach of the peace. Using ambiguous common-law precedents and the courts' traditional role as custodians of the public morals, judges in Connecticut, Pennsylvania, and Massachusetts assumed the right to suppress what they deemed to be harmful to public morality. Judge Jasper Yates in the critical 1815 Pennsylvania decision of Commonwealth v. Sharpless explained this newfound prerogative: "The destruction of morality renders the powers of government invalid, for government is not more than the public order; it weakens the bond by which society is kept together. The corruption of the public mind, in general . . . must necessarily be attended with the most injurious consequences and in such instances, courts of justice are, or ought to be, schools of morals," Commonwealth v. Sharpless, 2 S. & R. 102, 103 (Pa. 1815). The legislatures of Connecticut, New Hampshire, Massachusetts, and New Jersey hastened the outlawing of obscenity by enacting statutes. In 1842 Congress joined the bandwagon by banning the importation of obscene books. For discussion of the acts see Commonwealth v. Holmes, 17 Mass. 336 (1821); Knowles v. State, 3 Day 103 (Conn. 1808). See generally C. Thomas Dienes, *Law, Politics, and Birth Control* (Urbana, Ill., 1972), pp. 21–22; Robert W. Haney, *Comstockery in America: Patterns of Censorship and Control* (Boston, 1960), p. 18. Though few precedents existed in England on obscenity, the 1837 obscene publications statute, Lord Campbell's Act, clearly established the right of English authorities to prosecute such cases.

6   Charles Knowlton, *A History of the Recent Excitement in Ashfield* (Ashfield, Mass., 1834), p. 17; Sidney Ditzion, *Marriage, Morals and Sex in America* (New York, 1953), pp. 318–22.

7   Prosecutor quoted in Ditzion, *Marriage, Morals and Sex*, p. 320, and see Dienes, *Law, Politics, and Birth Control*, pp. 25–26; Raymond Lee Muncy, *Marriage and Sex in Utopian Communities in Nineteenth Century America* (Bloomington, Ind., 1975), pp. 160–92.

8   William Alcott, *The Physiology of Marriage* (New York, 1855), pp. 180–81; for publication information see Freyer, *Birth Controllers*, p. 105; and see Smith, "Family Limitation," 119–56; Caroll Smith-Rosenberg and Charles Rosenberg, "The Female Animal: Medical and Biological Views of Woman and Her Role in Nineteenth Century America," *JAH* 60 (1973):343–48; Anne F. Scott, "Women's Perspective on Patriarchy in the 1850s," *JAH* 61 (1974):55–57.

9   Degler, *At Odds*, p. 220. The most comprehensive account of abortion in nineteenth-century America is James C. Mohr, *Abortion in America, The Origins and Evolution of National Policy* (New York, 1978). I have relied on it in the following pages and generally concur with Mohr's assessments of the nature of the change in abortion policy. Yet, as will be clear, I think his central thesis, that antiabortion became the dominant American abortion policy in the century primarily because of a crusade by the medical profession, ignores related family-law changes and simplifies the character of legal change.

10   Theodoric Beck, *Elements of Medical Jurisprudence*, 2 vols. (Philadelphia, 1823), 1:207; on the often related issue of infanticide see Peter C. Hoffer and N. E. H. Hull, *Murdering Mothers: Infanticide in England and New England, 1558–1803* (New York, 1981), p. 65; Douglas Greenberg, *Crime and Law Enforcement in Colonial New York, 1691–1776* (Ithaca, N.Y., 1974), pp. 117–18; State v. McKee, 1 Add. 1 (Pa. 1791), this case included a detailed note on legislation dealing with infanticide; and for a general discussion of the subject see Maria W. Piers, *Infanticide* (New York, 1978).

11   Bernard Dickens, *Abortion and the Law* (London, 1966), pp. 20–23; Glanville Williams, *The Sanctity of Life and the Common Law* (New York, 1968); Cyril C. Means, Jr., "The Law of New York Concerning Abortion and the Status of the Foetus, 1664–1968: A Case of Cessation of Constitutionality," *NYLF* 14 (1968):411–21.

12   Coke, *The Second Part of the Institutes of the Laws of England* (London, 1620), p. 20; William Blackstone, *Commentaries on the Laws of England*, 4 vols. (London, 1765–69), 1:129.

13   43 Geo. III, ch. 58; Dickens, *Abortion and the Law*, pp. 23–25; Commonwealth v. Bangs, 9 Mass. 369 (1812); and see Leon Radzinowicz, *A History of English Criminal Law and Its Administration from 1750*, 4 vols. (London, 1938), 1:506 note 39, 631; Hoffer and Hull, *Murdering Mothers*, p. 87.

14   The statutes are discussed in Eugene Quay, "Justifiable Abortion, Medical and Legal Foundations," *GeoLJ* 49 (1960):173–255; 395–538; Mohr, *Abortion in America*, chaps. 2, 5.

15   9 Geo. IV, chap. 31; 7 Will. IV., and 1 Vic., chap. 85. See Dickens,

Abortion and the Law, pp. 25–28; Jeffrey Weeks, *Sex, Politics, and Society* (London, 1981), pp. 70–71.

16 Means, "The Law of New York," 441–53; Mohr, *Abortion in America*, pp. 26–31.

17 Cooper v. State, 2 Zab. 52, 54, 58 (N.J. 1849). The Pennsylvania Supreme Court refused to agree to this interpretation of the common law. The judges argued that abortion was indictable when it occurred at any time during gestation, see Mills v. Commonwealth, 13 Pa. 631, 632 (1850). In the *Mills* decision, the court admitted the existence of the Massachusetts precedent in favor of the quickening rule, but countered that it was not "the law in Pennsylvania, and never ought to be any- where." Rather, the justices maintained: "It is not the murder of a living child which constitutes the offense, but the destruction of gestation, by wicked means and against nature. The moment the womb is instinct with embryo life, and gestation has begun, the crime may be perpetrated." The reasoning of the court was rejected by other jurists and the case had little influence. Its impact could even be doubted in Pennsylvania; in 1860 the first state law on the subject specified separate punishments for unquickened and quickened abortions.

18 Cooper v. State, 121–22, 130–31; Ibid., 2 Zab. 58.

19 State v. Murphy, 3 Dutch. 112, 114 (N.J. Law 1858); and see Wilson v. State, 2 Ohio 319, 321 (1853); Commonwealth v. Wood, 11 Gray 85 (Mass. 1858); State v. Howard, 32 Vt. 380 (1859).

20 State v. Murphy, 3 Dutch. 114, 115 (N.J. Law 1858); State v. Howard, 32 Vt. 399 (1859).

21 Clarke v. Clarke, 2 H. Bl. 399, 401, 126 Eng. Rep. 617, 618 (1795); Francis Wharton, *A Treatise on the Criminal Law of the United States*, 4th ed. (Philadelphia, 1857), p. 537; Storer quoted in Alfred Taylor, *Medical Jurisprudence*, 5th U.S. ed. (Philadelphia, 1861), p. 441.

22 Cooper v. State, 56–57. For a discussion of fetal property rights see David W. Louisell and John T. Noonan, "Constitutional Balance," in *The Morality of Abortion*, ed. John T. Noonan (Cambridge, Mass., 1971), pp. 720–30; Tapping Reeve, *Law of Baron and Femme* (New York, 1816), pp. 295–96; James Kent, *Commentaries on American Law*, 4 vols. (New York, 1826–30), 4:412. Antebellum cases on the subject include Pemberton v. Parke, 5 Binn. 601 (Pa. 1813); Cottin v. Cottin, 5 Martin 93 (La. 1817); Marsells v. Thalhimer, 2 Paige 35 (N.Y. 1830); Hall v. Hancock, 15 Pick. 255 (Mass. 1834); Harper v. Archer, 43 Amer. Dec. 472 (Miss. 1845).

23 Smith v. State, 33 Me. 48 (1851); and see Commonwealth v. Grover, 16 Gray 602 (Mass. 1860); Amos Dean, *Medical Jurisprudence*, 2nd ed. (Albany, N.Y., 1873), p. 109.

24 Quay, "Justifiable Abortion," 436–37; Mohr, *Abortion in America*, pp. 39–41; and see Kathlyn G. Milman, "Note: Abortion Reform, History, Status, Prognosis," *CWRLR* 21 (1970):528–29.

25 State v. Vawter, 7 Blackf. 592 (Ind. 1845); People v. Stockham, 1 Parker's Crim. Rep. 424 (N.Y. 1853); Commonwealth v. Barrows, 176 Mass. 17, 18 (1860); and see Commonwealth v. Jackson, 15 Gray 187 (Mass. 1860); Holliday v. People, 9 Ill. 111 (1847); and for the judicial acceptance of the death of a woman from an abortion as a crime see Commonwealth v. Brown, 14 Gray 419 (Mass. 1860).

26 Advertisement cited in Gordon, *Women's Body*, p. 54.

27 *The Wonderful Trial of Caroline Lohman, Alias Restell*, 3rd ed. (New York, 1848), p. 5.

28 Orson Squire quoted in Gordon, *Women's Body*, p. 58.

29 Abrams v. Foshee, 3 Ia. 274, 281; Smith v. Gaffard, 33 Ala. 168 (1858); Bissell v. Cornell, 24 Wend. 354 (N.Y. 1840).

30 Mohr, *Abortion in America*, p. 144.

31 U.S. v. Hudson and Goodwin, 7 Cranch 32 (U.S. 1812); and see Morton Horwitz, *Transformation of American Law* (Cambridge, Mass., 1977), chap. 1; Lawrence Friedman, *A History of American Law* (New York, 1973), pp. 254–56; William Nelson, *The Americanization of the Common Law* (Cambridge, Mass., 1975), pp. 10, 38–39, 110–11.

32 Degler, *At Odds*, p. 235.

33 Smith, "Family Limitation," 123. For a transatlantic analysis of sexual attitudes during this period see Peter T. Cominos, "Late Victorian Sexual Responsibility and the Social System," *International Review of Social History* 8 (1971):18–48, 216–50.

34 Mohr, *Abortion in America*, p. 50, and see chap. 4 in general; Buffalo physicians quoted in ibid., p. 89; Augustus K. Gardner, *Conjugal Sins Against the Laws of Life and Health and their Effects Upon the Father, Mother, and the Child* (New York, 1876), p. 117; and see William Wallings, *Sexology* (Boston, 1876), pp. 55–65; Alcott, *The Physiology of Marriage*, pp. 184–85.

35 Mohr, *Abortion in America*, pp. 31, 39–41; Quay, "Justifiable Abortion," 436–37.

36 Horatio Robinson Storer and Franklin Fiske Heard, *Criminal Abortion: Its Nature, Its Evidence, and Its Law* (Boston, 1868), p. 10; and see Ditzion, *Marriage, Morals and Sex*, pp. 345–46.

37 Dean, *Medical Jurisprudence*, p. 126; Storer and Heard, *Criminal Abortion: Its Nature*, p. 10; Andrew Nebinger, *Criminal Abortion: Its Extent and Prevention* (Philadelphia, 1870), p. 10; John Ashton, *Book of Nature* (New York, 1865), p. 63; and see Beck, *Medical Jurisprudence*, pp. 113–14; Germain Grisez, *Abortion, The Myths, The Realities*

in the Argument (New York, 1970).

38 Storer and Heard, *Criminal Abortion: Its Nature*, pp. 6, 7.

39 *New York Times*, 23 August 1871, p. 6; Nebinger, *Criminal Abortion: Its Extent*, p. 29; and see Gordon, *Women's Body*, pp. 51–57; Mohr, *Abortion in America*, pp. 176–82.

40 Quay, "Justifiable Abortion," 451–87; Mohr, *Abortion in America*, pp. 123–43; Degler, *At Odds*, p. 231.

41 Means, "The Law of New York," 454–90; Cobel v. People, 5 Parker Crim. Rep. 348 (N.Y. 1862); medical society petition quoted in Means, "The Law of New York," note 117.

42 The New York legislation is described in Means, "The Law of New York," 458–90; and see Quay, "Justifiable Abortion," 500–1. The cases are discussed in Mohr, *Abortion in America*, pp. 215–19.

43 Evans v. People, 49 N.Y. 86 (1872); and see Means, "The Law of New York," 483–98.

44 Mohr, *Abortion in America*, pp. 227–28.

45 Quay, "Justifiable Abortion," 447–520; Mohr, *Abortion in America*, chaps. 8, 9.

46 Means, "The Law of New York," 436–37.

47 Gardner, *Conjugal Sins*, pp. 35, 31, 101; Wallings, *Sexology*, p. 74; and see Dio Lewis, *Chastity, or Our Secret Sins* (Philadelphia, 1874), pp. 89–109.

48 Paul S. Boyer, *Purity in Print: The Vice-Society Movement and Book Censorship in America* (New York, 1968), pp. 2–22; for a biographical sketch of Comstock see Heywood Broun and Margaret Leech, *Anthony Comstock: Roundsman of the Law* (New York, 1927).

49 U.S. Stat. at Large, XVII, 598–600. For analyses of the bill's passage see Margaret M. Goodart, "Contraception: The Secular Controversy, 1830–1937," (Ph.D. diss., University of California, Davis, 1975), 77–82; Mary Ware Dennett, *Birth Control Laws* (New York, 1926), pp. 19–45; Carol Flora Brooks, "The Early History of the Anti-Contraception Laws," *AQ* 18 (1966):3; and see in general Dorothy G. Fowler, *Unmailable, Congress and the Post Office* (Athens, Ga., 1977), pp. 55–72.

50 William J. McWilliams, "Laws of New York on Birth Control: A Survey," *BCRev* 14 (1930):46–47, 61–63; Dienes, *Law, Politics, and Birth Control*, pp. 43–51.

51 Brooks, "Early History," 6–9.

52 Brooks, "Early History," 9–13; "Comment: The History and Future of the Legislative Battle Over Birth Control," *CLQ* 42 (1964):279.

53 Lewis, *Chastity*, p. 183.

54 Comstock quoted in Broun and Leech, *Anthony Comstock*, p. 165.

55 Storer and Heard, *Criminal Abortion: Its Nature*, p. v; and see the

assessment of San Francisco superior court judge Edward A. Belcher, "Criminal Abortion," *Criminal Law Magazine and Reporter* 17 (1893): 141–50.

56 F. A. Harris, "A Case of Abortion with Acquittal," *Boston Medical and Surgical Journal* 104 (1881):346–50; and for the judicial reaction see Holland v. State, 131 Ind. 568 (1891); State v. Schverman, 70 Mo. Ap. 518 (1897); State v. McIntyre, 19 Minn. 93 (1872); State v. Drake, 1 Vroom 422 (N.J. 1863).

57 People v. Aiken, 66 Mich. 460, 480–81; and see Commonwealth v. Railing, 113 Pa. 37 (1886); People v. Olmstead, 30 Mich. 431 (1874); State v. Young, 55 Kan. 349 (1895); Morton Keller, *Affairs of State* (Cambridge, Mass., 1979), p. 516. The diversity of legislative language and the vagaries of judicial decision making also prevented the uniform treatment of abortionists. The discrepancies were quite evident in the often critical distinction between supplying and using abortion devices. Thus although the Indiana courts considered a catheter an abortion device, the Iowa bench refused to agree to such a contention by the state. State v. Sherwood, 75 Ind. 15 (1881); State v. Forsythe, 78 Ia. 595, 597 (1889); and see People v. Crichton, 6 Parker Crim. Rep. 363 (N.Y. 1864); Eggart v. State, 40, Fla. 527 (1898).

58 Lamb v. State, 67 Md. 524, 535 (1887); State v. Moothart, 109 Ia. 130, 134 (1899); and see Hauk v. State, 148 Ind. 238 (1897); State v. Lee, 69 Conn. 186, 193–94 (1897); State v. Morrow, 40 S.C. 221 (1893); Jones v. State, 70 Md. 326 (1889); Eckhart, et al. v. People, 22 Hun. 525 (N.Y. 1880).

59 Physician quoted in Gordon, *Women's Body*, p. 57.

60 Commonwealth v. W., 3 Pitts. 463 (Pa. 1871); Slattery v. People, 76 Ill. 217, 219 (1875); and see Commonwealth v. Leach, 156 Mass. 99 (1892); Rhodes v. State, 128 Ind. 189 (1890); People v. Van Zile, 73 Hun. 534 (N.Y. 1893); People v. Sessions, 58 Mich. 594 (1886).

61 Hays v. State, 40 Md. 633; Commonwealth v. Brown, 121 Mass. 69; and see Commonwealth v. Harvey, 103 Mass. 451 (1869); Commonwealth v. Blair, 126 Mass. 40 (1878); People v. McDowell, 63 Mich. 229 (1886); Commonwealth v. Sholes, 13 Allen 554 (1866); State v. McLeod, 136 Mo. 109 (1896).

62 Storer and Heard, *Criminal Abortion: Its Nature*, p. 145, and see p. 97. The refusal of a woman to testify often destroyed the state's case. That occurred in the 1899 prosecution of George Quinn. Rose Haughey first complained of Quinn's attempt to perform an abortion on her to Delaware authorities, but then she refused to testify against him at his trial. The case collapsed and the court freed Quinn. State v. Quinn, 2 Pennw. 339 (Del. 1899); and see Harold N. Mayer, "The Medico-Legal Relation

of Abortion," *MLJ* 9 (1891–92):40–41; Means, "The Law of New York," 428.

63   Commonwealth v. Snow, 116 Mass. 47 (1874); Watson v. State, 9 Tex. Ap. 237, 244 (1880); and see State v. Owens, 22 Minn. 238 (1875); Dunn v. People, 29 N.Y. 523 (1864); Moore v. State, 37 Tex. Crim. 552 (1897).

64   John Wigmore, *A Treatise on the Law of Evidence* (Boston, 1905), 3: 2755–56; and see Frazer v. People, 54 Barb. 306 (N.Y. 1863); State v. Hyer, 39 N.J. 598 (1877); Commonwealth v. Brown, 121 Mass. 69 (1876); State v. Carey, 76 Conn. 342, 352 (1904). In some jurisdictions the courts were so intent on convicting abortionists that they let women speak from the grave by accepting the dying declarations of abortion victims. Such declarations were exceptions to the general rules of evidence, which mandated that a defendant had the right to face his or her accuser. American courts differed on the admissibility of the statements. The key to the evidentiary loophole was that it could only be used in cases of homicide. Since some state statutes did not treat the death of the woman as homicide, it was blocked in several jurisdictions. Other judges were apprehensive about the equity of such evidence. But many courts, and the legislatures of New York and Pennsylvania, authorized the use of dying declarations in abortion trials. For cases on the subject see State v. Harper, 35 Ohio St. 78 (1878); People v. Davis, 56 N.Y. 95 (1874); State v. Baldwin, 79 Ia. 714 (1890); State v. Dickinson, 41 Wis. 299 (1877); State v. Keeper, 70 Ia. 478 (1886); State v. Pearce, 56 Minn. 226 (1894); Montgomery v. State, 80 Ind. 338 (1881); Commonwealth v. Keene, 7 Pa. Sup. Cts. 293 (1898).

65   Storer and Heard, *Criminal Abortion: Its Nature*, p. 144.

66   State v. Cave, 33 Tex. Crim. Rep. 335 (1894); and see Bassett v. State, 41 Ia. 303 (1872); State v. Montgomery, 71 Ia. 630 (1887); State v. Magnell, 3 Pennw. 307 (Del. 1901); State v. Fitzgerald, 49 Ia. 260, 261 (1878); Commonwealth v. Morrison, 16 Gray 224 (Mass. 1860); Dougherty v. People, 1 Col. 514; State v. Owens, 22 Minn. 238 (1875); State v. Van Houten, 37 Mo. 357 (1866); State v. Dean, 85 Mo. Ap. 473 (1900).

67   Moody v. State, 17 Ohio St. 111, 112 (1866); and see State v. Fitzporter, 93 Mo. 390 (1887); State v. Stokes, 54 Vt. 179 (1881); State v. Lee, 69 Conn. 186 (1897); State v. Meek, 70 Mo. 355 (1879); Willey v. State, 46 Ind. 363 (1874).

68   Henry Wright, *Marriage and Parentage*, 3rd ed. (Boston, 1855), p. 133; Edward Bliss Foote, Jr., *The Radical Remedy in Social Science* (New York, 1886), pp. 24–25; and see Storer and Heard, *Criminal Abortion: Its Nature*, pp. 102–3; Beasley v. People, 89 Ill. 571 (1878); State v.

Clements, 15 Ore. 237, 248 (1887); Clarke v. People, 16 Col. 511 (1891). For a general discussion of Wright's ideas see Lewis Perry, *Childhood, Marriage and Reform, Henry Clarke Wright, 1797–1870* (Chicago, 1980).

69 Bradford v. People, 20 Hun. 309, 311 (N.Y. 1880); and see State v. Moore, 25 Ia. 128 (1868); Earl v. People, 99 Ill. 123 (1881); Scott v. People, 141 Ill. 195 (1892); Howard v. People, 185 Ill. 552 (1900); Harchard v. State, 79 Wis. 357 (1891).

70 Isaac M. Quimby, "Introduction to Medical Jurisprudence," *AMAJ* 9 (1887):164.

71 State v. Slagle, 92 N.C. 653 (1880); Commonwealth v. Taylor, 132 Mass. 261 (1882); and see Commonwealth v. Wood, 11 Gray 85 (Mass. 1858); Commonwealth v. Follanlbee, 155 Mass. 274 (1892); Commonwealth v. Tibbetts, 157 Mass. 519 (1893); Power v. State, 48 N.J. Law 34 (1886). For examples of courts that still relied on the quickening rule see Mills v. Commonwealth, 13 Pa. 630 (1850); Mitchell v. Commonwealth, 78 Ky. 204, 209–10 (1879); Taylor v. State, 105 Ga. 846 (1898); and see Joel P. Bishop, *Commentaries on the Law of Statutory Crimes*, 6th ed. (Boston, 1877), p. 425; Quay, "Justifiable Abortion," 503.

72 Alcott, *The Physiology of Marriage*, p. 184.

73 State v. Emerich, 13 Mo. App. 492, 497 (1883), and for the retrial and his second conviction see Ibid., 87 Mo. 110 (1885); see also People v. Abbott, 116 Mich. 263 (1898); State v. Reed, 45 Ark. 333 (1885); State v. Watson, 30 Kan. 281 (1883).

74 In tort, property, and criminal law, fetal rights remained contingent upon either birth or statutes creating special legal prerogatives. In an 1891 Indiana bastardy decision, the state supreme court ruled that "until a child is wholly born, and has obtained a separate existence it is but a *foetus in utero*, and not a human being within the meaning of the law authorizing proceedings for the maintenance of bastard children after their birth," Robinson v. State, 128 Ind. 397, 398 (1891). Seven years earlier in the influential tort opinion of *Dietrich* v. *Northhampton*, Justice Oliver Wendell Holmes, Jr., of the Massachusetts Supreme Judicial Court had argued that the "unborn child was part of the mother" when it was injured during pregnancy, and thus had no separate claim for compensation, Dietrich v. Northhampton, 139 Mass. 14, 17 (1884). For other discussions of these issues see Patterson v. Buey, 1 ALRec 566 (Ohio, 1878); Canfield v. State, 56 Ind. 168 (1877); James M. Kerr, "Action by an Unborn Infant," *CLJ* 61 (1905):364–72; Lawrence Tribe, "Childhood, Suspect Classifications, and Conclusive Presumptions: Three Linked Riddles," *LCP* 39 (1975):21–22.

75 Degler, *At Odds*, p. 247.

76 Frederick J. Taussig, *The Prevention and Treatment of Abortion* (St.

Louis, 1910), pp. 78–80; and see Gordon, *Women's Body*, pp. 57–60.

77   "Abortion," *MLJ* 7 (1889):170–81; Junius C. Hoag, "Abortion and the Law," *MLJ* 8 (1890–91):126.

78   U.S. v. Whittier, 28 Fed. 591, 592 (C.C.E.D. Mo. 1878); Commonwealth v. Leigh, 15 Phila. 376, 377 (Pa. 1881); and see U.S. v. Bott, 24 Fed. Cas. 1204 (C.C.D., N.Y. 1879); Dienes, *Law, Politics and Birth Control*, p. 63; Loren P. Beth, *The Development of the American Constitution, 1877–1917* (New York, 1971), p. 210; Alvah W. Sulloway, *Birth Control and Catholic Doctrine* (Boston, 1959), p. 13. For an analysis of the Connecticut experience see Griswold v. Connecticut, 381 U.S. 479 (1965).

79   Broun and Leech, *Anthony Comstock*, pp. 273–74; Anthony Comstock, "Lotteries and Gambling," *NAR* 154 (1892):217.

80   U.S. v. Bott, 24 Fed. Cas. 1204 (Fed. Cas. #14,626, 1873), the same ruling also upheld U.S. v. Whitehead. For a critical commentary on the *Bott* ruling see D. M. Bennett, *Anthony Comstock and his Career of Crime and Cruelty* (New York, 1878), pp. 329–31.

81   U.S. v. Kelly, 26 Fed. Cas. 128 (U.S., C.C., C.D. Nev., 1876; Fed. Cas. #15,514, 1876).

82   U.S. v. Popper, 98 Fed. 423 (U.S. D.C. N.D., Cal. 1899); Queen v. Hicklin, 3 Q.B. 360, 371, 11 Cox C.C. 19, 20 (1868).

83   Ex parte Jackson, 96 U.S. 727, 736, 737 (U.S. 1877); U.S. v. Harmon, 45 Fed. 414, 423 (D.C. Kan. 1891); and see U.S. v. Clarke, 38 Fed. 732 (U.S. D.C. E.D. Mo. 1889).

84   Comstock quoted in Broun and Leech, *Anthony Comstock*, p. 156, and see chap. 11 in general; see also James F. Morton, Jr., "A Little Chapter of the Early History of Anti-Contraception Laws," *Medical Critic and Guide* 20 (1917):258–60; Anthony Comstock, *Traps for the Young* (New York, 1882), p. 137; Brooks, "Early History of Anti-Contraception Laws," 4–5.

85   Bennett, *Anthony Comstock and his Career of Crime*, p. 1037; Freyer, *Birth Controllers*, pp. 194–97; Dienes, *Law, Politics and Birth Control*, pp. 68–71; Ditzion, *Marriage, Morals and Sex*, pp. 171–80. Some of the antivice tactics also proved unsettling to the courts. The use of decoy letters in particular stirred some judges to protest that defendants were being caught by entrapment. Judge Dillon, for example, threw out one case because the authorities had used decoy letters. But most courts and legal writers accepted the use of the ploy to catch sellers of banned goods. Comstock himself vigorously defended the letters. For a discussion of the subject see U.S. v. Whittier, 28 Fed. Cas. 591, 593; U.S. v. Katmeyer, 16 Fed. 760, 763–64 (U.S. C.C. E.D. Mo. 1883); Bates v. U.S., 10 Fed. 92 (U.S. Ore. 1884); Anthony Comstock, *Frauds Exposed* (New York, 1880), p. 532; Boyer, *Purity in Print*, pp. 9–15.

86 Edward Foote quoted in Gordon, *Women's Body*, p. 168; U.S. v. Foote, 25 Fed. Cas. 1140, 1141 (U.S. S.D. N.Y. 1876); Edward Bliss Foote, *Plain Home Talk* (New York, 1882), p. 876; and see Brooks, "The Early History of Anti-Contraception Laws," 22–23.

87 Halstead v. Nelson, 36 Hun. 149 (N.Y. 1885); and see McWilliams, "Laws of New York," 46–47.

88 For the most thorough discussions of the birth-control movement in the twentieth century see Gordon, *Women's Body*, Part III; David M. Kennedy, *Birth Control in America, The Career of Margaret Sanger* (New Haven, Conn., 1970); James Reed, *From Private Vice to Public Virtue, The Birth Control Movement and American Society Since 1830* (New York, 1978).

89 The legislation is assessed in Fowler, *Unmailable*, pp. 101–2. The New York legislation is quoted in Sulloway, *Birth Control and Catholic Doctrine*, pp. 22–23.

90 Commonwealth v. Allison, 227 Mass. 57, 62 (1917); and see Commonwealth v. Gardner, 300 Mass. 373 (1938); J. Prentiss Murphy, "The Allison Case," *Survey* 37 (1916–17):266–67, 345–47.

91 People v. Sanger, 222 N.Y. 192 (1918); Dienes, *Law, Politics, and Birth Control*, pp. 99–100; Gordon, *Women's Body*, p. 189; and see Margaret Sanger, *An Autobiography* (New York, 1958), pp. 224–50; Kennedy, *Birth Control*, pp. 75–88.

92 Blossom, "Some Medico-Legal Aspects of the Birth Control Question," *MLJ* 33 (1908):117; and see Dr. Alfred W. Herzog, "Editorial: Contraception," *MLJ* 34 (1916):10; T. D. Crothers, "Birth Control," *MLJ* 33 (1916):10–11; James P. Lichtenberg, "Instability of the Family," *AAPS* 34 (1900):97–105; Goodart, "Contraception," 89–113. Judicial endorsement of the medical exemption reached its highest and most authoritative expression in the 1936 decision of U.S. v. One Package, which accepted the legality of doctors importing and distributing contraceptives. 86 Fed. 2nd. 737 (1936); and see Young's Rubber Co. v. Lee, 41 Fed. 2nd. 103 (1930); David v. U.S., 62 Fed. 2nd. 473 (1933); Sulloway, *Birth Control and Catholic Doctrine*, pp. 28–31; Dienes, *Law, Politics, and Birth Control*, pp. 108–15. For cases upholding the banning of contraceptives see U.S. v. Pupke, 133 Fed. 243 (U.S. D.C. E.D. Mo., 1904); Winters v. U.S., 201 Fed. 845 (1912); Ackley v. U.S., 200 Fed. 217 (1912); State v. Hollinshead, 77 Ore. 473 (1915); State v. Nelson, 7 Conn. Supp. 262 (1939).

93 John Stoddard, "Foeticide—Suggestions Toward Its Suppression," *Detroit Review of Medicine and Pharmacy* 10 (1875):653; Bennett, *Anthony Comstock and his Career of Crime*, p. 1068; and see Helen Clarke, *Social Legislation* (New York, 1940), p. 152; Foote, *Radical Remedy*, p. 25; Gordon, *Women's Body*, p. 108; Alice Stockham, *To-*

kology, A Book for Every Woman, 2nd ed. (New York, 1911), pp. 245–48; John Humphrey Noyes, *Male Continence* (Oneida, N.Y., 1872), pp. 6–15.

94 Mohr, *Abortion in America*, pp. 237–45; John S. Haller and Robin W. Haller, *The Physician and Sexuality in Victorian America* (Urbana, Ill., 1974), pp. 117–18, 249; Kennedy, *Birth Control*, p. 137.

95 Elizabeth Duffey, *The Relations of the Sexes* (New York, 1876), p. 204; Foote, *Radical Remedy*, p. 89.

Chapter 6

1 James Kent, *Commentaries on American Law*, 4 vols. (New York, 1826–30), 2:214; for a general discussion of illegitimacy and the law see Shirley Foster Hartley, *Illegitimacy* (Berkeley, Ca., 1973).

2 R. H. Helmholz, "Bastardy Litigation in Medieval England," *AJLH* 13 (1969):361.

3 William Blackstone, *Commentaries on the Laws of England*, 4 vols. (London, 1765–69), 1:454–60; and see Frederic Maitland, *Roman Canon Law in the Church of England* (London, 1898), pp. 53–55; Sir Frederick Pollock and Frederic Maitland, *History of English Law*, 2 vols. (London, 1895), 2:167–68; William Bartless, "Illegitimacy and Legislation," *ALRev* 54 (1920):576–77; Lawrence Stone, *Family, Sex, and Marriage* (London, 1977), pp. 516–48.

4 18 Eliz. ch. 3 (1601); and see Sophonisba P. Breckinridge, *Family and the State* (Chicago, 1934), pp. 415–18; Horace H. Robbins and Francis Doak, "The Family Property Rights of Illegitimate Children: A Comparative Study," *ColLR* 30 (1930):316–17; Arthur Calhoun, *A Social History of the American Family*, 3 vols. (Cleveland, 1917), 1:317–18; John Demos, *Little Commonwealth* (New York, 1970), pp. 109–10; Dominik Lasok, "Virginia's Bastardy Laws: A Burdensome Heritage," *WMLR* 9 (1967):411–12; Robert Semmes, *Crime and Punishment in Early Maryland* (Baltimore, 1938), pp. 187–201.

5 Hendrik Hartog, "The Public Law of a County Court: Judicial Government in Eighteenth Century Massachusetts," *AJLH* 20 (1976):301, and see generally 299–308; see also Henry Banfield, "Morals and Law Enforcement in Colonial New England," *NEQ* 5 (1932):443–47; William Nelson, *The Americanization of the Common Law* (Cambridge, Mass., 1977), pp. 37–39, 118; Mary S. Benson, *Women in Eighteenth Century America* (1935, reprint, Port Washington, N.Y., 1966), pp. 228–30; Lasok, "Virginia's Bastardy Laws," 409–13; James Ely,

"American Independence and the Law: A Study of Post-Revolutionary South Carolina Legislation," *VLR* 26 (1973):965–66.

6   Daniel Smith and Michael Hindus, "Premarital Pregnancy in America," *JIH* 5 (1975):537–39, 549; George Howard, *Matrimonial Institutions*, 3 vols. (Chicago, 1904), 2:193; Marcus Wilson Jernegan, *Laboring and Dependent Classes in Colonial America* (New York, 1931), pp. 151–65; Edward Capen, *The Historical Development of the Poor Law of Connecticut* (New York, 1905), pp. 39–40, 80–81; Julia Spruill, *Women's Life and Work in the Southern Colonies* (Chapel Hill, 1938), pp. 273, 317–20; Lasok, "Virginia's Bastardy Laws," 411, 416–20.

7   Robert Wells, "Illegitimacy and Bridal Pregnancy in Colonial America," in *Bastardy in Comparative History*, ed. Peter Laslett (London, 1976), pp. 355–56; and see Laslett, "Introduction"; Peter Hoffer and N. E. H. Hull, *Murdering Mothers* (New York, 1981), pp. 127–31, 166–68.

8   Benjamin Franklin, "The Speech of Polly Baker," in *The American Tradition in Literature*, 5th ed., ed. Sculley Bradley, Richmond Croom Beatty, E. Hudson Long, and George Perkins (New York, 1981), pp. 176–78.

9   Tapping Reeve, *Law of Baron and Femme* (New York, 1816), p. 274; and see Zephaniah Swift, *A System of Laws of the State of Connecticut* (New Haven, 1795), p. 212.

10 Daniel Scott Smith, "The Long Cycle in American Illegitimacy and Premarital Pregnancy," in *Bastardy in Comparative History*, ed. Laslett, p. 372.

11 Chirac v. Reinecker, 2 Pet. 613, 621 (U.S. 1829); Senser v. Bower, 1 Pa. 450 (1834); and see Reeve, *Baron and Femme*, p. 272; Douglas' Lessee v. Sanderson, 2 Dall. 116 (Pa. 1791); Jackson v. Cooley, 8 Johns. 128 (N.Y. 1811). For examples of the judicial use of the new rules see Henderson v. Cargill, 31 Miss. 367 (1856); Clapier v. Banks, 10 La. 60 (1836); Hunter v. Whitworth, 9 Ala. 965 (1846); Starr v. Peck, 1 Hill 270 (N.Y. 1841). Paralleling their policy in matrimony, judges placed great reliance on the treatment of a child by its parents and other family members; thus reputation and the statements of deceased parents could aid claims of legitimacy. See generally Simon Greenleaf, *A Treatise on the Law of Evidence*, 3 vols. (Boston, 1852), 1:122–23; Jackson v. Boneham, 15 Johns. 226 (N.Y. 1818); Elliott v. Peirsol, 1 Pet. 328 (U.S. 1828); Stein v. Bowman, 13 Pet. 209 (U.S. 1839); Greenwood v. Spiller, 2 Scam. 502 (Ill. 1840); Saunders v. Fuller, 4 Hump. 516 (Tenn. 1844); Emerson v. White, 29 N.H. 482 (1854); Kenyon v. Ashbridge, 35 Pa. 157 (1860); Birney v. Hann, 3 A.K. Marsh. 322 (Ky. 1821). For expression of judicial doubts about the rules see Johnson v. Johnson, 1 Des. 595 (S.C. 1797); Vaughan v. Rhodes, 2 McCord 227 (S.C. 1822);

Lessee of Speed v. Brooks, 7 J.J. Marsh. 119 (Ky. 1832); North v. Valk, 20 Ala. 548 (1852); Green v. Green, 14 La. An. 39 (1859).

12 Blackstone, *Commentaries*, 1:457; and see William Hooper, *The Law of Illegitimacy* (London, 1900), pp. 13–19.

13 For a general discussion of these issues see John Wigmore, *A Treatise on the Law of Evidence*, 3 vols. (Chicago, 1904), 3:2764; "Note: The Lord Mansfield Rule and the Presumption of Legitimacy," *MdLR* 16 (1956): 80–81; Commonwealth v. Stricker, 1 Browne Appendix 47, 48–50 (Pa. 1801); Dennison v. Page, 29 Pa. 420, 424 (Pa. 1857); Bowles v. Bingham, 3 Munf. Appendix 599, 602–3 (Va. 1803); Ibid., 11 Munf. 492 (Va. 1811). Generally only overwhelming proof could disprove a husband's paternity, see for example Cross v. Cross, 3 Paige 139, 140 (N.Y. 1832), where a husband proved he had lived apart from his wife for eighteen months prior to the birth of the child at issue; and see Commonwealth v. Wentz, 1 Ashm. 269 (Pa. 1808–30); Commonwealth v. Shepherd, 6 Binn. 283 (Pa. 1814); Reeve, *Baron and Femme*, p. 272; Kent, *Commentaries on American Law*, 2:211–12. In the case of Van Aernam v. Van Aernam, 1 Barb. Chan. 375, 376 (N.Y. 1846), the New York tribunal even refused the right of a married woman to admit her adultery as conclusive proof of her child's illegitimacy: "And courts should not be permitted to unsettle the title to property, to put the status of any one in jeopardy, by speculating upon the mere probabilities in favor of the illegitimacy of a child, who might or might not have been begotten by the husband of its mother." For other decisions in which strict evidentiary rules were used to promote legitimacy see Tate v. Penne, 7 Martin N.S. 548 (La. 1829); Vernon v. Vernon's Heirs, 6 La. An. 242 (1851); Sisco v. Harmon, 9 Vt. 129 (1837); Parker v. Way, 15 N.H. 45 (1844); Cannon v. Cannon, 7 Hump. 410 (Tenn. 1846); State v. Wilson, 10 Ire. 131 (N.C. 1849); State v. Herman, 13 Ire. 502 (N.C. 1852); Ratcliff v. Wales, 1 Hill 63 (N.Y. 1848); People v. Overseers of the Poor of Ontario, 15 Barb. 296 (N.Y. 1853); Greenleaf, *Evidence*, 2:144–46.

14 Reeve, *Baron and Femme*, p. 271; Davis v. Henderson, 2 Yates 289 (Pa. 1798).

15 Blackstone, *Blackstone's Commentaries*, ed. St. George Tucker (Richmond, Va., 1803), 2:440, 446; Arthur Calhoun, *Social History of the American Family*, 2:264; Stones v. Keeling, 5 Call 143, 146–47 (Va. 1804).

16 Hartwell v. Jackson, 7 Tex. 576 (1850); and see Brown v. Westbrook, 27 Ga. 102 (1859); Helen Clarke, *Social Legislation* (New York, 1940), p. 106.

17 Blackstone, *Blackstone's Commentaries*, ed. Tucker, 2:446, 453; Nathan Dane, *A General Abridgement of American Law*, 9 vols. (New

York, 1823–29), 2:245; Kent, *Commentaries on American Law*, 2:211; and see James Dundas White, "Legitimation by Subsequent Marriage," *LQR* 36 (1920):256; Sir Dennis Fitzpatrick, "Legitimation by Subsequent Marriage," *JCL*, N.S., 22 (1905):43.

18 Timothy Walker, *Introduction to American Law* (Philadelphia, 1837), p. 233. In 1822, the year before Dane's volume appeared, William Griffith's survey of state laws revealed that eleven states had adopted the new policy. They included several southern states, Virginia, Georgia, Alabama, and Maryland; former civil-law colonies such as Missouri, Mississippi, and Louisiana; the frontier commonwealths of Ohio, Indiana, and Kentucky; and one lone New England State, Vermont, William Griffith, *Annual Survey of American Law* (New York, 1822), vols. 2, 3, passim.

19 Wisconsin statute cited in Reeve, *Baron and Femme*, 3rd ed., p. 404 note. One investigator discovered 171 petitions for legitimation submitted to accept legitimation by marriage, forty of these petitioners actually had wed the mother of their now legal heir. Guim Griffis Johnson, "Courtship and Marriage in North Carolina," *NCHR* 8 (1931):392–93; and see Harriet Daggett, *Essays on Family Law* (Baton Rouge, La., 1935), pp. 25–28; Robert Bremner, et al., *Children and Youth in America*, 3 vols. (Cambridge, Mass., 1970–74), 1:368–69.

20 Sleigh v. Strider, 5 Call 439, 443 (Va. 1805); and see Stevenson's Heirs v. Sullivan, 5 Wheat. 207 (U.S. 1820); U.S. v. Stewart, 15 Tex. 226 (1855); Carroll v. Carroll, 20 Tex. 731 (1858). But if no statute existed, judges steadfastly refused to abrogate the common law and adopt the civil. See for example Bow v. Nottingham, 1 N.H. 260 (1818). In the same manner, if a father's acknowledgment of his child was clearly proven, courts in states using the civil-law method of legitimation by public acknowledgment assisted its recipients in their inheritance claims. Estate of Sanford, 4 Cal. 12 (1851); Pigeau v. Duvernay, 4 Martin, O.S. 265 (La. 1816); Jones v. Hunter, 2 La. An. 254 (1847); In the matter of Mina Celina, 7 La. An. 162 (1854).

21 McCormick v. Cantrell, 7 Yerg. 615, 623, 624 (Tenn. 1835).

22 Swanson v. Swanson, 2 Swan. 446, 453–54, 454–55 (Tenn. 1855); and see Edmonson v. Dyson, 7 Ga. 512 (1849); Lee v. Shankle, 6 Jones 313 (N.C. 1859); Perry v. Newsom, 1 Ire. Eq. 28 (N.C. 1840). Disputes over the inheritance rights of legitimated children arose when their fathers died intestate or when wills merely designated children without specifying both legitimate and legitimated offspring. But, as Justice Peck had noted, men were granted the power to devise their estate to their illegitimate children even if they were not legitimated. Though these bequests were challenged as inducements to immorality and obstacles to matrimony, they were also defended as proper and commendable

compensation for the loss of family rights. South Carolina appears to have gone the farthest in this regard. A colonial act, still valid after the Revolution, had formalized the process by allowing a man to give up to a quarter of his estate to his mistress and natural child. Most states placed no limit on such bequests and the courts endorsed them as valid legal acts. This policy protected the male prerogative to aid his illegitimate child without altering his marital status. It was the final way a bastard could gain access to his or her father's estates. Kent, *Commentaries*, 2:214; Bunn v. Winthrop, 1 Johns. Chan. 329 (N.Y. 1815); Harster v. Gibson, 4 Deasu. Chan. 139, 142–43 (S.C. 1810); Pratt's Lessee v. Flamer, 5 Harr. & John. 10 (Md. 1820); Collins v. Hoxie, 9 Paige 81 (N.Y. 1841).

23 Eleanor Boatright, "The Political and Civil Status of Women in Georgia, 1783–1860," *GaHQ* 25 (1941):317.

24 Zephaniah Swift, *Digest of the Law of Evidence*, 2 vols. (N.Y. 1810), 1:47–48. For general discussions of nineteenth-century illegitimacy law see Rollin C. Hurd, *A Treatise on the Right of Personal Liberty, and on the Writ of Habeas Corpus and the Practice Connected With It* (Albany, N.Y., 1858), pp. 522–27; Lewis Hochheimer, *A Treatise Relating to the Custody of Infants, Including Practice and Forms* (Baltimore, 1889), pp. 104–5; James Schouler, *The Law of Domestic Relations* (Boston, 1870), pp. 382–92.

25 Wright v. Wright, 2 Mass. 109, 110 (1806).

26 People v. Landt, 2 Johns. 375, 376 (N.Y. 1807).

27 Kent, *Commentaries*, 2:215–16; and see Hudson v. Hills, 8 N.H. 417, 418–19 (1836); Dalton v. State, 6 Blackf. 357 (Ind. 1842); Acosta v. Robin, 7 Martin N.S. 387 (La. 1829); Hurd, *Personal Liberty and Habeas Corpus*, p. 530.

28 Rex v. Delaval, 3 Burr. 1435 (K.B. 1763); People v. Kling, 6 Barb. 368–369 (N.Y. 1849); and see Carpenter v. Whitman, 15 Johns. 208 (N.Y. 1818); Wright v. Bennett, 7 Ill. 587 (1845); McGunigal v. Mong, 5 Pa. St. 269 (1847); Schouler, *Domestic Relations*, pp. 382–85. The issue of child custody is discussed more thoroughly in chapter 7. For a general analysis of the nineteenth-century expansion of the writ of *habeas corpus* see William F. Duker, *A Constitutional History of Habeas Corpus* (Westport, Conn., 1980).

29 Canaan v. Salisbury, 1 Root 155 (Conn. 1790). Petersham v. Dana, 12 Mass. 428, 432 (1815); Kent, *Commentaries*, 2:214. Another Connecticut decision made the point even more emphatically, Bethlem v. Roxbury, 20 Conn. 298 (1850): "The feudal and repulsive doctrine of the common law, that a bastard child has no parent, no protector, not even a mother, has never been found in this state"; and see Newton v. Braintree, 14 Mass. 382 (1817); Wynkoop v. New York City, 3 Johns. 15 (N.Y.

1808); Canton v. Bently, 11 Mass. 442 (1814); Hebron v. Marlborough, 2 Conn. 19 (1816); Danbury v. New Haven, 5 Conn. 584 (1825); Woodstock v. Hooker, 6 Conn. 36 (1825); Westfield v. Warren, 3 Halst. 249 (N.J. 1826).

30 Bloomfield v. Chagrin, 5 Ohio 316 (1832). For examples of the application of class and culturally biased rules see Philadelphia v. Bristol, 6 S. & R. 502 (Pa. 1819); Boylston v. Princeton, 13 Mass. 381 (1816); Manchester v. Springfield, 15 Vt. 385 (1843); Commonwealth v. Fee, 6 S. & R. 255 (Pa. 1820); Robalina v. Armstrong, 15 Barb. 247 (N.Y. 1852); Bustamento v. Analla, 1 N.M. 255 (1857); Moritz v. Garnhart, 7 Watts 302 (Pa. 1838); Byrne v. Love, 14 Tex. 81 (1855); and see Maxwell Bloomfield, *American Lawyers in a Changing Society, 1776–1876* (Cambridge, Mass., 1976), pp. 122–35, who argues that the poor were bypassed in an overall liberalizing trend in antebellum family law. Though I agree in part, I think Bloomfield fails to pay significant attention to the gender, cultural, and entrepreneurial biases that impinged on the rights of family members in all classes.

31 Blackstone, *Commentaries*, 1:455; and see Schouler, *Domestic Relations*, pp. 281–82; Cooley v. Dewey, 4 Pick. 93 (Mass. 1826).

32 The statute can be found in 12 Henning. 688 (1785); Stanley Katz, "Republicanism and the Law of Inheritance," *MLR* 76 (1976):1–29; Thomas Jefferson, *Papers of Thomas Jefferson*, 18 vols., ed. Julian Boyd et al. (Princeton, N.J., 1950–71), 2:393; Edward Dumbauld, *Thomas Jefferson and the Law* (Norman, Ok., 1978), chap. 7.

33 Kent, *Commentaries on American Law*, 2:213–14. The acts are cited in Griffith, *Annual Survey*, vols. 1, 2, passim; Reeve, *Baron and Femme*, 2nd ed., p. 275; Ibid., 3rd ed., pp. 400–4; Schouler, *Domestic Relations*, p. 381.

34 Stevenson's Heirs v. Sullivan, 5 Wheat. 260, 262 (U.S. 1820); and for other interpretations see Lange v. Richous, 6 La. 560 (1834); Earle and McNier v. Dawes, 3 Md. Chan. 230 (1849); Kelly's Heirs v. McGuire and Wife, 15 Ark. 555 (1855).

35 Flintham v. Holder, 1 Dev. Eq. 349, 351 (N.C. 1829); Little v. Lake, 8 Ohio Rep. 289 (1838); Miller v. Stewart, 8 Gill. 128, 131–32 (Md. 1849); and see Bacon v. McBride, 32 Vt. 585 (1860); Black v. Cartmell, 10 B. Monroe 188 (Ky. 1849); Bent's Adm'r v. St. Vrain, 30 Mo. 268 (1860).

36 Brown v. Dye, 2 Root 280, 281 (Conn. 1795); Woodstock v. Hooker, 6 Conn. 36 (1825); and for a full analysis of the subject in Connecticut see Dickinson's Appeal from Probate, 42 Conn. 492 (1875).

37 Tapping Reeve, *A Treatise on the Law of Descent* (New York, 1825), p. 96; Kent, *Commentaries*, 2:212–13; and see Burlington v. Fosby, 6 Vt. 83 (1834); Kent v. Barker, 2 Gray 535 (Mass. 1854).

38   Garland v. Harrison, 8 Leigh 368, 369, 372 (Va. 1837); and see Bennett
     v. Toler, 15 Grat. 588 (Va. 1860); Ash v. Way, 2 Grat. 203 (Va. 1845);
     Lewis v. Eutsler, 4 Ohio St. 355 (1854). As in the rest of family law,
     race played a special role in illegitimacy. Colonial statutes and authori-
     ties, especially in the south, often penalized black mothers and their
     baseborn offspring more severely than whites. Only those blacks who
     escaped both slavery and poverty could derive any benefit from the post-
     Revolutionary changes. Southern courts took particular care to ensure
     that claims for freedom could not be founded in pedigree arguments
     based on white ancestors or paternal attempts to free their illegitimate
     offspring. See generally Melinda and Sarah v. Gardner, 24 Ala. 719
     (1854); Howard v. Howard, 6 Jones 235 (N.C. 1858); State v. Watters, 3
     Ire. 455 (N.C. 1843); Davis v. Calvert, 5 Gill & John. 269 (Md. 1833);
     Chancellor v. Milly, 9 Dana 23 (Ky. 1839); Raby v. Batiste, 27 Miss.
     731 (1854); Mima Queen v. Hepburn, 7 Cranch 290, 297 (U.S. 1813);
     Negro John Davis v. Wood, 1 Wheat. 6 (U.S. 1816); Vaughan v. Phebe,
     1 Martin & Yerger 5 (Tenn. 1827); Lorenzo Greene, *The Negro in
     Colonial New England* (New York, 1942), pp. 126, 202; James John-
     stone, *Race Relations in Virginia* (Amherst, Mass., 1980, reprint of
     1934 diss.), pp. 167, 294–95, 11–12; Harry D. Kruse, *Illegitimacy:
     Law and Social Policy* (Indianapolis, Ind., 1971), p. 13; Daggett, *Essays
     on Family Law*, pp. 25–28; Lasok, "Virginia's Bastardy Laws," 416–18.
39   Laws of Ohio, Chap. XLII, 1805; Laws of Ohio, Act of February 2,
     1824, Sec. 6; and see Hartog, "Public Law of a County Court," 308;
     Lasok, "Virginia's Bastardy Laws," 423; Ely, "American Independence
     and the Law," 955–66; Schooner v. Commonwealth, Litt. Sel. Cas. 88,
     90–91 (Ky. 1809).
40   Hinman v. Taylor, 2 Conn. 357, 362 (1817); Reeve, *Baron and Femme*,
     p. 277. For a discussion of the rights of fathers in these trials see
     Moncrief v. Ely, 19 Wend. 405 (N.Y. 1838); Justices v. Chapman, 16
     Ga. 89 (1854); and see generally Smith v. Minor, 1 Cox 19 (N.J. 1790);
     Dunwiddie v. Commonwealth, 1 Hardin 290 (Ky. 1808); Comstock v.
     Weed, 2 Conn. 155 (1817); Mather v. Clark, 2 Aiken 209 (Vt. 1827).
41   State v. Goode, 10 Ire. 49, 51–52 (N.C. 1849); and see State v. Lee, 7
     Ire. 265 (N.C. 1847). For discussions and application of the various
     tools used to judge paternity, such as mothers' accusations (including
     those made during labor) and the likeness of the child see Williams v.
     Blincoe, 5 Litt. 171, 173 (Ky. 1824); Hitchcock v. Grant, 1 Root 107
     (Conn. 1789); Warner v. Willey, 2 Root 490 (Conn. 1796); Stiles v.
     Eastman, 21 Pick. 132 (Mass. 1838); Blake v. Junkins, 35 Me. 433
     (1853); Savage v. Reardon, 11 Gray 376 (Mass. 1858); Jacobs v. Pol-
     lard, 10 Cush. 287 (Mass. 1852); Beals v. Furbish, 39 Me. 469 (1855);
     Dennett v. Kneeland, 6 Greenl. 460 (Me. 1830); Bacon v. Harrington, 5

Pick. 63 (Mass. 1827); Commonwealth v. Cole, 5 Mass. 515 (1809); Loring v. O'Donnell, 12 Me. 27 (1835); R. R. v. J. M., 3 N.H. 135 (1825); Davis v. Salisbury, 1 Day 278 (Conn. 1804); State v. Bowles, 7 Jones 579, 580 (N.C. 1860); Wright v. Hicks, 15 Ga. 160 (1854); Cannon v. Cannon, 7 Hump. 410 (Tenn. 1846); Gilmanton v. Ham, 38 N.H. 108 (1859); Keniston v. Rowe, 16 Me. 38 (1839); Swift, *A System of Laws*, p. 208; Reeve, *Baron and Femme*, pp. 279, 635; ibid., 3rd ed., 408 note; Theodoric Beck, *Elements of Medical Jurisprudence*, 2 vols. (Philadelphia, 1823), 1:306–7, 631; Ernst Freund, *Illegitimacy Laws of the United States* (Washington, D.C., 1919), p. 40; Charles Doering, "Evidence: Admissibility of Evidence of Resemblance Where Paternity is at Issue," *CLQ* 11 (1925–26):380–85; Nelson, *Americanization of the Common Law*, pp. 25–26, 76. Perhaps the most notorious antebellum illegitimacy case based on the issue of resemblance was the 1808 trial of Alexander Whistelo, a black coachman. Lucy Williams, a mulatto, accused him of fathering her illegitimate child. The New York City Overseers of the Poor prosecuted him. However, the "color of the child was somewhat dark, but lighter than the generality of mulattoes" and its "hair was stringy, and had none of the peculiarities of the negro race." Whistelo denied paternity. After a lengthy trial, in which the medical knowledge of the day was paraded before the mayor's court, Whistelo was found innocent, Commissioners of the Almshouse v. Whistelo, 3 Wheeler Crim. Cas. 194, 204 (N.Y. 1808); and see State v. Long, 9 Ire. 488 (N.C. 1849); Hudson v. Taghkanac, 13 John. 244 (N.Y. 1816); Watkins v. Carlton, 10 Leigh 560 (Va. 1840).

42 Morse v. Pineo, 4 Vt. 281 (1832); and see Spears v. Forrest, 15 Vt. 435 (1843); Ginn v. Commonwealth, 5 Litt. 390 (Ky. 1824); O'Brien v. State, 14 Ire. 409 (N.C. 1823); Crawford v. State, 7 Bax. 41 (Tenn. 1872); William M. Rockel, "Evidence in Bastardy Cases," *CLJ* 18 (1884):305–7.

43 David Stewart, *A Digest of the Law of Husband and Wife as Established in Maryland* (Baltimore, Md., 1881), p. 138.

44 For an argument proposing that the suits were not class biased see Schooner v. Commonwealth, Litt. Sel. Ca. 88, 90 (Ky. 1809). For examples of the use of the law to protect local budgets see Spalding v. Felch, 1 Root 319 (Conn. 1791); Benedict v. Roberts, 2 Root 496 (Conn. 1797); Commonwealth v. Clark, 2 Mass. 155 (1806); Johnson v. Randall, 7 Mass. 340 (1811); Cooper v. State, 4 Blackf. 316 (Ind. 1837); Duncan v. Commonwealth, 4 S. & R. 449 (Pa. 1818); Sheffer v. Republican, 3 Yeates 39 (Pa. 1800); Bennett v. Hall, 1 Conn. 417 (1815); Reeve, *Baron and Femme*, 2nd ed., pp. 281–83; Ibid., 3rd ed., p. 411 note; Freund, *Illegitimacy Laws*, p. 42; Robert Ireland, *The County Courts in Antebellum Kentucky* (Lexington, Ky., 1972), p. 29.

45 Mauer v. Mitchell, 9 W. & S. 69 (Pa. 1845); *Mauer* overruled Shenk v. Mingle, 13 S & R. 28 (Pa. 1825). And see Coleman v. Frum, 3 Scam. 378, 380 (Ill. 1842); Wiggins v. Keizer, 6 Ind. 252 (1855); Kent, *Commentaries*, 2:216–17. Courts retained the right to supervise private settlements, and poor-law officials to sue the putative father if the mother refused to do so. See for example Burgen v. Straughan, 7 J.J. Marsh 583, 584–85 (Ky. 1832); State v. Harshaw, 3 Dev. & Bat. 371 (N.C. 1839); Hollister v. White, 2 Conn. 338 (1817); Woodkirk v. Williams, 1 Blackf. 110 (Ind. 1820); Dickerson v. Gray, 2 Blackf. 230 (Ind. 1829); Sherman v. Johnson, 20 Vt. 567 (1848); Phillippi v. Commonwealth, 18 Pa. St. 116 (1851).

46 Frank Fessenden, "Nullity of Marriage," *HLR* 13 (1899–1900):110; Arnold v. Cheeseborough, 58 Fed. 833 (U.S. C.C. N.Y. 1893); Orthwein v. Thomas, 127 Ill. 554, 562–63 (1889); and see Kaise v. Lawson, 38 Tex. 160 (1873); Illinois Land Co. v. Bonner, 75 Ill. 315 (1874); Moore v. Hegeman, 92 N.Y. 521 (1883); Drinkhouse's Estate, 151 Pa. 294 (1892); Eloi v. Mader, 1 Rob. 581 (La. 1841); Scott v. Hillenberg, 85 Va. 245 (1888); Grant v. Mitchell, 83 Me. 23 (1890); Bothick v. Bothick, 45 La. An. 1382 (1893); Matter of Seabury, 1 App. Div. 232 (N.Y. 1896); Fox v. Burke, 31 Minn. 319 (1883); Strode v. Magowan's Heirs, 2 Bush. 621 (Ky. 1865); Frederic Stimson, *American Statute Law* (Boston, 1886), Sec. 6620–22; Chester Vernier, *American Family Laws*, 4 vols. (Stanford, Ca., 1931–38), 4:150–52.

47 Tioga v. South Creek, 75 Pa. 433, 437 (1874); Egbert v. Greenwalt, 44 Mich. 245, 248 (1880).

48 Wigmore, *Evidence*, 2:2768; "Notes," *UPLR*, N.S., 64 (1924–25):73–74; "Note: The Lord Mansfield Rule as to Bastardizing the Issue," *MLR* 3 (1930):79–87; Richard Burgee, "The Lord Mansfield Rule and the Presumption of Legitimacy," *MdLR* 16 (1956):236–44. As they always had, the legal presumptions of legitimacy generated voluminous litigation, see for example Herring v. Goodson, 43 Miss. 392 (1870–71); State v. Rose, 75 N.C. 239 (1876); Shuler v. Bull, 15 S.C. 421 (1881); Wilson v. Babb, 18 S.C. 59, 70 (1882); Phillipps v. Allen, 2 Allen 453 (Mass. 1861); Miller v. Anderson, 43 Ohio St. 473 (1885); State v. Romaine, 58 Ia. 46 (1882); Kleinhart v. Ehlers, 39 Pa. St. 439 (1861); Bailey v. Boyd, 59 Ind. 292 (1877); Harrington v. Barfield, 30 La. An. 1297 (1878); Goodwin v. Owen, 55 Ind. 243 (1876); McNeely v. McNeely, 47 La. An. 1321 (1895); Pottsford v. Chittenden, 56 Vt. 49 (1866); Goss v. Froman, 89 Ky. 318 (1889); Dean v. State, 29 Ind. 483 (1868); Kearny v. Denn, 15 Wall. 51 (U.S. 1872); Bussom v. Forsyth, 32 N.J. Eq. 277 (1880); Hemmenway v. Towner, 1 Allen 209 (Mass. 1861); Commonwealth v. Reed, 5 Phila. 528 (Pa. 1864); Moseley v. Eakin, 15 Rich. 324 (1868); Mink v. State, 60 Wis. 583 (1884); State v.

McDowell, 101 N.C. 734 (1888); Scanlon v. Walshe, 81 Md. 118 (1895); Bell v. Terr, 8 Okl. 75 (1899); Schouler, *Domestic Relations*, 5th ed., pp. 444–50; Joel Bishop, *New Commentaries on the Law of Marriage and Divorce*, 2 vols. (New York, 1891), 1:504–6.

49 Stimson, *American Statute Law*, Sec. 6631–36; U.S. Census Bureau, *Special Reports: Marriage and Divorce in the United States, 1867 to 1906* (Washington, D.C., 1908–1909), p. 670; Vernier, *American Family Laws*, 4:156–89; Frederic Stimson, *The Law of the Federal and State Constitutions of the United States* (Boston, 1908), pp. 293, 194, 308; Morris Ploscowe, *Sex and the Law* (New York, 1951), pp. 106–12.

50 Watts v. Owen, 62 Wis. 512, 517 (1885); and see Succession of Navarro, 24 La. An. 298 (1872); Green v. Green, 126 Mo. 17 (1894); Heckert v. Hile's Adm'r, 90 Va. 390 (1894); Wright v. Lore, 12 Ohio St. 619 (1861); McColla v. Bane, 45 Fed. 828 (U.S.C.C.D. Ore. 1891); Henneger v. Lomas, 145 Ind. 287 (1896); Caldwell v. Miller, 44 Kan. 12 (1890); but for a different position see Dare v. Dare, 52 N.J. Eq. 195 (1893); Blacklaws v. Milne, 82 Ill. 505 (1876).

51 Andrews v. Page, 3 Heisk. 653, 666 (Tenn. 1871); and see Bishop, *New Commentaries*, 1:291–95.

52 Gregley v. Jackson, 38 Ark. 487, 493–94 (1882); Cantelou v. Doe, 56 Ala. 519 (1876); and see Allen v. Allen, 8 Bush. 490 (Ky. 1871); Woodward v. Blue, 107 N.C. (1890); Butler v. Butler, 161 Ill. 451 (1896). Southern courts generally construed the legitimating provisions quite liberally. Significantly, judges decided that the acts applied not only to the offspring of couples who had continued to live as husband and wife, but also to the children of slave unions in which one or both of the parties had died before acquiring their freedom. Adams v. Adams, 36 Ga. 236 (1867); White v. Ross, 40 Ga. 339 (1869); Neel v. Hibard, 30 La. 808 (1878); Dingle v. Mitchell, 20 S.C. 202 (1883); Fitchett v. Smith's Adm'r, 78 Va. 524 (1884); Davenport v. Caldwell, 10 S.C. 317 (1877); Smith v. Perry, 80 Va. 563 (1885); and for similar conclusions see Morris v. Williams, 39 Ohio St. 554 (1883).

53 Hawbecker v. Hawbecker, 43 Md. 516, 520 (1875); and see Brewer v. Hamor, 83 Me. 251 (1891); Dayton v. Adkisson, 45 N.J. Eq. 603 (1889); In re Matthias' Estate, 63 Fed. 523 (U.S. C.C.D. Wash. 1894). The other major civil-law method of legitimation, the father acknowledging the child through a special act or legal process, did not generate as much support. Fewer states provided for such procedures; and even when they did, the child's inheritance rights were much more restricted than when the parents actually wed. The courts dealt with the acts warily as well, in part because their method of legitimation only made a child an heir rather than including the offspring in the paternal family. See for example, McGunnigle v. McKee, 77 Pa. St. 81 (1874); McKamie v.

Baskerville, 86 Tenn. 459, 562 (1887); Brock v. State, 85 Ind. 397 (1882); Blair v. Howell, 68 Ia. 619 (1886); Hughes v. Knowlton, 37 Conn. 429 (1870); Hutcheson Investment Co. v. Caldwell, 157 U.S. 65 (1894); Williams v. Williams, 11 Lea 652 (Tenn. 1883); Crane v. Crane, 31 Ia. 296, 304 (1871); Pina v. Peck, 31 Cal. 359 (1866); Estate of Pico, 52 Cal. 84 (1877); Estate of Jessup, 81 Cal. 408 (1889); Blythe v. Ayres, 96 Cal. 532 (1892); "Comment: Parent and Child, Legitimation Through Acts, Definition of 'Family'," *CalLR* 2 (1913–14):78–80; Willoughby v. Motley, 83 Ky. 297 (1885); Cox v. Rash, 82 Ind. 519 (1882); Appeal of Edwards, 108 Pa. 283 (1885); Hicks v. Smith, 94 Ga. 809 (1894); Hartinger v. Ferring, 24 Fed. 15 (C.C. N.D. Ia. 1885); Vernier, *American Family Laws*, 4:178–82.

54   Chapman v. Handley, 7 Utah 49, 55, 57–75 (1890); Cope v. Cope, 137 U.S. 682, 687 (1891), and see Cope v. Cope, 7 Utah 63 (1891); Pratt's Estate, 7 Utah 278 (1891); Kimball Young, *Isn't One Wife Enough?* (New York, 1951), p. 441; Howard, *Matrimonial Institutions*, 2:476–77. For cases in which the racial line was drawn in legitimation disputes, see Greenhowe v. James' Ex'or, 80 Va. 636 (1885); Clements v. Crawford, 42 Tex. 601 (1875); Hart v. Hoss and Elder, 26 La. 90 (1874); Succession of Colwell, 34 La. An. 265 (1882); Succession of Hebert, 33 La. An. 1099 (1881); Daggett, *Essays on Family Law*, pp. 28–35; Charles S. Magnum, Jr., *The Legal Status of the Negro* (Chapel Hill, 1940), pp. 264–65. For Indian children who were generally excluded from this discrimination, see Buchanan v. Harvey, 35 Mo. 276 (1864); Boyer v. Dively, 58 Mo. 510 (1875); Kobogum v. Jackson Iron Co., 76 Mich. 498 (1889); however, where the law banned such marriages children remained without rights, Estate of Walker, 5 Ariz. 70 (1896).

55   Schouler, *Domestic Relations*, p. 381; Stimson, *American Statute Law*, Sec. 3151; Vernier, *American Family Laws*, 4:190–92; and see Dickenson's Appeal from Probate, 42 Conn. 491, 511–12 (1875).

56   Opdyke's Appeal, 49 Pa. 373, 379 (1865); and see McBride v. Patterson, 78 N.C. 412 (1878); Estate of Magee, 63 Cal. 414 (1883); Bales v. Elder, 118 Ill. 436 (1887); Estate of Wardell, 57 Cal. 484 (1881); Howell v. Tyler, 91 N.C. 207 (1884); Kingsley v. Broward, 19 Fla. 722 (1883); Haraden v. Larrabee, 113 Mass. 430 (1873); Jackson v. Jackson, 78 Ky. 390 (1880); Miller v. Williams, 66 Ill. 91 (1872); Neal's Appeal, 92 Pa. 193 (1879); Keeler v. Dawson, 73 Mich. 600 (1889); Pettus & Lott v. Dawson, 82 Tex. 18 (1891); Croan v. Phelps' Adm'r, 94 Ky. 213 (1893); Hawkins v. Jones, 19 Ohio St. 22 (1869); Estate of Ditche, 11 Phila. 15, 18 (Pa. 1875); Steckel's Appeal, 64 Pa. 493 (1870); Burton v. Elyton Land Co., 84 Ala. 384 (1887); Stimson, *American Statute Law*, Sec. 3151; Vernier, *American Family Laws*, 4:190–92.

57   Hochheimer, *Custody of Infants*, 2nd ed., p. 105; Freund, *Illegitimacy*

Laws, p. 43; Hochheimer, *Custody of Infants*, 2nd ed., pp. 104–5; In re Lewis, 88 N.C. 31, 33–34 (1883); and see State v. Noble, 70 Ia. 174 (1886). The English were much more reluctant to concede women this right, see "Notes," *ALJ* 27 (1883):203; Hochheimer, *Custody of Infants*, 2nd ed., pp. 104–5; Schouler, *Domestic Relations*, pp. 448–50. American courts not only granted mothers custody but considered the putative father the next rightful claimant, see Barea v. Roberts, 34 Tex. 544, 557 (1870–71); Pote's Appeal, 106 Pa. St. 574 (1884); Gabriel Woerner, *A Treatise on the American Law of Guardianship* (Boston, 1897), pp. 135–36.

58 County of Dodge v. Kemnitz, 32 Neb. 238 (1891); and see Marshall v. Reams, 32 Fla. 499 (1893); In re Nofsinger, 25 Mo. App. 116 (1887); U.S. v. Saugauge, 91 Fed. 490 (1899); Jones v. Emmert, 62 Ind. 533 (1878); Pratt v. Nitz, 78 Ia. 33 (1876); Jones v. Hart, 62 Miss. 13 (1884).

59 For a discussion of the Indiana statute see Stanton v. State, 6 Blackf. 83 (Ind. 1841); Adams v. Adams, 59 Vt. 158, 161 (1877); and see Stephen H. Marcus, "Equal Protection: The Custody of the Illegitimate Child," *JFL* 11 (1971):1–48.

60 William M. Rockel, "Evidence in Bastardy Cases," *CLJ* 18 (1884):305.

61 Francis v. Commonwealth, 3 Bush. 4, 7 (Ky. 1867); and see Musser v. Stewart, 21 Ohio St. 353 (1871); Vernier, *American Family Laws*, 4: 206–8; Joel Bishop, *Commentaries on the Law of Statutory Crimes*, 2 vols. (Boston, 1877), 1:368; Clarke, *Social Legislation*, p. 326. Only three states had no support provisions: Virginia, Alabama, and Texas; for the Virginia policy see Lasok, "Virginia Bastardy Laws," 323.

62 Rockel, "Evidence in Bastardy Cases," 306.

63 State v. Beatty, 66 N.C. 648, 650–51 (1872); and see Commonwealth v. Weaver, 9 Dist. Rep. 427 (Pa. 1899); Davis v. Herrington, 53 Ark. 5 (1890); Hook v. Pratt, 78 N.Y. 371 (1879); Glidden v. Nelson, 15 Ill. App. 297 (1884); Billingsley v. Clelland, 41 W.Va. 234 (1895); Todd v. Weber, 95 N.Y. 181 (1884); Schouler, *Domestic Relations*, pp. 451–52. States also used, and the courts upheld, the right to prosecute delinquent fathers if a mother failed to charge him. Women were then compelled to testify at the hearings. The rights of the parties were altered, though, by the gradual abolition of the old common-law prohibition of the testimony of interested parties. The change not only undermined the need for the old common-law test of declarations by women during childbirth, it also expanded the evidentiary scope of the hearings. Community fiscal concerns still dominated, however. For various cases and discussions of these issues see Morris v. Swaney, 7 Heisk. 591 (Tenn. 1872); State v. Ginger, 80 Ia. 574 (1890); Eddy v. Gray, 4 Allen 435 (Mass. 1862); State v. Britt, 78 N.C. 439 (1878); Paull v. Padelford, 16 Gray 263

(Mass. 1860); Jones v. People, 53 Ill. 366 (1870); State v. Crouse, 86 N.C. 617 (1882); Wheelright v. Greer, 10 Allen 389 (Mass. 1865); People v. Carney, 29 Hun. 47 (N.Y. 1883); Clark v. Bradstreet, 80 Me. 454 (1888); Young v. Makepeace, 103 Mass. 50 (1869); Jones v. Jones, 45 Md. 144 (1876); Vernier, *American Family Laws*, 4:208–15; Bishop, *New Commentaries*, 1:506–7; "Note: Admissibility of Evidence of Resemblance," *CLQ* 11 (1925–26):380–85; Payne v. Gray, 56 Me. 317 (1868); Booth v. Hart, 43 Conn. 182 (1879); Robbins v. Smith, 47 Conn. 182 (1879); Heath v. Heath, 58 N.H. 292 (1878); Richmond v. State, 19 Wis. 307 (1865); Leonard v. Bolton, 148 Mass. 66 (1888); Robbins and Doak, "Family Property Rights," 326–27.

64   Freund, *Illegitimacy Laws*, p. 42. For a detailed analysis of turn-of-the-century bastardy proceedings see W. Logan McCloy, "The Laws of Pennsylvania Relating to Illegitimacy," *Journal of Criminal Law and Criminology* 7 (1916–17):512–21; and see Francis W. Laurent, *The Business of a Trial Court, 100 Years of Cases* (Madison, Wisc., 1959), pp. 38–41.

65   Florence Kelley, "On Some Changes in the Legal Status of the Child Since Blackstone," *IR* 13 (1882):96.

66   Morton Keller, *Affairs of State* (Cambridge, Mass., 1977), p. 463.

67   Emma O. Lundberg and Katharine Lenroot, *Illegitimacy as a Child Welfare Problem*, Part I (U.S. Child's Bureau, Washington, D.C., 1920, Publication No. 66), pp. 26, 47–48; Juvenile Protective Association of Chicago, *The Care of Illegitimate Children in Chicago* (Chicago, 1913), pp. 4–12.

68   Susan Tiffin, *In Whose Best Interest? Child Welfare in the Progressive Era* (Westport, Conn., 1981), p. 171, and see generally chap. 7 which is the most thorough recent examination of illegitimacy in early twentieth-century America; Kate Waller Barrett quoted in ibid., p. 171; statement on "illegitimate parents" in *Standards of Legal Protection for Children Born Out of Wedlock* (U.S. Child's Bureau, Washington, D.C., Publication No. 77, 1921), p. 7.

69   D. H. Van Doren, "Rights of Illegitimate Children Under Modern Statutes," *ColLR* 16 (1916):700, 700–1.

70   McCloy, "The Laws of Pennsylvania," 525; and see Vernier, *American Family Laws*, 4:206–8.

71   Rev. Edward J. O'Brien, *Child Welfare Legislation in Maryland, 1634–1936* (Washington, D.C., 1937), pp. 7–8; Vernier, *American Family Laws*, 4:208–18; Clarke, *Social Legislation*, p. 312.

72   Berkeley Davis, "The Passing of Illegitimacy," *LN* 19 (1913):145.

73   The 1921 study is discussed in Mildred B. Mudgett, *Results of Minnesota's Laws for the Protection of Children Born Out of Wedlock* (U.S. Child's Bureau, Washington, D.C., 1924, Publication No. 28),

pp. 217–20; and see Carl A. Heisterman, "State Supervision of Children Born Out of Wedlock," in *Family and the State*, ed. Sophonisba Breckinridge (Chicago, 1934), p. 484; Ibid., pp. 476–84, 450; Bremner et al., ed., *Children and Youth*, 2:178. England finally joined the movement as well. In 1926, after years of debate and unheeded demands for reform, Parliament radically changed the law. The new act provided for legitimacy by the subsequent marriage of a bastard's parents, though excluding adulterous relations, and granted these children new maternal property rights. See generally T. E. James, "The Illegitimate and Deprived Child: Legitimation and Adoption," in *A Century of Family Law*, ed. Ronald Graveson and F. R. Crane, (Cambridge, 1957), pp. 43–45; Jeffrey Weeks, *Sex, Politics, and Society* (New York, 1981), p. 208.

74 Bradley Hull, cited in *Standards of Legal Protection for Children Born Out of Wedlock*, 82–93; and for Freund's acknowledgment of those prejudices see Freund, *Illegitimacy Laws*, p. 27.

75 Bell v. Terry & Tench Co., 177 App. Div. 123, 163 N.Y. Supp. 733 (1917).

76 Emma O. Lundberg, *Children of Illegitimate Birth and Measures for their Protection* (U.S. Child's Bureau, Washington, D.C., 1926), p. 11.

Chapter 7

1 For a general discussion of custody law see P. H. Pettit, "Parental Control and Guardianship," in *A Century of Family Law*, ed. Ronald Graveson and F. R. Crane (Cambridge, 1957), pp. 56–57; Sir Frederick Pollock and Frederic Maitland, *History of English Law*, 2 vols. (Cambridge, 1895), 2:436–47; Robert H. Mnookin, "Child Custody Adjudications: Judicial Functions in the Face of Indeterminancy," *LCP* 39 (1975):226–93; Joseph Goldstein, et al., *Beyond the Best Interests of the Child* (New York, 1973); Jamil Zainaldin, "The Emergence of a Modern American Family Law: Child Custody, Adoption, and the Courts, 1796–1851," *NLR* 73 (1979):1038.

2 Jay Fliegelman, *Prodigals and Pilgrims: The American Revolution Against Patriarchal Authority, 1750–1800* (New York, 1982), p. 95; for a general discussion of the issue see William Blackstone, *Commentaries on the Laws of England*, 4 vols. (London, 1765–69), 1:442.

3 David Hoffman, *Legal Outlines* (Baltimore, 1836), pp. 155, 156, 156–57; William Blackstone, *Blackstone's Commentaries on the Laws of England*, ed. George Sharwood, 5 vols. (Philadelphia, 1860), 2:452;

and see Blackstone, *Commentaries*, 1:438, 456, 462; Richard Morris, *Studies in the History of American Law* (New York, 1930), pp. 126–200; Maxwell Bloomfield, *American Lawyers in a Changing Society, 1776–1876* (Cambridge, Mass., 1976), pp. 97–99.

4   Massachusetts act cited in Arthur Calhoun, *A Social History of the American Family*, 3 vols. (Cleveland, 1917), 1:77; and see Mary Benson, *Women in Eighteenth Century America* (1935, reprint, Port Washington, N.Y., 1966), pp. 239–44; Lorena S. Walsh, "Child Custody in the Early Colonial Chesapeake: A Case Study" (paper presented at the Berkshire Conference on Women's History, Vassar College, June 1981); Mary Beth Norton, *Liberty's Daughters* (Boston, 1980), pp. 46–57.

5   Fliegelman, *Prodigals and Pilgrims*, p. 197; Howard Neil Cozen, "English Background: Origins of *Parens Patriae*" *SCaLR* 22 (1970):147–51; George Rossmer, "Parens Patriae," *OreLR* 4 (1955):236–38; Douglas R. Rendleman, "Parens Patriae: From Chancery to Juvenile Court," *SCaLR* 23 (1971):205–23; Joseph Story, *Commentaries on Equity Jurisprudence* (Boston, 1836), chap. 35; Gabriel Woerner, *A Treatise on Guardianship* (Boston, 1897), pp. 2–4; Blackstone, *Commentaries*, 3:427.

6   Rex v. Delaval, 3 Burr 1434 (K.B. 1763); and see John C. Hurd, *A Treatise on the Right of Personal Liberty and on the Writ of Habeas Corpus* (Albany, N.Y., 1858), pp. 453–72.

7   Prather v. Prather, 4 Desau. 33, 34, 44 (S.C. 1809); and see Anonymous, 4 Desau. 94 (S.C. 1820); and for a later acceptance of this power see Ex parte Hewitt, 11 Rich. Law 326 (S.C. 1858). In England the trend became more convoluted when Mansfield's successors questioned his broad ideas of judicial discretion and once again gave primacy to paternal custody claims. See Hurd, *Personal Liberty and Habeas Corpus*, pp. 467–72; Lewis Hochheimer, *A Treatise Relating to the Custody of Infants* (Boston, 1870), p. 395; Pettit, "Parental Control," 56–58.

8   Lawrence M. Friedman and Robert V. Percival, "Who Sues for Divorce? From Fault through Fiction to Freedom," *JLS* 5 (1976):69; and see Nelson M. Blake, *The Road to Reno* (Syracuse, N.Y., 1962), pp. 1–120; Lawrence Friedman, *A History of American Law* (New York, 1970), pp. 179–84. For the most thorough localized study of divorce in nineteenth-century America see Robert L. Griswold, *Family and Divorce in California, 1850–1890* (Albany, N.Y., 1982). Griswold's analysis supports the broader national trends posited in this and the preceding chapters.

9   Commonwealth v. Addicks, 5 Binn. 520, 522 (Pa. 1813); Commonwealth v. Addicks, 2 S. & R. 174, 176, 177 (Pa. 1815).

10 Bedell v. Bedell, 1 Johns. Chan. 605 (N.Y. 1815); and see Friedman and Percival, "Who Sues for Divorce?," 69; Codd v. Codd, 2 Johns. Chan.

141 (N.Y. 1816); Clark v. Clark, Wright 225 (Ohio 1833); Richmond v. Richmond, 1 Green Chan. 90 (N.J. 1838); Griswold, *Family and Divorce in California*, pp. 29–32.

11 Commonwealth v. Briggs, 16 Pick. 203, 204 (Mass. 1834). However such rights evaporated when the father was found to be unfit. Thus in the case of State v. Smith, 6 Greenl. 462 (Me. 1830), evidence that a father was immoral, insolvent, and had been pronounced guilty in a paternity suit, led the court to reject his claim for custody. The court added for good measure: "[T]he parental feelings of a mother toward her child are naturally as strong and generally stronger than those of the father."

12 James Kent, *Commentaries on American Law*, 4 vols. (New York, 1826–30), 2:193, 194; Kent quoted in Norton, *Liberty's Daughters*, p. 5; Story, *Equity Jurisprudence*, 2:596–97. For an assessment of the changing nature of divorce see Griswold, *Family and Divorce in California*.

13 2 Revised New York Statutes 562, art. 2 (1830); Ahrenfeldt v. Ahrenfeldt, 1 Hoffm. Chan. 497, 502 (N.Y. 1840). And see People v. Chagaray, 18 Wend. 637, 641 (N.Y. 1836); People v. Nickerson, 19 Wend. 16 (N.Y. 1837); People v. Mercein, 25 Wend. 64 (N.Y. 1840); People v. Mercein, 3 Hill 399, 322 (N.Y. 1842); People v. Mercein, 8 Paige 47 (N.Y. 1830); State v. King, 1 Ga. Dec. 93 (1841).

14 *Report of the D'Hauteville Case* (Philadelphia, 1840), pp. 292–93, 293, 234, and see pp. 47–50. Ellen and her parents tried to get legislation curtailing the custody rights of alien husbands. Such a bill passed the New York Legislature, but was vetoed by Governor William H. Seward. His veto message stressed that such a diminution of paternal rights could be used against native fathers as well: "[W]ho would not revolt at the idea that the Chancellor should have the power to enter the family circles of our citizens, and, without convicting the parent of neglect or omission of duty, overrule parental authority and separate helpless children from unoffending parents upon the arbitrary pretext of promoting the child's life." Rhode Island, though, where Ellen and her family summered, seemed to harbor no such fears and passed the law she sought in 1841. Seward cited in *Report of the D'Hauteville Case*, p. 50; *The Petition of Henry C. DeRham to the General Assembly of Rhode Island in the D'Hauteville Case* (Providence, R.I., 1841).

15 A Member of the Boston Bar, *Review of the D'Hauteville Case* (Boston, 1841), p. 41, and see pp. 25, 37.

16 Joel Bishop, *Commentaries on the Law of Marriage and Divorce* (Boston, 1852), pp. 517–18, 525–26; and see Tapping Reeve, *The Law of Baron and Femme* (New York, 3rd ed., 1846), pp. 448–49, notes.

17 Reeve, *Baron and Femme* (New York, 1816), p. 295; and see Kent,

Commentaries, 2:219–31; Francis Hilliard, *Elements of the Law* (New York, 1835), pp. 24–25.

18 Reeve, *Baron and Femme*, pp. 295, 319; Kent, *Commentaries*, 2:224–26; Hollingsworth's Appeal, 51 Pa. 518 (1866); Eldridge v. Lippincott, 1 Coxe's Law 397 (N.J. 1795); Fields v. Law, 2 Root 310 (Conn. 1796); Kline v. Beebe, 6 Conn. 494 (1827). In colonial Maryland, to take the most egregious example of the diminution of widows' rights, a statute authorized local authorities to take the child of a Protestant father from his Catholic widow, see Julia Spruill, *Women's Life and Work in the Southern Colonies* (Chapel Hill, 1938), pp. 345–46.

19 In the Matter of Van Houten, 2 Green Chan. 220, 226 (N.J. 1835); and see Copp v. Copp, 20 N.H. 284 (1850); Williamson v. Jordan, Busb. Equity 40 (N.C. 1852); Fullerton v. Jackson, 5 Johns. Chan. 277 (N.Y. 1821); Corrigan v. Kiernan, 1 Bradf. 203 (N.Y. 1850).

20 Armstrong v. Stone, 9 Gratt. 102, 107 (Va. 1852); Striplin v. Ware, 36 Ala. 87, 90, 89 (1860); and see Lea v. Richardson, 8 La. An. 94 (1853); People v. Wilcox, 22 Barb. 178 (N.Y. 1854); Leavel v. Bettis, 3 Bush 74 (Ky. 1867); Carlisle v. Tuttle, 30 Ala. 613 (1857); Porch v. Fries, 3 C.E. Green 204 (N.J. 1867); Baily v. Morrison, 4 La. An. 523 (1849); Delacroix v. Boisblanc, 4 Mart. O.S. 715 (La. 1817); Hochheimer, *Custody of Infants*, pp. 18–19; Woerner, *Guardianship*, pp. 102–4. For invocations of the older rule see Stenbrook v. McColm, 7 Halst. Law 97 (N.J. 1830); State v. Cheeseman, 2 South. 445 (N.J. 1819); Huie v. Nixon, 6 Porter 77 (Ala. 1837); Holley v. Chamberlain, 1 Redf. 333 (N.Y. 1860); Webb v. Webb, 5 La. An. 595 (1850); Hovey v. Morris, 7 Blackf. 559 (Ind. 1845).

21 Caroline Dall, *The College, the Market, and the Court* (Boston, 1867), p. 293. For the most extensive discussion of woman's sphere in antebellum America see Nancy Cott, *The Bonds of Womanhood* (New Haven, 1971). For the most compelling analysis of the intellectual sources of a new vision of women's legal rights tied to the new feminine sphere see Norma Basch, *In the Eyes of the Law* (Ithaca, N.Y., 1981).

22 Linda Kealey, "Introduction," in *A Not Unreasonable Claim, Women and Reform in Canada, 1880s-1920s*, ed. Linda Kealey (Toronto, 1979), p. 8.

23 The "Declaration" is in Elizabeth Cady Stanton, et al., *History of Woman Suffrage*, 6 vols. (New York, 1872–1922), 1:71; and see E. C. Strauder, *Address to the Legislature of New York* (Albany, 1854), pp. 14–16. These demands were repeated in women's rights platforms for the rest of the century, see *History of Woman Suffrage*, 1:105, 194, 241, 2:254–55, 260–61, 4:563, 579–89, 5:776–79. For a general assessment of the use of "feminine qualities" as a means of advanc-

ing women's rights, see Daniel Walker Howe, "Victorian Culture in America," in *Victorian America*, ed. Daniel Walker Howe (Philadelphia, 1976), pp. 26–27, and see Eleanor Flexnor, *Century of Struggle, The Woman's Rights Movement in the United States*, rev. ed. (Cambridge, Mass., 1975), Part I; Carl Degler, *At Odds* (New York, 1980), chap. 13.

24 Nichols's story is in Stanton, et al., *History of Woman Suffrage*, 1:174–78.

25 *Tribune* account quoted in Bell Squire, *The Woman Movement in America* (Chicago, 1911), p. 46; James Schouler, *A Treatise on the Law of Domestic Relations* (Boston, 1870), pp. 17, 18. For similar expressions of concern see Stanton, et al., *History of Woman Suffrage*, 3:152.

26 Samuel Sewall, *The Legal Condition of Women* (Boston, 1869), pp. 14–15; Schouler, *Domestic Relations*, 5th ed., p. 166; William Wallings, *Sexology* (Boston, 1876), p. 39. For an excellent discussion of the differences between political and domestic rights see Ellen Carol Dubois, *Feminism and Suffrage, The Emergence of an Independent Woman's Movement in America, 1848–1869* (Ithaca, N.Y., 1978).

27 Chandler and the 1877 Address cited in Stanton, et al., *History of Woman Suffrage*, 2:152, 3:419; Caroline Dall, *Woman's Rights Under the Law* (Boston, 1861), pp. 59–60. For continued feminist agitation for custody rights see Stanton, et al., *History of Woman Suffrage*, 2:102, 799, 3:419; Rheta Childe Dorr, *What Eight Million Women Want* (Boston, 1910).

28 The 1860 and 1861 acts are described in Stanton, et al., *History of Woman Suffrage*, 1:686–87, 747–78, and see in general chap. 14; Bell Squire, *The Woman Movement in America*, p. 89. For discussions of the property reforms which accompanied these custody changes see Basch, *In the Eyes of the Law*, chap. 6; Peggy A. Rabkin, *Fathers to Daughters, The Legal Foundations of Female Emancipation* (Westport, Conn., 1980), chap. 13.

29 People v. Brooks, 35 Barb. 85, 91 (N.Y. 1861); and see People v. Boice, 39 Barb. 307, 309–10 (N.Y. 1862).

30 Connolly is quoted in William Leach, *True Love and Perfect Union* (New York, 1980), p. 180; Dorr, *What Eight Million Women Want*, p. 110.

31 Stanton, et al., *History of Woman Suffrage*, 4:chaps. 24–72; and see Jeannie C. Wilson, *The Legal Rights and Duties of Women* (New York, 1913), for a larger assessment of turn-of-the-century women's legal rights.

32 George Bishop, *Every Woman Her Own Lawyer* (New York, 1858), p. 181; and see Joel Bishop, *Commentaries on the Law of Marriage and Divorce*, pp. 517–18, 525–26; Isaac Redfield, "Recent Developments in English Jurisprudence," *ALReg*, N.S., 4 (1865):137.

33 State v. Baird and Torrey, 21 N.J. Eq. 384, 388 (1869); and see Ibid., 18 N.J. Eq. 194 (1867); Landis v. Landis, 39 N.J. Law 274 (1877); State v. Kirkpatrick, 54 Ia. 373, 375 (1880).

34 Anonymous, 55 Ala. 428, 432–33, 433 (1876); and see Matter of Pray, 60 Howard Pr. 194, 194–95 (N.Y. 1881); McKim v. McKim, 12 R.I. 462, 466 (1879); Latham v. Latham, 300 Gratt. 364, 387 (1878); Matter of Watson, 10 Abb. N.C. 215 (1882); Greenwood v. Greenwood, 84 Minn. 203 (1901); Stickel v. Stickel, 18 App. D.C. 150 (1901); Tytler v. Tytler, 15 Wy. 319 (1906).

35 Carr v. Carr, 22 Gratt. 168, 174 (Va. 1872), and see Bennett v. Bennett, 43 Conn. 313 (1876). For a more detailed look at this judicial approach see the series of divorce suits in the 1830s and 1840s in which Ohio, New York, and Delaware courts split the custody of children, giving the older ones to the father and the younger ones to the mother. Jeans v. Jeans, 2 Harr. 142 (Del. 1835–39); Dailey v. Dailey, Wright 514 (Ohio 1834); Leavitt v. Leavitt, Wright 719 (Ohio 1834); Laurie v. Laurie, 9 Paige 234 (N.Y. 1841); and see State v. Paine, 4 Hump. 523 (Tenn. 1843). In awarding custody, the courts relied very heavily on a fault doctrine as well as their beliefs in sexual differences. In suits instigated under a writ of *habeas corpus* after a legal or informal separation, judges took pains to ascertain the cause of the marital split-up. By determining fault, courts acted on the assumption that a spouse who unjustifiably left his or her mate would also be less likely to be a reliable parent. Moreover, they were unwilling to allow custody law to be used to sanction marital breakdowns. People v. Olmstead, 27 Barb. 9, 31, 32 (N.Y. 1832); State v. Stigall, 2 Zabr. 286 (N.J. 1849); Magee v. Holland, 3 Dutch. 86 (N.J. 1858); People v. Rhoades, 24 Barb. 521 (N.Y. 1857); Bryan v. Bryan, 34 Ala. 516 (1859); Lindsey v. Lindsey, 14 Ga. 657 (1854). In 1882, a St. Louis attorney summarized the potent changes that the tender years doctrine had spawned: "It is in respect to children of very tender years that the most latitude in discretion is usually exercised; in all other respects the only proper course is to adhere rigidly to the rules of law respecting parental rights and, as far as the nature of the proceedings will admit, to those of equity in the appointment of guardians." *Habeas Corpus*: Custody of Infants," *CLJ* 15 (1882):384. England pursued a similar policy, though through Parliament, not the courts, see Pettit, "Parental Control and Guardianship," 69–70.

36 Acts cited in Alice Paul, *Outline of the Legal Position of Women in Pennsylvania* (Philadelphia, 1911), pp. 31–32; and see Robinson v. English, 34 Pa. 328 (1859); Landis v. Landis, 39 N.J. Law 274, 279 (1877); Matter of Viele, 44 How. Pr. 14 (N.Y. 1872).

37 Lindsey v. Lindsey, 14 Ga. 657 (1854); and see Matter of Viele, 44 How. Pr. 14 (N.Y. 1872).

38   Lelia Robinson, *The Law of Husband and Wife* (Boston, 1899), p. 47.

39   William O'Neill, *Divorce in the Progressive Era* (New Haven, 1967), chap. 7; and see Friedman, *History of American Law*, pp. 436–40; Morton Keller, *Affairs of State* (Cambridge, Mass., 1977), pp. 468–72. For the most thorough recent assessments of nineteenth-century divorce proceedings on the local level see Elaine May, *Great Expectations: Marriage and Divorce in Post-Victorian America* (Chicago, 1980); Griswold, *Family and Divorce in California*.

40   The statistics on divorce are in Friedman and Percival, "Who Sues for Divorce?," esp. 78–79; Griswold, *Family and Divorce in California*, p. 153; Elaine May, "The Pursuit of Domestic Perfection: Marriage and Divorce in Los Angeles, 1890–1920," (Ph.D. diss., U.C.L.A., 1975), 239–40; and see a table describing custody awards in May's subsequent book based on her dissertation, *Great Expectations*, p. 173.

41   *Domestic Relations*, 5th ed., p. 393; and see English v. English, 31 N.J. Eq. 543, 547 (1879); Green v. Green, 52 Ia. 403 (1879); McBride v. McBride, 1 Bush. 15 (Ky. 1866); Bush v. Bush, 37 Ind. 164 (1871); In re Bort, 25 Kan. 308 (1881); In re Delano, 37 Mo. Ap. 185 (1885); Stetson v. Stetson, 80 Me. 483 (1888); Kline v. Kline, 57 Ia. 386 (1881); Howard, *Matrimonial Institutions*, 3:28–30, 90–95, 158–63; Hochheimer, *Custody of Infants*, pp. 93–98; Thomas C. Carrigan, "The Law and the American Child," *The Pedagogical Seminary* 18 (1911):126–30; Herbert Goodrich, "Custody of Children in Divorce Suits," *CLQ* 7 (1921):1–10.

42   Bishop, *New Commentaries on the Law of Marriage and Divorce*, 2 vols. (New York, 1891), 2:465; Cocke v. Hannum, 39 Miss. 423, 438–39, 439. The pervasive use of fault in determining custody was evident in Massachusetts divorce statutes passed in the late 1850s, which stipulated: "On the principle that the rights of the parents to their children, in the absence of misconduct, are equal . . . the happiness and welfare of the children are to determine the care and custody." Such a directive to the courts meant awarding custody to the faultless party, who was generally the wife. For a discussion of this and subsequent acts see Henry H. Sprague, *Women Under the Law of Massachusetts*, 2nd ed. (Boston, 1903), 77–85. Hansford v. Hansford, 10 Ala. 561 (1846); Hunt v. Hunt, 4 Greene 216 (Ia. 1854); Fitler v. Fitler, 33 Pa. 50 (1859); Helden v. Helden, 7 Wis. 256 (1858); Cook v. Cook, 1 Barb. Chan. 639 (N.Y. 1846); Wand v. Wand, 14 Cal. 512 (1860); Levering v. Levering, 16 Md. 313 (1860); Kingsberry v. Kingsberry, 3 Harr. 8 (Del. 1839–43); Lusk v. Lusk, 28 Mo. 91 (1859); Miner v. Miner, 11 Ill. 43 (1849); Lemunier v. McClearly, 37 La. An. 133 (1885); Sherwood v. Sherwood, 56 Ia. 608 (1881); Welch v. Welch, 33 Wis. 534 (1873); Cole v. Cole, 23 Ia. 433 (1867); Wakefield v. Ives, 35 Ia. 238 (1872); People v. Allen, 40

Hun. 611 (N.Y. 1886); Bishop, *Commentaries on Marriage and Divorce*, p. 519.

43   Helden v. Helden, 7 Wis. 296, 303 (1858); Crimmins v. Crimmins, 64 How. Pr. 103, 105, 106 (N.Y. 1882); and see Lambert v. Lambert, 16 Ore. 485 (1888); Jackson v. Jackson, 8 Ore. 402 (1880); Kremelburg v. Kremelburg, 52 Md. 553 (1879).

44   Uhlmann v. Uhlmann, 17 Abb. N.C. 236, 264 (N.Y. 1885); Schouler, *Domestic Relations*, 6th ed., 2:2034–35; and see People v. Hickey, 86 Ill. Ap. 20 (1899); Umlauf v. Umlauf, 27 Ill. Ap. 375 (1888); Reeves v. Reeves, 75 Ind. 342 (1881); Goodrich v. Goodrich, 44 Ala. 670 (1870); Scoggins v. Scoggins, 80 N.C. 318 (1879); Draper v. Draper, 68 Ill. 17 (1873); Hewitt v. Long, 76 Ill. 399 (1875); Dubois v. Johnson, 96 Ind. 6 (1884); Bishop, *New Commentaries*, 2:466–67.

45   Commonwealth v. Hart, 14 Phila. 352, 357 (Pa. 1881); John Norton Pomeroy, *A Treatise on Equity Jurisprudence*, 3 vols., 2nd ed. (San Francisco, Ca., 1892), 3:2013; and see Keller, *Affairs of State*, pp. 461–64; Joseph Kett, *Rites of Passage* (New York, 1977), Part II.

46   These conflicts also point out some of the deeper changes at work within the law of parent and child. At the heart of those developments was a gradual separation of the parental responsibility to support his or her offspring from the filial obligation of service. The decline of that older property-based concept of parental rights was evident in 1890 when the Iowa Supreme Court severed service from support by granting a seventeen-year-old daughter the right to call on her parents for medical care even though she lived apart from them. The justices decided that the "obligation of support is not grounded on the duty of the child to serve, but rather the inability of the child to care for itself." By severing parental duties from natural rights and filial responsibilities, the law encouraged child dependency by expanding the obligations of parents and contracting those of their offspring. Porter v. Powell, 79 Ia. 151, 158 (1890).

47   Nichols v. Giles, 2 Root 461 (Conn. 1796).

48   Matter of Waldron, 13 Johns. 417 (N.Y. 1816).

49   U.S. v. Green, 3 Mason 482 (U.S. C.C. R.I. 1824, Fed. Case #15, 256).

50   In the Matter of Mitchell, 1 Charlton 489, 494–95, 496 (Ga. 1836).

51   State v. Hand, 1 Ohio Dec. 238, 242, 244 (1848).

52   The judicial position on informal transfers of custody was fully summarized in the 1858 New Hampshire decision of State v. Libby, 44 Me. 469 (1858): "It is quite apparent that there may be cases where the father's conduct is such, as by permitting tacitly or by express agreement, another to assume and discharge for many years the duties of parent to his child, that he could not afterward attempt to reclaim his child in good

faith, nor without subjecting to serious hazards its interests and happiness. In such a case the award of the custody of the child would not be consistent with the exercise of a sound judicial discretion." See also Hutson v. Townsend, 6 Rich. Eq. 249 (S.C. 1854); People v. Cooper, 8 How. Pr. 288 (N.Y. 1853); Ex parte Williams, 11 Rich. 452 (S.C. 1852); Ex parte Schumpert, 6 Rich. 244 (S.C. 1853); Commonwealth v. Cool, 2 Chest. Co. Rep. 304 (Pa. 1884); Enders v. Enders, 164 Pa. 266 (1894); Winslow v. State, 92 Ala. 78 (1890); Hurd, *Personal Liberty and Habeas Corpus*, pp. 540–48; "Relinquishment of Parent's Right to Custody of Child to Third Person," *VaLJ* 6 (1882):470–79; Woerner, *Guardianship*, pp. 18–19, 36–38; Paul Sayre, "Awarding Custody of Children," *UChiLR* 9 (1941–42):476–77; Schouler, *Domestic Relations*, p. 343; Bishop, *New Commentaries*, 2:455–56; Jacobus TenBroek, *Family Law and the Poor: Essays by Jacobus TenBroek*, ed. Joel Handler (Westport, Conn., 1974), pp. 81–92.

53   Chapsky v. Wood, 26 Kan. 650, 653, 656, 657 (1881); and see In re Vance, 92 Cal. 195 (1891); Green v. Campbell, 35 W.Va. 699 (1891); "State v. Bratton," *ALReg*, N.S., 15 (1876):359; Sheers v. Stein, 75 Wis. 44 (1889); Washaw v. Gimble, 59 Ark. 351 (1887); Jones v. Darnall, 103 Ind. 569 (1885); Hochheimer, *Custody of Infants*, p. 16.

54   Hoxsie v. Potter, 16 R.I. 374, 377 (1888); and see Bonnett v. Bonnett, 61 Ia. 199 (1883); Commonwealth v. Barney, 4 Brew. 408 (Pa. 1872).

55   Estate of Linden, 1 Myr. Prob. 215, 224 (Cal. 1878); Verser v. Ford, 37 Ark. 27, 30, 31 (1881); and see Sturtevant v. State, 15 Neb. 459 (1884); McKender v. Green, 13 Col. App. 270 (1884); "Relinquishment of Parent's Rights of Custody of Children to a Third Party," *VaLJ* 6 (1882), 470–1; Sayre, "Awarding Custody," 680–88.

56   Legate v. Legate, 87 Tex. 248, 251; and see Stringfellow v. Somerville, 95 Va. 701 (1898). For parents, perhaps the most grievous custody disputes were those in which children were granted a chance to choose their homes. Though by the common law a child could not exercise such a choice until the years of discretion (generally twelve for girls and fourteen for boys), the courts often relaxed the rule and allowed younger but more mature children to have a voice in custody proceedings. Children's wishes were not automatically granted; judges were well aware of the fears spawned by altering settled routines. Yet when the courts did endorse children's wishes, they became decisive factors in the final custody decision. See for example, In re Gates, 95 Cal. 461, 462 (1892); Henson v. Walts, 40 Ind. 170 (1872); Moore v. Christian, 56 Miss. 408 (1879); Ellis v. Jesup, 11 Bush. 403 (Ky. 1875); People v. Porter, 23 Ill. App. 196 (1886); Woerner, *Guardianship*, pp. 20–21; Bishop, *New Commentaries*, 1:458–59; Gideon T. Banti, "Habeas Corpus: Custody of Infants," *CLJ* 15 (1882):281. By placing child welfare at the center of

all custody determinations, the nineteenth-century bench rearranged the rights of all those who claimed parental status. The effect of the judicial commitment to the best-interests-of-the-child standard was to make custody a case-by-case decision in which parenthood became a trust, subject to broad judicial supervision and external standards of fitness. For examples of this approach and discussions of its implications see In the Matter of Scarritt, 76 Mo. 565, 585 (1882); Hochheimer, *Custody of Infants*, p. 22; Carrigan, "Law and the American Child," 171–72; State v. Richardson, 40 N.H. 272 (1860); Commonwealth v. Branyan, 8 Pa. County Court Rep. 80 (1890); Taylor v. Jeter, 33 Ga. 195 (1862); State v. Sharpe, 25 Ind. 495 (1865); Voullaire v. Voullaire, 45 Mo. 602 (1870); McGlennan v. Margowski, 90 Ind. 150 (1883); Miller v. Wallace, 76 Ga. 479 (1886); Woerner, *Guardianship*, pp. 18–19. Judicial reluctance to disturb the custody of children by taking them from their new homes reinforced the bench's more traditional disinclination to support the claims of parents of questionable fitness. The rules of the common law allowed the bench to deny custody to parents who violated commonplace notions of fitness. Judges used the rules against mothers and fathers shown to be intemperate, itinerant, unstable, and, most important, lacking by judicial reckoning a proper concern for their offspring. As always, fathers most easily transgressed the boundaries of parental fitness, but mothers could fail the tests as well. See generally In re Blackburn, 41 Mo. App. 622, 633–34 (1890); Commonwealth v. Smith, 1 Brew. 547, 549, 551 (Pa. 1868); Matter of Schroeder, 65 How. Pr. 194 (N.Y. 1883); Maples v. Maples, 49 Miss. 393 (1873); Bryan v. Lyon, 104 Ind. 227 (1885); People v. Brown, 35 Hun. 324 (N.Y. 1885); Drumb v. Keen, 47 Ia. 435 (1877); Bently v. Terry, 59 Ga. 555 (1877); Smith v. Bragg, 68 Ga. 650 (1882); Hienman's Appeal, 11 Pitts. L.J., N.S., 171 (Pa. 1880).

57 For a general discussion of the family-bound concept of apprenticeship see Edmund Morgan, *The Puritan Family* (Boston, 1944), pp. 68, 75–88; Bernard Bailyn, *Education in the Forming of American Society* (Chapel Hill, N.C., 1960), pp. 29–36; John Demos, *A Little Commonwealth* (New York, 1970), pp. 71–75; Kett, *Rites of Passage*, pp. 22–31.

58 Reeve, *Baron and Femme*, pp. 283–84; Homer Folks, *The Care of Destitute, Neglected, and Delinquent Children* (New York, 1902), pp. 28–29; Jacobus TenBroek, *Family Law and the Poor*, ed. Joel Handler (Westport, Conn., 1964), pp. 32–33; Robert Ireland, *The County Courts in Antebellum Kentucky* (Lexington, Ky., 1972), pp. 21–22; Bloomfield, *American Lawyers*, pp. 22–35.

59 Reeve, *Baron and Femme*, p. 279; Kent, *Commentaries*, 2:266 note, and see 2:202–4; and see Reeve, *Baron and Femme*, 2nd ed., p. 342 note.

60 Bailyn, *Education in American Society*, pp. 30–31; and see Morton Horwitz, *Transformation of American Law* (Cambridge, Mass., 1977), pp. 207–8; F. Raymond Marks, "Detours on the Road to Maturity: A View of the Legal Conception of Growing Up and Letting Go," *LCP* 39 (1975):81–84.

61 Matter of M'Dowles, 8 Johns. 328 (N.Y. 1811); U.S. v. Bainbridge, 1 Mason 71, 73 (U.S. C.C. Mass. 1816, Fed. Cas. #14,497); GFR, "The Rights and Liabilities of Parents," *ALReg* 46 (1853):647 and see the dissenting opinion in State v. Taylor, 2 Penning. 352, 354 (N.J. 1808); Respublica v. Kepple, 2 Dallas 197 (Pa. 1793); Day v. Everett, 7 Mass. 144 (1810); Irvins v. Norcross, 2 Penning. 710 (N.J. Law 1812); Commonwealth v. Moore, 1 Ashm. 123 (Pa. 1827); Velde v. Levering, 2 Rawle 269 (Pa. 1830); Pierce v. Massenburg, 4 Leigh 493 (Va. 1833); People v. Pillow, 1 Sandf. 672 (N.Y. 1848); Harper v. Gilbert, 5 Cush. 417 (Mass. 1850); Musgrove v. Kornegay, 7 Jones 71 (N.C. 1859); Brotzman v. Burnell, 5 Wharton 158 (Pa. 1839). For cases involving maternal rights see Commonwealth v. Hamilton, 6 Mass. 273 (1810); Commonwealth v. Murray, 4 Binn. 487 (Pa. 1812); Commonwealth v. Coxe, 1 Ashm. 71 (Pa. 1831); Burk v. Phips, 1 Root 487 (Conn. 1793); Commonwealth v. Crommie, 8 W. & S. 399 (Pa. 1845); Ballard v. Edmonston, 2 Cranch 419 (U.S. C.C. D.C. 1823); Commonwealth v. Eglee, 6 S. & R. 340 (Pa. 1821); Osborn v. Allen, 2 Dutch. 388 (N.J. 1857); Curtis v. Curtis, 5 Gray 535 (Mass. 1855).

62 Warner v. Smith, 8 Conn. 14, 18 (1830). The courts also insisted that indentures follow statutory guidelines, especially that they be written, not verbal, agreements. Apprentices too were compelled to live up to their freely agreed bargains. For cases involving these procedural issues see McGrath v. Herndon, 4 T.B. Monroe 480 (Ky. 1827); Stewart v. Rickets, 2 Hump. 151 (Tenn. 1840); Walters v. Morrow, 1 Houst. 527 (Del. 1855–58); Lyon v. Whitmore, 2 Penning. 619 (N.J. 1811); Eastman v. Chapman, 1 Day 30 (Conn. 1800); Commonwealth v. Wilbank, 10 S. & R. 416 (Pa. 1823); Squire v. Whipple, 1 Vt. 69 (1827); Commonwealth v. Harrison, 11 Mass. 63 (1814); Peters v. Lord, 18 Conn. 337 (1847); Banks v. Metcalfe, 1 Wheeler Crim. Cas. 381 (N.Y. 1823); Page v. Marsh, 36 N.H. 305 (1858); Maltby v. Harwood, 12 Barb. 374 (N.Y. 1852); Harney v. Owen, 4 Blackf. 337 (Ind. 1837); Boaler v. Cummines, Fed. Cas. #1,584 (U.S. C.C. E.D. Pa. 1853).

63 Reeve, *Baron and Femme*, p. 344; and see Paul H. Douglas, "American Apprenticeship and Industrial Education," *Columbia University Studies in History, Economics, and Public Law* 95 (1920–21):248.

64 Davis v. Coburn, 8 Mass. 299, 305–6 (1811); Commonwealth v. Deacon, 6 S. & R. 526, 529 (Pa. 1821); and see Hall v. Gardner, 1 Mass. 172 (1804); Ayer v. Chase, 19 Pick. 556 (Mass. 1837); Commonwealth

v. King, 4 S. & R. 109 (Pa. 1818); Hudnut v. Bullock, 3 A.K. Marsh 299 (Ky. 1821); Nickerson v. Howard, 19 Johns. 113 (N.Y. 1821); Stringfield v. Heiskell, 2 Yerg. 546 (Tenn. 1831); Versailles v. Hall, 5 La. 281 (1833); Vickere v. Pierce, 12 Me. 315 (1835); Haley v. Taylor, 3 Dana 221 (Ky. 1835); Lobdell v. Allen, 9 Gray 377 (Mass. 1857); Huffman v. Rout, 2 Met. 50 (Ky. 1859); Kent, *Commentaries*, 2:265, 333; Hochheimer, *Custody of Infants*, pp. 111–12.

65 Commonwealth v. Conrow, 2 Pa. 402, 403 (1835); and see Horwitz, *Transformation of American Law*, p. 308; Thorp v. Rankin, 19 N.J. Law 36 (1842); Lawrence Stone, *Family, Sex, and Marriage in England, 1500–1800* (London, 1977), pp. 362–63. Even guardians, the most legally supported surrogate parents, were not given the full rights of natural ones. They had fewer obligations and correspondingly fewer rights. Guardians had no responsibility to support their ward and the ward, upon coming of age, could select the guardian. For a full discussion of the subject see Hochheimer, *Custody of Infants*, pp. 7–80; Woerner, *Guardianship*, pp. 158–64. For a general assessment of the changes in apprenticeship see Kett, *Rites of Passage*, pp. 145–52.

66 The Etna, 1 Ware 474, 476–77, 481 (U.S. C.C. Me. 1838).

67 For general discussions of poor relief see Ivy Pinchbeck, "The State and the Child in Sixteenth Century England," *BJS* 7 (1956):273–85; E. M. Leonard, *The Early History of English Poor Relief* (London, 1900), pp. 215–300; Marcus Wilson Jernegan, *Laboring and Dependent Classes in Colonial America, 1607–1783* (New York, 1931), pp. 10, 88, 114–27; Stefan A. Risenfeld, "The Formative Era of American Public Assistance Law," *CalLR* 43 (1955):175–233; Bloomfield, *American Lawyers*, pp. 99–104; David Rothman, *The Discovery of the Asylum* (Boston, 1971), chaps. 2, 7; Rendleman, "Parens Patriae," 131–33.

68 Commonwealth v. Jones, 3 S. & R. 158, 163 (Pa. 1817); Stanton v. State, 6 Blackf. 83, 84 (Ind. 1841); and see Bloomfield, *American Lawyers*, pp. 131–32; Reeve, *Baron and Femme*, pp. 283–84; Folks, *Care of Destitute Children*, pp. 28–29; Ireland, *County Courts*, pp. 21–22; Kent, *Commentaries*, 2:255; Timothy Walker, *Introduction to American Law* (Philadelphia, 1837), p. 272; Woerner, *Guardianship*, pp. 113–17; Johnson v. State, 21 Tenn. 282, 283 (1840); Kettlas v. Gardner, 1 Paige 488 (N.Y. 1829); Nicholson's Appeal, 20 Pa. 50 (1852); Farrer v. Clark, 29 Miss. 195 (1855); Foster v. Mott, 3 Bradf. 409 (N.Y. 1855); In the Matter of Pierce, 12 How. Pr. 532 (N.Y. 1856); Darnall v. Mullikin, 8 Ind. 152 (1856); Cozine v. Van Horn, 1 Bradf. 143 (N.Y. 1850).

69 Warner v. Swett and Way, 7 Vt. 446 (1835); and see Jefferson v. Letart, 3 Ohio 99, 102–3 (1827); Bloomfield v. Chagrin, 5 Ohio 316 (1832);

Vernon v. Smithville, 17 Johns. 89 (N.Y. 1819); Randolph v. Braintree, 10 Conn. 436 (1838). For a different view of these issues, see Oxford v. Rumney, 3 N.H. 331 (1825); for examples of cases in which the settlement laws were not used to break up families see Dedham v. Natick, 16 Mass. 135 (1819); Northfield v. Roxbury, 15 Vt. 622 (1843); Paterson v. Bryan, 23 N.J. Law 394 (1852); Folks, *Care of Destitute Children*, p. 28; Bloomfield, *American Lawyers*, pp. 123–26. Free black children faced the most drastic curtailment of their rights. Some states abolished educational requirements for them, others gave masters the right to indenture black children regardless of parental finances. In apprenticeship, as in much of family law, blacks were treated as the most subservient of the poor. For cases and discussions of this subject see Rachel v. Emerson, 6 B. Monroe 280 (Ky. 1845); Lamb v. Lamb, 4 Bush. 213 (Ky. 1860); Clinkinbeard v. Clinkinbeard, 3 Met. 330 (Ky. 1860); Smith v. Elwood, 4 Cranch 670 (U.S. C.C. D.C. 1836); Lea v. White, 4 Sneed 73 (Tenn. 1856); for a contrasting analysis see Comas v. Reddish, 35 Ga. 236 (1866); Graham v. Graham, 1 S. & R. 330 (Pa. 1815); Prue v. Hight, 6 Jones 265 (N.C. 1859); Futrell v. Vann, 8 Ire. Law 402 (N.C. 1848); Tucker v. Magee, 18 Ala. 99 (1850); Graham v. Kinder, 11 B. Monroe 60 (Ky. 1850); Moore v. Ann, 9 B. Monroe 36 (Ky. 1848); Demar v. Simonson, 4 Blackf. 132 (Ind. 1835); Bakers v. Winfrey, 15 B. Monroe 499 (Ky. 1854); William McDowell, "Free Negro Legislation in Georgia," *GaHQ* 16 (1932):35; Jeffrey Brackett, *The Negro in Maryland* (Baltimore, 1889), pp. 198, 219–20.

70   State v. Brearly, 2 South. 556 (N.J. 1819); Bloomfield, *American Lawyers*, p. 132; and see Glidden v. Unity, 30 N.H. 104 (1855); Rolfe v. Rolfe, 15 Ga. 451 (1854); Parsons v. Hand, Litt. Sel. Cas. 220 (Ky. 1816); Powers v. Ware, 2 Pick. 451 (Mass. 1824); for a different view see Curry v. Jenkins, 1 Hardin 493 (Ky. 1808); Reidell v. Morse, 19 Pick. 358 (Mass. 1837). For attempts to impose the protective requirements of apprenticeship, such as education and nurture, upon reluctant masters see In re Goodenough, 19 Wis. 274 (1865); Butler v. Hubbard, 5 Pick. 250 (Mass. 1827); Burnham v. Chapman, 7 Me. 385 (1840); Himes v. Howes, 13 Met. 80 (Ky. 1847); Commonwealth v. Edwards, 6 Binn. 202 (Pa. 1813); Williams v. Finch, 2 Barb. 208 (N.Y. 1848); Phelps v. Culver, 6 Vt. 430 (1834); Kent, *Commentaries*, 2:262; Sophonisba R. Breckinridge, *Illinois Poor Law and its Administration* (Chicago, 1939), pp. 29–30.

71   See generally Folks, *Care of Destitute Children*, pp. 4–24, 35–36, 111–26, 250–53; Rothman, *Discovery of the Asylum*, chap. 9; Bremner, et al., *Children and Youth in America*, 3 vols. (Cambridge, Mass., 1970–74), 2:671; Hochheimer, *Custody of Infants*, pp. 116, 122; Henry Thurston, *The Dependent Child* (New York, 1930), pp. 45–46, 78–79, 104–

5, 120–21; Commonwealth v. M'Keagy, 1 Ashm. 248, 250, 253 (Pa. 1831); People v. Kearney, 19 How. Pr. 493 (N.Y. 1860); Mason P. Thomas, Jr., "Child Abuse and Neglect, Part I, Historical Overview, Legal Matrix, and Social Perspective," *NCLR* 50 (1973):293–95; Stephen B. Presser, "The Historical Background of the American Law of Adoption," *JFL* 11 (1971):447–86.

72   Ex parte Crouse, 4 Whart. 9, 11, 11–12 (Pa. 1839); and see Steven Schlossman, *Love and the American Delinquent: The Theory and Practice of 'Progressive Juvenile Justice,' 1825–1920* (Chicago, 1977), chaps. 2–3.

73   Pollock and Maitland, *History of English Law*, 2:254; Glanville, quoted in ibid.; for the most thorough assessments of the origins of American adoption laws see Presser, "American Law of Adoption," 445–70; Zainaldin, "The Emergence of a Modern American Family Law"; see also John Francis Brosman, "The Law of Adoption," *ColLR* 22 (1922):332–35; Leo Albert Huard, "The Law of Adoption: Ancient and Modern," *VLR* 9 (1956):743–77; Helen L. Witmer, et al., *Independent Adoptions: A Follow-Up Study* (New York, 1963), pp. 21–23.

74   Witmer, et al., *Independent Adoptions*, p. 19. Both Presser and Zainaldin comment on the lack of publicity that surrounded the enactment of adoption. The same was true for many of the statutory innovations in family law discussed in this volume. This silence suggests both that the changes had judicial origins and were later merely formally brought into family law by codification and that by the time the legislators did so the innovations had become widely accepted.

75   Van Dane v. Vreeland, 3 Stock. 370, 380–81 (N.J. 1857).

76   Joseph Ben-Orr, "The Law of Adoption in the United States: Its Massachusetts Origins and the Statute of 1851," *NEHGR* 130 (1976):265–67; for other examples of the private acts see Witmer, et al., *Independent Adoptions*, p. 29; Presser, "American Law of Adoption," 464.

77   "Discussions: de Code Civil dans le Conseil d'Estate," *ALReg* 2 (1809): 477, and see 477–82; Huard, "Adoption: Ancient and Modern," 747–48; James A. Burgea, "Adoption in Louisiana: Its Past, Present, and Future," *LoyLR* 3 (1945):5; Carl Babier, "A Historical Comment on the Substantive Adoption Law of Louisiana," *LoyLR* 15 (1965):298.

78   Vidal v. Comagere, 13 La. An. 516, 519 (1838); and see Fuselier v. Masse, 4 La. 423 (1832); Moore v. Estate of Moore, 35 Vt. 98 (1862); Teal v. Sevier, 26 Tex. 516 (1863); Tutorship of Upton, 16 La. An. 175 (1861).

79   Witmer et al., *Independent Adoptions*, pp. 30–31; George Sims, "Comment: Adoption by Estoppel, History and Effect," *BayLR* 15 (1963): 162–63; Catherine McFarland, "The Mississippi Law of Adoption," *MissLJ* 10 (1938):240.

80   Cited in Babier, "A Historical Comment on the Adoption Law of Louisiana," 298–301; New York Commissioners of the Code, *The Civil Code of the State of New York* (Albany, N.Y., 1865), p. 36; and see William P. Letchworth, "The History of Child-Saving in the State of New York," in *History of Child-Saving in the United States*, ed. Committee on the History of Child-Saving Work (New York, 1893), pp. 184–85; Justus S. Stearns, *Laws Relating to the Support of Poor Persons* (Lansing, Mich., 1900), pp. 41–43; Phillip O. Jochimsen, "The Statute to Legalize the Adoption of Minor Children," *ALJ* 8 (1873):653–57; Witmer, et al., *Independent Adoptions*, pp. 30–31.

81   William H. Whitmore, *The Law of Adoption* (Boston, 1876), pp. iii, 30–31, 74, 75, 77, 85.

82   The Massachusetts and Pennsylvania legislation is cited in Witmer, et al., *Independent Adoptions*, p. 31; Wolf's App., 10 Sad. 93 (Pa. 1888); and see Parsons v. Parsons, 101 Wis. 76, 80 (1898). Although welfare considerations set the scope of the adoption laws, federalism allowed for significant variation in the qualifications to be met by prospective members of artificial families. Most states limited adoption to minors, and insisted that the adoptive parent be an adult, often several years older than the child. States also normally required the consent of both spouses. But many added their own caveats. Montana, Louisiana, Nevada, and Texas formally banned adoptions between whites and racial minorities. The New England states specifically prohibited the adoption of close blood relatives. Several others banned the adoption of illegitimate children by their fathers. Whitmore, *Law of Adoption*, pp. 73–79; Brosman, "The Law of Adoption," 335–37; Jack Greenberg, *Race Relations and American Law* (New York, 1959), pp. 351–52; Walter Waddington, "Adoption of Children Under Seventeen in Louisiana," *TLR* 36 (1962): 1201–32; Chester Vernier, *American Family Laws*, 4 vols. (Stanford, Cal., 1931–38), 4:281–92.

83   Almon G. Shepard, "Adoption Without Consent of Natural Parents," *CC* 17 (1911):396; and see Johnson v. Terry, 34 Conn. 259 (1867).

84   Schiltz v. Roenitz, 86 Wis. 31, 40 (1893); and see Humphrey, 137 Mass. 84 (1884); Furgeson v. Jones, 17 Ore. 204 (1888); People v. Congden, 17 Mich. 351 (1889); Taylor v. Deseve, 81 Tex. 246 (1891); Booth v. Van Allen, 7 Phila. 410 (Pa. 1870); Luppie v. Winans, 37 N.J. Eq. 245 (1883); Gibson, 154 Mass. 378 (1891); Ex parte Clark, 87 Cal. 638 (1891); Ex parte Chambers, 80 Cal. 216 (1889); In re Clements, 78 Mo. 352 (1883); Woodruff v. Conley, 50 Ala. 304 (1874); Burger v. Frakes, 67 Ia. 460 (1885); Succession of Forstall, 25 La. An. 340 (1873); Woerner, *Guardianship*, p. 26.

85   California statute cited in TenBroek, *Family Law and the Poor*, 120;

Lally v. Fitzhenry, 85 Ia. 49 (1892); Matter of Larson, 31 Hun. 540 (N.Y. 1884); In re McCormick, 108 Wis. 234 (1900); Parsons v. Parsons, 101 Wis. 76 (1898); Fouts v. Pierce, 64 Ia. (1844); In re Bush, 47 Kan. 264 (1891); Brown's Adoption, 25 Pa. Superior Ct. 259 (1904); Baskette v. Streight, 106 Tenn. 549 (1901).

86 Woodward v. Woodward, 87 Tenn. 644, 659 (1889); and see Godine v. Kidd, 64 Hun. 585 (N.Y. 1892); Virgin v. Marwick, 97 Me. 578 (1903); Tilley v. Harrison, 91 Ala. 295 (1890); Coffer v. Scroggins, 98 Ala. 342 (1892–93); Foley v. Foley, 61 Ill. App. 577 (1895); Martin v. Aetna Life Insurance Co., 73 Ore. 25 (1881); Von Beck v. Thomsen, 44 App. Div. 373 (N.Y. 1899); Lunay v. Vantyne, 40 Vt. 501 (1868).

87 Whitmore, *Law of Adoption*, p. iii.

88 Hochaday v. Lynn, 200 Mo. 456, 464 (1906).

89 Long v. Hewitt, 44 Ia. 363, 367 (1876); and see Tyler v. Reynolds, 53 Ia. 146, 148 (1880); Shearer v. Weaver, 56 Ia. 578 (1881); Gill v. Sullivan, 55 Ia. 341 (1880); Succession of Vollmer, 40 La. An. 593 (1888); White v. Dotter, 73 Ark. 130 (1904). Judges were particularly intent on limiting the use of customary and private-law adoptions; they often tightly controlled the rights that flowed from such acts. See generally Matter of Thorne, 155 N.Y. 140 (1898); Carroll v. Collins, 6 App. Div. 106 (N.Y. 1896); Davis v. Hendricks, 99 Mo. 478 (1889); Stanley v. Chandler, 53 Vt. 619 (1881); King v. Davis, 91 N.C. 142 (1884); Non-She-Po v. Wa-Win-Ta, 37 Ore. 213 (1900); McCulley's Appeal, 10 Weekly Notes 80 (Pa. 1881); Ballard v. Ward, 89 Pa. 358 (1879).

90 J. B. Varnum, "Adoption," *ALJ* 8 (1873):383.

91 Cited in William Bullock, *Law of Domestic Relations of the State of New York* (Albany, N.Y., 1898), p. 50; Nugent v. Powell, 4 Wy. 173, 187 (1893); and see In re Masterson's Estate, 108 Wash. 307, 308 (1919); Simmons v. Burrell, 8 Misc. 388 (N.Y. 1894); Fosburgh v. Rogers, 114 Mo. 122 (1893); In the Matter of Newman, 75 Cal. 213 (1888); Bancroft v. Bancroft, 53 Vt. 9 (1880); Brown v. Brown, 101 Ind. 340 (1884); Power v. Halfley, 85 Ky. 671 (1887); Clark v. Clark, 76 N.H. 551 (1913); Martin v. Long, 53 Neb. 694 (1898); Sharkey v. McDermott, 91 Mo. 647 (1887); Vernier, *American Family Laws*, 4:408–12; "Legislation: Legislation and Decisions on Inheritance Rights of Adopted Children," *IaLR* 22 (1936):145–54; Albert M. Kales, "Rights of Adopted Children," *IlLR* 9 (1914):149–79; Presser, "American Law of Adoption," 507–10.

92 Schafer v. Eneu, 54 Pa. 304, 306 (1867); Phillips v. McConica, 59 Ohio St. 1, 8 (1898).

93 Upson v. Noble, 35 Ohio St. 655 (1880); Safford v. Houghton's Estate, 48 Vt. 236 (1876); Quigley v. Mitchell, 41 Ohio St. 375 (1884); Warren

v. Prescott, 84 Me. 483 (1892); Jenkins v. Jenkins, 64 N.H. 487 (1887); Clarkson v. Hatton, 143 Mo. 47 (1898); Beaver v. Crump, 76 Miss. 34 (1898); Wyeth v. Stone, 144 Mass. 441 (1887); Helms v. Elliot, 89 Tenn. 446 (1890); Atchison v. Atchison, 89 Ky. 488 (1890); Moran v. Stewart, 122 Mo. 295 (1894); Krug v. Davis, 87 Ind. 590 (1882); Isenhour v. Isenhour, 52 Ind. 328 (1876); Barnes v. Allen, 25 Ind. 222 (1865); Nulton's Appeal, 103 Pa. 286 (1883); Succession of Hosmer, 37 La. An. 839 (1885); Kales, "Rights of Adopted Children," 149–50; Gabriel Woerner, "Legal Status of Adopted Children," *CLJ* 31 (1890):69–70; for a different view of the issue see Sewall v. Roberts, 115 Mass. 262, 275 (1874); Stearns v. Allen, 183 Mass. 404 (1903); Johnson's Appeal, 88 Pa. 346 (1879).

94 Wagner v. Varner, 50 Ia. 532, 534 (1879); and see Whitmore, *Law of Adoption*, pp. 80–81; Vernier, *American Family Laws*, 4:411.

95 Hole v. Robbins, 53 Wis. 514, 520 (1881); and see Barhizel v. Ferrel, 47 Ind. 335 (1874); Reinders v. Koppelmann, 68 Mo. 482 (1878); Commonwealth v. Powell, 16 Weekly Notes 297 (Pa. 1885); Murphy v. Portum, 95 Tenn. 605 (1895); Succession of Unforsake, 48 La. 546 (1896); Whitmore, *Law of Adoption*, pp. 81–82; Vernier, *American Family Laws*, 4:413–52.

96 Joseph Newbold, "Jurisdictional and Social Aspects of Adoption," *MinnLR* 11 (1927):608.

97 Vernier, *American Family Laws*, 4:279–80; Witmer, *Independent Adoptions*, pp. 34–36; Ida Parker, *"Fit and Proper," A Study of Legal Adoption in Massachusetts* (Boston, 1927); but see Annie Hamilton Powell, "The Adopted," *Harper's Weekly* 113 (1906):927–33, for a fictional account of the plight of adopted children.

98 For a general assessment of the effort see Keller, *Affairs of State*, pp. 464–68.

99 Anthony Platt, *The Child Savers* (Chicago, 1969); Ellen Ryerson, *The Best-Laid Plans, America's Juvenile Court Experiment* (New York, 1978), chaps. 1–4; Schlossman, *Love and the American Delinquent*, chaps. 4–9; Grace Abbott, *The Child and the State*, 2 vols. (Chicago, 1938), 2:Part II; Thurston, *Dependent Child*, pp. 136–75; Robert Mennel, *Thorns and Thistles: Juvenile Delinquents in the United States, 1825–1940* (Hanover, N.H., 1973), chaps. 1–3; Vernier, *American Family Laws*, 3:112–38; David Rothman, *Conscience and Convenience, The Asylum and its Alternatives in Progressive America* (New York, 1980), Part III; Stephen Wood, *Constitutional Politics in the Progressive Era* (Chicago, 1971); Miriam Langsam, *Children West: A History of the Placing Out of the New York Children's Aid Bureau* (Madison, Wis., 1964); Susan Tiffin, *In Whose Best Interest? Child Welfare in the Pro-*

gressive Era (Westwood, Conn., 1981).

100 Rose Holman Smith quoted in *History of Child-Saving*, p. 189; Rice quoted in *History of Child-Saving*, p. 75.

101 Folks, *Care of Destitute Children*, p. 105; Miriam Van Waters, *Parents on Probation* (New York, 1927), p. 166.

102 Minot Savage, "The Rights of Children," *Arena* 6 (1892):13–14; Kate D. Wiggins, "Children's Rights," *Scribner's Magazine* 12 (1892):243.

103 Ernst Freund, *The Police Powers* (Chicago, 1904), p. 248; and see Christopher Tiedeman, *Limitations of the Police Power* (St. Louis, 1886), p. 554; Schouler, *Domestic Relations*, pp. 332–33; Vernier, *American Family Laws*, 4:17–18.

104 Savage quoted in Keller, *Affairs of State*, p. 469. Enlarged maternal rights made inroads into guardianship as well. The most obvious and telling example was the decreasing right of husbands to appoint a guardian by will. By the first decades of the twentieth century, twenty-one states gave married women the right either to overrule the choice of such testamentary or to make such appointments themselves. Four other states authorized widows to use the testamentary power if their husbands had not chosen to exercise it. And in other states judicial decisions and maternally biased common-law doctrines weakened paternal testamentary power by upholding judicial notions of parental fitness. See generally Lord v. Hough, 37 Cal. 657 (1869); Wardwell v. Wardwell, 9 Allen 518 (Mass. 1865); Carpenter v. Harris, 51 Mich. 223 (1883); Matter of Schmidt, 77 Hun. 201 (N.Y. 1894); Thompson v. Thompson, 55 How. Pr. 494 (N.Y. 1876); Hill v. Hill, 49 Md. 450 (1878); Matter of Reynolds, 11 Hun. 41 (N.Y. 1877); Wilkinson v. Deming, 80 Ill. 342 (1875); Succession of Farrelly, 47 La. An. 1667 (1895); McKinney v. Noble, 37 Tex. 731 (1872–73). For a different analysis see Ex parte Bell, 2 Tenn. Chan. 327 (1875); for a thorough judicial discussion of these issues see Ingalls v. Campbell, 18 Ore. 461, 464 (1889); and see Woerner, *Guardianship*, pp. 58–60; George Bayles, *Women's Legal Status* (New York, 1902), pp. 98–99.

105 Dahlgren quoted in Stanton, et al., *History of Woman Suffrage*, 3:152; Schouler, *Domestic Relations*, 5th ed., p. 166; and see James Schouler, "Universal Marriage," *SLR* 7 (1881):532–43; George A. O. Ernst, *The Legal Status of Married Women in Massachusetts* (Boston, 1895), pp. 24–32. For a discussion of revolutionary ideas of sovereignty see Gordon Wood, *The Creation of the Republic, 1776–1787* (Chapel Hill, 1969), p. 9.

106 *Law Review* quoted in Keller, *Affairs of State*, p. 470; Linda Kerber, *Women of the Republic* (Chapel Hill, 1980), chap. 5; William Holdsworth, *History of English Law*, 16 vols. (London, 1903–66), 1:467–68.

107   Roscoe Pound, "Individual Interests in Domestic Relations," *MLR* 14 (1916):182, and see 183–84. For detailed summary of custody-law standards see Pomeroy, *Equity Jurisprudence*, 3:2012–13.

108   Robert Grant, *Law and the Family* (New York, 1919), pp. 181–82, 182, 183, v–vi.

Chapter 8

1   James Schouler, *A Treatise on the Law of Domestic Relations* (Boston, 5th ed., 1895), p. 9.

2   For a more general statement of this theme see Michael Grossberg, "Who Gets the Child? Custody, Guardianship, and the Rise of a Judicial Patriarchy in Nineteenth Century America," *FS* 9 (1983):235–60; see also Janet Rifkind, "Toward a Theory of Law and Patriarchy," *Harvard Women's Law Journal*, 3 (1980):83–95.

3   For the most thorough analysis of the character and makeup of the nineteenth-century bench see Kermit Hall, *The Politics of Justice: Lower Federal Judicial Selection and the Second Party System, 1829–1861* (Lincoln, Neb., 1979); Kermit Hall, "Constitutional Machinery and Judicial Professionalism: The Careers of Midwestern State Appellate Court Judges, 1861–1899," in *The New High Priests*, Lawyers in Post-Civil War America, ed. Gerard Gawalt (Westport, Conn., 1984), 29–49.

4   See for example, Joel Bishop, *New Commentaries on the Law of Marriage and Divorce*, 2 vols. (New York, 1891), 1:420.

5   Joel Bishop, *Commentaries on the Law of Married Women*, 2 vols. (Boston, 1871), pp. 74–75, 75.

6   Joel Bishop, *Common Law and Codification* (Chicago, 1888), pp. 3, 3–4; and see generally, Morton Keller, *Affairs of State* (Cambridge, Mass., 1977), chap. 9.

7   Isaac Redfield, "The Responsibilities and Duties of the Legal Profession," *ALReg*, N.S., 10 (1871):547; and see Bishop, *New Commentaries*, 2:181.

8   For the examination of the development of other substantive areas of the law that have served as models for this analysis of family law see Lawrence Friedman, *Contract Law in America* (Madison, Wis., 1965); G. Edward White, *Tort Law in America, An Intellectual History* (New York, 1980).

9   For an analysis of nineteenth-century commercial law that complements this study, see Charles McCurdy, "Justice Field and the Jurisprudence

of Government-Business Relations: Some Parameters of *Laissez Faire*
Constitutionalism, 1863–1897," *JAH* 61 (1975):970–1005.

10   Beyond the increase in books, articles, and courses devoted to family
law, perhaps the most graphic example of its growing specialization can
be found in the work of Joel Bishop. A comparison of his first presentation of the law of marriage and divorce in 1852 with his thorough 1891
revision documents the subject's growth. Bishop's lengthy introduction
to the latter volume also places the law in a larger political and professional context that he apparently had not thought to be relevant in 1852.

11   Elinor Nims, *The Illinois Adoption Law and its Administration* (Chicago, 1928), p. xiii. For a recent discussion of the limits of the nineteenth-century state see Stephen Skowronek, *Building a New American
State: The Expansion of National Administrative Capacities, 1877–1920*
(New York, 1982).

12   Lelia Robinson, *The Law of Husband and Wife* (Boston, 1899), p. 45.

13   In re Burrus, 136 U.S. 586, 593–94 (1890); and see Barber v. Barber, 63
U.S. 582 (1858); Thomas I. Cooley, *Michigan, A History of Government* (Boston, 2nd ed., 1905), pp. 227–28; "Note: Federal Jurisdiction
of 'Domestic Relations' Cases," *JFL* 7 (1967):309–17.

14   For general discussions of these rules see Morton Horwitz, *The Trans-
formation of American Law* (Cambridge, Mass., 1977), p. 246; Joseph
Story, *Commentaries on Conflicts of Law* (Boston, 1834), pp. 94–118;
Ibid., (Boston, 3rd ed., 1846), pp. 96, 232–33; Ernest Lorenzen and
Kurt H. Nadleman, "Justice Story's Contribution to American Conflicts
of Law: A Comment," *AJLH* 5 (1961):230–53; David Engdahl, "Full
Faith and Credit in Merrie Olde England: New Insight for Marriage
Conflicts Law from the Thirteenth Century," *ValLR* 5 (1970):1–25; Eng-
dahl, "Proposal for a Benign Revolution in Marriage Law and Marriage
Conflicts Law," 58–116; Paul Finkelman, *An Imperfect Union, Slavery,
Federalism, and Comity* (Chapel Hill, N.C., 1981), pp. 13–14; Anthony
Bland, "The Family and the Conflicts of Law," in *A Century of Family
Law* (Cambridge, 1957), ed. Ronald Graveson and F. L. Crane, ed.,
pp. 274–80.

15   *Commentaries on Marriage and Divorce*, 5th ed., pp. 317–18. For the
debate over these issues see William L. Snyder, *The Geography of
Marriage: Or Legal Perplexities of Wedlock in the United States* (New
York, 1899); Charles Stuart Welles, *The Apotheosis of Christ, or, The
New Marriage* (New York, 1884); "History of Efforts to Secure a Uniform Law on Marriage and Divorce," *Congressional Digest* 6 (1927):
183–209; League for the Protection of the Family, *Annual Report, 1891–
1907* (Boston, 1892–1908); Chester Vernier, *American Family Laws*,
4 vols. (Stanford, 1931–38), 1:209–13; Mary Richmond and Fred S.
Hall, *Marriage and the State* (New York, 1929), pp. 188–206; William

O'Neill, *Divorce in the Progressive Era* (New Haven, Conn., 1967), pp. 238–53.

16 Elizabeth Cady Stanton, et al., *History of Woman Suffrage*, 6 vols. (New York, 1872–1922), 2:152; Lelia Robinson, *The Law of Husband and Wife*, p. 52.

17 Dike's statement is in National League for the Protection of the Family, *Annual Report, 1888* (Boston, 1889), p. 20.

18 Elaine May, *Great Expectations, Marriage and Divorce in Post-Victorian America* (Chicago, 1980), p. 58; Florence Kelley, "On Some Changes in the Legal Status of the Child Since Blackstone," *IR* 12 (1882):96, 97.

19 Chandler quoted in William Leach, *True Love and Perfect Union* (New York, 1980), p. 89.

20 For discussions of these broader issues see Leach, *True Love and Perfect Union*; Christopher Lasch, *Havens in a Heartless World* (New York, 1977); W. Norton Grubb and Marvin Lazerson, *Broken Promises, How Americans Fail Their Children* (New York, 1982).

21 Isaac Redfield, "Comment," *ALReg* 19 (1871):372, 374, 357; People v. Turner, 55 Ill. 280 (1870); and see Douglas Rendleman, "Parens Patriae: From Chancery to the Juvenile Court," *SCLR* 23 (1971):233–36.

22 For general discussions of the paternalistic bias of nineteenth-century American law see Linda Kerber, *Women of the Republic* (Chapel Hill, N.C., 1980), chap. 5; Norma Basch, "Invisible Women: The Legal Fiction of Marital Unity in Nineteenth-Century America," *FS* 5 (1979): 346–66.

23 I would like to thank Dirk Hartog for helping me clarify this vital point.

24 Kelley, "Some Changes in the Legal Status of the Child," 84.

25 Mary Greene, "The American Mother's Right to Her Child," *ALRev* 52 (1918):371–82.

26 Fitzhugh quoted in Paul Conner, "Patriarchy: Old World and New," *AQ* 17 (1965):54.

27 For a useful discussion of the power of legal fictions see Lon Fuller, *Legal Fictions* (Stanford, Ca., 1967); see also G. Edward White, *Patterns of American Legal Thought* (Indianapolis, Ind., 1978), chap. 1.

28 Richard Hofstadter, *Age of Reform* (New York, 1955), p. 155; and see generally Burton J. Bledstein, *The Culture of Professionalism, The Middle Class and the Development of Higher Education in America* (New York, 1976); Robert Wiebe, *The Search for Order, 1877–1920* (New York, 1967), especially chap. 5.

29 Thurston, Flexner, and Tuthill quoted in Susan Tiffin, *In Whose Best Interest? Child Welfare in the Progressive Era* (Westport, Conn., 1982), pp. 220–21; and see David Rothman, *Conscience and Convenience, The*

Asylum and its Alternatives in Progressive America (Boston, 1980), Part III.

30 Jacques Donzelot, *The Policing of Families*, trans. Robert Hurley (New York, 1979), p. 103.

31 Dike's statement is in National League for the Protection of the Family, *Annual Report, 1900* (Boston, 1901), p. 14; Arthur Calhoun, *Social History of the American Family*, 3 vols. (Cleveland, 1917), 3:169, and see generally chap. 8.

32 For general discussions of these changes see Mary Ann Glendon, *State, Family, and Law* (Oxford, 1977); Joseph Goldstein, Anna Freud, and Albert J. Solnit, *Beyond the Best Interests of the Child* (New York, 1973); Karen DeCrow, *Sexist Justice* (New York, 1974); Leo Kanowitz, *Women and the Law, The Unfinished Revolution* (Albuquerque, N.M., 1979); "Children and the Law," *LCP* 39 (1975):1–293; Eva R. Rubin, *Abortion, Politics, and the Courts, Roe v. Wade and its Aftermath* (Westport, Conn., 1982).

INDEX

Maternal preference: and bastardy law, 208–11; and child custody, 244, 250, 253, 281–85, 382 (n. 11). *See also* Child custody, law of; Maternal rights; Paternal rights; Women

Maternal rights, 235–36, 238; and feminine sphere, 238–39; and guardianship, 242–43, 397 (n. 104); and maternal feminism, 244; and child custody, 244–47, 253; and spousal rights, 281–85. *See also* Paternal rights; Patriarchy; Women

Matrimonial republicanism, 19

May, Elaine (historian): on women's emancipation, 55; on maternal custody awards, 251; on consequences of reform, 297

May, Samuel (reformer): on gender spheres, 5; on seducers, 47; on maternal rights, 246

Medical restrictions, nuptial, 149–52. *See* Marriage, legal prohibitions on

Merrick, E. T. (judge): on adoption, 271

Michigan, legislation: on nuptial medical tests, 150; on adoption, 278

Michigan, Supreme Court of: on abortion procedure, 180; on nonaccess and bastardy, 220

Milford v. *Worcester* (marriage), 71–72

Miller, Samuel (judge): on state domestic-relations jurisdiction, 295

Mills v. *Commonwealth* (abortion), 359 (n. 17)

Minnesota, legislation: on bastardy, 232

Minnesota, Supreme Court of: on common-law marriage, 89

Minnesota Law Review: on common-law marriage, 101

Miscegenation, 136. *See also* Interracial marriage

Mississippi, Court of Errors and Appeals: on custody and divorce, 251–52

Mississippi, Supreme Court of: on nuptial rights, 89; on nuptial sanity, 147

Missouri, Court of Appeals: on abortion punishments, 185–86

Missouri, Supreme Court of: on breach of marriage promise, 46, 55; and defense of common-law marriage, 95–96; on nuptial presumptions, 98–99; on adoption and inheritance, 275–76

Mohr, James (historian): and nineteenth-century abortion, 170, 358 (n. 9)

Mormons (Church of Jesus Christ of Latter Day Saints): and nuptial restrictions, 121–26; and bastardy law, 223–24; compared to Shakers, 346–47 (n. 47). *See also* Marriage, legal prohibitions on

Morrow, Prince A. (physician): on nuptial regulation, 149

Moss v. *Moss* (marriage, GB), 119

Nash, Frederic (judge): on bastardy procedures, 216–17

Nebinger, Andrew (physician): on quickening, 172; on abortion reform, 172–73

Nebraska, legislation: on bastardy suits, 221

Nebraska, Supreme Court of: on bastardy suits, 226

Nevada, Supreme Court of: on marriage age, 143

Newbold, Joseph (lawyer): on nature of adoption, 278

New England Divorce Reform League (also National League for the Protection of the Family): origins, 90; role in late nineteenth-century nuptial reform, 91–92. *See also* Dike, Rev. Samuel

New Hampshire, Supreme Court of: on common-law marriage, 74; on nuptial ceremonies, 77

New Jersey: divorce in, 238

New Jersey, legislation: on parental child custody, 247, 248

New Jersey, Supreme Court of: and abortion prosecutions, 162–64, 165; advice to parents, 330 (n. 40); on restraint of marriage, 338 (n. 1)

New York, Court of Appeals: on abortion and physicians, 184

New York, legislation: on breach of promise, 50; on marriage age, 107; on impotence, 109; on abortion, 162, 173–75; on contraception, 177; on child custody, 240–41, 246; controversy over custody law, 246–47; on adoption, 272, 276–77

New York Moral Reform Society, 11

New York State Women Suffrage Society: on maternal custody rights, 246

New York Times: on nuptial reform, 97; and banning abortion, 173